THINK
ROCK

•KEVIN J. H. DETTMAR•

Creative Editor
Pomona College

Boston   Columbus   Indianapolis   New York   San Francisco   Upper Saddle River
Amsterdam   Cape Town   Dubai   London   Madrid   Milan   Munich   Paris   Montréal   Toronto
Delhi   Mexico City   São Paulo   Sydney   Hong Kong   Seoul   Singapore   Taipei   Tokyo

Editorial Director: Craig Campanella
Editor in Chief: Sarah Touborg
Acquisitions Editor: Richard Carlin
Editorial Project Manager: David Nitti
Editorial Assistant: Tricia Murphy
Director of Marketing: Brandy Dawson
Executive Marketing Manager: Wendy Gordon
Senior Marketing Manager: Kate Stewart Mitchell
Marketing Assistant: Kyle VanNatter
Full-Service Project Management: Michael Egolf and Adam Noll
 (Words & Numbers, Inc.)
Senior Managing Editor: Ann Marie McCarthy
Assistant Managing Editor: Melissa Feimer
Project Manager: Barbara Taylor-Laino
Copy Editor: Gabrielle Durham (Words & Numbers, Inc.)
Proofreader: Words & Numbers, Inc.
Senior Operations & Manufacturing Supervisor: Nick Sklitsis
Senior Operations Specialist: Brian K. Mackey
Line Art Illustrations: Words & Numbers, Inc.

Manager of Design Development: John Christiana
Art Director, Text and Cover Design: Laura Gardner
Manager, Visual Research: Beth Brenzel
Manager, Rights and Permissions: Zina Arabia
Image Permission Coordinator: Cynthia Vincenti
Photo Researchers: Lee Scher and Kathy Ringrose
Manager, Cover Visual Research & Permissions: Karen Sanatar
Back Cover: istock
Director of Media Production: Tim Armstrong
SSA Associate Director of Media Production: Diane Hynes
Senior Media Editor: David Alick
Media Project Manager: Rich Barnes
Advanced Media Project Manager: Robert White
Advanced Media Project Manager: Michael Forbes
Media Project Manager: Jessica Bodie Richards
Composition: Words & Numbers, Inc.
Printer/Binder: Courier Kendallville
Cover Printer: Lehigh-Phoenix Color

> To teach rock & roll is to court disaster; this book is
> for my students, who have always been gentle &
> generous, and have taught me well.

This book was set in 8.5/12 Helvetica Neue Light.

Credits and acknowledgments borrowed from other sources and reproduced, with permission, in this textbook appear on appropriate pages within text (or on pages 314–318).

Library of Congress Cataloging-in-Publication Data available upon request from the Library of Congress

10 9 8 7 6 5 4 3 2 1

Prentice Hall
is an imprint of

www.pearsonhighered.com

ISBN 10: 0-205-77299-4
ISBN 13: 978-0-205-77299-5
Exam Copy ISBN 10: 0-205-79496-3
Exam Copy ISBN 13: 978-0-205-79496-6

BRIEF CONTENTS

CONTENTS

04

05

06

10

11

12

14

SMOOTH SOUNDS, SLICK PACKAGING: THE PERSISTENCE OF POP (1994–) 246

CONTENTS

13

HIP-HOP AND RAP (1973–) 226

My sincere thanks go out to Richard Carlin, editor extraordinaire, for inviting me to imagine this book with him. It's easy to criticize histories of rock, all of which (including this one) get it wrong in important ways. It takes guts to put your money where your mouth is, though—courage I wouldn't have had without Richard's support.

A big shout out, too, to David Nitti at Prentice Hall, and Mike Egolf at Words & Numbers, for their patient good humor. Working on this book has been intensely collaborative, and no author could hope for a better, more supportive collaborative team. And finally, my humble thanks to those writers at Words & Numbers who put vibrant flesh onto the bare bones of my outline. Shown a valley of dry bones, the Lord asks the prophet Ezekiel, "Can these bones live?"; if *these* bones manage to come alive, it's owing first and foremost to their hard work and dedication.

Finally, I would like to thank Cliff Adams at the College-Conservatory of Music and the University of Cincinnati, Chuck Archard at Rollins College, Theo Cateforis at Syracuse University, Kevin Holm-Hudson at the University of Kentucky, Steve Waksman at Smith College, and Eric Wallack at Owens State Community College. Their reviews of the manuscript have helped immensely to make the book what it is today.

ABOUT THE CREATIVE EDITOR

KEVIN J. H. DETTMAR is W. M. Keck Professor and Chair of English at Pomona College. He is the author or editor of a number of books on modernist literature and culture, and the culture of rock & roll, including *Reading Rock & Roll: Authenticity, Appropriation, Aesthetics; Is Rock Dead?;* and *The Cambridge Companion to Bob Dylan.* He is general editor of the *Longman Anthology of British Literature,* and editor of the Oxford University Press book series, Modernist Literature & Culture.

"Dear Sir:

The other day I turned on a Frank Sinatra program and I noted the shrill whistling sound, created supposedly by a bunch of girls cheering. Last night as I heard Lucky Strike produce more of this same hysteria I thought: how easy it would be for certain-minded manufacturers to create another Hitler here in America through the influence of mass-hysteria! I believe that those who are using this shrill whistling sound are aware that it is similar to that which produced Hitler. That they intend to get a Hitler in by first planting in the minds of the people that men like Frank Sinatra are O.K. therefore this future Hitler will be O.K."

—Anonymous letter to the FBI, August 13, 1943

"I have carefully noted the content of your letter and wish to thank you for volunteering your comments and observations in this regard."

—John Edgar Hoover, September 2, 1943

John Edgar Hoover's response to the anonymous writer concerned about Frank Sinatra's influence on millions of young people seems dismissive. However, this letter launched a five-decade FBI investigation of Sinatra's life and influence. Sinatra, a smooth crooner who rocketed to stardom, worried the FBI with his social and political influences, particularly on the teenage population. Sinatra was known to socialize with people from organized crime, and the FBI worried about what type of message his impressionable audience would get from his songs. During Sinatra's time (and especially today), teens were huge consumers of the music industry, often determining the hottest artists and breathing life into new music genres, like rock & roll. The worry expressed by this anonymous writer would only be multiplied a hundredfold when teens came forth as a major market for a new and more disturbing musical style: rock & roll.

THE PREHISTORY OF ROCK & ROLL

CHAPTER 01

3

WHAT WERE THE FIRST INFLUENCES OF ROCK & ROLL?

There are many competing stories about the "birth" of rock & roll, but one thing is certain: the audience that nurtured it was the postwar boom generation of teenagers. So, what brought rock & roll on the scene? There are numerous contributing factors, from the evolution of the way music was performed, heard, and ultimately popularized to the transition from live performances to records as a major distribution method of popular music to the new technologies, such as radio networks and electrical recording, that made it possible for music to be heard from coast to coast and beyond. Rock & roll seemed to combine all of these influences with the collective energy of the postwar generation. Chapter 2 deals with these competing stories of rock & roll's "birth" more closely, but first it is important to recognize the musical conditions leading up to the decade after World War II—the era that birthed rock & roll.

Mongrel Genealogy: The Ancestors of Rock & Roll

Although the end of World War II is considered the cradle of rock & roll, the genre's roots can be traced back to the late 1800s. Rock & roll's parentage is like a family tree turned upside-down. Instead of having just two sources, rock & roll contains elements—either culturally or musically—of Tin Pan Alley, jazz, blues, folk, country, and rhythm & blues—sometimes in bits, and often all at once. For this reason, no musical chart could contain the new genre; the hits of Elvis seemed to climb up three or four of the *Billboard* charts at once. Some of the contributing popular music genres that led to rock & roll originated in the United States, while others hailed from foreign shores.

A SHEET-MUSIC ECONOMY AND A NEW MASS-MARKET

Mass-produced sheet music made up the bulk of the music publishing business in the late 19th and early 20th centuries. Although recording and reproducing sound were still scratchy at best, printing sheet music was much easier. For the first time in history, a single song could be mass-produced and then sell thousands of copies in a single urban area, something practically impossible with the oral folk tradition and certainly never so profitable. Sheet music sales took off in the early part of the century. Between 1890 and 1909, sales more than tripled; and by 1910, sales totaled 30 million copies (Starr and Waterman 2003, 29). Because a single song sold for anything from 25 to 60 cents (roughly about five to thirteen dollars in today's dollar value), volume was essential to this method of publication.

Tin Pan Alley

Tin Pan Alley referred to the many new publishing houses that were opening in lower Manhattan, on 28th Street between Fifth and Sixth Avenues. In the early 1900s, the first major wave of Jewish Eastern European immigrants began many of these publishing houses, which were so popular that they challenged even the established publishers. While the older publishers generally made their money by publishing European-style parlor songs and classical scores, this collection of newer publishers broke into the business with mass-produced popular songs. At first, these songs were performed in vaudeville theaters as a

<<< **78 r.p.m. records** *represented the beginning of the transition* **from written to recorded music.**

The Prehistory of Rock & Roll (1950)

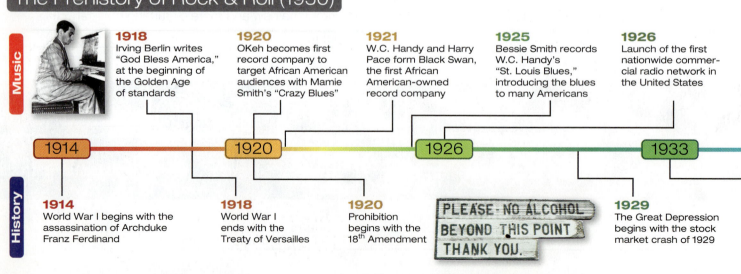

Music

1918
Irving Berlin writes "God Bless America," at the beginning of the Golden Age of standards

1920
OKeh becomes first record company to target African American audiences with Mamie Smith's "Crazy Blues"

1921
W.C. Handy and Harry Pace form Black Swan, the first African American-owned record company

1925
Bessie Smith records W.C. Handy's "St. Louis Blues," introducing the blues to many Americans

1926
Launch of the first nationwide commercial radio network in the United States

1914 — 1920 — 1926 — 1933

History

1914
World War I begins with the assassination of Archduke Franz Ferdinand

1918
World War I ends with the Treaty of Versailles

1920
Prohibition begins with the 18th Amendment

PLEASE · NO ALCOHOL BEYOND THIS POINT THANK YOU.

1929
The Great Depression begins with the stock market crash of 1929

part of variety shows before later integration with a new form of entertainment: Broadway musicals.

Tin Pan Alley—so called because of the sound of dozens of pianos playing all kinds of tunes at once—was once the center of the popular sheet music publishing world. Composers and lyricists churned out popular songs that were then copied and published in-house. **Song pluggers** were paid to get specific publishers' songs played and purchased then hawked the tunes all over the city. During the day they went to big department stores such as Macy's or Woolworth's to play their tunes for customers, and

at night to vaudeville venues where they tried to convince performers to incorporate new songs into their acts. This last method sometimes involved bribing vaudeville performers to perform particular songs in the hopes of increased exposure and therefore higher sheet music sales.

Irving Berlin, a song plugger who eventually became one of the most famous popular songwriters of all time, got his start by being paid to sing along with composer Harry von Tilzer's songs when they were being performed in vaudeville halls. The hierarchical structure of Tin Pan Alley was later somewhat replicated in the Brill Building on Broadway, where aspiring songwriters would work in small cubicles to write songs for various labels and artists (see Chapter 4).

Printed Music Becomes Primary

Tin Pan Alley, in its goal to publish music *for* the people but not necessarily *by* them, represented a huge shift in popular music and mass media that in some ways continues to this day. Composers wrote specifically for a popular audience. One successful writer, Harry von Tilzer, advised his younger colleagues to keep the range of their melodies small so that they could be sung by almost anyone (Starr and Waterman, 2003, 30).

In the late 1800s and early 1900s, the method of distribution for popular music was printed music. This allowed for mass distribution of the score of a single song or tune; however, distribution of a single

<<< Tin Pan Alley **was sometimes referred** to as a "songwriting ghetto" **because of the** cramped, tiny rooms **where songwriters worked.**

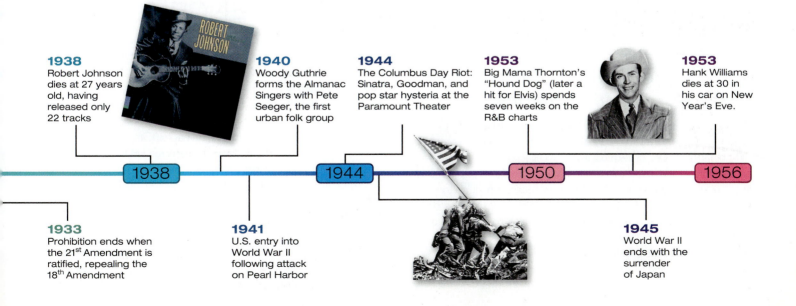

1938
Robert Johnson dies at 27 years old, having released only 22 tracks

1940
Woody Guthrie forms the Almanac Singers with Pete Seeger, the first urban folk group

1944
The Columbus Day Riot: Sinatra, Goodman, and pop star hysteria at the Paramount Theater

1953
Big Mama Thornton's "Hound Dog" (later a hit for Elvis) spends seven weeks on the R&B charts

1953
Hank Williams dies at 30 in his car on New Year's Eve.

1938 — 1944 — 1950 — 1956

1933
Prohibition ends when the 21st Amendment is ratified, repealing the 18th Amendment

1941
U.S. entry into World War II following attack on Pearl Harbor

1945
World War II ends with the surrender of Japan

RAGTIME a "rag" is a derivation of an African American term describing the process of syncopating a piece of music.

SYNCOPATED describing the state in which the accent of a measure of music falls either between the beat or on a beat not normally accented.

STANDARDS songs with predictable forms written during the Golden Age that were commonly interpreted by many performers.

R.P.M. revolutions per minute, or the speed at which a record rotates on a turntable; the quicker the speed, the less information can be encoded per square inch of vinyl.

RADIO NETWORK a series of linked commercial radio stations, allowing for live broadcasts to be transmitted across the country.

ELECTRICAL RECORDING method of recording that utilizes an amplified microphone to capture and transmit sound to an electromechanical record engraver.

CROONING an exaggerated style of singing that developed with the invention of the electric microphone, allowing for more intimacy than was previously possible with acoustic megaphones.

performance was not yet possible. In this way, the score preceded the performance, something that had been commonplace in classical music but was now available in popular music as well. This mass production had a few downsides that led to homogenization; customers of varying skills had to be able to play the scores themselves, so innovation and virtuosity did not generally sell well. Although the music incorporated elements of other styles such as **ragtime** music, it still tended to be simpler than the highly **syncopated** rags of Scott Joplin.

THE "GOLDEN AGE" OF TIN PAN ALLEY: 1920s AND 1930s

Tin Pan Alley's "Golden Age" is the source of many of the **standards** that we have today, including some that have been reinterpreted and replayed for almost a century now. These songs were a part of the Broadway musicals of that era, which had by and large replaced vaudeville theaters as the primary proponents of new popular music. However, for much of the early part of the Golden Age, the musicals were merely vehicles for the songs; the shows themselves were largely forgettable. Where present-day Broadway show tunes often expand on the thoughts of a particular character, a song like "I Got Rhythm" employs a vaguer lyricism, making it possible for other performers to reinterpret it. Golden Age songs tend toward thematic and formal conservatism and sometimes employ nostalgic elements—a hit for Depression audiences looking for an escape. In many ways, these standards bear much greater resemblance to modern-day pop and rock songs than to today's Broadway show tunes.

Golden Age Successes

The greatest artists of the Golden Age wrote many songs and scores for Broadway stage musicals, and the songs themselves have generally outlasted the musicals. Many of the composers are still very well known: Irving Berlin ("God Bless America," "White Christmas"), Richard Rodgers with both Lorenz Hart and Oscar Hammerstein II (the musical *Oklahoma!* in 1943), Cole Porter (the musical *Kiss Me Kate*), and the brothers George and Ira Gershwin ("I Got Rhythm," the musical *Porgy and Bess*). These composers' diverse output ranged from Berlin's decidedly prolific career—899 songs still in print in 1969 (Starr and Waterman 2003, 64)—to the double entendres and witty social commentary of the Ivy League-educated Cole Porter. George Gershwin, who also composed the orchestral work *Rhapsody in Blue*, did much to bring the classical and popular audiences together, while Richard Rodgers, writing the songs for many hit musicals, worked to develop the Broadway musical as a coherent art form. These composers exemplify the work ethic and versatility that were required to succeed as a Tin Pan Alley writer.

>>> Irving Berlin, **the most prolific of the Tin Pan Alley composers, has many songs that are** still popular today.

HOW DID NEW TECHNOLOGIES INFLUENCE MUSICAL STYLES?

Technological Breakthroughs Create a New Audience

Between 1900 and the mid-1930s, the most influential form of dissemination for music moved from printed sheet music to 78 **r.p.m.** records to radio broadcasts. One of the most significant effects of this transition from printed to recorded music was a shift in how audiences received music. In the past, people had used sheet music to perform popular songs at home, with audiences standing around the piano, a middle-class parlor staple. Now, however, people were able to listen to the radio or to records, changing both the economics and the production of music.

During the Great Depression, radio was favored over the phonograph, Radio was free to listen to, and with the start of commercial radio in 1920 and **radio networks** in 1926, listeners could tap into national sources of information and entertainment. In fact, the Depression hurt the record companies so much that their sales dove from $106 million in 1921 to $6 million in 1933 (Gillet 1996, 4). Record sales of the new "swing" music by big bands made up much of the recovery in sales to $44 million by 1939, but it was the post-war boom that really improved the health of the recording industry. The audience that emerged at the end of the war was a much younger one than had previously existed. Teenagers now had money to spend, and much of this money went to music.

RECORDING TAKES HOLD

With the development of commercial radio and record players, music listening became at least potentially a private activity. In 1919, the Victor Company released the first hit song ever popularized as a recording *before* it was issued as sheet music. Later that same year, the Victor Company

Black Swan Records

Although recording technologies were becoming increasingly popular for music distribution, in 1920, there were no recording studios that would allow African American artists to record their work. To remedy this, in 1921, Harry Herbert Pace created the Pace Phonograph Corporation, Inc, later renamed Black Swan Records. Pace believed that there was a large market for these artists' work, although he had not been able to convince the large recording studios: "Companies would not entertain any thought of recording a colored musician or colored voice. I therefore decided to form my own company and make such recordings as I believed would sell" (Scott 2001).

Pace signed on artists such as Fletcher Henderson, Ethel Waters, and Revella Hughes, and consumers quickly proved that Pace had been correct in his beliefs. However, this success came with a cost. After the completion of a successful tour, other recording companies began signing African American singers, and Black Swan lost its competitive edge. Pace closed its doors in 1924. However, this company took a major step in helping African American artists break into the recording industry and paved the way for the rock & roll artists to come.

produced the first record to sell more than a million copies. In this recording—the Selvin Novelty Orchestra's "Dardanella"—listeners could hear "Oriental"-sounding banjos and saxophones, sounds that would certainly have been difficult to transcribe as piano-based sheet music.

Even though more musicians began recording their work, most performers continued to see live performance and sheet music as their main way to make a buck. However, practical home sound reproduction—products such as the radio and the phonograph—continued to improve, making recorded music a cheaper, more viable option for personal listening. In the mid-1920s national record sales overtook sheet music for the first time ever. Because rock & roll revolved around the recording studio, this commercial feat marks a momentous shift in the conditions that would lead to the emergence of the genre.

POPULAR MUSIC AND THE NATIONAL SCENE

In 1926, the National Broadcasting Company (NBC) launched one of the first nationwide commercial radio networks in the United States, heralding the beginning of a new market for popular music. Now listeners in Chicago could hear live performances by singers in New York, laying the groundwork for national music celebrity. Radio networks and mass-distributed phonographs allowed for regional artists to reach a wider audience without necessarily displacing or destroying regional scenes.

However, the lack of any electric amplification required an exaggerated style of singing; the nuance of today's recording was impossible with the acoustic megaphones that vocalists had to use. In the days of acoustic recording, the entire band played into a large megaphone, with the singer at the front; a needle engraved the record mechanically in one take, with no mixing board—a fixture in any modern recording studio. In this early studio, the singer practically had to shout over the band to be heard on the recording. By the 1920s, the development of **electrical recording**, which utilized an amplified microphone to capture and transmit sound information to an electromechanical record cutting mechanism, allowed singers to sing at a more natural volume. Without having to shout, singers could deliver performances that gave vocal recordings a novel feeling of intimacy. This pseudo-intimacy led to a new style of singing, called **crooning**, begun by Bing Crosby and developed by two of the great crooners: Frank Sinatra and Nat "King" Cole.

ROCK TECHNOLOGY ▶▶▶ Electrical Recording

The electrical recording system marked a huge change in American popular music. Without having to shout into a large, acoustic megaphone, singers could now convey a large range of emotion and intimacy in their recordings. Crooners such as Bing Crosby, Frank Sinatra, and Nat "King" Cole used this refined amplification technology to concentrate on pitch and sensitivity in their interpretations, leading to a wide variety of singing styles.

Although this originality was supposedly the goal, Sinatra wrote in 1974 that "everybody was trying to copy the Crosby style—the casual kind of raspy sound in the throat," but it occurred to Sinatra that "maybe the world didn't need another Crosby." Sinatra developed a new technique centered on the electric microphone, in which the microphone was more like an instrument than an accessory to the natural human voice. Indeed, for Sinatra the microphone was an extension of his singing technique. He modeled his technical control of the microphone after instrumentalists in much "the way that Tommy [Dorsey] played his trombone." (Starr and Waterman, 2003, 158–159). Without the need to shout into a megaphone, Sinatra could afford to sing an entire phrase without taking a breath. The expressive qualities of this *bel canto* singing, modeled after the Italian operatic style, were a huge hit with audiences across the United States (Morris, 2009).

The new technology also allowed for national stardom on unprecedented levels. Crosby and other crooners were arguably the first national superstars, in part because listeners felt a connection to their personal lives through the intimacy of their voices.

WHAT MUSICAL STYLES PREFIGURED ROCK & ROLL?

THE JAZZ CRAZE

Beginning around World War I, an influential "jazz craze" swept both the United States and Europe. This jazz craze followed a short-lived ragtime craze led by composer Scott Joplin. Joplin began by studying classical music theory, but while working as a café pianist developed a style that improvised on themes of well-known songs. These "rags" caught on because of their heavy rhythmic syncopation, which was practically unknown in most music popular among white audiences.

Jazz, born in New Orleans of Caribbean and African influences, also relied heavily on syncopation. New Orleans was home to many populations and cultures, particularly French, the people who lived there often came together for weekend musical performances in city parks or town hall dances. These gatherings allowed people from diverse backgrounds to share their various music styles with one another. The proximity of New Orleans to the Caribbean also contributed to jazz's growth in the city, as it brought high-energy dance bands that added loud percussion, wind, or brass instruments to the more standard lineup of string bass, guitar, violin, or even banjo. These dance bands did what ragtime pianists did to the rhythms of European marches—except they did it all at once, improvising together. Their music crossed racial lines, as white audiences sought out the illicit thrills of the hybrid African American **hot music** in the Tenderloin district of New Orleans. Jazz specifically targeted a dance audience, and the genre caught on like wildfire.

A Victim of Its Own Success

Paul Whiteman's Ambassador Orchestra was the most commercially successful jazz ensemble of the 1920s. Although Whiteman was an excellent businessman who helped defend jazz against its mostly white detractors, his orchestra played a non-threatening, severely attenuated form of the music originally imported from New Orleans to white audiences around the United States. This early example of white mainstreaming of African American music was replicated again and again throughout the 20th century. Whiteman's staggering 150 top-selling records between 1920 and 1934 set the stage for hits such as Elvis's "Hound Dog."

In 1931, American novelist F. Scott Fitzgerald described the Jazz Age: "It was an age of miracles, it was an age of art, it was an age of excess, and it was an age of satire" (Fitzgerald 1996, xvi). Indeed, Fitzgerald's writing gives a good picture of what could be called America's first youth-culture phenomenon. Usually rich and carefree, Fitzgerald's flappers saw jazz as a way to rebel against their parents' 19th-century morality, but African Americans were nowhere to be seen. Whiteman's Orchestra was relevant in this regard, particularly because it promised some contact with the exotic, exciting new musical form, without actually requiring any contact with the people who were truly responsible for it. Although it is easy to get caught up denigrating this generation for its exclusion of African Americans—Whiteman's band was completely white, made "multicultural" by its mixture of European heritages—it did set the stage for the upcoming swing bands, some of whom were pioneers in integration.

THE SWING BANDS GET IN THE MOOD

In the late 1920s, a new style of jazz music called "swing" sprang up. Led by celebrity bandleaders, swing bands were more like Paul Whiteman's Orchestra in size and like Dixieland dance bands in their emphasis on professionalism.

MAJOR SWING BANDS AND BANDLEADERS

In 1939, the Glenn Miller Orchestra ruled the charts for 12 weeks with "In the Mood," a 12-bar blues-based swing tune. **William "Count" Basie**, a blues pianist and bandleader, exemplified the Kansas City blues style. Bandleader Duke Ellington took a unique experimental approach to his band, developing new instrumental combinations and harmonies. His fusion of various elements of American music from the minstrel song to ragtime to Tin Pan Alley to the blues in his own style made him one of the most important musicians and composers of the 20th century.

Famed trombonist Tommy Dorsey led several bands during his career. Dorsey—who often played ballads—had a pure tone and a gift for phrasing that some consider unmatched to this day. Dubbed the "King of Swing" by radio stations, **Benny Goodman** was a clarinetist. His popularity among the white population soared despite Goodman being the first major bandleader to integrate his band, hiring African American pianist Teddy Williams, guitarist Charlie Christian, and vibraphonist Lionel Hampton.

∧
∧ Paul Whiteman's Ambassador
∧ Orchestra **achieved unprecedented commercial success.**

The Big Band Singers Go Solo

Although the big bands struck a chord with listeners amidst the increased

The Columbus Day Riot in 1944 was the first example of pop hysteria. Sinatra had bought out his contract with Tommy Dorsey's band, and in 1942 he debuted with Benny Goodman's band at the Paramount Theater. By 1944 when they returned for another concert, Sinatra had become a huge sensation. Thirty thousand fans showed up for tickets at the 3,600-seat Paramount Theater. When audience members—many teenage girls included—refused to leave after the first show, there was a riot. Sinatra's fans followed him everywhere, sometimes falling into a "Sinatrance." As the quote from the concerned anonymous writer at the beginning of this chapter predicted—albeit a bit too rashly—this was just the beginning of what would become a series of celebrity pop stars.

optimism at the end of the Great Depression, they did not last through the end of World War II for myriad reasons. During the war, band members were drafted into the army, and the wartime audience was more focused on supporting the troops than on attending dances. It became expensive for bands to tour, and wartime gas rationing made fueling vehicles difficult. Meanwhile, public tastes changed and the big band audience for shrunk. Even as the big bands declined, however, the singers who had performed with them took off. The most charismatic singers, such as Nat "King" Cole, Rosemary Clooney, and Frank Sinatra, went solo, and the new crooner era revisited the standards of the Golden Age just as the big bands had before them.

Nat "King" Cole introduced the world to the idea of the still widely imitated drumless trio with Cole on piano, accompanied by guitar and bass. The most successful African American recording star of the post-war decade, Cole enjoyed crossover success by scoring hits on both the race (rhythm & blues) and pop charts. Like Cole, Rosemary Clooney and Peggy Lee had their starts in the swing era and became successful solo artists. Both recorded with the illustrious Frank Sinatra—quite possibly the first "teen idol" in American popular music—during their careers.

Race Records and the Blues

If Tin Pan Alley catered to mostly white, middle-class audiences shopping for sheet music at department stores, then the blues did just the opposite originally. Music labels originally referred to blues and jazz records as **race records**, although this was not necessarily intended as a derogatory term. As some of the first recordings made by and for African Americans, race records initially catered to black audiences in the rural South. The first African American-owned record company, Black Swan, was founded in 1921 to record and distribute such recordings. Entering the record business proved difficult for Black Swan, however, as many white-owned companies attempted to hamper Black Swan's success. For example, one white-owned company bought out a local pressing plant to stop Black Swan

from manufacturing race records. Despite such obstacles, Black Swan found a way to produce its first record. The company's success provided it with the resources to buy its own pressing plant, eliminating all obstacles from the company's competitors. By the 1920s, Southern music such as the blues reached new audiences because of migration from the South to Northern cities including Chicago. These changing demographics opened up new markets, as people moving to the cities still wanted to hear Southern-influenced music, and people remaining in

Breakdown of "Race Music" Record Releases in the 1920s and 1930s

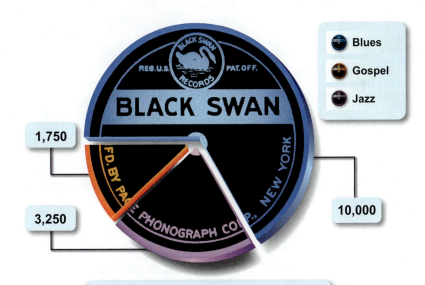

- Blues
- Gospel
- Jazz

1,750

3,250

10,000

Total "race music" records: 15,000

Source: St. James Encyclopedia of Popular Culture, "Race Records," http://findarticles.com/p/articles/mi_g1epc/is_tov_2419101005.

> **"Race music"** was the general term used for all music, including jazz, gospel, and the blues, aimed at an African American audience.

HILLBILLY RECORDS the country music of the rural South; analogous to "race records" in terms of the audience targeted.

COUNTRY BLUES a rough style of blues performed by Robert Johnson and others; also called "delta blues," after the Mississippi Delta.

RIFF a repeated musical phrase, used often in jazz and swing music, and later in rock & roll.

rural communities often had friends in the city who introduced them to new hit records.

Migration also expanded the audience for **hillbilly**, or country music, aimed toward white, rural audiences rather than toward the more general pop record audiences. Although blues and country were targeted at segregated—and therefore limited—markets under the labels of "race" and "hillbilly" music, the effects of the migration carried these styles, formerly limited to the South, to a much larger, national audience.

SURPRISE HITS FIND A MARKET

In 1920, the OKeh Record Company planned to have Jewish American singer Sophie Tucker record the blues song "Crazy Blues." When Tucker became ill, Perry Bradford, the song's composer, persuaded OKeh to bring in African American singer Mamie Smith to record the song. The record company was pleased when this decision resulted in a surprise hit song. Although the record company was based in New York, its director Ralph Peer—who was responsible for the term "race music"—made trips to the South, bringing equipment with him and setting up studios on the road. This was a new effort to tap into underserved markets, as the major labels primarily focused on white, urban audiences. When Mamie Smith recorded "Crazy Blues" and OKeh advertised it in black communities, it sold a profitable 7,500 copies. In 1921, W.C. Handy and Harry Pace founded Black Swan, while Paramount Records opened in 1922 as the second white-owned company to market race music in addition to its other music offerings. These small-label successes inspired the major labels to enter the "race record" field: Columbia in 1923, Vocalion/Brunswick in 1926, and even Victor, who had rejected Mamie Smith in 1920, in 1927.

Because African American musicians rarely received radio exposure and live venues were subject to segregation, records were the primary source of musical exchange between black and white audiences. Because of this, records were in very high demand beginning in 1920 and eventually culminating in 1927 with around 500 race records released yearly. However, these artists were often paid far less than their white counterparts, and their songs, which had not previously been published, were then owned by record companies, which collected royalties without giving any money to the artists.

COUNTRY BLUES

Country blues began in the rural South around the Mississippi Delta and East Texas. Although there were many different styles of country blues recorded in the South, this region produced the most popular and influential style: delta blues. Country blues began as a purely oral tradition, passed down in a flexible form by musicians who changed both the lyrics to suit their own experiences and the music to fit those lyrics. The lyrics were not only personal but also gritty, both in content and in singing and instrumental style.

Even though the 12-bar blues tunes of the swing era hold to steady, written forms, the non-notated nature of country blues often led musicians to add or subtract beats at will, ending up with odd numbers of bars. Some innovative country blues forms could be based just on a single **riff** (with no accompanying chords), or just move between two chords. Most of all, country blues was fundamentally rough, employing vocal slides and styles much closer to speech than traditional singing, with songs that seemingly had no origin or finished rendition. A few country blues musicians managed to find widespread success, albeit well after they had died.

Blind Lemon Jefferson, Robert Johnson, and Muddy Waters

A few important figures in the history of country blues stand out, for both their representative approaches to the blues and their influences on later forms of music. Blind Lemon Jefferson was born in East Texas in 1897. He released his first recordings in 1926, and although he died poor in 1929—Paramount Records denied him royalties—he was one of the first stars of the genre, marketed as "old-fashioned blues" well after other artists had popularized a smoother form of blues.

Although Jefferson was the first star, Robert Johnson and Muddy Waters were probably most influential on later rock musicians. Johnson died young, living from 1911 to 1938 and releasing just 22 songs, which sold poorly during his lifetime. He was primarily an entertainer, but many of his blues songs were not necessarily indicative of the type of blues being played by many other musicians at the time. However, he did achieve success posthumously and inspired many contemporary musicians decades after his death; Eric Clapton covered Johnson's song "Crossroad Blues," and many guitarists, from Jimmy Page (Led Zeppelin) to Keith Richards (the Rolling Stones) emulated his guitar licks. Part of the reason for this was the mythology surrounding Johnson and other blues players of his time; it was rumored that Johnson had sold his soul to the devil in exchange for his guitar-playing skills and that he would turn his back to audiences in performance so that they couldn't see what his fingers were doing. However great the myths, the music persisted as something even greater for decades to come.

Muddy Waters was the only one of these three musicians to leave the Mississippi Delta. While in Mississippi in the late 1930s, Alan Lomax,

∧ ∧ ∧ **Robert Johnson was mythologized after his death at a young age, and** he strongly influenced later rock musicians.

a collector of folksongs in the 1930s and early 1940s, recorded Waters for the Library of Congress. Shortly after making those recordings, Waters moved to Chicago, picked up an electric guitar, and by the early 1950s was the most popular blues musician in Chicago. (You will read more about Lomax and his field recordings of musician Lead Belly in Chapter 5.) These early field and commercial recordings of country blues artists are the beginning of the knowable history of the music—the rest is in the songs themselves.

"CLASSIC" BLUES AND THE SMOOTHER SOUND

The "classic" blues of the early 20th century differed from their country counterparts. Although influenced by the styles of the Mississippi Delta, they were filtered through the lens of Tin Pan Alley and the sheet music publishing industry. Because of this, the strong structures of the Tin Pan Alley songs made their way into the construction of the country blues, and blues forms including 12-bar and 16-bar structures were finalized. As European notation did not account for the multitude of sounds that blues singers produced, much less the bends and bottleneck slides that were the trademarks of blues guitar, the publication of blues in sheet music format led to a homogenizing and smoothing of the delta blues' roughness. Initially, the blues songs that actually made it to publication were mostly written by professional composers seeking to make a profit by marketing these songs to mostly middle-class audiences. Mamie Smith's recording of "Crazy Blues," the surprise hit for OKeh records, was one of these blues songs. However, even though it was a hit with both black and white audiences, "Crazy Blues" did not quite achieve the huge crossover success that **W.C. Handy** did.

When Bessie Smith recorded W.C. Handy's "St. Louis Blues" in 1925, it was the first time many Americans— white and black alike— had ever heard some

W.C. HANDY one of the most successful African American Tin Pan Alley composers, and the artist responsible for bringing some version of the blues to a wide audience.

version of the blues. Bessie Smith, joined by Gertrude "Ma" Rainey, performed classic blues songs mostly for working-class African American populations in Chicago and New York. W.C. Handy himself was one of the forces behind the popular blues movement, both as a co-founder of Black Swan records and as a composer and lyricist, his "St. Louis Blues" foremost among them. However, the difference between Smith's recording of Handy's song and the country blues of Johnson is unmistakable: The strong chord changes alone make it more European in feel, and the form is a solid 12-bar unit rather than the mostly arbitrary forms of country blues artists.

St. Louis Blues

Handy's achievement is not to be understated; the poet T.S. Eliot called the song's opening line, "I hate to see the evening sun go down," the most perfect line of iambic pentameter verse in the English language. Shakespeare, Milton, Wordsworth, and Eliot

>>> **The blues was a mixture of many styles and influenced a variety of other musical genres.**

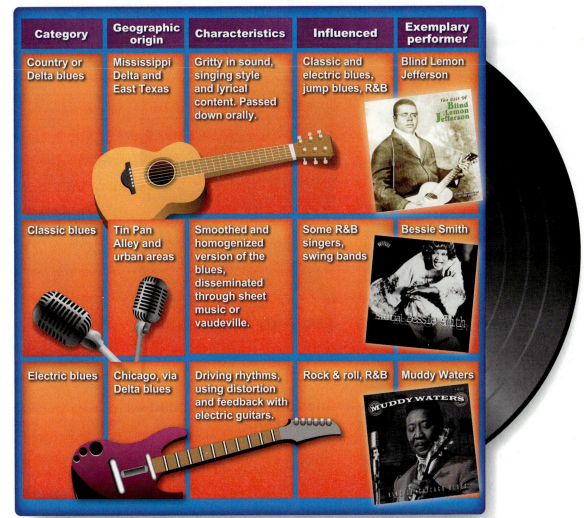

Category	Geographic origin	Characteristics	Influenced	Exemplary performer
Country or Delta blues	Mississippi Delta and East Texas	Gritty in sound, singing style and lyrical content. Passed down orally.	Classic and electric blues, jump blues, R&B	Blind Lemon Jefferson
Classic blues	Tin Pan Alley and urban areas	Smoothed and homogenized version of the blues, disseminated through sheet music or vaudeville.	Some R&B singers, swing bands	Bessie Smith
Electric blues	Chicago, via Delta blues	Driving rhythms, using distortion and feedback with electric guitars.	Rock & roll, R&B	Muddy Waters

himself used iambic pentameter meter, which has lines that are five "feet" with an unstressed syllable followed by a stressed syllable. Eliot gave credence to the idea that an African American artist could be as artistically successful as the canonical writers of the English language.

Handy's version of the blues soon became popular among both black and white communities. Performances like Bessie Smith's retained strong elements of the blues tradition, such as the prominent use of **blue notes** and the free rhythmic syncopation that Smith adds to Handy's already-syncopated rhythms. Certainly, Handy's version was a huge hit with white audiences, but it was also a hit with black audiences as well.

HOW DID CROSSOVER HITS PAVE THE WAY FOR ROCK & ROLL?

Blues Goes Electric

By the end of World War II, traditional delta blues had more or less died out. However, when Muddy Waters moved from the delta to Chicago, he began using an electric guitar to be heard over the noise of the crowds in the city's tiny blues clubs. This Chicago-style "electric blues" employed the bottleneck slides of delta blues but had a driving pulse from the heavy rhythm section of bass, piano, and drums. Just as Robert Johnson managed to get otherworldly sounds from his guitar, Waters's technique of eliciting new harmonic effects with his slide certainly prefigured rock & roll's use of the electric guitar as a special effect as much as an instrument. Waters's sound was more urban than that of his country blues predecessors, with its driving beat and use of modern sound capabilities.

Folk Begins with the Depression

The Great Depression all but wiped out the markets for race records, and African American families especially had very little extra money to spend on records. Network radio grew to fill the gap, but exposure on these radio networks was generally restricted to white musicians. Although the commercial blues was nearly destroyed and generally saccharine Tin Pan Alley songs tended to fill radio broadcasting, hillbilly music had measured success relative to other genres with 25 percent of the total market (Starr and Waterman 2003, 113). Because blues artists couldn't get radio play and the race record companies were either going under or being bought up, the only real proponent of working-class concerns such as poverty, mass migration, and economic disaster was hillbilly music, soon to become known as country music.

During the Depression, millions of rural poor were displaced, moving across the country or moving to the cities. Country music flourished

as a result, alternating nostalgia and idealization of rural life with a realistic accounting of the problems facing many people. **Woody Guthrie**, a particularly talented young country musician, charged his music with political relevance, developing a form of folk music that was emulated for decades thereafter.

WOODY GUTHRIE

Woodrow Wilson "Woody" Guthrie was one of the foremost early folk musicians, beginning his career singing hillbilly music but becoming more political after his time as an impoverished migrant traveling from Oklahoma to California. Guthrie's music reflected experiences from his nomadic lifestyle as he crisscrossed the country. He eventually headed north and east to New York, where he took a decidedly political stance with his music. He wrote the politically charged songs "This Land is Your Land" and "Talking Dust Bowl Blues," and once the Depression was over, he was mostly known as a protest singer.

In 1940 in New York, Guthrie joined Pete Seeger's Almanac Singers, which sustained Guthrie's political approach. Guthrie's populist appeal was clear, but he didn't achieve success until later in life. You will read more about Guthrie and his work in Chapter 5.

∧
∧ **Woody Guthrie** finally
∧ settled in New York **after traveling all around the country** during the Depression.

URBAN FOLK: FROM GUTHRIE TO SEEGER

The Almanac Singers disbanded in 1942, but two of them—Lee Hays and **Pete Seeger**—recruited two other musicians and formed the Weavers in 1949. The first "urban" folk group, the Weavers had huge hits playing folk songs by such artists as Lead Belly and Woody Guthrie. The Weavers borrowed from the aesthetics of the hillbilly music of the rural United States, but they were New Yorkers in their urban lyrics and cosmopolitan sensibilities. Their hits ranged from the early Guthrie folk tunes to "Wimoweh (The Lion Sleeps Tonight)," an adaptation (and accidental misspelling of "Mbube," Zulu for "lion") of a South African song.

TOP OF THE CHARTS
WHAT'S HOT!
APRIL 11, 1945

1. "Dream" – Pied Pipers
2. "There, I've Said It Again" – Vaughn Monroe Orchestra
3. "If I Loved You" – Perry Como
4. "The More I See You" – Dick Haynes
5. "Sentimental Journey" – Les Brown Orchestra
6. "I Don't Care Who Knows It" – Harry James Orchestra
7. "You Belong to My Heart" – Bing Crosby
8. "Bell Bottom Trousers" – Tony Pastor Orchestra
9. "Gotta Be This or That" – Benny Goodman Orchestra

Mary (for more on folk music, see Chapter 5). In this way, their aura of independence paradoxically allowed record companies to profit from their appeal to urban, educated markets.

The Beginning of Country

As millions of Americans moved from rural areas to urban centers, they sang about two things: the past and the present. The songs were nostalgic for times before the mechanization of agriculture, but they were also evocative of the restless, migrant nature of rural displacement. At the aesthetic roots of country music was a strong link to the English folk ballad tradition, much like the urban folk music that would come later. The narrative of these ballads contrasts sharply with the lyrical Tin Pan Alley tunes; the ballads often mention specific names and places and are passed down through folk traditions, rather than published and copyrighted.

The first star of country music, somewhat analogous to Robert Johnson in the blues tradition, was Jimmie Rodgers, "The Singing Brakeman." Like Johnson, Rodgers died young; he contracted tuberculosis and passed away at age 27. He hung out with hobos and cowboys, collecting their songs and writing his own songs about them. Rodgers's "blue yodel" recordings, or songs that combined blues music with yodeling, reflected the reckless attitudes of the hobos and cowboys with whom he associated, making him an early prototype of the "too fast to live, too young to die" mythology of rock stars. Rodgers's 13 blue yodel recordings (all named "Blue Yodel") were simply numbered "No. 11" or "No. 8 [Muleskinner Blues]." Although he accompanied himself on guitar, his playing never reached the level of Johnson or other blues musicians; rather, it maintained the lyric-driven folk tradition, with the guitar as an accompanying instrument.

THE CARTER FAMILY

The Carter Family were perhaps the most important performers in country music's early history. They were made up of A.P. "Doc" Carter, his

Although his façade was folksy, banjo player and songwriter Pete Seeger was politically active to the point that he and two of the other Weavers were accused of being Communists during the McCarthy era. This mix of world music, political activism, and rural instruments confounded the record labels. Seeger and the rest of the Weavers placed a premium on authenticity and operating outside the system. Nevertheless, after Decca Records dropped them from their label amid accusations of communism, the Weavers did not again make the pop charts. However, their music paved the way for the future success of other urban folk performers, including Bob Dylan and Peter, Paul, and

CLASSIC RECORDINGS ▶▶▶

"GOODNIGHT IRENE," by The Weavers (written by Lead Belly)

The Weavers' biggest hit, "Goodnight Irene," reached number one on the pop charts in 1950. Written by Huddie "Lead Belly" Ledbetter, the song has a tangled history. Lead Belly originally learned the tune from his uncle and added verses as he pleased throughout his life, including his stints in prison. He was pardoned in 1923, but ended up in prison again until he recorded "Irene" with Alan Lomax for the Library of Congress in 1934. He later received his pardon for good behavior and sang "Goodnight, Irene" as his theme song until his death in Manhattan in 1949.

The Weavers' version was more suited for a sing-along than Lead Belly's, especially the repeating chorus, "Irene goodnight, Irene goodnight." This probably helped them reach the top of the pop charts. In addition, they omitted the final verse of Lead Belly's song, with its reference to the distraught lover using morphine to ease his pain. That same article described the Weavers' version as "prettied up and cut in half." Indeed, the Weavers and their record label did not necessarily intend this song to be as big as it was; it was a **B-side** to another one of their hits, "Tzena, Tzena, Tzena."

During this era, B-sides were largely considered "filler" tracks. Most groups were releasing **singles**, which were usually 45 or 78 r.p.m. records with about three minutes of possible music on each side. These usually contained an A-side featuring the song that the group was promoting and a B-side to fill the extra space. As technology began to improve, **albums**, or collections of songs on a slower-turning, larger record (33 1/3 r.p.m.), began to replace singles. However, these albums were initially just collections of unrelated singles, and it was not until some of the conceptual albums outlined in Chapter 6 that they began to have real coherence and structure. The term "B-side" is still used today to refer to recorded tracks that did not make the original album; many bands put out whole albums of B-sides from previous recording sessions.

THE WEAVERS
1949–1953

Goodnight Irene

Population Change from Migration, 1900–1930

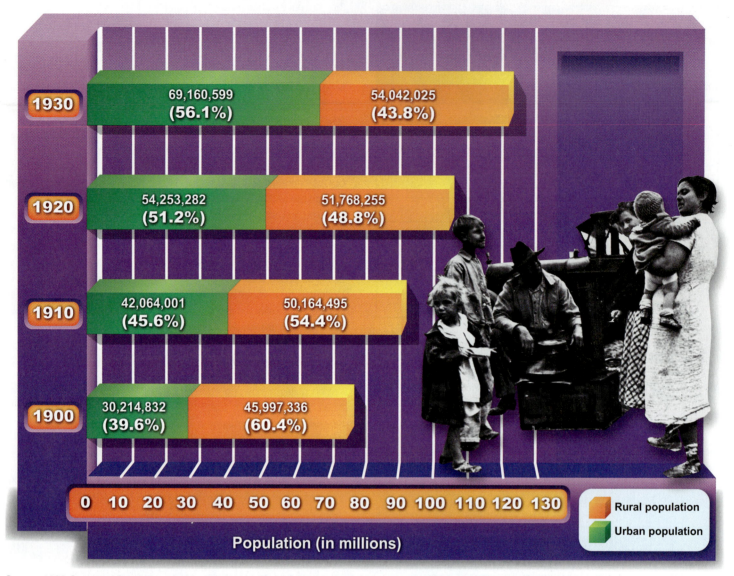

1930 69,160,599 **(56.1%)** 54,042,025 **(43.8%)**

1920 54,253,282 **(51.2%)** 51,768,255 **(48.8%)**

1910 42,064,001 **(45.6%)** 50,164,495 **(54.4%)**

1900 30,214,832 **(39.6%)** 45,997,336 **(60.4%)**

0 10 20 30 40 50 60 70 80 90 100 110 120 130

Population (in millions)

Rural population

Urban population

Source: 1990 Census of Population and Housing. "1990 Population and Housing Unit Counts: United States," (CPH-2); and 1980 PC80-1-1, http://www.census.gov/population/www/censusdata/hiscendata.html.

∧
∧ **Between the years 1900 and 1930,** the U.S. population shifted **from a** majority in
∧ rural areas **to a** majority in urban areas.

wife, Sara, and his sister-in-law, Maybelle. They recorded 300 songs, primarily between 1927 and 1941, and owed much to the folk tradition. Initially, Ralph Peer recorded them for RCA's record label. A.P. sang bass and collected and arranged the folk tunes he found in the country, then copyrighted them regardless of whether he had actually composed them. When Peer's company published the songs, he split the profits in half with A.P.

However, there were other reasons for the Carters' success. Maybelle, who played guitar, was primarily responsible for the guitar style that is associated with country music today: The chords are strummed on the higher strings on the off beats to accompany the singing with melodic "fills" on the bass strings in between. The Carters could be considered a parallel to the Sacred Harp tradition of singing;

unlike earlier country styles, where the guitar was merely a background accompaniment, this new style of music included sections where the guitar took a prominent role in the song. Their singing was also meant to be interactive and included audience participation rather than having the vocalist simply sing at listeners (Ellertson 2005). This added to the highly vocal, sing-along feel of country and western music, which remained influential in the genre.

ROY ACUFF, SINGING COWBOYS, AND CROSSOVER HITS

The swing era was called that for a reason—big bands filled the pop charts—but country music charts were still in a category all their own, and only occasionally did crossover hits find a popular audience. This was in part because the pop charts were concerned with the large urban centers, and the audience for country music lived mostly in the rural South. However, throughout the first third of the century, many rural Southerners were moving to these urban centers to escape the economic and ecological catastrophe of the Dust Bowl. This audience was ripe for the **crossover** hits that would eventually find their way into the standard repertoire of popular singers like Bing Crosby.

One of the first crossover hits, Roy Acuff's 1936 "Great Speckled Bird" took its name and theme from a Bible verse, which probably helped it become so successful. In addition, the song was based on a traditional melody that was repeated for each verse. Other crossover hits emerged because of the influence of Hollywood film. As Hollywood capitalized on the mythology of the West, associating it with the future and opportunity while still retaining traditional sounds, the "Singing Cowboy" persona became popular. Gene Autry was the first to become successful; by the time he played a small role in a Western film, he had already been a successful hillbilly performer. In this new role, he developed the image of the singing cowboy, both allowing country music to reach a wider audience and making it possible for later country music stars like Roy Rogers to be successful.

HYBRID STYLES: WESTERN SWING AND COUNTRY-LITE

Another side effect of Depression-era mass migration took things one step further than the crossover hits of the singing cowboys. One new style, "Western swing," arose in the mid-1930s when Bob Willis and his Texas Playboys began playing country-influenced swing music (or swing-influenced country music) in Oklahoma and the vicinity, eventually becoming very popular in California after World War II. Although Willis's songs were mostly derived from old country and fiddle tunes, his string band—including a banjo and guitars—was backed up by a full swing orchestra of trumpets, saxophones, and a rhythm section. The arrangements owe quite a bit to the swing music of the time, even though they may not have swung themselves.

Patti Page was a singer who did not necessarily have the same hybrid qualities as Bob Willis, but she drew on influences from country

VVV Technological developments in the early 20th century transformed the landscape of American popular music.

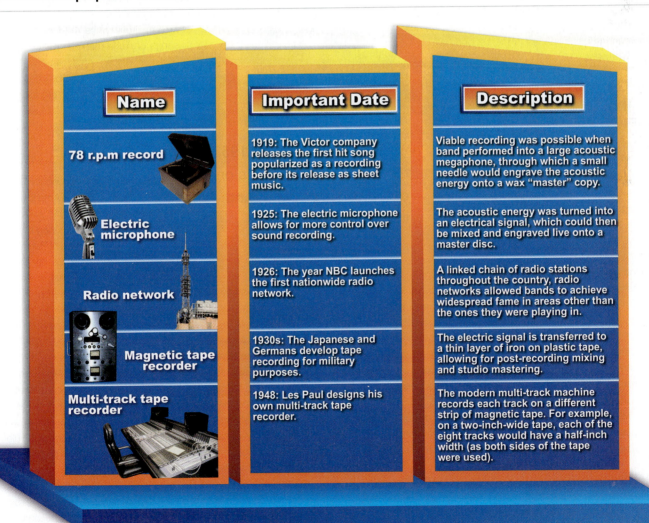

Name	Important Date	Description
78 r.p.m record	1919: The Victor company releases the first hit song popularized as a recording before its release as sheet music.	Viable recording was possible when band performed into a large acoustic megaphone, through which a small needle would engrave the acoustic energy onto a wax "master" copy.
Electric microphone	1925: The electric microphone allows for more control over sound recording.	The acoustic energy was turned into an electrical signal, which could then be mixed and engraved live onto a master disc.
Radio network	1926: The year NBC launches the first nationwide radio network.	A linked chain of radio stations throughout the country, radio networks allowed bands to achieve widespread fame in areas other than the ones they were playing in.
Magnetic tape recorder	1930s: The Japanese and Germans develop tape recording for military purposes.	The electric signal is transferred to a thin layer of iron on plastic tape, allowing for post-recording mixing and studio mastering.
Multi-track tape recorder	1948: Les Paul designs his own multi-track tape recorder.	The modern multi-track machine records each track on a different strip of magnetic tape. For example, on a two-inch-wide tape, each of the eight tracks would have a half-inch width (as both sides of the tape were used).

music to become successful on the popular charts. In fact, Page was one of the most successful female singers of the 1950s, sometimes with cloying novelty songs such as "The Doggie in the Window." However, her biggest hit was a pop arrangement of a country song, "The Tennessee Waltz." This recording sold six million copies, on the strength of Southern nostalgia and sentimentality. Page sings harmony with herself on this recording, using **multi-track tape recording** to layer vocal parts, a process that would become standard for most music produced in the second half of the 20th century.

BLUEGRASS AND INSTRUMENTAL PROFICIENCY

Although bluegrass could not explicitly be called a backlash against the mainstreaming of country music, its style was focused on one of the original instrumental combinations: the **string band**. The label **bluegrass** comes from Bill Monroe's group formed in 1938, the Blue Grass Boys. The Blue Grass Boys' focus was a dual goal of both reaching back to the roots of the Southern, Anglo-American string band while maintaining a high level of instrumental proficiency. The tempos were fast and the music is primarily for instrumentalists, rather than the moderate tempos and lyrical lines of most pop tunes. There were also improvised solos, melding the format of African American blues and jazz with the Southern string band sound. However, there was a distinct style of singing that went with bluegrass music often called "high lonesome" singing. Practiced by the Carter Family, this style that reached back to the traditional singing of the Appalachian Mountains. Bluegrass music never had much commercial potential, however. Its focus on the instrumentalists, the unique singing, and the open-ended format assumed a degree of familiarity among its audience that did not translate well to the mass market.

Genre-Bending Country Hits

There was one true country music star whose songs translated across the charts, and that was **Hank Williams**. Williams had 36 Top 10 country records between 1947 and 1953. When he died at the age of 30, his songs went on to become hits for all kinds of performers. Williams was born devastatingly poor in Alabama, but after performing on the street as a child, he got his own radio show and started the band the Drifting Cowboys at age 16. Although he was greatly successful by his mid-20s, he became dependent on alcohol and painkillers and died from a heart attack in the back of his car on New Year's Day, 1953. Much like Jimmie Rodgers, Williams's early death only heightened the intrigue of his life and work.

Even though Hank Williams's recording career was short, he is considered by many as the most important country star of all time. He melded traditional country music, with its fiddles and string-band setup, with modern and forward-looking instruments like the steel guitar. The drawl of his voice set the tone for much of the lonesome sound of country music, since his Southern twang made the sound of the words as important as their meaning. He included honky-tonk themes in his songs, with lyrics about doing wrong and having wrong being done. However, his recording career was only part of the reason for his success. His songs themselves went on to become huge hits for performers across the charts, especially mainstream pop musicians; it seemed as though his songs instantly appealed to a wide audience if the country twang was replaced with a mainstream pop sound. The young performer Tony Bennett even recorded one of Williams's songs, "Cold, Cold Heart," which stayed at number one on the pop chart for six weeks. His other hits are familiar in many incarnations as well, among them "Lovesick Blues," "Your Cheatin' Heart," and "I'm So Lonesome I Could Cry." This process of mainstream, urban white musicians covering the songs of niche markets—whether Southern white or African American "race music"—would only be amplified after producers managed to label the next big thing in African American music: rhythm & blues.

> ∧
> ∧ **Before his death in 1953,**
> ∧ Hank Williams **was one of the** most popular **and** influential country **music** performers.

Rhythm & Blues

As big bands declined in popularity, **rhythm & blues** restored an African American character to the swing style. Where swing took the blues and orchestrated it, using blues riffs and devices with the discipline of Paul Whiteman's band, R&B reached back to the ecstatic energy of New Orleans jazz. R&B bands still had horns—usually a couple of saxophones and brass—but they added a driving, bluesy electric guitar and hard-hitting drums to the mix. The "rhythm" part of rhythm & blues was the thriving energy, while the "blues" was the soulful singing style.

When the term "rhythm & blues" was first coined, it was meant to refer to all music made by or specifically for an African American audience. After the war, the major record companies in the "race market" realized that it was time to pick a new name to describe their target audience—perhaps something more euphemistic than "race." The record companies tried out different names, but in 1949 Billboard—with no particular explanation—changed the name of its "race" charts to "rhythm & blues." To this day, Billboard's "R&B/Hip-Hop" chart is almost exclusively dominated by African American artists. Even as the musical style has evolved into something worlds apart from the early rhythm & blues, the chart describes an audience as much as a musical style. Rhythm & blues became a catchall phrase for many different styles of music, much as rock & roll would later.

Louis Jordan

Louis Jordan and his Tympany Five was one of the most successful jump bands of the era and a clear forerunner of rock & roll. Jordan's band was a downsized swing bang,consisting of piano, string bass, drums, trumpet, and tenor saxophone, with Jordan both playing saxophone and singing. Jordan's singing had a lighter feeling then the shout and cry vocals of much of the earlier, bluesier R&B music, and his humorous, expressive vocals were his hallmark. Much of Jordan's popularity can be attributed to his vocal delivery. His voice clearly articulates each word, removing the slurred delivery that was popular with R&B singers of the era. This clear articulation undoubtedly helped his music gain footing with white audiences, as he only rises to a near shout in the last line of his hit "Choo-Choo Ch' Boogie." His most popular song, "Choo-Choo Ch' Boogie" followed the 12-bar blues structure of W.C. Handy's "St. Louis Blues" or Glenn Miller's "In the Mood." However, in Jordan's hands the form regains more of the original blues character and driving rhythm of African American R&B while still retaining the popular appeal of Miller and Handy.

Yet, certain writers have noticed that his lyrics can be read in a way that shows their appeal to black audiences. The lyrics contain "joking complaints about women of fate," while also "implying an unjust society" (Gillet 1996, 134). Whatever the reason for Jordan's widespread popularity, he was clearly influential on the future of music; major rock & roll figures such as Chuck Berry and James Brown have cited him as a primary influence (Starr and Waterman 2003, 170).

One of these R&B styles relied on a heavily downsized swing band and had a dynamic, energetic style that became known as "jump blues." The jump blues combos centered primarily on a strong rhythm section consisting of piano, guitar, bass, and drums with one or two saxophones. Rooted in the driving left hand of the pianist, the rhythm recalled the boogie-woogie patterns of the early part of the century.

The Dominoes and Doo-wop

Another strain of rhythm & blues in the years leading up to rock & roll was the "vocal harmony" group, described today as "doo-wop." A precursor to these vocal harmony groups was the Mills Brothers. Their 1942 hit "Paper Doll" spent an incredible 36 weeks on the pop charts. But it was the Dominoes, featuring the young tenor Clyde McPhatter, who successfully moved the vocal harmony format away from the smoother sound of the Mills Brothers and closer to the harder sounds of black gospel. Drawing heavily on the gospel tradition, this secular group appealed to an audience that grew up with a similar style of music in the black gospel church. The style paid off, as their 1952 hit "Have Mercy Baby" was in the top spot of the R&B charts for 10 weeks.

WOMEN AND RHYTHM & BLUES

The R&B charts of the early 1950s weren't just dominated by male groups. Some women had widespread success, among them Big Mama Thornton and Ruth Brown. Thornton was a powerful physical figure who delivered the first line of her first big hit with an earthy growl, "You ain't nothin' but a hound dog." "Hound Dog" was, in fact, written explicitly for her by two white college kids, Jerry Leiber and Mike Stoller, who went on to achieve success in the early days of rock & roll. This recording, which was on the R&B charts for seven weeks in 1953, is vastly different from the recording that would be made just three years later by Elvis Presley, after rock & roll had officially been born. Thornton's version sits at a slower tempo, and her singing is closer to the snarl of early blues artists than to Elvis's, which evokes Louis Jordan's cooler, ironic delivery. Either way, Thornton created her own interpretation of this song that gave it early and influential success.

Ruth Brown was about as far away from Thornton in style as possible while still occupying the very same charts. Her song "Mama, He Treats Your Daughter Mean" was written by professionals and recorded with horns and a full band, rather than Thornton's sparse setup of only a rhythm section and an electric guitar. However, Brown brought a gospel sound to her R&B recordings that clearly helped her audience appeal; "Mama" was in the top spot of the R&B charts for five weeks in 1953 and even reached number 23 on the pop charts—an impressive feat for any African American artist at the time.

Post-war Crossovers Become Rock & Roll

Despite all the genre distinctions of the decade after World War II, the crossover phenomenon was increasingly common. For example, Ray Charles combined features of gospel and country into a nascent R&B style in "I Got a Woman." This synthesis proved to be influential on later generations of performers. In any case, the music of the post-war decade would not be able to maintain its separateness for long, as was made clear by performers such as Louis Jordan, drawing on swing music, or Woody Guthrie, plying folk with a new urban sensibility. With the new, younger generation of teenage audiences and performers, music soon developed into what would seem—to an earlier audience—like a series of inexplicable crossover hits.

Review

Summary

WHAT WERE THE FIRST INFLUENCES OF ROCK & ROLL?   4

• The lyrical styles of Tin Pan Alley and Broadway show tunes moved away from the narrative tradition and toward a style of singing that could be interpreted differently by many performers. This departure allowed for "cover" songs, where one artist would play a song previously performed by an earlier artist.

• The music of the Tin Pan Alley's "Golden Age" included standards, or thematic songs that often employed nostalgic elements, making it possible for listeners to escape the dreariness of life around them due to the Great Depression.

HOW DID NEW TECHNOLOGIES INFLUENCE MUSICAL STYLES?   6

• Between 1900 and the mid-1930s, a shift occurred in the ways music was disseminated to the population. This transition moved from printed to recorded music, which helped make music more of a public event than a private one.

• The pseudo-intimacy of the electric microphone allowed for listeners to develop emotional connections to performers.

• The national radio networks allowed bands to earn fame in areas where they weren't even playing. This phenomenon led bands to play more for the radio exposure than for the actual audience in attendance.

• Higher-quality recording techniques made the previously inaccessible blues music of the Mississippi Delta viable as an influence on other styles. Also, since African American artists were generally not played on the radio, records became the primary method of dissemination.

WHAT MUSICAL STYLES PREFIGURED ROCK & ROLL?   8

• Paul Whiteman's Ambassador Orchestra was an early example of white mainstreaming of African American music. This would become practically standard, especially in the early years of rock & roll, when white artists would record toned-down versions of African American songs.

• Musical styles such as swing, the blues, and country blues all influenced the rock & roll genre.

• Robert Johnson's recordings would go on to influence generations of rock & roll musicians, playing a large part in the musical styles of later bands.

HOW DID CROSSOVER HITS PAVE THE WAY FOR ROCK & ROLL?   12

• The mass migration of people from rural to urban areas during the Great Depression caused an influx of new styles. Among these was Muddy Waters's "electric blues" out of Chicago, which melded the delta blues with modern electric guitar techniques.

• There were many hybrid styles of country music that also came out of this migration, including Bob Willis and his Texas Playboys with Western swing, Patti Page with pop covers of country songs, and Roy Acuff with "Great Speckled Bird," a traditional song with a popular, patriotic theme.

• The "jump blues" of Louis Jordan was riff-based with blues roots. Louis Jordan's blending of the popular swing music with the energy of the solo singer R&B acts would go on to influence early rock & roll.

Key Terms

Tin Pan Alley area of Manhattan around 28th Street where much of the sheet music for the popular vaudeville tunes of the early 20th century were written   4

song pluggers employees of Tin Pan Alley publishing companies paid to promote their employers' songs around the city, in places ranging anywhere from department stores to saloons   5

Irving Berlin one of the most successful Tin Pan Alley songwriters; wrote "God Bless America" and "White Christmas," as well as the music for "Annie, Get Your Gun"   5

ragtime a "rag" is a derivation of an African American term describing the process of syncopating a piece of music   6

syncopated describing the state in which the accent of a measure of music falls either between the beat or on a beat not normally accented   6

standards songs with predictable forms written during the Golden Age that were commonly interpreted by many performers   6

r.p.m. revolutions per minute, or the speed at which a record rotates on a turntable; the quicker the speed, the less information can be encoded per square inch of vinyl   6

radio network a series of linked commercial radio stations, allowing for live broadcasts to be transmitted across the country   6

electrical recording method of recording that utilizes an amplified microphone to capture and transmit sound to an electromechanical record engraver   7

crooning an exaggerated style of singing that developed with the invention of the electric microphone, allowing for more intimacy than was previously possible with acoustic megaphones   7

hot music a catch-all term to describe jazz at its beginning; it referred to the driving, syncopated rhythms of the Dixieland dance bands   8

William "Count" Basie the pianist and bandleader most closely allied with the blues tradition, exemplified the Kansas City style in that he was inspired by the blues   8

Benny Goodman one of the most successful swing band leaders, and a pioneer in integrating his band   8

race records any record marketed toward a predominantly African American audience   9

hillbilly records the country music of the rural South; analogous to "race records" in terms of the audience targeted   10

country blues a rough style of blues performed by Robert Johnson and others; also called "delta blues," after the Mississippi Delta   10

riff a repeated musical phrase, used often in jazz and swing music, and later in rock & roll   10

W.C. Handy one of the most successful African American Tin Pan Alley composers, and the artist responsible for bringing some version of the blues to a wide audience   11

blue notes "bent" notes, or notes slightly flat of a normal note as played on a piano; played in the country blues era by either stopping the string with a bottleneck slide or bending the string on the fret   12

Woody Guthrie a pioneer of "urban folk," he combined traditional folk music with an urban, cosmopolitan sensibility   12

Pete Seeger played with Woody Guthrie in the Almanac Singers; later went on to form the first commercially successful urban folk group, the Weavers   12

B-side the opposite side of a record relative to the "A-side" of a single   13

single a 78 or 45 r.p.m. record, containing an A-side and a B-side; usually the A-side was the one referred to as the "single"   13

album a collection of songs on a 45 or 33 1/3 r.p.m. record   13

crossover a hit popular with multiple audiences; for example, Roy Acuff's "Great Speckled Bird" was a hit with both popular and country audiences   15

multi-track tape recording the process of recording multiple "tracks" (often each a single instrument) onto different sections (by width) of a reel of magnetic tape; allows for independent control of each instrument after it has already been recorded, and also lets performers "double" themselves on a different track, a process called "overdubbing"   16

string band a country band, usually with banjo, mandolin, guitars, fiddle, string bass, or any combination thereof   16

bluegrass style of music that melded the format of African American blues and jazz with the Southern string band sound, and featured instrumentalists and "high lonesome" singing   16

Hank Williams considered one of the most important country singers, he had a string of hits until his early death in 1953 at age 30   16

rhythm & blues term describing many different styles of blues-influenced music and used as a euphemism for "race records" after Billboard stopped using the term in 1949; often abbreviated R&B   16

Louis Jordan a pioneer of "jump blues," who also had a huge influence on rock & roll   17

Sample Test Questions

1. Which new technology facilitated the style of singing called "crooning"?
   a. the phonograph
   b. the electric microphone
   c. the national radio network
   d. the electric guitar

2. Which big band leader exemplified the bluesy, Kansas City style of swing?
   a. Glenn Miller
   b. Duke Ellington
   c. Benny Goodman
   d. Count Basie

3. Which style of blues was often written in sheet music form?
   a. delta blues
   b. classic blues
   c. electric blues
   d. rhythm & blues

4. What was NOT an explicit influence on Woody Guthrie's "urban folk" style?
   a. the Tin Pan Alley songs played on national radio networks
   b. country and hillbilly music
   c. the Dust Bowl and the Great Depression
   d. the English ballad tradition

5. What was NOT a goal of the development of "bluegrass" music?
   a. to give country music more commercial potential
   b. to reach back to the roots of country music
   c. to take instrumental proficiency to a high level
   d. to bring back the traditional country string band

ANSWERS: 1. b; 2. d; 3. b; 4. a; 5. a

ESSAY

6. Discuss how the development of Broadway musicals affected Tin Pan Alley song styles.

7. Pick one new technology mentioned in this chapter and discuss its influence on musical style.

8. Pick a musical style from before the 1930s and discuss its influence on 1930s swing bands.

9. How did the "race records" market encourage or hamper African American musical expression?

10. What are some styles of early 1950s R&B that foreshadow the beginning of rock & roll?

WHERE TO START YOUR RESEARCH PAPER

For an overview of the many styles of blues and associated artists, go to http://www.allmusic.com

For more information on Alan Lomax's recording project and folk musical styles, go to http://www.culturalequity.org/index.jsp

For an extended biography of Benny Goodman, go to http://www.bennygoodman.com/about/biography2.html

For an in-depth look at recording technology with historical pictures, go to http://www.recording-history.org/HTML/musictech1.php

For a timeline of the life of Louis Jordan, go to http://www.louisjordan.com/timeline.aspx

For a video montage of Hank Williams's performances, go to http://www.cmt.com/artists/az/williams_sr_hank/videos.jhtml

Remember to check www.thethinkspot.com for additional information, downloadable flashcards, and other helpful resources.

"A crowd

of about 6,000 persons, dissatisfied because they could not buy tickets to the Moondog Coronation Ball at the Arena, pushed down doors and entered, adding their number to the 10,000 already inside last night, creating such a confined mass of humanity that the police had to call off the event.

"Police Captain William Zimmerman said 10,000 tickets had been sold beforehand to the entertainment. Alan Freed, a WJW disc jockey, was master of ceremonies. The frustrated gathered outside, unable to buy tickets at $1.75, their number increasing to about 6,000, the captain said.

"About 9:30, they stormed the arena, knocking down four panel doors, brushing police aside, and poured inside. Some two hours and 30 policemen later, Capt. Zimmerman called it a night. He said movement was almost impossible.

"A 20-year old West Sider was arrested for fighting. He alleged another man provoked it by pulling his hair. Emmet Greshen, 25, of 10205 North Boulevard, N.E., was gouged by a man who said: "I'm coming through." He was treated at St. Vincent Charity Hospital for a wound on the left cheek.

"After ordering the ball ended, Chief Zimmerman asked the crowd to leave. Police stood by as they slowly and reluctantly filed out."

—"Moondog Ball is Halted as 6,000 Crash Arena Gate,"
Cleveland Plain Dealer, March 22, 1952

THE "BIRTH" OF ROCK & ROLL
(1951–1955)

WHERE DID ROCK & ROLL COME FROM?

On the night of March 21, 1952, something big was happening, but no one really knew what to call it. Cleveland disc jockey **Alan Freed**, whose WJW show appealed to white hipsters and black R&B fans, had spent weeks publicizing "The Moondog Coronation Ball," which would feature popular artists Paul Williams and Tony Grimes, among others. The 10,000-seat arena was sold out; 6,000 angry, boisterous fans were left outside trying to get in. Paul Williams barely got through his first song before the police closed the arena. The rock concert was born, and the first concert riot immediately followed.

Freed's organizational skills could be faulted on that night, but his vision was impeccable. For years, a new music had been sweeping across the country, which would eventually become rock & roll. More importantly, a huge, untapped audience of young fans was clearly ready to receive what these rock & rollers were offering. These were young Americans who not only wanted to listen to the music, but who wanted to listen to it together, with a crowd of their peers who were also in on these revolutionary new sounds. Concerts like this would soon be spreading across the country. From New York to San Francisco, enthusiastic musical celebrations would cater to whooping, sometimes raucous, and often out-of-control young audiences for whom the old rules no longer fit. In 1955, Freed would host the **First Rock & Roll Ball** in New York City. By then, young Americans, both black and white, would make up the audience. The unrestrained crowds were becoming regular "riots" at jam-packed Elvis Presley concerts. America was changing. So was popular music.

The History of the Term

Like the music itself, the term "**rock & roll**" went through several important evolutions before it was used to describe a musical style. The first recorded pairings of those words appeared in 1912 in a spiritual, "The Camp Meeting Jubilee." There, the lyrics give the phrase "rock & roll" a religious overtone: "We've been rocking and rolling in your arms/Rocking and rolling in your arms/In the arms of Moses." By 1922, in Trixie Smith's "My Man Rocks Me (with One Steady Roll)," the phrase is used quite differently, to describe the act of intercourse: "My man rocks me with a steady roll/There's no slippin' once he takes hold." Smith's music is unmistakably jazz, but the transition from the religious hymns to secular and even sexually suggestive music becomes central to the evolution of rock & roll.

Over the next few decades, the words "rock & roll" continued to appear in many popular jazz and R&B songs. In 1937, Chick Webb and Ella Fitzgerald used the phrase in their hit "Rock it for Me." As this music became more popular, the use of the term as a genre of music gradually became more acceptable. The "King of Rock & Roll", Elvis Presley, tended to refer to his music as "hillbilly music" or "country" when he began to play it in 1954. But by 1956, with a string of films, including *Rock, Rock, Rock* (1956), *Don't Knock the Rock* (1956), and *Mister Rock and Roll* (1957) the phrase was firmly established in the lexicon of American popular culture. Alan Freed, the influential DJ who helped popularize the term, defined it in his 1956 film *Rock, Rock, Rock:* "Rock & Roll is a river of music that has absorbed many streams: rhythm and blues, jazz, rag time, cowboy songs, country songs, folk songs. All have contributed to the big beat" (Guralnick 1994, 175).

<<< **Disc jockey and promoter Alan Freed** is credited with popularizing the term **"rock & roll."**

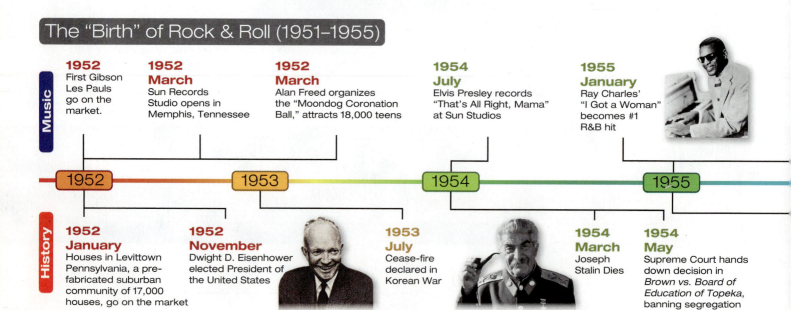

The "Birth" of Rock & Roll (1951–1955)

Music

1952
First Gibson Les Pauls go on the market.

1952 March
Sun Records Studio opens in Memphis, Tennessee

1952 March
Alan Freed organizes the "Moondog Coronation Ball," attracts 18,000 teens

1954 July
Elvis Presley records "That's All Right, Mama" at Sun Studios

1955 January
Ray Charles' "I Got a Woman" becomes #1 R&B hit

1952 — 1953 — 1954 — 1955

History

1952 January
Houses in Levittown Pennsylvania, a pre-fabricated suburban community of 17,000 houses, go on the market

1952 November
Dwight D. Eisenhower elected President of the United States

1953 July
Cease-fire declared in Korean War

1954 March
Joseph Stalin Dies

1954 May
Supreme Court hands down decision in *Brown vs. Board of Education of Topeka*, banning segregation

The Evolution of Rock & Roll

The history of rock & roll is a history of beginnings: in dive bars, clubs, record studios, and places where, suddenly, things came together in ways that they hadn't come together before. In 1954, Elvis Presley went across town from his Southern Memphis home to visit the **Sun Studio** at 706 Union Street, where he recorded his first demo record. Within six months, he was playing in front of screaming, fainting fans. In a cramped, underground club in Hamburg, West Germany, called the Star Club, manager Brian Epstein watched a skiffle group called the Silver Beatles polishing their act in nightly performance. One year later, the Beatles would conquer the world. One afternoon in 1975, a young man named John Lydon walked into the SEX fetish clothing shop with "I Hate" scribbled on his Pink Floyd T-shirt and, in a brief audition, sang "I'm Eighteen" by Alice Cooper. Malcolm McLaren, owner of the shop and manager of the Sex Pistols, knew he had a phenomenon on his hands. New Yorkers might contend that it all began on August 14, 1974, on their side of the Atlantic, at the small Bowery dive CBGB/OMFUG, where a ragged band of skinny, leather-jacketed kids called the Ramones made their inauspicious debut. Then, all of these theories might be shouted down by someone arguing that the roots of rock & roll, and the music itself, were born in the Mississippi Delta in the late teens, where a new, harder version of the blues was born. They would all be right. Rock & roll has always been a history of beginnings.

1950s AMERICA: A CHANGING COUNTRY

Rock & roll isn't an organism; it is a musical and social practice. It wasn't conceived, and it doesn't have a single point of origin. That's because, as a form of popular music, rock & roll grew out of many different influences: rockabilly, rhythm & blues, blues, country, and soul all claim parentage. Structurally, rock & roll is a simple form of music, based on harmonies and beats that are relatively easy to learn. But the origins of rock & roll reveal that it is as complex as the nation that engendered it.

On the surface, the 1950s was a simple time. In 1952, World War II general Dwight D. Eisenhower had been elected president. The war

ALAN FREED Cleveland disc jockey and radio personality known as "Moondog" and credited with bringing rock & roll to a mainstream teenage audience.

FIRST ROCK & ROLL BALL a highly successful rock concert held in New York City and organized by Freed, noteworthy for its integrated audience.

ROCK & ROLL a term first used to describe sexual intercourse that, in the 1950s, became the term for the popular, youth-oriented music trend that was sweeping the nation.

SUN STUDIO Memphis recording studio run by Sam Phillips that became the focus point for the crossover of music from R&B to rock & roll.

MISSISSIPPI DELTA location in the American South, where the acoustic delta blues would first emerge with singers like Robert Johnson and Son House.

he helped win had ended, and, in the process, the United States had become the economic and military leader of the free world. The Korean War, meanwhile, was beginning to come to a stalemate. Americans enjoyed a stable, expanding economy. Senator Joseph McCarthy's communist witch-hunt was in full swing, attempting to stamp out any ideology that might threaten that stability. The country's self-image—immortalized in the weekly TV show "Leave it to Beaver", which ran from 1957 to 1963—was of an expanding, white middle class in a world of suburbs and picket fences.

But beneath the surface, the post-war United States was changing radically. The second wave of the Great Migration was changing the racial makeup of the country. Poverty and Jim Crow laws were driving large numbers of African Americans from the South to seek out opportunities and jobs in Northern cities. From 1940 to 1950, 214,000 southern African Americans arrived in Chicago, most of them from the **Mississippi Delta**. Between 1940 and 1960, the African American population of Chicago increased from 278,000 to 813,000 (Szatmary 2010, 5). They brought their blues roots and transformed the music into a more beat-driven, electronically amplified version of the delta blues, which became the basis for rock & roll.

Around this same time, a different kind of younger population was emerging. Because of the post-war "baby boom," the number of teenagers in the United States increased from 5.6 million to 11.8 million

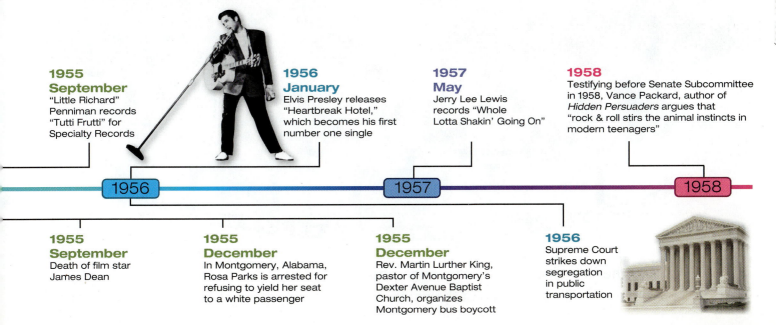

1955 September "Little Richard" Penniman records "Tutti Frutti" for Specialty Records

1956 January Elvis Presley releases "Heartbreak Hotel," which becomes his first number one single

1957 May Jerry Lee Lewis records "Whole Lotta Shakin' Going On"

1958 Testifying before Senate Subcommittee in 1958, Vance Packard, author of *Hidden Persuaders* argues that "rock & roll stirs the animal instincts in modern teenagers"

1956   **1957**   **1958**

1955 September Death of film star James Dean

1955 December In Montgomery, Alabama, Rosa Parks is arrested for refusing to yield her seat to a white passenger

1955 December Rev. Martin Lurther King, pastor of Montgomery's Dexter Avenue Baptist Church, organizes Montgomery bus boycott

1956 Supreme Court strikes down segregation in public transportation

JAMES DEAN American actor who first achieved popularity in the film *Rebel Without a Cause*, created one of the first personas of the rebellious American teenager, and was admired by Elvis Presley.

CHESS RECORD STUDIO Chicago recording studio partly responsible for the "Chicago Sound," a new, beat-oriented R&B sound that would eventually become rock & roll.

MUDDY WATERS migrating blues musician who was among the first to integrate amplified electric guitar sounds into music and record songs that would become rock & roll standards.

45 seven-inch vinyl record with a single and a backing song ("B-side") that made rock & roll songs available to the youth market.

LEO FENDER radio repairman who revolutionized the guitar sound by developing a solid-bodied electric guitar.

RAY CHARLES soul singer whose full-throated vocal style in the early 1950s would influence rock & roll singing style.

from 1946 to 1960 (Szatmary 2010, 21). This young sector of the population—with more money to spend and an increasing curiosity about the new African American music that was beginning to spread around the country—would become the market for rock & roll. They were also forming a new sense of identity, as film stars like **James Dean** and Marlon Brando embodied the image of rebellious, misunderstood youth, itching to escape the confines of picket-fence suburbia.

As this teenage population was growing rapidly, the barriers between black and white cultures were slowly falling. In the 1954 Supreme Court decision *Brown vs. Board of Education*, segregation in schools in the United States was declared unconstitutional. Movie theaters and concert halls were gradually being desegregated. By 1955, when rock & roll was riding the crest of its first wave of popularity, the audiences were frequently integrated. This new flexibility and willingness to cross racial boundaries in search of entertainment would expand the rock & roll audience.

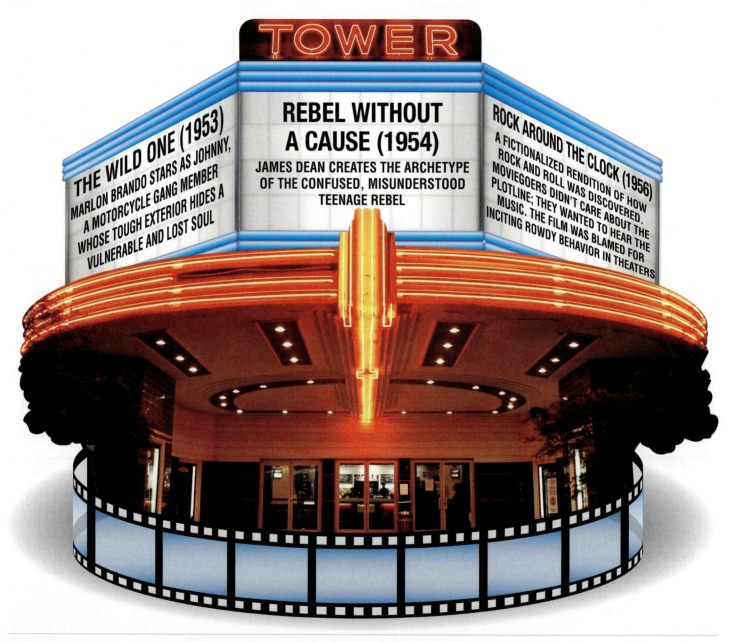

TOWER

THE WILD ONE (1953)
MARLON BRANDO STARS AS JOHNNY, A MOTORCYCLE GANG MEMBER WHOSE TOUGH EXTERIOR HIDES A VULNERABLE AND LOST SOUL

REBEL WITHOUT A CAUSE (1954)
JAMES DEAN CREATES THE ARCHETYPE OF THE CONFUSED, MISUNDERSTOOD TEENAGE REBEL

ROCK AROUND THE CLOCK (1956)
A FICTIONALIZED RENDITION OF HOW ROCK AND ROLL WAS DISCOVERED. MOVIEGOERS DIDN'T CARE ABOUT THE PLOTLINE; THEY WANTED TO HEAR THE MUSIC. THE FILM WAS BLAMED FOR INCITING ROWDY BEHAVIOR IN THEATERS

∧ In the 1950s, the booming American teenage population began to find role models and
∧ social influences in films directed at the youth market.

Throughout the 1940s, the 78-rpm record ruled the roost. That large, shellacked record was relatively expensive for the teenage market, however, and it had the additional drawback of being very easy to break. When **45s** hit the market in 1950, they offered a less breakable alternative to the 78. Typically, a 45-rpm record featured a hit on one side and a lesser-known song on the other, the B-side. Although the 33 1/3-rpm record came into use

at roughly the same time, the album format would not become popular until the mid-60s, when bands like the Beatles would use the longer-playing format artfully. Throughout the 1950s, however, the word "record" is generally understood to mean a 45. Presley's first four records were actually two-song 45s and 78s. His first full-length album, which was released in March 1956, was a collection of greatest hits.

◀◀◀

A CHANGING MUSIC

The **Chess Record Studio**, located at 2120 South Michigan Avenue on the South Side of Chicago, played a central role in developing the sound that would later evolve into rock & roll. Founded in 1950 by Jewish immigrants Leonard and Phil Chess, Chess Records took on artists who latched onto a more powerful, rhythm-based sound that was becoming popular in the African American market.

Muddy Waters, a migrant himself from Mississippi, recorded his first disc for Chess Records, "I Can't Be Satisfied." His singles, including "Rollin' Stone," "Hoochie Coochie Man," and "I Just Want to Make Love to You," have become standards for rock bands to this day. Chester "Howlin' Wolf" Burnett brought a rawness and edge, along with a powerful, curtain-chewing performance style to the delta blues sound. His compositions, such as "Smokestack Lightnin'" and "Moanin' at Midnight," have been covered by the Yardbirds, Led Zeppelin, and Jimi Hendrix. Ellas Bates, whose stage name, "Bo Diddley," was given him by Leonard Chess, brought his famous "Bo Diddley" beat to the music—a staggering, almost primal African beat that set his music apart from other blues performers.

By 1950, an amplified, beat-driven version of the blues attracted the attention of local DJs and young musicians across the country. Eventually, it would spread to the other side of the Atlantic, where young music fans like Mick Jagger and Keith Richards were eagerly lapping it up. When they first toured the United States as the Rolling Stones in 1964, they paid tribute to the influence Chess Records had on their career by recording their instrumental "2120 South Michigan Avenue" at the studio.

The Solid-Bodied Electric Guitar

With their migration to Chicago, blues artists brought a harder, aggressive sound to the softer, personalized delta blues style. Playing in ensembles in small clubs required amplification of guitars. Migrating blues artists, including Muddy Waters and Bo Diddley, were among the first to integrate a highly amplified electric sound into their music. In 1946, radio repairman **Leo Fender** took the electric guitar to another level when he developed the Fender Esquire, the first commercially successful, solid-bodied electric guitar. Later, a new type of guitar—the Telecaster—would evolve from the Esquire. Unlike traditional acoustic guitars, these guitars had a solid wooden body. The sharper, harder guitar sound integrated tightly with the drumbeat, building the rhythmic intensity. Guitarists began using riffs—short, repeated fragments of melody—to become key and memorable parts of each song. Songs like Bo Diddley's "I'm a Man" and Muddy Waters's "Mannish Boy" brought the electronic guitar riff to the forefront of the ensemble, giving it a prominence equal to, if not greater than, the vocals themselves.

<<< The Great Migration and the solid-bodied electric guitar, **like this Fender Esquire,** helped traditional blues evolve into a **more aggressive and amplified, rhythm-oriented rhythm & blues style.**

HOW DID ROCK & ROLL FIRST EMERGE IN THE UNITED STATES?

The First Rock & Roll Records

There are several contenders for the distinction of being the first rock & roll song. But, in the quickly evolving musical world they were born into, none of them was known as "rock & roll" songs to begin with. Just as important as the songs themselves are the transitions they went through before becoming known as rock & roll hits and the blend of musical styles that went into their composition.

"I'VE GOT A WOMAN": GOSPEL MEETS R&B

Ray Charles may not have ever wanted to be classified as a rock & roller, but his memorable "I Got a Woman" has had a profound influence on rock & roll vocals. Born in 1930, Charles grew up in the segregated South. He grew up listening to the blues, R&B, and gospel music, which would have a deep impact on his musical career. At the young age of

"I GOT A WOMAN" by Ray Charles

Growing up in a religious Southern family, Ray Charles was immersed in a rich culture of gospel and country music from an early age. So, it's no surprise that he would later incorporate aspects of both types of music within his songs. Although his early songs did well, it was the song "I Got a Woman" that would rocket Charles to the spotlight. When it was released in 1955, it quickly rose to the top of the R&B charts. Unlike his earlier works, "I Got a Woman" was a blend of gospel, blues, and rock. In the song, Charles focused on portraying emotion and showing his inner feelings through his movement and his playing. His vocals blended the passion of gospel with blues lyrics. The result was a song that broke the color barrier and topped the charts. More importantly, however, was that this song was a predecessor of an entirely new genre of music: soul.

seven, Charles had lost all of his sight, and he was sent away to a school for the deaf and blind. It was at this school that he received the formal musical training that would help the gifted boy hone his talent and learn to work with the skills that he had shown from an early age.

Charles' career as a musician started out as a pianist in an all-white hillbilly band, and then progressed to emulate the smoother pop of Nat "King" Cole. However, in the early 1950s, all of that changed. With his legendary "I Got a Woman," Charles abandoned his earlier crooning style and took on a rougher, more muscular tone that mixed blues with gospel styling. Although Charles is credited as a co-writer of the song, he identifies it as a reworking of the gospel tune "Jesus Is All the World to Me." According to rock critic Peter Guralnick, the song had a seminal impact on the rock & roll singing technique: "the very stratagem of adapting a gospel song, putting secular lyrics to it, and then delivering it with the attendant fanfare of a Pentecostal service was, simply stated, staggering" (1994).

∧∧∧ Ray Charles's full-throated singing style was **a model for rock & roll singers** such as Elton John.

R&B charts, where it stayed for six months in 1948.

"ROCKET '88": ROCK & ROLL MEETS THE AUTOMOBILE

"**Rocket '88**," attributed to "Jack Brenston and his Delta Cats," was actually recorded by guitarist/soul great Ike Turner and his band, the Kings of Rhythm. When Turner and his band recorded the piece, it hit the top spot in the R&B charts in 1951. The song is the original tribute to what would become a long-standing relationship between the rock & roller and his beloved automobile. This relationship created the stereotype of a "greaser" and his car, usually a hot rod, cruising down the road for the sheer joy of driving and having nothing else to do. "Rocket '88" is one of the first of many car-inspired and hot rod themed songs. You'll learn more about the the wave of hot rod music in the 60s when in Chapter 5.

"Rocket '88" is also considered seminal in rock & roll for its pioneering use of guitar distortion. According to legend, the "fuzz" on guitarist Willie Kizart's guitar was an accident, caused by a blow that the amplifier took in transit on the way to Memphis, where the song was recorded at the legendary Sun Studios. Producer Sam Phillips, known for his improvisational approach to studio technology, decided to use the damaged amp for the roughness and edge that it added to the guitar sound. The gamble paid off, and Turner's version of "Rocket '88" reached the top of the R&B charts, where it stayed for five weeks in 1951. This pioneering use of distortion would later become a staple in rock & roll music.

"GOOD ROCKIN' TONIGHT": R&B MEETS THE PARTY ANIMAL

When first written and recorded in 1947 by blues artist Roy Brown (1925–1981), "**Good Rockin' Tonight**" enjoyed only moderate success on the R&B charts. The lyrics' emphasis on partying and sexual exuberance—"Have you heard the news? There's good rockin' tonight!"—was a departure from the mellower, somewhat downbeat Southern blues sound. Brown himself, in an interview in Robert Palmer's *Dancing in the Streets,* is unapologetic about the sexual undertones of the song: I had my mind on this girl in the bedroom. I'm not going to lie to you. Listen, man, I wrote them kind of songs. I was a dirty cat" (1996, 15)

Later that same year, "Good Rockin' Tonight" was brought even closer to what we now call rock & roll by the more primal and driving version by Wynonie Harris (1915–1969). Harris helped popularize the "shouting" style of rock & roll, which would dispose of melody entirely at points, as the singer reached emotional peaks. This vocal technique fit with Harris's own reputation as a hard-driving, hard-living singer. Harris's version of "Good Rockin' Tonight" shot up to the top of the

The First Rock & Roll Singers

As rock & roll became louder, faster, and more energetic, the traditional role of the singer changed. Not only did the singer have to sing, but he or she also became a showman who would communicate the exuberant, emotive nature of the song to a younger audience. As the music became more driven and more energized, the role of the singer as a charismatic rock persona evolved. Younger, crazier singers were in the spotlight. Instead of just playing the music or singing the lyrics, it was their job to communicate the sense of abandon, joy, or insanity in the music itself.

THE FABULOUS LITTLE RICHARD

For many, Richard Penniman, aka **Little Richard,** is the apotheosis of the no-holds-barred singer. His bisexuality, flamboyant dress, and outrageous mannerisms are as much a part of his legend as his musical innovations. Little Richard, present at the birth of rock & roll, incorporated many of the contradictory impulses and influences that have brought rock & roll to its heights and its depths.

Penniman was born in Macon, Georgia, in 1932 to a family of devout Seventh Day Adventists. His uncles were preachers, and his father sold bootleg whiskey (Romanowski 1995, 590). He started out as a gospel singer and, as he grew up, began to sing with circuses and traveling sideshows. When his father was shot in a brawl, Penniman took up singing full time to support himself and his family. By 1951, at the age of 19, he had turned from gospel to R&B and cut his first record. He toured black nightclubs, performing rhythm and blues numbers. By the early 1950s, with his backing band the Upsetters, Penniman began to cultivate an image as a sex-crazed, hard-partying piano pounder. Little Richard's onstage behavior became a central part of the show. He was the prototypical bisexual glam rocker: his pompadour, eye shadow, lipstick, and clothing were among the first in rock & roll to provoke, shock, and awe.

Penniman's personality was more complex, however, than his onstage persona. Throughout his career and despite his reputation as a wild child, Penniman felt the pull of his religious roots. In 1957,

^^ Little Richard's music ^^ and personality **challenged the boundaries between sex and music.**

>>> In the early 1950s, the divisions between R&B sales and pop sales were largely erased as R&B music entered mainstream American culture.

when his songs were hitting the charts, Penniman suddenly renounced rock & roll and returned to Alabama (see Chapter 4 for more details). He later returned to rock & roll on the revival circuit, but the tension between religion and "the devil's music" has remained a part of his life as a performer.

Tutti Frutti, Sex, and Sales

"**Tutti Frutti,**" which eventually became Little Richard's 1955 hit, offers a peek at the earlier, sexually explicit roots of rock & roll. For most of us today, it's a harmless party song. But when music like this first arrived on the scene, its openly sexual content offended the mores of middle-class America. With its pounding piano and intense accompaniment, this song helped pioneer a rock & roll musical style that, instead of resolving, built up to an explosive finale. The original lyrics are explicit enough that, even by today's standards, they would probably merit a parental alert. Producer Robert Blackwell at Specialty Records hired a local songwriter to replace the original words with more innocuous, nonsense lyrics before it was recorded. The song, in its cleaned-up

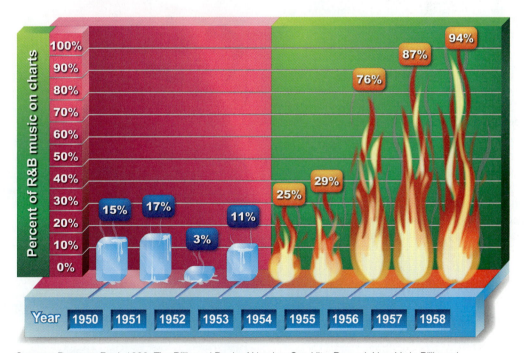

Popularity of R&B on the Billboard Charts

Percent of R&B music on charts

Year	1950	1951	1952	1953	1954	1955	1956	1957	1958
	15%	17%	3%	11%	25%	29%	76%	87%	94%

Sources: Bronson, Fred. 1988. The Billboard Book of Number One Hits. Rev. ed. New York: Billboard Publications. Ennis, Philip. 1992. The Seventh Stream: The Emergence of Rocknroll in American Popular Music. Hanover. NH: Wesleyan University Press.

form was a legendary hit, which sold 200,000 copies in the week and a half after its release and hit number two on the Billboard R&B charts in 1956 (Szatmary 2010, 18). Rock & roll artists since Little Richard have had their work cut out for them: balancing oblique sexual double entendres with marketability. Rock & roll is often undeniably about sex, but it's also about getting radio play in a country where FCC regulations rule.

>>> **The multi-talented Chuck Berry** is a singer, songwriter, and guitarist.

his words as he sang, and his songs' subject matter was about his audience and their experiences. Disc jockey Alan Freed immediately noticed the crossover appeal. While getting a co-writer's credit on the song, Freed also promoted the song heavily. "Maybellene" made its way to number ten on Billboard charts. Berry followed that up with a string of other hits: "Roll Over Beethoven," "School Day," "Rock and Roll Music," "Sweet Little Sixteen," "Johnny B. Goode," and "Reelin' and Rockin.'"

With "Johnny B. Goode," he wrote one of the first rock & roll autobiographies: A young man living near New Orleans who couldn't read

CHUCK BERRY PLAYS, SINGS, AND DUCK WALKS

Like Little Richard, **Chuck Berry** helped create a persona that would become essential to the rock & roll world. Born in St. Louis in 1927, Berry had roots in gospel music as a child. In his autobiography, he writes, "Our family lived a block and a half from our church, and singing became a major tradition in the Berry family. As far back as I can remember, mother's household chanting of those gospel tunes rang through my childhood. . .Looking back, I'm sure that my musical roots were planted, then and there" (Szatmary 2010, 18).

After spending four years in reform school and working on a General Motors assembly line, Berry developed his guitar licks on the St. Louis barroom circuit. He and his fellow band members Ebby Hardy and Johnnie Johnson became local fixtures by 1955, when Berry made the jump to Chicago and the Chess Label. His first song, "Ida Red," was later renamed "Maybellene." With that tune, Berry was the first black musician to successfully break into the field of white pop music.

Berry broke the color barrier in a new way: by integrating country music into R&B. When asked about what he thought contributed to the success of the song, Berry stated that he had written and performed the song to appeal to a white pop audience; he carefully enunciated

>>> **Many of the rock & roll stars of the 1950s** made important musical and stylistic contributions to the genre.

Major Influences on Rock & Roll

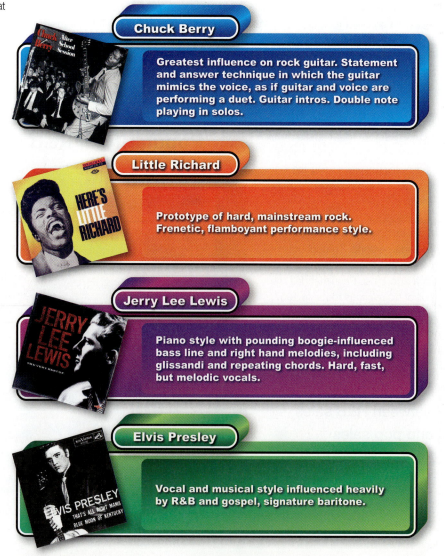

Chuck Berry
Greatest influence on rock guitar. Statement and answer technique in which the guitar mimics the voice, as if guitar and voice are performing a duet. Guitar intros. Double note playing in solos.

Little Richard
Prototype of hard, mainstream rock. Frenetic, flamboyant performance style.

Jerry Lee Lewis
Piano style with pounding boogie-influenced bass line and right hand melodies, including glissandi and repeating chords. Hard, fast, but melodic vocals.

Elvis Presley
Vocal and musical style influenced heavily by R&B and gospel, signature baritone.

Sun Studio

At Sun Studio in Memphis, Tennessee, rock & roll first crossed the color barrier. Unlike other recording studios, which were predominantly white, both black and white artists were able to record their greatest hits within the Sun Studios. For artists like Johnny Cash, Elvis Presley, Ike Turner, Jerry Lee Lewis, Junior Parker, and Howlin' Wolf, this small, one-story building on Union Street was a melting pot for rockabilly, blues, rock & roll, bluegrass, R&B, and country.

Sam Phillips opened Sun Studio in 1950. A 28-year-old native of Florence, Alabama, Phillips, after several years of working as a radio announcer, manager, and broadcast engineer, found himself attracted to the possibilities that the quickly changing African American music scene had to offer. In its early years, Sun Records recorded work by black musical artists. With his partner, Marion Keisker, Phillips opened his doors to African American artists who had been turned away or ignored entirely by major labels.

The studio itself was small, with only a 20 by 30 foot room for performers, plus a small control room. The microphones had been purchased from an army surplus sale, and the recording setup was bare bones. Phillips recorded on 16-inch acetate disks, and he carefully analyzed the sounds by feeding them back through the board. He was also the first person to use slapback delay, a

∧
∧ By 1957, **Sun Studio's label, Sun**
∧ **Records,** had become a hitmaker with artists including (from left to right) **Jerry Lee Lewis, Carl Perkins, Elvis Presley, and Johnny Cash.**

process that allowed him to enhance the sound of the instruments and the vocals. This process and Phillips's intense attention to getting the perfect sound would draw a wide range of artists and music fans, both black and white.

In the mid-1950s, as Phillips attracted white musicians, including Roy Orbison and Johnny Cash, the studio became a nexus of sorts for a mixture of R&B and country. In the early 1950s, Phillips had noted that, if he could find a white man who was able to sing black music, he would "make a billion dollars" (Garelick 2003). Although he never made a billion dollars, he did find the man he was looking for: Elvis Aaron Presley, a young man just out of high school, who lived just across town in another part of Memphis.

After a series of other successful artists after Elvis, Phillips sold the studio in 1969. Today, the studio has two functions. By day, it is a popular tourist spot where people can view recording equipment and learn a little more about the great artists who recorded there. At night, the studio returns to its original purpose, and artists are able to use the facilities for recording purposes.

and write but was a masterful guitar player. Since then, countless rock & rollers, including Bruce Springsteen, Bob Dylan, and Keith Richards, have used the form of the rock & roll self-portrait to cultivate their own identity as rebels or antiheroes who escaped the dreariness of everyday life in search of fame, danger, and the open road.

Berry also added a level of showmanship to his live performances that guitar players had not previously been known for. Berry brought the guitarist/composer into the spotlight. During the seemingly endless touring of his early career, Berry made famous the guitarist's "duck walk." This acrobatic type of dancing is where the guitarist stands on one leg, then shuffles the other foot back and forth while playing his guitar. Berry said that he first performed this move in concert, when he was trying to hide wrinkles in his suit. The audience loved it, so he did it again and again, and soon it was part of his musical routine. Many later guitar players—Ted Nugent, Angus Young of AC/DC, and Pete Townsend of the Who among them—would choreograph their guitar playing with similar moves.

ELVIS AARON PRESLEY

Elvis Presley was born in Tupelo, Mississippi, in 1936, to Vernon and Gladys Presley. His father changed jobs and addresses frequently, and, in 1948, moved in search of better fortunes to Memphis, Tennessee. With the move to Memphis, Presley was living less than a mile away from **Beale Street**, a vibrant musical hub for black R&B musicians.

TOP OF THE CHARTS
WHAT'S HOT!
1956
1. "Don't be Cruel" – Elvis Presley
2. "Hound Dog" – Elvis Presley
3. "Singing the Blues" – Guy Mitchell
4. "Wayward Wind" – Gogi Grant
5. "Heartbreak Hotel" – Elvis Presley
6. "Rock & Roll Waltz" – Kay Starr
7. "The Poor People of Paris" – Les Baxter
8. "Memories are Made of This" – Dean Martin
9. "Love Me Tender" – Elvis Presley
10. "My Prayer" – The Platters

From an early age, Presley was an aspiring singer and musician, who absorbed the musical culture of the South. He would listen ceaselessly to R&B stations on the radio, and, according to legend, head over to Beale Street, where he would be seen thumbing through records and absorbing the exuberant musical atmosphere. As a teenager, he was quiet and polite, but was a flamboyant dresser with a greased-back pompadour, colored shirts, and an upturned collar.

When he graduated from Humes High School in 1953, Presley went to work at a machinists' shop. His career as a recorded singer began on July 18, 1953, when he walked into Sam Phillips's Sun Studio to record a 45 as a birthday present for his mother. He paid $4 and walked away with two recorded ballads: "My Happiness," backed by "That's When Your Heartaches Begin." Sam Phillips wasn't present at the time, but Phillips's assistant and radio personality, Marion Keisker scribbled a note on the master tape: "Good ballad singer. Hold."

Elvis Hits
the Airwaves

Several months later, Phillips invited Presley to a recording session. The ballad, "Without You," didn't go over very well. Finally, on July 5, 1954, Phillips gave Presley one last chance. With guitar player Scotty Moore and bass player Bill Black, they tried out a few country ballads. That session didn't go well until they took a break, and Presley, on a whim, launched into a version of **Arthur Crudup**'s "That's All Right, Mama," one of his favorite tunes. Moore and Black both joined in, and Phillips, listening from the booth, realized that he had a hit. Just a few days later, the recording was released as a single.

Arthur "Big Boy" Crudup was born in Mississippi in 1905 and worked as a laborer in construction sites, sawmills, and in the fields. He started his singing career later than many of the other rock & roll musicians, in his 30s, when he headed up to Chicago with a gospel group called the Harmonizing Four. In 1939, he turned to playing guitar and singing the blues. In the mid-1940s, he got several record deals and composed a number of songs that became R&B standards, and, later, rock & roll classics: "Rock Me Mama," "My Baby Left Me," and "That's All Right, Mama." As the songs became R&B hits, Crudup was repeatedly cheated out of royalties by his unscrupulous producer and record label. By the 1950s, Crudup, discouraged, returned to working the fields.

But in the mid-1940s, Crudup had one big fan: Presley. As a teenager, he would listen to Crudup's music on the radio. Quoted in an interview, he pays tribute to one of his primary influences, "Down in Tupelo, I used to hear old bluesman Arthur Crudup bang his box the way I do now, and I said, if I ever got to the place where I could feel all old Arthur felt, I'd be a music man like nobody ever saw" (Guralnick 1994, 289).

When the recording of "That's All Right, Mama" hit the airwaves on local DJ Dewey Phillips's (no relation to Sam) "Red Hot and Blue" radio show, the response was overwhelming. By July 19, when the record was officially released—backed by the country standard "Blue Moon of Kentucky"—5,000 orders had been made for the record. Within a month it was at the top of the Memphis charts. The success took Elvis by surprise, but he was just the singer Sam Phillips had been waiting for: a white man who could credibly sing R&B. On the day of the single's release, when switchboards on Memphis radio stations were lit up with requests for "That's All Right, Mama," a nervous Presley had to be hunted down in a Memphis movie theater to hear how well his song was being received. Dewey Phillips conducted the first interview with Presley. The interview was unremarkable except for the fact that Phillips repeatedly asked the nervous Presley what high school he had gone to. Hume High School, as most listeners would understand, was an all-white school. Phillips wanted to make sure that the audience understood that this talented new singer, who played black music, was actually white.

A Star Is Born

Presley's live performances would set the standard for rock & roll. While guitarist Scotty Moore and bassist Bill Black kept the beat going, Presley's dynamic, knee-wiggling, hip-thrusting performances radiated charisma and energy in a way that few other white performers had before. According to one account by country singer Bob Luman, "The cat came out in red pants and a green coat and a pink shirt and socks. And he had this sneer on his face and he stood behind the mike for five minutes, before he made his move. Then he hit the guitar a lick. . .and

Presley's performance style became as famous as his music.

these high school girls were screaming and fainting and running up to the stage. (Guralnick 1994, 182). The responses from his young, mostly female audiences, were legendary: screaming crowds of women grabbing at his clothes or ripping his shirt off him.

A year of nearly constant touring followed, including numerous appearances on the Louisiana Hayride, a country radio show that transmitted over much of the southern and western United States. By the end of 1955, Presley had recorded five 45s for Sun Records, and his reputation had grown across the country. In the fall of 1955, in search of a more national audience, Presley hired the promoter/ex-carnival barker, 45-year-old "Colonel" Tom Parker as his manager. Parker arranged for RCA to buy out Presley's Sun contract for $40,000. From 1956 until 1958, under Parker's management, Presley began to diversify his career and tone down his delivery in search of a more mainstream audience.

When Presley was drafted in 1958, his career was put on hold. When he returned to the United States two years later, rock & roll had been replaced by a more generic pop sound, and, in addition to returning to recording music, Presley focused on his acting career. From 1960 to 1968, Presley appeared in about 31 movies, which were critically panned but financially lucrative.

In 1968, he returned to the stage with his "Comeback" show, an hour-long Christmas special that was a mix of live and recorded music. This show was meant to bring Elvis back into the musical scene after a seven-year hiatus. His fans were thrilled with his return, and the success of this show ultimately relaunched his musical career. He went touring again and released another popular album, *Burning Love* (1972). However, after the release of this album, his musical career once again declined. He eventually retired to his home, Graceland, where died in 1978 at the age of 42.

Presley's Sun years—and the five single records he recorded with them—broke the color barrier in American popular music. For the first time, rockabilly, country, and R&B all came together successfully in a musical form that was inclusive, flexible, and exciting. Presley's Louisiana Hayride shows, his Sun Sessions, as well as the tours across the South, are legendary—and not just for the screaming teeny-boppers, but also because rock & roll was at that moment a work in progress.

Flashpoints ISSUES in ROCK

For many, rock & roll played a big role in bringing the United States closer to racial integration. By playing the songs that were once only heard in dive bars and black sections of Mississippi Delta towns, white rock musicians spread the word about a rich musical heritage that, until then, had been largely ignored. But as white singers like Presley rocketed to fame with tunes like "Good Rockin' Tonight," the original black composers remained, for the most part, in poverty. Presley undoubtedly brought his own sensibility and tone to the song, and he wasn't shy about bragging about it, reportedly saying, "The colored folks been singing it and playing it just like I'm doin' now, man, for more years than I know. . .[but] nobody paid it no mind 'til I goosed it up" (Guralnick 1994, 289). However, the question remains: Who deserves credit for inventing rock & roll?

In the Jim Crow South, blues singers like Crudup or Joe Brown—who both wrote songs that became hits for Presley—were exploited by agents and record labels. Presley and other white artists were often generous with their praise of these singers, but the benefits of that added tribute rarely translated into cash. Two years after recording "That's All Right, Mama," Presley was financially set for life. Crudup, however, had lost the rights for the song to an unscrupulous manager. In 1968, after years of working in the fields and trying in vain for decades to retrieve back royalties for his music, Crudup stated his case presciently: "I was born poor, I live poor, and I'm going to die poor."

Royalties and Rights

This may explain the ambivalent relationship between musicians such as Berry and the white rock stars who made millions from versions of their songs. On one hand, rock & roll is credited for breaking down the color barrier and giving African-American musical compositions the recognition they deserved. But some also consider rock & roll to be commercial exploitation of an indigenous American culture. It's a question that arises when, for instance, *Saturday Night Live* comedians Dan Aykroyd (1952-) and John Belushi (1949–1982) made millions by aping Chicago singers as the Blues Brothers. Originally a skit on *SNL*, the two dressed up in suits and played humorous songs based on old R&B classics. Did rock & roll break the color line, or did it just exploit it?

>>> **Arthur Crudup composed "That's All Right, Mama,"** Elvis Presley's first Sun record. **It rocketed Presley to fame and fortune,** but Crudup had to return to farming the fields later in his career.

JERRY LEE LEWIS

Part of Presley's appeal as a popular entertainer was his ability to skirt the borders of propriety while maintaining the persona of the teetotaling, milk-and-cookies-loving mama's boy. Ed Sullivan, the host of a television show that featured popular musicians of the day, had doubts about Presley. However, when a rival television program's ratings soared, Sullivan invited Presley on his show. After the young rock & roller performed, Sullivan admitted that he had been charmed by the young man's politeness and deference. The same could not be easily said of **Jerry Lee Lewis**. Known as the "Killer," Lewis was, to many, the white Little Richard. His personal life was as chaotic as Penniman's: By the age of 21, when he was recording his first hits for the Sun label, he had already been married three times, and he would be married another three times. His roots were in blues, country, and gospel music. Like Penniman, he had grown up in a troubled but intensely religious environment. Before choosing a musical career, he spent a year studying for the ministry at Southwestern Bible School. Then, attracted by the Sun label, Lewis came to Memphis to show Sam Phillips what he had. Phillips was impressed: "He played the piano with abandon. A lot of people do that. But I could hear between the stuff that he played and that he didn't play, that spiritual thing" (Szatmary 1995, 36).

Lewis's first Sun single, "Crazy Arms" reached the lower spots of the country charts. He also played as a session musician for artists such as Johnny Cash and Carl Perkins. As a pianist, Lewis is credited with bringing the piano to rockabilly. His intense, unique playing style integrated a percussive backbeat—punctuated by rolls—into the R&B style. During performances he would dance on his piano, kick it, and once he even set it on fire. With a driving, off-the-wall performance on *The Steve Allen Show* in July 28, 1957, Lewis got national attention. As a result, his song, "Whole Lotta Shakin' Going On" climbed immediately to number three on the Billboard charts. A month later, he recorded "Great Balls of Fire" and seemed destined for stardom on the level of Presley.

Lewis may have been the first white bad boy in rock & roll. His unquestionable talent was matched by relationship and drinking problems. It was an image that worked—for a while. His percussive, boogie-influenced piano style, along with his legendary sexual appetite, was more offensive than the more mild-mannered Presley to adults. Both Presley and Lewis came from the poor, white South, but Lewis seemed to take that as a badge of honor. Noted rock critic Robert Palmer called him the "original rock & roll rebel."

Like most rebels, "the Killer" never offered his young audience a way out, but he offered a brief escape. . .and, in his brief career, it became clear that this new teenage audience was ready to shell out their pocket change for that chance to challenge the somewhat staid, middle-class version of the world.

CARL PERKINS

When Elvis Presley left Sun Records for RCA in 1955, Sam Phillips began looking for a replacement. For a moment, it seemed that **Carl Perkins** was

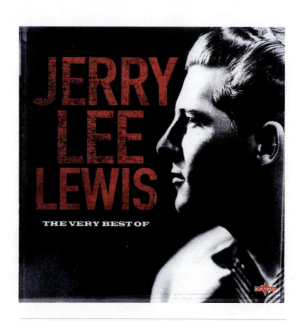

∧
∧
∧ After his performance on *The Steve Allen Show,* **Jerry Lee Lewis's "Whole Lotta Shakin' Going On"** hit number three in the Billboard charts.

the one. Perkins was born in poverty in Tennessee, and he got his first exposure to gospel and blues sounds as he picked cotton alongside African American share-croppers. At the age of 14, Perkins scraped up the three dollars he needed to purchase a new guitar. His guitar playing was influenced by the styling of blues musician Muddy Waters and bluegrass great Bill Monroe. Encouraged by Presley's early success, Perkins signed with Sun Records. After a disappointing first record, according to legend, Perkins penned the lyrics for the 1956 hit "Blue Suede Shoes" on a potato sack. The song rocketed to the top of country, R&B, and pop charts. The B-side, "Honey, Don't" also did well in its own right.

Despite his skills as a composer, however, Perkins, already a father of three at 22, lacked the star quality and charisma of Presley. However, this was not the only roadblock in his path to stardom. Tragedy struck when, while driving to New York City for a potentially career-making appearance on the *Perry Como Show,* Perkins and his brother, Jay, were gravely injured in a car crash. The long period of hospitalization and Perkins's slow recuperation stopped his career in its tracks. He would have to endure the indignity of watching his song "Blue Suede Shoes" make its television debut on Tommy Dorsey's *Stage Show* being sung by none other than Elvis Presley.

Despondent, and combating alcoholism, Perkins eventually left Sun Records. His career slowed considerably throughout the early 1960s. But Perkins's talents as a songwriter would return to the public eye when, in 1964, the Beatles recorded "Honey Don't," "Everybody's Trying to Be My Baby," and "Matchbox." Although he never became a star at Presley's level, Perkins is still remembered as one of early rock & roll's most talented songwriters.

"THAT'S ALL RIGHT"/"BLUE MOON OF KENTUCKY" by Elvis Presley

When they first came out, LP records were not considered "albums" so much as they were a collection of singles hits on one record. Many of the early rock & roll artists did not release albums as we know them today until much later, instead focusing on singles records with the occasional B-side song. Elvis didn't release his first LP records until 1956, and even then, it was a collection of his past singles hits rather than a cohesive group of songs.

Instead, it was Elvis's first Sun single record, "That's All Right"/ "Blue Moon of Kentucky" (1954), which launched his musical career.

Both songs were cover songs—"That's All Right" was originally an R&B/jazz song by Arthur Crudup, and "Blue Moon" was a country blues song written by Bill Monroe. Elvis's renditions of the songs combined elements of blues, jazz, country, rockabilly, and rock that blended into a unique "pop" sound. It was this new sound that attracted listeners who were both white and black. For songs like "That's All Right," Elvis's rendition helped popularize black music for a white audience.

HOW WAS ROCK & ROLL MARKETED?

Selling the Music

The music and the stars have their place in rock & roll history. But in an art form whose origins were so widespread, it was the promoters who managed to package it neatly into the rock & roll format and turn it into a marketable product. They were the visionaries—people who saw the possibilities in a music that, in the early 1950s, was regarded as a passing fad by many Americans. Rock & rollers are interested in making music; promoters want to sell it. But as a social phenomenon, rock & roll in its early years was as much about spreading the news and finding a growing audience as it was about playing the music. Rock & roll got its start because of several visionary promoters who managed to spread the news to an audience that caught on enthusiastically.

AM RADIO

As networks began to turn toward television in the mid-1940s, the radio airwaves were opening up across the country and offering audiences everywhere exposure to R&B hits. By 1950, smaller independent radio stations were popping up all over the country—with some of the same results that "indie" bands would have in later years. The new local stations reflected the musical tastes of their locale. (Stuessy & Lipscomb 2008, 56) DJs prided themselves on their ability to detect local talent and send new and promising artists to the top of the local charts. They looked to some of the new independent labels for inspiration and new talent. **AM radio** had become a primary medium for the discovery and promotion of rock & roll.

ALAN FREED: FINDING THE AUDIENCE

Born in 1921, Alan Freed was a promoter who helped turn rock & roll into an industry and a commodity that could be sold on a level that Presley, in 1954, would never have imagined. Sam Phillips, it is said, saw the possibilities in the music. Freed was a successful businessman who, as a

∧
∧ Transistor radio gave young Americans **the chance**
∧ **to listen to the hits outside the living room.**

Cleveland DJ, was able to foresee the possibilities of integration in rock & roll. He played to an audience of "hipsters"—the growing crowd of young white fans of black music. That sector of the young American audience has propelled many commercial ventures since then. For Freed, the diversity of the music and the American population presented the economics of the future.

Freed was one of the first to create television and films built exclusively around rock & roll. In 1956, Freed appeared in a series of teen movies, including "Rock around the Clock," and "Go Johnny Go," that predated the appeal of video. After a successful run in Cleveland, Freed was offered a DJ job in New York City, where his radio show, "The Big Beat," reached an even larger audience. Freed, with his hipster slang was one of the first to use rock & roll to key into the white teenage market. Freed's own career would come to a premature halt in 1960, when he was convicted in a "payola" scandal, but his legacy—that rock & roll offers white teenagers the chance to get a little crazy—became the driving economic force in the music for years to come. We'll discuss this scandal at further length in Chapter 3.

Freed also found creative ways to sell this "big beat" by using the media to attract various possible markets. To attract potential concertgoers, Freed brought the "rock concert" into the American vernacular by organizing several major shows in the mid-1950s. As Freed recognized, these concerts offered a sense of community for the young population that no other market could replicate. These concerts would become the mainstay of the rock & roll economy. Freed died in 1965, but had he lived a few more years, he would have seen the phenomenon he nurtured turn into a cultural marking point, as the concert at Woodstock would create the identity for an entire American generation.

DJ DEWEY PHILLIPS: FINDING THE TALENT

In 1950, **Dewey Phillips** was a 24-year-old radio celebrity for radio station WHBQ broadcasting in Memphis, Tennessee. He played late nights on weekdays and Saturdays and spent his days working in a record store on South Main Street, just a few blocks away from Beale Street in Memphis—the center of a thriving musical culture, which would later grab the attention of Presley. In his early years, Phillips played black music on his radio show, and his audience was almost exclusively black (Guralnick 1994, 99). It was one of the most popular shows on Memphis radio.

Dewey was the DJ who would give Presley his initial boost. He developed a close association with Sam Phillips, the owner and producer

∧ ∧ In the 1950s, **independent labels Chess and Sun** played essential roles in assembling and recording artists whose work would become **the foundation of rock & roll.**

"Colonel" Tom Parker: Selling the Superstar

At first glimpse, **Tom Parker** would seem to be an unlikely candidate for the rock & roll business. In 1955, he was a heavyset, balding, middle-aged man, with a curious background as a carnival barker and, later, as the founder of a pet cemetery. He was never a Colonel, and, until late in life, never admitted that he had been born in the Netherlands. He had a reputation in the music industry—he had already been manager of country singers Eddy Arnold and Hank Snow—as a controlling, forceful promoter who protected and cultivated his stars into long-term investments. When he met Presley in 1955, the young man's popularity was still peaking, but even Presley himself worried that it wouldn't last.

Parker offered Presley a way out; instead of rising and falling with his position in the Billboard charts or with the musical fashion, he was convinced that Presley could be marketed as a personality and an icon. When Parker persuaded RCA to purchase the rights to Presley's recordings from Sun Records for $35,000—an unprecedented sum for a recording artist—Parker set about selling Presley's music and image on a national level.

Parker took an all-business approach to his new charge. By 1957, he focused on recreating him as a marketable popular icon with mass appeal across age groups. This involved toning down his rebel image, thereby increasing his appeal to an adult audience. He also started marketing products with the Presley label: buttons, posters, shirts, signs, and books. Instead of selling the music, Parker was selling the persona of the star.

In Parker's view, rock stars could be their own worst enemy: Their unpredictability was part of their appeal, but it could also bring their careers to an early halt. Chuck Berry, Jerry Lee Lewis, and Little Richard had all lost control of their careers at points. To insulate him from publicity but keep his image alive, he turned Presley from a rock star to a film actor. From 1960 to 1968, Presley would star in 31 films, most of them safe, B-grade movies that would deliver exactly what his audience wanted.

Even among his detractors, Parker is considered a visionary—the first person to see what controlled, marketable commodities rock & roll stars could become. His promotional genius would be imitated six years later by Brian Epstein, who managed to sell an entire group—the Beatles, whom we will discuss in Chapter 6—as personalities. For Presley the person, the strategy isolated him from the audience that gave him strength, as well as from the music he loved. In 1968, chafing at the bit, Presley would defy the Colonel's own advice by returning to the stage in his legendary comeback performance, which was broadcast live in parts on national television. For Elvis the rock & roll icon, though, history speaks for itself. As the Colonel himself has wryly noted, Elvis continued to be a marketable item long after his death.

for Sun Records, who had long been searching for a white audience. This close association was what gave rock & roll its pulse and speed. Promoters could discover talent and would then enlist DJs like Dewey to play a record. And so, when in July 1954, Sam Phillips gave Dewey a copy of "That's All Right, Mama" sung by an unknown singer, Dewey was able to spread the word.

DJs like Dewey prided themselves on their ear for talent. As Sam Phillips is quoted, "When he picked a damn record, he didn't want to be wrong. . .'Cause when he went on the air, he just blabbed it right out, 'It's gonna be a hit, it's gonna be a hit, it's the biggest thing you ever heard" (Guralnick 1994, 99).

The personalities of rock & roll were a large part of what drew so many people to the genre. Because of this, record companies were able to cash in on names like Elvis and Little Richard because they added a face to go with the music. However, these big companies were often less than scrupulous in their dealings with musicians, and scandal within the establishments of music was practically inevitable.

Summary

WHERE DID ROCK & ROLL COME FROM? 22

- The term "rock & roll" originally referred to sexual intercourse. As applied to music, it, in many ways, retains this association.

- Rock & roll evolves as R&B starts to move northward with the Great Migration, and the music starts to appeal to white Americans.

- With racial barriers being broken down in the United States, an increasing number of young baby boomers, and rebellious personas like James Dean as portrayed in films, rock & roll had a ready and willing audience.

- The solid-bodied electric guitar changes music by offering a more aggressive, amplified sound.

HOW DID ROCK & ROLL FIRST EMERGE IN THE UNITED STATES? 25

- Ray Charles's "I Got a Woman" introduces the full-throated gospel voice to R&B.

- Joe Turner's "Good Rockin' Tonight," later covered by Wynonie Harris, is one of the first "shouting" songs. It would eventually be covered by Elvis Presley.

- "Rocket '88" by Ike Turner brings two additional elements to the sound. It brings guitar distortion and the long-standing relationship between the rock & roller and his beloved automobile.

- Little Richard belts out the first highly sexed, somewhat off-the-wall hits. His persona of the oddball, who wears lipstick, makeup, and strange clothing, will become a rock & roll prototype for later glam-rockers and others.

- Chuck Berry is one of the first rock & roll singers/composers/ guitarists. For the first time, the guitar player is the front man, and his guitar playing, with leads and trademark "moves," becomes essential to the persona.

- Sam Phillips at Sun Records Studios first records R&B singers, and later brings in country and hillbilly music. He looks for the perfect mix: a white singer who can absorb all these influences.

- Elvis Presley walks in to Sun Studio and records "That's All Right, Mama," which turns him into a local star overnight.

- Jerry Lee Lewis cultivates more of a "bad boy" image and is often referred to as the "white Little Richard"

- Carl Perkins composes "Blue Suede Shoes" and starts to challenge Presley on the Billboard charts.

HOW WAS ROCK & ROLL MARKETED? 33

- Promoters have been essential to the industry of rock & roll. They took a music with complex roots and managed to package it for mass consumption.

- Alan Freed is generally credited with bringing the term "rock & roll" into popular usage. He managed to merge the music with television and film industries, creating a format and audience that will keep growing.

- Dewey Phillips, the Tennessee DJ, is one of many local DJs who found inspiration and local talent in R&B. He introduced talents like Elvis Presley to a mainstream audience.

- "Colonel" Tom Parker managed to market and control the rock personality. He recreated Elvis Presley, turning him from being a rocker to a sort of persona who is everything to everybody.

Key Terms

Alan Freed Cleveland disc jockey and radio personality known as "Moondog" and credited with bringing rock & roll to a mainstream teenage audience *22*

First Rock & Roll Ball a highly successful rock concert held in New York City and organized by Freed, noteworthy for its integrated audience *22*

rock & roll a term first used to describe sexual intercourse that, in the 1950s, became the term for the popular, youth-oriented music trend that was sweeping the nation *22*

Sun Studio Memphis recording studio run by Sam Phillips that became the focus point for the crossover of music from R&B to rock & roll *23*

Mississippi Delta location in the American South, where the acoustic delta blues would first emerge with singers like Robert Johnson and Son House *23*

James Dean American actor who first achieved popularity in the film *Rebel Without a Cause*, created one of the first personas of the rebellious American teenager, and was admired by Elvis Presley *24*

Chess Record Studio Chicago recording studio partly responsible for the "Chicago Sound," a new, beat-oriented R&B sound that would eventually become rock & roll *25*

Muddy Waters migrating blues musician who was among the first to integrate amplified electric guitar sounds into music and record songs that would become rock & roll standards *25*

45 seven-inch vinyl record with a single and a backing song ("B-side") that made rock & roll songs available to the youth market *25*

Leo Fender radio repairman who revolutionized the guitar sound by developing a solid-bodied electric guitar *25*

Ray Charles soul singer whose full-throated vocal style in the early 1950s would influence rock & roll singing style *25*

(continued)

"Good Rockin' Tonight" one of the first rock & roll songs about sex, which popularized the "shouting" style of rock & roll when recorded by Wynonie Harris *26*

"Rocket '88" song recorded by Ike Turner and his band in 1951, pioneered the use of distortion *26*

Little Richard born Richard Penniman in 1932, a flamboyant rock & roll showman with major 1950s hits, including "Long Tall Sally" and "Tutti Frutti" *27*

"Tutti Frutti" an early rock & roll song popularized by Little Richard after its original sexually explicit lyrics were tamed into nonsense sounds *27*

Chuck Berry born 1926, a pioneer of rock & roll guitar *28*

Sam Phillips head of Sun Studio, responsible for helping launch the career of Elvis Presley *29*

Elvis Presley born in Mississippi in 1936, one of the first white musicians to popularize black R&B and blues songs with credibility *29*

Beale Street Memphis, Tennessee, cultural center for African-American music *29*

Arthur "Big Boy" Crudup born in 1905 in Mississippi, he wrote "That's All Right, Mama," the song that would launch Elvis Presley's career, although he received little credit or compensation for it *30*

Jerry Lee Lewis born in 1935, pioneering pianist, vocalist, and bad boy during the early days of rock & roll *32*

Carl Perkins born in 1932, singer-guitarist who composed the hit "Blue Suede Shoes" *32*

AM radio broadcasting technology that provides high-fidelity sound over radio airwaves *33*

Dewey Phillips Memphis disc jockey who helped popularize Elvis Presley's music *34*

"Colonel" Tom Parker Elvis Presley's manager who marketed him as an icon rather than just a musician *35*

Sample Test Questions

1. In what city did disc jockey Alan Freed hold his first "Moondog" concert?
   a. New York City
   b. Cleveland
   c. Chicago
   d. Atlanta

2. Which of these factors did NOT contribute to the popularization of rock & roll?
   a. the Great Migration
   b. the popularity of R&B
   c. the Cold War
   d. the increased prosperity of the white middle class

3. Which of these statements is correct?
   a. Elvis Presley was born in Memphis.
   b. Chess Records was located in New York City.
   c. Muddy Waters was born in Mississippi.
   d. Chuck Berry grew up in New Orleans.

4. Which of the following was the first song to break the pop charts' color barrier?
   a. "Maybellene"
   b. "Honey, Don't"
   c. "I Got a Woman"
   d. "That's All Right, Mama"

5. Which song was written by Joe Turner?
   a. "Good Rockin' Tonight"
   b. "Hound Dog"
   c. "Johnny B. Goode"
   d. "Tutti Frutti"

ESSAY

6. Discuss the impact of the Great Migration on rock & roll.

7. What factors led to a greater audience for rock & roll in the 1950s?

8. How did the persona of the rock singer evolve?

9. What techniques did managers use to promote rock & roll?

10. How did R&B singers influence early rock & roll?

WHERE TO START YOUR RESEARCH PAPER

For an overview of the origins of rock & roll, go to
http://www.britannica.com/EBchecked/topic/1485091/rock-and-roll

For an in-depth biography of the artists, go to
http://www.allmusic.com or http://www.rollingstone.com/artists

To research past and present Billboard 100 charts, go to
http://www.billboard.com.

To learn more about the origins of R&B, go to
http://www.nostalgiacentral.com/music/merseybeat.htm

Answers: 1. b; 2. c; 3. c; 4. a; 5. a

Remember to check www.thethinkspot.com for additional information, downloadable flashcards, and other helpful resources.

Psychologists

suggested yesterday that while the rock 'n' roll craze seemed to be related to "rhythmic behavior patterns" as old as the Middle Ages, it required full study as a current phenomenon.

One educational psychologist asserted that what happened in and around the Paramount Theatre yesterday [a rock & roll show starring disc jockey Alan Freed and the screening of the rock & roll movie "Don't Knock the Rock"] struck him as "very much like the medieval type of spontaneous lunacy where one person goes off and lots of other persons go off with him. . . ."

Meanwhile, a parallel between rock 'n' roll and St. Vitus Dance has been drawn by Dr. Joost A. M. Meerlo, associate in psychiatry at Columbia University, in a study just completed for publication. . . .

Dr. Meerlo described the "contagious epidemic of dance fury" that "swept Germany and spread to all of Europe" toward the end of the fourteenth century. It was called . . . St. Vitus Dance (or Chorea Major), he continued, with its victims breaking into dancing and being unable to stop. The same activity in Italy, he noted, was referred to as Tarantism and popularly related to a toxic bite by the hairy spider called tarantula.

"The Children's Crusades and the tale of the Pied Piper of Hamelin," Dr. Meerlo went on, "remind us of these seductive, contagious dance furies."

Dr. Meerlo described his first view of rock 'n' roll this way: Young people were moved by a juke box to dance themselves "more and more into a prehistoric rhythmic trance until it had gone far beyond all the accepted versions of human dancing."

Sweeping the country and even the world, the craze "demonstrated the violent mayhem long repressed everywhere on earth," he asserted.

He also saw possible effects in political terms:

"Why are rhythmical sounds and motions so especially contagious? A rhythmical call to the crowd easily foments mass ecstasy: 'Duce! Duce! Duce!' The call repeats itself into the mind of all reasonable inhibitions . . . as in drug addiction, a thousand years of civilization fall away in a moment."

Dr. Meerlo predicted that the craze would pass "as have all paroxysms of exciting music." But he said that the psychic phenomenon was important and dangerous. He concluded in this way:

"Rock 'n' roll is a sign of depersonalization of the individual, of ecstatic veneration of mental decline and passivity.

"If we cannot stem the tide with its waves of rhythmic narcosis and of future waves of vicarious craze, we are preparing our own downfall in the midst of pandemic funeral dances.

"The dance craze is the infantile rage and outlet of our actual world. In this craze the suggestion of deprivation and dissatisfaction is stimulated and advertised day by day. In their automatic need for more and more, people are getting less and less."

—Milton Bracker, *New York Times*, February 23, 1957

THE ESTABLISHMENT STRIKES BACK (1954–1960)

CHAPTER 03

HOW DID ROCK & ROLL DIVIDE THE GENERATIONS?

The *New York Times* article exemplifies a common theme in 1950s news: Rock & roll was an illness or psychological disturbance rather than just a new kind of music. It was a demon that had stolen their children, and parents wanted to know how to fight it. In the eyes of the older generation, rock & roll prompted an abandonment of traditional values, inspiring irreverence, wild dancing, and sexual impropriety.

American teenagers, on the other hand, felt inspired and almost desperate for the fast, rhythmic beats, the unencumbered dance moves, and the freedom inspired by rock & roll music. Caught up in the new dance "craze," teenagers across the country wiggled and shook to rock & roll. The music changed not only what teenagers listened to—it changed what they thought and how they expressed themselves. Teenagers weren't trying to restrain their passions, and their parents were not happy.

Rock Gets Its First "Black Eye"

In 1953, Dwight D. Eisenhower took office as the President of the United States. The Great Depression and World War II were in the past. Americans had rebuilt their lives and turned their focus to progress in schools, careers, and the home. Beneath this drive was the Cold War and fear of communism. Racial tensions also simmered just beneath society's surface. Much of the country was still segregated. Schools were soon to be integrated, but whites and African Americans continued to live in separate areas and often existed culturally independent of one other.

Rock & roll was one of the first distinct movements in teen culture to emerge in the United States. Teens were also emerging as a financially lucrative demographic. They had plenty of free time; they drove cars and had disposable income from jobs or allowances. These factors meant they were often viewed as aimless and unprincipled to the point where some teenagers became characterized as rebellious juvenile delinquents. The teens most often cast in these roles by the suspicious older generation typically belonged to ethnic minorities or to the working class, and they lived in cities and suburbs more often than rural areas. Teen rebels such as James Dean and Marlon Brando epitomized the juvenile delinquent of the era.

Most teenagers listened to popular, or **pop music**, singers like **Frank Sinatra**. Rock & roll music, however, was displacing pop music as the most popular music for teens across the country. Disc jockeys like Alan Freed—about whom you read in Chapter 2—helped foster the movement. Freed said of rock & roll, "It's the rhythm that gets the kids. They are starved for music they can dance to after all those years of crooners" (DeCurtis 1992, 46). Because rock & roll began as an underground movement identified with the African American community and because its audience was known for rowdiness, the older generation and the press quickly came to associate rock & roll with juvenile defiance and delinquency.

BLACKBOARD JUNGLE

One film in particular influenced older Americans' increasingly negative view of rock & roll. Richard Brooks' *Blackboard Jungle*, based on Evan Hunter's novel by the same title, was released in the spring of 1955. The film portrays troubled and violent juvenile delinquents making their own rules in an inner-city U.S. high school. Richard Dadier, played by Glenn Ford, is an idealistic teacher who is determined to reach his confrontational and volatile students. The explosive Artie West, played by Vic Morrow, leads the juvenile delinquents. In one scene, West pulls a knife and challenges Dadier to kick him out of class. Dadier refuses to give up on these students that everyone else has forgotten.

The movie's depiction of adolescents as a threat to the established social order was a common social issue of the time. President Eisenhower, in a State of the Union address given in 1955, declared an emergency: "To help the states do a better job, we must strengthen their resources for preventing and dealing with juvenile delinquency. I shall propose federal legislation to assist the states in dealing with this nationwide problem" (Dawson 2005, 120). In *Blackboard Jungle*, a written introduction appears on screen before the opening credits roll: The scenes and incidents depicted here are fictional. However, we believe that public awareness is a first step toward a remedy for any problem. It is in this spirit and with this faith that *Blackboard Jungle* was produced (Doherty 2002, 110).

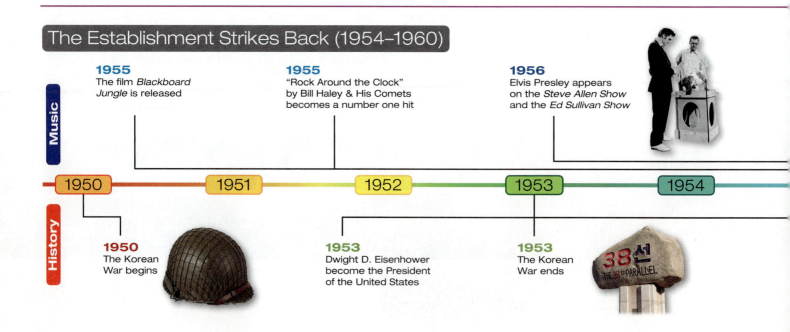

The Establishment Strikes Back (1954–1960)

Music

1955
The film *Blackboard Jungle* is released

1955
"Rock Around the Clock" by Bill Haley & His Comets becomes a number one hit

1956
Elvis Presley appears on the *Steve Allen Show* and the *Ed Sullivan Show*

1950 | 1951 | 1952 | 1953 | 1954

History

1950
The Korean War begins

1953
Dwight D. Eisenhower become the President of the United States

1953
The Korean War ends

As the statements fade, the credits begin to the sounds of "Rock Around the Clock" by Bill Haley and His Comets.

Although the film went on to be nominated for four Oscars, its scathing social commentary immediately spawned controversy. Groups of teachers, the American Legion, and even the Girl Scouts condemned the movie (Altschuler 2003, 32). Many cities were angered over the portrayal of public schools. The movie upset officials in New Brunswick, New Jersey, enough that they refused to show it unless it included a disclaimer stating that the school in the film was unlike any found in their town. In March 1955, the *Hollywood Reporter* reported that a group who called itself the Institute of Public Opinion sent postcards to film critics, warning them that the film was "anti-public schools" and that it was pure fiction; no schools as bad as the school in the movie could possibly be found in the United States (TCM 2009).

THE TEENAGE NATIONAL ANTHEM

The press and others didn't object only to the social commentary of the film, they objected to its music; "Rock Around the Clock" blared, in sharp contrast to the bland opening music for other films. At the first notes, many teenaged audience members sprang to their feet, cheering and dancing in the aisles, even ripping theater seats from the floor in some

POP MUSIC shortened name of "popular music".

FRANK SINATRA American singer popular in the 1940s and 1950s.

BLACKBOARD JUNGLE controversial film that showed juvenile delinquency in the 1950s and connected it with rock & roll through the use of its opening song "Rock Around the Clock".

> ∧ ∧ ∧ The themes and violence in *Blackboard Jungle* influenced people's opinions on rock & roll.

cases. Singer Frank Zappa said of watching the film that he heard Bill Haley "playing the Teenage National Anthem and it was LOUD. I was jumping up and down" (Altschuler 2003). Some theaters ran the first reel in silence to prevent destruction of their property; others banned the movie altogether in fear of the wild vandalism characteristic of its audiences both inside and outside the theaters. In many venues, police were planted in the aisles and outside to deter any violence. Hearing the song in connection with the juvenile delinquents in the film and seeing the vandalism the song inspired, rock & roll's critics were armed with more evidence of the new music's perils.

Ironically, rock & roll—the music perceived in the wake of the film's popularity to be an illness plaguing America's teenagers—was a late addition to the film. Originally, the juvenile delinquents in *Blackboard Jungle* were to be characterized as pop-music enthusiasts, as were many teenagers of the time. As the film neared

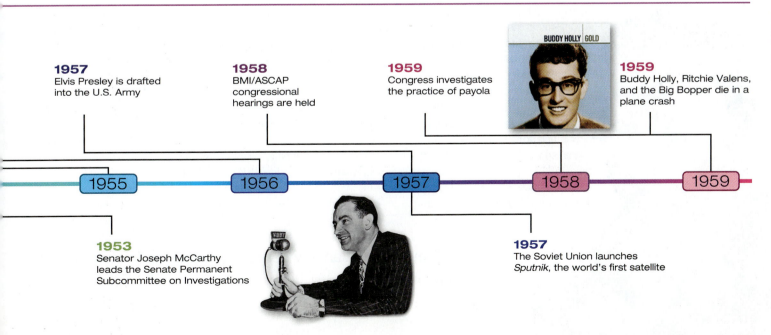

1957 Elvis Presley is drafted into the U.S. Army

1958 BMI/ASCAP congressional hearings are held

1959 Congress investigates the practice of payola

1959 Buddy Holly, Ritchie Valens, and the Big Bopper die in a plane crash

1955　1956　1957　1958　1959

1953 Senator Joseph McCarthy leads the Senate Permanent Subcommittee on Investigations

1957 The Soviet Union launches *Sputnik*, the world's first satellite

TOP OF THE CHARTS
WHAT'S HOT!
JULY 9, 1955

1. "Rock Around the Clock" – Bill Haley and His Comets
2. "Cherry Pink and Apple Blossom White" – Perez Prado
3. "Blossom Fell/If I May" – Nat (King) Cole
4. "Unchained Melody" – Les Baxter
5. "Learnin' the Blues" – Frank Sinatra
6. "Something's Gotta Give" – McGuire Sisters
7. "Honey-babe" – Art Mooney
8. "Hard to Get" – Giselle McKenzie
9. "Unchained Melody" – Al Hibbler
10. "It's a Sin to Tell a Lie" – Somethin' Smith & the Redheads

completion, however, Elvis Presley became the world-renowned icon of rock, and the popularity of rock & roll skyrocketed. To maintain cultural relevance, Brooks knew he needed a rock & roll song in the film to legitimize the portrayal of the juvenile delinquents. According to Peter Ford, son of *Blackboard Jungle*'s lead actor Glenn Ford, the idea for using the song "Rock Around the Clock" came when the elder Ford borrowed his son's record of the single. Rather than rewrite any scenes, Brooks added the track to the opening and closing credits, forever associating the tumultuous juvenile delinquents with rock.

WHAT EFFECT DID SCANDALS HAVE ON ROCK?

Another "Black Eye" for Rock: ASCAP vs. BMI

Until the 1940s, the **American Society of Composers, Authors, and Publishers (ASCAP)** held nearly all publishing rights to recorded music. They demanded high royalties and often battled radio stations over payment for broadcasting their music. ASCAP even advised songwriters not to allow their music to be played on the radio because ASCAP placed a greater value on live performances. At the end of the 1930s, ASCAP dramatically increased their royalty fees, which alienated radio broadcasters. In the early 1940s, the situation escalated to the point that radio broadcasters boycotted ASCAP music and formed a new music licensing company, **Broadcast Music Incorporated (BMI)**, as a means to fight ASCAP's licensing monopoly.

Until the formation of BMI, ASCAP ruled as the established power in the licensing industry and was able to determine which musicians' songs would be played on the radio. ASCAP predominately selected established musicians who brought a large songwriter's catalogue for licensing.

As a result, music made by racial minorities or musicians from lower- and working-class backgrounds were often denied licensure and access to ASCAP's services. Thus, African American rhythm & blues musicians, country & western musicians, and emerging rock & roll singers all swarmed to BMI upon its formation. BMI's profits skyrocketed, and the songs they owned soon dominated the music charts. In fact, by 1955, BMI licensed 80 percent of all music played on the radio (Altschuler 2004, 134).

Starting as early as 1953, a group called the Songwriters of America, which was largely made up of ASCAP members, fought against BMI's new power. These ASCAP members argued that they were not getting radio play because the radio executives that owned stock in BMI played only BMI-licensed songs on their stations. In 1958, ASCAP asked Congress to pass a bill that would prevent broadcasters from owning any stock in BMI to remove this conflict of interest and end the involvement of radio networks in music publishing and promotion. Soon, a congressional committee was organized to investigate and examine BMI's alleged conflict of interest.

Witnesses such as songwriter **Oscar Hammerstein II** were eager to support ASCAP. Hammerstein testified that BMI and its control over the radio-station owners had duped the public into liking "poor" music. Hammerstein went on to insist that the American public were being forced into listening to music they didn't necessarily like by BMI stock-owning radio executives. The public still enjoyed the classics, he argued, but they weren't given the chance to hear them. **Arlan Coolidge**, chairman of the Department

<<< ASCAP members Alan Jay Lerner, Ira Gershwin (pictured), and Virgil Thompson filed a lawsuit against BMI and other major networks for influencing what was played on the radio.

Payola and the Corruption of Teenagers:
How Conservatives Made a Case Against Rock and Roll

of Music at Brown University, also testified, asking for legislation to end the "monopolistic control" over the music that was being played on the radio, television, and jukeboxes. Coolidge stated that as soon as the hold the industry had over teens ended, people would find that teens really did prefer more classical, traditional music—such as the music proffered by ASCAP.

Journalist and social critic **Vance Packard** made ASCAP synonymous with the clean, wholesome culture desired by many in the United States. Packard testified before Congress that BMI was flooding the airways with poor music and obscene, sexually charged lyrics—the music responsible for the corruption of American teenagers. Packard's testimony reflected a common fear among many Americans and politicians: that rock was poison and had no value or place in the American society.

BMI, however, argued that it was merely trying to provide licensure to those who would otherwise be shut out of the music industry. BMI held an open-door policy and signed musicians who were ignored by ASCAP, while ASCAP required artists to have a minimum of five hit singles as a prerequisite of membership. Also unlike ASCAP, BMI's musicians were given equal royalties for radio play and live performances. Other witnesses for BMI also testified that many radio stations had relationships with both BMI and ASCAP. In addition, they argued, radio stations played BMI songs, especially rock & roll, not because these songs were owned by BMI, but because rock & roll was popular.

In the end, ASCAP didn't get the proposed changes in legislation that they wanted, as Congress decided BMI had not locked ASCAP out of airplay. ASCAP, however, was not ready to back down. They would soon find another way to attack BMI and rock music.

The Payola Scandal

In October 1959, Congress began hearings into quiz-show scandals, finding that TV game shows were sometimes rigged to allow popular contestants to return week after week. In the midst of the quiz show uproar, ASCAP asked House Oversight Subcommittee Chairman Oren Harris, an Arkansas Democrat, to investigate what it claimed were BMI's unlawful practices of using "payola" to ensure that their songs would be played on the radio. **Payola** (which combines the words "pay" and "Pianola"—the

trademark name for a player piano) refers to the practice of paying disc jockeys and other radio executives to play certain records. Sometimes, DJs were paid in cash; other times they were given rights to records or were sent on extravagant vacations. At the time, payola was not a federal crime, though it was considered illegal in several states.

Once Congress announced its intention to hold hearings on payola, radio stations began firing many of the disc jockeys implicated in the practice; others quit to avoid being linked to the scandal. Well-known local disc jockeys such as Joe Niagara of WIBG Philadelphia and Murray "The K" Kaufman of WINS New York were called to testify before Congress. In their testimonies they were "asked to confess their sins, which began with playing rock & roll in the first place, and only ended with the taking of money" (DeCurtis 1992, 63). Members of the Congressional committee made no effort to hide their distaste for and bias against rock & roll.

Many of the witnesses—including presidents of record companies and distribution centers—testified that payola was the only reason rock & roll was popular. They contended that rock & roll's popularity was a farce, that ratings were based solely on payola, and that there was no way rock music would survive unless the machine of payola fed it. Some of the witnesses were angry about the payola system and hoped to gain back the power they once had. They were tired of competing against the power that rock music seemed to hold over radio play.

ALAN FREED AND DICK CLARK

Alan Freed and Dick Clark became two of the main targets of the payola investigation. Both men had TV shows popular with teen audiences. Both men were instrumental in the promotion of rock music. Freed and Clark had two very different experiences in the hearings, however, which were influenced by their public personas.

Freed was very popular with teenagers and African Americans; his peers, however, found him to be controversial. He supported the original hits made by African Americans, and not the sanitized covers made for white audiences. His shows had racially integrated audiences and often resulted in violence and even in riots. He was characterized as the "bad boy" of rock and was viewed as an instigator of teenage rebellion.

Flashpoints ISSUES in ROCK   Payola

The established powers of the 1950s and the older generation were terrified of what had become of American culture, the music industry, and music itself. They claimed the only possible explanation for the growth and popularity of such bad music was payola and its wide reach throughout the industry.

However, payola, though a new term, was not a new practice in the industry. Before the 1950s Congressional hearing got underway, *Billboard* magazine published an article arguing that the new term referred to an old practice, one that had been part of the music industry since the vaudeville days of the 1920s and that had flourished during the big band days of the 1930s and 1940s, when popular singers and bands were paid to perform certain songs on stage.

Payola in the 1950s was different from the payola of previous years, however. Rock & roll was easier to obtain: it was produced on inexpensive 45 records and was readily accessible on the radio or on popular television shows, meaning the public was less reliant on live performance to enjoy music. Teenagers as a demographic with purchasing power created an audience susceptible to the influence of popular disc jockeys and radio stations, and music labels sought to exploit that influence to drive sales.

Payola was also a means by which small independent record labels (those that often signed rock & roll and African American musicians) could compete with the major labels to get their records on the air. By using payola, these small labels flourished in the 1950s, breaking the established labels' monopoly on the music industry. To fight the new power and influence of the small independent labels, the big labels pushed for congressional hearings and tried to prove that the popularity of rock music was a farce. Indeed, as we discuss in this chapter, the payola hearings themselves were "rigged" to favor industry insiders like Dick Clark, while punishing "bad" influences like Alan Freed, pictured.

When the payola scandal came to light, Freed had little chance of surviving the hearings unscathed. When radio and TV executives gave Freed a statement to sign in which he would deny the acceptance of payola, Freed refused. He felt that signing this acknowledgment would be an insult; he wasn't going to play the game his employers wanted. During the hearings, Freed claimed the payments he received were consultation fees, not pay-for-play payments. The committee and much of the public didn't believe him, and he was charged with violating New York's bribery laws.

On November 11, 1959, in one of his final shows, Freed thanked the music industry and the fans for their support over the years and left by saying, "this is not good-bye, it's just good night" (Media of Alan Freed 1998). But it was good-bye: His days in the industry were over. Both ABC-radio and WNEW-TV promptly fired him, and Freed never recovered either financially or professionally. He was blacklisted from the music industry and jailed.

In contrast, Dick Clark, aided by his employer, ABC, spent a great deal of time and effort in his preparation for the hearings. Prior to the hearings, Clark had financial stakes in publishing houses, independent record labels, distributors, and even a record-processing plant. Before he testified, he divested himself of several record companies at the request of ABC. In addition, he came to the hearings prepared. He hired a statistician to show that he played records because they were popular and not because he would retain a profit.

Clark also testified that the work of the committee would be helpful to the music industry and that he was willing to follow any guidelines the committee set. During his testimony, he was evasive and claimed ignorance, but he never lost his composure. He explained that he got caught up in rock & roll as a business opportunity. He was in the music industry—where else would he invest his money? Clark claimed he didn't know if any of his firms or businesses had used payola because he wasn't in the practice of tracking his finances. The occasions on which he did accept gifts, he did so because he was unsure how to return them.

The committee had a strong case against Clark. They even supplied a complex web of diagrams that showed the music industry with Dick Clark at the center of the web (DeCurtis 1992). The government also had its own statisticians undermine the work of Clark's statistician. Yet Clark, with his clean-cut image, was not brought up on charges. Although he had to sell nearly all of his holdings in the industry, he survived with his career and reputation intact (for more information on Dick Clark, see Chapter 4).

∧∧∧ Many disc jockeys were **brought before Congress** to testify about the extent of **the payola scandal.**

THE END OF PAYOLA

The committee looking into payola eventually discovered that over $263,000 was paid to 207 broadcasters, mostly disc jockeys, in 42 cities (Martin & Segrave 1993, 75–77). The payola hearings affected all facets of the music industry. Based on the hearings, Congress amended the Federal Communications Act, making it illegal to use bribery to ensure airplay. The industry was restructured, and the distribution of music became easier to control. The small, unregulated record labels that succeeded during the payola era could no longer compete in the post-hearing industry. They didn't have the resources needed to lure new talent and could not compete with the promotional capabilities of major labels.

The congressional committee members at the payola hearings also made it very clear that rock & roll would no longer be tolerated. The committee advised against the procurement and distribution of rock and claimed that the music lacked merit as a financial investment. In the hearings, the committee worked hard to prove that rock music existed only because of payola and therefore wasn't popular enough to receive airplay. They also pointed out that radio stations would be responsible for what their disc jockey employees played. If a DJ played any unsavory music such as rock, the radio station would be held accountable. As a result, some disc jockeys were no longer allowed to select records to play on their shows and instead were required to play songs chosen by radio executives. Some stations even forbade use of the terms "disc jockey" and "rock & roll" on the air to further distance themselves from the scandal. Radio stations and record companies were quick to play more "acceptable," melodic music.

After many executives lost their jobs due to the payola scandal, the new representatives

>>> **Payola** was a factor in the massive **increase in record sales** in the 1950s.

who replaced them were hired for their conservative reputations and judgments. These newcomers were afraid to take a risk on any new music or talent that might cause trouble. With the congressional hearings and changes that ensued, rock music had gotten another "black eye."

Increase in Record Sales in the 1950s

$700,000,000
$600,000,000
$500,000,000
$400,000,000
$300,000,000
$200,000,000
$100,000,000

$603,000,000

$213,000,000

1954   1959

IN WHAT OTHER WAYS WAS ROCK MUSIC ATTACKED IN THE 1950s?

Attack of the Musical Mainstream

Even before the hearings and scandals of the late 1950s, music industry representatives were proclaiming the end of rock at the same time as the rock movement spread across the nation. As early as 1956, Mitch Miller, a director of **Artists and Repertoire (A&R)** for Columbia Records, reported that, "Quality show tunes are pushing Rock 'n' Roll back into its proper place" (Dettmar 2006, 49). Miller's views were representative of those of the music establishment of the time and circulated throughout the industry and media. He felt, as did much of the establishment, that rock would quickly fade, and any admission of its popularity would only extend the fad.

THE PLAN OF ATTACK

Miller proposed a plan to allow the popular music industry to fight off the undesirable interest in rock & roll. He wanted representatives in the industry to essentially ignore rock and the purchasing power of the teen demographic, and keep their focus on **MOR**, or middle-of-the-road, music aimed at a more sophisticated, adult audience.

Some critics had a hard time trusting his plan, however. First, it was hard to argue against the impressive profits to be made by selling not just rock music but also the merchandise affiliated with rock singers. When MOR artist Frank Sinatra was at his most popular, merchandise carrying his name or image was insignificant in scope and sales. In contrast, when Elvis Presley was at his peak, about $22 million dollars worth of merchandise had been sold (Austen 2005, 14). You could buy Elvis Presley shoes, skirts, T-shirts, handkerchiefs, lipstick, pillows, and more. Second, radio executives did not want to lose listeners by ignoring requests for rock music. Even though some industry players agreed with Miller, for others, ignoring rock was just too risky.

Those who did agree with Miller went on the offensive. Reporters published near-constant dismissals of rock & roll as a low form of music that any fool could play, and termed it worthless and infantile. In interviews, respected popular musicians disparaged rock music. **Pablo Casals**, a highly regarded cellist, said that rock & roll was "against art, against life. It leads away from the exaltation and elevation of spirit that should spring naturally from all good music" (Dettmar 2006, 54).

Music producers also used aggressive marketing tactics intended to bring about the end of rock and to provide a return to safe, mainstream music. Some encouraged bans on rock music, while others had radio stations advertise that they were unaffiliated with subversive music. Companies played MOR recordings and promoted cover songs in the hopes that they could transform rock into popular, mainstream music. Many of these cover records were remakes by white singers of popular songs made by African Americans. (See Chapter 4 to read more about the practice of hijacking of hits.) Producers also increased access to other types of music, such as calypso, folk music, and **novelty records**. These schemes were all concocted to divert the public's attention away from rock & roll and to focus it on "safer" forms of music.

Dick Clark and MOR

During this time, Dick Clark offered a clean-cut version of rock that adults and the powers-that-be embraced. In contrast to the often volatile audiences at Alan Freed's shows, Clark's hit show, *American Bandstand*, demonstrated the ideal MOR version of rock music. His show featured well-dressed dancers without the stereotypical T-shirts and motorcycle jackets worn by juvenile delinquents. The dancers also kept their distance from each other, demonstrating none of the raucous, sexual moves often associated with rock. Clark and the representatives of the show preferred to show MOR artists, many of whom had some sort of financial relationship with the show (Garofalo 2008). Although Clark is sometimes portrayed as a "sellout" for his part in domesticating rock & roll, many of his guests later became inductees to the Rock & Roll Hall of Fame.

ROCK & ROLL AND THE RED SCARE

In the 1950s, fear of the invasion of communism and the atomic bomb gripped Americans. In Washington, D.C., **Senator Joseph McCarthy** held highly publicized hearings on supposed communist infiltration of industries and organizations throughout the United States, ranging from the Army to the entertainment industry. The hearings incited fear, and, as a result, people across the country supported government investigation into any person or aspect of culture that appeared to be related to communism. In fact, in a poll taken in 1954, 78 percent of Americans thought that reporting the friends and neighbors they suspected of being communists to government authorities was important—even if innocent people were implicated or hurt in the process of investigation (Altschuler 2003, 7).

Anyone could be suspected of being a communist sympathizer. People lived in fear of being accused of communism and took oaths and signed contracts to prove their democratic principles. Those accused were blacklisted and ostracized. People were highly sensitive about anything that could be even remotely misconstrued as communism, and they viewed any kind of dissent from the norm as a possible indication of communist tendencies. People felt anxious, paranoid, and vulnerable.

CLASSIC / RECORDINGS ▶▶▶

LET'S ALL SING WITH THE CHIPMUNKS by Alvin and the Chipmunks

Novelty songs—humorous songs—have appealed to the public and become popular at least since the late 1800s. One of the famous novelty records of the 1950s came from a group called Alvin and the Chipmunks. In 1958, songwriter **Ross Bagdasarian** began experimenting with the playback speed on recordings. He found that if vocals were sped up, the effect was a comical, chirping tone. Bagdasarian also experimented with overtracking—that is, recording one voice and then adding another on top. In one early experiment, Bagdasarian recorded himself singing in three-party harmony, and then sped up the results. Due to the high pitch this produced, he attributed the record to cartoon chipmunks he named Alvin, Simon, and Theodore. In 1958, under the name "David Seville," he released his recording of the Chipmunks as a Christmas novelty record, "The Chipmunk Song (Christmas Don't Be Late)." This song spent four weeks at the top of the music charts. In time, Bagdasarian would also introduce the Chipmunks in a popular television show.

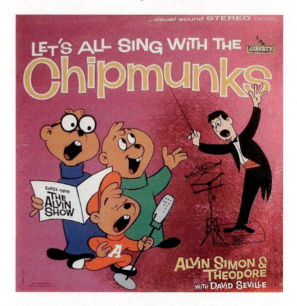

The paranoia of the time was easily projected onto rock & roll. After all, it was a music linked to African Americans, juvenile delinquents, and the lower class—all factions viewed as a threat to the middle class. To parents in the 1950s, rock was mind control powered by the rhythmic beats of sexualized dancing. These characteristics lulled middle-class teens into a weakened state that deprived them of thought, reason, and individuality. For many, it was therefore easy to accept the notion that rock was a transparent communist plot intended to infiltrate middle-class America. The paranoia induced by this fear of communism served to convince many that rock & roll's teenage listeners were easily manipulated into mindless automata of the communist agenda.

The fear that rock & roll was yet another vehicle to indoctrinate Americans in the communist agenda had far-reaching effects that continued for the next 20 years. In the 1970s, the hit television series **Happy Days** intentionally portrayed only the innocent and fun-loving aspects of the 1950s. The show centered on the Cunninghams, a traditional middle-class family in Wisconsin. Fonzie, or "the Fonz," played by Henry Winkler, was the only leather-clad character and did not fit the bill of a thug-like juvenile delinquent. The rest of the teenagers wore letterman's sweaters,

bobby socks, and poodle skirts. They were concerned with love, school, and hanging out at the diner. Over the course of the series, viewers watched the mild-mannered, middle-class teens grow into respectable, law-abiding adults.

In this idyllic fictionalization of 1950s youth, two prominent themes from the 1950s—rock & roll and communism—are glossed over, and their effects on life at the time is ignored. Although Richie, Potsie, Ralph, Fonzie, and the rest of the teens listened to rock & roll on the show, the music was symbolically tamed, contained within the jukebox of Al's Diner. The music did not inspire the teens to rebellion; they remained close to their parents and maintained traditional, middle-class values. Communism is completely absent from the show. The deletion of both of these formative cultural issues from the 1950s echoes the anxiety induced by rock and the paranoia that communist reinforcements and plots could still be at work.

Rock & Roll and Communism

The paranoia and fear engendered by the Red Scare led many to believe that **rock & roll was a communist plot** to control the minds of American teens.

WHAT NEARLY KILLED ROCK & ROLL?

Domestication and the Near Death of Rock Music

Unlike radio, television had a completely different take on rock. Rather than ban it or ignore it, television embraced it. In doing so, television offered audiences a sanitized version of rock that was acceptable and domesticated. Television's format offered audiences the rock musicians they craved while controlling and censoring what people saw and heard.

ELVIS PRESLEY MEETS TELEVISION

Elvis Presley was one of the most popular rock stars of the 1950s, yet he was considered too racy for the mainstream. His hip-thrusting gyrations were expected during his concerts, and as he began to be booked for television shows, his fans expected more of the same. When asked about the way he moved, Presley once said, "Some people tap their feet, some people snap their fingers, and some people sway back and forth. I just sorta do 'em all together, I guess" (Elvis Presley Enterprises 2009).

It wasn't until Presley's second appearance on the *Milton Berle Show* that television executives and television-show hosts would find it necessary to control how rock musicians were portrayed on TV. During the show, Presley sang an extended version of "Hound Dog" complete with a slow, sexually charged stroll. He "seemed wicked and crafty as he flirted with the camera and contorted his body" (Austen 2005, 11). The audience in the studio went crazy, while the people who watched from home—as well as television executives—were shocked by his audacious performance. Television executives who didn't like Presley were now furious. Presley was highly criticized for his performance, with newspapers reporting that he was "appalling," "nauseating," and "couldn't sing a lick" (Martin & Segrave 1993, 63). Presley's song, however, skyrocketed to the top of the charts, and the *Milton Berle Show* got huge ratings.

Presley on the *Steve Allen Show*

Presley was scheduled to appear on the *Steve Allen Show* shortly after his appearance on Berle's show. However, NBC assured the public that Presley would not be shown grinding or dancing inappropriately. In short: Steve Allen was ready to take on Presley.

Allen did not hide his lack of admiration for rock & roll. His show even included a comedy skit in which he gave dramatic readings of rock song lyrics intended to reveal them as tasteless and trite. Years later, Allen said about Presley, "A beautiful sound he never had. . . .it was chiefly his face, a cuteness, a likability" (Austen 2005).

A buzz of anticipation surrounded Presley's big appearance on the show, and Allen didn't want any of Presley's signature hip-shaking seen on air. Allen and NBC executives intended to prevent a recurrence of the provocative gyrations that had caused such uproar, and thus found a way to televise a harmless, desexualized Presley, even going so far as to introduce the "new Elvis Presley" (Dettmar 2006). By having Presley appear in a full tuxedo and perform the song that had caused a sensation on the *Milton Berle Show*, "Hound Dog," as a serenade to a tuxedo-clad basset hound, Presley appeared to mock his own performance on Berle's show. Later in the show, Elvis broke further from his sexy image by playing a simpleton named "Tumbleweed Presley" in a western skit.

Presley on the *Ed Sullivan Show*

Even though the anticipated Presley was not the one shown on the *Steve Allen Show*, the episode out-rated its competitor, the *Ed Sullivan Show*. In response, Presley was quickly booked for three appearances on the *Ed Sullivan Show*.

<<< **Television shows** such as the *Steve Allen Show* **sought ways to domesticate rock.**

ROCK PLACES

Washington, D.C.

Given the overall climate of the 1950s, it comes as no surprise that Washington, D.C., would have an influence on rock & roll. It was the start of the Cold War, and government leaders were consumed with the fight against communism. They were focused on accumulating weapons, spreading democracy, and reaching their goal to be the first nation to explore space. In addition, many government representatives were convinced that rock music was part of a plot to undermine and weaken American society. If you can't control your own people, how can you influence the world?

D.C. was also the site of the music establishment's obvious fight against rock & roll, where government committees listened to testimony in the 1958 BMI-ASCAP hearings and,

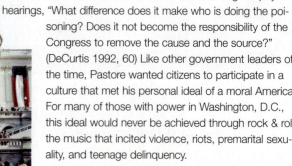

soon after, the Legislative Oversight Subcommittee of the House Committee on Interstate and Foreign Commerce investigated payola. During each of the hearings, testimony was met with the preconceived agenda of congressional committee members, whose main goal was to reduce and eliminate the influence of rock & roll. As Senator John Pastore of Rhode Island stated during the payola hearings, "What difference does it make who is doing the poisoning? Does it not become the responsibility of the Congress to remove the cause and the source?" (DeCurtis 1992, 60) Like other government leaders of the time, Pastore wanted citizens to participate in a culture that met his personal ideal of a moral America. For many of those with power in Washington, D.C., this ideal would never be achieved through rock & roll, the music that incited violence, riots, premarital sexuality, and teenage delinquency.

ELVIS PRESLEY by Elvis Presley

Elvis Presley had a series of hits, many of which reached the top of the charts. These hits were released as singles, the inexpensive record format teens most often purchased at that time. There was little need to produce an album, especially for a rock musician unlikely to attract sales from older Americans. However, in 1956, RCA's director of A&R, Steve Sholes, was convinced that Presley could sell a rock album, especially since Presley's recent television appearances had made him a world-renowned rock star.

The resulting 12-track album, titled *Elvis Presley,* released in 1956, included "Blue Suede Shoes," "Tutti Frutti," and "Blue Moon." The album was cut after two recording sessions, both of which had taken place early in 1956, prior to Presley's famed televi-

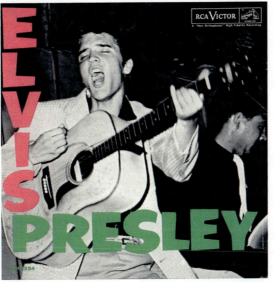

sion appearances. The album, which is demonstrative of Presley's varied influences, including rockabilly, rhythm & blues, and country & western, rapidly rose in the charts and became the first rock & roll album to reach number one. Fans quickly bought copies, and RCA made over 1 million dollars in sales from the album.

Many Presley supporters were not surprised by the fans' reaction to the album. The adoration showered on Presley had become a phenomenon in and of itself. Even today, he is often considered one of the greatest entertainers of all time and has sold more records across the world than any other singer. He also holds records for the most Top 10 hits and the most weeks at number one.

Prior to the highly rated Allen show, Sullivan had vowed never to book Presley, claiming he wasn't a suitable act for family television. But when his competitor drew viewers by booking Presley, Sullivan changed his mind rather quickly. He tried to save face with claims that he had based his criticism of Presley on secondhand reports, not on his personal experience. After hearing tapes of Presley, Sullivan said he decided the rock star wasn't so bad after all, though it was certainly not his favorite music. Unlike Presley's appearance on the *Steve Allen Show*, Presley would be allowed to dance or gyrate on Sullivan's show: however, the viewers at home would never see it.

On September 9, 1956, Sullivan—recuperating at home from an automobile accident—watched stand-in Charles Laughton host Presley's first appearance on his show. Presley opened with "Don't Be Cruel," followed by "Love Me Tender." Sullivan's camera operators used camera angles to show—or not show—what they wished viewers at home to see. Some shots showed Presley from above the waist, others shot him from behind, and still others zoomed in to frame Presley's face. By selecting camera angles, the *Ed Sullivan*

Show was able to censor which moves the audience at home would see and therefore provide TV viewers with a domesticated version of Presley. The show was a huge success: that night, over 80 percent of U.S. television viewers watched the *Ed Sullivan Show* (Martin & Segrave 1993, 64). Although Presley's first appearance did include brief shots showing him from head-to-toe and allowed viewers to see a few of the singer's trademark moves, most hip gyrations were obscured by drums or microphones. In Presley's subsequent two appearances, he would only be filmed above the waist.

"CLEAN TEENS" IN FILM

Like television producers, movie executives also sought ways to domesticate rock to appease the fears of the older generation while still capitalizing on the disposable income of the teen demographic. Some films, such as Alan Freed's *Rock Around the Clock* and *Don't Knock the Rock,* did show the side of rock that brought anxiety to the older generation, but movie executives increasingly felt pressure from the public and therefore began promoting rock movies deemed "clean." One critic describes the new teen films as "light, breezy, romantic, and frankly escapist" (Doherty 2002, 159). These movies focused on middle-class American teens who grappled with themes such as becoming part of a social clique and passing exams, as well as de-sexualized romantic themes centered on such tame concerns as securing a date for the big dance. If there are juvenile delinquents in these films, they often realize the error of their ways, and by the end of the film, they are reconciled with strong, traditional morals. Some of the more famous teen movies include Pat Boone's *April Love* and *Tammy and the Bachelor* with Debbie Reynolds. Publicity for these films often touted their lack of juvenile delinquents or highlighted them as "family" pictures, and their soundtracks didn't feature rock &

<<< "Clean teen" films presented a **sanitized version of rock music** that supported **the values of older generations of Americans.**

JUKEBOX a machine used to play records often found in clubs, diners, and restaurants in the 1950s.

RITCHIE VALENS a rock & roll musician famous for "La Bamba"; killed in a plane crash.

BIG BOPPER a rock & roll musician also known as Jiles Perry Richardson; killed in a plane crash.

BUDDY HOLLY a rock & roll musician who influenced later generations; killed in a plane crash.

DON MCLEAN a musician who wrote the song "American Pie" and coined the phrase "the day the music died".

roll. These clean teen films also delivered the subtle message that teenagers were not a rebellious bunch seeking to overturn traditional American culture.

Rock's Deathbed

The latter part of the 1950s had been hard on rock. The music establishment, ASCAP, and the government achieved a dramatic dampening of rock & roll with the payola scandal, and large record companies regained their domination of the airwaves and played anything *but* rock & roll. The older generation and the established powers were back in control, regulating both the industry and the musical culture in America. Those people who still craved rock & roll were hard-pressed to find it, between MOR music promotions and the frequent banning of rock tracks on radio stations. Moreover, as you'll see, many of the best-known rock personalities had left the industry or had been forced out by scandal.

JERRY LEE LEWIS

Jerry Lee Lewis was one of the first rock musicians to lose ground as a star. His outrageous personality and performances had made his one of the faces of rock most despised by the conservative middle-class watchdogs. They made no secret of their desire to get him out of rock, so it was no surprise when he was forced to stop performing after his 1957 marriage to his 13-year-old third cousin, Myra Gale, was revealed to the public. For months the marriage had been kept a secret from the public. Lewis's representatives at Sun Records knew the announcement of his bride's age would cause problems, and they worked tirelessly to convince Lewis not to announce it. Lewis, however, didn't think his fans would mind, and in 1958, he introduced his bride, claiming she was 15 years old, while he was on tour in England.

Reporters soon uncovered Gale's true age along with the revelation that Lewis wasn't even divorced from his second wife at the time he married Gale, which meant his marriage wasn't even legal. The fallout was devastating. The British press asked the public to boycott his shows, claiming the singer was a danger to young girls. They also wanted Lewis

to be deported. At the concerts that people did attend, Lewis was met by angry crowds screaming that he was a "cradle-robber" (Martin & Segrave 1993). The concert tour was canceled after three appearances, and Lewis returned to the United States.

Back home, Lewis suffered a similar public outcry. He tried to salvage his career, remarrying Gale to ensure the marriage's legality. Lewis even paid for an open letter in the magazine *Billboard*, expressing his hope that the bad publicity wouldn't destroy his career. But there was little support for Lewis at the end of the conservative 1950s. He was quickly blacklisted from radio stations, and people stopped attending his shows.

THE DAY THE MUSIC DIED

The year 1959 held yet another devastating event for rock audiences. It was the year that rock lost **Ritchie Valens**, Jiles Perry Richardson (known as the **Big Bopper**), and **Buddy Holly**. In the winter of 1959, these three performers were part of the "Winter Dance Party" tour through the Midwest. Ritchie Valens, a Hispanic singer from California, rose to stardom with his hits "La Bamba" and "Donna." His songs were at the top of the charts, and he had a top billing on the "Winter Dance Party" tour. The Big Bopper brought in large crowds as well with "Chantilly Lace" and his infamous catch phrase "Hellooo, baby!" Buddy Holly, known for "Peggy Sue" and "That'll Be the Day," joined the tour in need of money. He rocked the stage with his classic black horn-rimmed glasses and drew crowds with his appeal and charm.

While on the tour, the performers grew tired of long, cold bus rides from venue to venue. After their performance on February 3, 1959, Buddy Holly chartered a plane to take himself and his bandmates, Waylon Jennings and Tommy Allsup, to the next stop in Minnesota. During the final preparations for the flight, Jennings and Allsup gave up their seats to Ritchie Valens and the Big Bopper. Shortly after takeoff from Mason City, Iowa, the plane crashed in a cornfield. All three passengers and the pilot were killed.

Many, including musician **Don McLean**, felt that the tragic event was "the day the music died." In McLean's song "American Pie," released in 1971, he symbolically unfolds the evolution of popular music, starting with the death of rock legend Buddy Holly.

McLean was not alone in his sentiments, and many felt that rock had lost three of its most important members in the plane crash.

ROCK ON HIATUS

While Jerry Lee Lewis dropped from sight and Buddy Holly's life was cut tragically short, other rock stars disappeared for short periods, although they continued to sell records.

Chuck Berry was a rocker who spent about two years away from the industry. As noted in Chapter 2, Berry was a controversial figure in the anxiety-ridden climate of the 1950s—he was African American and a

ROCK TECHNOLOGY ▶▶▶ Jukebox

Through all the ups and downs in rock & roll history, one of the most iconic symbols of the 1950s was a technology that almost possesses its own personality: the **jukebox**. One of the first manufacturers of the jukebox was Chicago's J. P. Seeburg Company. Early jukeboxes held only 20 selections; however, as the jukebox soared in popularity after World War II, Seeburg found ways to add more records. In fact, Seeburg was one of the first companies to offer a 100-selection capability, which gave the jukebox its classic look. Records were positioned vertically and encased in transparent plastic so customers could see selections as they were played. Lights,

chrome piping, and sometimes bubbles were added and quickly made the jukebox an object to be both heard and seen. Some of the most famous jukeboxes include the 1952 Seeburg M100C, the 1954 Seeburg HF100R, and the 1954 Rock-Ola 1438 Comet.

The jukebox became a gathering point in clubs, bars, and diners, bringing people together at a time when the increasingly popular phonograph allowed people to listen to music in the privacy of their homes. The jukebox therefore allowed the appreciation of music to be a shared activity, much like a live performance.

Buddy Holly

Although Buddy Holly (born Charles Hardin Holley) had a short career in rock & roll—he died at the age of 22 and had experienced success for just 18 months—he influenced rock music for the next 30 years. Some of the many musicians Holly inspired include the Beatles, the Rolling Stones, Bob Dylan, Linda Ronstadt, the Hollies, and Elvis Costello. It was not just the fact that he wrote his own songs that influenced future rockers; Holly also was one of the first rockers to use a variety of studio techniques in his songs.

As early as high school, Holly was playing in a band. Soon after high school he played as the opening act for musicians on tour when they passed through his hometown of Lubbock, Texas. In those early performances, he played country & western music. In 1955, he even opened for Elvis Presley, and in 1957,

he had his own number one hit, "That'll Be the Day," as a member of the Crickets. In total, Holly released three studio albums before this death, including hits such as "Oh, Boy" and "Peggy Sue." Numerous compilation albums were released following Holly's death.

Holly and his band were not just popular in the United States. In England, where they spent a month on tour, their popularity rivaled that of Elvis. In 1976, Paul McCartney purchased the rights to Holly's prolific song catalogue and organized a tribute to Holly, known as "Buddy Holly Week." Holly was further immortalized in the film about his life, *The Buddy Holly Story*, and he was inducted into the Rock Hall of Fame in 1986.

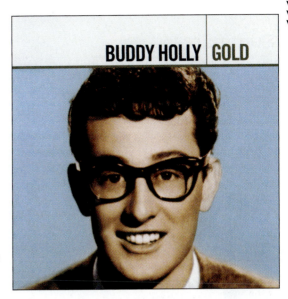

rock & roller. Berry's career flourished throughout the 1950s until it came to a sudden halt in 1959.

While on tour in Mexico, Berry met Janice Escalante, a 14-year-old girl. Berry brought her to St. Louis to work in his nightclub, Club Bandstand. One night, police picked up Escalante as a prostitute after she allegedly solicited someone for sexual favors. Escalante recounted her link to Berry. Authorities were quick to prosecute Berry for his violation of the Mann Act, the law that prohibited the transportation of minors across state lines for immoral purposes. Berry was found guilty and sentenced to prison and a fine of $5,000. Although he was released two years later, the press took advantage of this opportunity to use Berry's race and alleged depravity as another example of the immorality of rock & roll. Even though Berry's career was tarnished, he continued to sell records while he served his prison term and would later return to rock after his release.

During this tumultuous period, Elvis Presley also was on hiatus. However, this break from the rock scene didn't tarnish his career; rather, it improved his standing in the public eye. Presley took a short break from rock & roll in two very different ways. His manager, Tom Parker, orchestrated the first. Parker recognized that the so-called "bad repu-

tation" of rock & roll musicians had helped Presley achieve stardom. However, now that Presley was at the top of rock, Parker knew he needed to change his reputation if his appeal was to continue to spread into adult audiences. Parker therefore slowly shifted the focus of Presley's career toward film, as mentioned in Chapter 2.

Presley's second break from rock occurred in 1957, when he was drafted into the U.S. Army. While serving as a soldier from 1958 to 1960, Presley remained in the public eye. Cameras and reporters followed him from his first Army haircut to his transfer to basic training in Texas. Parker also made sure that Presley's music and films did not go unnoticed, releasing a backlog of records and Presley's film *King Creole*. Presley's popularity grew with adult audiences. He was now a model citizen, considered by many a patriot. His reputation changed from the sexually charged rocker to a more sophisticated musician. Once his service was over, he quickly transitioned back to the music and film industry.

By the end of 1959, rock & roll's decline in popularity made it seem less threatening to the mainstream. Rock quietly slipped from the headlines into the background to be played only on the phonographs of die-hard fans.

Demise of Rock & Roll

- Payola scandal
- Decrease of small labels
- Promotion of MOR and other types of music
- Loss of rock & roll singers

The setbacks of the late 1950s led all but the most ardent fans to believe that **rock & roll was dead.**

Review

Summary

HOW DID ROCK & ROLL DIVIDE THE GENERATIONS? 40

- American teens emerged as a demographic.
- Teens are characterized as undisciplined and rebellious.
- A fraction of teen society becomes characterized as juvenile delinquents with crime, rebellion, and violence as their only intent.
- Teenagers begin to listen to the rhythm & blues music once only associated with African Americans. The sexually charged lyrics and dance moves jar the adult population, which leads them to draw the conclusion that rock music is primitive and base.
- *Blackboard Jungle* cements the link between teenage rebellion and rock & roll.

WHAT EFFECT DID SCANDALS HAVE ON ROCK? 42

- ASCAP launches its campaign to fight BMI and rock & roll.
- BMI holds the rights to the most popular music of the time, which further perpetuates the fight with ASCAP.
- The established powers in the music industry and the government launch congressional hearings on payola.
- Alan Freed is arrested in the payola scandal, while Dick Clark leaves nearly unharmed.
- Small record companies are forced to close doors or sign with large companies due to the effects of payola on the music industry.

IN WHAT OTHER WAY WAS ROCK MUSIC ATTACKED IN THE 1950s? 45

- Mitch Miller launches his plan to eliminate rock from the radio through the promotion of MOR music, cover records, novelty records, and new forms of music.
- Radio stations ban rock music, and the media continue their assault on the evils of rock, attempting to link it with communism.
- Television shows such as *American Bandstand* show a cleaner version of MOR rock music.

WHAT NEARLY KILLED ROCK & ROLL? 48

- Musicians sing cover songs to compete with the more volatile rock music.
- Elvis Presley's image is domesticated by television through strategic camera operations.
- At the request of the public, movie executives clean up teen movies by focusing on light themes.
- Little Richard, Jerry Lee Lewis, Buddy Holly, Ritchie Valens, the Big Bopper, Chuck Berry, and Elvis Presley have all left the rock & roll stage for one reason or another. This is a signal to some that rock has died.

Key Terms

pop music shortened name of "popular music" *40*

Frank Sinatra American singer popular in the 1940s and 1950s *40*

Blackboard Jungle controversial film that showed juvenile delinquency in the 1950s and connected it with rock & roll through the use of its opening song "Rock Around the Clock" *40*

American Society of Composers, Authors, and Publishers (ASCAP) a membership association that held nearly all publishing rights to recorded music until the 1940s *42*

Broadcast Music Incorporated (BMI) a membership association formed as a response to ASCAP's music licensing monopoly *42*

Oscar Hammerstein II an American songwriter who testified for ASCAP in the ASCAP-BMI hearings of 1958 *42*

Arlan Coolidge a chairman at the Department of Music at Brown University who supported legislation in the music industry in the late 1950s *42*

Vance Packard a journalist and social critic in the 1950s who took part in the ASCAP-BMI hearings of 1958 *43*

payola the practice of play for pay on radio stations *43*

Artists and Repertoire the division in a record company that is responsible for the acquisition of new talent *45*

MOR middle-of-the-road, or popular music *45*

Pablo Casals a Spanish cellist and conductor *46*

novelty record a humorous parody *46*

Ross Bagdasarian a songwriter and creator of Alvin and the Chipmunks *46*

Senator Joseph McCarthy a Wisconsin senator who held hearings on alleged communists in the 1940s and 1950s *46*

Happy Days a television show in the 1970s that portrayed a sanitized version of life in the 1950s *47*

jukebox a machine used to play records often found in clubs, diners, and restaurants in the 1950s *50*

Ritchie Valens a rock & roll musician famous for "La Bamba"; killed in a plane crash *50*

Big Bopper a rock & roll musician also known as Jiles Perry Richardson; killed in a plane crash *50*

Buddy Holly a rock & roll musician who influenced later generations; killed in a plane crash *50*

Don McLean a musician who wrote the song "American Pie" and coined the phrase "the day the music died" *50*

Sample Test Questions

1. Why did *Blackboard Jungle* cause controversy?
   a. It was the first "teen" movie.
   b. It showed juvenile delinquency.
   c. It proved all teens were rebellious.
   d. It showed the inexperience of teachers.

2. What was one of the main reasons ASCAP fought against BMI?
   a. BMI took all of their clients.
   b. ASCAP wanted more record companies.
   c. ASCAP had lost control over the industry.
   d. BMI ended rock & roll.

3. What two key people testified at the payola hearings?
   a. Chuck Berry and Elvis Presley
   b. Elvis Presley and Dick Clark
   c. Alan Freed and Dick Clark
   d. Alan Freed and Jerry Lee Lewis

4. Why was rock music considered a communist plot?
   a. Rock music was feared to be a form of mind control.
   b. Rock music was started in the Soviet Union.
   c. Rock music led to rioting.
   d. Rock music was played at large gatherings.

5. Which of the following rock stars left the music industry to serve in the military?
   a. Chuck Berry
   b. Elvis Presley
   c. Ritchie Valens
   d. Jerry Lee Lewis

ESSAY

1. What psychological traits are evident in Dr. Joost A.M. Meerlo's analysis of the dance craze in the 1950s?
2. What factors led the establishment to fear rock music in the 1950s?
3. Describe how BMI and rock music changed the music industry.
4. Compare and contrast Alan Freed and Dick Clark.
5. Analyze two different personas associated with rock in the 1950s.

WHERE TO START YOUR RESEARCH PAPER

For a history of rock & roll in the 1950s, go to
http://www.rockhall.com/teach/sti-lesson-5

For an overview on BMI and the hearings with ASCAP, go to
http://www.fundinguniverse.com/company-histories/Broadcast-Music-Inc-Company-History.html

For an in-depth biography on Alan Freed, go to
http://www.alanfreed.com

For an in-depth biography on Elvis Presley, go to
http://www.elvis.com

To find more information on selected musicians from the 1950s, go to
http://www.rockhall.com

ANSWERS: b, 2. c, 3. c, 4. a, 5. b

Remember to check www.thethinkspot.com for additional information, downloadable flashcards, and other helpful resources.

"Viewers

who are beyond voting age are not likely to derive much pleasure from 'American Bandstand,' the disk jockey show that began yesterday on Channel 7.

"Those who have been voting for quite a few years may, in fact, find this ninety-minute session of music and dancing to be something of an ordeal.

"Presiding over the show, which originates in Philadelphia, is Dick Clark, a well-groomed young man richly endowed with self-assurance. Mr. Clark is inclined, when expressing agreement with guests on his program to use contemporary idioms such as 'Crazy,' 'I'm with you,' and 'Ah, too much.'

"Yesterday's program began with Elvis Presley's interpretation of 'Teddy Bear.' Some of the subsequent records were less atrocious, but most of the lyrics were not memorable. The words of one song ran something like this:

> Let the four winds blow,
> Let them blow, blow, blow.
> From East to the West.
> I love you the best.

"During the program, the studio from which it was televised was crowded with energetic teenagers who danced as the records were played. They were an attractive group of youngsters. The girls wore pretty gowns and the boys were dressed conservatively. There were no motorcycle jackets and hardly a sideburn in the crowd.

"The quality of the dancing, however, was poor. There was also a shortage of boys. Quite a few girls had to dance with other girls, and some of them looked grim about it.

"The format of the program is almost identical to that of a show that has been conducted in here over Channel 9 by Ted Steele. The young set dances to records on that program, too.

"This kind of television is not for adults, particularly those who have fond memories of Hal Kemp and Glen Gray. They won't care at all for 'American Bandstand.'"

—J. P. Shanley, "TV: Teen-Agers Only," *New York Times*, August 6, 1957

AMERICAN BANDSTAND, TEEN IDOLS, AND RACE LINES (1957–1961)

CHAPTER 04

HOW DID WHITE COVER ARTISTS "HIJACK" RECORDS BY AFRICAN AMERICAN ARTISTS?

J. P. Shanley's comments about the lack of motorcycle jackets and sideburns among the *American Bandstand* teenagers shed light on the new brand of rock & roll that was emerging in the late 1950s. A far cry from the suggestive lyrics and greasy images of the earlier rockabillies, the teen idols promoted on popular teen music show *American Bandstand* helped bring a respectability to rock & roll that appealed to teens and parents alike. Dick Clark demanded that teenagers on his show follow strict dress codes, banning "sexy" dances, and refusing to use the term "going steady." Launching the careers of squeaky-clean teen idols such as Frankie Avalon, Clark repackaged rock & roll as a non-threatening, family-friendly form of music and sold it to the masses. The teen idols promoted on *American Bandstand* would reign supreme in the charts until the arrival of the British Invasion bands in 1964.

Cover Versions

Prior to the 1950s, cover versions of songs were nothing new. It was advantageous for songwriters and music publishers to have as many artists as possible perform their new songs to gain exposure and maximize performance royalties. But as records began to replace sheet music and live performances, it became more important to identify cover versions as such. Record labels chose whether or not to cover a particular song the way newspaper editors chose whether or not to cover a particular story, and frequently several versions of a song hit the charts at the same time. Thus, rather than referring to a song that had previously been performed or recorded, the term **cover version** alluded to current performances of songs that were expected to become hits. Because most stores only stocked particular labels—R&B for black audiences, mainstream pop for white audiences—decision makers at individual record labels tried to ensure

that they recorded a version of all potential hits, "covering" the market for each song.

HIJACKING HITS

When industry heads recognized the growing popularity of African American R&B songs among white listeners during the 1950s, they tried to capitalize on the trend by producing alternate versions of the hits using white artists. Sanitizing the songs for the mainstream market, they replaced any lyrics that referenced sex, alcohol, or drugs, and used clean-cut white singers to front the performance. The release of a cover by a white artist on the heels of a hit by a black performer was known as **hijacking** a hit, and black artists recording for independent labels were usually the victims of this practice. Because the major recording labels had superior distribution channels and promotional abilities, hijacked hits frequently outsold original performances. As a result, the term "cover version" began to imply a lack of originality, exploitation, and unfair competition.

One of the earliest "hijackers" was the King himself. Elvis's 1954 version of "That's All Right, Mama" was a cover of blues singer Arthur Crudup's 1946 recording. Although the lyrics did not need sanitizing for white middle-class consumers, as noted in Chapter 2, disc jockeys took pains to let their audiences know that Elvis was white. During a radio interview, Memphis DJ Dewey Phillips asked Elvis which high school he had attended—a euphemistic way of clarifying for listeners in that time of segregation that despite his soulful voice, the singer was Caucasian.

PAT BOONE

The second biggest-selling artist of the 1950s after Elvis, **Pat Boone** (a direct descendant of 18th-century pioneer Daniel Boone)

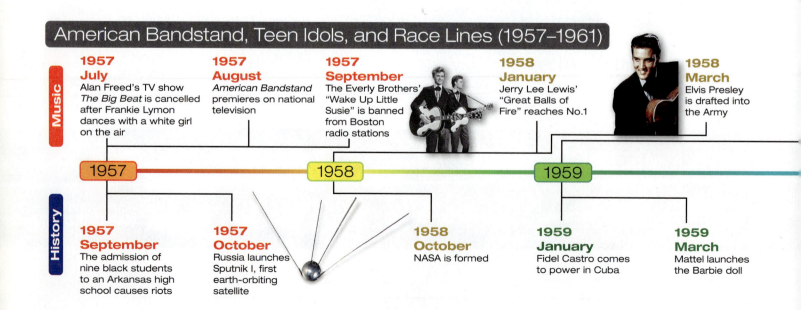

American Bandstand, Teen Idols, and Race Lines (1957–1961)

Music

1957 July
Alan Freed's TV show *The Big Beat* is cancelled after Frankie Lymon dances with a white girl on the air

1957 August
American Bandstand premieres on national television

1957 September
The Everly Brothers' "Wake Up Little Susie" is banned from Boston radio stations

1958 January
Jerry Lee Lewis' "Great Balls of Fire" reaches No.1

1958 March
Elvis Presley is drafted into the Army

1957   **1958**   **1959**

History

1957 September
The admission of nine black students to an Arkansas high school causes riots

1957 October
Russia launches Sputnik I, first earth-orbiting satellite

1958 October
NASA is formed

1959 January
Fidel Castro comes to power in Cuba

1959 March
Mattel launches the Barbie doll

established his rock & roll career by reworking classic R&B hits. College-educated with neatly combed hair, a gleaming smile, and all-American looks, Boone was the essence of white, middle-class America. With his trademark white buck shoes and smooth, polished style, Boone made rock & roll safe and unthreatening. His cover of Fats Domino's "Ain't That a Shame" became his first number one hit in September 1955 (the original reached number one on the R&B charts the same year but only made number ten on the pop charts), and a 1956 cover of Ivory Joe Hunter's "I Almost Lost My Mind" became his second.

Boone recorded numerous cover versions of songs first credited to African American artists, including Little Richard. Famous for his frenetic performance style, Little Richard appealed to both white and black teens, but his songs were often banned from white radio stations that favored more acceptable cover versions. Boone's 1956 version of "Tutti Frutti" outsold the original and went gold, even though Little Richard had already sanitized the lyrics for his version of the song. Little Richard attempted to foil Boone by increasing the tempo of his next song so Boone would not be able to keep up, but Boone's sterile version of "Long Tall Sally" also went gold, although this time it did not outsell the original and only made number eight on the U.S. pop charts.

BILL HALEY

Credited with producing some of the earliest rock & roll hits, **Bill Haley and His Comets** began their musical career performing

bluesy country and western songs. Initially known as Bill Haley and the Saddlemen, the band ventured into rock & roll in 1951 with a cover of Ike Turner's "Rocket 88" recorded just a few months after the original. The song became a regional hit in the Northeast, and the band followed up a year later with a cover of Jimmy Preston's 1940s R&B song "Rock the Joint." Renaming themselves Bill Haley and His Comets, the band covered Big Joe Turner's "Shake, Rattle, and Roll" in 1954, replacing sexual phrases from the original with fashion statements and moving action from the bedroom to the kitchen. The song reached number seven on the charts and sold over a million copies between late 1954 and early 1955. The re-release of

<<< Pat Boone built a career by sanitizing classic rock & roll hits, **selling more records in the 1950s than every other artist except Elvis Presley.**

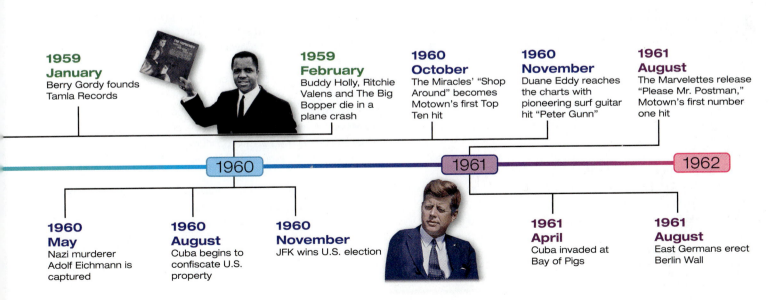

1959 January
Berry Gordy founds Tamla Records

1959 February
Buddy Holly, Ritchie Valens and The Big Bopper die in a plane crash

1960 October
The Miracles' "Shop Around" becomes Motown's first Top Ten hit

1960 November
Duane Eddy reaches the charts with pioneering surf guitar hit "Peter Gunn"

1961 August
The Marvelettes release "Please Mr. Postman," Motown's first number one hit

1960   1961   1962

1960 May
Nazi murderer Adolf Eichmann is captured

1960 August
Cuba begins to confiscate U.S. property

1960 November
JFK wins U.S. election

1961 April
Cuba invaded at Bay of Pigs

1961 August
East Germans erect Berlin Wall

Covering the Music of Chuck Berry

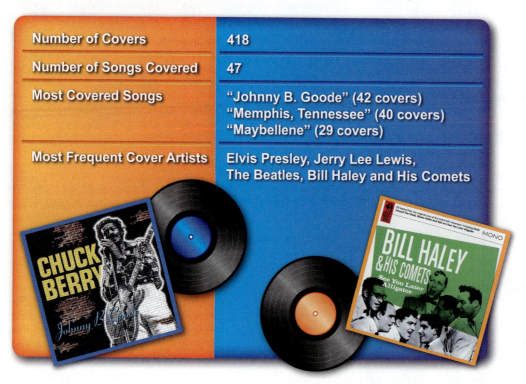

Number of Covers	418
Number of Songs Covered	47
Most Covered Songs	"Johnny B. Goode" (42 covers) "Memphis, Tennessee" (40 covers) "Maybellene" (29 covers)
Most Frequent Cover Artists	Elvis Presley, Jerry Lee Lewis, The Beatles, Bill Haley and His Comets

∧∧∧ **One artist frequently covered by** Bill Haley and His Comets was Chuck Berry. **However, Haley wasn't the only one. The songs of Chuck Berry** are actually among the most covered in music history.

"Rock Around the Clock" in the spring of 1955 (following the song's use in the opening credits of the film *Blackboard Jungle*) launched the band into rock & roll history, selling 25 million copies worldwide and remaining at the number one spot on the pop charts for eight weeks.

IMPLICATIONS OF WHITE-BREAD POP

Did the 1950s cover artists rip off the original R&B performers or introduce American teens to a whole new genre of music? Although some teens preferred cover versions of R&B songs, many were turned on to original recordings as a result of mainstream airplay of covers. Little Richard called Pat Boone "the man who made me a millionaire," while Fats Domino's definitive version of "Ain't That a Shame" soon became more popular than the cover version, bringing Domino's music to the mass market half a dozen years after his first major recording. However, many African American artists were financially disadvantaged by the "hijacking" trend (see *Flashpoints: Issues in Rock* on page 66), and Boone's sanitized versions of earlier R&B tracks were often

---

Flashpoints ISSUES in ROCK

The Exploitation of African American Talent

Hijacking hits was standard industry procedure as the popular music market was driven by the consumption of songs rather than artists' individual renditions of them; the practice acquired racial undertones in the 1950s. Larger music labels hijacked R&B hits as a means of exploiting African American talent, using their financial might to promote white cover versions at the expense of original recordings. As a result, many 1950s R&B artists were denied the royalties they were due from the hits of this period. In some cases, black songwriters were forced to accept "co-writers" in order to gain airplay or promotion of a song.

One of the most notable casualties of hijacking was R&B singer LaVern Baker, who was signed with then small-time label Atlantic Records. Marketed as a pop singer, her songs held wide appeal and were thus vulnerable to hijacking. When Baker's 1955 hit "Tweedle Dee," reached the charts, Mercury Records quickly released its own version by pop singer Georgia Gibbs. Gibbs's version (assisted by Mercury's considerable marketing budget and by the reluctance of pop radio stations to play "race records") outsold Baker's recording, causing her to lose an estimated $15,000 in royalties. Incensed that

Gibbs's version was a note-for-note cover, Baker petitioned Michigan State Representative Charles Diggs, Jr., in an attempt to revise the Copyright Act of 1909 to make it illegal to copy an arrangement verbatim without permission. The lawsuit was unsuccessful, and the following year, Gibbs released a carbon copy version of Baker's "Tra La La," reaching number 24 on the pop disc-jockey charts, where Baker's original had failed to chart. Enraged, Baker took out a life insurance policy before one of her flights, naming Gibbs as the sole beneficiary and writing her a letter explaining that the policy was to provide for her should she be deprived of the opportunity to copy Baker's songs and arrangements in the event of her untimely death (Gibbs was apparently not amused).

Did the sanitization of African American hits during the 1950s primarily exploit talented songwriters and musicians, or did it open the door for teens to discover a wealth of previously unheard-of artists? As teen listeners began to distinguish between originals and pale imitations, these covers became signposts that increasingly led them to seek out the original versions—but the practice of hijacking hits undoubtedly left many black singers and songwriters financially behind.

dismissed as white-bread pop, lacking the feeling and authenticity of the originals.

Squeaky-Clean Teen Idols

As discussed in Chapter 3, during the conservative Eisenhower era, parents viewed rock & roll as a dangerous influence and linked the music with sexuality and juvenile delinquency. Wholesome, clean-cut singers such as Pat Boone provided an alternative face for rock & roll. The stripped-down version of the music became more acceptable to nervous parents. This acceptance grew during 1956 and 1957 with the release of films such as *Rock Around the Clock*; *Rock, Rock, Rock*; and *Don't Knock the Rock*. The films featured influential disc jockey Alan Freed, who was known for favoring original R&B recordings over white cover versions and is often credited with opening the door to white acceptance of African American music. These films effectively captured the social upheaval surrounding rock & roll. In particular, *Don't Knock the Rock*—a story about a vilified rock & roll hero banned from playing in his hometown until his supporters convince local parents otherwise—did much to defend rock & roll, emphasizing its wholesome image. This legacy of rock and roll as a positive influence on youth continues today, through Disney's *High School Musical* franchise.

^^^ Alan Freed's roles in films such as *Don't Knock the Rock* did much to broaden the acceptance of rock & roll among dubious white audiences.

AMERICAN BANDSTAND

This chapter opened with a *New York Times* review of *American Bandstand* that suggested the show was not to everyone's liking, but in the 1950s the show quickly became a hit with teens, serving as a launching pad for teen idols including Frankie Avalon, Bobby Darin, and Paul Anka.

Originally called *Bandstand*, the program launched in 1952 on ABC network affiliate WFIL-TV in Philadelphia and showcased teenagers dancing to hit records. Host Bob Horn was fired after being arrested for drunk driving during an anti–drunk-driving campaign sponsored by WFIL's owner, the *Philadelphia Inquirer*. The station chose news announcer **Dick Clark** to replace Horn. Clark approached the music with an open mind, commenting, "The more I heard the music, the more I enjoyed it, the more I understood the kids.... I knew that if I could tune into them and keep myself on the show I could make a great deal of money" (Clark and Robinson 1976, 50). At 27, Clark was more than a decade older than the teenagers on the show, but youthful looks and unflappable delivery made the "perpetual teenager" a natural presenter. In August 1957, ABC picked up the show for national broadcast and

renamed it *American Bandstand*. The weekday afternoon show drew an initial audience of eight million viewers, which grew to 20 million within two years. A few months after the network debut, show dancers were receiving 15,000 letters a week, along with gifts ranging from stuffed animals to jewelry. As the show's popularity increased, mail increased to 45,000 letters a week and the program's ratings equaled the combined ratings for two rival network shows in the same time slot.

Formula for Success

American Bandstand had little competition from other shows in the 1950s. Rock & roll was rarely heard on national television networks, which were linked to major record companies and therefore primarily geared toward pop music. Popular weekly television show *Your Hit Parade* (which aired between 1950 and 1959) hired cover artists to perform renditions of the previous week's Top 10 pop songs, but the cover versions paled next to the live rock & roll performances becoming popular in the late 1950s. As songs became linked to particular artists, the format of *Your Hit Parade* became obsolete. *American Bandstand* featured original recordings by original artists, with clean-cut, all-American youngsters showing viewers at home the latest dance steps, from the Twist to the Mashed Potato. Every show featured a performance by an artist lip-synching his or her latest hit onstage—a practice that brought the show constant censure from critics, but had little impact on its popularity. By 1959, *Your Hit Parade* was off the air and *American Bandstand* was a family favorite.

Family Values

As noted in the *New York Times* review that opened this chapter, Dick Clark maintained a strict moral code on the show. In an interview with *TV Guide* in September 1958, Clark said, "We don't try to preach to anybody, but we help to set a good example for the people watching at home" (Shore and Clark 1985, 14). The potential for daily television broadcasts to reach millions of people nationwide helped disseminate an image of rock & roll as wholesome, non-threatening music, keeping it alive in the face of parental opposition, albeit in a watered-down form.

Dick Clark

Famous for hosting *American Bandstand*—the longest running music show in television history—Dick Clark, the "world's oldest teenager," began his career in radio. Born in upstate New York in 1929, he studied advertising and radio at Syracuse University, landing a part-time job during his senior year as an announcer for country station WOLF, before working for his station-manager father at WRUN in Utica, New York. In 1952, he took a job as a disc jockey at WFIL-AM in Philadelphia, first doing station IDs, commercials and news, and then spinning pop records on his own show. Four years later, he moved to WFIL-TV to host popular local dance show *Bandstand*.

Largely through Clark's initiative and business savvy, *Bandstand* transformed from a local telecast into a national phenomenon. Realizing that teenagers were a key part of a booming economic market and had $9 billion a year to spend, Clark drummed up advertising support for the show, securing a lucrative contract with Beecham Spearmint Gum and earning himself a reputation as a highly effective salesman through his on-show pitches.

Further branching out from his presenting duties, Clark invested in various record companies and bought partial copyrights to more than 160 songs. During the 1950s, he held shares in 33 music-related corporations, including publishers, recording companies, and pressing plants. Despite an obvious conflict of interests (many of the artists who recorded for companies in which Clark owned shares frequently appeared on *American Bandstand*), Clark escaped the 1959 payola investigation (see Chapter 3) largely unscathed. Agreeing to sell his outside interests, he was admonished solely for accepting a fur stole and expensive jewelry from a record company executive. Once again benefiting from his clean-cut, wholesome appearance, Clark was described as a "fine young man" by the chairman of the federal committee that investigated him.

Often contrasted with contemporary disk jockey Alan Freed, Clark is frequently dismissed as a promoter of what music historian Reebee Garofalo describes as "schlock rock"—commercially appealing but bland songs that moved away from the roots of rock & roll, emphasizing the artists' visual appearance over their musical abilities. The regional accents of the rock & rollers gave way to homogenized voices that sang of teenage love rather than sex, and songs rich with frenetic improvised riffs were replaced by tracks full of lavish instrumentals (Garofalo 2008, 146). While Freed promoted original African American R&B performers on his radio show, Clark launched the careers of attractive but hitherto unknown Philadelphia-bred youths whom he promoted and cast as stars of *American Bandstand*. The regular appearances of these overnight sensations on the show undoubtedly contributed to their success, which likely would have been far less prominent without national exposure. Although Clark himself points out that over two-thirds of the people initiated into the Rock & Roll Hall of Fame had their television debuts on *American Bandstand* (Schipper, 1990, p. 70), he was largely responsible for transforming rock & roll from the energized hits of 1956 into the bland, homogenized "teen pop" chart toppers of 1959.

Clark's career continued to flourish throughout the lifetime of *American Bandstand* (which aired until 1989). Retaining his youthful looks, the golden boy of rock & roll went on to produce spin-off show *Where The Action Is*, hosted the game show *The $10,000 Pyramid* (and four of its later versions) and the family entertainment program *TV's Bloopers and Practical Jokes*, and covered the New Year's Eve celebrations in New York's Times Square for more than three decades.

>>> **Dick Clark's wholesome appearance and suave manners reassured parents** *that rock & roll was safe and unthreatening.*

WHAT WAS THE IMPACT OF TEEN IDOLS?

Teen Idols

In the late 1950s, the success of *American Bandstand* made Philadelphia a center for male **teen idols**. Hopefuls from Philadelphia (and from around the country) used boy-next-door good looks to appeal to teenage fans. A safe alternative to Elvis's "dangerous" sexuality, the *American Bandstand* teen idol was a carryover from the days of 1930s and early 40s crooner Frank Sinatra: Gentle delivery, pleasant lyrics, and a squeaky-clean image made teen idols the nice boys of rock & roll.

One of the most prolific "schlock rock" idols was 16-year-old **Fabian**, a Philadelphia teen whose resemblance to Elvis Presley drew the attention of Bob Marcucci, co-owner of Chancellor Records. Despite two years of singing lessons (Chancellor Records actually ran a "teen idol"

school in which they indoctrinated artists into show business by teaching them how to behave both onstage and offstage), Fabian was barely able to sing a note, a fact that did not stop Dick Clark from promoting him on *American Bandstand* in 1959. Breaking into the Top 10 with "Turn Me Loose," Fabian went on to produce eight Top 40 hits.

Among the more talented Philadelphian idols managed by Bob Marcucci, **Frankie Avalon** first caught the eye of a talent scout because of his trumpet skills, and he scored 1959 hits "Venus" and "Why" through repeated appearances on *American Bandstand*. Avalon reached the Top 10 seven times in a two-year period. When his recording career began to flag, he set his sights on Hollywood, starring in a number of surfing movies during the 1960s and returning to the big screen for a cameo performance as Teen Angel in the hit musical *Grease* in 1978.

1. "The Battle of New Orleans" – Johnny Horton
2. "Mack the Knife" – Bobby Darin
3. "Personality" – Lloyd Price
4. "Venus" – Frankie Avalon
5. "Lonely Boy" – Paul Anka
6. "Dream Lover" – Bobby Darin
7. "The Three Bells" – The Browns
8. "Come Softly to Me" – The Fleetwoods
9. "Kansas City" – Wilbert Harrison
10. "Mr. Blue" – The Fleetwoods

TEEN IDOL white teen heartthrob of the 1950s.

FABIAN manufactured teen idol from Philadelphia, promoted on *American Bandstand*.

FRANKIE AVALON teen idol famous for hit songs "Venus" and "Why;" later crossed into the film industry.

BRILL BUILDING center of music production in the 1950s, housing record companies, songwriters, and publishers.

NEIL SEDAKA performer and songwriter known for hits about the joys and angst of teenage love.

PAUL ANKA Canadian songwriter and performer associated with the Brill Building sound.

RICKY NELSON teen idol who used his role on the TV sitcom *The Adventures of Ozzie and Harriet* to promote his music.

THE EVERLY BROTHERS country-influenced duo famed for their vocal harmonies.

THE BRILL BUILDING BUNCH

By the mid-1950s, corporate America had taken notice of rock & roll. The **Brill Building** consolidated the groups of music producers, record companies, songwriters, and performers, who traditionally gathered along a New York street in the Tin Pan Alley days. Located at 1619 Broadway, the Brill Building emerged as the one-stop center of professional songwriting and publishing formulated to cater to the new rock & roll market. The Brill Building sound, characterized by the records of Neil Sedaka and Paul Anka, spoke directly to teenagers with innocent, catchy lyrics about teenage love and loss.

Neil Sedaka was a classical music student who teamed up with schoolmate Howie Greenfield to write some of the catchiest teen pop tunes of the 1950s. Initially signed by Aldon Music to write songs for performers such as Connie Francis, Sedaka soon began recording his own material, typically singing about the joy and angst of teenage love. In 1959, RCA signed him and he had a string of hits over the next three years, including "Breaking Up Is Hard to Do," "Calendar Girl," "Happy Birthday, Sweet Sixteen," and "Oh! Carol."

Canadian singer **Paul Anka** had his first hit at the age of 16 with "Diana" in 1957. He produced six more Top 10 songs between 1958 and 1960, including "Puppy Love," "Lonely Boy," and "Put Your Head on My Shoulder." "Puppy Love" is reflective of the typical teen idol hits during this time period, portraying teenage love as

infatuation rather than sexual desire. Anka also had considerable success as a songwriter. His composition "My Way" became a hit for numerous artists of all stripes, including Frank Sinatra, Elvis Presley, and Sid Vicious.

MUSICAL FAMILIES

For some teen idols, music was a family business. **Ricky Nelson** established himself as a television star at a young age, playing himself and starring with his real-life family on the TV sitcom *The Adventures of Ozzie and Harriet*. Focusing on a white middle-class suburban family in the 1950s, the show originally began as a radio program featuring Nelson's bandleader father and vocalist mother, who made a name for themselves with their comedic boy-girl banter. When the show moved to television, with Ricky and his brother David joining the act, Ricky's musical roots shone through. The show served as a platform to promote Nelson's music, and his rendition of Fats Domino's "I'm Walking" made it into the Top 20, while the flip side, "A Teenager's Romance," reached number two. Signed by Imperial and promoted as a respectable Elvis Presley, Nelson released 36 *Billboard* Hot 100 tracks between 1957 and 1961 before losing popularity in the wake of the British Invasion.

Like Nelson, the **Everly Brothers** began their musical careers as part of a family act. The children of Midwestern country stars Ike and Margaret Everly, Don and Phil toured with their parents around the South and Midwest and performed on the family radio show. Their performance of "Bye Bye Love" sent them soaring onto the charts in 1957, and the brothers followed the single with a stream of hits, including "All I Have to Do Is Dream," "Cathy's Clown," and "Bird Dog." Despite their pleasant harmonies and soft, non-aggressive style, the brothers did not entirely escape the attack on rock & roll, and their 1957 hit "Wake Up Little Susie" was banned from Boston radio stations for its "suggestive" lyrics.

<<< The Everly Brothers were part of the squeaky-clean teen idol clan of the 1950s, although their hit song "Wake Up Little Susie" was banned in Boston for its "risqué" lyrics.

WHAT WERE THE EARLY INFLUENCES OF SURF MUSIC?

SURF MUSIC music popularized by the surfing culture in California and characterized by twanging guitar riffs and high harmony vocals.

DUANE EDDY instrumentalist whose innovative guitar work laid the foundation for future rock guitarists.

TWANG reverberating, treble-heavy guitar sound.

TREMOLO lever on an electric guitar that produces a wavering effect in a musical tone.

DICK DALE musician who worked with guitar manufacturer Leo Fender to develop the reverberation unit that gave surf music its distinctive sound.

FENDER STRATOCASTER popular electric guitar introduced in 1954.

PICKUP small microphone attached to vibrating surface that captures mechanical vibrations and converts them into an electric signal.

SHOWMAN AMP Fender amp with more than 100 watts of power, enabling the electric guitar to be played at high volume.

REVERB UNIT device that simulates the way sounds naturally reflect and fade away in enclosed spaces.

DOUBLE STOP two notes played together; rock & roll guitar technique pioneered by Chuck Berry.

Surfing U.S.A.

If the teen idols played up the respectable aspect of white, middle-class rock & roll, surf musicians played up the fun. Centered in Southern California, an area with an abundance of natural resources and a booming postwar population, the carefree sport of surfing began to gain popularity in the late 1950s. In 1959, the year that surfing birthplace Hawaii joined the

Gnarly	a large or difficult wave
Gremmy	an inexperienced surfer
Hang 10	surfing with 10 toes over the edge of the board
Hodad	a "non-surfer"
Surf's Up	a wave that is high enough to surf on
Wipe Out	to fall off the board while surfing
Woody Wagon	a wood-sided wagon that carried surfers and their boards to the beach

∧∧ Surfers in the 1950s developed their own culture and language.

United States, two Californian surfboard companies replaced the heavy wooden boards with new lightweight versions that were easier to handle. The release of the surfing movie *Gidget* the same year further popularized the sport. Surfing developed its own subculture, incorporating the look—bleached blond hair, deep tans, and cutoff shorts; the lingo—surfers would run into the "soup" (foaming water near the beach) on their "polys" (surfboards) in an attempt to impress the "bunnies" (girls); and the must-have accessories including expensive cars, such as T-birds or Corvettes.

Reflecting these themes of affluence and consumption, **surf music** was a short-lived phenomenon that nonetheless had considerable influence on rock & roll history. Developing from the instrumental hits of the late 1950s by artists such as Duane Eddy, Link Wray, and the Ventures, surf music was characterized first by its twanging guitar riffs and later by its high harmony vocals. Although it had mostly petered out by 1964, the music that energized the California surfing culture laid the foundations for several later genres, including garage rock, heavy metal, thrash, and grunge.

EARLY SURF

Although technically not a "surf guitarist," instrumentalist **Duane Eddy's** stylistic innovations played an important role in the development of surf music. His influence can be heard on many tracks, including the Beach Boys' "Surfin' USA." Eddy introduced "**twang**"—the sharp, reverberating guitar sound—by picking on the low strings, turning up the **tremolo**, and running the signal through a tube amplifier equipped with a tremolo or reverb effect. Promoting the guitar from its traditional support role to a solo instrument by constructing instrumentals with strong melodies, Eddy created the powerful, driving sound heard in his popular 1960 cover of the *Peter Gunn* theme song. Other early contributors to the surf music sound included rockabilly musician Link Wray, instrumental rock band the Ventures, British band the Shadows, and surfing enthusiast Dick Dale and His Del-Tones.

Born in Lebanon, **Dick Dale** moved to the Southern Californian coast as a teenager and joined the surfing crowd. A keen guitarist, Dale worked closely with Leo Fender, creator of the first solid-body electric guitars, to help develop amplification and reverberation equipment that gave much of surf music its distinctive sound (see *Rock Technology* on this page). He attempted to musically reproduce the feeling he had while surfing, creating a vibrating, pulsing sensation on the low strings of his guitar with the aid of a tremolo effect and accompanying it with a thunderous beat supplied by backup musicians.

Popular live performances at the Rendezvous Ballroom in Balboa, California, and the release of regional hit "Let's Go Trippin'" in 1961 and classic surf instrumental "Misirlou" in 1962 earned Dale and his band a contract with Capitol Records, who dubbed him the "King of the Surf Guitar." Although the band failed to make waves nationally, their pioneering guitar sound caught on and surf rock came to national prominence the following year with the all-Californian Beach Boys and fellow surf rockers Jan and Dean (see Chapter 5).

ROCK TECHNOLOGY ▶▶▶ The Fender Stratocaster, Fender Amp, and Fender Reverb Unit

Designed by guitar manufacturer Leo Fender, the **Fender Stratocaster**, commonly known as the "Strat," is a much-copied model of electric guitar that is still in production today. Its deep upper-body cutaways made the high frets more accessible and reduced the guitar's weight. The original Strat offered musicians a choice of three **pickups** controlled by a three-way toggle switch to create three different sounds. Guitarists quickly established that by setting the switch *between* positions they could mix sounds from two pickups, creating the snarling nasal tones associated with 1950s rock music. The discovery prompted Fender to introduce models with five-way toggle switches, expanding the range of the guitar. The Strat's bright, twangy tone was perfect for the surf music sound popularized by Dick Dale.

Frequently asked to road test Fender's creations, Dick Dale blew up more than 40 amps and speakers with his extremely loud, aggressive guitar playing before Fender developed the **Showman amp**. With more than 100 watts of power, the amp and its accompanying 15-inch speaker finally enabled Dale to blast his power chords at full volume. Although the surf sound was associated with the flowing sounds of a **reverb unit**—a device that simulates the way sounds naturally reflect and fade away in enclosed spaces—Dale's early hits were cut without the use of the reverb effect. Dale first experimented with reverb to sustain his singing, rather than the sounds from his guitar, and when Dick Dale and Leo Fender began experimenting with spring reverb in the electric guitar, Fender had to license a design the Hammond Organ Company had originally developed to enhance the sound of their electric organ. When Fender unveiled the Fender Reverb Unit in 1961, the warm, watery tone it provided naturally evoked surfing, and reverb immediately became a hit among the surf bands of the early 1960s.

◀◀◀ **With its streamlined, modern look,** *the Fender Stratocaster offered several practical advantages* **over rival models.**

HOW DID MOTOWN ORIGINATE?

R&B Lives On

Although racial prejudice during the 1950s marginalized black artists on film, television, and radio, African American artists continued to shape rock & roll history. Aided by disc jockeys such as Alan Freed, who refused to play cover versions on his radio show, the music of Chuck Berry and Little Richard reached a generation of teenagers hungry for rock & roll.

CHUCK BERRY

Throughout the 1950s, Chuck Berry had a string of hits on the pop charts. Singing about the frustrations and freedoms of the teenage years ("School Days," "Sweet Little Sixteen," "Almost Grown"), Berry spoke to the emerging teen culture with songs about the everyday concerns of their lives: school, girls, cars, and the problems of growing up. He also slyly addressed racial and class issues in his music ("Brown Eyed Handsome Man," "No Money Down"), and the storytelling element to his lyrics far surpassed the nonsense syllables that comprised many 1950s rock songs.

However, Berry's primary contribution to the rock & roll scene was his unique guitar style with its trademark licks and **double-stopped** riffs—when a guitarist plays two strings at once. His distinctive intros were widely imitated by numerous

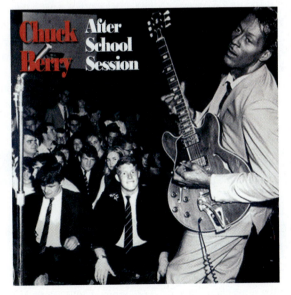

∧∧∧ *One of the pioneers of rock & roll,* **Chuck Berry's popularity remained consistent among both white and black audiences** *in the 1950s.*

artists, from the Beach Boys to the Rolling Stones—the Beach Boys' "Surfin' U.S.A." was so close to Berry's "Sweet Little Sixteen" that Berry threatened to sue and was given songwriting credit on all subsequent releases of the track on compilation albums. Stones' guitarist Keith Richards acknowledged Berry's influence on his own musical career when he inducted the legend into the Rock & Roll Hall of Fame in 1986, stating, "It's hard for me to induct Chuck Berry, because I lifted every lick he ever played!"

LITTLE RICHARD

Often mentioned in the same breath as rock & roll founding fathers Chuck Berry and Jerry Lee Lewis, flamboyant rocker Little Richard was the self-proclaimed "King and Queen of Rock and Roll." As noted earlier in this chapter, Richard was a victim of hit hijacking; however, his popularity was never overshadowed by the success of his cover artists. By the time Pat Boone covered "Long Tall Sally" in 1957, it was apparent that both black and white audiences preferred the real thing. Richard's whooping, shouting vocals, falsetto *woo woos* and wild piano banging on the break out hit "Tutti Frutti" set the style for a string of hits in 1956 and 1957, including "Good Golly, Miss Molly," "Slippin' and Slidin'" and "Jenny, Jenny." Many later bands, including the Beatles and the Rolling Stones, cited

Richard as an influence, adopting his frenetic, head-shaking theatrics on stage. Others, such as David Bowie, Prince, and Boy George, took on Richard's gender-bending proto-glam rock style, a trend that would remain popular over the next three decades.

Little Richard was everything conservative 1950s parents feared; a flamboyant, bisexual rocker who frequently participated in post-concert orgies with members of his audience. Ironically, Richard's own religious upbringing caused an internal conflict between hell-raising and piety, and in 1957, he quit his rock career at the height of his success to enroll in a Bible college in Alabama. However, his call to religion was not as strong as his call to rock & roll, and by 1962, Richard was touring Britain with two aspiring British rock groups: the Beatles and the Rolling Stones. Stones' lead singer Mick Jagger later described Richard's performance style as "hypnotic, like an evangelistic meeting where, for want of a better phrase, Richard is the disciple and the audience the flock that follows" (White 1984, 119).

ETTA JAMES

Like Little Richard, R&B singer **Etta James** grew up singing gospel songs in a Baptist church choir. Her no-holds-barred singing style influenced many white rockers of the 60s, including Janis Joplin and Keith Richards, and she bridges the gap between R&B and rock & roll.

Discovered by bandleader Johnny Otis while singing in San Francisco in a vocal trio called the Peaches, James moved to L.A. to pursue a recording career. Under Otis's guidance, James wrote and recorded "Roll With Me, Henry" (later renamed "The Wallflower" because the original title was considered too racy for radio airplay), which topped the R&B charts for four weeks in 1955. An "answer

song" to Hank Ballard's hit "Work With Me Annie," James's version was covered by LaVern Baker's nemesis, pop singer Georgia Gibbs. Like Baker, James was displeased to hear that her original recording had been outsold, until Otis explained to her that she would receive one-third of the songwriting royalties, the rest to be divided between Otis and Ballard. Strictly speaking, Otis deserved little of the royalty money for "Roll With Me, Henry," having little to do with the song's composition. Along with many other artists, James's financial naïveté was frequently exploited by her record companies, which purchased the publishing rights to her songs for as little as $25, enabling them to keep 50 percent of all future royalties.

Following the success of her first hit, 14-year-old James toured the R&B circuit with Little Richard, witnessing some of his infamous post-concert parties. In 1960, she signed with Chicago-based Chess Records, scoring 10 chart-making R&B hits through 1963, including the soulful, jazz-tinged number two hit "At Last." Remaining with the groundbreaking label for 16 years, she ultimately launched 30 singles onto the R&B singles chart, ranking her the third most prolific female R&B hitmaker of her era, after Aretha Franklin and Dionne Warwick.

Doo-wop

Despite their influence on musical history, Chuck Berry and Little Richard were in the minority as black artists playing pure rock & roll. Most of the successful black artists of the 1950s belonged to doo-wop groups. Originating from the vocal groups of the 1940s, **doo-wop** was a derivative of R&B combined with jazz and gospel influences. Primarily consisting of urban African American male vocal harmony groups, doo-wop began on the streets of New York City, where groups of young black men unable to afford instruments would sit around and make up songs. The genre was typified by nonsense lyrics such as "sha-na-na-na-na" or "do-be-do-be-do," and groups usually consisted of a wide range of voices, including a falsetto or lead tenor, a second tenor, and a baritone bass. Most groups deemphasized instrumentation and relied on vocal harmonies to sing soft ballads about youth and young love.

Countless doo-wop groups formed in the 1950s, often modeling themselves on the Ravens, a popular six-man group led by Jimmy Ricks. The Ravens spawned dozens of doo-wop groups named after

CLASSIC RECORDINGS ▸▸▸

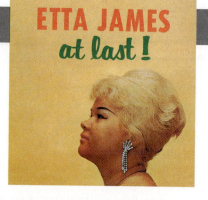

AT LAST! by Etta James

Released in 1961, James's debut album with Chess Records' Argo subsidiary propelled her to crossover stardom with its mixture of blues, soul, and R&B. Produced by Phil and Leonard Chess, the album included crooning rock ballad "My Dearest Darling," lush violin-backed sounds on "Trust in Me" and "At Last," and Willie Dixon's bawdy blues classic "I Just Want to Make Love to You." It exhibited the impressive range of James's stylistic capabilities.

James recorded several of the album's duets with Harvey Fuqua of the Moonglows, with whom she had a romantic and professional relationship. Although their romantic relationship was brief, Fuqua, who was 10 years older than James, continued his role as James's mentor at Chess, Motown, and other labels.

Reaching number 68 on the pop album chart, *At Last!* featured four singles that made the pop and R&B charts in 1960 and 1961, including James' signature title track. It also ranked number 116 in *Rolling Stone*'s top 500 greatest albums of all time. In 1993, James was inducted into the Rock & Roll Hall of Fame, described by *Rolling Stone* as "a singer of unprecedented power and appeal."

Young, inexperienced doo-wop groups
such as Frankie Lymon and the
Teenagers **were often exploited by
unscrupulous** record company executives.

> **V V V Young, inexperienced doo-wop groups** such as Frankie Lymon and the Teenagers **were often exploited by unscrupulous** record company executives.

birds, including the Larks, the Robins, the Flamingos, the Crows, the Orioles, the Falcons, and the Penguins. Of these, the Penguins were the most widely known, with their chart-topping 1955 hit "Earth Angel." Other groups named themselves after the cars they saw on the streets of New York or Philadelphia—the Cadillacs, the Impalas, the Fiestas, and the Eldorados.

ONE-HIT WONDER GROUPS

Of the few doo-wop groups that managed to achieve chart success, most were one-hit wonders, disappearing into obscurity after a single pop hit. Competing cover versions and the instability of small independent record labels took their devastating toll on fledgling groups, whose youth and inexperience often caused them to make poor business decisions. Often agreeing to be paid by recording session rather than by the number of records, young doo-wop artists who were happy just to get a record deal essentially gave away the rights to

>>> Berry Gordy's Motown record empire **was the largest African American-owned corporation in the United States** until its 1988 purchase by MCA, **and it paved the way for a multitude of successful** black record executives and producers.

their original songs and signed contracts allowing record companies to pay studio and promotional costs with artists' royalties. One classic example of this type of exploitation is the story of Frankie Lymon and the Teenagers, a New York group that rose to fame in 1956 with "Why Do Fools Fall in Love" when lead singer Frankie Lymon was just 13 years old. Producer George Goldner paid Lymon an allowance of $24 a week, with the rest of the royalties and performance fees supposedly going into a trust fund. When Lymon later attempted to collect the cash, he found there was little to claim. The destitute former teen star eventually died of a heroin overdose in a Harlem tenement at the age of 25.

Although most of the doo-wop groups proved to be one-hit wonders, it was the individual recordings of these one- and two-hit groups that would define the doo-wop style. Characterized by the yearning lead vocals of the Penguins' "Earth Angel," the plaintive "doo-wop doo-wah" refrain in the Five Satins' "In the Still of the Night," and the vocal imitations of instruments such as the double bass in the Marcels' "Blue Moon," the smooth charm of the doo-wop groups flowed through to the Motown bands of the early 1960s.

Beginnings of Motown

If doo-wop was primarily centered in New York City, **Motown** unequivocally belonged to Detroit. Its founder was former boxer and automobile worker **Berry Gordy**, a tough, middle-class black man from Detroit who started his career in the music industry as a producer and songwriter. Favoring jazz over the black R&B and gospel hits emerging in the 1950s, Gordy ran a small jazz record store in the mid-1950s and wrote songs for local R&B acts. His association with Golden Gloves boxing champion and R&B singer Jackie Wilson gave him his first break in 1957 when Brunswick Records bought a song he wrote called "Reet Petite" for Wilson to record. Over the next couple of years, Gordy wrote all of Wilson's biggest hits, including the million-selling "Lonely Teardrops," "That's Why (I Love You So)," and "I'll Be Satisfied." During this time, Gordy established the Jobete Music Publishing Company (named after his three children, Hazel Joy, Berry, and Terry), and began to produce records, including the Miracles' "Got a Job."

In 1959, 31-year-old Gordy borrowed $800 from his family and started his first record company, **Tamla Records**. The following year, Gordy founded the Motown Record Corporation in a rented eight-room house at 2648 West Grand Boulevard, which he optimistically named "Hitsville USA." The building—which featured a recording studio no bigger than a suburban living room—would soon house not only Motown Records, but also subsidiary labels Tamla, Gordy, and Soul.

Gordy scored a minor hit with Tamla's first release, "Come to Me" by R&B singer Marv Johnson. During his first year of operation, Gordy also co-wrote and produced Barrett Strong's hit "Money," which reached number two on the R&B chart. Unable to keep up with the demands of national production and distribution, Gordy relied on United

later explained to *Rolling Stone* magazine, "I worked on the Ford assembly line and I thought, 'Why can't we do that with the creative process?' You know, the writing, the producing, the artist development. . . And when you got through and you came out of the door, you were like a star, a potential star" (Palmer 1995, 86).

THE SOUND OF YOUNG AMERICA

Both black and white audiences flocked to the Motown sound, which combined elements of pop and soul to create an upbeat new sound. Noting the tendency for soul records to top the R&B charts but fall short in the pop charts, Berry Gordy styled his artists according to a set formula aimed at commercial success across a wider audience. Songs had to be danceable, upbeat, and non-threatening, omitting any mention of the drugs and alcohol associated with R&B culture. Gordy's Motown hits were characterized by carefully arranged harmonies, gospel-style call and response vocals, tambourines, hand-clapping, blaring horns, and driving bass lines that took simple, catchy pop tunes to a sophisticated level. The "Sound of Young America"—a phrase adopted as the Motown label logo—was an instant success, rolling hits off its assembly line throughout the late 1950s and 1960s. The music successfully crossed racial boundaries; Gordy later noted that 70 percent of all Motown hits were sold to white listeners.

Artists and Chess Records for help, until young singer-songwriter William "Smokey" Robinson convinced him that Motown should distribute its own records.

Despite being undercapitalized, Gordy took Robinson's advice, co-writing and distributing the million-selling "Shop Around" by Smokey Robinson and the Miracles in 1960. The song reached the number one spot on the R&B chart and number two on the pop chart, establishing Motown as an important independent company. Within seven years, the Motown Record Corporation had become a national powerhouse, selling more singles than any other independent or major company and boasting a wealth of talent that included Marvin Gaye, the Temptations, the Supremes, and the Four Tops.

Presiding over the entire in-house operation, Gordy was in control of not only the Motown and Tamla labels, but also the Hitsville USA studio, Jobete Publishing, and International Talent Management (ITM), a personal management company that provided fledgling artists with etiquette lessons and performance training. His success resulted from a combination of talent, ambition, and innovation, the last epitomized by the development of ITM. Realizing that many of his vocalists had been raised in Detroit's inner-city neighborhoods and housing estates and were lacking in social and professional finesse, Gordy turned Motown into a type of finishing school. Hiring experienced teachers in music theory, choreography, and charm-school poise, he ensured that his protégés would be prepared for the finest Hollywood supper clubs, modeling the star-making process after the automobile industry in which he had once worked. Gordy

THE SUPREMES

One of Motown's greatest successes, the **Supremes'** rags-to-riches tale began in Detroit's low-income Brewster housing project, where Diana Ross was introduced to a local female vocal group. Ross, along with Mary Wilson, Florence Ballard, and Betty Travis, accompanied male vocal trio the Primes (later the Temptations) on stage and became known as the Primettes. In 1960, the Primettes won a high school talent contest and began pestering Berry Gordy for an audition with his new record company. Gordy believed the girls were too young and told them to return once they finished high

<<< **Berry Gordy's Motown Empire** became one of the top record-producers in the country.

Detroit

Situated on the Detroit River in the state of Michigan, **Detroit** is traditionally associated with the auto industry. From the early 1900s, assembly-line jobs in auto plants attracted immigrants from Europe and newcomers from the American South. In the 50-year period leading up to World War I, Detroit's population exploded by 1,200 percent. Industrial plants created jobs, but not housing; the sudden shift in demographics caused racial tension between existing white communities and incoming blacks. Tensions heightened during the 1940s, and despite Franklin Roosevelt's Fair Employment Practices Committee, nearly one third of defense plants opened during World War II refused to hire African American workers. In

1943, a strike at the Packard plant contributed to the eruption of three days of race riots, which led to the deaths of 34 people, most of them African American. For many, including Berry Gordy, Detroit was a city of hardship and racial discrimination. Until Gordy was six years old, his family lived in rat-infested home where the eight Gordy children shared three beds between them.

Despite its reputation as an industrial city, the Motor City had a thriving club scene, with a strong tradition of gospel and jazz rising from the African American neighborhood known as "Paradise Valley." Detroit drew touring bebop artists and world-famous jazz performers. Before Motown, Paradise Theatre was a top venue on the **Chitlin Circuit** and attracted performers Nat King Cole, Duke Ellington, and Billie Holiday.

In 1960, Detroit had the fourth largest African American population in the country. The city harbored a wealth of talent but offered few opportunities. Hopeful recording artists had to travel to Chicago, Philadelphia, or New York to make records. When Berry Gordy founded the Motown Record Corporation in the heart of Detroit, he tapped a gold mine of local talent. Detroit-born artists Jackie Wilson, Smokey Robinson, Diana Ross, and the Four Tops all got their big break at 2648 West Grand Boulevard, earning the company its moniker "Hitsville USA."

By the time Motown left Detroit for Los Angeles in 1968, its historical legacy was established. Today, fans from around the globe flock to the Motown Historical Museum every year to see exhibitions chronicling the history of Motown.

school, but relented a year later, signed the group with the encouragement of Ross's former neighbor, Smokey Robinson, and changed their name to the Supremes.

Gordy initially had little success with his new act. Their first two singles, issued on the Tamla label, went nowhere, while the next three barely made the bottom of the Hot 100 chart. By the end of 1963, the group, now consisting of Diana Ross, Florence Ballard, and Mary Wilson, still had not scored a major hit record. Their Motown colleagues began to refer to them as the "no-hit Supremes." Bringing in songwriting team Brian Holland, Lamont Dozier, and Eddie Holland, Gordy finally discovered the formula for the Supremes' success. The group released "Where Did Our Love Go" while touring on the Dick Clark Caravan of Stars, and the song reached number one. The Supremes were moved from the opening act to the prestigious closing spot on the show, and the song became the prototype for a consecutive string of number one hits. By the

end of 1965, the Supremes had scored six number one songs ("Where Did Our Love Go," "Baby Love," "Come See About Me," "Stop! In the Name of Love," "Back in My Arms Again," and "I Hear a Symphony"), all of which were written by Holland, Dozier, and Holland. Typifying the Motown sound, the tracks featured a lead singer (Ross) with vocal backup and strong orchestration, consisting of strings, brass, sax, keyboards, and percussion. The songs all had a strong beat, reinforced by hand claps, and often shifted key toward the end of the track ("I Hear a Symphony," "Baby Love").

The Supremes' success was particularly impressive in light of heavy competition from the British Invasion bands between 1964 and 1966 (see Chapter 6). The group ranks third behind the Beatles and Elvis Presley in 1960s chart performance, with a total of 12 number one hits and 11 other Top 40 hits. Berry Gordy carefully promoted the songs, organizing appearances on mainstream television programs such as *The Ed Sullivan Show*, *The Dean Martin Show*, and *The Tonight Show*. Having run the group through his etiquette training camp, Gordy reinforced Motown's slick, high-class

<<< **When the Supremes were assigned to the** writer/producer team of Holland-Dozier-Holland in 1964, **Motown discovered a successful formula that would result in** a string of five consecutive number one hits.

image by favoring performance venues such as the Copacabana in New York and the exclusive Las Vegas hotels. In the mid-1960s, the Supremes became the poster group for the image Motown craved: elegant, professional, and precisely coordinated to appeal to mainstream audiences.

The legacy of the Supremes can be heard over the decades in the work of countless other female vocal groups, including the Pointer Sisters, LaBelle, and Destiny's Child. The Supremes' story was the model for the hit Broadway musical *Dreamgirls*.

THE TEMPTATIONS

Berry Gordy's production-line approach achieved a similar level of success with the **Temptations**. Originally formed from two Detroit-based vocal harmony groups—the Primes and the Distants—Gordy signed the quintet to Motown in 1961 and renamed them the Temptations. As with the Supremes, Gordy shaped his new group into the Motown image, replacing their casual clothes with matching suits and neatly cropped hairdos, and enlisting the help of Motown choreographer Cholly Atkins to revamp their stage show.

Like the Supremes, the Temptations achieved only moderate success before 1964, releasing a string of non-charting singles. Their luck changed when they were teamed with Motown legend Smokey Robinson, reaching number 11 on the charts with "The Way You Do the Things You Do" in 1964 and hitting the number one spot a year later with "My Girl," Robinson's answer to the Mary Wells hit "My Guy." The group's dual lead singer format (a throwback to earlier black groups such as the Ravens) enabled Robinson to maximize the complementary sounds of Eddie Kendrick's wispy falsetto and David Ruffin's gruff baritone. Arranging complex vocal harmonies in both ballads and dance songs, Robinson helped the Temptations pour out a steady stream of hits, including "Since I Lost My Baby" and "Get Ready," before producer Norman Whitfield

> ∧
> ∧ **Channeling the vocal styles of**
> ∧ **the earlier doo-wop groups,**
>
> the Temptations were the most popular male Motown group of the 1960s.

replaced him in 1966. The most popular Motown male group of the decade, the Temptations ultimately charted 37 Top 40 hits, including four number one songs. Their refined, tailored style and carefully choreographed dance steps set the bar for all future male vocal groups, including the Delfonics, the Jackson Five, and, more recently, 1990s Motown act Boys II Men.

THE FOUR TOPS

Unlike the Supremes and the Temptations, which both underwent several changes in their lineups, the **Four Tops** were one of the most stable and consistent groups to emerge from Motown, retaining all four original members for over four decades. Signed to Motown in 1963 with nearly 10 years of experience under their belts, the Detroit natives—lead vocalist Levi Stubbs, baritone Renaldo "Obie" Benson, first tenor Abdul "Duke" Fakir, and second tenor Lawrence Payton—grew up together in the 1940s. Modeling themselves on vocal harmony group the Ink Spots, the Four Aims, as they were initially known, recorded briefly on Chess, Columbia, and Riverside Records before being lured to Motown by Berry Gordy.

Under the guidance of Motown's top songwriting and production team Holland-Dozier-Holland, the Four Tops reached number 11 in the pop charts in 1964 with the pleading, gospel-tinged "Baby I Need Your Loving," a track that perfectly suited Stubbs's leonine tenor. A succession of hits quickly followed, including "I Can't Help Myself" and "Reach Out I'll Be There," which both reached the number one spot on the charts. By the time the group moved to ABC-Dunhill Records in 1972, they had placed 17 hits in the Top 40 and Levi Stubbs had established himself as an international star (despite turning down numerous offers for a solo career). His distinctive voice and pleading vocal style inspired both singers and songwriters; in 1986, English songwriter Billy Bragg paid tribute to the emotional power of Stubbs's voice in his song "Levi Stubbs' Tears."

Like the Supremes and the Temptations, the Four Tops owed much of their polished style and slick choreography to the team at the Motown finishing school, which cultivated the Tops' image to boost their crossover appeal. Although Motown successfully tapped into the tastes of both black and white audiences, the bands did not entirely escape the racial tensions of the Civil Rights era. Tours of the southern states often involved racially charged incidents, including both verbal abuse and physical violence. Otis Williams of the Temptations recalled being shot at by a car full of white men while touring with the Four Tops and other Motown acts. The groups also encountered clubs in South Carolina that strung a rope across the middle of the floor to divide black and white patrons. "There were far too many scenes like that to recount," Williams later said (Posner 2002, 107).

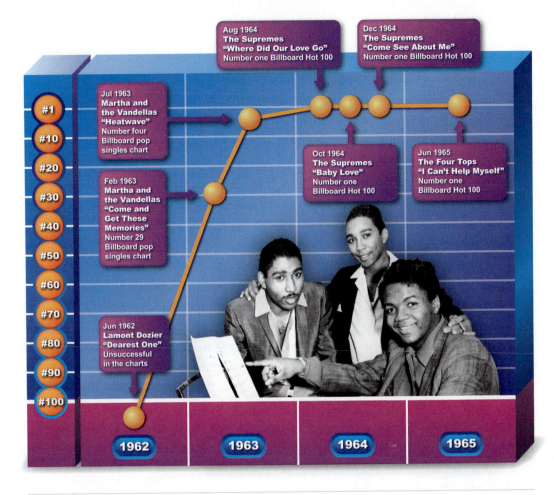

Aug 1964
The Supremes
"Where Did Our Love Go"
Number one Billboard Hot 100

Dec 1964
The Supremes
"Come See About Me"
Number one Billboard Hot 100

Jul 1963
Martha and the Vandellas
"Heatwave"
Number four Billboard pop singles chart

Feb 1963
Martha and the Vandellas
"Come and Get These Memories"
Number 29 Billboard pop singles chart

Oct 1964
The Supremes
"Baby Love"
Number one Billboard Hot 100

Jun 1965
The Four Tops
"I Can't Help Myself"
Number one Billboard Hot 100

Jun 1962
Lamont Dozier
"Dearest One"
Unsuccessful in the charts

#1 #10 #20 #30 #40 #50 #60 #70 #80 #90 #100

1962 1963 1964 1965

∧∧∧ Songwriting team Brian Holland, Lamont Dozier, and Eddie Holland wrote more than fifty Top 10 pop or R&B hits during their highly successful collaboration.

"Dancing in the Street," a call for youthful solidarity that was one of the dozen Top 40 hits the group recorded before disbanding in 1971.

The Funk Brothers

Like many of the Motown groups, Martha and the Vandellas received backing support from the company's in-house session musicians, who dubbed themselves the **Funk Brothers**. Many of the key band members came to Motown as members of pianist Joe Hunter's combo, including bassist James Jamerson (often seen as the linchpin of the band) and drummer Benny Benjamin. Helping enforce Berry Gordy's strict quality control, the Funk Brothers ensured consistency of sound across all Motown groups. Motown recordings had a simple, heavily accented backbeat accompanied by baritone sax, tambourines, and handclaps—a musical pattern present on all the major hit singles. Aware that he had created a highly successful formula and determined not to stray from it, Gordy purged any elements of raw R&B, gospel, or soul from his recording sessions and stringently avoided controversial lyrics until he reluctantly allowed the Supremes' provocative "Love Child" in 1968 and Marvin Gaye's politically charged "What's Going On" in 1971.

MARTHA AND THE VANDELLAS

Motown's girl group alternative to the Supremes, **Martha and the Vandellas** had an earthier sound than the demure vocals of Diana Ross or sultry tones of teen solo artist Mary Wells. Influenced by Clara Ward's gospel sound and jazz singer Billie Holiday, lead vocalist Martha Reeves began singing with the Del-Phis in 1960, releasing an unsuccessful single with Chess Records the following year.

In 1961, Motown's William "Mickey" Stevenson spotted Reeves performing at the Detroit nightclub Twenty Grand. She had earned a three-day booking there after winning a local talent contest. Stevenson hired her as his secretary, and Reeves and her group sang backing vocals in recording sessions whenever they were needed (most notably for fellow Motown artist Marvin Gaye on "Pride and Joy" and "Hitchhike"). In 1962, Martha and the Vandellas, named after Detroit's Van Dyke Street and Reeve's favorite singer Della Reese, were offered a contract of their own. The group soared into the charts the following year with their second single, "Heat Wave," a Holland-Dozier-Holland dance hit that reached number four and was soon joined in the Top 10 by "Quicksand." Martha and the Vandellas scored their biggest hit with 1964's summertime anthem

THE JACKSON FIVE

Taking Motown into its second decade, the **Jackson Five** were the last big hit-making group to emerge from Berry Gordy's formulaic assembly line before artists such as Stevie Wonder and Marvin Gaye took the label in a more individualized direction. Introduced to Gordy in the late 1960s, the Indiana-born quintet, led by 11-year-old Michael Jackson, had a fresh, youthful sound that appealed to a wide audience. Under Gordy's guidance, the brothers—Michael, Tito, Jermaine, Marlon, and Jackie—made music-business history when their first four singles shot to number one in 1970. Much of their material (including smash hits "I Want You Back" and "ABC") was written by the Corporation, a songwriting team put together by Berry Gordy to replace Motown's recently departed Holland-Dozier-Holland. Quickly recognized as a merchandising bonanza, the Jackson Five publicists promoted everything from dolls to an animated Saturday-morning cartoon show, a fact that often caused the group to be dismissed as "bubblegum soul." Despite their lightweight reputation, the Jackson Five were far more talented than they were given credit for. Although the group was one of the earliest examples of a modern boy band, consisting of five adolescents whose image was specifically packaged and marketed by a record label for crossover pop success, it also launched the explosive solo career of pop icon Michael Jackson.

Review

HOW DID WHITE COVER ARTISTS "HIJACK" RECORDS BY AFRICAN AMERICAN ARTISTS? 56

• Prior to the 1950s, covering songs was advantageous for songwriters, because having as many artists cover their material as possible maximized performance royalties. Cover versions referred to current performances of songs that were expected to become hits.

• During the 1950s, it became common practice for record companies to take original material from African American artists, clean up the lyrics, and front the song with a clean-cut white performer to make the music more acceptable to white audiences. When the cover version was released on the heels of a hit, taking focus and financial success away from the original, it was known as hijacking a hit. Pat Boone, Bill Haley, Elvis Presley, and Georgia Gibbs were popular white cover artists associated with this practice.

• The practice of hijacking hits exploited African American artists and cost them royalties, but it also increased people's interest in listening to original recordings.

WHAT WAS THE IMPACT OF TEEN IDOLS? 60

• Teen idols became hugely popular in the 1950s. Their success was partly due to heavy promotion on popular television music show *American Bandstand*, which aired nationally starting in 1957. Hosted by Dick Clark, the show reinforced strong moral values through its strict dress code and clean-cut image. It presented rock & roll as wholesome and non-threatening.

• Many teen idols came from Philadelphia, the home of *American Bandstand*. These included "schlock rock" star Fabian and "Venus" singer Frankie Avalon. Others, such as Neil Sedaka and Paul Anka, emerged from New York's Brill Building. Teen idols Ricky Nelson and the Everly Brothers achieved success through their musical family roots.

• The teen idols were primarily known for their clean-cut image, good looks, and wholesome reputation. Although they were chosen primarily for their appearance, most had some musical talent.

WHAT WERE THE EARLY INFLUENCES OF SURF MUSIC? 62

• Surf culture developed in southern California in the late 1950s. Surf music drew on the instrumental hits of artists such as Duane Eddy, Link Wray, and the Ventures.

• Surf music was characterized first by twanging guitar riffs and later by high harmony vocals.

• Guitar innovations by Duane Eddy (the twang) and Dick Dale (experiments on the Fender Stratocaster) gave surf music its distinctive sound.

• Surf music had mostly petered out by 1964, but it laid the foundations for several later genres, including garage rock, heavy metal, thrash, and grunge.

HOW DID MOTOWN ORIGINATE? 63

• Although white teen idols dominated the pop charts in the late 1950s, African American music continued to flourish with rock & rollers Chuck Berry and Little Richard, the soulful Etta James, doo-wop groups, and early Motown.

• Motown was founded by producer and songwriter Berry Gordy, who was associated with Detroit artists Jackie Wilson and Smokey Robinson.

• Gordy organized the company as a production line, with in-house writing and production teams, choreographers, etiquette coaches, and a session band. For maximum crossover appeal, he gave all the artists a slick, professional image and ensured that all singles had a consistent sound.

• Within seven years, Motown was an industry powerhouse, featuring artists such as the Supremes, the Temptations, the Four Tops, and Martha and the Vandellas. Many Motown hits can be attributed to the top songwriting team Holland-Dozier-Holland.

Key Terms

cover versions current performances of songs that were expected to become hits (later acquired negative connotations related to lack of originality and exploitation) *56*

hijacking release of a cover by a white artist on the heels of a hit by a African American performer *56*

Pat Boone second-biggest selling artist of the 1950s after Elvis, popularized R&B hits for mass audiences *57*

Bill Haley and His Comets covered several popular R&B songs in the early 1950s, best known for "Rock Around the Clock," one of the earliest rock & roll songs *57*

American Bandstand national televised dance party that ran from 1957 to 1989 and launched the careers of many clean-cut teen idols *59*

Dick Clark presenter of *American Bandstand* who helped popularize rock & roll among the white middle classes *59*

teen idol white teen heartthrob of the 1950s *60*

Fabian manufactured teen idol from Philadelphia, promoted on *American Bandstand 60*

Frankie Avalon teen idol famous for hit songs "Venus" and "Why;" later crossed into the film industry *60*

Brill Building center of music production in the 1950s, housing record companies, songwriters, and publishers *61*

Neil Sedaka performer and songwriter known for hits about the joys and angst of teenage love *61*

Paul Anka Canadian songwriter and performer associated with the Brill Building sound *61*

Ricky Nelson teen idol who used his role on the TV sitcom *The Adventures of Ozzie and Harriet* to promote his music *61*

The Everly Brothers country-influenced duo famed for their vocal harmonies *61*

surf music music popularized by the surfing culture in California and characterized by twanging guitar riffs and high harmony vocals *62*

Duane Eddy instrumentalist whose innovative guitar work laid the foundation for future rock guitarists *62*

twang reverberating, treble-heavy guitar sound *62*

tremolo lever on an electric guitar that produces a wavering effect in a musical tone *62*

(continued)

Dick Dale musician who worked with guitar manufacturer Leo Fender to develop the reverberation unit that gave surf music its distinctive sound *62*

Fender Stratocaster popular electric guitar introduced in 1954 *63*

pickup small microphone attached to vibrating surface that captures mechanical vibrations and converts them into an electric signal *63*

Showman amp Fender amp with more than 100 watts of power, enabling the electric guitar to be played at high volume *63*

reverb unit device that simulates the way sounds naturally reflect and fade away in enclosed spaces *63*

double stop two notes played together; rock & roll guitar technique pioneered by Chuck Berry *63*

Etta James influential female R&B singer whose career spans from the 1950s to the present day *64*

doo-wop musical genre influenced by gospel, jazz, pop, and blues, and performed by urban vocal harmony groups *64*

Motown style of music originating in Detroit that combined elements of soul, jazz, and pop *65*

Berry Gordy founder of Motown *65*

Tamla Records music label owned by Berry Gordy, subsidiary of Motown Records *65*

The Supremes Motown's most successful female vocal group, later known as Diana Ross and the Supremes *66*

Detroit Midwestern city in which Motown originated *67*

Chitlin Circuit collective name given to a number of performance venues throughout the eastern and southern United States that

catered to African American artists and audiences during the period of racial segregation *67*

The Temptations Motown male vocal quintet that achieved chart success in the 1960s with several hits written by Smokey Robinson *68*

The Four Tops Motown male vocal quartet known for its longevity; achieved success under the guidance of songwriting team Holland-Dozier-Holland *68*

Martha and the Vandellas earthier girl-group alternative to the Supremes, achieved hit status with "Dancing In the Street" *69*

The Funk Brothers Motown's in-house session musicians; ensured a consistency of sound across all the Motown groups *69*

The Jackson Five Motown's youngest superstars who took the recording empire into its second decade with their brand of funky pop-soul *69*

Sample Test Questions

1. Why did the term "cover version" begin to acquire negative connotations?
   a. It implied that the performer was lazy or untalented.
   b. It did not earn the cover artist as much money as the original artist.
   c. It became associated with the practice of hijacking hits.
   d. It became associated with the dangerous, threatening image of rock & roll.

2. Which of these factors did NOT contribute to the success of *American Bandstand*?
   a. clean-cut image of performers and presenter
   b. lack of competition from other music shows
   c. the use of an in-house cover band
   d. one live performance on every show

3. Which of these statements is correct?
   a. Most of the doo-wop groups enjoyed long, successful careers.
   b. Paul Anka used his success on a television sitcom to promote his music.
   c. LaVern Baker successfully sued Georgia Gibbs for copying her arrangements.
   d. Motown transcended the color barrier, selling most of its hits to white listeners.

4. Early surf music was primarily characterized by
   a. twanging guitar riffs.
   b. tambourines and handclaps.
   c. vocal harmonies.
   d. a strong backbeat.

5. Which of these factors did NOT contribute to the financial exploitation of African American artists in the 1950s?
   a. artists' youth and inexperience
   b. the banning of "race records" on radio
   c. the promotional power of major record labels versus independent labels
   d. laws requiring record companies to own publishing rights for all songs released

ANSWERS: 1. c; 2. c; 3. d; 4. a; 5. d

ESSAY

6. Discuss the practice of hijacking hits and examine the positive and negative effects this had on the original artists.

7. How did the teen idols and *American Bandstand* presenter Dick Clark shape rock & roll in the late 1950s and early 1960s?

8. Discuss the factors that contributed to the success of Motown in the early 1960s.

9. What pioneering guitar techniques were developed and perfected in the surf music era, and how did surf music influence future genres?

10. How did racial tensions during the Civil Rights era affect performers and the development of rock & roll in the 1950s and 1960s?

WHERE TO START YOUR RESEARCH PAPER

For a detailed history of *American Bandstand*, go to http://www.museum.tv/archives/etv/A/htmlA/americanband/americanband.htm

For general information about teen idols in the 1950s, go to http://www.statemaster.com/encyclopedia/Teen-idol

For information about the history of the Brill Building's talent, go to http://www.history-of-rock.com/brill_building.htm

To research past and present *Billboard* 100 charts, go to http://www.billboard.com/bbcom/index.jsp

To learn more about the history of surf music, including information about individual artists, go to http://www.surfmusic.com/history.htm

For more information about the origins of the Fender Stratocaster, go to http://www.theguitarhistory.com/stratocaster-history.html

For specific information about individual doo-wop groups, go to http://www.history-of-rock.com/doo.htm

For more information about the history of Motown, go to http://www.history-of-rock.com/motown_records.htm

To find out about the Motown industry as it exists today, go to http://www.motown.com

Remember to check www.thethinkspot.com for additional information, downloadable flashcards, and other helpful resources.

"The guitars

flooded into seaside Newport, R.I., last week on a twanging tide. In shopping centers, in roadside ditches, on car bumpers, in open car trunks, in historic Touro Park, on sticky Second Beach at 3 in the morning they glittered to the eye and ear. And then they fell silent and were carried by the thousands to Freebody Park, site of the third Newport Folk Festival.

"The audience was young, mostly teenagers who seemed to travel in pairs. One came from Colorado in a home-made jalopy, another from Texas in a Jaguar. They came on scooters, bicycles, in boats, and on foot. They wore dirty chinos cut off at the knees and sloppy sneakers, and they seldom washed. But they carried 2-quart bottles of milk, instead of beer, and got into few accidents or altercations with the police. . . .

"The folk fans learned how from a diverse roster of talent, from the almost purely commercial (Peter, Paul, and Mary) to the uncommercially pure (Bessie Jones and the Sea Island Singers), playing Bluegrass, blues, gospels, chanteys, and songs of protest. The range was wide because this was the first folk festival run by the performers themselves. Offering only $50 a performance to all comers, famous and obscure, the festival committee still managed to attract some top drawers, although one folk fan observed some of the best came "as an act of contrition for going commercial."

"The folkniks loved them all, but some they loved more than others. All paid obeisance to Pete Seeger, who is their patron saint. . . .

"The queen of the folk is Joan Baez and at this festival she informally named a crown prince, the 22-year-old Bob Dylan, a slight, reedy balladeer and backwoods poet with fluffy hair, a scared look in his small eyes, and a cry of anguish in his big voice and in his strong songs. The crowd applauded every time his name was mentioned. 'The most important folk singer today,' declared Peter Yarrow, of Peter, Paul and Mary. 'I feel it, but Dylan can say it,' said Joan Baez. 'He's phenomenal.'"

—"The Milk Drinkers," *Newsweek,* August 12, 1963

CHANGIN' TIMES
(1962–1966)

CHAPTER 05

WHAT IS FOLK MUSIC?

FOLKNIKS musicians and followers of the 1960s folk revival.

NEWPORT FOLK FESTIVAL a major annual folk music concert that has launched numerous folk careers.

FOLK REVIVAL the repopularization and modernization of traditional folk music that took place in the United States during the 1950s and 1960s.

FOLK ROCK genre of music combining characteristics of folk music and rock & roll that emerged in 1965.

FOLK MUSIC simple, sincere music with roots in working-class and African American genres.

LEAD BELLY an African American folksinger who was one of the first to bring traditional folk music to a mainstream audience.

The **folkniks** at the **Newport Folk Festival** in 1963 weren't like other rock & roll fans. They weren't screaming teenage girls, and they didn't tout rebellion—just change. But the **folk revival** of the 1960s wasn't just a momentary calm in the storm of rock & roll. In the tradition of its working-class roots, folk songs were often written in protest, and in the 60s, that meant civil rights. As folk music began to become more popular, a tension developed between black folksingers and white promoters, "pure" and commercial artists, songwriters and song interpreters. Folk music enjoyed plenty of controversy, and the folkies definitely had some things they wanted to say.

As the reluctant leader of this folk movement, Bob Dylan had a finger on all of these pulses, despite continued efforts to outrun his own innovations. With his harmonica at his lips and his tongue in his cheek, Dylan made a career out of constantly changing course and keeping both his fans—more of them screaming teenage girls every day—and the press on their toes. Regardless of whether he wanted to admit it, Dylan played an enormous role in creating the genre of **folk rock** and ushering in the era of the singer-songwriter, two enduring musical archetypes that stand strong today.

Folk's Roots

Unlike the sharp bass lines and smooth saxophones of 1950s rock music, folk songs relied on little more than an honest voice and a trusty guitar to create their enduring melodies. With roots in the rural and working-class United States of the early 20th century, **folk music** in many ways exemplifies the adjectives *simple* and *sincere*. Many of the songs were idealistic, their lyrics including political message that called for social change. African Americans' reinterpreting gospels into blues songs, workers' bemoaning union rights to the tunes of protest, and Appalachian family bands' blowing on jugs in the backyard all contributed to the folk music tradition. During the Great Depression, these voices found no mainstream outlet, despite the earlier musical surge caused by the emergence of the commercial recording industry and radio broadcasts in the 1920s. Instead, these homespun musicians wove their own musical landscape.

FOLK CROSSES THE COLOR LINE

Some place the birth of the 1960s folk revival to the moment in 1934 in Philadelphia, when a group of wealthy, white academics were introduced to a black ex-con from Mississippi. John and Alan Lomax, a father-and-son folklorist team with the Library of Congress, arranged for Huddie Ledbetter—commonly known as **Lead Belly**—to perform at the Modern Language Association's annual conference. Lead Belly later traveled with John and Alan to New York City, where his songs about prison life, unrequited love, and a rough life in the South garnered attention from the newspapers and influential people in the recording industry.

Lead Belly's introduction to Northern white society helped make his folk music style accessible to a world that otherwise would have never been exposed to it. Although John Lomax deserves accolades for this feat, his purported treatment of Lead Belly didn't break the same racial barriers. He controlled Lead Belly's clothing and song choices, forcing him to fit a stylized stereotype of what he thought a black ex-con from the South should be. Not only did he treat Lead Belly more like a personal assistant than a significant artist, Lomax also pocketed two-thirds of Lead Belly's earnings and included his name on the credits of many of Lead Belly's songs, despite having little to no artistic involvement with them (Lankford 2005, 10).

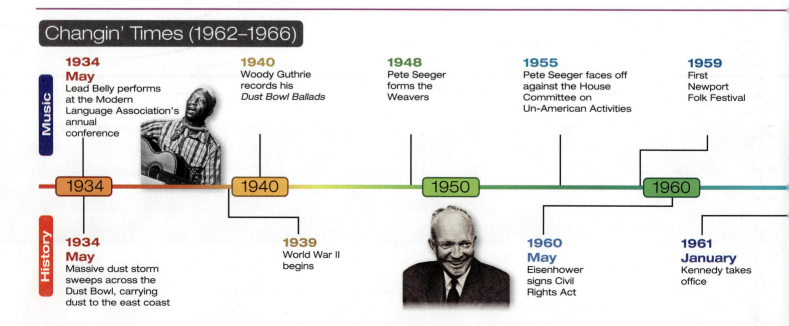

Changin' Times (1962–1966)

Music

1934 May
Lead Belly performs at the Modern Language Association's annual conference

1940
Woody Guthrie records his *Dust Bowl Ballads*

1948
Pete Seeger forms the Weavers

1955
Pete Seeger faces off against the House Committee on Un-American Activities

1959
First Newport Folk Festival

History

1934 May
Massive dust storm sweeps across the Dust Bowl, carrying dust to the east coast

1939
World War II begins

1960 May
Eisenhower signs Civil Rights Act

1961 January
Kennedy takes office

1934   1940   1950   1960

Still, without this pairing, rock & roll may have never had some of the enduring classics that Lead Belly first recorded with Lomax: "Midnight Special" was later recorded by Creedence Clearwater Revival and Eric Clapton, among others; artists as diverse as Frank Sinatra and the Grateful Dead later recorded "Goodnight, Irene"; and what Lead Belly recorded as "In New Orleans" later became both Bob Dylan's and the Animals' hit "House of the Rising Sun." Furthermore, the influence of African American folksingers like Lead Belly helped tie together the folk revival with the Civil Right Movement in the 1960s.

Folk Gets Political

Although early folk songs may have touched on the plights of the poor, African Americans, cowboys, and struggling farmers, it wasn't until folk music gained a broader mainstream audience that its songs turned political in an effort to bring about change.

WOODY GUTHRIE

Around the same time that Lead Belly was bringing African American folk music to new audiences, Woody Guthrie was doing the same for working-class protest songs. With their mother hospitalized for Huntington disease and their father in Texas paying off an old debt, Guthrie and their seven siblings were essentially orphans, forced to beg and do odd jobs to survive. Eventually, Guthrie traveled west to California alongside the migrant workers known as Okies. Guthrie was no stranger to being a downtrodden, working-class outsider, and these experiences made him sympathetic to the populist, socialist, and communist political groups he encountered in California.

By 1939, Guthrie had landed in New York City, where he became friends with Lead Belly and won the

approving eye of the city's left-leaning activists and artists. His 1940 recording *Dust Bowl Ballads* popularized the **protest song**, championing the underdog and the poor, whom Guthrie felt deserved more from their country. Seeking to capture these voices, he even penned the well-known song "This Land Is Your Land" as a new version of the national anthem. With his rudimentary guitar playing and dusty-voiced vocals, Guthrie embodied the folk performance style and became the iconic image of the American folksinger.

PETE SEEGER

Although today we remember Guthrie primarily for his solo work, he spent part of his career playing as part of folk group the **Almanac Singers**, which he formed with Pete Seeger in 1940. As you learned in Chapter 1, the Almanac Singers embraced the leftist progressive politics of their day, often performing at union rallies, workers strikes, and protests (Lornell 2004, 136). Seeger belonged to the Communist Party, and many of the Almanac Singers' early 1940s songs reflected that party's views of U.S. President Franklin Roosevelt. For example, the Almanac Singers' 1941 album *Songs for John Doe* criticized Roosevelt for enacting a peacetime military draft, a position shared by the then-pacifist Communist Party. However, after Nazi Germany invaded the Soviet Union and thus forced a change in the Communist party line, Seeger and company followed suit. The Almanac Singers' album *Dear Mr. President* reversed the group's previous positions on Roosevelt's policies, and both Guthrie and Seeger served in the armed forces during World War II.

∧∧∧ **Politically tinged lyrics** transformed Pete Seeger's songs from **simple folk tunes into protest music.**

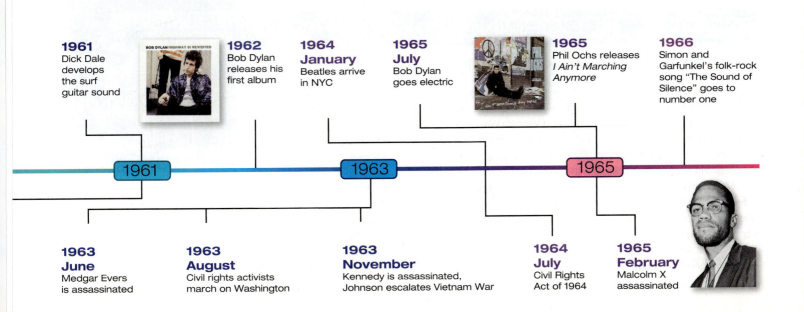

1961
Dick Dale develops the surf guitar sound

1962
Bob Dylan releases his first album

1964 January
Beatles arrive in NYC

1965 July
Bob Dylan goes electric

1965
Phil Ochs releases *I Ain't Marching Anymore*

1966
Simon and Garfunkel's folk-rock song "The Sound of Silence" goes to number one

1961   1963   1965

1963 June
Medgar Evers is assassinated

1963 August
Civil rights activists march on Washington

1963 November
Kennedy is assassinated, Johnson escalates Vietnam War

1964 July
Civil Rights Act of 1964

1965 February
Malcolm X assassinated

Baez's long career epitomizes one of the revolutions that characterized the folk revival. Up to the early 1960s when Dylan began to record albums featuring primarily his own work, folksingers had largely been interpreters of traditional songs. Baez remained true to this form even as many of her contemporaries shifted toward the singer-songwriter model ushered in by her collaborator. Although she gradually began writing her own songs and adding additional instrumentation to her albums, Baez tended to succeed most when she covered songs that spotlighted her striking soprano, such as the Band's "The Night They Drove Old Dixie Down." Her efforts to produce entirely original work culminated with the 1975 album *Diamonds and Rust*.

THE LIGHTER SIDE OF FOLK

The folk revival of the 1960s repeated many of the trends and conflicts of the folk popularization in the previous decade. Despite a return to politically oriented protest music, a commercial market for the lighter style of folk such as that mastered by the Kingston Trio continued to thrive. In fact, the Kingston Trio managed to score a few more hits during the 1960s, including 1961's "Where Have All the Flowers Gone?" Other new

> Λ
> Λ
> Λ **Manager Albert Grossman**
> thought that a group combining a handsome musician (Peter), a lanky comedian (Paul), and a blonde beauty (Mary) would be the perfect combination for success.

groups also achieved folk music commercial success with tunes delivered in a sunnier style.

Peter, Paul, and Mary

Music executive Albert Grossman—who would later manage Bob Dylan—engineered a folk sensation when he brought together Peter Yarrow, Noah Paul Stookey, and Mary Travers to form **Peter, Paul, and Mary** in 1961. The combination of the group's somewhat artificial beginning, their long-term relationship with major record label Warner Brothers, and their glossy sound has encouraged many music critics to place Peter, Paul, and Mary firmly on the commercial side of folk. Indeed, the group had great commercial success interpreting folk songs, including Seeger's "If I Had a Hammer" and Dylan's "Blowin' in the Wind," for mainstream audiences.

However, despite their commercial origins, the group wasn't a vapid trifle. The Greenwich Village-bred Travers had long been politically active, and Peter, Paul, and Mary participated in the seminal 1963 March on Washington alongside widely acknowledged activists such as Seeger and Dylan. Six years later, Yarrow helped organize another March on Washington, and by then the three musicians had attended numerous Vietnam War protests. In fact, because their audience-pleasing song styling engaged non-traditional folk audiences in

CLASSIC RECORDINGS ▸▸▸

I AIN'T MARCHING ANYMORE by Phil Ochs

"Singing journalist" **Phil Ochs** was a fixture on the Greenwich Village folk circuit during the early 1960s (Buckley 2003, 742). His protest songs won him a slot at the pivotal 1963 Newport Folk Festival, although Ochs—unlike Dylan, to whom he has been often compared—never diversified his career or achieved lasting success. However, Ochs was simply amused rather than appalled when Dylan challenged the folk world by plugging his heretofore-acoustic guitar at the 1965 Newport Folk Festival (Ochs 1967).

In 1965, Ochs released his second album *I Ain't Marching Anymore*. Despite the shift of folk music away from it acoustic roots toward the burgeoning rock scene, the album played to Ochs's traditional protest song roots. *I Ain't Marching Anymore* challenged such varied topics as the racially divided South, the escalating Vietnam War, the death penalty, and labor unions, as well as offering an elegy for assassinated President John F. Kennedy.

Although most classify the album as traditional folk, Ochs included only three songs that drew on existing material for inspiration. Instead,

the bulk of the album offers original protest works, including the title song, a direct, unapologetic confrontation of the United States' history of military atrocities that later became an anthem for the anti-Vietnam War generation.

Although Dylan may have received the lion's share of the credit, Ochs also contributed significantly with such folk hallmarks as irony, humor, originality, and a certain literariness to rock & roll. Although the protest singer had little commercial success, his subversive lyrics and activities caught the attention of the FBI, a fact that only came to light after Ochs committed suicide in 1976 as a result of personal struggles with depression and paranoia (May 2009).

their protest songs, the group may have had a broader political impact than typically credited. Certainly, Peter, Paul, and Mary have proved their lasting relevance through the continuing success of the members' joint and solo careers (Eder 2009).

The Mamas and the Papas

Singing quartet **The Mamas and the Papas**—made up of husband-and-wife team John and Michelle Phillips, as well as Cass Elliot and Denny Doherty—had established roots in traditional folk music well before coming together. John Phillips had been a member of the Journeymen, Elliot of the Big Three, and Doherty of the Halifax Three. The Mamas and the Papas also had ties to the folk-pop band Lovin' Spoonful, which had hits with "Do You Believe in Magic" and "You Didn't Have to Be So Nice."

The Mamas and the Papas' John Phillips arranged dual male and female harmonies and their sunny disposition even in the face of somber subjects made them a standout act. Emblematic of the commercial side of folk, the group released five albums between 1965 and 1968 and had 10 hit singles, including "California Dreamin'" and "Monday, Monday." Although the group had split up by 1969 (reuniting again briefly in 1972 to fulfill contractual obligations to their record label), the hippies of the Summer of Love embraced their colorful musical harmonies, distinctive sartorial styles, and idealizations of California (Rock and Roll Hall of Fame 2007).

Meanwhile, at the Beach

While folk music dominated the Greenwich Village scene, other musical styles also thrived during the 1960s. In straightforward rock & roll, the Elvis Presley-style performer model remained a driving force. On the West Coast, a group of musicians began exploring themes and sounds even more distanced from the heartfelt protest of the Greenwich Village folkniks.

While folksingers spent the 1960s advocating for the working class, protesting the Vietnam War, and championing the civil rights movement, middle-class musicians in southern California's suburbs began releasing songs that celebrated their easygoing lifestyle, unhindered consumption, and material affluence. Hollywood banked on the mass appeal of this beach-centric lifestyle with films such as 1963's *Beach Party* and 1965's *Beach Blanket Bingo* and the mid-1960s television series *Gidget* starring Sally Field. Ironically—but perhaps typically—the movie and music industries' versions of the surf lifestyle had very little to do with the sport itself. Similarly, while surf music may have started out as an expression of the California beach lifestyle, it later shifted away from mere surfing to influence the psychedelic and progressive rock sounds of the 1970s.

Jan and Dean

As you learned in Chapter 4, Dick Dale was the first to start making waves on the surf rock scene. With his reverberating sounds and new style of music, other artists were soon taking the plunge and also adapting a surfer rock style. Jan Berry and Dean Torrence, two high school friends from Southern California who got their start playing music together in Berry's parents' garage-cum-recording studio, found fame as **Jan and Dean**. Often overshadowed by their friends and collaborators, the **Beach Boys**, the duo and their musical signif-

PHIL OCHS a traditional folksinger best known for his protest songs.

PETER, PAUL, AND MARY a folksinging ensemble that achieved success by performing traditional folk songs and Dylan songs in a more accessible style.

THE MAMAS AND THE PAPAS a harmonic quartet emblematic of commercial folk.

JAN AND DEAN surf rock band that collaborated with the Beach Boys.

BEACH BOYS surf rock band that went on to help launch psychedelic and prog rock.

icance are frequently underestimated. In the makeshift studio, Berry experimented with using echo-delay effects and splicing techniques to create a final version of one song from multiple takes. Although these techniques are now standard in any recording studio, they were revolutionary in the late 1950s—especially for a teenager working in his parents' garage.

The duo achieved minor successes with "Jennie Lee" (1958), "Baby Talk" (1959), and "Heart and Soul" (1961). However, it was their musical friendship with the Beach Boys that provided them with their first bona fide hit. Brian Wilson, the leader of the Beach Boys band, collaborated with Berry on the lyrics of "Surf City," a song that took Jan and Dean to the top of the charts. The Beach Boys also passed on Dale's surf guitar style and encouraged Jan and Dean to ramp up their harmonies. At performances together, the Beach Boys often played as Jan and Dean's backing band, and Brian continued to write and perform with his friends for many years. These efforts helped spare the duo from being eclipsed when the British Invasion began in 1964. In fact, rather than seeing their popularity slip that year, Jan and Dean had two summertime hits: "Little Old Lady from Pasadena" and "Ride the Wild Surf."

TOP OF THE CHARTS
WHAT'S HOT!
SEPTEMBER 4, 1965

1. "Help" – The Beatles
2. "Like a Rolling Stone" – Bob Dylan
3. "California Girls" – The Beach Boys
4. "Unchained Melody" – The Righteous Brothers
5. "It's the Same Old Song" – Four Tops
6. "I Got You Babe" – Sonny and Cher
7. "You Were On My Mind" – We Five
8. "Papa's Got a Brand New Bag" – James Brown
9. "Eve of Destruction" – Barry McGuire
10. "Hold Me, Thrill Me, Kiss Me" – Mel Carter

SURFER GIRL by the Beach Boys

The Beach Boys' 1963 album *Surfer Girl* helped lay the groundwork for both surf music and the Beach Boys' sound in years to come. By establishing surf music as a craze and staking out the Beach Boys' place in music just months before the British Invasion changed the face of American music, *Surfer Girl* allowed the Beach Boys to endure the onslaught of UK talent during a period when many other bands wilted in their shadows. *Surfer Girl* also offered a tantalizing glimpse into Brian Wilson's blossoming genius as a songwriter and producer.

The album's title track displayed Wilson's songwriting talent to great commercial success, with the ballad reaching number seven on the U.S. charts. The catchy "Little Deuce Coupe," one of the band's several car songs, reached number 15. Many of the other songs on the album are filler typical of the surf style and failed to impress critics. However, "In My Room" is perhaps the first Beach Boys' song that portends the artistic achievements that were yet to come from the Beach Boys, and Wilson in particular. These achievements would be fully realized in their later album, *Pet Sounds* (1966).

The song also veers quite far from the typical carefree, fun-in-the-sun attitude of surf music. The somber feelings and desire for solitude expressed in "In My Room" reveal Wilson as a songwriter whose sincerity and authenticity would help him compete with the music yet to come out over the rest of the decade, and beyond. Unfortunately, it also hinted at the inner turmoil that would ultimately lead to the downfall of Wilson and to the demise of the Beach Boys as well.

THE BEACH BOYS

The Beach Boys pooled Brian Wilson's talent with that of his brothers Dennis and Carl, cousin Mike Love, and friend Al Jardine. Together, this group sang some of the most intricate and recognizable harmonies in rock & roll. In 1961, they released the local hit "Surfin'" under their original band name, the Pendletones. On the strength of this track, Capitol Records signed the freshly renamed Beach Boys and soon released their full-length debut, *Surfin' Safari*. This album and its two 1963 follow-ups, *Surfin U.S.A.* and *Surfer Girl*, helped solidify the surf music genre and bring it to a national audience. Both *Surfin U.S.A.* and *Surfer Girl* cracked the Top 10 in 1963, establishing the Beach Boys as surf music hit makers.

By 1964, the popularity of the British Invasion put an end to the short-lived surf craze. Although many other surf musicians continued to record and release albums, the Beach Boys greatly outstripped their contemporaries in terms of long-range success. Despite its brief life span, surf rock did have a lasting impact on rock & roll. With its celebration of excess and its willingness to adapt and experiment with newly available technology, surf music's legacy to rock & roll was a new way of thinking for artists dreaming up new ways to translate sounds from a songwriter's imagination to the recorded medium.

Hot-Rod Music

Around the same time that musicians were singing about hitting the beach, still others were singing about hitting the highways. Another phenomenon of Southern California, **hot-rod music** focused on the "greaser" subculture among the youths of the area. Despite being from the same area, however, the hot-rodders were in fierce competition with and generally disliked the surfers. They loved cars and speed, particularly hot rods, and would participate in drag racing and customizing their cars. These greasers also had a distinct style: black leather biker jackets, jeans, and slick, greased back hair. The movie *Grease* is a perfect example of the greaser image.

Although this social group got its start in the 1950s listening to rebellious singers like Elvis Presley and Eddie Cochran, there were several bands in the 1960s that captured the greaser ideology. Ronnie and the Daytonas released the song "Little GTO" in 1964, which was their first big hit of a series of hot-rod songs. Another popular hot-rod band was the Rip Chords, with songs like "Hey Little Cobra" (1963) and "Three Window Coupe" (1964). The Hondells recorded "Little Honda" in 1964, which made the Top 10 list. The Beach Boys would later record their own cover of "Little Honda," although they also wrote songs such as "409" (1962), "Little Deuce Coupe" (1963), and "Fun Fun Fun" (1964).

HOW DID FOLK MUSIC INFLUENCE EMERGING ROCK & ROLL GENRES?

Folk Collides with Rock

While groups like Peter, Paul, and Mary were finding success by softening Dylan's biting tunes, other groups were achieving equally strong results by making those same songs rock harder. After 1964, folksingers had to find ways to compete with the explosion of excitement ushered in with the British Invasion. They started using electric instruments and used stronger drum accompaniment. They took elements from songs that had made the British Invasion so successful to incorporate into their own works. This new approach to folk music created not only a new genre—folk rock—but also another rift in the folk scene, as many folkniks questioned whether folk could, in fact, rock.

DYLAN AND THE BRITS

Of course, Dylan wasn't doing anything new when he plugged in. Plenty of musicians were already playing music—even folk music—with electric guitars. Dylan's electric transformation stemmed from a response to the influential music coming from the United Kingdom. With the massive impact of the British Invasion on American rock & roll, Dylan realized that he needed to do something drastic to sustain his artistic and commercial momentum.

The Beatles

Although he wouldn't admit it at the time, Dylan was a Beatles fan. The so-called serious musicians who traveled in Dylan's circles thought the Beatles were a passing fad soon to be left behind when their teenaged fans found new pop idols. But Dylan appreciated how the British quartet handled chords and harmonies. Equally, the Beatles respected and enjoyed Dylan's work, attending one of his concerts on the UK tour that followed the blowout at the 1965 Newport Folk Festival.

Unquestionably, the Beatles contributed to Dylan's decision to add a layer of rock & roll to his music. The influence—like the admiration—was mutual. According to rock lore, Dylan introduced the Beatles to marijuana, and their subsequent use of mind-altering drugs left its stamps on albums such as *Rubber Soul* and *Sgt. Pepper's Lonely Hearts Club Band*. Dylan's attention to poetically crafted lyrics also had an effect on Beatles' John Lennon's own songwriting.

The Animals

Part of the British Invasion, the Animals were a rhythm & blues-based band that scored a hit in both the United States and the United

Kingdom with their 1964 version of Dylan's "House of the Rising Sun." Their first single, "Baby, Let Me Take You Home," was also an interpretation of a Dylan song, "Baby Let Me Follow You Down." When Dylan heard the Animals' recordings of traditional folk songs in an unapologetically rock & roll style, he was intrigued by the possibilities of the form. Although some others worried that money-grubbing rock music could contaminate folk, Dylan realized that bringing the two genres together would have a revolutionary impact on music (Scaduto 1973, 204).

THE BYRDS

If the Animals were folk-inspired rockers, then the **Byrds** were rock-inspired folkies. The California-based band was well-known on the U.S. folk circuit for their recordings of works by other folk artists, including Dylan and Seeger. Dylan's "Mr. Tambourine Man" served as the title track for the Byrds' debut album and provided the group with a pan-Atlantic hit in 1965. Appearing that same year, the Byrds' successful follow-up

ISSUES in ROCK

Dylan Plugs In

They should have seen it coming. Dylan's 1964 *Another Side of Bob Dylan* showed an obvious stylistic transition, including both the protest songs that had helped him establish his career and the surrealistic songs that would mark the next phase of it. In 1965, he released two albums: *Bringing It All Back Home*, a half-acoustic, half-electric album, and *Highway 61 Revisited*, which laid out a full-on electric assault. But when Dylan took the stage at the 1965 Newport Folk Festival wearing a black leather jacket, carrying an electric guitar, and backed by musicians from the Paul Butterfield Blues Band, the audience didn't suspect that their acoustic hero of the past two years was about to turn his back on that sound.

Dylan and his backing band had barely rehearsed because Dylan was trying to keep his live electric debut under wraps. He knew that many people in the audience would not approve of his switching from classic acoustic guitar to an electric guitar. Some fans felt that acoustic instruments were what kept the music "pure." So, it was perhaps unsurprising that, when they launched into "Maggie's Farm" and "Like a Rolling Stone" un-soundchecked and underrehearsed, the performance was a mess. The audience

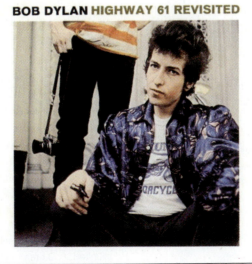

responded with unenthusiastic applause, boos, and even heckling. Dylan played one more song with the backing band before they all left the stage. At the urging of Peter Yarrow, Dylan returned to the stage with Yarrow's acoustic guitar and a borrowed harmonica. After playing a none-too-subtle message about his stylistic changes in "It's All Over Now, Baby Blue," he left the stage and never again returned to the Newport Folk Festival (Shelton 1986, 301–304).

Criticisms abounded: Dylan was a traitor, a sellout, a Judas. The singer had always enjoyed toying with the press and expectations, so it's difficult to clearly define his intentions when he plugged in. Dylan claims that he was simply following his own artistic path and denies being upset at the ensuing jabs. Others, however, have stated that Dylan was highly distraught and even in tears the night after he played. Even the audience's reaction is ambiguous—were they actually crying out against Dylan going electric or just against the cacophonous effects of Dylan and his backing band going on unrehearsed? Only one thing is certain: When Dylan went electric, sparks flew.

The Award for Best Folk Recording Goes To...

1960	The Kingston Trio, The Kingston Trio At Large
1961	Harry Belafonte, "Swing Dat Hammer"
1962	Belafonte Folk Singers, Belafonte Folk Singers at Home and Abroad
1963	Peter, Paul, and Mary, "If I Had a Hammer"
1964	Peter, Paul, and Mary, "Blowin' in the Wind"
1965	Gale, Garnett, We'll Sing the Sunshine
1966	Harry Belafonte, An Evening With Belafonte/ Makeba
1967	Cortelia Clark, Blues in the Street
1968	John Hartfod, Gentle on My Mind
1969	Judy Collins, "Both Sides Now"

∧
∧ Although folk music wielded varying levels of mass appeal throughout the 1960s, some
∧ of the most influential folk artists of the decade, including Bob Dylan, were not recognized at the Grammy Awards.

album relied on this same formula, employing an adaptation of Seeger's "Turn! Turn! Turn!" as its title track.

The Byrds' influence on rock & roll first stemmed from their contribution to the establishment of folk rock as an independent genre. In doing this, they became a model for combining the rebellious nature of rock with the purpose-driven music of folk. Once folk rock was established, however, their style became restless. Quickly drawn toward the rising sounds of psychedelic rock, the Byrds' experimental sounds encouraged the electronic manipulation of music that later became integral to some forms of rock music. The Byrds were also a major influence on the country rock genre, releasing *Sweetheart on the Rodeo* just a few months before Dylan released his own country rock album, *Nashville Skyline*, in 1969.

THE TURTLES

Originally a surf rock band called the Crossfires, the **Turtles** refashioned and renamed themselves the Tyrtles in homage to fellow Californians the Byrds. This misspelled homage was amended before the Turtles had a hit with their glittery version of Dylan's "It Ain't Me Babe" in 1965. Despite their subsequent hits with "Happy Together,"

"You Know What I Mean," and "She's My Girl," the Turtles were ultimately unsuccessful in trying to keep up with the ever-changing styles of the time.

SIMON AND GARFUNKEL

Although **Simon and Garfunkel** became one of folk rock's most popular duos, their big break was more the work of producer Tom Wilson than of the artists themselves. Paul Simon and Art Garfunkel were childhood friends who first gained attention playing as a duo under the moniker Tom and Jerry before recording the first Simon and Garfunkel album, *Wednesday Morning, 3 A.M.* (1964). When the sounds of British Invasion overpowered this traditional folk debut, the two musicians went their separate ways for a time.

However, this separation did not last long, and the duo was reunited. A DJ remixed their song "Sounds of Silence" with rock instrumentation, reviving interest in the song. This new mix inspired Columbia to have Tom Wilson—who had also been involved with the electrification of Dylan—record new backing for the song. This new version of the song proved to be immensely popular; "The Sound of Silence" became a number one folk-rock hit in 1966.

Buoyed by the success of the new rock version of the song, the duo reformed and worked with Wilson on their follow-up album. Simon and Garfunkel released the albums *Sounds of Silence* and *Parsley, Sage, Rosemary, and Thyme,* both of which embodied many of the pair's best-known characteristics, in the same year. Their unparalleled harmonies were equally haunting whether singing about loneliness ("I Am a Rock"), the inevitability of fleeting time ("Leaves That Are Green"), or enjoying whatever life has to offer ("The 59th Street Bridge Song [Feelin' Groovy]"). Simon's songwriting could be literary ("Richard Cory"), ironically self-aware ("A Simple Desultory Phillipic [Or How I Was Robert McNamara'd Into Submission]"), or at once powerful and delicate ("The Dangling Conversation").

Simon and Garfunkel recorded only two other studio albums. One of rock's first concept albums, the quirky and artistic *Bookends* preceded the duo's orchestral swansong, *Bridge Over Troubled Water*. In 1968, Hollywood tapped into Simon and Garfunkel for the popular soundtrack to the film *The Graduate*; inspired by the film, the song "Mrs. Robinson" gave the pair another hit. When the two disbanded in the early 1970s, it had been on difficult terms. Simon went on to have a hugely successful solo career, while Garfunkel did some recordings with other artists in addition to his solo work. It wasn't until 1981 that the duo reunited and performed for a live audience in New York's Central Park. Their relationship continued on somewhat shaky terms over the years, although they performed together for charity shows and a brief tour in the Far East in 1993.

The Rise of the Singer-Songwriter

In the summer of 1966 and at the apex of his career, Dylan suffered a motorcycle accident and secluded himself in Woodstock, New York, to recuperate. Just before disappearing from the limelight, Dylan released *Blonde on Blonde*, another masterful album that featured the poetic lyrics and literary allusions that helped make the importance of personal, sincere, and meaningful—if cryptic—lyrics a major part of Dylan's legacy. The attention that artists such as Dylan and Simon paid to lyrics, along with the one-man-band tradition of folksingers, paved the way for a new breed of rock & roll stars: **singer-songwriters**. These artists came to dominate rock & roll after the ebb of the British Invasion.

THE CANADIAN INVASION

In the late 1960s, the United States welcomed an influx of talented musicians from Canada. Although the British invaders had largely already established careers at home with a hit or two under their belts,

THE TURTLES folk-rock band that began as surf rock band and later had a hit with Dylan's "It Ain't Me Babe."

SIMON AND GARFUNKEL highly successful folk-rock act that paved the way for later singer-songwriters.

SINGER-SONGWRITERS musicians who write and perform their own songs, which often feature personal and sincere lyrics.

NEIL YOUNG a singer-songwriter and rock musician who was a part of the Canadian Invasion and achieved popularity as part of the group Crosby, Still, Nash, and Young.

∧
∧
∧
Simon and Garfunkel are **one of the most commercially and critically successful folk-rock acts of all time,** with five gold or platinum albums, ten Top 30 singles, and six Grammy awards under their caps.

the musicians of the Canadian Invasion instead often came to the United States to begin their careers. Attracted by the Greenwich Village scene, strong record labels, and an enthusiastic U.S. audience that always seemed ready to gobble up the next big thing, these Canadian imports steadily worked their way across the border.

Neil Young

The son of a single mother, **Neil Young** (pictured in this chapter's Rock Technology feature) spent his high school years in a working-class suburb of Winnipeg, Manitoba. In the mid-1960s, Young moved to Southern California, where he joined the eclectic folk-rock band Buffalo Springfield. The band's second album featured two solo tracks from Young that showed off his signature folk-rock/country-rock style. After Buffalo Springfield disbanded, Young began a long and successful solo career peppered with hits such as "Cinnamon Girl," "Down By the River," and "Heart of Gold."

In the late 1960s, Young joined forces with David Crosby, formerly of the Byrds; Steven Stills, a fellow Buffalo Springfield alum; and Graham Nash, a veteran of British group the Hollies to form the supergroup Crosby, Stills, Nash, and Young (CSNY). Soon, CSNY recorded the classic album *Déjà Vu*. In the tradition of folk protest songs, CSNY followed up the hit album with the single "Ohio," a song about the national guard shootings of students at Kent State University during an anti–Vietnam War protest.

After leaving CSNY, Young achieved continued solo success by experimenting with a multitude of musical styles, some more successful than others. In the late 1980s, Young's style relied heavily on electric guitar feedback, and he hired avant-garde band Sonic Youth to open for his *Ragged Glory* tour. With the advent of grunge music in the early 1990s, Young was dubbed the "Godfather of Grunge," a testament to his enduring influence on artists like Nirvana's Kurt Cobain and Pearl Jam's Eddie Vedder (see Chapter 12). Young's

ROCK TECHNOLOGY ⟫⟫⟫ The Harmonica Neck Rack

Thinking of the phrase "one-man band" might summon up an extreme image of a musician with cymbals strapped to his knees, bells on his feet, maracas on his elbows, a guitar strapped to his front, and a drum to his back. Certainly, the busking tradition has encouraged the development of innovative ways for one person to play the roles of many musicians while still allowing for mobility.

Many of these contraptions are admittedly a little absurd, but the **harmonica neck rack**, or harp rack, was vital to folk musicians who commonly played the guitar and harmonica in addition to singing. By wrapping around the singer's neck or shoulders, the neck rack held the harmonica in front of the singer's mouth until he or she was ready to play it. Although Dylan made the neck rack famous, the device has a long tradition; the 1902 Sears, Roebuck, and Co. catalog offered a neck rack for just 30 cents. However, similar instruments such as the Chinese *sheng* or the Japanese *sho* instruments date back to 110 BCE,

so it's likely that folksingers were fashioning holders from metal or wood centuries before they were available through mail order.

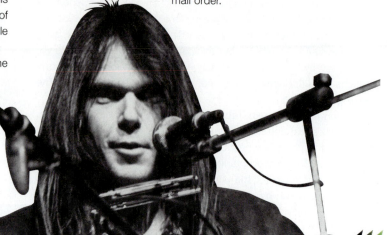

career, spanning more than five decades, shows the flexibility afforded to singer-songwriters, who write and perform their own songs and can therefore adapt their styles to suit personal or popular changes, which is well suited to an enduring career.

Joni Mitchell

While still on the folk circuit in Canada, Young met another folksinger with whom he would collaborate while playing with CSNY. After teaching herself to play guitar with a Pete Seeger instructional book, **Joni Mitchell** moved to Detroit from her native Toronto, Ontario. There, her distinctive, trilling singing style and poignant songwriting skills garnered her much attention. Soon, she was filling up clubs in New York City.

Mitchell's first three albums met with critical and commercial acclaim. Her third album, *Ladies of the Canyon*, included the hit single "Big Yellow Taxi," an environmentalist's anthem, and "Woodstock," about the legendary 1969 festival. The connections between Mitchell and CSNY ran deep. Crosby had produced her first album, and she was romantically involved with Nash, who penned "Our House" about their congenial cohabitation.

Like other singer-songwriters, Mitchell's career features stylistic experimentations. While her earlier albums are largely acoustic and folk-inspired, her later albums exhibit jazz, avant-garde, and world music influences. This diversity has attracted many other musicians to Mitchell's songs, and interpretations and covers are common.

Judy Collins

One of Mitchell's best-known interpreters is **Judy Collins**. As part of the Greenwich Village scene, Collins got her start strumming traditional folk and protest songs on her guitar during the early 1960s. Only later did she make her mark as a song interpreter. Although not herself Canadian, Collins played an essential role in bringing wider attention to emerging Canadian singer-songwriters such as Mitchell

and Leonard Cohen. She was also notable for her social activism and her relationship with Stills, which inspired the CSNY song "Suite: Judy Blue Eyes."

Leonard Cohen

"Suzanne," one of Collins's biggest hits, was written by **Leonard Cohen**. During the late 1950s and early 1960s, Cohen established himself as a poet and novelist in his native Canada. In 1967, he moved to the United States and landed in the avant-garde world of Andy Warhol's Factory. However, Cohen's singer-songwriter style did not fit neatly into those of his contemporaries, and he himself remained something of an outsider, spending much of the 1960s living in Hydra, Greece.

Cohen drew inspiration from U.S. and European folk and country music as well as from legendary Warhol protégé Nico, the sometimes chanteuse for the Velvet Underground. Cohen's debut album in 1967, *Songs of Leonard Cohen*, established his dark, introspective style that combines hauntingly stark instrumentals with Cohen's signature baritone. The album also gave a small taste of the subject matter that dominated his oeuvre, from sex and longing to religion and spirituality to power and isolation. Tinged with extreme sincerity, Cohen's lyrics are often intensely personal and delivered with visceral honesty and dry humor. Cohen's first album ends with a nearly minute-long atonal, guttural cry for a lost love, while "Dress Rehearsal Rag" from 1971's *Songs of Love and Hate* is an anthem of self-hatred and suicide. But Cohen also rose from these dark depths with a smirk on songs like "Don't Go Home With Your Hard-On" and "Chelsea Hotel." Cohen's second album, *Songs From a Room*, featured "Bird on a Wire." Popularized by Collins, this song was also recorded by Dave Van Ronk.

Although Cohen has generally received greater levels of popular and critical attention in Canada and Europe than in the United States, he remains one of the most significant and respected singer-songwriters of his generation among his musical peers. In 1994, singer-songwriter Jeff Buckley made waves with his cover of Cohen's "Hallelujah," and Cohen continues to gain new fans even today as more modern musicians release covers of his classic songs.

Rock Before the Invasion

From 1962 to 1966, music played an important role in America's political and social development. Political activists like Woody Guthrie and Pete Seeger used folk music as a medium for their political views, while singers like Bob Dylan used acoustic and later electric instruments as they tried to explore a blending of traditional folk music with the burgeoning rock & roll genre. On the West Coast, hot-rodders and surfers focused on a more pop-sounding rock & roll, focusing on an all-American lifestyle. From coast to coast, the music of America was changing with the times and the improving technologies. The music that came out of this era had powerful messages and catchy tunes that would make singers and bands famous around the world.

But America wasn't the only place where music was changing. In Great Britain, American rock & roll had found a new audience, and it wasn't long until the American style of music was played by British bands, but with a new twist. In the mid-1960s, some of these British songs made their way into America, and soon a flood of music would come pouring over the Atlantic in what is now called the British Invasion.

HARMONICA NECK RACK a device that wrapped around a singer's neck to hold a harmonica in front of the mouth to enable performers to sing while playing guitar and harmonica.

JONI MITCHELL singer-songwriter who was a part of the Canadian Invasion and whose long and stylistically diverse career is representative of how singer-songwriters often experimented with different musical styles throughout their careers.

JUDY COLLINS song interpreter who popularized many Joni Mitchell and Leonard Cohen songs.

LEONARD COHEN Canadian poet, novelist, and musician whose style is marked by dark, personal lyrics.

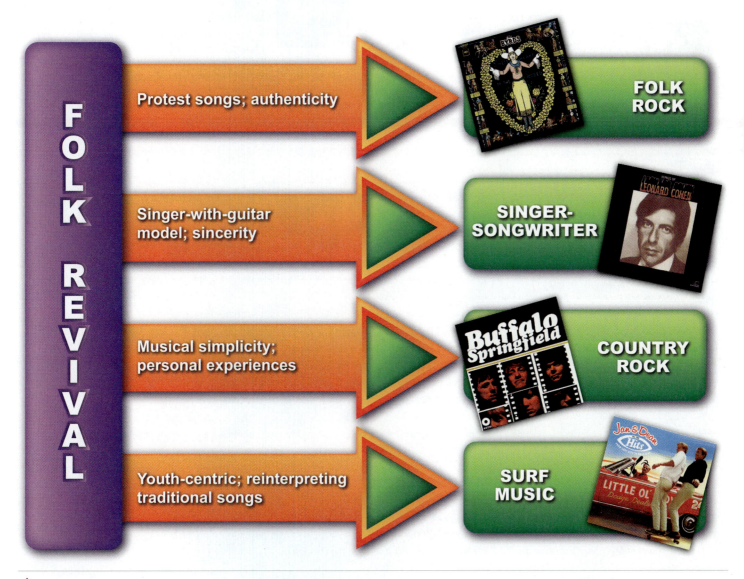

The folk revival of the 1960s **influenced different styles of music in various ways.**

Review

Summary

WHAT IS FOLK MUSIC? 74

- Folk is simple, sincere music with roots in working-class and African American America.
- Protest songs dealing with civil rights, workers' rights, and other political issues are fixtures of folk.
- Folk music usually features a singer with just a harmonica and guitar.
- Lead Belly introduced audiences to African American folk music, while Woody Guthrie introduced them to the plights of the working class.

HOW DID THE SPIRIT OF THE 1960s CHANGE FOLK MUSIC? 77

- The political climate of the 1960s made audiences receptive to politically oriented music. Many folksingers were active in the civil rights movement and later in Vietnam War protests.
- Bob Dylan served as a Woody Guthrie for the 1960s and brought folk to wider audiences. He also adapted it to suit the folk-rock and singer-songwriter trends that came later in the decade.

- Commercial and pop-folk acts tried to capitalize on the interest in folk music by making it appeal to a mainstream audience. This created a rift between commercial and so-called "pure" folksingers.
- At the same time, the carefree sounds of surf music captured other listeners. Prominent surf rock artists included the Beach Boys, Dick Dale and the Del-Tones, and Jan and Dean.

HOW DID FOLK MUSIC INFLUENCE EMERGING ROCK & ROLL GENRES? 82

- Folk rock combines elements of both folk music and rock & roll. It was the source of another rift among folksingers, who argued whether folk should be contaminated by rock.
- Dylan's influence on folk music stressed the importance of lyrics in rock & roll, paving the way for singer-songwriters. Many singer-songwriters, such as Neil Young, Joni Mitchell, and Leonard Cohen came to the United States from Canada in what was termed the Canadian Invasion.

Key Terms

folkniks musicians and followers of the 1960s folk revival 74

Newport Folk Festival a major annual folk music concert that has launched numerous folk careers 74

folk revival the repopularization and modernization of traditional folk music that took place in the United States during the 1950s and 1960s 74

folk rock genre of music combining characteristics of folk music and rock & roll that emerged in 1965 74

folk music simple, sincere music with roots in working-class and African American genres 74

Lead Belly an African American folksinger who was one of the first to bring traditional folk music to a mainstream audience 74

protest song a type of folk song that uses music to deliver a topical message 75

The Almanac Singers politically progressive U.S. folk act featuring Woody Guthrie and Pete Seeger 75

The Weavers a prominent folk group formed by Pete Seeger 76

The Kingston Trio an early popular folk band that gained popularity by eschewing political topics 76

Bob Dylan legendary musician who began as a folksinger, ushered in folk rock, and enjoyed a long and versatile career 77

hootenanny an informal folk music event featuring various musicians 78

basket houses venues at which performers were paid by passing a hat or basket around the audience 78

Dave Van Ronk a club owner and central figure in the Greenwich Village folk scene 78

John Hammond Columbia Records producer and talent scout responsible for helping integrate music and launch the career of Bob Dylan 79

Joan Baez a traditional folksinger and social and political activist who went on to have a career as a singer-songwriter 79

busking performing music on the street for money 79

Phil Ochs a traditional folksinger best known for his protest songs 80

Peter, Paul, and Mary a folksinging ensemble that achieved success by performing traditional folk songs and Dylan songs in a more accessible style 80

The Mamas and the Papas a harmonic quartet emblematic of commercial folk 81

Jan and Dean surf rock band that collaborated with the Beach Boys 81

Beach Boys surf rock band that went on to help launch psychedelic and prog rock 81

hot-rod music similar to surf music, West Coast music that revolved around cars and the greaser lifestyle 82

The Byrds an early folk-rock band that achieved success by injecting elements of rock into Dylan songs 83

The Turtles folk-rock band that began as surf rock band and later had a hit with Dylan's "It Ain't Me Babe" 84

Simon and Garfunkel highly successful folk-rock act that paved the way for later singer-songwriters 84

singer-songwriters musicians who write and perform their own songs, which often feature personal and sincere lyrics 85

Neil Young a singer-songwriter and rock musician who was a part of the Canadian Invasion and achieved popularity as part of the group Crosby, Still, Nash, and Young *85*

harmonica neck rack a device that wrapped around a singer's neck to hold a harmonica in front of the mouth to enable performers to sing while playing guitar and harmonica *86*

Joni Mitchell singer-songwriter who was a part of the Canadian Invasion and whose long and stylistically diverse career is representative of how singer-songwriters often experimented with different musical styles throughout their careers *86*

Judy Collins song interpreter who popularized many Joni Mitchell and Leonard Cohen songs *86*

Leonard Cohen Canadian poet, novelist, and musician whose style is marked by dark, personal lyrics *86*

Sample Test Questions

1. Which of the following most likely influenced Dylan's decision to "go electric"?
   a. Dylan's encounter with the Beatles and hallucinogenic drugs
   b. Dylan's appreciation for the Animals' interpretations of his songs
   c. Dylan's desire to distance himself from his collaborations with Baez
   d. Dylan's political shift away from the civil rights movement

2. Along with Dylan, which of the following songwriters impacted singer-songwriters by stressing the importance of poetic lyrics?
   a. Joan Baez
   b. Neil Young
   c. Paul Simon
   d. Art Garfunkel

3. Which of the following was most important in enabling folksingers and singer-songwriters to perform as solo acts?
   a. harmonica neck rack
   b. hootenanny
   c. busking
   d. basket houses

4. Which musician was credited with creating the surf guitar sound?
   a. Jan Berry
   b. Brian Wilson
   c. Dean Torrence
   d. Dick Dale

5. Who is known as the Mayor of MacDougal Street?
   a. Dave Van Ronk
   b. Brian Wilson
   c. John Hammond
   d. Bob Dylan

ESSAY QUESTIONS

6. What was the relationship between singer-songwriters and the traditions and styles of folk music?

7. How might historical events taking place in the United States during the 1960s have encouraged the growth of diverse musical styles?

8. How did issues of race influence folk musicians and their work?

9. Select a contemporary musician and explain how that musician's style reflects the folk tradition.

10. Compare and contrast how the British Invasion affected surf music and folk rock.

WHERE TO START YOUR RESEARCH PAPER

For video resources about folk's roots, go to
http://www.pbs.org/americanrootsmusic

For extensive information about Woody Guthrie, go to
http://www.woodyguthrie.org/index.htm

For more information about Bob Dylan, including a collection of lyrics to every song, go to http://www.bobdylan.com

For more information about the Library of Congress's American Folklife Center and the recordings of John and Alan Lomax, go to
http://www.loc.gov/folklife

For more information about the Newport Folk Festival, including lineups for current festivals, go to http://www.folkfestival50.com

For more information about singer-songwriters, go to
http://www.britannica.com/EBchecked/topic/545826/singer-songwriter

For a history of surf music, go to
http://www.legendarysurfers.com/surf/legends/lsc212.html

For information and news about Paul Simon's solo career, go to
http://www.paulsimon.com

ANSWERS: 1. b; 2. c; 3. a; 4. d; 5. a

Remember to check www.thethinkspot.com for additional information, downloadable flashcards, and other helpful resources.

HOW DID BRITISH BANDS INFLUENCE ROCK IN THE 1960s?

Just months before the *New York Times* article was written, few Americans had heard of the Beatles. Despite the innovative styles of girl groups and the nascent Motown scene, among others, rock & roll was at a standstill. The hits of Elvis Presley, Chuck Berry, and Jerry Lee Lewis were a distant memory—the U.S. charts in the early 1960s were primarily dominated by the music industry's prefabricated teen idols.

Meanwhile, the assassination of beloved president John F. Kennedy in November 1963 sent shock waves through American society and sapped the national mood. America's teenagers were ready for the energizing, hopeful young band that landed in New York in 1964, and the Beatles subsequent success gave American teenagers a taste for the exciting new sounds coming out of Britain. Over the next two years, dozens of British rock groups charted tracks on the U.S. pop rankings, paving the way for numerous future developments in popular music. Unbeknownst to the apprehensive quartet arriving in New York in February 1964, they were about to kick-start a whole new era in music: the British Invasion.

The Skiffle Craze

Wherever it was "born," in the early 1960s, rock & roll was clearly an American product. Exported around the world, the music of American stars such as Jerry Lee Lewis and Buddy Holly was particularly popular in Britain, where many aspiring rock musicians tried to imitate their American counterparts.

Although some achieved success in their own country, few British artists were able to peddle their brand of rock music on the other side of the Atlantic. Prior to 1964, only Cliff Richard, the Tornadoes, and Lonnie Donegan had appeared on the U.S. charts. Of these, **Lonnie Donegan** proved to be the biggest influence on British bands of the 1960s. Known as the "King of Skiffle," Donegan's 1954 Lead Belly cover "Rock Island Line" reached the Top 20 in the United States—a rare feat for a British artist at that time.

Donegan's version of Dixieland jazz and country blues engendered a simple, accessible musical style known as **skiffle**. Composed of a crude guitar, homemade bass, a suitcase played with whisk brooms, and a washboard strummed with thimbles, the band's music acquired the term "skiffle," after Dan Burley and His Skiffle Boys, a Chicago-based band from the 1940s. The term was originally used as slang for a rent party, in which poor, urban families would get together, play music with whatever instruments they could find (or improvise), and then pass around a hat to collect money for whoever's turn it was to pay the rent.

<<< **Prior to 1964, Lonnie Donegan was one of the few British acts to successfully chart hits across the Atlantic.**

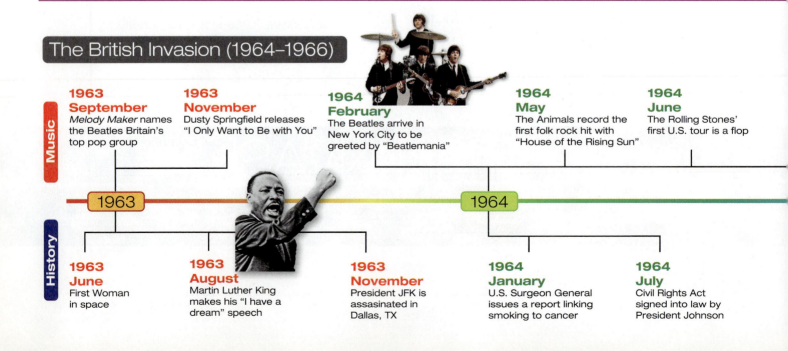

The British Invasion (1964–1966)

Music

**1963
September**
Melody Maker names the Beatles Britain's top pop group

**1963
November**
Dusty Springfield releases "I Only Want to Be with You"

**1964
February**
The Beatles arrive in New York City to be greeted by "Beatlemania"

**1964
May**
The Animals record the first folk rock hit with "House of the Rising Sun"

**1964
June**
The Rolling Stones' first U.S. tour is a flop

1963   1964

History

**1963
June**
First Woman in space

**1963
August**
Martin Luther King makes his "I have a dream" speech

**1963
November**
President JFK is assassinated in Dallas, TX

**1964
January**
U.S. Surgeon General issues a report linking smoking to cancer

**1964
July**
Civil Rights Act signed into law by President Johnson

Donegan's success in the UK inspired hundreds of poor British youths to hunt down cheap guitars, banjos, and washboards and start their own skiffle bands. Skiffle required little musical schooling and, more importantly, it prepared wannabe rock stars to play amplified, blues-based American rock & roll. Mick Jagger, Jimmy Page and John Lennon all began their musical careers in skiffle bands.

MERSEYBEAT

In the UK, **Liverpool** became the first hotbed of the "beat boom." Its role as an industrial port exposed the city to influential rock & roll imports from the United States, which had an enthusiastic audience among the city's youth. Inspired both by the influx of American rock & roll records and by the newly accessible skiffle style, Liverpudlian teenagers were galvanized into picking up their own instruments and forming bands. In the early 1960s, several hundred beat groups were active on Merseyside, competing for recognition at local venues. **Merseybeat** (named after the Mersey River in Liverpool), or "beat" music, combined skiffle, doo-wop, and soul, to create a popular genre of music typified by groups such as Gerry and the Pacemakers, the Searchers, the Merseybeats, and—most prominently—**the Beatles**.

The Beatles and Beatlemania

On February 7, 1964, four young English musicians from Liverpool stepped off a plane at Kennedy International Airport in New York City to be greeted by a crowd of 200 reporters and photographers, 100 police officers, and 4,000 screaming fans, who lined the rooftop observation deck of the airport's International Arrivals Building. As fans chanted, "We love you Beatles, oh yes we do," the four lads—John, Paul, George, and Ringo—sporting their trademark suits and mop-top haircuts, were

ushered inside the airport for their first press conference. Reporting on the manic scene, CBS news anchor Walter Cronkite stated, "The British Invasion this time goes by the code name Beatlemania."

Cronkite wasn't exaggerating—disc jockeys all over the United States played Beatle records nonstop, occasionally pausing to announce "Beatle time" and "Beatle temperature." The *Ed Sullivan Show*, which hosted the Beatles two days after their arrival, received 50,000 applications for seats in an auditorium that only seated 700 people. An estimated 74 million Americans (34 percent of the population) watched the broadcast—the largest audience ever recorded for an American television program (Gould 2007, 3–4).

By the time the Beatles left New York for London on February 16, few Americans could

<<< By the time the Beatles arrived at New York's Kennedy Airport in February 1964, "Beatlemania" was sweeping the nation.

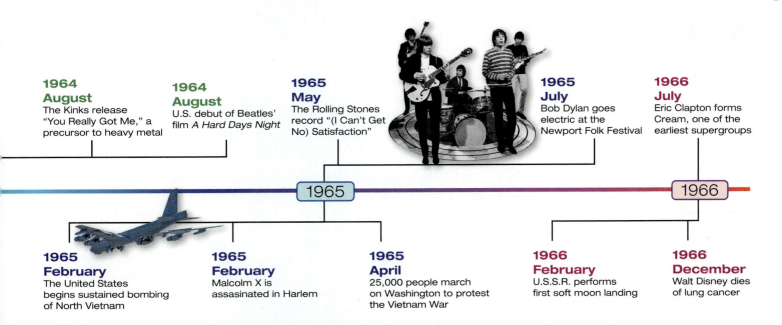

1964 August
The Kinks release "You Really Got Me," a precursor to heavy metal

1964 August
U.S. debut of Beatles' film *A Hard Days Night*

1965 May
The Rolling Stones record "(I Can't Get No) Satisfaction"

1965 July
Bob Dylan goes electric at the Newport Folk Festival

1966 July
Eric Clapton forms Cream, one of the earliest supergroups

1965

1966

1965 February
The United States begins sustained bombing of North Vietnam

1965 February
Malcolm X is assassinated in Harlem

1965 April
25,000 people march on Washington to protest the Vietnam War

1966 February
U.S.S.R. performs first soft moon landing

1966 December
Walt Disney dies of lung cancer

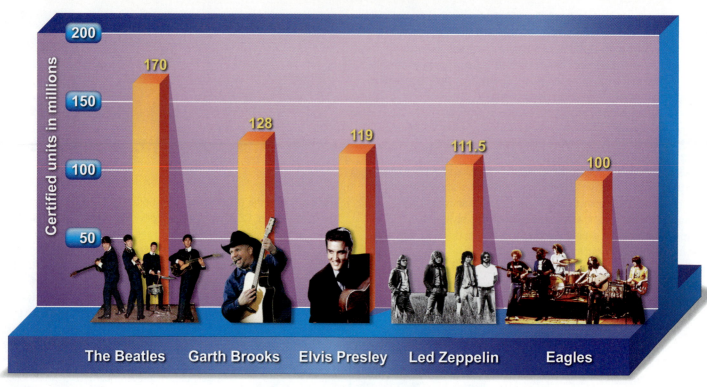

The Beatles — 170
Garth Brooks — 128
Elvis Presley — 119
Led Zeppelin — 111.5
Eagles — 100

Certified units in millions

Source: Recording Industry Association of America, "Gold and Platinum: Top Selling Artists," http://www.riaa.com/goldandplatinumdata.php?table=tblTopArt.

In 1999, the Recording Industry Association of America named the Beatles the top recording artists of the 20th century. To date, the Fab Four have sold more than 170 million albums in the United States alone.

claim ignorance of the Beatles. Featured on the covers of *Life*, *Look*, and *The Saturday Evening Post*, the band also occupied the first and second positions for both singles and albums on the U.S. record charts. "I Want to Hold Your Hand" hit number one on February 1 and stayed there for seven weeks, giving way to "She Loves You" on March 21. Two weeks later, "Can't Buy Me Love" took the number one spot. On March 28, 1964, the Beatles placed 10 singles in the Top 100, beating Elvis Presley's nine Top 100 singles in December 1956. By mid-April 1964, this figure had increased to 14 Beatles singles in the Top 100 (Bronson 1988, 145). The trade journal *Billboard* later estimated that 60 percent of the singles sold in the first quarter of 1964 were Beatles recordings (Belz 1972, 145).

ROCK PLACES

Liverpool

Until as late as 1962, the idea that Liverpudlians might flood the British and American music charts with hit singles was laughable. The British music industry was firmly centered in London, while Liverpool was primarily known for its comedians. However, the sense of working-class solidarity and fierce patriotism within the port city spurred local musicians, inspired by the American rhythm & blues records brought back by sailors, to make the most of their collective enthusiasm. The publication of the newspaper *Mersey Beat*, founded by John Lennon's friend Bill Harry in 1961, further helped promote the local music scene (although Harry was primarily interested in promoting the Beatles), and the vast number of musical venues provided an outlet for local talent. Among these venues, Liverpool's **Cavern Club** was to become the most famous. Originally featuring jazz performers when it opened in 1957, the Cavern Club was swept up in the skiffle craze and, in the early 1960s, became the spawning ground for the sounds of Merseybeat. John Lennon debuted at the Cavern Club in the Quarrymen in 1957, with Paul McCartney joining the band onstage a year later. However, it was after the Beatles' return from Hamburg in 1960 that the renamed band became firm club favorites, establishing the Cavern Club as one of the world's most famous live music venues.

In 2001, *The Guinness Book of Records* declared Liverpool the World Capital of Pop because of the record-breaking number of chart-topping hits to emerge from the city. Today, the Cavern Club continues to host live music, in addition to attracting hundreds of thousands of Beatles fans every year, excited to see the stage on which their idols once played.

ORIGINS OF THE BEATLES

By the time Beatlemania reached the United States, it was already well underway in Britain. Late in 1963, Ed Sullivan had witnessed more than 15,000 screaming Beatles fans descend on London's Heathrow airport to welcome the band home from a trip abroad. He quickly booked them as headliners for three consecutive shows in the States, even though they had yet to make an impact on the U.S. charts.

Although the Beatles landed on U.S. soil with a bang, their rise to fame in Britain was a somewhat slower process. Originally a skiffle band named the Quarrymen, founded by John Lennon and his school friends in 1957, the group soon added Paul McCartney to their lineup, followed by George Harrison a year later. As the founding members began to drift away, the core group briefly changed its name to Johnny and the Moondogs, then the Silver Beetles, and finally the Beatles (paying tribute to Buddy Holly's band the Crickets). By this time, Lennon's art school friend Stuart Sutcliffe had joined the band on bass, although he could barely play the instrument, and local drummer Pete Best was asked to join (primarily because he owned a full drum set).

In 1961, the group traveled to Hamburg, Germany, for a job playing at the Star Club, a small bar where the band performed grueling sets through the night. While in Germany, they were hired to back up singer Tony Sheridan on one of his records; at the session, they also cut their first record, "My Bonnie," released that same year. When the Beatles returned from Germany, Sutcliffe stayed behind, leaving McCartney to take over his bass guitar duties (Sutcliffe died from a brain hemorrhage in 1962). There would be one more change to the Beatles' lineup when drummer Ringo Starr replaced the less experienced Pete Best in 1962—a consequence of signing with EMI's Parlophone label. With a recording contract in place and its lineup solidified, the band's success was imminent. Within a year, the Beatles had two number one albums on the UK charts—*Please Please Me* and *With the Beatles*. By 1963, Britain's best-loved rock band had arrived.

∧ ∧ ∧ **Manager Brian Epstein** was responsible for cleaning up the Beatles' image. **He died in 1967 of an accidental drug overdose.**

BRIAN EPSTEIN

Much of the Beatles' success can be attributed to the canny efforts of manager Brian Epstein. A successful salesman in his father's music shop, Epstein took pride in his ability to fulfill any customer's request, no matter how obscure. When local teens began to ask for the Beatles' recording of "My Bonnie," Epstein was stumped. His customers told him that the band was playing at the nearby Cavern Club, so he decided to check them out. Although Epstein had little knowledge of the music or its fans, he appreciated the Beatles' complete indifference to the opinions of their audience. Epstein met with the band several times, eventually convincing them to bring him on board as their manager in 1961 for the attractive sum of 25 percent of all net revenues.

Epstein's first task was to clean up the Beatles' image to make them appealing to the general public. He replaced their 1950s Rocker image

of leather jackets and slicked-back hair with a more professional look, and he told them not to smoke or swear on stage. Having been turned down by nearly every British music label, Epstein contacted George Martin, the head of EMI subsidiary label Parlophone Records. The company was a small fish in the music business pond, known for comedy and light music, but Martin had ambitions to increase its respectability. Sensing the potential for a fresh new sound, he offered Epstein a one-year, four-song contract, promising the Beatles a royalty of one penny per double-sided single sold. In September 1962, the Beatles recorded their first British release, "Love Me Do" and "P.S. I Love You."

THE ROAD TO AMERICA

In September 1963, a *Melody Maker* poll showed that the Beatles were the top British pop group. Their fourth big hit, "She Loves You," made it to the number one slot on the basis of advance orders, and a television appearance on *Sunday Night at the London Palladium* in October gained them national exposure. When John Lennon made his famous quip to the Royal Family during the 1963 Royal Variety Performance a month later, asking the people in the cheaper seats to clap their hands and those upstairs to "rattle their jewelry," the British press went wild. Even respectable British newspapers, which had previously paid little attention to Beatlemania, began to sit up and take notice. Interviews and articles portrayed the band as innocent, cheeky, and lovable, and their charm and quick wit seemed to unite Britons of all ages, classes, and educational backgrounds.

The furor in Britain did not go entirely unnoticed across the Atlantic. After the Royal Variety Performance in London, both *Time* and *Newsweek* ran articles on the Fab Four, with *Newsweek* describing their sound as "one of the most persistent noises heard over England since the air-raid sirens were dismantled." Despite worldwide press attention, George Martin had little success persuading EMI-owned Capitol Records to release a Beatles record in the United States. In November 1963, Brian Epstein flew to New York in an attempt to convince the record company to change its mind. Capitol hesitantly agreed to release "I Want to Hold Your Hand" in January 1964 (later moving the release date up to December 1963 when American disc jockeys began playing the record on the radio). Epstein convinced promoter Sid Bernstein to present the Beatles in concert at Carnegie Hall and then began a $50,000 crash publicity campaign, plastering five million "The Beatles Are Coming" stickers on walls, lampposts, and phone booths in every state.

By the time the Beatles touched down in New York City on February 7, 1964, "I Want to Hold Your Hand" was at the number one spot in the

George Martin

One of the most successful record producer in the history of popular music, George Martin came from fairly humble roots. Born into a working-class London family in 1926, he developed an early love for music, forming his own dance band at the age of 15 called George Martin and the Four Tune Tellers. After leaving school, Martin served as a pilot in the Royal Navy during World War II. When the war ended, Martin left military service to pursue his musical career, studying classical composition at the London Guildhall School of Music. He was working as a professional musician when the BBC offered him a job in its music library.

In 1950, Martin left the BBC to work as an assistant to the head of Parlophone Records. When his boss retired in 1955, Martin became the youngest producer (at the age of 28) ever to be put in charge of an EMI label. He soon made a name for himself in comedy records, producing recordings by Peter Ustinov, Peter Sellers, and Spike Milligan.

It was Martin's comedy producing background that helped forge a warm rapport with the Beatles when he agreed to an audition session. Sensing the group's potential, he committed Parlophone to a year-long contract, ultimately beginning an eight-year relationship with the Beatles. Under Martin's tutelage, the band replaced drummer Pete Best with Ringo Starr and quickened the tempo of second single "Please Please Me," sending it to the top of the UK charts in February 1963. Martin went on to sign a slew of other successful artists, including Gerry and the Pacemakers, Billy J. Kramer and the Dakotas, and Cilla Black.

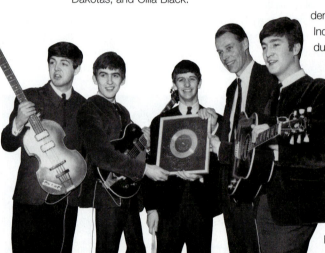

But it was Martin's production work with the Beatles that was his greatest achievement during this period. Both Lennon and McCartney turned to the producer to help them achieve the sounds that they wanted to create, particularly as the group matured and began experimenting with studio effects. Martin's contributions included simple tricks like double-tracking lead vocals on early recordings (such as Paul McCartney's lead on "Can't Buy Me Love") to adding different instrumental textures (the baroque trumpet on "Penny Lane") to the famous swirling orchestral climax at the end of "A Day in the Life."

Martin left EMI in 1965 to found independent production company AIR (Associated Independent Recording) with three fellow producers. The move finally earned him some well-deserved royalties (denied to him by EMI despite his run of success over the previous two years). When the Beatles disbanded in 1970, Martin continued to work with a diverse array of artists, ranging from Kenny Rogers to the Bee Gees, and on many different projects, ranging from film scores to TV shows. In 1996, Martin was awarded a knighthood by the British crown—the first member of his profession to be so honored.

TOP OF THE CHARTS
WHAT'S HOT!
APRIL 4, 1964

1. "Can't Buy Me Love" – the Beatles
2. "Twist and Shout" – the Beatles
3. "She Loves You" – the Beatles
4. "I Want to Hold Your Hand" – the Beatles
5. "Please Please Me" – the Beatles
6. "Suspicion" – Terry Stafford
7. "Hello, Dolly!" – Louis Armstrong
8. "Shoop Shoop Song" – Betty Everett
9. "My Heart Belongs to Only You" – Bobby Vinton
10. "Glad All Over" – Dave Clark Five

charts and, as seen in *The New York Times* article at the beginning of the chapter, Beatlemania had well and truly swept the United States. Just as Elvis had in the preceding decade, the mop-topped Beatles tapped into the repressed energy of American middle-class teens and gave them an outlet through the mass hysteria of Beatlemania.

In July of that year, the band capitalized on their musical success by releasing the full-length motion picture *A Hard Day's Night*, a thinly fictionalized account of two days in the life of the Beatles. The film comically documented (and subtly promoted) Beatlemania, conveying a sense of how it felt to be on the inside. Its portrayal of the Beatles as four wacky, unpretentious, and likable lads from Liverpool crystallized the Beatles' hold on the public imagination, turning an overheated craze into an enduring love affair. Although the main purpose of the film was to sell records, it also pulled in $5.8 million in U.S. ticket sales within six weeks, grossing around $14 million worldwide.

The Beatles' success in the United States can partly be attributed to the postwar baby boom, which created millions of teenagers in the 1960s searching for an identity. In a country that had been ripped apart in November 1963 by the assassination of JFK, the Beatles provided America's youth with a sense of unity and optimism.

Encouraged by the enthusiastic embrace of their fans, the Beatles built on their success by experimenting with new musical styles on albums such as *Rubber Soul* (see *Classic Recordings* on page 99) and *Sgt. Pepper's Lonely Hearts Club Band* (see Chapter 7). As their teenage fans matured, so too did the Beatles' music. The Fab Four's enormous popularity gave them the freedom to pursue whatever creative direction struck their fancy, and as a result their music enjoyed the somewhat unusual distinction of being both popular and avant-garde until the group disbanded in 1970.

British Invasion Bands of the First Wave

The Beatles' success on the other side of the Atlantic gave Americans a taste for all things British. Within the next two years, dozens of British Invasion bands successfully charted in the United States, forever changing the history of rock & roll. Among the most notorious of these were the bad boys of rock & roll—the Rolling Stones.

THE ROLLING STONES

While the Beatles were playing at Liverpool's Cavern Club, the **Rolling Stones** were trying to make a name for themselves in London. Unlike their Liverpudlian counterparts, who listed Presley, Holly, and Little Richard as their influences, the Rolling Stones went back to the roots of rock & roll, particularly Chicago blues. There was an active blues subculture in London at the time, popularized by Alexis Korner and Cyril Davies (former members of the Chris Barber Band). Korner and Davies formed Blues Incorporated and landed a regular Saturday night gig at the **Ealing Club** in London— a basement venue that attracted R&B enthusiasts, including Keith Richards, Mick Jagger, and Brian Jones.

Forming a loose band called the Blue Boys, school friends Jagger and Richards often attended sessions at the Ealing Club in the hope that they might get a chance to perform. Although Korner was less than impressed by Jagger's vocal performances, it was at the Ealing Club that Jagger and Richards were first introduced to guitarist Brian Jones. The trio joined forces, and together with bass guitarist Dick Taylor and drummer Mick Avory, they debuted at the Marquee Club on July 12, 1962, as the Rolling Stones (naming themselves after a song by blues singer Muddy Waters). Living in a rundown apartment in the slightly seedy district of King's Road, the band played wherever work could be found through the rest of 1962. By early 1963, Taylor and Avory had been replaced by Bill Wyman on bass and jazz enthusiast Charlie Watts as their regular drummer, solidifying a lineup that has remained intact (more or less) for over four decades.

∧∧∧ Former Beatles publicist Andrew Loog Oldham cultivated the Stones' "bad boy" image counter to the Beatles' clean-cut look.

Andrew Loog Oldham

In 1963, publicity manager Andrew Loog Oldham (former publicity man for Bob Dylan and the Beatles) approached the Rolling Stones about becoming their manager. Decca Records executive Dick Rowe, who famously rejected the Beatles, was not about to make the same mistake twice and signed the band on the recommendation of George Harrison. In May of that year, the Stones recorded their first single, covers of Chuck Berry's "Come On," with Muddy Waters' "I Wanna Be Loved" on the flip side.

When the band first appeared on British television show *Thank Your Lucky Stars* to promote their new record (which reached number 21 on the British chart), they looked like a carbon copy of the Beatles. On Oldham's advice, they dressed in checkered suits with velvet collars and matching ties and trousers—the manager's attempt to tidy up the band in the same way that Brian Epstein had done with the Beatles. However, Oldham quickly changed his tactic and began marketing the Stones in the opposite image of their Liverpudlian counterparts. He encouraged them to grow their hair longer, to reject matching clothes, and to appear scruffy and unclean. Oldham purposely built an image of "surliness, squalor, rebellion, and menace" (Norman 1984, 113), engineering a media blitz by inciting the press with outrageous quotes and phrases from the band. One of Oldham's lines to the press—"Would you let your daughter marry a Rolling Stone?"— was picked up by *Melody Maker* in 1964, which ran an article using the question as its headline. The article went on to describe the Stones as "symbols of rebellion. . . against the boss, the clock, and the clean-shirt-a-day routine." The British *Daily Express* labeled the group as "boys any self-respecting mother would lock in the bathroom." The Stones embraced their new reputation, scowling at the camera and insulting journalists with flippant replies during interviews.

The Stones Invade the United States

By 1964, the Rolling Stones were hugely successful in the UK, having reached the Top 15 with a version of Lennon and McCartney's "I Wanna Be Your Man," and the number three spot with Buddy Holly's "Not Fade Away." The group's self-titled debut album received 100,000 advance orders, rocketing it to the top of the charts upon its release in May 1964. Now notorious for their bad behavior, the Stones' reputation was solidified with a number of sensationalist articles in the British press, culminating in a story about the band members receiving fines for urinating in public.

Despite their UK successes, the Stones' first U.S. tour did not go anywhere nearly as well as expected. Greeted by hundreds, rather than thousands, of fans upon their arrival (who did not chase them around Manhattan in a frenzy), the band received scant attention in the American press, and their first prime-time TV appearance on *The Hollywood Palace* was marred by sarcastic comments made by the host, Dean Martin. The rest of the June 1964 tour proved to be equally unsuccessful, with the band playing to mostly empty seats. Aside from a couple of sell-out concerts at Carnegie Hall at the end of the tour, the Stones' first attempt to conquer the United States was a failure.

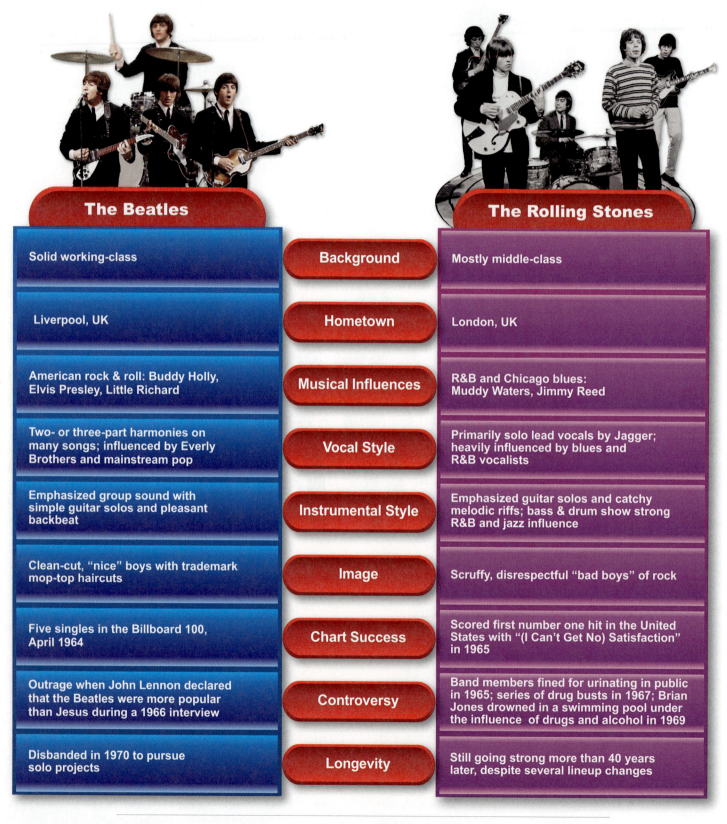

The Beatles		The Rolling Stones
Solid working-class	**Background**	Mostly middle-class
Liverpool, UK	**Hometown**	London, UK
American rock & roll: Buddy Holly, Elvis Presley, Little Richard	**Musical Influences**	R&B and Chicago blues: Muddy Waters, Jimmy Reed
Two- or three-part harmonies on many songs; influenced by Everly Brothers and mainstream pop	**Vocal Style**	Primarily solo lead vocals by Jagger; heavily influenced by blues and R&B vocalists
Emphasized group sound with simple guitar solos and pleasant backbeat	**Instrumental Style**	Emphasized guitar solos and catchy melodic riffs; bass & drum show strong R&B and jazz influence
Clean-cut, "nice" boys with trademark mop-top haircuts	**Image**	Scruffy, disrespectful "bad boys" of rock
Five singles in the Billboard 100, April 1964	**Chart Success**	Scored first number one hit in the United States with "(I Can't Get No) Satisfaction" in 1965
Outrage when John Lennon declared that the Beatles were more popular than Jesus during a 1966 interview	**Controversy**	Band members fined for urinating in public in 1965; series of drug busts in 1967; Brian Jones drowned in a swimming pool under the influence of drugs and alcohol in 1969
Disbanded in 1970 to pursue solo projects	**Longevity**	Still going strong more than 40 years later, despite several lineup changes

∧
∧ **The** contrasts between the Beatles and the Rolling Stones **led**
∧ **to a vigorous rivalry among their many fans.**

A second tour of the States, beginning in October 1964, proved far more successful, with the Stones appearing on Beatlemania launchpad *The Ed Sullivan Show*. Although publicly denouncing the band for their lewd behavior and declaring that the Stones would never be allowed back on his show, Sullivan privately acknowledged that the band had received the most enthusiastic applause he had ever heard. Although parents were horrified at the band's raunchy lyrics and crude behavior, rebellious American teenagers enjoyed the fact that the Stones were not universally liked. Whereas the Beatles were clean-cut, personable fellows, the Stones were dangerous and street-tough.

Satisfaction

Despite having achieved massive popularity, Oldham began pushing Richards and Jagger into moving away from blues-dominated cover songs and writing their own material. Their first original single, "Tell Me (You're Coming Back)" reached the U.S. Top 40 in June 1964, but it wasn't until the band's third U.S. tour in the spring of 1965 that a moment of creative genius rocketed the group to superstardom. While resting in a motel room, Richards strummed a catchy riff on his guitar and Jagger improvised some words. The resultant "(I Can't Get No) Satisfaction," a rebellious song about teenage aggression and frustration, reached the top of the U.S. charts that summer, becoming the band's first international number-one hit. "(I Can't Get No) Satisfaction" developed the Stones' signature style of big, bluesy riffs and cynical,

KINKS London band that popularized the power chord.

provocative lyrics, solidifying both their public persona and their trademark sound.

Although the Stones attempted to branch out and experiment with new sounds on their 1967 album *Their Satanic Majesties Request*, their efforts at musical innovation were not as well received as the Beatles'. After this setback, the Stones returned to what they knew best—mainstream, blues-based rock & roll—and have continued to enjoy popularity and commercial success up to the present day. Though notable for their longevity and their many hits, perhaps one of the Stones' greatest contributions to rock history is their cultivation of the "bad boy" image. The Stones set the standard for outrageous, anti-social behavior and hedonistic excess—an achievement that has shaped the development of rock & roll to a degree that few bands can claim to match.

THE KINKS

On St. Patrick's Day in 1963, Ray and Dave Davies, brothers from the working-class Muswell Hill region of London, formed a band with bassist Peter Quaife and former Stones drummer Mick Avory. Naming themselves the **Kinks** (from their habit of wearing fake leather capes and "kinky" boots

CLASSIC RECORDINGS ▶▶▶

RUBBER SOUL by the Beatles

The same year that the Rolling Stones defined their trademark sound with "(I Can't Get No) Satisfaction," the Beatles began their departure from their pop rock roots and ventured into new territory with their sixth studio album, *Rubber Soul*. Released in December 1965, the George Martin-produced album showcased a marked evolution in lyrical sophistication, influenced in part by the folk rock of Bob Dylan and the Byrds.

Rubber Soul introduced fans to a more mature and imaginative Beatles than they had heard before. The song "Norwegian Wood (This Bird Has Flown)" showcases the band's musical experimentation. Pairing Lennon's Dylan-inspired lyrics with the exotic melodies of Harrison's sitar (an Indian string instrument that Harrison discovered during the filming of *A Hard Day's Night*), the song recounted one of Lennon's extramarital affairs—a stark contrast to the innocence of early hits like "I Want to Hold Your Hand."

The Beatles' fans met the band's new direction with enthusiasm—*Rubber Soul* replaced the Beatle's previous album, *Help!*, at the top of the charts, where it remained for eight weeks. Considered to be one of the best albums of all time by many critics, *Rubber Soul* also influenced the development of psychedelic rock and encouraged the Beatles' contemporaries to experiment with new musical styles and sounds.

AFTERMATH by the Rolling Stones

Released in the States toward the end of the British Invasion in June 1966, *Aftermath* was the Rolling Stones' sixth American album. A major artistic breakthrough for the band, the LP was the first full-length release consisting entirely of original material. It was also the first Stones' album to be recorded entirely in the United States (at the legendary RCA studios in Hollywood) and the first album that the band released in stereo.

The release of *Aftermath* helped define the Rolling Stones as the bad boys of rock & roll, with their sneering, misogynistic (or at the very least chauvinistic) lyrics in "Under My Thumb" and "Stupid Girl." It was also notable for its musical experimentation and unusual (for rock records) timbres, with Brian Jones's use of the sitar throughout "Paint It Black" giving the song an "exotic" flavor; the album also features the marimba on "Under My Thumb," the harmonica on "High and Dry" and

"Goin' Home," and the dulcimer on "Lady Jane."

Although its impact was somewhat dulled by the simultaneous release of the Beatles' *Revolver* and Bob Dylan's *Blonde on Blonde*, *Aftermath* peaked at number two and remained on the U.S. charts for 50 weeks, eventually going platinum. In 2003, it was voted number 108 on *Rolling Stone* magazine's list of 500 greatest all-time albums.

POWER CHO

DISTORTION
voltage exceed

ROCKERS Bri
cles, and Ame

MODS fashion
and rode custo

WHO London
opera, *Tommy*
performances.

ROCK OPER/
multiple parts.

SYNTHESIZE
to produce a v

ANIMALS Nor
R&B and credi

HERMAN'S H
their novelty B

on stage), the
debuted with Li
Tall Sally," follow
titled, "You St
group finally hit
Really Got Me,'
U.S. Top Ten in
noisier, more dy
gle prominently
chord—a chord
root and fifth o
technically not
contains only tw
three). Played o
the power cho
to compensate
ture of a full cl
Davies experime
by cutting the sp
fier with a razor
ing them with
effect was a p
metal music, a
riffs became a
later bands. His
credited as one
known for his qu
a dash of satire
and "Dedicated

Having co
and All of the N
the Kinks were
British Invasion
the summer of
American Fede
group for unpro
onstage). Preve
was cut off fror
British Invasion.

HOW DID THE HIPPIE MOVEMENT INFLUENCE ROCK MUSIC IN THE LATE 1960s?

The word "**hippie**" probably came from the "hipsters" of the 1940s, a subculture that lived in (often) self-induced poverty and prided itself on keeping up-to-date with trends and the new jazz. Although it has never been quite clear whether the word is positive or pejorative, by the time "The Hippies" hit newsstands in early July 1967, the **Summer of Love** was already in full swing. Just six months after the Human Be-In in San Francisco's Golden Gate Park—a gathering of 20,000 people organized to protest the banning of LSD in California—"Turn on, tune in, drop out," the phrase coined by **Timothy Leary**, was no longer the exclusive phenomenon of the Haight-Ashbury district of San Francisco. With releases from the Beatles, the Grateful Dead, the Doors, Donovan, Jefferson Airplane, Pink Floyd, Love, Moby Grape, Cream, the Moody Blues, and the Jimi Hendrix Experience, psychedelic music was dominating the charts. Over the next three years, a small group of unconventional hippies from Northern California would lead a revolution in popular music and culture, from fashion to food to politics—a group whose legacy continues today.

>>> In 1964, **Ken Kesey and a group of friends calling themselves "Merry Pranksters"** took a cross-country trip to New York City in a "psychedelic" bus.

Rock's Alliance with the Counterculture

The hippies were driven and inspired by a distinctly West Coast counterculture, characterized by writer and political activist **Ken Kesey**. Kesey is probably best known for his novel *One Flew Over the Cuckoo's Nest*, based partly on his experiences working in a veteran's hospital, but in the 1960s he formed a crucial link between the Beat Generation and the hippies. After growing up in Oregon, Kesey moved to San Francisco in 1958 to study creative writing at Stanford University. Kesey's parties, called "Acid Tests," had a profound

The Summer of Love and Psychedelic Rock (1967–1969)

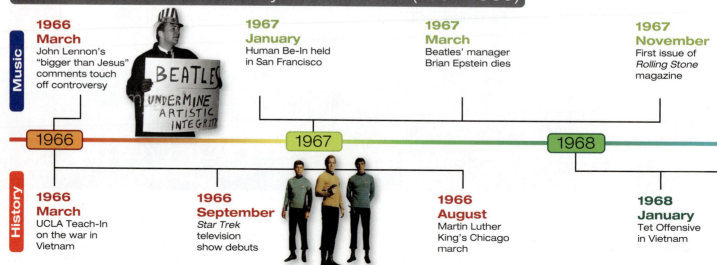

Music

1966 March
John Lennon's "bigger than Jesus" comments touch off controversy

1967 January
Human Be-In held in San Francisco

1967 March
Beatles' manager Brian Epstein dies

1967 November
First issue of *Rolling Stone* magazine

1966 · 1967 · 1968

History

1966 March
UCLA Teach-In on the war in Vietnam

1966 September
Star Trek television show debuts

1966 August
Martin Luther King's Chicago march

1968 January
Tet Offensive in Vietnam

influence on the counterculture trendsetters of the Bay Area during the transition from the Beat Generation to the hippie youth movement. The West Coast counterculture had been defined by the **beatnik** generation, when countercultural writers such as Jack Kerouac made California (and San Francisco especially) a home. With the arrival of Kesey and the group that formed around him, the Merry Pranksters, San Francisco once again became a locus for a new generation's counterculture.

HIPPIE OPPOSITION TO THE VIETNAM WAR

While the hippies in the Haight were tuning in, turning on, and dropping out, America's involvement in the war in Vietnam—and the stirrings of public opposition—continued to escalate. On March 8, 1965, 3,500 U.S. Marines were deployed to South Vietnam, beginning the ground war phase of American involvement. Although much of the "straight world,"—that is, the non-hip world—in the United States initially supported the war in Vietnam as part of the larger struggle against the spread of communism, the hippies, with their ethos of love and peace, showed their opposition in street protests, anti-war art and music, and "happenings." Rock music had replaced folk as the music of protest.

By 1968, the military draft was in full force, there were half a million U.S. troops in Vietnam, and protests and college campuses were increasing in strength and numbers. At the same time, many U.S. servicemen in

HIPPIE a member of the counterculture of the 1960s.

SUMMER OF LOVE summer 1967, a time at which the hippie era was at its peak.

TIMOTHY LEARY American writer, psychologist, and vocal advocate of psychedelic drug use.

KEN KESEY American writer and political activist associated with 1960s counterculture.

BEATNIK a member of the Beat Generation, an anti-establishment literary and cultural youth movement of the 1950s.

BARRY MCGUIRE American singer-songwriter most famous for his hit "Eve of Destruction".

GRATEFUL DEAD American rock band formed in 1965.

JERRY GARCIA guitarist of the Grateful Dead.

PEDAL STEEL GUITAR type of electric guitar played horizontally; pedal steel is mostly commonly heard in U.S. country music.

BOB WEIR rhythm guitarist for the Grateful Dead.

IGOR STRAVINSKY 20th-century Russian composer.

JOHN COLTRANE American jazz saxophonist and composer.

Vietnam were finding in popular music a reflection of their own worries and frustrations—blasting **Barry McGuire**'s "Eve of Destruction" and Jefferson Airplane songs in the middle of the jungle on their transistor radios and portable record players.

WHAT PATTERNS EMERGE WHEN COMPARING THE LEADING BANDS OF THE 1960s?

The Grateful Dead

Although many of the influential bands of the period drew inspiration from the drug culture, and from LSD in particular, few were more strongly identified with drug use than the **Grateful Dead**. **Jerry Garcia** formed the Warlocks in 1964, and the band began playing live in 1965. Initially, they were very much a blues-oriented band, as Garcia's background was in bluegrass and acoustic folk. However, after the Rolling Stones and the

Beatles debuted, the Dead began to throw rock into the mix as well, experimenting with psychedelic elements.

The Dead's singular music was as much the result of their varied backgrounds as of artistic experimentation within the band itself. Jerry Garcia's lifelong love was bluegrass and country music, and he also played banjo and **pedal steel guitar**. Rhythm guitarist **Bob Weir** has cited classical composer **Igor Stravinsky** and jazz saxophonist **John Coltrane** as influences. Bass guitarist Phil Lesh was a classically trained

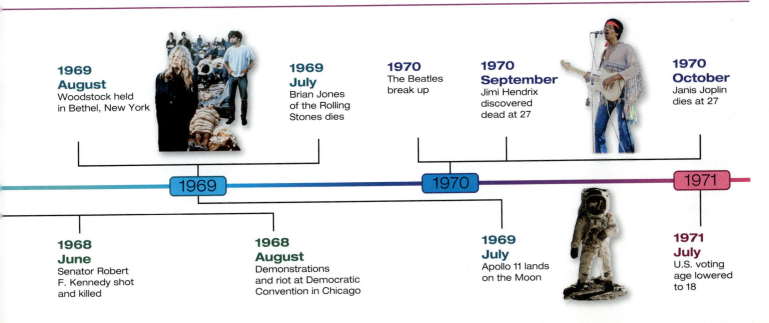

1969 August Woodstock held in Bethel, New York

1969 July Brian Jones of the Rolling Stones dies

1970 The Beatles break up

1970 September Jimi Hendrix discovered dead at 27

1970 October Janis Joplin dies at 27

1969   1970   1971

1968 June Senator Robert F. Kennedy shot and killed

1968 August Demonstrations and riot at Democratic Convention in Chicago

1969 July Apollo 11 lands on the Moon

1971 July U.S. voting age lowered to 18

trumpeter. Keyboardist Ron "Pigpen" McKernan was a blues player, and original drummer Bill Kreutzmann had a jazz background. Later drummer Mickey Hart studied with Nigerian drummer Babatunde Olatunji and frequently made use of a wide variety of unusual percussion instruments, including non-Western and orchestral percussion.

Their 1969 album *Aoxomoxoa* was a monument of studio experimentation. However, unlike experimenting during live shows, experimenting in the studio was expensive, and *Aoxomoxoa* left the band $100,000 in debt. The first track on the album, "St. Stephen," combines the metaphysical lyrics of longtime collaborator Robert Hunter with the melodic lyricism of both Garcia's voice and his guitar. Through all of their songs, Garcia's guitar was just as much a driving melodic force as the sung melodies themselves.

THE GRATEFUL DEAD LIVE

The Grateful Dead's long mellow jams were perfect for an audience under the influence of LSD, and the varied elements of their sound created a genre—the "jam band"—all its own. Because of their fusion of everything from jazz to country, and their literary, self-referential and metaphysical lyrics, manager **Bill Graham** said of the band, "They're not the best at what they do, they're the only ones that do what they do," (Graham & Greenfield 2004). To this extent, the Grateful Dead eschewed studio recording and commercial radio for "street parties" and long, improvisational jam sessions. The Dead also encouraged, or at least condoned, bootleg recordings of their concerts as long as the tapes were traded, not sold. Dead fans, or "dead heads," became connoisseurs of the band's many bootleg recordings. No show was ever the same, reflecting the band's improvisation, spontaneity, and interaction with the audience. The Dead toured and played live nearly constantly, and thousands of these concerts have been recorded as bootlegs.

Since live concerts were such an important part of the Dead's existence, it was no surprise that their soundman, **Owsley Stanley**, was a crucial part of the band. Stanley was the Dead's audio engineer, and in the early 1970s he designed and built the Dead's sound system for tours, called the "Wall of Sound." The sound system allowed each musician a separate input and the engineer more control over mixing the sound for a live audience.

The Dead toured continually until Jerry Garcia died of a heart attack in 1995. As one of the earliest and longest-lasting bands of the era,

∧∧∧ **The Grateful Dead's 1969 live album** *Live/Dead* **captured** the band's strengths of improvisation and spontaneity.

the Grateful Dead's impact on popular culture and the music business cannot be overstated. The band sold an enormous number of records and tickets over these four decades, while maintaining a commitment to artistic experimentation and personal exploration. Without support from commercial radio, the Dead became one of the most successful and enduring rock bands of all time.

Jefferson Airplane

The first San Francisco band of the era to achieve wide commercial success, **Jefferson Airplane** started when Marty Balin began both a band and a club in 1965 to play a hybrid style of folk and rock. This initial band went through a few incarnations, but their debut album *Jefferson Airplane Takes Off* (1966) only reached number 128. However, in mid-1966 the band recruited a young former model and singer/songwriter named **Grace Slick**. Slick was one of the lead singers of the Great Society, a popular San Francisco band, when she was asked to join the Airplane. She brought two songs with her: "White Rabbit" and "Somebody to Love," both of which would quickly become anthems of the time and launch Jefferson Airplane into the commercial stratosphere.

"White Rabbit," with its lyrics referencing the Lewis Carroll novel *Alice in Wonderland*, was a quintessential expression of rock's drug culture. Juxtaposing Carroll's hallucinatory imagery with the vivid story of an acid trip, Alice's experience within the psychedelic wonderland is enlightening, even though some images themselves are disturbing. Released as a single after "Somebody to Love," "White Rabbit" became the band's second Top Ten hit, rising to number eight on the Billboard Hot 100 in 1967. These two tracks helped the album *Surrealistic Pillow* (1967) go gold within six months. Slick was soon considered one of the era's most influential women in rock, an icon of female strength, intelligence, and independence.

Thanks to their manager, Bill Graham, Jefferson Airplane was the only band to have performed at all three of the era's defining festivals: Monterey (1967), Woodstock (1969), and Altamont (1969). They also headlined the Human Be-In (1967) in Golden Gate Park, one of the era's signal events protesting the ban on LSD. Through this period, one of Jefferson Airplane's most experimental albums was *After Bathing at Baxter's*, released in late 1967, only ten months after *Surrealistic Pillow*. The album explored the far reaches of psychedelia in music, and the band was largely given free reign to produce themselves without creative constraint. To this end, the album was not nearly as commercially successful as *Surrealistic Pillow*, but it represents an example of the "studio craft" that would become important in the era.

In late 1970, Marty Balin left the band, and since they did not have a new album to release they instead released a compilation, titled *The Worst of Jefferson Airplane* (1970), which had platinum sales. The band members continued to pursue side projects, and eventually evolved into the arena rock band Jefferson Starship. Balin rejoined, but both he and Slick left in 1978 after their tour to support the platinum-selling album *Earth* (1978). Although the band went through many

San Francisco

During the Gold Rush of the late 1840s and early 1850s, San Francisco became the largest city in California. Ever since, it has welcomed a diverse population from across the country and around the world and has remained a melting pot with a legendary tolerance for nonconformist lifestyles and attitudes. Like many seekers before them, the hippies found a welcome home in the Bay Area.

By the early 1960s, poets, artists, and musicians began moving to San Francisco's **Haight-Ashbury** neighborhood in search of cheap rent and a hospitable environment.

1967's Summer of Love would become one of the defining moments of the 1960s, when as many as 100,000 hippies descended on Haight-Ashbury, making it the worldwide center of the hippie movement. The folk, rock, and psychedelic music created there became the soundtrack of a generation.

incarnations, it was their first two hits—"White Rabbit" and "Somebody to Love"—that defined the nascent hippie culture of San Francisco from its inception.

Moby Grape

Moby Grape was founded by two Jefferson Airplane exiles: once drummer, now guitarist Skip Spence, and the Airplane's first manager, Matthew Katz. Like the Dead, Moby Grape was democratic: All band members wrote and sang lead and backup vocals on their debut album. Moby Grape's three-guitar lineup was nearly unique in rock, and each guitarist—Jerry Miller, Peter Lewis, and Skip Spence—developed a distinctive role in the intertwining guitar "crosstalk" that distinguished the band's sound.

Moby Grape struggled commercially despite being one of the most critically admired of the San Francisco bands. Even with the terrible marketing of the band's debut, involving the simultaneous release of multiple singles, Moby Grape's self-titled 1967 album still managed to win over fans at the time, and critical praise has only increased over the years. The year 1967 culminated with Moby Grape's troubled appearance at the Monterey Pop Festival

Fillmore Auditorium
1805 Geary

Jefferson Airplane
2400 Fulton

Human Be-In
Golden Gate Park

The Grateful Dead
710 Ashbury

Janis Joplin
112 Lyon

Fillmore West
10 S. Van Ness

In 1967, many considered Haight-Ashbury, home of the Grateful Dead, Janis Joplin, and Jefferson Airplane, the hippest neighborhood in the world.

D.A. PENNEBAKER American documentary filmmaker who created the seminal documentary *Monterey Pop*.

BIG BROTHER AND THE HOLDING COMPANY influential psychedelic rock band from San Francisco.

JANIS JOPLIN singer and songwriter, lead singer of Big Brother and the Holding Company.

JIMI HENDRIX influential guitarist and member of the Jimi Hendrix Experience.

CHAS CHANDLER the Animals' bassist and manager of Jimi Hendrix.

and legal wrangling that kept their performance out of **D. A. Pennebaker**'s seminal documentary *Monterey Pop*. Things would only get worse for the band. During the recording of their second album, *Wow/Grape Jam* (1968), in New York, Spence came into the studio wielding an axe (presumably to attack drummer Don Stevenson), a breakdown likely triggered by drug use. He was hospitalized for six months in a psychiatric facility.

Although they broke up in 1969, Moby Grape reunited occasionally to record and perform through the 1990s, both with and without original members Spence and bassist Bob Mosley. However, because of legal disputes with Katz, they could not always use the name "Moby Grape," and so many of these albums remain practically unheard. In 1998, Spence died after a long struggle with mental illness.

Janis Joplin

In its earliest incarnation, **Big Brother and the Holding Company** was a successful band in the Bay Area, playing instrumental psychedelic rock as the house band at the Avalon Ballroom. The band had a solid psychedelic history—founder Peter Albin had once played with Jerry Garcia and Ron McKernan—but their manager Chet Helms thought they needed a strong vocalist to attract a wider audience and remembered a young singer named Janis Joplin from his days as a show promoter in Texas.

In 1966, **Janis Joplin** was living in Port Arthur, a small East Texas city on the bank of Sabine Lake, where she had grown up. A few months earlier, friends had raised the money for Joplin's bus ticket home after she'd spent a productive but difficult year in the Haight, singing, writing music, and taking dangerous amounts of drugs. It took some convincing from Helms before Joplin decided to return to the Haight, this time for good. At first, it wasn't a perfect fit. Big Brother was an experimental psychedelic band, while Joplin was a singer steeped in traditional blues. Some fans weren't happy with the new direction, and it didn't help that Joplin was still learning how to front a loud rock band.

Big Brother (and, to a greater extent, Joplin) came to national and international attention with their appearance at the Monterey

^ ^ ^ Janis Joplin's trailblazing work in the male-dominated rock music scene has inspired countless other female rockers.

Pop Festival in June 1967 and in a documentary film of the concert released the next year. In particular, Joplin's performance of the blues song "Ball and Chain" became one of the highlights of the film of the festival, earning them a deal with Columbia Records. This performance characterized Joplin's interpretive style, oscillating between soft and intense and near-shrieks. More than just a standard white singer coopting of the blues, Joplin's active reinterpretation of Big Mama Thornton's classic secured her place in rock history.

Their second album *Cheap Thrills* ("*Sex, Dope and*" was dropped from the beginning of the title after complaints from Columbia) was recorded in the spring and released in early summer of 1968. Propelled by the smash single "Piece of My Heart," it reached number one on the Billboard charts two months after it was released and held the spot for eight nonconsecutive weeks. By the end of the summer, Joplin's management convinced her to strike out on her own. Her last performance with the band was on December 1, 1968. Three weeks later, she was in Memphis with her new band, soon to be called the Kosmic Blues Band.

I Got Dem Ol' Kozmic Blues Again Mama! was released in 1969 to heightened anticipation and generally mixed reviews. Joplin and the Kosmic Blues Band played Woodstock that same year, but by the end of 1969, the band was finished. Joplin's drug use was increasing, and she had added heroin to the mix, fuelling the downward spiral she had tried to escape in Port Arthur a few years earlier. Joplin formed a new band, and her Full Tilt Boogie Band played festivals through the summer of 1970 before decamping to Los Angeles in the fall to record a new album. Joplin died of a heroin overdose before all the tracks were completed, but *Pearl*, released in 1971, went on to become the most successful album of her career, with the posthumous number one hit "Me and Bobby McGee."

Jimi Hendrix

By consensus one of the greatest rock guitarists ever, **Jimi Hendrix** was born in Seattle, Washington, in 1942. He spent years honing his guitar playing skills on the so-called "chitlin circuit," working as a sideman for R&B artists including Little Richard and the Isley Brothers. Yet, constrained by the format of the music and his status as a supporting player, his wild genius had few opportunities to shine. Hendrix knew he was destined for bigger things, and in 1966 he left home to start his own band.

While playing in a club in New York, Hendrix was eventually discovered by **Chas Chandler**, bassist for the Animals. The Animals were about to call it quits, and Chandler was searching for talent to manage and produce. Chandler brought Hendrix to London and signed him to a management and production deal, then helped Hendrix find musicians for his new band, the Jimi Hendrix Experience.

Hendrix, along with bassist Noel Redding and drummer Mitch Mitchell, recorded the singles "Hey Joe" and "Purple Haze" in 1966 and 1967, both of which reached the Top 10 in the United Kingdom. The Experience released their debut album *Are You Experienced?* in 1967, which they supported with an extensive European tour. It was during this period that Hendrix first set his guitar on fire during a live performance. This stunt, along with his ability to play the guitar with his teeth and behind his back, grabbed massive attention for the band. The album reached number two (right behind the Beatles' *Sgt. Pepper's Lonely Hearts Club Band*).

The Jimi Hendrix Experience got their big break in the United States when they played at the Monterey International Pop Music Festival in June of 1967. After Monterey, Hendrix's stunning series of performances at Bill Graham's **Fillmore** in San Francisco set the stage for the band's next masterpiece, *Axis: Bold as Love* (1967). Hendrix and his engineers experimented with various studio effects, and Hendrix added new guitar effects to his arsenal, including a **wah-wah pedal**. The album includes the classic tracks "Little Wing" and "If 6 Was 9."

The band's final studio album was a double LP, *Electric Ladyland* (1968), a sprawling, often experimental series of songs that showcased Hendrix's virtuosity and a new thematic complexity to the lyrics. *Electric Ladyland* includes some of the strongest music of Hendrix's career, notably a brilliant cover of Bob Dylan's "All Along the Watchtower."

>>> Hendrix's performance at Woodstock in 1969 included his now-legendary rendition of "The Star-Spangled Banner."

Hendrix died in September of 1970 after choking on his own vomit, in an episode related to sleeping pills. However, the vast amount of live and unreleased studio material has made possible the near-continual release of material from the Hendrix archives. Al Hendrix, Jimi's father, hired Hendrix's original producer to remaster the original three albums, which were rereleased in 1997.

The Doors

While the Bay Area was a hotbed of new music, there was also a white-hot music scene 400 miles to the south in Los Angeles. In 1966, **the Doors** were the house band at the now-famous club Whisky A Go Go on the Sunset Strip. A hard rock powerhouse, fusing blues, heavy rock, and Eastern mysticism, and fronted by the darkly charismatic **Jim Morrison**, the Doors would become one of the most popular and enduring rock bands of the era.

The Doors formed in 1965 with a chance meeting between two UCLA film school alumni, Morrison and Ray Manzarek. The final lineup featured Morrison on lead vocals, Manzarek on keyboards, guitarist Robby Krieger, and

CLASSIC RECORDINGS ▶▶▶

THE DOORS by the Doors

The Doors recorded their self-titled debut in August 1966. The band recorded most of the album, including the 11-and-a-half-minute "The End," live in the studio, without the help of overdubbing and layering tracks that was popular at the time. The second single from the album, a truncated version of "Light My Fire," sold over a million copies and held the number one spot on the Billboard charts for three weeks in 1967. The band was set to perform the hit on the Ed Sullivan Show, but Sullivan did not want the word "higher" sung on the air. After agreeing to change the lyric, the band performed the song as it was and were banned from the show for life. *The Doors* introduced the world to the band's distinct fusion of rock, blues, and poetry, and established them as one of the preeminent hard rock bands of the time and a commercial force in music.

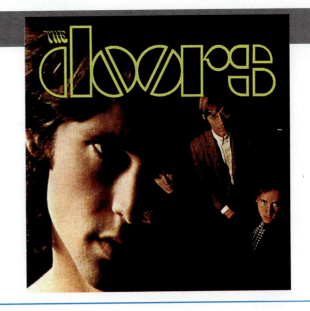

drummer John Densmore. To make up for the lack of a bass player during live shows, Manzarek played bass lines on a Fender Rhodes piano bass with his left hand. Morrison's lyrics were the first thing that caught Manzarek's interest, and they were equally compelling to the Doors' fans. A sort of literary rock band, the Doors took their name from Aldous Huxley's book about psychedelic drugs, *The Doors of Perception*, the title of which refers to a line by 19th-century poet William Blake. Morrison became a type of Romantic visionary, a rock poet who approached life according to another line by Blake: "The road to excess leads to the palace of wisdom."

The Doors were signed to Elektra Records after Arthur Lee, guitarist and singer for the group Love, recommended the band to the label's president. A few days later, the Doors were fired from their Whisky gig when an apparently tripping Morrison profanely recounted the scandalous details of the classical Greek drama *Oedipus Rex* to the crowd during the band's performance of their song "The End."

The Doors returned to the studio for their next album, *Strange Days* (1967), which featured two of their most popular songs, "People Are Strange" and "Love Me Two Times." Morrison's drunken stage antics culminated in Miami in 1969, when he reportedly exposed himself on stage and was subsequently arrested, charged with indecency and obscenity.

After 1969's poppier *Soft Parade*, the band returned to form in 1970 with

their fourth LP, *Morrison Hotel*, and fans and critics greeted the heavier rock of the album favorably. Their fifth, *L.A. Woman* (1971), included the singles "L.A. Woman," "Love Her Madly," and "Riders on the Storm" and cemented the band's return to rock superstar status. After completing *L.A. Woman*, Morrison left the band for Paris. He died of an apparent drug overdose, and the band failed to continue without him. Morrison's status was already legendary at the time of his death and has only continued to grow since.

∧∧∧ Arthur Lee's band Love was one of the first interracial bands in rock.

Love

An idiosyncratic musical genius, **Arthur Lee** had been bouncing around the Los Angeles music business as a session player when, at the age of 20, he met fellow songwriter and singer Bryan MacLean. They formed the band Love, and over the course of three albums perfected a distinctive amalgam of folk, rock, blues, jazz, and orchestral pop. Although they failed to make much of a dent with the American public beyond a cult following, they provided an inspiration for other L.A. bands, broke down social barriers as one of the first interracial rock groups, and left behind a body of work that overshadows the troubled life of its leader.

Inspired by British bands like the Rolling Stones and American folk rockers the Byrds, Love was signed by Elektra and released a self-titled debut in

ROCK PEOPLE

Bill Graham

Concert promoter Bill Graham was born Wolfgang Grajonca in Berlin in 1931; by the age of 11, he was a foster child living in the Bronx. He fought in the Korean War, earning a Bronze Star and a Purple Heart, and later moved to San Francisco. He tried to make it as an actor, but while managing the San Francisco Mime Troupe, he decided to put on a benefit concert for the group. The concert featured San Franciscan band Jefferson Airplane and the poets Lawrence Ferlinghetti and Allen Ginsberg and was hugely successful, both from an artistic and an economic standpoint.

He continued producing shows, coupling musicians like Miles Davis with the

Grateful Dead and fostering local psychedelic artists, using their artwork as concert promotion materials. His two venues, the Fillmore (San Francisco) and the Fillmore East (New York) were legendary; the Allman Brothers' *Live at the Fillmore East* was recorded just months before the venue closed in 1971. Janis Joplin and Jimi Hendrix both played live at the Fillmore early in their careers, gaining crucial exposure. Later in his life, he focused on benefit concerts, including Philadelphia's Live Aid and Amnesty International's "Conspiracy of Hope." He died in 1991 in a helicopter crash.

1966. It wasn't until their second album, the wildly psychedelic *Da Capo*, released in January 1967, that the band would have a Top 40 hit, "Seven & Seven Is." Although the recording of the album was fraught with the problems of Lee's and MacLean's deteriorating relationship, *Forever Changes*, released in November 1967, was a landmark of rock: powerful, dark, and subtle, featuring tasteful horn and string arrangements. The band broke up shortly after, and although Lee kept recording under the name Love, MacLean and the other band members were completely absent. Lee recorded one solo album and a few as Love through 1974, after which he essentially stopped recording.

ARTHUR LEE lead singer and guitarist for Love.

FRANK ZAPPA prolific American rock musician and composer.

EDGARD VARÈSE 20th-century French experimental composer.

WATTS RIOTS large-scale race riot that took place in Watts, California, in August 1965.

ACID TRIP the mind-altering experience of LSD.

13TH FLOOR ELEVATORS a band that pioneered psychedelic rock; fronted by singer Roky Erickson.

Frank Zappa

Frank Zappa was one of rock's most eclectic geniuses and unlikeliest stars. A prolific composer, his influences included 1950s doo-wop groups and avant-garde composers like Igor Stravinsky and **Edgard Varèse**. Zappa was also a virtuosic guitar player, record producer, and a groundbreaking entrepreneur who carved out a career in music by bucking the system. Zappa released over 60 albums during his lifetime, recording for MGM and Reprise Records before forming his own label, Barking Pumpkin.

Zappa began writing classical music while he was still in high school, and at the same time he played drums and then guitar in R&B bands. After a brief attempt at studying music at junior college, Zappa worked a variety of odd jobs before being hired to score the low-budget feature film *Run Home Slow* in 1965. He used the money he made to build a recording studio and formed a band to play his songs. Zappa and the Mothers of Invention released the double album *Freak Out!* on MGM's Verve label in 1966, a postmodern concept album satirizing music industry conventions. He also experimented with meaningful social commentary, including a song about the **Watts riots** called "Trouble Every Day."

In 1967, Zappa released *Absolutely Free*, which jumped from rock to free-form jazz to a rock opera called "Brown Shoes Don't Make it." However, their album *We're Only in it for the Money* (1968) would cement Zappa's status as a master of satire. The album's song titles are ironic questions, like "What's the Ugliest Part of Your Body?" with a reprise seemingly skewering the reprise of *Sgt. Pepper's* title track. Yet, the album wasn't just a joke; it was also a remarkable example of studio craft. Zappa showed on *Money* that he, like the Beatles, could use splicing, studio effects, and seemingly-out-of-place sounds, while satirizing the Beatles' commercial success.

Zappa continued developing the formula used in *Freak Out!*, his "freakish" mix of genre-bending satire. He experimented with doo-wop as early as *Freak Out!*'s "Go Cry on Somebody Else's Shoulder," but devoted an album to it with *Cruising with Ruben and the Jets* (1968). *The Grand Wazoo* (1973) was a foray into large-scale jazz-rock, with credits listing 27 musicians. Zappa succeeded as a bandleader and arranger, as well as a satirist and artist in his own right.

13th Floor Elevators

Hailing from Austin, Texas, **13th Floor Elevators** were pioneers of the psychedelic sound whose career was tragically cut short by lead singer Roky Erickson's drug arrest and subsequent hospitalization. Erickson had written the 13th Floor Elevators' lone hit, "You're Gonna Miss Me," in 1965 for another Austin band, but recording the song with the Elevators brought him fame. Featuring Erickson's haunted yowl, Stacy Sutherland's weaving guitar lines, and Tommy Hall's percussive jug playing, the new version was a hit in Austin and led to the band signing with the Houston record label International Artists. The single was rereleased and reached number 56 on the pop charts in 1966.

The band made frequent trips to California, touring and sharing bills with Quicksilver Messenger Service, the Great Society with Grace Slick, and Moby Grape. They returned to Texas in 1967 to record their psychedelic masterpiece, *Easter Everywhere*, which featured a cover of Bob Dylan's "It's All Over Now, Baby Blue" and the Grape classic "I've Got Levitation." In all, the band released four LPs and seven 45s until they were derailed by Erickson's hospitalization.

ROCK TECHNOLOGY ▶▶▶ Lysergic Acid Diethylamide (LSD)

Commonly known as acid, LSD fueled the acid-rock movement of the mid- to late 1960s, especially on the West Coast, serving as an inspiration to artists and their audiences. An "acid trip" might include the perception of glowing colors, time distortion, loss of identity, and feelings of euphoria. Many proponents of LSD claim the effects are spiritual and mind-expanding when taken in the proper setting and with the right frame of mind.

Swiss chemist Albert Hofmann synthesized LSD in 1938 from ergot, a fungus that grows on rye. Hofmann discovered LSD's psychoactive properties after accidentally absorbing some of the drug. Hofmann's employer, Sandoz Laboratories, began marketing LSD as a psychiatric pharmaceutical in 1947, but after it was adopted by members of the counterculture as a recreational drug, LSD was made illegal throughout most of the world and was banned in the United States in 1966. However, this did not stop the spread of the drug's popularity: The Grateful Dead's soundman, Owsley Stanley, continued to be one of San Francisco's primary LSD producers. Likewise, it was a large part of the rock festival scene, as Wavy Gravy's advice against dropping the brown acid at Woodstock.

SYD BARRETT founding member of Pink Floyd.

PINK FLOYD English band that began as a psychedelic band.

HUMAN BE-IN rock and cultural festival held January 14, 1967, in San Francisco's Golden Gate Park.

SIT-INS nonviolent occupations of an area for the purpose of protest.

RAM DASS American Hindu spiritual teacher.

ALLEN GINSBERG American poet and member of the Beats.

GARY SNYDER Pulitzer Prize-winning American poet, essayist, and social activist.

MONTEREY INTERNATIONAL POP MUSIC FESTIVAL three-day concert held in 1967 that was attended by 200,000 people.

WOODSTOCK MUSIC & ART FAIR iconic rock festival held in 1969 near Woodstock, New York; viewed by many as the highpoint of the psychedelic-hippie era.

Pink Floyd

The Tea Set began in 1964 as four former architecture students: Nick Mason, Roger Waters, Richard Wright, and Bob Klose. **Syd Barrett** joined the band as their lead guitarist soon after, and the band changed their name to "The Pink Floyd Sound," inspired by two American blues musicians, Pink Anderson and Floyd Council. The more jazz-oriented Klose left as Barrett's

>>> **Syd Barrett recorded only one album,** Pink Floyd's 1967 debut LP, *The Piper at the Gates of Dawn,* **before succumbing to LSD-induced mental illness.**

surrealism began to dominate the band's musical approach, and their name was shortened to **Pink Floyd**.

The group signed with EMI and released their debut album, *The Piper at the Gates of Dawn*, in August 1967, today considered one of the pinnacles of psychedelic rock. The album was almost entirely written by Barrett and features surreal lyrics and music ranging from experimental pieces to more traditional, folk-inspired songs. Producer Norman Smith also experimented with a variety of studio techniques on *Piper*, including tape editing, feedback, reverb, stereo panning, echo effects, and the heavy use of electronic keyboards. The album was a hit in the United Kingdom, where it peaked at number six. As the band's commercial fortunes improved, Barrett's mental health deteriorated, in part because of heavy LSD use. Barrett would become catatonic on stage, so guitarist David Gilmour was brought in as a second guitarist. The band wanted Barrett to write, even if he couldn't perform, but that didn't work either, and in 1968, the band made the painful decision to fire their leader and friend.

The following years would be their most commercially successful, even without their fallen genius-in-residence. In 1975, the band recorded *Wish You Were Here*, a tribute to Barrett featuring one of Pink Floyd's longest and most popular songs: the nine-part "Shine On You Crazy Diamond." Barrett made a surprise appearance during the recording of the song, though his old band mates barely recognized him, as he had gained weight and shaved off all of his hair. This brief reunion was the last time the band would see Barrett, who retreated to the English countryside until his death in 2006. In the meantime, Pink Floyd would go on to continued success, as you will read in Chapter 8.

HOW DID MUSIC FESTIVALS DEFINE THE HIPPIE ERA?

Rock and the Counterculture

As examples of some of the hippie era's casualties might suggest, the best political and artistic hopes were sometimes compromised or cut short by the desire to "drop out" of society, its structures, and mores. Indeed, many of its brightest stars—Janis Joplin, Jim Morrison, and Jimi Hendrix—died before their 30th birthdays. Many more burst onto the scene displaying profound talent, but failed to achieve their full potential. And while the hippies were one of the largest and most visible subcultures in the United States during the late 1960s—making major impacts on popular culture in music, fashion, literature, theater, film, and TV—their genuine desire was to protest not just Vietnam, but mainstream U.S. culture in general.

The Festivals

Although the hippie movement energized a new anti-establishment culture of music, personal and sexual freedom, spirituality, and social revolution around the world, the era's utopianism manifested itself most successfully in its music festivals.

THE HUMAN BE-IN

A prelude to the Summer of Love was the **Human Be-In** on January 14, 1967, which gathered over 20,000 hippies in San Francisco's Golden Gate Park to protest a new California law banning the use of LSD. The primary organizer of the event, artist Michael Bowen, coined the name from the many "**sit-ins**" sweeping the country as a means of nonviolent political protest. Speakers included counterculture icon Timothy Leary, spiritual teacher **Ram Dass**, poets **Allen Ginsberg** and **Gary Snyder**, and social activist and comedian Dick Gregory. Bands including Jefferson Airplane, the Grateful Dead, and Quicksilver Messenger Service provided the music. Despite the drug's new illegality, the Grateful Dead's Owsley Stanley supplied the crowds with a superior form of LSD called "White Lightning."

THE MONTEREY INTERNATIONAL POP MUSIC FESTIVAL

The **Monterey International Pop Music Festival** was a three-day concert held from June 16 to June 18, 1967. Two years before Woodstock, over 200,000 people gathered at the Monterey County Fairgrounds in Monterey, California, for a celebration of peace and love and listened to an incredible array of artists and bands that reads, with some notable exceptions, like a who's who of the era's top acts. The bill was groundbreaking multicultural and genre-agnostic, mixing folk, R&B, rock, blues, jazz, soul, and pop.

Monterey was the first rock festival to be widely promoted and was the subject of *Monterey Pop*, the acclaimed documentary by filmmaker D.A. Pennebaker. The festival and the film launched the careers of many who played. It not only introduced many audiences to Janis Joplin and Otis Redding, but it was also the first major U.S. appearance by Jimi Hendrix and the Who. The list of "no's" and no-shows for the festival is almost as impressive: the Beatles (who had already quit touring), the Kinks (who were refused a work visa), the Beach Boys, Dionne Warwick, the Impressions, Cream, Donovan (who had visa problems relating to a drug arrest), and Captain Beefheart. And although the Rolling Stones didn't play Monterey due to legal troubles in the United Kingdom, guitarist Brian Jones was on hand to introduce Hendrix.

THE ISLE OF WIGHT FESTIVALS

On August 31, 1968, a pastoral British island became the site of the first Isle of Wight Festival, drawing 10,000 fans to see rock acts such as Jefferson Airplane. It was the start of what would become one of the biggest music festivals ever staged.

The second year of the Isle of Wight Festival drew an estimated 300,000 attendees, approximately three times the island's population. Held on August 30 and August 31, 1969, the lineup included the Band, Bob Dylan, and the Who, among others. With its massive crowds and all-star bill, the 1969 Isle of Wight Festival was considered an incredible success. The 1970 Isle of Wight Festival was the largest and most infamous of the early festivals, with an estimated attendance of over 600,000, exceeding even the crowds at Woodstock the previous year. Held from August 26 to August 31, 1970, the stellar lineup featured

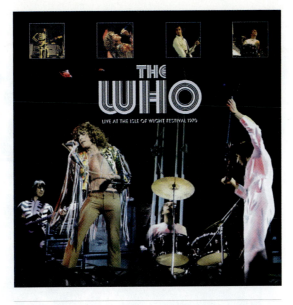

∧
∧
∧ The Who's performance at **the 1970 Isle of Wight Festival** lasted nearly two hours and **included the entirety of their 1969 rock opera,** *Tommy.*

more than 50 acts, including the Who, Jimi Hendrix, Miles Davis, the Doors, Emerson, Lake and Palmer (playing their second gig), Joni Mitchell, Leonard Cohen, and Jethro Tull.

A majority of fans showed up without tickets, expecting to get in. The "free" show at Woodstock the year before had led fans to expect that all festivals' acts should perform for free. Authorities and festival organizers were overwhelmed. The impractical site that was forced on organizers at the last minute, disgruntled fans, and myriad logistical problems associated with staging a festival for 600,000 attendees led to an atmosphere that Joni Mitchell described as the "hate-the-performer" festival (RTE Radio, 1983). The next year, the British Parliament passed the "Isle of Wight Act" to prevent gatherings of more than 5,000 people on the island without a license, ensuring that 1970's festival would be the last event of its kind for 32 years.

THE WOODSTOCK MUSIC & ART FAIR

Billed as "An Aquarian Exposition: 3 Days of Peace & Music," the **Woodstock Music & Art Fair** was held from August 15 to August 17, 1969, on Max Yasgur's dairy farm about 40 miles from the town

TOP OF THE CHARTS
WHAT'S HOT!
NOVEMBER 16, 1968

1. *Electric Ladyland* – Jimi Hendrix
2. *Cheap Thrills* – Big Brother & The Holding Company
3. *Time Peace/The Rascals' Greatest Hits* – The Rascals
4. *Feliciano!* – Jose Feliciano
5. *The Second* – Steppenwolf
6. *The Time Has Come* – The Chambers Brothers
7. *The Crazy World of Arthur Brown* – The Crazy World of Arthur Brown
8. *Are You Experienced?* – Jimi Hendrix
9. *Wheels of Fire* – Cream
10. *Gentle On My Mind* – Glen Campbell

>>> **Tickets for Woodstock** cost $18 in advance and $24 at the gate **for all three days of the festival.** About 186,000 tickets were sold in advance, but **an estimated 500,000 attended.**

of Woodstock, New York. From humble—and commercial—beginnings, Woodstock would become an iconic moment in rock history and the beginning of the end of the hippie era.

Unlike many of the important festivals that had come before it, Woodstock was first and foremost conceived of as a profit-making business venture. The organizers had first considering using their funds to build a recording studio in the Woodstock area, but eventually agreed on the idea of hosting an outdoor festival that would attract some of the biggest names in the music business. But with no track record, they had difficulty signing acts.

Creedence Clearwater Revival was the first band to agree to perform, at a cost of $10,000. The band was at the peak of its commercial success, having just that year released their third album, *Green River*, which featured the singles "Bad Moon Rising," "Lodi," "Green River," and "Commotion." After booking CCR, organizers found that the floodgates opened. Woodstock featured performances by Ravi Shankar, Arlo Guthrie, Joan Baez, the Grateful Dead, Janis Joplin with the Kozmic Blues Band, the Who, Jefferson Airplane, the Band, and Jimi Hendrix.

However, shifting venues and logistical problems led to a number of difficulties for Woodstock's organizers. The concert was originally scheduled to be held at a 300-acre industrial park, but nearby residents opposed the project. Organizers eventually settled on a nearby dairy farm with a sloping hill for viewing the stage, which was constructed at the bottom. The farm also featured a pond that became famous when fans used it for skinny-dipping.

The Most Famous Event in Rock History

The late selection of a venue made it impossible to both fully enclose the area and complete the stage before the scheduled start of the festival. Fans were already arriving early—and in larger numbers than expected. The decision was made to finish the stage instead of fencing the entire area, and the "free" Woodstock concert

was born. It also didn't help that people broke down those fences that were erected, while the ticket booths to be placed at the entrances were sitting on trucks in massive traffic jams along the New York State Thruway.

Expecting around 200,000 people, the organizers were overwhelmed by the approximately 500,000 fans that eventually arrived. First aid, food, and sanitation were in short supply. The weather was also a problem. Rain before and during the festival turned the hills and fields of Yasgur's farm muddy and slick. Despite the problems, a generally peaceful attitude reigned at Woodstock. Yasgur later described the event as a success that could teach the rest of America about overcoming adversity (Spitz 1989, 477).

There were a number of high-profile acts that missed what would become one of the defining moments in rock history. From the peaceful mud-soaked hill to the decision to put the members of a hippie commune, the Hog Farm, in charge of security—they said they would use

ISSUES in ROCK

The 27 Club

The "27 Club" is a pop culture concept that groups together important rock musicians who died at the age of 27. Three of the most famous "members" of the 27 Club are Jim Morrison, Jimi Hendrix, and Janis Joplin.

After recording *L.A. Woman*, Morrison flew to Paris for a break from the limelight. Freed from the responsibility of shepherding the album to completion, Morrison returned to drinking heavily, and on July 3, 1971, he was found dead in the bathtub of his Paris apartment. French law did not require an autopsy without evidence of foul play, and the official account is that he died of heart failure. However, there is circumstantial evidence that he died of a heroin overdose in a nightclub, most notably depicted in a book by club owner Sam Bennett (Walt 2007).

Joplin died in Los Angeles on October 4, 1970, of a heroin overdose before completing all the tracks of her album *Pearl*, although the album would yield the hit "Me and Bobby McGee." Hendrix died in a hotel room in London on September 18, 1970—only a year after his legendary appearance at Woodstock—asphyxiating on his vomit after an apparent overdose of sleeping pills.

Although many of the artists of the hippie era attributed at least some of their creativity to drug use, there have been many highly creative and successful artists before and since who did not take drugs. Could the same music have been created without the use of drugs, particularly LSD?

The rock & roll lifestyle claimed the lives of many talented musicians in the late 1960s and early 1970s, including the members of the so-called "27 Club."

BRIAN JONES
Died July 3, 1969
Found drowned in swimming pool

JANIS JOPLIN
Died October 4, 1970
Overdosed on heroin

JIMI HENDRIX
Died September 18, 1970
Overdosed on sleeping pills

JIM MORRISON
Died July 3, 1971
Causes unknown (probable heroin overdose)

seltzer and cream pies as their weapons (Gravy 2002)—Woodstock seemed like a singular event, even expanding on Monterey. In addition, the artists that did play achieved some of the most noteworthy and famous performances of their careers. From Hendrix's rendition of "The Star-Spangled Banner" to Richie Havens' "Freedom," the performances were legendary. It also helped that many of these performances were captured in the 1970 film, *Woodstock*, which won the Academy

Award for Documentary Feature that year. The film featured both Hendrix's and Havens's performances, further immortalizing the festival in the mythology of rock history.

THE ALTAMONT SPEEDWAY FREE FESTIVAL

The **Altamont Speedway Free Festival** was held on December 6, 1969, at a motor sports racetrack located in Alameda County in northern California. Originally planned for Golden Gate Park in San Francisco, site of the Human Be-In, the festival was moved when it was discovered that an NFL football game was scheduled for the same weekend. Organized by the Rolling Stones, the bill also included the Flying Burrito Brothers, Crosby, Stills & Nash, Santana, Jefferson Airplane, and the Grateful Dead.

Estimated Music Festival Attendance, 1967–1970

Monterey International Pop Music Festival (1967) 200,000

Altamont Speedway Free Festival (1969) 300,000

Human Be-In (1967) 20,000

Woodstock Music & Art Fair (1969) 500,000

Isle of Wight Festival (1970) 600,000

Λ Λ Large outdoor music festivals like **Woodstock and the Isle of Wight** defined the hippie era.

Described at the time as "Woodstock West," after the ground-breaking festival in New York four months earlier, Altamont would shake the conviction of many in the hippie movement that peace and love would always win out. It was an event marred by violence, most notably the controversial stabbing death—caught on film—of a young man in the crowd named Meredith Hunter.

Approximately 300,000 people attended the concert, and again, due to shifting venues and larger-than-expected crowds, the organizers were overwhelmed and underprepared. Because the stage was only four feet high, the Stones felt they needed security to keep the crowds off it, so they "hired" about 300 members of the **Hells Angels Motorcycle Club**, paying them with beer.

Hell Breaks Loose

The show began peacefully, but as the day progressed, the crowd and the Angels became more agitated. Fistfights broke out, and a fan punched Mick Jagger as he arrived. The violence and tension continued to increase. Local musician Denise Jewkes, who was six months pregnant, was onstage watching the show when she was hit in the head by an empty beer bottle thrown from the crowd; she suffered a fractured skull. Marty Balin, co-lead singer for Jefferson Airplane, was knocked unconscious by a blow to the head and was taken by helicopter to a local hospital. The Dead refused to go on and left.

By the time the Stones took the stage at sundown, the Hells Angels had armed themselves with sawed-off pool cues and chains and were riding motorcycles through the crowd. Thousands surged toward the stage, and some especially rowdy fans attempted to climb over the Angels to get to the Stones. Despite Mick Jagger's pleas to the crowd to "cool down," the worst was yet to come.

Filmmakers Albert and David Maysles shot footage of the festival for their 1970 documentary feature about the Stones' 1969 U.S. tour, *Gimme Shelter*. The Maysles' footage shows 18-year-old Meredith Hunter approaching the stage and being surrounded by eight Hells Angels. Hunter pulls a revolver from his jacket while his girlfriend tries to take the gun from him, and the crowd around them flees in horror. Suddenly, a Hells Angel named Alan Passaro rushes forward with a knife, swipes at Hunter's gun, and stabs him multiple times in the back, killing him. The Stones, unaware of the fatal stabbing, continued playing eight more songs to finish their set. Passaro was arrested and tried for murder, but was acquitted after a jury saw the footage and decided he acted in self-defense.

For many observers, the events in Altamont marked the end of the hippie era. Although Monterey, just two years earlier, had been a completely peaceful event with little security, it seemed that the "Summer of Love" was now over. In contrast to Woodstock emcee Wavy Gravy's promise of breakfast in bed for 400,000, and with Hells Angels running "security" instead of hippies, Altamont seemed less like "Woodstock West" and more like Woodstock's evil doppelgänger.

HOW DID THE RISE OF STUDIO CRAFT CHANGE ROCK MUSIC?

The Rise of Studio Craft

Studio technology had come a long way since the 1960s. Although the technology is nearly ubiquitous today due to digital processing, clever musicians, producers, and engineers were just discovering ways to create new sounds, enhance existing sounds, and produce music that sounded like nothing that came before.

PET SOUNDS

Pet Sounds was the eleventh studio album by the Beach Boys, released May 16, 1966, on Capitol Records (for more on the Beach Boys, see Chapter 5). At a time when most albums were recorded essentially live in the studio and consisted of a collection of singles, the band's songwriter, bassist, and vocalist Brian Wilson envisioned the album as a cohesive work, much like an opera or Broadway musical. He also recognized the almost limitless potential of the modern recording studio to create new sounds, dense textures, and the layered production that a live band could never achieve. Widely considered one of the most influential pop records ever released, *Pet Sounds* was produced over several months in the studio after Wilson stopped touring to focus his creative energies on writing and recording.

Wilson constructed elaborate vocal harmonies by layering multiple takes, and he supplemented the band's keyboards and guitars—played here by studio musicians—with sound effects and other "instruments," including bicycle bells and dog whistles. *Pet Sounds* was a game-changer, a high-water mark of rock recording that inspired other artists to re-imagine their own music and process in the studio. Eric Clapton said of the album, "I consider *Pet Sounds* to be one of the greatest pop LPs to ever be released. It encompasses everything that's ever knocked me out and rolled it all into one" (Bacon & Badman 2004, 139).

Although Wilson modeled his approach in the studio on Phil Spector's "Wall of Sound," he has credited the initial impetus for *Pet Sounds* as a desire to respond to the Beatles' *Rubber Soul*. "It felt like it "all belonged together," Wilson says, "and I was very impressed. I said, 'That's it. I really am challenged to do a great album'" (Wilson 2007).

Most of the songs on the album, with the exception of "Sloop John B," were written between December 1965 and January 1966. While Wilson worked on what would become *Pet Sounds*, fellow band members Mike Love, Dennis Wilson, brother Carl Wilson, and Al Jardine recuperated from the band's heavy touring schedule with vacations in Japan and Hawaii. When they returned to record their vocals, they were stunned by Wilson's change in musical direction and his abandonment of their winning formula of girls, cars, and beaches that had made them a major commercial success. Wilson had not only used session musicians to record most of the music, but he had begun working with lyricist Tony Asher to help him achieve his new vision of the Beach Boys.

Inspiration came full circle when the Beatles first heard *Pet Sounds*. Paul McCartney said,

"It was *Pet Sounds* that blew me out of the water. ... it may be going overboard to say it's the classic of the century ... but to me, it certainly is a total, classic record that is unbeatable in many ways." (BrianWilson.com)

>>> **Following** the release of the Beach Boys' *Pet Sounds* in May 1967, many bands began experimenting with conceptual albums.

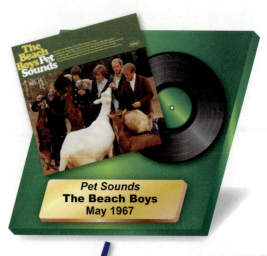

Pet Sounds
The Beach Boys
May 1967

The layered sounds of *Pet Sounds* certainly prefigured one of the Beatles' largest artistic successes to come: In 1967, *Sgt. Pepper's Lonely Hearts Club Band* would dominate the charts with a similar approach to sound and cohesive structure of the album.

SGT. PEPPER'S LONELY HEARTS CLUB BAND

Released June 1, 1967, *Sgt. Pepper's* was recorded over a 129-day period beginning in December 1966. The album marks the end of the Beatles' touring regimen and the beginning of a wildly productive period of studio experimentation (for more on the Beatles, see Chapter 6). Even if they had wanted to tour—and they didn't—the Beatles wouldn't have been able to reproduce the studio effects of *Sgt. Pepper's* live. They were now creating albums for their own sake, not as a collection of singles to be promoted on radio or reproduced for a live audience.

Along with producer George Martin, the Beatles expanded the palette of acceptable sounds in rock music with their LP. They hired experienced studio musicians and used orchestral and non-Western instruments, including the **sitar** and **tambura**. The techniques—later skewered in Frank Zappa's *We're Only in it for the Money*—included the circus sounds of

Days of Future Passed
The Moody Blues
November 1967

S.F. Sorrow
The Pretty Things
December 1968

The Who Sell Out
The Who
December 1967

The Kinks Are the Village Green Preservation Society
The Kinks
November 1968

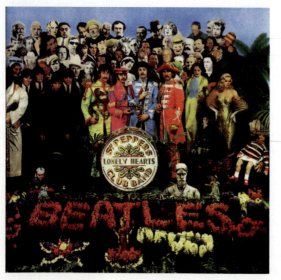

<<< **The Beatles'** landmark 1967 concept album, *Sgt. Pepper's Lonely Hearts Club Band,* helped push rock music in surprising and exciting new directions.

"Mr. Kite," the pseudo-big band on "When I'm 64," and the psychedelic masterpiece "Lucy in the Sky with Diamonds." "Flanging," one of many techniques used on "Lucy," appeared on the earlier *Revolver* and is sometimes likened to the sound of two voices singing at once. These space-age studio effects were a staple of psychedelia.

Lennon and McCartney's lyrics were equally adventurous and sophisticated; gone were the days of "Love Me Do." Now the Beatles were writing about everyday, working-class life, pastoral England, and the experiences of childhood. The loose concept for *Sgt. Pepper's* has the Beatles standing in for the fictitious band of the title, fronted by one "Billy Shears." This alter ego allowed them the creative freedom to experiment beyond the restrictive expectations of a world steeped in Beatlemania.

Sgt. Pepper's was a huge international commercial success, eventually spending 27 weeks in the number one slot on the U.K. Album Chart and 15 weeks at the top of the American Billboard 200. It was also highly acclaimed by the music press and won four Grammy awards in 1968, including Album of the Year and Best Engineered Recording, Non-Classical.

A British Blues Revival and Folk Goes Electric

As the Beatles expanded the boundaries of rock to include music from all over the world, another group of musicians from Britain were delving deeper into the blues. The blues still had power: Otis Redding's and Janis Joplin's performances at Monterey attest to that. Now that rock had been around for a while, these blues players fused it again with its blues roots and managed to share the charts with the Beatles' eclectic *Sgt. Pepper's*. While American bluesmen and women had found a welcoming (and welcome) audience in the United Kingdom, it took a generation of mostly white British blues players to make the music a commercial success. By employing modern studio techniques and electric instruments, British bands like the Rolling Stones and the Yardbirds helped build huge audiences for blues-influenced rock & roll (for more on the Yardbirds and the Rolling Stones, see Chapter 6).

JOHN MAYALL & THE BLUESBREAKERS

British blues guitarist John Mayall was born in 1933 in an English town near Manchester. Mayall has mentored some of rock's most important musicians, including Eric Clapton, Jack Bruce, and Aynsley Dunbar, to name just a few. He started his band, The John Mayall Bluesbreakers, in the 1960s, and the legendary *Bluesbreakers with Eric Clapton* LP was released in the United Kingdom on July 22, 1966. This album served as both Mayall's commercial breakthrough and as former Yardbirds guitarist Clapton's launching pad to superstardom; like most of Mayall's protégés, Clapton soon left, and the lineup was short-lived. Mayall's style of blues was not quite the blues-rock of the Yardbirds, and so when Clapton left the Yardbirds to play more blues-oriented music, Mayall was the logical place to turn. Mayall has since had a long and productive career, and performed with the Bluesbreakers until 2008.

∧
∧
∧ Cream's 1967 album *Disraeli Gears* fused blues with psychedelic rock.

CREAM

British blues-rock band Cream is often considered the first "supergroup," although most of the acclaim for the individual members would result from their time in Cream and later bands. Clapton was probably the most famous at the time, but his stints in the Yardbirds and the Bluesbreakers only hinted at his enormous potential. Both singer Jack Bruce and drummer Ginger Baker had come from the Graham Bond Organization, a successful British R&B outfit with the band's namesake on vocals and organ. Bruce, Baker, and Clapton were tired of being sidemen in other people's bands. The name "Cream" was derived from the notion that the trio was the "cream of the crop" of British musicians. The band recorded four albums in two years, beginning with 1966's *Fresh Cream*, which

featured mostly blues covers, to 1968's *Wheels of Fire*, which saw the band moving closer to progressive rock. The supergroup's collaboration was fleeting, however, as animosity between Baker and Bruce forced the band apart in 1968.

SPENCER DAVIS GROUP AND TRAFFIC

The British Spencer Davis Group wasn't exactly a blues band, but keyboardist and singer Steve Winwood's soulful vocals and band originals like "Gimme Some Lovin'" and "I'm a Man" skillfully incorporated electric blues, as well as elements of American gospel and soul music. Winwood eventually left to form Traffic with guitarist Dave Mason, horn player Chris Wood, and drummer Jim Capaldi. The band's debut, *Mr. Fantasy*, was released in 1967 and incorporated a variety of elements cribbed from everything from the Beatles' *Sgt. Pepper's* to Delta blues. Mason was fired, and then invited back. In 1968, the band followed up with the classic *Traffic*, an LP split between Mason's folk-rock and Winwood's blues-rock jams, before Mason left for good and Winwood dissolved the band. Winwood went on to join Blind Faith, another of Eric Clapton's short-lived supergroups, in 1969, before reviving Traffic and releasing several more albums before finally breaking up in 1974.

FAIRPORT CONVENTION AND PENTANGLE

Fairport Convention is a British electric folk band formed in 1967. Featuring guitarist, singer, and songwriter **Richard Thompson** and the powerful vocals of **Sandy Denny**, the band truly made an impact with its fourth album, released in 1969, entitled *Liege & Lief*. Widely regarded as the album that launched the English folk rock movement, *Liege & Lief* listed six traditional songs and three originals written in a similar style, played with modern electric instruments. The album made it to number 17 on the U.K. album chart.

Like Fairport Convention, Pentangle was a British folk band, although they generally eschewed the use of electric instruments. Built around two guitar virtuosos, Bert Jansch and John Renbourn, Pentangle explored a variety of music beyond folk, experimenting with psychedelia, jazz, and pop. The band reached its commercial pinnacle with 1969's *Basket of Light* and scored a minor hit with the single "Light Flight," which was used as the theme song for a BBC show.

Summary

HOW DID THE HIPPIE MOVEMENT INFLUENCE ROCK MUSIC IN THE LATE 1960s? 112

- Writer Ken Kesey held LSD-fueled parties he called "Acid Tests" featuring the jamming of the Warlocks, which went on to become the Grateful Dead.
- Many of the influential bands of the period drew inspiration from the drug culture generally, and LSD in particular.
- "The Haight" became a center of 1960s hippie counterculture and was the home of the Grateful Dead, Jefferson Airplane, and Big Brother and the Holding Company.

WHAT PATTERNS EMERGE WHEN COMPARING THE LEADING BANDS OF THE 1960s? 113

- The Grateful Dead's music was a fusion of disparate elements—from jazz to country—and their literary, self-referential lyrics often seemed to wrestle with the metaphysical.
- San Francisco band Jefferson Airplane's "White Rabbit" was a quintessential expression of rock's drug culture.
- Like the Grateful Dead, Moby Grape was democratic. All band members wrote and sang lead and backup vocals on their debut album.
- Janis Joplin's unique vocals came to international attention with her appearance at the Monterey Pop Festival with the band Big Brother and the Holding Company.
- Jimi Hendrix's final album, *Electric Ladyland*, was a sprawling, often experimental series of songs that showcased Hendrix's virtuosity and a new thematic complexity to lyrics.
- Fronted by Jim Morrison, the Doors fused blues, rock, and Eastern mysticism.
- Over the course of three albums, the band Love perfected a distinctive amalgam of folk, rock, blues, jazz, and orchestral pop.
- Frank Zappa was one of rock's most eclectic geniuses whose influences included 1950s doo-wop and avant-garde composers like Igor Stravinsky and Edgard Varèse.

- 13th Floor Elevators were pioneers of the psychedelic sound, and one of the most innovative psychedelic rock bands of the 1960s was Pink Floyd.

HOW DID MUSIC FESTIVALS DEFINE THE HIPPIE ERA? 120

- The Human Be-In on January 14, 1967, gathered over 20,000 hippies in Golden Gate Park to hear music and protest a new California law banning the use of LSD.
- The Monterey International Pop Music Festival was a three-day concert held in 1967 whose bill was groundbreaking multicultural and genre-agnostic, mixing folk, R&B, rock, blues, jazz, soul, and pop.
- 1970's Isle of Wight Festival featured an impractical site, disgruntled fans, and a myriad of logistical problems. Joni Mitchell described it as the "hate-the-performer" festival.
- The huge crowds that arrived overwhelmed the organizers of the Woodstock Music & Art Fair, but despite its problems, a peaceful attitude reigned.
- The violence at the Altamont Speedway Free Festival signaled the end of the era.

HOW DID THE RISE OF STUDIO CRAFT CHANGE ROCK MUSIC? 125

- On *Pet Sounds*, the Beach Boys' Brian Wilson recognized the potential of the modern recording studio to create new sounds, dense textures, and the layered production that a live band could never achieve.
- *Sgt. Pepper's* was recorded over a 129-day period and used studio effects that the Beatles wouldn't have been able to reproduce live.
- However, two lower-tech kinds of music—blues and folk-rock—were also popular at the time.

Key Terms

hippie a member of the counterculture of the 1960s *112*

Summer of Love summer 1967, a time at which the hippie era was at its peak *112*

Timothy Leary American writer, psychologist, and vocal advocate of psychedelic drug use *112*

Ken Kesey American writer and political activist associated with 1960s counterculture *112*

beatnik a member of the Beat Generation, an anti-establishment literary and cultural youth movement of the 1950s *113*

Barry McGuire American singer-songwriter most famous for his hit "Eve of Destruction" *113*

Grateful Dead American rock band formed in 1965 *113*

Jerry Garcia guitarist of the Grateful Dead *113*

pedal steel guitar type of electric guitar played horizontally; pedal steel is mostly commonly heard in U.S. country music *113*

Bob Weir rhythm guitarist for the Grateful Dead *113*

Igor Stravinsky 20th-century Russian composer *113*

John Coltrane American jazz saxophonist and composer *113*

Bill Graham highly successful concert promoter who managed many of the most important rock acts of the 1960s *114*

Owsley Stanley sound engineer for the Grateful Dead and underground LSD chemist *114*

Jefferson Airplane San Francisco based-band fronted by Grace Slick *114*

Grace Slick lead singer of Jefferson Airplane *114*

Haight-Ashbury a district in San Francisco associated with 1960s counterculture and psychedelic rock bands *115*

Moby Grape a popular psychedelic band in the 1960s *115*

D.A. Pennebaker American documentary filmmaker who created the seminal documentary *Monterey Pop* *116*

Big Brother and the Holding Company influential psychedelic rock band from San Francisco *116*

Sample Test Questions

1. Which U.S. city was known as the birthplace of the hippie movement?
   a. Los Angeles
   b. Lodi
   c. Santa Monica
   d. San Francisco

2. What were the Grateful Dead first called?
   a. Moby
   b. The Tea Set
   c. Big Brother and the Holding Company
   d. The Warlocks

3. Which festival signaled the end of the hippie era?
   a. The Woodstock Music & Art Fair
   b. The Human Be-In
   c. The Altamont Speedway Free Festival
   d. The Bonnaroo Music Festival

4. Arthur Lee was the leader of which band?
   a. The Doors
   b. 13th Floor Elevators
   c. Love
   d. Cream

5. Which album showcases satire aimed at rock?
   a. Frank Zappa's *Freak Out!*
   b. The Doors' *The Doors*
   c. Jefferson Airplane's *Surrealistic Pillow*
   d. The Beatles' *Rubber Soul*

ANSWERS: 1. d; 2. d; 3. c; 4. c; 5. a

ESSAY

6. Discuss the impact of LSD and other drugs on rock & roll.
7. What pioneering studio techniques did the Beach Boys and the Beatles introduce in the late 1960s?
8. Why did so many bands of the era originate in San Francisco?
9. Discuss the rise of studio craft and how it affected popular music.
10. Choose one of the influential bands of the era and discuss its musical influences.

WHERE TO START YOUR RESEARCH PAPER

For an in-depth biography of Ken Kesey, go to
http://www.britannica.com/EBchecked/topic/755155/Ken-Kesey

For an in-depth biography of the Beach Boys, go to
http://www.rollingstone.com/artists/thebeachboys/biography

For an in-depth biography of the Beatles, go to
http://www.rollingstone.com/artists/thebeatles/biography

For an overview of the Doors, go to http://www.allmusic.com

To research past and present *Billboard* 100 charts, go to
http://www.billboard.com/bbcom/index.jsp

To learn more about Frank Zappa, go to
http://www.rollingstone.com/artists/frankzappa

For more information about the origins of psychedelic rock, go to
http://www.britannica.com/EBchecked/topic/481546/psychedelic-rock

For an overview of the history of rock music, go to
http://encarta.msn.com/encyclopedia_761558548/rock_music.html

Remember to check www.thethinkspot.com for additional information, downloadable flashcards, and other helpful resources.

"Four albums

later, David Bowie has come to the forefront of the new music of the new image 70s. His move to RCA Records resulted in the highly acclaimed 'Hunky Dory' album, which received unprecedented critical huzzas. . .at least unprecedented until the release of Bowie's 'The Rise and Fall of Ziggy Stardust and the Spiders from Mars,' an album that has elicited such quotable quotes as 'A stunning work of genius' (*Circus*), 'A strong, moving, powerful piece of rock and roll,' (*LA Times*), 'The Elvis of the 70s' (Lillian Roxon of the *N.Y. News*) and 'David Bowie is one bitch of a rocker' (Ron Ross in Words & Music). And too, there is the interesting prognostication of Nancy Erlich in the *N.Y. Times*: 'The day will come when David Bowie is a star and the crushed remains of his melodies are broadcast from Muzak boxes in every elevator and hotel lobby in town'. . .

"In 1972, David Bowie—with his supercharged band The Spiders from Mars—began a series of gigs in the United Kingdom and the United States. It has been a while since the hyper-kinetic Bowie has been seen on stage, and the audience response has been a killer. One UK writer describes the Bowie phenom like this: 'Bowie. . .dressed first as Harlequin meets Star Trek, and then in Garboesque white satin. He has a painted white face, a haircut from Clockwork Orange and moves like a marionette. For the next few months his picture will be in every magazine. And yet—amazingly enough—he is a remarkable performer'. . .

"David Bowie has often been described as the darling of the avant garde, but now it has become clear that he has moved into the greater arena and his impact is overall. . .invading areas previously thought the property of the 'Puppy Love' school of music, and too, shaking up the ears of the rock purists.

"David Bowie will go where he wishes to go—as he always has. Armed with his two RCA Records albums and his phenomenal band, it is certainly that, to quote Words & Music, 'David and company. . . will kick more sonic ass than any group since the Stones.' And what does David Bowie say? 'Look out you rock and rollers. . .' That's what he says."

—RCA Press Kit, 1972

SIRENS, SOUL SINGERS, AND SELLOUTS (1967–1975)

WHAT WERE THE MUSICAL RESPONSES PRODUCED BY THE SOCIAL CRISES OF THE LATE 1960s?

DAVID BOWIE early 1970s glam rocker who took the image to extremes, creating controversial, glittery onstage personas such as Ziggy Stardust.

SOFT ROCK melodic rock music that stresses themes of vulnerability in a confessional, introspective style.

JAMES TAYLOR successful 1970s singer-songwriter whose music exemplified the introspective, self-oriented style of soft rock.

Materializing from a cloud of dry ice, wearing a tight-fitting, glimmering jumpsuit, sequined hunting boots, and orange-tinted hair, **David Bowie's** bisexual, space-age persona of Ziggy Stardust epitomized early 1970s rock & roll excess. In embracing the theatrical side of music, Bowie—along with fellow glam rockers Lou Reed, Iggy Pop, and Mott the Hoople—took rock & roll in an elaborate new direction. Meanwhile, the race riots of the late 1960s and protests against the Vietnam War were leading other artists along two divergent musical paths: the militant protest songs of Jefferson Airplane and the Grateful Dead, and the calming, escapist music of easy listening bands such as the Eagles. A third movement, emerging in the wake of the 1964 Civil Rights Act, latched onto the new wave of African American pride and kick-started a soul revival through the sounds of Aretha Franklin, Johnny Taylor, and Otis Redding. The diverse musical trends and tastes that developed during the late 1960s would help establish the 1970s as one of the most vibrant and dynamic decades in rock history.

Protest Versus Soft Rock

By 1968, the United States had stationed 542,000 troops to Vietnam, and civil unrest on the home front was rife. Clusters of students on major university campuses began demonstrating against the war, initially conducting hippie demonstrations—such as the levitating of the Pentagon in October 1967—although gradually these protests becoming more radical. When the United States stepped up its aerial bombing campaign of North Vietnam in 1968, students began occupying university buildings to protest the war, and resistance to police interference often erupted into violence. Meanwhile, race riots were shaking the urban centers of Detroit, Chicago, San Francisco, and Atlanta. The murder of Dr. Martin Luther King, Jr., in April 1968 sparked further outbursts of violence across the country.

Radicalized by these social crises, many young Americans turned not to the folk-based protest music of the early 1960s, but to the harder sounds of psychedelic rock. Bands such as the Grateful Dead and Jefferson Airplane became the new, acid rock-fused voices of the protest movement. As mentioned in Chapter 7, Jimi Hendrix's screeching, feedback-laden rendition of "The Star-Spangled Banner" during the final set of Woodstock in August 1969 captured the militant spirit of an angry, alienated American youth.

However, these same political events drove other artists in a dramatically different musical direction. The murders of four student protesters at Kent State University in May 1970 by Ohio National Guardsmen, the continuation of a seemingly endless war, and the threat of a major recession created a somber, conservative mood among many Americans that was reflected in popular music. Turning away from the pounding, angry sounds of psychedelic rock, many artists instead created an apolitical hybrid of pop, folk, and rock that was intended to comfort, rather than challenge, its audience. This new genre became known as **soft rock**, or easy listening.

EASY LISTENING ARTISTS

Introspective, confessional songs that incorporated themes of everyday life, love, and relationships made up much of early 1970s soft rock. Focusing on their own personal experiences, singer-songwriters adopted a 1960s folk style to sing about their first loves and the painful experience of unrequited passion.

James Taylor

Among the most successful of the 1970s soft rock stars was mellow folk rocker **James Taylor**, a Boston singer-songwriter originally signed to the Beatles' Apple label by producer Peter Asher in 1968. Despite the appear-

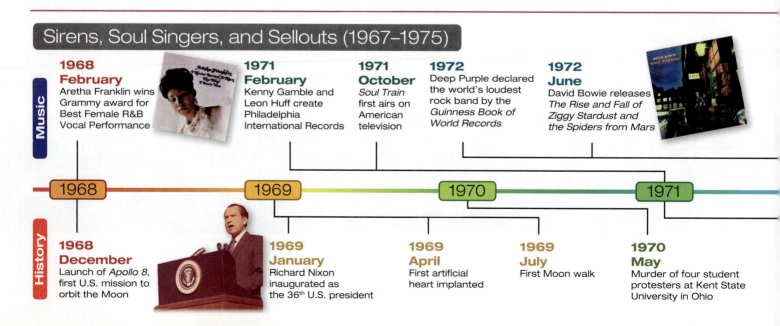

Sirens, Soul Singers, and Sellouts (1967–1975)

Music

1968 February
Aretha Franklin wins Grammy award for Best Female R&B Vocal Performance

1971 February
Kenny Gamble and Leon Huff create Philadelphia International Records

1971 October
Soul Train first airs on American television

1972
Deep Purple declared the world's loudest rock band by the *Guinness Book of World Records*

1972 June
David Bowie releases *The Rise and Fall of Ziggy Stardust and the Spiders from Mars*

1968   1969   1970   1971

History

1968 December
Launch of *Apollo 8*, first U.S. mission to orbit the Moon

1969 January
Richard Nixon inaugurated as the 36th U.S. president

1969 April
First artificial heart implanted

1969 July
First Moon walk

1970 May
Murder of four student protesters at Kent State University in Ohio

ance of Paul McCartney and George Harrison as backup musicians, Taylor's self-titled 1968 debut created few waves. However, a new contract with Warner Brothers changed all that. His 1970 album *Sweet Baby James* reached the Top Five and remained on the album chart for more than two years, becoming one of the definitive releases of the soft rock genre. The album's hit song "Fire and Rain," about such personal issues as Taylor's own psychiatric struggles and the suicide of a friend, exemplified the turn toward introspection and narcissism among singer-songwriters of the 1970s—a transition that drew much criticism from rock & roll purists. In his 1971 diatribe "James Taylor Marked for Death," music critic Lester Bangs fantasized about disemboweling the musician with a broken bottle of Ripple wine. Despite his critics' negative reactions, Taylor went on to enjoy nothing less than gold album sales for the next 11 years. Many of his hits were cover versions—Carole King's "You've Got a Friend" (1971), Marvin Gaye's "How Sweet It Is (To Be Loved By You)" (1975), and Jimmy Jones' "Handy Man" (1977). Taylor also frequently collaborated with many other folk and easy listening artists, including Art Garfunkel and Carly Simon.

Carly Simon

The connection between fellow confessional songwriter **Carly Simon** and James Taylor was personal as well as professional. Daughter of Richard Simon, the cofounder of Simon & Schuster publishers, Carly Simon initially attempted to launch her recording career with Bob Dylan's manager, Albert Grossman, in the 1960s. Following the recording of four unreleased tracks, Simon signed with Elektra Records in 1970, hitting the Top 30 with her self-titled debut album a year later. In 1972, she married James Taylor and reached the top of the singles charts with "You're So Vain"—a song that fueled endless speculation regarding its unnamed, narcissistic subject. Two years later, Simon collaborated with Taylor on the Top Five single

CARLY SIMON singer-songwriter married to James Taylor.

CAROLE KING singer-songwriter from Brill Building group of early 1960s who went on to enjoy solo success with top-selling album *Tapestry*.

"Mockingbird," from the gold-selling album *Hotcakes*. A brief career lull ended in 1977 with the release of "Nobody Does It Better," the theme song from the James Bond movie *The Spy Who Loved Me*. Suffering from stage fright, Simon later stopped performing live and started a successful career as a composer, winning an Oscar for Best Original Song for "Let the River Run" (from 1988's *Working Girl*). She continued to diversify throughout the 1990s and 2000s, writing a number of children's books as well as several collections of new material.

Carole King

Carole King, one of the Brill Building stable of singer-songwriters in the early 1960s, became involved with the New York folk scene after she divorced her husband, Gerry Goffin, with whom she had collaborated on many early 1960s hits. Although her 1970 debut failed to gain much attention, King's second solo album *Tapestry* (1971) became a huge hit, reaching number one and staying there for 15 weeks. The album, which included the inaugural version of "You've Got a Friend" along with number one hit singles "It's Too Late" and "So Far Away," remained on the charts for six years and sold more than 20 million copies, making it the number one pop album of the era. Using simple piano accompaniments and a team of talented backup singers, including Joni Mitchell and James Taylor, the quiet, reflective *Tapestry* helped popularize the singer-songwriter genre of the 1970s. King's chart successes continued throughout the release of albums *Music* (1971), *Rhymes &*

∧
∧ In the wake of the Vietnam
∧ War, **folk rock artists such as James Taylor** turned away from political protest songs and **instead wrote introspective ballads.**

1972 August
Stax Records hosts Wattstax Music Festival in L.A. to commemorate the seventh anniversary of the Watts riots

1973 March
Pink Floyd release *The Dark Side of the Moon*, which becomes the longest-running chart album in history

1973 May
Led Zeppelin break previous concert attendance records by performing to a crowd of 57,000 in Tampa, Florida

1975 October
Bruce Springsteen appears on the covers of both *Time* and *Newsweek*

1975 December
Stax Records forced into bankruptcy

1972   1973   1974   1975

1971 April
Charles Manson receives death sentence

1972 February
First hand-held calculator, priced at $395

1973 December
Homosexuality removed by the American Psychiatric Association from its list of mental disorders

1974 August
President Nixon resigns over the Watergate affair

1975 April
Last U.S. troops leave Vietnam

Reasons (1972), and *Wrap Around Joy* (1974), but her musical career began to wane in the early 1980s. King has not had a Top 40 hit since she released the 1980 LP *Pearls*, a collection of songs written during her partnership with Goffin.

Country Influences

Although some artists took their inspiration from 1960s folk music, others attempted to escape the unsettling political climate and return to the simple values of pre-war rural living by turning to Americana as extolled in country music. In the early 1970s, a new sound began to emerge on the West Coast, characterized by vocal harmonies, pedal steel guitars, and a soft rock backbeat. Of all the bands to adopt this brand of country-influenced rock, one managed to catapult the genre to a global phenomenon: the **Eagles**. Formed in 1971, the group comprised of bassist Randy Meisner, guitarist Bernie Leadon, drummer Don Henley, and guitarist Glenn Frey, all of whom had individually toured as members of Linda Ronstadt's backing group.

The band became one of the most popular groups of the 1970s, achieving five number one singles, fourteen Top 40 hits, and four number

Easy Listening Artists of the 1970's

Artist	Influences	Popular Recordings	Notable Facts
Neil Diamond	Emerged out of Brill Building era	"Cherry, Cherry" (number six, 1966), "Sweet Caroline" (number four, 1969), "Cracklin' Rosie" (number one, 1970)	Third most successful adult contemporary artist ever (after Elton John and Barbra Streisand)
Jimmy Webb	Burt Bacharach	"Wichita Lineman" (number three, 1968), "By the Time I Get to Phoenix" (number 26, 1967), "Up, Up, and Away" (number seven, 1967)	Earned Record of the Year and Song of the Year at the 1968 Grammy Awards for "Up, Up, and Away"
John Denver	Folk background; touches of country and soft rock	"Take Me Home Country Roads" (number two, 1971), "Rocky Mountain High (number nine, 1973), "Sunshine on My Shoulder" (number one, 1974)	Humanitarian interests include ecological causes, space exploration, and anti-nuclear power groups
Linda Ronstadt	Folk and country	"When Will I Be Loved" (number two, 1975), "You're No Good" (number one, 1975)	Credited with bringing the works of Buddy Holly, Elvis Costello, and Chuck Berry to a mass audience
The Carpenters	Soft rock/pop	"We've Only Just Begun" (number two, 1970), "Close to You" (number one, 1970)	Karen Carpenter died of cardiac arrest in 1983 after a long struggle with anorexia.
Burt Bacharach and Hal David	Songwriters associated with Dionne Warwick; throwbacks to Tin Pan Alley/Brill Building era	"Walk On By" (number six, 1964), "Wishin' and Hopin'" (number six, 1964), "What the World Needs Now Is Love" (number seven, 1965)	Bacharach and David worked on several Broadway productions, including 1968 musical *Promises, Promises*.

∧
∧ The easy listening artists of the 1970s fused elements of folk, rock, pop, and country music.

one albums—including *Their Greatest Hits 1971–1975*, which according to the Recording Industry Association of America (RIAA) is the best-selling album in U.S. history, having been certified 29 times platinum.

Transporting country music from the American heartland to the laid-back West Coast, the Eagles embraced the hedonism of 1970s California. Their signature song "Take It Easy"—a rousing track extolling the joys of life on the road—together with the material on 1976 album *Hotel California* created visions of faded blue jeans, suede jackets, mirrored sunglasses, palm trees, ocean views, convertibles, and a relaxed lifestyle that appealed to American youth. Straddling the line between country ("Hollywood Waltz," "Lyin' Eyes") and mainstream rock ("One of These Nights," "Too Many Hands"), the Eagles helped define the broadly popular sound that became known as classic rock.

THE EAGLES country rock band that straddled the line between mainstream rock, folk rock, and country rock; produced the best-selling album in U.S. history.

STAX RECORDS Memphis record label founded in 1960 by brother-and-sister team Jim Stewart and Estelle Axton; Motown's main rival.

WATTSTAX MUSIC FESTIVAL L.A. music concert held in 1972 to commemorate the Watts riots; popularity reflected growing market appeal of African American artists.

SOUL TRAIN first black-oriented music variety show on American television; ran for 35 years.

ARETHA FRANKLIN gospel-influenced Queen of Soul; achieved huge crossover success among white audiences in the late 1960s and early 1970s.

WHO TOOK PART IN THE SOUL REVIVAL?

The Soul Revival Takes Flight

The civil rights movement in the 1960s sparked renewed interest in soul music. Many African Americans equated the genre with black dignity and pride. A newfound black consciousness prompted many adherents to wear their hair in more natural afro styles, to refer to one another as "soul brothers" and "soul sisters," and to describe traditional African American foods such as candied yams, cornbread, and black-eyed peas as "soul food."

WATTSTAX MUSIC FESTIVAL

In August 1972, Memphis's **Stax Records** held a concert at the L.A. Coliseum to commemorate the seventh anniversary of the Watts riot—a race riot in the Watts neighborhood of Los Angeles that lasted for six days and resulted in the deaths of 34 people, including 25 African Americans. To encourage as many members of the black community to attend as possible, Stax sold the tickets for just one dollar. This helped fill the 100,000 person-capacity L.A. Coliseum and led to the largest gathering of African Americans since the 1963 civil rights march on Washington, D.C. Due to the large turnout some viewed the concert, known as the **Wattstax Music Festival**, as the "black Woodstock." Although it did not garner as much media coverage as Woodstock, Wattstax demonstrated the growing market appeal of African American musicians. The lineup featured a wide cross-section of the Stax Records roster: gospel performers such as the Rance Allen Group ("Lying on the Truth" and "I Got to Be Myself") and the Staple Singers ("I'll Take You There" and "Respect Yourself"), bluesmen such as Little Milton ("Walking the Back Streets and Cryin' " and "That's What Love Will Make You Do") and Albert King ("Laundromat Blues" and "Born Under a Bad

Sign"), and R&B artists such as Johnny Taylor ("I Had a Dream," "I've Got to Love Somebody's Baby"). The soulful Isaac Hayes ("Theme from *Shaft*," "Never Can Say Goodbye") ended the festival on a high note with a high-powered set.

RIDING ON THE *SOUL TRAIN*

If Wattstax was the black Woodstock, *Soul Train* was the black *American Bandstand*. The first black-oriented music variety show on American television, *Soul Train* began its syndicated run in October 1971. Initially limited to seven cities—including Detroit, Los Angeles, and Philadelphia—the weekly show gained popularity and spread to 25 markets in 1972. Hosted by Chicago radio announcer Don Cornelius, *Soul Train* featured performances by soul and R&B acts, appearances by guest hosts, and dance numbers by the Soul Train Gang. This group of fashionably dressed young dancers competed for prizes during a game called "The Soul Train Scramble" and showed off their individual talents during the formation of the "Soul Train Line." Although soul music as a genre waned in popularity, episodes of *Soul Train* were produced for 35 years, until 2006.

Soul Train did much to bring African American popular culture into diverse American households during the 1970s. Notable guests from the era included: husband and wife R&B duo Ashford & Simpson ("Don't Cost You Nothing"), rock & roll pioneer Chuck Berry ("Johnny B. Goode"), Motown diva Diana Ross ("Ain't No Mountain High Enough"), Chicago-based soul group The Chi-Lites ("Have You Seen Her"), the "Godfather of Soul" James Brown ("Papa's Got a Brand New Bag"), and one of the biggest personalities in soul—Aretha Franklin.

ARETHA FRANKLIN

Known as "Lady Soul" and the "Queen of Soul," Memphis-born, Detroit-bred **Aretha Franklin** was one of the most important crossover artists of the late 1960s and early 1970s. Discovered by Columbia Records

>>> **James Brown, the "Godfather of Soul,"** was just one of many notable guests on the long-running **music variety show** *Soul Train.*

Philadelphia

In 1971, the City of Brotherly Love set the tone for a new brand of soul with the formation of **Philadelphia International Records**. Created by songwriting and producing duo Kenny Gamble and Leon Huff, the record label released songs that emphasized smooth vocals embellished with lush instrumental arrangements provided by strings and horns. Applying their formula to bands such as the O'Jays and Harold Melvin & the Blue Notes, Gamble and Huff produced the distinctive Philadelphia Sound, or **Sweet Philly Soul**, that immediately began to dominate the R&B charts. Scoring its first hit with the O'Jay's

"Back Stabbers" in 1972, Philadelphia International sold 10 million singles within its first nine months of operation. By 1975 it had become the second-largest African American-owned business in the United States, surpassed only by Motown.

Unlike other producers, Gamble and Huff helped write many of songs they produced. Often these songs reflect concerns prevalent in the African American community ("Survival," "For the Love of Money," and "Livin' for the Weekend") as well as the Philadelphia ideals of peace and brotherhood ("Love Train" and "Put Your Hands Together"). In 1974, Gamble and Huff were asked to create a theme song for *Soul*

Train. Using their house band, MFSB (Mother, Father, Sister, Brother), the duo created the number one hit song "T.S.O.P. (The Sound of Philadelphia)." Gamble and Huff later said that the theme song was written to "reflect . . . the sound and spirit of the City of Brotherly Love, the freedom at Independence Hall, the vibrations of the Liberty Bell, or the locomotive rhythm of a SEPTA subway train."

Today, visitors to Philadelphia can view the engraved brass plaques acknowledging the influence of Gamble and Huff on the city's Avenue of the Arts, a short walk from the studio that recorded much of the music released by Philadelphia International.

---

talent scout John Hammond in 1960, she initially recorded show tunes such as "If I Would Ever Leave You" with limited success. When her contract with Columbia expired in 1966, Franklin signed to Atlantic Records under the tutelage of music producer Jerry Wexler, who developed her into a soul singer. Within a few months, Franklin's first Atlantic album—*I Never Loved a Man (the Way I Love You)*—reached number two on the charts, with its title song becoming a Top 10 hit. But it

>>> **"Respect,"** on Aretha Franklin's breakthrough album *I Never Loved a Man the Way I Love You*, became an **anthem for both the civil rights and feminist movements.**

was a recording of Otis Redding's "Respect" that really put Lady Soul on the map. Released amidst the 1967 Detroit race riots, the song's call for recognition and appreciation signaled a renewed sense of black pride. Adopted both by the civil rights and the feminist movements,

"Respect" sold more than one million copies and became Franklin's first number one song.

During the next two years, Franklin placed seven out of her next eight singles in the Top 10. The albums *Aretha Arrives* (1967), *Aretha: Lady Soul* (1968), and *Aretha Now* (1968) all made the Top Five. The gospel-charged renditions of "Chain of Fools," "Think," and "Baby, I Love You" helped earn Franklin the first of many Grammy Awards, for Best Female R&B Vocal Performance, in 1968. In total, Franklin has won 18 Grammy awards, placed 20 singles at the top of the R&B chart, and provided a vocal inspiration for countless contemporary divas, including Toni Braxton, Mariah Carey, Whitney Houston, and Mary J. Blige.

WHAT WERE THE EARLY INFLUENCES OF GLAM ROCK?

The Origins of Glam

In the early 1970s, the United States exited the Vietnam War, the military draft ended, and former protesters began to focus on careers and settling down with families. However, rising gas prices and increased inflation helped create an economic recession that ended a long period of steady economic growth. This caused many people to focus not on the larger issues of social or political injustice, but rather on their own economic problems. Turning inward, many struggling baby boomers sought comfort in spiritual renewal, self-help books, and therapy. Others took advantage of the loosening sexual boundaries of the era by engaging in

wife swapping or joining sex clubs. Noting this shift from activism to selfish individualism, writer Tom Wolfe labeled the 1970s the "me" decade.

Musically, this ideological shift manifested not just in the confessional, introspective musings of the easy listening artists that you have read about earlier, but also in the extravagant self-indulgence of the glam rockers. Characterized by a flamboyant, often androgynous look that incorporated glittery costumes and heavy makeup, **glam rock** fused elements of hard rock and pop. Largely a British phenomenon (with exceptions such as KISS and Alice Cooper), glam rock established itself as a major musical presence through acts such as Slade, The Sweet, David Bowie, Elton John, and Gary Glitter. Although a short-lived movement, particularly in the United States, glam rock permanently challenged traditional notions of masculinity and femininity. The glitzy, extravagant aspects of the genre resurfaced in 1980s hair bands such as Def Leppard, Poison, and Mötley Crüe.

THE VELVET UNDERGROUND

Although the extravagant, cross-dressing image of the glam rockers was distinctly British, some of glam's musical influences came from the American garage bands of the 1960s. **The Velvet Underground** laid the groundwork for many future rock & roll genres, including glam, garage, and punk. Despite relatively poor album sales and unimpressive chart performances, the group became one of the most influential bands in rock history. Such diverse rockers as the New York Dolls, the Sex Pistols, Roxy Music, and U2 have named the group as a major inspiration.

Formed in New York City in 1965, the Velvets comprised vocalist and guitarist Lou Reed, keyboardist and viola player John Cale, guitarist Sterling Morrison, and drummer Maureen "Moe" Tucker. The pop artist Andy Warhol became the band's manager and helped the band secure a record deal. Warhol also suggested they collaborate with the singer Nico. In 1967, the group released its debut, *The Velvet Underground and Nico*, featuring a Warhol-designed jacket with a peelable illustration of a banana. Embracing noise and chaos, the Velvets sang about the underside of American life and youth culture, including taboo subjects such as sexual deviancy ("Venus in Furs"), drug addiction ("Heroin"), and paranoia ("Sunday Morning"). Downplaying their middle-class roots—Reed had a B.A. in literature from Syracuse University and Cale had a prestigious classical music background—the Velvets went out of their way to disturb their audiences with their crudity. Said Cale, "We really wanted to go out there and annoy people" (Palmer 1995, 178).

After his bitter departure from the band in August 1970, vocalist **Lou Reed** withdrew from the limelight for two years before returning to enjoy a successful solo career. Influenced by glam rocker David Bowie, he began performing with bleached-blonde hair, makeup, and black fingernail polish. His 1973 Bowie-produced album *Transformer* featured the Top 20 hit "Walk on the Wild Side," a song about the misfits and transvestites in Andy Warhol's studio, known as the Factory. Reed's foray into glam rock ended the same year with the release of *Berlin*, a grim concept album charting the doomed relationship of a drug-addicted couple. The album fared poorly in the United States, although it later came to be recognized as one of Reed's best studio albums as a solo artist.

Andy Warhol

∧
∧ **The Velvet Underground** is
∧ credited as being one of **the most influential bands in rock history,** *inspiring many future glam,* *garage, and punk rock groups.*

bands and even formed a short-lived mime company before attaining musical success. This came in 1969 with the release of the existential "Space Oddity," which coincided with public excitement surrounding the first moon landing. The song became a Top Five hit in the United Kingdom, but was largely ignored in the United States until its re-release in 1973.

Around the turn of the 1970s, Bowie began experimenting with an androgynous image. In 1970 he posed for the album cover of *The Man Who Sold the World* in a dress, and in 1972 he declared himself bisexual to British magazine *Melody Maker*. This admission reflected changing social attitudes toward sexual orientation and also helped stir interest in Bowie's forthcoming album. After touring with T. Rex glam rocker Marc Bolan, Bowie began dyeing his hair orange. In 1972 Bowie unveiled the glittery alter ego Ziggy Stardust to coincide with the release of *The Rise and Fall of Ziggy Stardust and the Spiders from Mars*. This concept album chronicles the experiences of an alien rock superstar who attains fame just as Earth enters the last five years of its existence. Bowie's extravagant live show became a hit on both sides of the Atlantic, making him one of the few glam rockers to carve out a niche in the United States. He followed up his success with 1973 album *Aladdin Sane*, which topped the UK charts and made the U.S. Top 20. The album's title character—a schizoid androgyne with a distinctive lightning bolt painted on his face—was a pun on "a lad insane," a supposed reference to Bowie's schizophrenic brother, Terry.

DAVID BOWIE

The glittery, theatrical incarnation of David Bowie described in the RCA press release at the beginning of this chapter exemplifies 1970s glam rock excess. Born in London, Bowie played in a number of unsuccessful mod

MARC BOLAN

Many have attributed Bowie's creation of Ziggy Stardust to the influence of pioneering glam rocker **Marc Bolan**. Appearing on British television show *Top of the Pops* in 1970 wearing a satin jacket and eye makeup, heavy metal sound. Despite much hype, the group's first few albums fared poorly, and the band was on the verge of splitting up when they met David Bowie in March 1972. Offering to produce their next album, Bowie also provided the band with one of his songs, "All the Young Dudes." The track—which the group performed in nine-inch platform shoes, heavy mascara, and sequined costumes—became an instant success on both sides of the Atlantic, reaching number three in the United Kingdom and hitting the Top 40 in the United States. In the wake of the Greenwich Village Stonewall riots and the foundation of the Gay Activist Alliance in 1969, the song also became a gay anthem and the band obtained a cult gay following, particularly in the United States.

Bolan and his band T. Rex inspired a slew of artists to follow suit. Originally a hippie acoustic duo called Tyrannosaurus Rex, singer and guitarist Bolan and percussionist Steve Peregrin Took achieved an underground following in the late 1960s with their epic fantasy songs about elves, witches, and warriors. When Bolan and Took swapped their acoustic instruments for electric guitars, simplified their sound, and abbreviated the band's name to T. Rex in 1970, they scored their first UK hit with "Ride a White Swan." Ten consecutive UK Top 10 hits ensued. The fanatical reaction among British audiences caused the music press to coin the term "T.Rextasy." Although T. Rex never achieved such stature in the United States, they did reach the U.S. Top 10 in 1972 with "Bang a Gong (Get It On)."

MOTT THE HOOPLE

Like most 1970s glam rockers, the members of **Mott the Hoople** used glam rock's controversial androgynous image for shock value. Formed in the early 1960s, the band initially started out as a hard rock group that combined the cynicism of Bob Dylan with a

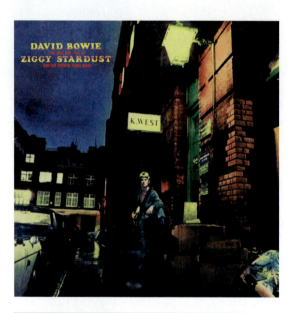

ʌ
ʌ **David Bowie adopted an**
ʌ **extravagant on-stage persona** for shows in support of his 1972 concept album, *The Rise and Fall of Ziggy Stardust and the Spiders from Mars.*

QUEEN

Taking the theatrical aspects of glam rock to the limit, **Queen** created an extravagant, mock-operatic sound that combined showy glam rock, heavy metal, and complex vocal harmonies. Embracing the excesses of the decade, the band put on hugely elaborate stage shows, complete with special effects such as flares, dry ice, and smoke bombs. However, the group's accessible sound and universal appeal made it one of the most successful bands in rock history. Current estimations of the band's total worldwide album sales range from 130 million to 300 million.

Originally formed in London in 1971 when guitarist Brian May and drummer Roger Taylor joined forces with vocalist **Freddie Mercury** (born Farok Bulsara), the group later added bassist John Deacon. Mercury chose the band name for its immediacy and visual potential; although he was aware that "queen" is a slang name for a homosexual, Mercury did not seek out an openly gay image. In fact, the singer did not reveal that he was gay until 1991, shortly before his death from AIDS complications. Nonetheless, he flirted with gender boundaries by using

Flashpoints ISSUES in ROCK   Rock as Perfomance Art

David Bowie's performances as Ziggy Stardust introduced an element of artifice into rock music that made it difficult for critics to distinguish between the real performers and their self-conscious, theatrical trappings. The adoption of various onstage personas was a giant leap away from the 1960s rock & rollers who had valued spontaneity and community with their audience as a means of proving their authenticity. Bowie mocked this 1960s-style earnestness by positively exalting in all that was artificial through his gender-bending outfits and larger-than-life performances.

Illustrating this concept of theatricality, in a 1972 interview with *Rolling Stone* Bowie said, "What the music says may be serious, but as

a medium it should not be questioned, analyzed, or taken too seriously. I think it should be tarted up, made into a prostitute, a parody of itself. It should be the clown, the Pierrot medium. The music is the mask the message wears—the music is the Pierrot and I, the performer, am the message."

The performance aspect of rock became increasingly dominant throughout the 1970s and 1980s—from the onstage theatrics of the heavy metal bands to the pop music videos that allowed postmodern artists such as Madonna to create new personas for themselves with every single they released.

Iggy Pop

Considered by many to be the godfather of punk, **Iggy Pop** explored the many facets of alternative rock, inspiring both 1970s punk bands and 1990s grunge acts. After forming **the Stooges** in 1968, Pop became known for his primitive stage antics. The Stooges recorded two proto-punk LPs that kick-started the punk rock genre, but had little commercial success. In 1971, the group disbanded, and Pop took a yearlong respite from music to recover from a heroin addiction. (You will learn more about the Stooges in Chapter 9.)

A meeting with David Bowie in 1972 convinced Pop to reassemble the Stooges, resulting in the explosive 1973 album *Raw Power*. Although the album received critical acclaim, it failed to ignite Pop's languishing career, and the Stooges soon broke up again.

However, two years later, Bowie again stepped in, prodding Pop to perform as a solo act. The ensuing albums *The Idiot* and *Lust for Life* featured Pop's scabrous vocals over a haunting Eurodisco beat. Working with Bowie, Pop recorded songs such as "Lust for Life," "The Passenger," and "China Girl," and won for himself a measure of critical and commercial success that he had never achieved with the Stooges. Throughout the mid-1970s, however, Pop battled various drug and mental health problems. By 1976, he had recovered enough to tour with Bowie, reinforcing his link to the glam tradition. Pop, now a punk legend, continues to perform today.

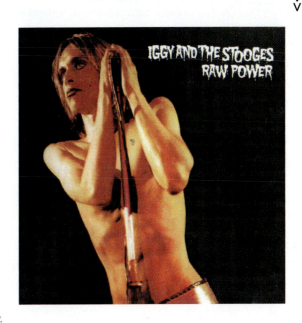

heavy eyeliner and black nail polish to create a glam rock image modeled after one of his idols, pop singer Liza Minnelli.

In 1973 and 1974, Queen developed a following in the United Kingdom. But it wasn't until the release of *A Night at the Opera* in 1975 that Queen attained widespread success in the United States. This break-through album, which contains the group's signature mock-operatic heavy metal song "Bohemian Rhapsody," made the U.S. Top 10 and quickly went platinum. Although music critics judged the band harshly—a *Rolling Stone* review labeled their 1979 album *Jazz* "fascist"—the group's popularity remained undiminished, and they released eight gold and six platinum

Eight Quintessential Glam Rock Albums

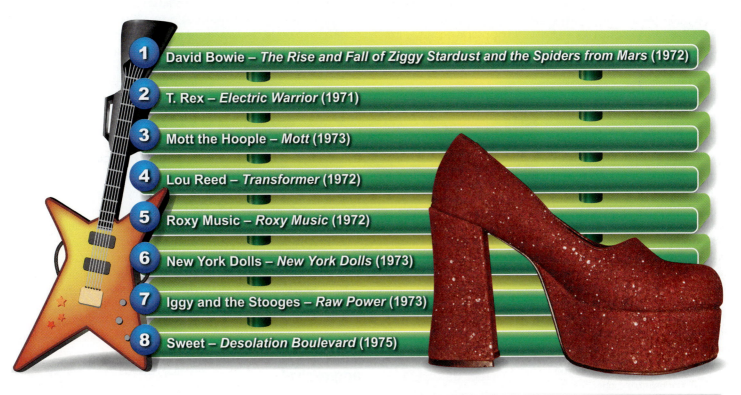

1. David Bowie – *The Rise and Fall of Ziggy Stardust and the Spiders from Mars* (1972)
2. T. Rex – *Electric Warrior* (1971)
3. Mott the Hoople – *Mott* (1973)
4. Lou Reed – *Transformer* (1972)
5. Roxy Music – *Roxy Music* (1972)
6. New York Dolls – *New York Dolls* (1973)
7. Iggy and the Stooges – *Raw Power* (1973)
8. Sweet – *Desolation Boulevard* (1975)

∧ According to *Entertainment Weekly* magazine, **Ziggy Stardust** tops the list of
∧ must-own glam rock albums.

records. The band's decadent, showy act was one of the clearest reflections of 1970s extravagance.

ELTON JOHN

If Queen marked a transition toward heavy metal, then **Elton John** bridged the gap between the sensitive singer-songwriters of the early 1970s and the extravagant rock stars that dominated the middle of the decade. Born Reginald Kenneth Dwight, the young pianist won a scholarship to the London Royal Academy of Music, where he studied for six years before joining blues group Bluesology as a teenager. In 1967, he changed his name to Elton John and teamed up with lyricist Bernie Taupin, beginning a prolific collaboration that has lasted to this day. Elton John's debut album *Empty Sky* (1969) achieved little commercial success, but the popular ballad "Your Song" helped propel his self-titled second album into the Top Five on the U.S. Billboard Pop chart. Between 1972 and 1976, John and Taupin charted 16 Top 20 hits in a row.

Although John's early albums established him as a commercial success, his wild stage performances provided the "wow" factor that elevated him to superstardom. Wearing flamboyant costumes such as sequined jumpsuits, platform shoes, ostrich feather boas, and $5,000 spectacles that spelled out his name in lights, John entertained his audience by doing handstands on his piano and kicking over his piano bench and performing the rest of his set standing at the piano. Occasionally, he even dressed in a Statue of Liberty costume or appeared on stage as Donald Duck. When it came to theatrical extravagance during the era of excess, Elton John was without peer.

WHAT LED TO THE RISE OF HEAVY METAL AND PROGRESSIVE ROCK?

The Rise of Heavy Metal

Although some performers thrived on excess and exemplified the "me" decade, others were expressing their anger and frustration with the establishment. The Watergate crisis of the mid-1970s contributed to increasing levels of distrust of the American government and the political system. Disillusioned with a corrupt administration, young people expressed their anger through increasingly harder forms of rock music. **Heavy metal**—characterized by extreme volume, distorted timbre, screeching vocals, emphatic beats, and extended guitar solos—provided an ideal outlet for adolescent frustration.

In the early 1970s, heavy metal evolved from the sound of harder, blues-based rock bands of the 1960s—such as the Rolling Stones, the Yardbirds, the Who, Iron Butterfly, and Steppenwolf (who coined the phrase "heavy metal thunder" in the hit 1968 anthem "Born to Be Wild"). The use of the deafening power chords popularized by the Kinks and the Who together with the maximum sonic distortion—as demonstrated by Steppenwolf—became the archetypal features of the genre. No longer perceived as an undesirable consequence of overdriving components, distortion became associated with extreme power. When an amplifier is overdriven, it creates both harmonic distortion and signal compression, with the latter causing sustain. Whereas a note played on a non-overdriven electric guitar fades quickly, a distorted guitar note can be held indefinitely without the loss of volume. Since sustaining anything requires effort, the metal guitarists' ability to blast out endless notes was an indication of tremendous power. Coupled with aggressive, screaming vocals, the early metal sound was one of angry rebellion—a premise reflected in lyrics that commonly dealt with themes such as violence, suicide, and the occult. In the early 1970s, three bands stood out as the prototypical heavy metal groups: Led Zeppelin, Black Sabbath, and Deep Purple.

∧ **Led Zeppelin's blues-inspired hard rock** ∧ helped establish the **aggressively powerful sound** that characterizes heavy metal.

LED ZEPPELIN

After the Yardbirds disbanded in 1968, guitarist Jimmy Page (see Chapter 6) recruited vocalist Robert Plant, bassist John Paul Jones, and drummer John Bonham to form the New Yardbirds. Having fulfilled the original bands' tour dates, the group rechristened themselves **Led Zeppelin**. (Popular mythology alleges that the name came about when the Who's drummer Keith Moon quipped that Page's new band would go over like a "lead zeppelin.") Signed by Atlantic Records, in 1969 the band released their self-titled debut album. With such slashing, amplified blues hits as Willie Dixon's "You Shook Me" and the band's bass-heavy signature performance piece "Dazed and Confused," the album reached number 10 on the U.S. charts. Each of the band's eight subsequent albums reached number one or number two on the pop charts, and the group, aided by manager Peter Grant, set concert attendance records all over the United States.

Despite Led Zeppelin's success, the rock press widely disparaged the band's albums, with *Rolling Stone* referring to their early LPs as a "thunderous, near-undifferentiated tidal wave of sound" (Bangs 1970). Seemingly undeterred by the negative reviews, Plant later acknowledged that, "acclaim always came from the street, never from the written critique" (Considine 1990, 59).

Unwilling to pigeonhole itself as a heavy metal band, Led Zeppelin experimented with Indian and Arab music, most notably on the Middle Eastern-tinged "Kashmir," as well as with folk, funk, reggae, and synthesizer pop. However, hard rock blues remained the band's main influence. Many of Page's guitar solos are based on melodic ideas derived from blues scales. Despite their reluctance to accept a heavy metal label, Led Zeppelin is frequently cited as the most influential and successful pioneer of the heavy metal genre.

BLACK SABBATH

Formed in Birmingham, England, **Black Sabbath** took a similar hard rock path as Led Zeppelin and was equally despised by the music press. The band formed from a group of working-class schoolmates: John "Ozzy" Osbourne (vocalist), Terry "Geezer" Butler (bassist), Tony Iommi (guitarist), and Bill Ward (drummer). Initially calling itself Earth,

the band got its musical start covering blues numbers by Howlin' Wolf and Muddy Waters. Gradually, they developed a heavier, more aggressive sound, slowing the tempo of their songs and accentuating the bass. Following a name change in 1969—Black Sabbath is the title of a song written by bassist Geezer Butler and a tribute to an old Boris Karloff horror movie—the band used distorted, repetitive guitar riffs combined with a sludgy tempo and heavy bass. Their 1970 self-titled debut sold moderately well but was lambasted by rock critics, who did not appreciate the direction the band appeared to be taking. Projecting anger, defiance, and aggression, Black Sabbath embodied the doom and gloom antiwar sentiment of the era, particularly on their second album *Paranoid* (1970), which featured tracks such as "War Pigs" and "Iron Man."

Along with war, the band pursued themes that included social chaos, good versus evil, the afterlife, and the supernatural. This latter interest often caused the band to be labeled as devil-worshippers or princes of darkness, although they insisted that their fascination with black arts was nothing more than morbid curiosity. Black Sabbath's gloomy outlook appealed to a post-hippie generation that was dealing with the realities of working-class life exacerbated by a downward-spiraling economy, high unemployment rates, the aftermath of war, and the prevalence of drug addiction. By the end of the 1970s, when Ozzy Osbourne left the band, Black Sabbath had produced five platinum albums and sold over eight million records. Many subsequent heavy metal bands—such as Metallica, Guns n' Roses, Iron Maiden, and Judas Priest—have cited the band as a major musical influence.

CLASSIC RECORDINGS ▶▶▶

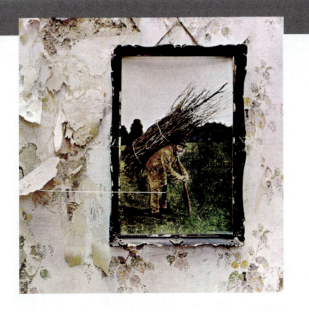

LED ZEPPELIN IV

Released in November 1971, Led Zeppelin's untitled fourth LP (commonly referred to as *Zoso*) crystallized the band's fusion of acoustic folk and heavy metal and became the defining sound of 1970s hard rock. Including many of the band's most beloved songs, such as "Rock and Roll," "When the Levee Breaks," and the masterful "Stairway to Heaven," the album became an instant commercial success, reaching number two on the *Billboard* Top 200 chart and topping the UK album chart. As of 2009, it is one of the best-selling albums in history, sharing the third spot on the RIAA top 100 albums list with Pink Floyd's *The Wall*. In 2003, *Rolling Stone* ranked the album 66th on its list of the 500 greatest albums of all time.

The album's sense of mysticism, compounded by its lack of title and the use of four runic symbols on the label and inside sleeve, reflected Page's fascination with mythology, religion, and the occult— a spirituality explored in the haunting, mandolin-driven folk ballad, "The Battle of Evermore" and in the classic "Stairway to Heaven." Frequently topping radio stations' most-requested lists, "Stairway" begins as a simple acoustic guitar-driven folk song and gradually builds to a climactic burst of guitar riffs and solos. Ironically, the song was never released as a single, a fact that did not prevent it from becoming the band's most popular recording. The length of "Stairway" is balanced by the equally lengthy "When the Levee Breaks." This song features a **backward echo** on the harmonica that displays the band's use of studio techniques. More than a decade later, the Beastie

Boys sampled "When the Levee Breaks" on their 1986 *License to Ill* album. This is one of the many examples of how Led Zeppelin's influence extended well beyond the boundaries of hard rock and heavy metal.

Led Zeppelin IV was one of the band's few albums to achieve positive critical acclaim. In the words of *Rolling Stone* magazine, the album contains tracks that "will probably be right up there in the gold-starred hierarchy of put 'em on and play 'em again" (Kaye, 1971).

DEEP PURPLE second-wave British Invasion band that shifted to heavy metal music midway through its career.

PROGRESSIVE ROCK musical genre associated with prominent keyboards, complex metric shifts, fantastical or abstract lyrics, and elements of classical, jazz, or world music.

DEEP PURPLE

Another band considered by many rock critics to be a pioneer of heavy metal is **Deep Purple**. Formed in England in 1967, the group gained early success with a cover of Joe South's "Hush." In 1969, the band fused classical and rock music in *Concerto for Group and Orchestra*, performed with the Royal Philharmonic Orchestra. When the album failed to sell in the United States, guitarist Ritchie Blackmore steered the band in

a more aggressive, guitar-dominated direction. The result was the rowdy, borderline-anarchic *Deep Purple in Rock* (1970), an ear-splitting cacophony of pounding drums, speedy guitar riffs, neo-classical keyboards, and shrill vocals. The album, which reached the Top Five in the UK charts, became one of the definitive sounds of 1970s heavy metal. In 1972, Deep Purple released *Machine Head,* which featured their biggest hit single "Smoke on the Water," a song inspired by the band's near-disastrous concert with Frank Zappa in Montreux, Switzerland, during which the venue burned to the ground. "Smoke on the Water" reached number four on the Billboard pop singles chart. Around this same time the *Guinness Book of World Records* declared that Deep Purple was the loudest band on earth. Having reached the height of its success, the band's popularity began to wane toward the end of 1973 following a series of personnel changes.

Like Led Zeppelin, Deep Purple has experimented with a variety of genres—from psychedelic rock to art rock—and therefore they also resist the heavy metal label. Strongly influenced by the works of J. S. Bach and

Rock Music Sound Meter

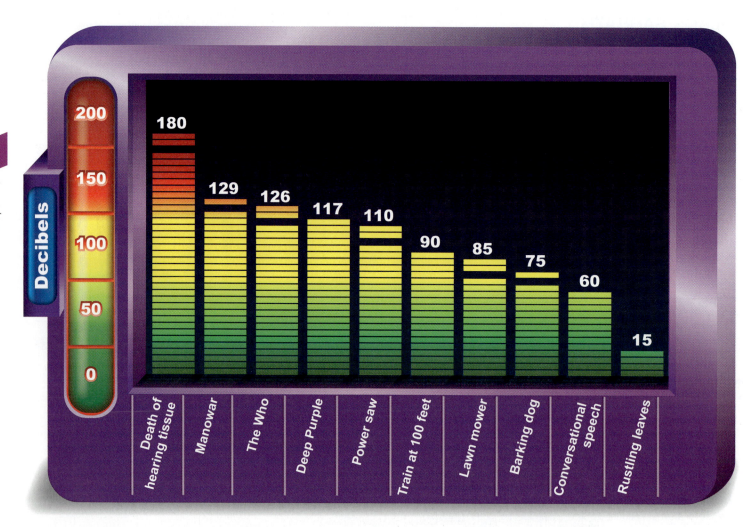

∧ **Deep Purple,** once the Guinness world record holder for **the loudest band,** topped out
∧ at 117 decibels in 1972. The band has since been **beaten by Manowar, KISS, and the Who.**
The *Guinness Book of Records* no longer includes a category for the world's loudest rock
band **for fear of promoting ear damage.**

other classical musicians—both Blackmore and organist Jon Lord had studied classical music in their youth—the group had a fuller, more complicated sound than many of their contemporaries. Despite the band's reluctance to accept and identify with the genre, many later heavy metal bands acknowledged Blackmore's guitar virtuosity as a major influence.

Progressive Rock

Evolving from psychedelic rock, **progressive rock** was an attempt to make rock with more artistic credibility. Primarily a British phenomenon that was taken very seriously in its country of origin but widely disparaged in the United States, progressive rock groups such as **Yes** and **Emerson, Lake and Palmer** created lengthy, complex musical works marked by prominent keyboards, complex metric shifts, fantastical or abstract lyrics, and elements of classical, jazz, or world music. Bands often created concept albums that told an epic story or dealt with one overarching theme that bore more resemblance to the types of themes found in classical literature, fantasy, or folklore than to the usual rock and pop subjects of love and loss.

An element of the 1970s excess that the glam rock crowd had glorified was also present in progressive rock. Bands often incorporated elaborate and flamboyant stage theatrics into their concerts. Among many stage effects, Pink Floyd performances featured crashing airplanes, a giant floating pig, and, during the 1980 *The Wall* tour, a 30-foot wall erected on stage between the band and the audience, which was torn down at the end of every show. Such excesses combined with its artistic ambitions, caused many critics to dismiss progressive rock as pretentious. The Yes entry in the *Rolling Stone Album Guide* reflects this: "Pointlessly intricate guitar and bass solos, caterwauling keyboards, quasi-mystical lyrics proclaimed in an alien falsetto, acid-dipped album cover illustrations: this British group wrote the book on art-rock excess" (Holm-Hudson 2002, 22). Many critics viewed the genre as a betrayal of the working-class, blues-oriented roots of rock & roll: Rock was supposed to rebel against the establishment, not aspire to the high-culture status of the bourgeoisie. Progressive rock was too complex, too ostentatious, and too concerned with art for art's sake to appeal to populist American reviewers.

However, the harsh criticism of progressive rock did not diminish the commercial successes of Yes, Emerson, Lake and Palmer, and other progressive rock groups during the early 1970s. In 1974, Emerson, Lake and Palmer earned five million British pounds through live appearances, a figure surpassed only by the Rolling Stones, the Who, and Led Zeppelin. Success on the album charts was equally prominent, with Yes charting five Top 10 albums between 1972 and 1977, and Pink Floyd releasing the longest-running chart album in history with 1973's *The Dark Side of the Moon*.

PROGRESSIVE ROCK AND ART ROCK

The term "progressive rock" is often used interchangeably with "art rock," although there are slight differences between the two genres. Whereas **art rock**, exemplified by such bands as the Velvet Underground and Talking Heads, has experimental or avant-garde influences, progressive rock focuses on traditional melodies

and classically trained instrumental techniques. However, the two styles frequently overlap, and their origins can be found in conceptually unified albums such as the Beatles' *Sgt. Pepper's Lonely Hearts Club Band* (1967). Both progressive rock and art rock are album-based—a fact illustrated by the successes of progressive rock bands on the album as opposed to singles charts. Both take advantage of the format's ability to include longer, more complex compositions.

The popularity of both styles diminished by the late 1970s with the advent of punk, which rejected the excesses of prog-rock and returned to the stripped-down, rebellious roots of rock & roll (see Chapter 9). Although it is often omitted from rock histories as an anomaly, progressive rock did not disappear entirely. Popular prog-rock bands such as Yes, Genesis, and Pink Floyd continued to chart throughout the 1980s, and a small wave of neo-progressive groups such as Marillion, Twelfth Night, and Pallas cropped up in the late 1980s and early 1990s, characterized by their use of digital synthesizers and virtuosic instrumental techniques.

YES

British band Yes is one of the most influential and enduring progressive rock groups, surviving the critical backlash against the genre and retaining its popularity during the punk rock era of the late 1970s.

Initially formed in 1968, the band went through several lineup changes in its early years, including the additions of guitarist Steve Howe and classically trained pianist Rick Wakeman. The latter, a flamboyant musician who used more than a dozen instruments, incorporated various synthesizers, an organ, several pianos, and an electric harpsichord into his considerable repertoire. With Howe's guitar pyrotechnics and Wakeman's stylish, complex keyboarding skills, the band achieved its breakthrough U.S. album *Fragile* (1971). This album made the Top Five on the Billboard Top 200 chart and included the hit "Roundabout," one of the few progressive rock songs to conquer the singles charts successfully. *Fragile* marked the beginning of a lengthy collaboration between Yes and artist Roger Dean, who designed fantasy-style cover artwork to reinforce the band's lyrics. Dean also later designed the band's touring stage sets, thereby helping consolidate the look that became an integral part of the group's identity. Following in the footsteps of the Beatles' *Sgt. Pepper*, several other progressive rock bands also used album art as part of the overall artistic concept; for example, Pink Floyd worked with art design group Hipgnosis to pioneer many innovative visual and packaging techniques.

<<< **Pink Floyd's live shows,** featuring elaborate special effects like this **giant floating pig,** were typical of the **ambitious progressive rock concerts** that critics in the 1970s **dismissed as pretentious.**

YES influential British progressive rock band featuring neoclassical structures and three-part harmonies.

EMERSON, LAKE AND PALMER British prog-rock band that was one of the earliest rock & roll supergroups.

ART ROCK experimental music genre with avant-garde influences that attempted to elevate rock music into an art form.

Among Yes's five Top Ten albums, *Close to the Edge* (1972) peaked highest, reaching number three on the *Billboard* Pop Album chart. Consisting of three extended cuts and a four-movement title suite, the album set a trend of structuring an album around a single epic song—a trippy, 20-minute track featuring rich harmonies, ethereal lyrics, and complex keyboard passages. Keyboardist Wakeman later went on to enjoy a successful solo career, recording such scholarly, classically influenced titles as *The Six Wives of Henry the VIII* (1973), *Journey to the Center of the Earth* (1974), and *The Myths and Legends of King Arthur and the Knights of the Round Table* (1975).

GENESIS

The members of prog-rock band **Genesis** met at secondary school in 1967 and initially played a folk-based progressive pop that had little mainstream appeal. Fans of psychedelic rock deemed it too poppy, fans of pop/rock acts such as the Bee Gees found it too complex, and fans of hard rock found it not heavy enough. The band was on the verge of breaking up when it released its second album, *Trespass* (1970). Featuring extended pieces with intricate, semi-orchestral arrangements by keyboard player Tony Banks and mystical lyrics from singer Peter Gabriel, the album proved to be an important stepping-stone in the band's musical progression despite its commercial failure.

[Around this time Genesis began to use masks, makeup, and props during their concerts, attracting a cult following. Gabriel frequently introduced the group's songs with surreal spoken introductions, setting up some of the more complex

∧ Genesis's **theatrical live shows** often
∧ included **elaborate costumes and props.**

material for the audience. Hitting the British Top Ten with three albums between 1972 and 1975, including the ambitious double concept album *The Lamb Lies Down on Broadway* (1974), the band maintained its popularity over the next two decades throughout several personnel changes, including Gabriel's departure and the shifting of vocal responsibilities to Phil Collins.

EMERSON, LAKE AND PALMER

One of rock & roll's earliest supergroups (see Chapter 6), the members of Emerson, Lake and Palmer came from three already successful bands. Consisting of guitarist Greg Lake (King Crimson), classically trained pianist Keith Emerson (The Nice), and drummer Carl Palmer (Atomic Rooster), ELP are credited with bringing progressive rock into mainstream popularity, creating a radio phenomenon, and paving the way for fellow progressive rock bands such as Yes, who became the band's main rival throughout the 1970s. The band made their debut appearance in August 1970 just a few days before appearing at the massive three-day Isle of Wight Festival. That same year, ELP made the Top 20 with their self-titled first album, a collection of instrumental and vocal pieces that featured extracts from classical composers including Bach and Bartók. The album's final track, the acoustic folk ballad "Lucky Man," became a hit on both sides of the Atlantic.

In 1971, the trio released the best-selling *Tarkus*, a dense concept album about a mechanized armadillo that battles other half-mechanical creatures and is eventually defeated by a mythical beast called a manticore. The same year, ELP released a live version of classical composer Modest Mussorgsky's *Pictures at an Exhibition*. Both albums reached the Top 10 in the United States and UK, and by 1973 the band had achieved enough recognition to create its own record label. The band had a string of successes, including the live album *Welcome Back My Friend to the Show That Never Ends* (1974), which included Bach's "Toccata." The group eventually split in 1979, unable to overcome the music press's sneering criticisms of prog-rock and an increasing public preference for punk rock and disco.

PINK FLOYD

As you read in Chapter 7, Pink Floyd began as a psychedelic rock band in the 1960s. However, after the departure of Syd Barrett in 1968, the group's sound began to change. With the addition of guitarist David Gilmour, the band began to explore a more somber and experimental form of rock. This new direction brought Pink Floyd success, with *Ummagumma* (1969) and *Atom Heart Mother* (1970) both reaching the UK Top Five.

However, the 1973 masterpiece *The Dark Side of the Moon* truly established the band as progressive rock superstars. This concept album reached number one on the album chart and remained on the *Billboard* Top 200 album chart for 741 weeks—over 14 years. Tackling themes of alienation, paranoia, and schizophrenia, *The Dark Side of the Moon* was bleak but approachable. Along with the standard electric guitars, bass, and drums, the band also used synthesizers, taped voices, and high production values to craft a seamless album, on which many of the songs lead into one another. Yielding two hit singles—"Money" and "Us and Them"—the album became a classic rock milestone that made Pink Floyd one of the biggest-selling acts of all time.

Unlike many prog-rock bands, Pink Floyd's success continued throughout the late 1970s and early 1980s, culminating with *The Wall* (1979), a bleak concept album that topped the U.S. chart for 15 weeks and produced one of the most complex and theatrical stage shows in the history of rock. Although the band began to unravel in the wake of *The Wall*, Pink Floyd produced several chart-topping albums in the 1990s (*The Division Bell* in 1994 and *P.U.L.S.E.* in 1995).

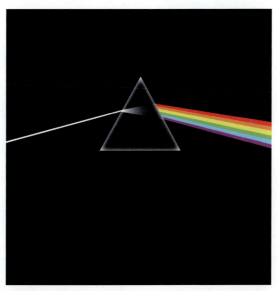

∧∧ Pink Floyd's progressive rock masterpiece **The Dark Side of the Moon stayed on the Billboard charts** for over 14 years.

like hooks and choruses of hard rock and heavy metal bands and the synthesizer solos and three- or four-part vocal arrangements favored by the progressive rock bands. Although some stadium rock bands took on the progressive rock themes of spiritual quests, fantasy, and folklore—as in Styx's "Come Sail Away" and "Lord of the Rings"—many stuck to the subject material favored by the hard rock bands of the early 1970s—sex, drugs, and rock & roll.

Rejecting both the complex rhythmic and harmonic techniques of progressive rock and the edginess and rage of heavy metal, the simple, catchy hooks of stadium rock appealed to the mainstream, making it a huge commercial success. Concerts typically featured large-scale special effects, including smoke machines and laser light spectaculars, as well as two-story mega amps and large video screens. Although British bands such as the Beatles, the Rolling Stones, Led Zeppelin, and the Who paved the way for stadium rock with their frenetic live performances at increasingly large venues, stadium rock was ultimately emblemized by American bands such as Kansas, Journey, Foreigner, Styx, and Boston, all of which sold out some of the world's largest music venues in the late 1970s and early 1980s.

Critics of stadium rock argued that the big arena rock bands were taking rock in an overcommercialized direction and putting music increasingly out of

MIKE OLDFIELD

Aptly demonstrated by *The Dark Side of the Moon*'s "On the Run," many progressive rock bands experimented with a form of electronic rock that later became known as synth pop or electropop. (You will learn more about synth pop in Chapter 10.) Characterized by a heavy reliance on high-tech synthesizers and electronic keyboards, electronic rock superimposed layers of sonic material to create complex "sound collages." One of the most successful artists to adopt this branch of art rock was composer **Mike Oldfield**, who rose to fame with the release of eerie conceptual album *Tubular Bells* (1972). Playing nearly 30 different instruments on the album, which contained countless overdubs, Oldfield fused a number of musical genres to create an intricate 49-minute composition. The album reached the number one spot on the UK charts and sold over 16 million copies globally, creating a market for the instrumental sounds of New Age music. An excerpt from *Tubular Bells* was chosen as the theme music for 1973 movie *The Exorcist*, consolidating the record's popularity.

Stadium Rock

During the mid-1970s, the popular genres of heavy metal, hard rock, and progressive rock converged to create a commercialized, radio-friendly form of rock music. Meant to be performed in large stadiums, **stadium rock** combined the guitar pyrotechnics and anthem-

TOP OF THE CHARTS
WHAT'S HOT!
APRIL 28, 1973

1. *The Dark Side of the Moon* – Pink Floyd
2. *Aloha from Hawaii via Satellite* – Elvis Presley
3. *Billion Dollar Babies* – Alice Cooper
4. *The Best of Bread* – Bread
5. *Houses Of The Holy* – Led Zeppelin
6. *The World Is a Ghetto* – War
7. *Masterpiece* – The Temptations
8. *Lady Sings the Blues* – Diana Ross
9. *The Beatles/1962–1966* – The Beatles
10. *The Beatles/1967–1970* – The Beatles

BRUCE SPRINGSTEEN U.S. musician who gave music fans a dose of realism and "authenticity."

MULTITRACK RECORDING recording with more than two tracks simultaneously to enable various musical elements to be recorded on separate tracks.

OVERDUBBING process of merging additional musical elements with previously recorded tracks.

touch with its fans. When playing such large venues, performers were unable to connect personally with their audiences. By the early 1980s the popularity of stadium rock bands began to wane, as audiences grew tired of the bombastic special effects and of being unable to see the actual performers on stage. The advent of MTV in the early 1980s made stadium rock largely irrelevant; declining ticket sales and album sales caused the music industry to tighten its belt, capping recording and production costs.

Heavy Metal

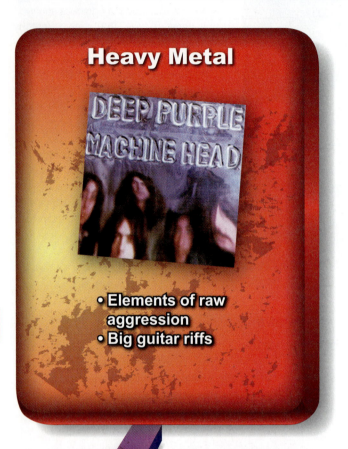

- Elements of raw aggression
- Big guitar riffs

Progressive Rock

- Concept albums
- Complex harmonies
- Fantasy themes
- Synthesizer solos
- Three- or four-part vocal arrangements

Stadium Rock

- Large-scale special effects in concert
- Big, anthemic hooks
- Commercially oriented

∧
∧ **Stadium rock** bands took elements of hard rock, heavy metal, and progressive rock to
∧ create a more radio-friendly genre of popular music.

BRUCE SPRINGSTEEN: THE FUTURE OF ROCK & ROLL?

During an era of escapism and excess, **Bruce Springsteen** provided rock & roll fans with a dose of realism that earned him the reputation as the new Bob Dylan. Springsteen's sincere insights into the heart of working-class America helped him forge a direct connection with his listeners—a connection missing from the impersonal live performances of the arena rock bands.

The son of a bus driver and a secretary, Springsteen grew up in Freehold, New Jersey, and played in a series of bands during his teenage years before going solo in the autumn of 1971. His first real break came a year later when he caught the attention of Columbia A&R representative John Hammond, who signed the young musician to the label. Springsteen's debut release *Greetings from Asbury Park, N.J.* (1973) initially went unnoticed, despite being touted by Columbia as a masterpiece by the "new Dylan." Selling mostly to fans on the Jersey shore, the album did not even make the Top 200 until the 1975 release of *Born to Run* reignited interest in Springsteen's earlier work. During his 1974 tour, Springsteen, performing with backup band the E Street Band, built a grassroots following. He received encouragement from *Rolling Stone* journalist Jon Landau, who wrote: "I saw the rock & roll future and its name is Bruce Springsteen." Springsteen

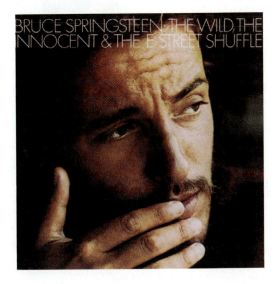

later hired Landau to coproduce *Born to Run,* which—aided by an unprecedented PR campaign that cost Columbia more than $200,000— reached the Top Five and earned Springsteen an enthusiastic mainstream audience.

Music critics applauded Springsteen's return to rock & roll's roots, and he appeared on the covers of both *Time* and *Newsweek* in October 1975. *Time* wrote, "Springsteen represents a regeneration, a renewal of rock. He has gone back to the sources, rediscovered the wild excitement that rock has lost over the past few years. . . Springsteen has taken rock forward by taking it back, keeping it young." With his earnest lyrics about unemployment, social issues, and the rage and frustrations of everyday working-class life, Springsteen stripped away the flashy, superficial veneers of glam and stadium rock and brought back the personal connection between audience and performer (see Chapter 11).

<<< **Bruce Springsteen** *eschewed the elaborate artistry of progressive rock in favor of a* **back-to-basics approach to rock & roll.**

ROCK TECHNOLOGY >>> Multitrack Recording

Prior to the invention of **multitrack recording**, musicians had to simultaneously play live together in a studio. The first commercially available tape recorders were monophonic, meaning that they only had one track on which to record sound. During the 1940s and 1950s, some musicians began to experiment with **overdubbing**. This process involves playing live music over a previous recording. The combination is recorded on a second tape. This process diluted the sound quality, however, and added a hissing tape noise that intensified with each successive overdub.

In 1953, guitarist Les Paul, who had been experimenting with overdubbing, commissioned the Ampex Corporation to build a custom recorder with eight parallel tracks to be inscribed on special one-inch-wide tape. By 1955, the company had produced the first commercial multitrack tape recorder. Although two-track recorders were in common use by the late 1950s,

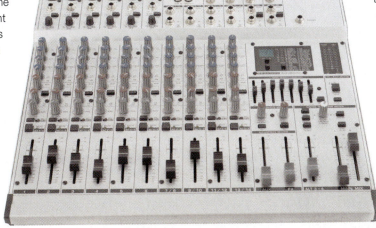

recording studios were slow to catch on to the latest developments in multitrack recording. As late as 1967, the painstaking process of connecting two four-track recorders to get eight tracks was used for the Beatles' *Sgt. Pepper* album, enabling the band to create the swirling circus sounds of "Being for the Benefit of Mr. Kite" and mix a 40-piece orchestra into "A Day in the Life." As studios moved from eight-track (the Beatles' *White Album,* 1968) to 16-track (Tommy James and the Shondells' *Crimson and Clover,* 1968) to 32-track recording (Steely Dan's *Gaucho,* 1980), albums increasingly became studio creations. Studio producers utilized mixing boards (pictured here) to shape the complex, multi-layered recordings. In the words of composer Brian Eno, the recording studio itself became a "compositional tool," enabling artists to build the intricate sounds of orchestral progressive rock and heavy metal that developed in the early 1970s.

Summary

WHAT WERE THE MUSICAL RESPONSES PRODUCED BY THE SOCIAL CRISES OF THE LATE 1960s? 132

• In the late 1960s, the Vietnam War and race riots radicalized some American artists, but others turned away from protest music toward an apolitical hybrid of pop, folk, and rock that was intended to comfort, rather than challenge, its audience—soft rock.

• Soft rock artists took on an introspective, confessional style that incorporated themes of everyday life, love, and relationships.

WHO TOOK PART IN THE SOUL REVIVAL? 135

• The civil rights movement of the 1960s sparked renewed interest in soul music, and in August 1972, the Wattstax Music Festival demonstrated the growing market appeal of African American artists.

• *Soul Train*, the first African American-oriented music variety show on American television, aired in 1971 and helped popularize many soul and R&B artists.

WHAT WERE THE EARLY INFLUENCES OF GLAM ROCK? 136

• The 1970s were labeled the "me" decade, an ideological shift that manifested musically in the extravagant self-indulgence of glam rockers.

• Glam rock fused elements of hard rock and pop and was characterized by a flamboyant, often androgynous look that incorporated glittery costumes and heavy makeup.

• Some of the musical influences for glam rock developed out of the American garage bands of the 1960s, including the Velvet Underground.

WHAT LED TO THE RISE OF HEAVY METAL AND PROGRESSIVE ROCK? 140

• Heavy metal—characterized by extreme volume, distorted timbre, screeching vocals, emphatic beats, and extended guitar solos—provided an ideal outlet for adolescent frustration during the government scandals of the 1970s.

• Progressive rock was a self-conscious attempt to elevate rock music to high-culture status by incorporating elements of cultivated musical influence.

• Stadium rock combined elements of heavy metal, hard rock, and progressive rock to create a commercialized, radio-friendly form of rock music.

Key Terms

David Bowie early 1970s glam rocker who took the image to extremes, creating controversial, glittery onstage personas such as Ziggy Stardust *132*

soft rock melodic rock music that stresses themes of vulnerability in a confessional, introspective style *132*

James Taylor successful 1970s singer-songwriter whose music exemplified the introspective, self-oriented style of soft rock *132*

Carly Simon singer-songwriter married to James Taylor *133*

Carole King singer-songwriter from Brill Building group of early 1960s who went on to enjoy solo success with top-selling album *Tapestry* *133*

The Eagles country rock band that straddled the line between mainstream rock, folk rock, and country rock; produced the best-selling album in U.S. history *135*

Stax Records Memphis record label founded in 1960 by brother-and-sister team

Jim Stewart and Estelle Axton; Motown's main rival *135*

Wattstax Music Festival L.A. music concert held in 1972 to commemorate the Watts riots; popularity reflected growing market appeal of African American artists *135*

Soul Train first black-oriented music variety show on American television; ran for 35 years *135*

Aretha Franklin gospel-influenced Queen of Soul; achieved huge crossover success among white audiences in the late 1960s and early 1970s *135*

Philadelphia International Records record label created by Philadelphia-based songwriting duo Kenny Gamble and Leon Huff that introduced the Sound of Philadelphia *137*

Sweet Philly Soul soul music originating from Philadelphia characterized by smooth vocals and lush orchestral sounds *137*

glam rock fusion of hard rock and pop characterized by performers' flamboyant, glittery costumes *137*

The Velvet Underground American garage band formed in the 1960s; considered one of the most influential groups in rock history for its substantial impact on punk, glam, and garage rock *137*

Lou Reed singer in the Velvet Underground, later began a solo career that incorporated the glam rock image *137*

Marc Bolan one of the early pioneers of 1970s British glam rock, lead singer of T. Rex *137*

Mott the Hoople American glam rock band that achieved a cult homosexual following in the 1970s *138*

Queen London glam rock band that created a mock-operatic sound and was known for its extravagant theatrical performances *138*

Freddie Mercury lead vocalist and frontman for Queen *138*

Iggy Pop American proto-punk rocker infamous for his wild onstage antics; did not achieve mainstream success until the mid-1990s *138*

The Stooges proto-punk 1970s band fronted by Iggy Pop *138*

Elton John singer-songwriter who first achieved popularity in the 1970s with his sensitive ballads and wild onstage antics *140*

heavy metal genre of music characterized by extreme volume, distorted timbre, screeching vocals, emphatic beats, and extended guitar solos *140*

Led Zeppelin influential 1970s heavy metal band led by former Yardbirds guitarist Jimmy Page *140*

Black Sabbath one of the defining 1970s heavy metal bands, fronted by "prince of darkness" Ozzy Osbourne *140*

backward echo effect obtained during mixing by placing the echo ahead of the sound *140*

Deep Purple second-wave British Invasion band that shifted to heavy metal music midway through its career *142*

progressive rock musical genre associated with prominent keyboards, complex metric shifts, fantastical or abstract lyrics, and elements of classical, jazz, or world music *142*

Yes influential British progressive rock band featuring neoclassical structures and three-part harmonies *143*

Emerson, Lake and Palmer British prog-rock band that was one of the earliest rock & roll supergroups *143*

art rock experimental music genre with avant-garde influences that attempted to elevate rock music into an art form *143*

Genesis British progressive rock band that provided a launching pad for singers Peter Gabriel and Phil Collins *144*

Mike Oldfield Composer who experimented with electronic rock, creating the legendary 49-minute instrumental composition *Tubular Bells* *144*

stadium rock commercialized genre of music that fused elements of progressive rock, hard rock, and heavy metal; designed to be performed in a large stadium *144*

Bruce Springsteen U.S. musician who gave music fans a dose of realism and "authenticity" *146*

multitrack recording recording with more than two tracks simultaneously to enable various musical elements to be recorded on separate tracks *146*

overdubbing process of merging additional musical elements with previously recorded tracks *146*

Sample Test Questions

1. Which musical genre in the late 1960s and early 1970s was characterized by its confessional, introspective style?
   a. psychedelic rock
   b. soul music
   c. soft rock
   d. progressive rock

2. Which of these factors led to a renewed interest in soul music?
   a. the Vietnam War
   b. the civil rights movement
   c. government scandals such as Watergate
   d. political events such as the Kent State massacre

3. Which of these statements is correct?
   a. Soft rock was a precursor to the American punk movement of the late 1970s.
   b. Glam rock was a self-conscious attempt to elevate rock music to high-culture status.
   c. Stadium rock fused elements of heavy metal, hard rock, and progressive rock.
   d. Progressive rock was characterized by a flamboyant, often androgynous look.

4. Multitrack recording enabled artists to
   a. layer and blend different recordings.
   b. produce longer concept albums.
   c. use guitar techniques such as distortion.
   d. experiment with digital synthesizers.

5. Which musical genre incorporated themes of violence, suicide, and the occult?
   a. heavy metal
   b. progressive rock
   c. glam rock
   d. stadium rock

ESSAY

6. Discuss the social and political factors that contributed to the fragmentation of rock in the late 1960s and early 1970s.

7. How were elements of the self-indulgent "me" decade reflected in music?

8. Discuss the origins and early influences of heavy metal music.

9. Compare and contrast the musical components of hard rock, progressive metal, and stadium rock.

10. What factors contributed to the demise of stadium rock?

WHERE TO START YOUR RESEARCH PAPER

For an overview of soft rock, including a list of artists and albums, go to
http://www.allmusic.com/cg/amg.dll?p=amg&sql=77:382

For an in-depth biography of David Bowie, go to
http://www.rollingstone.com/artists/davidbowie/biography

To learn about the history of *Soul Train*, go to
http://www.museum.tv/archives/etv/S/htmlS/soultrain/soultrain.htm

For more information about Philadelphia soul and the history of Philadelphia International Records, go to
http://www.gamble-huffmusic.com/home/

For more information about the origins of glam rock, go to
http://www.britannica.com/EBchecked/topic/234774/glam-rock

For more information about the origins of heavy metal, go to
http://www.britannica.com/EBchecked/topic/258947/heavy-metal

For more information about progressive rock and art rock, go to
http://www.allmusic.com/cg/amg.dll?p=amg&sql=77:374

ANSWERS: 1. c; 2. b; 3. c; 4. a; 5. a

Remember to check www.thethinkspot.com for additional information, downloadable flashcards, and other helpful resources.

HOW DID DISCO CHANGE THE MUSIC SCENE DURING THE 1970s?

WHAT WERE THE ORIGINS OF THE PUNK MOVEMENT IN AMERICAN MUSICAL CULTURE?

WHERE DID PUNK BEGIN?

HOW DID NEW WAVE EMERGE FROM THE DEATH OF PUNK?

"WINTERLAND

is traditionally associated with the Grateful Dead and is Bill Graham's home from home—he was there on Saturday night to watch the Pistols and collect some of the booty that the audience was throwing on stage.

"Sid Vicious strutted out, bass around his kneecaps, sneering invitingly at the curious and converted who have already begun throwing objects, either as gifts or as insults which the Pistols spent the evening encouraging. San Francisco already has the strongest punk scene outside of New York and Akron (!) and there are a number of leftovers from the Hookers' Ball to provide local color.

"Rotten and the rest lurched on stage, John leaning on the mic like the desperate cripple he imitated all night.

'Welcome to London!' he yells out and is greeted with cries of 'F–you, this is SF.'

"Outside, the band's bus has 'Pretty Vacant, England' written across it. A sign of pride, perhaps they've figured that it has to be London to work and knowing it can't be are determined to treat the assembled yanks as a busload of gullible tourists waiting to be gulled. . . .

"They lumber into 'God Save The Queen,' a leftover from the Jubilee. The playing is uncoordinated but loud and remains so during the hour-long set.

"Rotten is superb, hanging from the mic like a clothes-hanger, then leaping into a grotesque imitation of life while singing. Somehow, for all his cynicism, sneers and leathers, he maintains a pasty-faced innocence.

"He asks the audience to throw up some cameras, complaining that what has been thrown up so far is 'not good enough, is it?' Between numbers he searches the stage for worthwhile mementos which he stuffs into his pockets. At the end of the show he leaves, clutching three umbrellas.

"The Pistols have claimed frequently enough to be a peoples' band but I get the impression that they regard people as being an exclusively British species. Here they express nothing but contempt for their audience and seem to demand the same in return. . . .

"The Pistols' set and playing has absolutely no pacing or range. So, instead they make an art of ripping off their audience while keeping up a running commentary on what they're doing. 'F– you,' cries the audience in delight. They've got a nerve alright. Especially Mr. Rotten. They took their visas on liberal guilt, they're trying to steal the world."

—Mark Cooper, *Record Mirror,* 28 January 1978

DISCO, PUNK & NEW WAVE: STRANGE BEDFELLOWS (1973–1979)

CHAPTER 09

HOW DID DISCO CHANGE THE MUSIC SCENE DURING THE 1970s?

In January 1978, the **Sex Pistols** lurched across the lower half of the United States in a bizarre tour that eventually landed them at San Francisco's Winterland Palace. There, after a final, bewildering performance that concluded with a reprise of Iggy Pop's "No Fun," Rotten famously demanded, "Ever get the feeling you've been cheated?" (Charles Taylor, *Los Angeles Times*, December 24, 2006.) Although those words marked the end of the Sex Pistols, the question still hangs in the air for anyone who wonders if rock & roll has a way of exploiting the same fans upon whom it depends. Disco and punk made for strange bedfellows indeed, but during the 1970s both strove to return an increasingly corporate art form to the people.

Disco Dances In

By the mid-1970s, the rock & roll hierarchy was more or less fixed. Stadium rock powerhouses such as Led Zeppelin and the Eagles dominated the show, and slack-jawed audiences sat in amazement as the musicians strutted their stuff. But, in the early 1970s, disco had begun to put the spotlight back on the dance floor.

In the late 1960s and early 1970s, warehouse-sized clubs such as New York City's The Loft became mixing boards for the new dance sound. Disc jockeys and musicians used tape loops and drum machines to create a danceable groove that synched perfectly with the all-night party atmosphere of discotheques. However, the focus wasn't on the instrumentalists: it was on the dancers. The democratic dance floor was a pleasure dome that invited all people to join the fun.

THE PRODUCERS

Musically, disco drew on the funk-inflected soul of R&B and the hypnotic sounds of the late psychedelic era to create something more carefully orchestrated and mechanical. In traditional 1970s rock the songwriter or guitarist ran the show, but disco made the producer, armed with technology, the primary creative driver of the music.

Largely, mixers and arrangers defined the disco experience. Throughout the 1970s, Italian-born producer Giorgio Moroder pioneered disco sounds. His use of computerized music and orchestrated vocals helped artists such as The Three Degrees and Donna Summer bring dance music from the clubs to the airwaves. In partnership with Pete Bellotte, Moroder founded the Munich-based Musicland Studio, a central point in the evolution of the disco mix. There, he recorded tracks that gave disco a texture at once visceral, sensual, and futuristic. **Moog synthesizers**

<<< **Disco brought dancing back into popular music** for the first time in a decade.

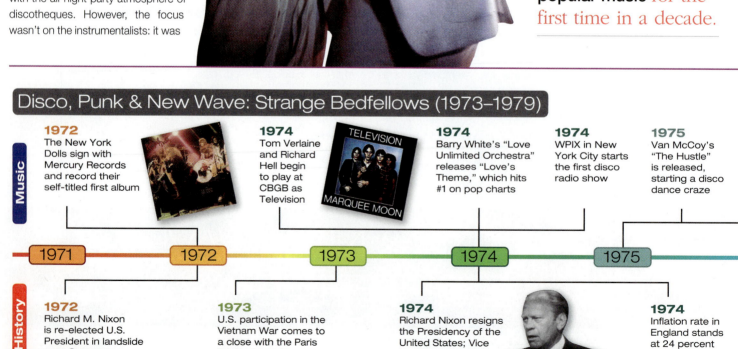

Disco, Punk & New Wave: Strange Bedfellows (1973–1979)

Music

1972
The New York Dolls sign with Mercury Records and record their self-titled first album

1974
Tom Verlaine and Richard Hell begin to play at CBGB as Television

TELEVISION
MARQUEE MOON

1974
Barry White's "Love Unlimited Orchestra" releases "Love's Theme," which hits #1 on pop charts

1974
WPIX in New York City starts the first disco radio show

1975
Van McCoy's "The Hustle" is released, starting a disco dance craze

1971 — 1972 — 1973 — 1974 — 1975

History

1972
Richard M. Nixon is re-elected U.S. President in landslide over Governor George McGovern

1973
U.S. participation in the Vietnam War comes to a close with the Paris Peace Accords

1974
Richard Nixon resigns the Presidency of the United States; Vice President Gerald R. Ford replaces him

1974
Inflation rate in England stands at 24 percent

added extra layering to the music. (You will learn much more about the influence of synthesizers on rock music in Chapter 10.) Anchored by a regular, mechanical drum machine beat, disco overcame dance music's earlier limitations.

DANCING AND DISCO

Disco was unapologetically about dancing in a way that nothing in rock addressed. The genre launched a series of dances including "The Box" or "**The Hustle**." By the mid-1970s, the crowd of aspiring dancers grew larger, inspired in part by John Travolta's moves in the popular film *Saturday Night Fever*. Because disco required more skill than dancing the Twist, dance schools popped up across the country to fill this new demand. Thanks to the appearance of the 12-inch single and the popularity of the solid, thumping bass line, songs could top 20 minutes before segueing into the next, and the next, and the next.

This focus on dancing made the beat itself the music's unique edge in a way that disco's lyrics—which were generally about the virtues of partying or boogie shoes—did not. Dancers won prestige by gaining entrance to highly exclusive clubs. Such locales as New York's **Studio 54**, the Sanctuary, the Haven, and the Odyssey became focal points of the new, night-clubbing society of disco fans.

DONNA SUMMER: QUEEN OF DISCO

Radio stations ignored disco until the mid-1970s, when the genre suddenly began to conquer the airwaves. **Donna Summer**, disco's first major crossover star, led this charge. Born in 1948 to devoutly Christian parents, Summer was still a relatively unknown singer when she started her solo career in 1974. However, she caught the attention of producers Moroder and Bellotte. The duo recorded Summer's "Love to Love You," which became the singer's first disco hit after Casablanca Records released it in November 1975, eventually

SEX PISTOLS British band that was one of the most influential groups in the punk movement.

MOOG SYNTHESIZER digital keyboard used to create background for disco hits.

"THE HUSTLE" partner dance that became popular during the disco era and was featured prominently in *Saturday Night Fever*.

STUDIO 54 famous Manhattan dance club that became the center of disco culture in the late 1970s.

DONNA SUMMER American singer who came to prominence during the disco era.

reaching #2 on Billboard's Top 100 chart. Backed by a synthesized accompaniment and the regular, steady beat that made disco famous, the song notoriously featured a moaning, wordless vocal that simulated a sexual encounter and ran for an entire side of Summer's first album.

Continued collaboration with Moroder and Bellotte maintained Summer's position as disco's reigning diva until 1979. In 1977, her song "I Feel Love" also hit #2 on the Billboard charts, and 1978's "Last Dance" not only reached #3 but also won Summer a Grammy. As opposed to the novelty of "Love to Love You," these later singles featured fuller lyrics and showed off Summer's vocal capabilities. By the time the disco revolution began to fade in 1979, Summer had begun to

<<< Donna Summer became disco music's **first genuine megastar.**

1975
While managing the disintegrating New York Dolls, Malcolm McLaren takes note of the new "punk fashion" then spreading among the New York underworld

1976
Sex Pistols release their debut single, "Anarchy in the U.K." "God Save the Queen" shortly follows

1977
Studio 54 opens

1977
The Sex Pistols headline the *Anarchy in the U.K.* tour with the Damned, the Clash, and Johnny Thunders' Heartbreakers

1979
Steve Dahl organizes Disco Demolition night at Comiskey Park

1976 | 1977 | 1978 | 1979 | 1980

1977
Queen Elizabeth's Silver Jubilee

1978
Jerry Falwell founds the Moral Majority

1979
Margaret Thatcher becomes Prime Minister of Great Britain

1980
Ronald Reagan elected President of the United States

In 1978, the single "Le Freak" from the group's second album *C'est Chic* spent five weeks at the top of the charts, selling over four million copies. That same year, *C'est Chic* went platinum. Followup album *Risque* appeared in 1979. This album featured "Good Times," another disco classic characterized by its thudding, minimalist beat. Chic's influence can be seen in the legacy of "Good Times"; the song inspired the rhythm of Queen's "Another One Bites the Dust" (1980) and appeared as the backing track for what is often cited as the first rap recording, Sugarhill Gang's "Rapper's Delight" (1979). (For more on Queen, see Chapter 8; for more on Sugarhill Gang, see Chapter 13.) After Chic disbanded in 1983, both Rogers and Edwards went on to careers as high-profile producers and musicians.

diversify into electronic music and even New Wave. (You will read much more about the New Wave sound in Chapter 10.) Even today, however, Summer remains best known as "The Queen of Disco," a singer who gave a face and a personality to a musical form previously associated with dance floors.

CHIC

Donna Summer may have been disco's queen, but the two musicians behind the group **Chic** were its most innovative and influential composers. Guitarist Nile Rodgers and bass player Bernard Edwards collaborated to create a stripped-down, funk-driven form of disco that funk, new wave, and hip-hop artists have imitated to the present. Both having trained in jazz, the two musicians met just out of high school in 1970. By the end of 1976, they had dabbled in New Wave music, playing in a band called Allah & the Knife Wielding Punks. In 1977, they formed Chic. Accompanied by vocalists Norma Jean Wright and Alfa Anderson, Chic recorded and released its first single "Dance, Dance, Dance" that same year on Buddah Records. When Atlantic Records signed them and rereleased "Dance, Dance, Dance," Chic hit the big time.

BARRY WHITE: THE SULTAN OF SOUL

Texas native **Barry White** began his career as an R&B producer. In the early 1970s, he assembled the Love Unlimited Orchestra, a girl group modeled on the Supremes. After hearing him record a three-song demo of his own, colleagues began to prod him to use his own inimitable bass to full advantage. When he joined 20th Century Records, White brought along Love Unlimited musicians to record the instrumental "Love's Theme," which went to reach number 1 on Billboard's pop charts in 1974 as one of disco's first big radio hits.

Once he added his own soulful voice to the mix, White created a distinctive, sexy, danceable sound. From 1974 to 1979, White enjoyed an uninterrupted string of hits, including disco/R&B classics such as "You're the First, the Last, My Everything" (1974), "I Can't Get Enough of Your Love" (1974), and "What Am I Gonna Do With You?" (1975). White's symphonic orchestration, which included as many as five guitars as well as a string and horn section, helped define the disco sound throughout the 1970s. White brought to disco not only his sexy baritone but also a new emphasis on romantic songs with sweeping melodies, while still maintaining the dance beat. Although he was one of the pioneers of

ROCK PLACES

Studio 54

When disco fever went mainstream in 1977, Studio 54—named for its location on Manhattan's 54th Street—was the genre's preeminent venue. Those who made it to the right side of the velvet rope could boast that they had reached the top of the disco mountaintop. They were, literally, dancing with the stars.

Partners Steve Rubell and Ian Shrager founded Studio 54 in 1977. The gregarious Rubell was often seen out in front of the club, separating the wheat from the chaff to mix the dance floor with the right combination of celebrities and attractive unknowns. From the moment the club opened in April 1977, it stood out as a playground for the famous and well connected. Countless New York celebrities including Mick and Bianca Jagger, Donald

and Ivana Trump, and Debbie Harry made appearances on Studio 54's opening night. For friends and foes alike, Studio 54 represented the hedonism of the **Me Decade**.

Studio 54 greeted its visitors with a large, glowing sign above the dance floor called "Man on the Moon with a Cocaine Spoon." While drugs in the 1960s had been ingested for their purportedly mind-expanding properties, the drugs of the disco era aimed to charge—and recharge—dancers' batteries throughout the night. Quaaludes left arms and legs feeling like rubber, and cocaine kept dancers on the floor for hours at a stretch. Long nights under the influence increased sexual promiscuity. Studio 54's dance floor wasn't just any stage; for dancers, it was the first stage in a courtship ritual that might end up in the legendary upper balcony of the

nightclub, a popular spot for sexual encounters.

Disco's drug culture—just like the one that had developed in the flower-power era—eventually became an oppressive and creatively stultifying force, as drugs overtook the central role previously accorded to music and dancing. The reputation of clubs as drug scenes also attracted the attention of the police, which led to numerous closures and legal actions. In fact, Studio 54's reputation caught up with it after only 33 months. In December 1979, federal agents burst in brandishing warrants. They found garbage bags full of cash as well as drug dealers' records. The club closed, and both Rubell and Shrager spent 13 months in jail. Although Studio 54 never reopened, it continues to symbolize an era of fast living and easy loving.

disco, White's career extended far beyond that. When he died in 2003, the "Sultan of Soul" had sold over 100 million albums.

SATURDAY NIGHT FEVER, HITMAKER

By the mid-1970s, Barry, Robin, and Maurice Gibb of Australian pop band the Bee Gees were in a creative and financial rut. Their early, Beatles-influenced pop sound infused with tightly arranged vocals had won them hits such as "New York Mining Disaster 1941" in 1967, but was no longer commercially viable. However, producer Robert Stigwood urged the brothers to try out **Barry Gibb**'s trademark falsetto on the emerging disco bandwagon. Two successful records followed: *Main Course* (1975) and *Children of the World* (1976), which included such hits as "Jive Talking" and "Nights on Broadway." But the Bee Gees didn't achieve superstar status until they composed and recorded the soundtrack for *Saturday Night Fever*, a film starring John Travolta as a Brooklynite with a dead-end job who gets his kicks on the dance floor.

The album succeeded beyond anyone's wildest dreams. In late 1977 and early 1978, the Bee Gees

had six number one hits including "How Deep is Your Love," "Staying Alive," and "Night Fever," giving them a dominance unmatched since the days of the Beatles' monopoly. "Staying Alive" represented the Bee Gees' disco peak: the arrangement swirled with dramatic strings and a heavy bass-drum beat, the lyrics told a dramatic story of urban survival, and the high-pitched harmonies gave the vocals a piercing quality that matched the staccato beat. Ultimately, the album sold over 40 million copies and became the highest-selling soundtrack in music history. The *Saturday Night Fever* soundtrack revived not only the Bee Gees' career, but also disco itself. By 1977, it appeared disco had run its course. But the combination of John Travolta, the Bee Gees, and *Saturday Night Fever* catapulted disco into the American mainstream.

KC and the Sunshine Band

Before the Bee Gees hit the charts with the *Saturday Night Fever* soundtrack, the racially integrated KC and the Sunshine Band gave disco its white face. Bandleader **Harry Wayne "KC" Casey** worked in human resources at KC records in Miami, Florida before finding his niche in music. Beginning in 1977, KC and the Sunshine

Disco's Wide Influence

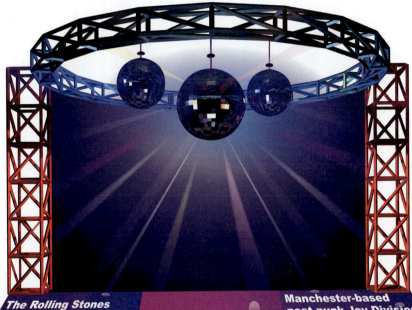

The Rolling Stones come out with a 12-inch version of "Miss You" in 1978, which takes them to the top of the charts.

Manchester-based post-punk Joy Division uses euro-disco and electronic sounds initiated by producer Giorgio Moroder.

Shortly after kissing the Sex Pistols goodbye, John Lydon's Public Image Limited, with bassist Jah Wobble, release "Death Disco," a bass-driven disco sound that will come to define post-punk.

Talking Heads strongly influenced by bass line of disco beat. Tina Weymouth's and Chris Frantz's side venture Tom Tom Club, hits the top of the R & B and disco charts in 1981.

Chic's "Good Times" is incorporated in Grandmaster Flash's and the Furious Five's 1981 rap hit, "The Adventures of Grandmaster Flash on the Wheels of Steel."

∧ Disco had a **surprising influence on conventional**
∧ **rock** in the late 1970s and early 1980s.

Trammps

Although the Trammps began as a group of R&B crooners in the early 1970s, their harmonious sound and joyful melodies captured the spirit of the disco era. Led by lead singer Jimmy Ellis, the group built on the Philly soul sound that you read about in Chapter 8, a combination of Motown, R&B, and funk. Soon, the Trammps made a pioneering crossover to disco. Their biggest hit, 1976's "Disco Inferno," shot up to number 11 on the Billboard pop charts in 1978 after being featured prominently in the film *Saturday Night Fever*. The Trammps' party-loving themes and harmonized voices brought lush vocal orchestration to the beat-driven disco sound. Although their success did not survive disco's decline, the Trammps are still remembered for adding a soulful, human element to the disco groove. Their hits "Soul Bones," "Ninety-nine and a Half," and "I Feel Like I've Been Livin' (On the Dark Side of the Moon)" figured prominently in any 1970s disco night, and *Where the Happy People Go* (1976) and *Disco Inferno* (1977) still stand as disco classics.

Band dominated the airwaves with a series of disco hits that mixed elements of funk and R&B. Their straightforward party songs, such as "Shake Shake Shake (Shake Your Booty)," "Do You Wanna Go Party," and "Boogie Shoes," became classics of the era. This last song—the group's biggest hit—got a boost from its slot on the megaplatinum *Saturday Night Fever* soundtrack.

The band's success was short but sweet. KC and the Sunshine Band racked up nine Grammy nominations and three awards, and sold millions of records, but nevertheless failed to survive the slow death of disco in the late 1970s.

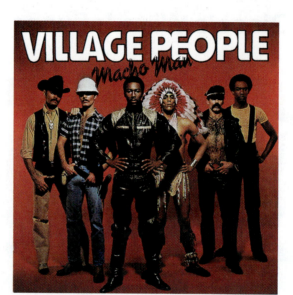

>>> **The Village People brought disco's gay subculture** to the American mainstream.

THE VILLAGE PEOPLE

Because American society largely condemned homosexuality, by the early 1970s gay men had begun to flock to establishments such as bathhouses, bars, and clubs that catered specifically to a homosexual, rather than a mainstream heterosexual, clientele. At about this time, disco culture thrived in gay nightclubs such as New York City's Sanctuary, leading to the creation of a

Flashpoints   ISSUES in ROCK   Disco vs. Rock & Roll

As disco's star rose in 1977, its influence began to infiltrate the conventional world of rock. Former Small Faces rock front man Rod Stewart embraced the era with "Do Ya Think I'm Sexy?" which shot to the top of the charts in 1979. That same year, the Grateful Dead drifted away from their usual psychedelic/country fare with the disco pulse of the title track from *Shakedown Street*, shocking many fans in the process. Even the Rolling Stones seemed to jump on the bandwagon, hitting number one in the United States for the first time in years with disco-influenced single "Miss You," on which Mick Jagger parodied Barry Gibbs' high-lead falsetto singing. However, the marriage between disco and rock & roll was not meant to last.

Many diehard rock fans were poised to strike back at disco's dominance of the airways and playlists. Chicago disc jockey **Steve Dahl** organized Disco Demolition night as part of a White Sox doubleheader at the city's **Comiskey Park** after losing his on-air slot at radio station WDAI when it took on an all-disco format. On the evening of July 12, 1979, Dahl invited baseball fans to bring unwanted disco records in exchange for a ticket price of only

98 cents. Between the games and amidst chants of "disco sucks," Dahl blew up the records. The explosion damaged the grass, and thousands of fans rushed the field, lighting fires, and starting fights. The second game of the doubleheader had to be cancelled and was ultimately forfeited. For disco haters, though, the night was a resounding success: Forces of anti-disco and rock & roll fans who had been confused by the recent musical trends had taken shape.

However, the "disco sucks!" message held a somewhat ominous undercurrent. The disco movement had briefly re-integrated white and black audiences and blurred the line between homosexual and heterosexual cultures. The **Disco Sucks** campaign, in a subversive way, rejected those postures by recruiting rock & roll's white, heterosexual audience. Although rock had a history of crossing boundaries, the anti-disco campaign encouraged listeners to return to a more segregated time when whites and blacks—and gays and straights—kept to their own music. Did Disco Demolition night really return to the basics of good old-fashioned rock & roll? Or was it instead a repudiation of all rock & roll was supposed to be?

>>> **Many consider the riots in Comiskey Park to be the end of the disco era.**

On July 21, 1979, four of Billboard's top five singles are disco hits . . .

. . . but on September 22, 1979, none are.

"Bad Girls" Donna Summer	"My Sharona" The Knack
"Ring My Bell" Anita Ward	"After the Love is Gone" Earth Wind and Fire
"Hot Stuff" Donna Summer	"The Devil Went Down to Georgia" Charlie Daniels Band
"Good Times" Chic	"Rise" Herb Alpert
"Makin' It" David Naughton	"Lead Me On" Maxine Nightingale

gay musical subculture. Founded in 1977 by composer Jacques Morali, the **Village People** targeted the gay audience with campy parodies of macho gay archetypes. Morali assembled six men to play the roles of cowboy, Native American, biker, soldier, policeman, and construction worker. When he put this motley crew in the studio, the Village People helped propel sounds of the gay clubs to a mass audience.

As the disco era was peaking in 1977 and 1978, the Village People issued a string of smash hits, including "Macho Man," "Y.M.C.A.," and "In the Navy." Their tongue-in-cheek references to gay culture were just subtle enough to attract gay audiences without endangering mass acceptance—so much so that the U.S. Navy planned to use megahit "In the Navy" in a recruiting commercial until officials realized that having a flamboyantly gay sextet singing the virtues of the Navy might be counterproductive.

WHAT WERE THE ORIGINS OF THE PUNK MOVEMENT IN AMERICAN MUSICAL CULTURE?

Punk Pre-History

Much as disco recalled the dance crazes of the early 1960s, punk rockers traced their origins to a handful of bands that were turning heads—if not selling many records—later in that decade. At the same time that many bands moved toward more elaborate, instrumentally complex formats, a smaller core of rock musicians worked to challenge the status quo with a more stripped-down, elemental sound. In Detroit, rock groups the MC5 and the Stooges fashioned a hard-edged, confrontational version of rock & roll that gained some notoriety. On the East Coast, New York City's Velvet Underground and the New York Dolls

explored interesting new directions both stylistically and artistically. In fact, these four bands were independently moving toward a shared style of rock & roll minimalism that influenced countless bands over the decades that followed.

IGGY POP AND THE STOOGES

Just a working class kid from Ypsilanti, Michigan, James Osterberg began his musical career playing drums in a garage band named the Iguanas during high school. But after watching the Doors' Jim Morrison perform at a 1967 University of Michigan show in nearby Ann

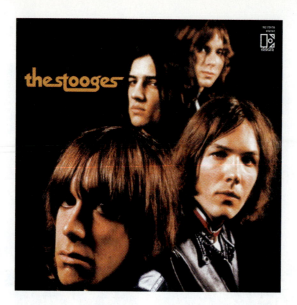

>>> The Detroit-based Stooges were a **seminal influence in American punk.**

Arbor, Osterberg decided to became a band front man. When he formed the Stooges with several other Ann Arbor friends that same year, Osterberg recreated himself as Iggy Pop: an offensive, sexually ambiguous, crowd-baiting, and weirdly charismatic rock anti-hero.

Although guitar heroes climbed into rock's stratosphere, Osterberg broke down barriers, rolling in broken glass and diving into his audience, allowing them to smear him with peanut butter and occasionally baiting them to attack him. Iggy and the Stooges deliberately offended middle-class American sensibilities with songs such as "Your Pretty Face is Going to Hell," "I Wanna Be Your Dog," "Loose," and "Down on the Street." The music itself was distorted and grindingly simplistic. With the albums *The Stooges* and *Fun House,* Stooges' guitarist Ron Asheton, drummer Scott Asheton, and bass player Dave Alexander brought a jazz-infused, R&B beat to the feedback-laden guitar sound that would, in later years, be imitated by other bands, including the Sex Pistols and Black Flag.

Collapse and Conquer

The Stooges' three records—*The Stooges* (1969), *Fun House* (1970), and *Raw Power* (1973)—remain proto-punk masterpieces, both for their in-your-face attitude and for their harsh, driving guitar work. Commercially, however, the band flopped. Prolific drug use and on-stage self-mutilation also took a toll. The Stooges' last show, recorded live in 1974 for the infamous album *Metallic KO* (released in 1977), concluded with Iggy Pop getting knocked unconscious by a bottle hurled by an angry fan. Shortly after the collapse of the Stooges, Pop put his career on hold to check himself into rehab in California. As you read in Chapter 8, an encounter with David Bowie propelled Pop to a career revival. The success of his work with Bowie reinforced Pop's place on the punk map and contributed to the lasting influence of the Stooges.

In 2003, the Stooges re-formed and began making a series of live appearances at major music festivals. Three years later, the group entered the studio for the first time in

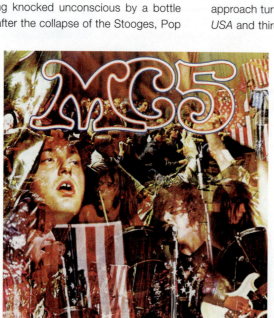

over three decades to record *The Weirdness* (2007), a still punky—if somewhat less lyrically compelling—sonic assault.

MOTOR CITY FIVE (MC5)

Fellow Michiganders, the MC5—properly the Motor City 5, a nod to their hometown of Detroit—offered a raw, full-on brand of rock & roll that later influenced bands including the Ramones, the Dead Boys, and the Heartbreakers (led by guitarist Johnny Thunders). The band earned its reputation and initial popularity for their high-speed, high-energy live rock & roll performances. Led by guitarists Fred "Sonic" Smith and Wayne Kramer, the group's two-guitar blitz also molded the later punk rock sound.

Playing in the Detroit area between 1965 and 1968, the MC5 developed a loyal local following as a live act. The chaotic but electrifying *Kick Out the Jams,* recorded at the Grandee Ballroom in Ann Arbor, Michigan, in October 1968, marked the band's recorded debut. Regarded by many rock critics as one of the genre's greatest live albums, *Kick Out the Jams* cracked the Billboard Top 30 in 1968 despite the refusal of some national retailers to stock the album because of its potentially offensive lyrics.

The MC5 was as uncompromising politically as they were artistically. Band manager John Sinclair, a political ally of Black Panther Huey Newton and founder of his own militant White Panther party, informed the group's controversial leftist political agenda. In the summer of 1968, the MC5 made a stir by playing in Chicago prior to the Democratic convention riots. Sinclair—under constant surveillance by federal agents—was eventually arrested and jailed for two years after offering two joints to a federal agent. Recorded without Sinclair's influence, the group's second album, *Back in the USA* (1970), has been celebrated as a pioneering hard-rock album. Its full-throttle guitar approach turned the MC5 into punk icons. However, both *Back in the USA* and third album *High Time* failed to live up to *Kick Out the Jams* commercially. After a farewell show at Detroit's Grandee Ballroom, the MC5 disbanded in 1972. Just five years later, many New York and London punk bands credited the MC5 as originators of the punk sound.

THE VELVET UNDERGROUND

As you read in Chapter 8, New York City's Velvet Underground pioneered a new brand of rock & roll: urban punk. In a marked departure from the popular

<<< **MC5 pioneered the punk rock sound** with albums like 1968's *Kick Out the Jams.*

sounds of the late 1960s, the Velvet Underground explored a bleak realism on their seminal debut, *Velvet Underground and Nico* (1967). Later punk artists drew inspiration from the group and its at times noisy, experimental work. Equally, by showing that bands could break new barriers artistically while still working within their own musical limitations, the Velvet Underground contributed to the punk aesthetic. German-born chanteuse Nico had a notoriously unmelodic singing voice, and Lou Reed was no Robert Plant. However, despite a limited vocal range, Reed employed one of the most distinctive, emotionally gripping voices in rock & roll. Guitarist John Cale, meanwhile, was not a virtuoso in the traditional sense. Instead of focusing on wailing solos, he used jarring dissonance to create a texture and background for the Velvet Underground's voice.

THE NEW YORK DOLLS

In their short, fast life, the New York Dolls brought a sense of style to proto-punk rock. Their music offered a somewhat accelerated—and louder—version of the Rolling Stones. Much like the MC5, however, what attracted attention was the group's live act. Singer David Johansen and band members Sylvain Sylvain, Johnny Thunders, Jerry Nolan, and Billy Murcia all appeared on stage

∧
∧ With their bizarre sense of
∧ style, the **New York Dolls**
would inspire later punks to use
clothes as a way of **offending
mainstream rock & roll tastes.**

wearing lipstick, wigs, platform shoes, fetish clothing, and anything else they could pick up at bargain-basement clothing stores or Salvation Army sales. In 1974, though, that marketing strategy did little for business. After just two albums—*New York Dolls* (1973) and *Too Much Too Soon* (1974)—Mercury Records dropped the band.

However, this theatricality did attract the attention of future Sex Pistols manager Malcolm McLaren, who helped the band organize shows in 1975. McLaren's efforts to re-energize the group ultimately fell flat. The New York Dolls broke up in 1975 and now rest comfortably in the pantheon of punk legends.

Singer David Johansen left the Dolls for an eclectic solo career that would take him from R&B to composing to the world of lounge music, scoring a Billboard Hot 100 hit with 1987's dance hit "Hot, Hot, Hot" under the pseudonym Buster Poindexter. Guitarist Johnny Thunders went on to form 1970s punk act the Heartbreakers before dying of a heroin overdose in 1991. Although McLaren's relationship with the Dolls was brief, its legacy was longer-lasting: the band's knack for attracting attention and audiences while spitting in the face of commonly accepted good taste inspired McLaren to form the Sex Pistols, as well as dozens of other punk bands in the emerging London scene.

ROCK PEOPLE

Patti Smith

Poet, punk, playwright, novelist, and mother, Patti Smith could have been tagged as the Bob Dylan of New York City's underground music movement. After dropping out of New Jersey's Glassboro State Teacher's College in 1967, Smith headed to New York City. There, she immediately began to develop artistic partnerships and personal relationships with such cultural figures as photographer Robert Mapplethorpe and playwright Sam Shepherd, with whom she co-wrote the play *Cowboy Mouth*. Her first single, "Hey Joe," combined spoken word poetry with hard-edged rock & roll, while B-side "Piss Factory" described Smith's own experiences working on an assembly line as a college student.

The tension between rock and poetry continued to provide material for Smith. Her John Cale-produced 1975 debut,

Horses, included some of punk's founding statements. Ranked number 44 on *Rolling Stone*'s 500 greatest albums of all time, *Horses* featured guitarist Tom Verlaine and infused punk with a memorable, politically outspoken, feminist voice. *Radio Ethiopia* (1976) and *Easter* (1978) followed, bringing Smith from the world of punk to the mainstream. *Easter's* "Because the Night," co-written with Bruce Springsteen, scored Smith a number 13 on the Billboard Hot 100 chart. But Smith's increased popularity never made her any less politically outspoken. Smith has backed the Green Party, protested the Iraq War, and provided the soundtrack for Barack Obama's 2008 Campaign for Change in the form of the song "People Have the Power."

WHERE DID PUNK BEGIN?

New York City

In the history of punk rock, rock venue CBGB has the iconic status that, say, Sun Records might have for early rock & rollers. This legendary—if low-rent—venue in lower Manhattan became a creative nexus for local bands throughout the 1970s. For example, when punk icon Patti Smith came to New York City in 1974 as an unwed mother and poet with a desire to sing, CBGB offered her the chance that few others would. In Chapter 10, you will learn more about CBGB's influence on the New York scene.

THE RAMONES

While Patti Smith offered Bob Dylan-style punk-rock lyricism, the **Ramones'** anthems ultimately defined 1970s New York punk music. The band itself had neither the auspicious art world credentials of the Velvet Underground or Patti Smith, nor their lyrical subtlety. In fact, their backgrounds diverged greatly; rather than art school dropouts, the Ramones were high school dropouts from Forest Hills, Queens, New York. Their original lineup—all of whom adopted the surname Ramone—included bassist Dee Dee Ramone, guitarist Johnny Ramone, vocalist Joey Ramone, and drummer Tommy Ramone.

The American Mini-Invasion, 1976–1977: Proto-Punk American Bands Cross the Atlantic

Group	Hometown	Style	Influence on Punk
The Ramones	New York City	Speed.	Other bands were suddenly playing their songs much faster.
Iggy Pop	Detroit	Frontman attitude.	Model for Johnny Rotten and other British punks.
Johnny Thunders and the Heartbreakers	New York City	Drugs. Johnny Thunders had his guitar style and lifestyle.	Heroin use spreads among British punks.
Wayne County and the Electric Chairs	New York City	Transexuality and androgyny.	Broke through the remaining taboos in punk music.

∧∧ American proto-punk bands strongly influenced the British punk scene.

Hey, Ho, Let's Go!

Their pioneering sound relied on three simple elements: a roaring but melodic blast of distorted guitar, Joey's whining vocals, and rapid-fire drumming. Without much in the way of solos or rhythm shifts, the songs clocked in at two minutes or less. However, this simplicity belied a subtle, strategic musical theory that might not be apparent at first listen. The Ramones believed that they were giving audiences what they really wanted out of rock & roll: a simple, fast beat, and a few words that they could chant along with. As rock stripped of all pretensions, it was a direct challenge to the intense musical complexity and heroic guitarists that dominated arena rock.

The formula worked brilliantly. The Ramones became the first New York punk band to get a recording contract, signing with Sire Records in 1975. Their 14-song debut includes such classics as "Blitzkrieg Bop," "Beat on the Brat," and "Now I Wanna Sniff Some Glue." Less offensive than playfully nonsensical, the album jammed all 14 tracks into only 30 minutes. Endless touring—including a trip to England in 1976—spread the word that primal, fast-forwarded rock & roll had a wide appeal.

The 1980s and Beyond

Unlike many of their contemporaries, the Ramones flirted with commercial success. Later records such as *Rocket to Russia* (1977) drew inspiration from bubblegum pop and surf rock. Songs like "Rockaway Beach" maintained the band's trademark speed, but softened their overall sound with harmonious guitar sounds and less abrasive lyrics. In 1980, the Ramones attracted the attention of producer Phil Spector, who had crafted his famous "wall of sound" to back up groups including the Supremes and the Beatles. Ensuing collaborative effort *End of the Century* peaked at number 44 on the *Billboard* charts in punk's biggest bid for the mainstream.

But the attempt to move toward the pop market was ultimately futile, and the Ramones proceeded to initiate another unfortunate practice that would become a tradition for aging punk legends: They toured relentlessly for two decades and put out a string of increasingly formulaic albums. Finally, they called it quits in 1995 with *Adios Amigos*.

London

In Great Britain, punk rock's roots were economic and artistic. London in 1975 simmered with discontent—and with good reason. High unemployment and an entrenched class system left many unconnected youth with little but dead-end jobs to aspire to. If the Beatles had offered distraction in 1964, then this 1970s generation was looking for something more elemental—a way of getting back at the society that had left them in the lurch. **Pub rock** bands powered by R&B energies that had sprung up around the city had offered some consolation, but with the advent of punk rock, the fire really started.

THE SEX PISTOLS

The story of the Sex Pistols begins in the King's Road boutique SEX, a purveyor of bondage gear and toys. Owner Malcolm McLaren was an aspiring band manager—the same Malcolm McLaren who had briefly established a relationship with the New York Dolls in New York City during their chaotic final year. He returned from New York with little to show for his efforts other than creative inspiration from the outrageous, cross-dressing affront to good taste that the Dolls represented. In 1974, he set up shop in London's Chelsea neighborhood with partner and famed punk fashion designer Vivienne Westwood. There, he saw a small but growing crowd of young, disaffected kids who were more than willing to extend their middle fingers in the direction of the self-satisfied, class-conscious British mind-set.

Enter Johnny Rotten

When McLaren noticed a young malcontent with rotten teeth named **John Lydon** hanging around the jukebox at his store, he knew he had spied the perfect front man. A trio of musicians including guitarist Steve Jones, drummer Steve Cook, and bass player Glen Matlock needed a singer, and the 19 year-old Lydon, wearing a T-shirt scribbled with the words "I Hate" written across the Pink Floyd emblem, passed his one-song audition—a version of Alice Cooper's "Eighteen"—with flying colors. McLaren decided that Lydon's grubby, snarling charisma suited the band perfectly. Lydon adopted the moniker "Johnny Rotten," and the rest is rock & roll history.

The Sound and the Fury

After a chaotic opening concert at St. Martin's School of Art, the Sex Pistols' reputation spread quickly. Rotten's venomous, electrifying performances struck a chord with audiences looking for an outlet for their anger. The message spread, and through the long hot summer of 1976, bands began sprouting up like weeds. Imagination and passion trumped talent as essential ingredients in punk rock. For the moment, boundaries of good taste and propriety had been broken down. As local magazine *Sniffin' Glue* laid out the magic formula: "This is a chord. This is another. This is a third. Now form a band." This message defiantly challenged the generation of guitar gods and megagroups that had come to dominate rock & roll.

> **The Ramones'** stripped-down rock & roll, with it's simple lyrics and blistering tempo, **defined New York punk.**

Winterland and After

Essentially banned from performing in their home country, the Sex Pistols set out to conquer the United States. By the time McLaren had lined up a U.S. tour, however, the band was disintegrating. After the final, disastrous show at San Francisco's **Winterland Palace**, the Sex Pistols finally imploded. Jones and Cook accompanied McLaren to Brazil to record a few songs with notorious British train robber Ronald Biggs, and bassist Sid Vicious settled in New York City's Chelsea Hotel with girlfriend Nancy Spungen. In New York, Vicious recorded one single, a haunting version of Frank Sinatra's "My Way." However, Spungen was soon found stabbed to death at the Chelsea, and Vicious was accused of manslaughter. Briefly imprisoned and then released on bail, Vicious died of a heroin overdose before he could stand trial. Meanwhile, Johnny Rotten returned to London where he once again assumed his birth name, John Lydon, and proclaimed that punk was dead.

After releasing the single "Anarchy in the U.K.," the four Sex Pistols made their television debut on *Today,* a respectable British evening interview show hosted by middle-aged announcer Bill Grundy. When Grundy pressed the Sex Pistols to live up to their reputation, they didn't disappoint, with guitarist Jones hurling a few choice epithets in Grundy's direction. The response was immediate and overwhelming. The following morning's headlines screamed about this new breed of foul-mouthed youth. But, by now, the Sex Pistols and McLaren were on a roll. Follow-up single "God Save the Queen," a mockery of British royalty, coincided with Queen Elizabeth II's 25th anniversary on the throne in an all-out declaration of war on British sensibilities. Despite being banned by the BBC, the single shot to number two in the pop charts. Banning proved to be a common way of dealing with the Sex Pistols; by mid-1977, all but a few British clubs had outlawed the band.

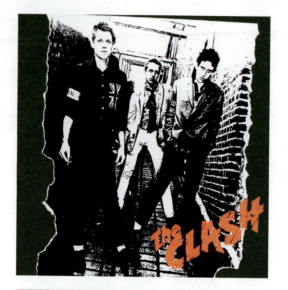

∧
∧ The Clash's politically charged
∧ lyrics set them apart from the other bands of the UK punk scene.

THE CLASH

If the Sex Pistols were harbingers of the end of rock & roll, then the **Clash** claimed boldly that they were the beginning of an era. Musically and politically brash, they

CLASSIC RECORDINGS ▶▶▶

NEVER MIND THE BOLLOCKS, HERE'S THE SEX PISTOLS
by the Sex Pistols

The Sex Pistols' debut album flaunts its bad manners, right down to its florescent pink cover and cutout lettering, a declaration of the band's primitive aesthetic. But over 30 years after its release, *Never Mind the Bollocks* stands the test of time as one of punk's true masterpieces. Despite the fact that guitarist Steve Jones and drummer Paul Cook revel in their amateur status, the work on this record is a tightly contained and executed whole. Certainly, Jones wasn't a guitar virtuoso by any traditional definition, but he and Cook managed to create a tightly controlled explosion of sound that could stop and start on a dime as Glen Matlock—who played bass on the album despite having already been replaced by Sid Vicious as the band's bassist—offered a surprisingly melodic counterpart.

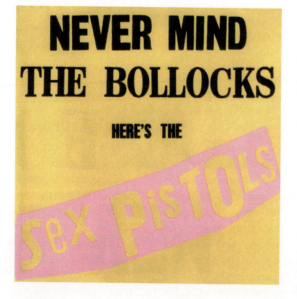

The opening chords of "Holidays in the Sun" hang for a moment before precisely clicking into gear. The song "Bodies" tumbles into overdrive, then pauses for a suspenseful moment before suddenly ramping up again. The guitar solo and minor chord structure of seminal single "Anarchy in the U.K." lend the song a mocking triumphalism particularly apt for its snarling derision.

Producer Chris Thomas attested that the album's recording was neither as raw nor as rushed as is popularly believed. Instead, it was carefully built on a wall of sound, layered with guitar riffs to offer the perfect backdrop to Rotten's snarling, sneering cry to chaos. Although the Sex Pistols are frequently spoken of in terms of their rush to self-destruction, *Never Mind the Bollocks* proves that they had musically coalesced.

TOP OF THE CHARTS
WHAT'S HOT!
APRIL 1, 1978

1. "Night Fever" – the Bee Gees
2. "Stayin' Alive" – the Bee Gees
3. "Lay Down Sally" – Eric Clapton
4. "Can't Smile Without You" – Barry Manilow
5. "Emotion" – Samantha Sang
6. "If I Can't Have You" – Yvonne Elliman
7. "I Go Crazy" – Paul Davis
8. "Love" – Andy Gibb
9. "Thunder Island" – Jay Ferguson
10. "Dust in the Wind" – Kansas

boundaries. A cover of reggae song "Police & Thieves," one of their early singles, firmly set the Clash apart in the punk rock movement.

Commercially, the Clash were by far the most successful of London's generation of punk bands. Their self-titled debut album won them a $200,000 advance from major label CBS. (The Sex Pistols, in their first contract with EMI, had reportedly been offered a comparably paltry $70,000.) Although *The Clash* entered the British charts at number 12, Columbia initially declined to distribute the album in the United States because it was too "crude." However, *The Clash* became immediately popular in the U.S. underground, selling over 100,000 copies as an import. When Columbia eventually did market the album in 1979, it went gold in the United States.

London Calling's New Sound

While the Sex Pistols and the British punk scene imploded, the Clash continued to expand its reach. The group's second album *Give 'Em Enough Rope* received only moderate response, but the Clash roared back with 1979 double album *London Calling*. An eclectic combination of pop and rock & roll styling, *London Calling* signaled the Clash's permanent departure from the world of punk in favor of rock & roll. The group's musical departure can be readily heard on opening track, rockabilly (a hybrid of country and rock) standard "Brand New Cadillac," while "Rudie Can't Fail" employs a horn section. Rising politicization informed many of the album's best-known songs. "London Calling" addresses themes such as unemployment, nuclear accidents, and rising drug use, and "Clampdown" is a call to arms against the forces of the status quo. "Lost in the Supermarket" bemoans continued poverty in an age of wealth. These richly themed songs and their instrumental textures inspired *Rolling Stone* to hail *London Calling* as one of the decade's best albums.

Followup album *Sandinista!* (1980) sprawled over three records with a more experimental, widely ranging view. The album was deliberately noncommercial, and the group itself had to make up for lost profits by paying back funds from royalties and tour support. Despite their leftist politics, the Clash moved farther into rock's mainstream. The 1982 dance number "Rock the Casbah" became an MTV hit, reaching number eight on the Billboard charts. The Clash toured with the Who, and their next album, *Combat Rock*, incorporated newer forms of music including funk and rap. This increasingly eclectic nature may have endeared the group to critics, but it ultimately cost the Clash its fan base. Internal rifts ensued. Joe Strummer fired Mick Jones in 1983, and the band disbanded entirely in 1986 after releasing a fourth album, *Cut the Crap*.

used their punk rock credentials not only to strip the sound down, but also to head in directions that confounded even their early admirers. In 1976, 23-year-old Joe Strummer (whose real name was John Mellor) was impressed by a Sex Pistols show when they opened for his band, the 101ers. Inspired by this new musical sound, Strummer, the son of an English diplomat, left the 101ers and formed the edgier, punkier Clash with fellow Londoners Mick Jones, Paul Simonon, and Tory Chimes.

Punk Pioneers

The Clash rode the same wave of punk feeling as the Sex Pistols, albeit with a different brand of sound and fury. However, the two groups spoke to the same audience; in fact, the Clash played its first gig with the Sex Pistols in July 1976, and later opened for them on the *Anarchy in the U.K.* tour. Although songs such as "White Riot" or "1977" with the high-amped guitar and fast, powerful delivery are easily tabbed as punk, the Clash from the beginning looked for inspiration outside punk's

HOW DID NEW WAVE EMERGE FROM THE DEATH OF PUNK?

New Wave Rears Its Head

Although the terms "New Wave" and "punk" had been synonymous in the London of 1976 and 1977, as punk began to peter out as a creative force, "New Wave" began increasingly to be identified with those who moved on—or moved to—a more commercial sound. Once it became its own segment of the rock scene in the late 1970s, the "New Wave" label could be credibly applied to a diverse mixture of music that was coming from both England and the United States. Artists such as British pub rocker Elvis Costello radiated some of Johnny Rotten's in-

your-face qualities, but also incorporated the pop sensibilities of Buddy Holly. Soon, Costello became associated with the more pop-driven sound that epitomized New Wave. Chapter 10 will explore the New Wave movement in greater depth.

PUBLIC IMAGE LIMITED

One of the first musicians to publicly break with punk was ironically enough the king of punk himself: John Lydon. Feeling that he had painted himself into a corner artistically as punk rocker Johnny

MY AIM IS TRUE by Elvis Costello

When Elvis Costello's *My Aim is True* came out in Great Britain in 1977, no one was sure what to make of it. Unquestionably, it was punk—or at least so declared the cover with its mean-looking, spiky haired guitar player wielding his ax like a machine gun. And equally, the audacity was pure punk; after all, not many rock & rollers have the guts to name themselves after the King of Rock & Roll.

Hard-driving music aside, Costello was almost audaciously comfortable breaking through punk into a new genre. The lyrics had traces of dark, mordant humor and a certain complexity that seemed to set the album at odds with

the punk movement. The darkly themed "Alison" is about shooting a girlfriend out of love for her, while "Mystery Dance" addresses premature ejaculation, not one of rock's most recurring themes—and a distinct shift from the reggae-infused challenge to Britain's right wing Nationalist Party, "Less than Zero." Creepy track "Watching the Detectives" pulls on a funky, keyboard-driven sound.

Critics wanted to call Costello punk, but found that *My Aim is True* pushed the boundaries of the genre's tail end in a way that made it something new. In fact, the album signaled the beginning of a career of a musician who, after 30 years, has never let himself be defined by any genre.

Rotten, Lydon did a U-turn and directed his iconoclastic streak against punk rock itself. As opposed to taunting rock & roll fans as in the past, Lydon's enemy of choice became the by-then status quo of punk rock.

By the end of 1978 and only a few months after the demise of the Sex Pistols, Lydon had formed a new band with Keith Levene and Jah Wobble. The trio originally considered the name Carnivorous Buttock Flies, but instead settled on Public Image Limited. The "Limited" was a conscious attempt to erase all vestiges of the Sex Pistols from his new career. Public Image Ltd. was not just a band, but also a business.

Distributed in film containers with three 12-inch singles, Public Image Ltd.'s second album, *Metal Box,* proved to be its seminal release. Despite the difficulties this packaging decision caused for the record companies and distributors, the album itself became a dominant foundation for the emerging New Wave sound. With Wobble's low-pitched, reggae-influenced bass, Levene's snarling guitar, and Lydon's somewhat echoing vocals, the album displayed a musical form that was at once challenging and danceable. After *Metal Box,* the band members went their separate ways, and Lydon turned his company into a one-person project.

GANG OF FOUR

With a dissonant, funk-driven musical form that managed to impress critics and win spins at rock clubs, Britain's Gang of Four came together in Leeds, England, in 1977. By turns cerebral—espousing a militant Maoist ideology—and visceral, the group produced a pounding, beat-driven sound anchored by the layered, distortion-driven atonality of guitarist Andy Gill. Instead of recalling stadium rock solos or even the bracing chords of the Sex Pistols, Gill's guitar line entered and left at will. Singer Jon King had a dry,

equally tuneless style that floated above the rhythm rather than simply engaging it.

Their first album *Damaged Goods* became a hit in England, and their next, *Entertainment!*, introduced them to a small but admiring U.S. audience. Such songs as "Your Love is Like Anthrax" and "To Hell with Poverty" challenged the audience with uncompromising politics. Although the Gang of Four came in at the tail end of punk, they were elemental to the fusion of black and white music that characterized later progressive rock. After several personnel changes, Gang of Four ended their short-lived career in 1983. However, their combination of metal and staccato riffs with funk and reggae beats influenced later bands including the Red Hot Chili Peppers and even 1980s punk rockers Fugazi.

X-RAY SPEX

Propelled by the tunelessly raw scream of teenage vocalist Poly Styrene, X-Ray Spex laid out a feminist message on first single "Oh Bondage Up Yours." The energetic, visceral song became a punk anthem and a rallying cry against the victimization of women. The full-length effort *Germ Free Adolescents* (1978) found Styrene exuberantly shouting her anti-consumerist lyrics over a punk rock sound explosion, with Rudi Thompson's saxophone wailing a melody over Jak Airport's distorted guitar and Paul Dean and B.P. Hurding's thrashing rhythms. Although Styrene soon left the group, ending X-Ray Spex's career, the seminal *Germ Free Adolescents* remains one of punk rock's most respected and influential albums.

THE SLITS

The **Slits** had a beginning not all that different from that of the X-Ray Spex. Jumping on the punk bandwagon in 1976, the group—fronted by 14-year-old singer Arianna Foster, or "Ari Up," won some notoriety when they toured with the Clash during the 1977 British *White Riot* tour. By the time their first album, *Cut*, debuted in 1979, their sound had moved from punk to a more polished, reggae-driven, and experimental sound. One of the most powerful feminist voices to arise from the postpunk era, the Slits enjoyed a brief career before disbanding for over 20 years. The group reformed with some of its original members in 2005.

THE AU PAIRS

Formed in Birmingham in 1978, the Au Pairs—vocalist/guitarist Lesley Woods, guitarist Paul Moad, bassist Jane Munro, and drummer Peter Hammond—equally employed postpunk's New Wave sound to approach and even deconstruct the world from a feminist viewpoint. Like the Gang of Four, their music was danceable; however, the dissonant guitar and occasionally hectoring vocals never lost their edge. Their first album, *Playing With a Different Sex* (1981), delivered classic postpunk rock while dismantling some of the assumptions about sexual relationships. On their next album, *Sense and Sensuality* (1982), the Au Pairs started to tinker with jazz and even disco. But by 1983, the band found themselves lacking a clear musical direction and broke up. However, their influence lived on: outspoken front woman Woods later inspired the bands of what would be called the "riot grrrl" movement in the United States. (You will learn more about this movement in Chapter 12.)

JOY DIVISION

Manchester band **Joy Division**, with their sorrowful but danceable sound, became one of British postpunk's best-known acts in the United States. Formed in 1976 after watching a Sex Pistols gig in

Manchester, Joy Division developed a sound rooted in the Velvet Underground's monotonous, sometimes droning beats. Named after the prostitutes' wing of Nazi concentration camps, Joy Division found a memorable front man in Ian Curtis, a charismatic melancholic whose gloomy lyrical quality drew on such influences as Jim Morrison and Iggy Pop.

After releasing two albums, 1979's *Unknown Pleasures* and 1980's *Closer*, Joy Division encountered both success and tragedy. With a U.S. tour on the horizon and the single "Love Will Tear Us Apart" recently recorded, Curtis' inner demons overtook him, and he hanged himself. Although Curtis' death brought about the end of Joy Division, "Love Will Tear Us Apart" rose to number 13 on the British charts, and Curtis, with his inimitable post-punk baritone, earned a place in the pantheon of dead rock stars. Remaining Joy Division members Bernard (Albrecht) Sumner, Peter Hook, and Stephen Morris teamed up with keyboardist Gillian Gilbert to form postpunk dance act New Order.

THE JAM

Another English band that started with the punks, the Jam successfully reached the rarified atmosphere of stardom. The Jam formed in 1975 with singer Paul Weller, bassist Bruce Foxton, and drummer Rick Butler. Dressed in sharp suits and ties, the Jam loudly reinterpreted the smooth rhythms of 1960s American R&B blended with the thrashing, energetic rock sounds of the Who. Although the group's 1977 debut, *In the City*, took only 11 days to record, two songs—"In the City" and "All Around the World"—broke the top 40 of the British charts. Followup effort *This is the Modern World* (1977) also graced the upper reaches of the charts.

As the band matured, Weller's increasingly narrative, complex songwriting found greater expression through hook-driven songs that maintained punk's sharp attitude while easing into a more melodic sound. Hits such as "That's Entertainment" presented Weller's tuneful, descriptive lyrics crooned over rhythmically strummed acoustic guitar riffs, while "Town Called Malice" reinterpreted the soul beats of the

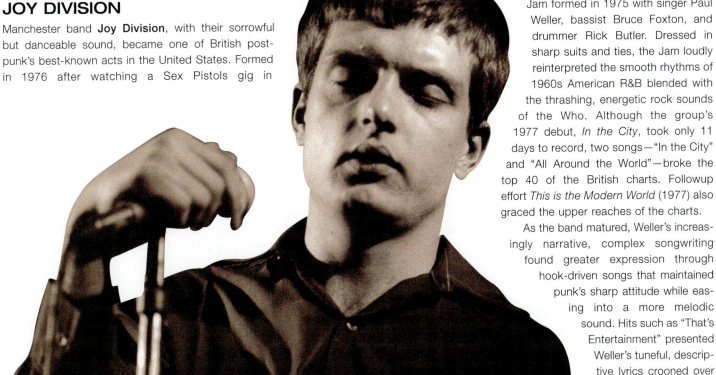

∧ ∧ ∧ Ian Curtis's bleak lyrics reflected **the Joy Division frontman's deep depression** in the years preceding his suicide.

In 1976, despite their rebellious, anti-authoritarian stance, bands such as the Clash and the Sex Pistols made their debuts on major labels. Rather than selling out, they were simply following the conventional wisdom of the era: For all their flaws, major labels were the best at distributing and producing records.

In January 1977, however, Buzzcocks singer Pete Shelly decided to go independent. Borrowing several hundred pounds from his father, Shelly recorded the Buzzcocks' debut EP *Spiral Scratch* for his own New Hormones record label. (You will learn more about this band in Chapter 10.) In an effort to demystify the entire recording process, the EP's liner notes contained an extended account of the production itself. Soon, the first 1,000 copies sold out. Later, through mail order distribution, the band managed to sell an impressive 18,000 copies. Although the Buzzcocks eventually signed with a major label as well, this do-it-yourself (DIY) approach to recording technology and distribution characterized the genre's enduring independence and started an indie revolution that long outlasted the punk era.

DIY went beyond self-producing records, however. Punk rock declared that anyone could be a musician or singer, regardless of so-called "talent." In the wake of big, professional rock bands, punk roared with minimally trained instrumentalists and singers whose voices were anything but refined. DIY extended to the band's stage fashion and make-up—many groups drew on the Salvation Army and other thrift stores for their clothing—and posters and flyers that resembled ransom notes. Punk rock was about returning music to the people and showing fans that anyone could be a star.

1960s for contemporary listeners. After the Jam disbanded in 1983, Weller embarked on a successful solo career marked by more popular hits.

TOM VERLAINE, RICHARD HELL, AND TELEVISION

Born Thomas Miller in Delaware in 1949, guitarist Tom Verlaine took his stage name in honor of French Symbolist poet Paul Verlaine. Although trained as a classical pianist, Verlaine turned his attention to rock & roll after hearing the Rolling Stones' "Nineteenth Nervous Breakdown." After moving to New York City in the late 1960s, Verlaine started his musical career when he and Lexington, Kentucky-bred bassist Richard Hell formed the Neon Boys. In 1973, the group expanded to include guitarist Richard Lloyd and took the name Television. As this band began to gather an underground following, Verlaine persuaded New York club CBGB to allow live bands to play. Frustrated by the band's direction, Hell left Television in 1975, initially joining forces with ex-New York Doll Johnny Thunders in the Heartbreakers before founding his own noteworthy group, Richard Hell & the Voidoids.

Television, however, soldiered on and in 1977 released the seminal punk album *Marquee Moon*. Although not a commercial success, the album remains recognized as a rock classic. With numbers such as "See No Evil" and title track, Verlaine's soundscapes blazed a trail for punk and post-punk rockers. After a disappointing second album, *Adventure*, Television disbanded in 1978 and Verlaine started a solo career, releasing albums including 1981's *Dreamtime* and 1987's *Flash Light*.

Throughout his career, Verlaine contributed to the wider music scene. In 1975, for example, he played guitar on Patti Smith's "Piss Factory." Although Verlaine never achieved marked commercial success, he is recognized as one of punk's truly great guitarists. Ever eclectic, Verlaine has sought inspiration in the sounds of jazz as well as those of rock & roll. His sharp guitar licks with lyrical, winding leads brought an edge and complexity to rock & roll music that influenced rock & roll guitarists for decades afterward. You will read more about his contributions to the development of New Wave in Chapter 10.

New Wave Goes Full Circle

By the early 1980s, the disco-punk era had gone full circle. Disco was dead. Punk, at least the English variety, had all but died out. In the United States, a commercially viable version of New Wave was emerging. The performers were idiosyncratic and quirky. But the music itself hearkened back to both disco and punk. Synth pop and dance pop were right around the corner, waiting to beckon a new generation of dance floor dwellers, and postpunk stood ready to pick up the shattered pieces of rock left in the wake of punk's destructive force.

Notable Postpunk and New Wave Bands, 1977–1981

Band	Sound	Notable Album
Public Image Ltd.	Low-pitched, reggae-influenced bass, snarling guitar, and echoing vocals	*Metal Box* (1979)
Gang of Four	Combination of metal and staccato riffs with funk and reggae beats	*Entertainment* (1979)
X-Ray Spex	Exuberant punk rock vocals, wailing saxophones, distorted guitars, and thrashing rhythms	*Germ Free Adolescents* (1978)
The Slits	Experimental, reggae-influenced postpunk	*Cut* (1979)
The Au Pairs	Postpunk rock with hectoring vocals and dissonant guitars	*Playing With a Different Sex* (1981)
Joy Division	Gloomy baritone vocals, droning beats	*Closer* (1980)
The Jam	Hook-driven songs with punk's attitude and energetic rock melodies	*This is the Modern World* (1977)
Television	Energetic, jazz-inspired guitar rock	*Marquee Moon* (1977)

∧
∧ As punk died out, a new wave of postpunk rockers
∧ emerged in the late 1970s and early 1980s.

Summary

HOW DID DISCO CHANGE THE MUSIC SCENE DURING THE 1970s?   152

● Disco was as much a social as a musical force. It was rooted in the culture of the 1970s and in night-clubs such as Studio 54. When disco entered the marketplace, it challenged some of the basic assumptions of rock & roll by returning to the dance floor. Musically, disco was orchestrated in a way that rock & roll wasn't. Producers such as Giorgio Moroder, who used electronic synthesizers and drum machines along with layered vocals to create an all-around effect, crafted the sound.

● Donna Summer was the pioneering vocalist of the disco era. The groups Chic, Trammps, The Village People, and KC and the Sunshine Band also helped bring disco into the mainstream. The *Saturday Night Fever* soundtrack played a major part in popularizing the disco movement in the United States.

● With the "Disco sucks" movement, rock & roll struck back at disco, creating a backlash against the diversity of disco and its listeners.

WHAT WERE THE ORIGINS OF THE PUNK MOVEMENT IN AMERICAN MUSICAL CULTURE?   157

● Several late 1960s bands were formative in their attempts to return to a stripped-down, more emotionally resonant brand of rock & roll. These bands included the Stooges, MC5, the Velvet Underground, and the New York Dolls.

WHERE DID PUNK BEGIN?   160

● Punk began to flourish in the artistically active atmosphere of 1970s New York City.

● Patti Smith was "punk's Bob Dylan" who mixed her eclectic musical taste with poetry to create seminal punk album *Horses*. The Ramones brought an enlightened primitivism to punk, stripping chords and lyrics down to an essential two-minute roar. They never reached the top of the charts, but their songs were essential to the form of the music.

● Punk came to England in the mid-70s. Heavily influenced by some of the formative U.S. bands, the punk movement was also a response to the troubled economic and social atmosphere of mid-70s Britain. Formed by Malcolm McLaren, The Sex Pistols had an anti-authority, pro-anarchy stance that provoked much reaction in England. After the group dissolved in 1978, Johnny Rotten claimed that punk was dead. However, the Clash took a different approach. Their music, including the popular album *London Calling*, embraced different styles as well as a leftist political approach.

HOW DID NEW WAVE EMERGE FROM THE DEATH OF PUNK?   163

● With the end of punk, a new wave of rock & rollers was born. Some of them were deliberately experimental, while others created more accessible music than punk and tried to infuse traditional pop with punk energy.

● John Lydon's Public Image Limited broke with punk, taking cues from disco and dub to create a haunting, industrial sound that would influence many of the no-wave bands of the 1980s.

● The Gang of Four became known for atonal, politically charged songs such as "To Hell with Poverty." Bands including The Slits and X-Ray Spex added an important female voice to New Wave. The Au Pairs and Joy Division were part of Manchester's industrial music scene. The Buzzcocks had an interesting mix of punk and pop elements that got radio airtime in England, even though their success was limited in the United States. Tom Verlaine's band Television, best known for the classic *Marquee Moon*, set the stage for American New Wave.

Key Terms

Sex Pistols British band that was one of the most influential groups in the punk movement   *152*

Moog Synthesizer digital keyboard used to create background for disco hits   *153*

"The Hustle" partner dance that became popular during the disco era and was featured prominently in *Saturday Night Fever*   *153*

Studio 54 famous Manhattan dance club that became the center of disco culture in the late 1970s   *153*

Donna Summer American singer who came to prominence during the disco era   *153*

Chic one of disco's most influential bands with hits including "Le Freak" and "Good Times"   *154*

Barry White R&B crooner, sex symbol, and songwriter whose recordings were influential during the disco era   *154*

Me Decade nickname given to the 1970s by writer Tom Wolfe that came to characterize the self-absorption and hedonism of the era   *154*

Barry Gibb lead singer for the Bee Gees whose trademark falsetto gave the group their distinctive sound   *155*

Harry Wayne "KC" Casey disco composer and singer of Top 10 hits including "Boogie Shoes" and "Shake Shake Shake (Shake Your Booty)"   *155*

Steve Dahl Chicago DJ who organized the Disco Demolition night at Chicago's Comiskey Park   *156*

Comiskey Park 1970s home of the Chicago White Sox and site of Disco Demolition Night   *156*

Disco Sucks anti-disco campaign that led the backlash against disco in 1979   *156*

Village People concept disco band 1970s that released hits including "Macho Man," "In the Navy," and "Y.M.C.A."   *156*

The Ramones quartet from Queens that created the template for short, fast punk rock songs *160*

pub rock back-to-basics rock movement that drew on country and blues influences and paved the way for punk, postpunk, and New Wave in the United Kingdom *161*

John Lydon singer for The Sex Pistols and later Public Image Limited who took the stage name Johnny Rotten *161*

Winterland Palace San Francisco concert hall where the Sex Pistols played their last show in January 1978 *162*

The Clash musically and politically brash British punk rockers *162*

The Slits all-female punk group led by 14-year-old singer Arianna Foster *164*

Joy Division British postpunk band featuring the somber lyrics and baritone vocals of troubled frontman Ian Curtis *165*

Sample Test Questions

1. Which American artist was known as the "Queen of Disco"?
   a. Robin Gibb
   b. Donna Summer
   c. Gloria Gaynor
   d. Patti Smith

2. Which of these factors did NOT contribute to rise of disco?
   a. the increasing popularity of dance clubs
   b. the development of computerized music
   c. the release of *Saturday Night Fever*
   d. the disbandment of the Beatles

3. Which of these statements is correct?
   a. Disco was primarily influenced by heavy metal.
   b. Elvis Costello emerged at about the same time as the Sex Pistols.
   c. The Clash's first record was a best seller in the United States.
   d. The Gang of Four was an American punk band.

4. In 1977, the Sex Pistol's song "God Save the Queen"
   a. caused a decline in record sales.
   b. caused outrage in Great Britain.
   c. created a rift within the band.
   d. became a number one hit in the United States.

5. Which album was credited as being one of the greatest live albums?
   a. The MC5's *Kick Out the Jams*
   b. The Clash's *London Calling*
   c. Donna Summers' *Love to Love You*
   d. The Bee Gee's *Saturday Night Fever*

ESSAY

6. Discuss the impact of the disco era on rock & roll.
7. What pioneering techniques did disco producers introduce in the 1970s?
8. What factors contributed to the "punk" phenomenon in Britain?
9. What effect did the Disco sucks movement have on rock & roll?
10. Choose one of the punk bands discussed in this chapter and discuss their influence on rock & roll today.

WHERE TO START YOUR RESEARCH PAPER

For an in-depth biography of Donna Summer, Chic, or Barry White, go to http://www.allmusic.com

For an in-depth biography of the Sex Pistols, go to http://www.rollingstone.com/artists/thesexpistols/biography

To research past and present Billboard 100 charts, go to http://www.billboard.com/bbcom/index.jsp

To learn more about punk, go to http://www.nostalgiacentral.com/music/merseybeat.htm

For information about individual punk bands, go to http://punkmusic.about.com/od/punk101/tp/punkbooklist.htm

ANSWERS: 1. b; 2. d; 3. b; 4. b; 5. d

Remember to check www.thethinkspot.com for additional information, downloadable flashcards, and other helpful resources.

HOW DID PUNK'S DESTRUCTIVE FOCUS CREATE NEW OPTIONS FOR LATER MUSICIANS?

WHAT ROLE DID BRITAIN PLAY IN CRAFTING THE NEW WAVE SOUND?

WHAT WAS THE PLACE OF DANCE MUSIC IN POST-PUNK AND NEW WAVE?

HOW DID MTV CHANGE THE WAY THAT MUSIC WAS RECEIVED?

"The scene

at our [Los Angeles] Whisky A-Go-Go show was curious. The audience consisted of young people making spectacularly misguided attempts to emulate London and New York punk style, all Halloween makeup and bin-liner dresses and a smattering of leather-skinned industry types in pressed denim, silver jewelry, and bouffant hair . . . but at least we were playing where people had actually heard of us.

"Three days later we found ourselves at a sparsely attended club in New Orleans—the atmosphere not helped by the fact that the audience were standing in a foot of water from a burst pipe. Our hotel rooms in the French Quarter had doors that had been kicked in on more than one occasion. The corridor carpet wore dark, tacky stains that were either ketchup or something more sinister. . . .

"The tour proceeded across the States, encountering every reaction from curiosity to hostility until we reached the more welcoming audiences of Boston, Philly, and, finally, New York City. We even played the legendary Stone Pony in Asbury Park but had to lock ourselves in the dressing room to escape a furious posse of Springsteen fans when I jokingly introduced The Attractions' own Bruce as 'the Real Future of Rock and Roll.'

"The following night we made our U.S. television debut on *Saturday Night Live*. The Sex Pistols had been scheduled for the show only to cancel after an alleged oversight regarding work permits. Needless to say the expected viewing figures for the debut of U.K. punk outrage were in our favour.

"We were getting pressure to perform a number from *My Aim is True*. I honestly believed that the words of 'Less than Zero' would be utterly obscure to American viewers. Taking a cue from an impromptu performance by Jimi Hendrix on a late '60s B.B.C. television show, I stopped this tune after a few bars and counted off an unreleased song, 'Radio, Radio.' I believed that we were just acting in the spirit of the third word of the show's title, but it was quickly apparent that the producer did not agree. He stood behind the camera making obscene and threatening gestures in my direction. When the number was over, we were chased out of the building and told that we would 'never work on American television again.' Indeed, we did not make another U.S. television appearance until 1980. Although this clip from *SNL* went on to be rerun on numerous occasions, I was not allowed back on the show until 1989."

—Elvis Costello, liner notes,
This Year's Model (1993 reissue)

NEW WAVE & SYNTH POP (1977–1987)

CHAPTER 10

HOW DID PUNK'S DESTRUCTIVE FOCUS CREATE NEW OPTIONS FOR LATER MUSICIANS?

POSTPUNK music in the immediate aftermath of punk rock that recognizes either punk's influence or the way in which punk denied other influences.

NEW WAVE the British movement that came out of punk, also associated with U.S. bands like the Talking Heads.

SYNTH POP an originally British movement that used synthesizers instead of guitars, drawing heavily on European styles.

ELVIS COSTELLO seminal British New Wave/postpunk musician who combined the sarcasm and energy of punk with a biting lyrical style.

DAVID BYRNE lead singer and producer of the Talking Heads who later went on to a long-lasting solo career.

TALKING HEADS American postpunk band who met at the Rhode Island School of Design and were part of the developing New York postpunk scene, often playing at CBGB.

Postpunk, New Wave, synth pop, and the other genres that came out of the short-lived punk explosion harkened a new musical order. Certainly, this sound was post-something, but no one could quite figure out what exactly that "something" was. After punk managed to destroy what it was against—that is, everything—the genre itself imploded without anointing an obvious successor. Thus, the *post* of postpunk did not necessarily mean music derived from punk aesthetics or politics; rather, it meant music that could not have existed had punk's wrecking ball not cleared the way.

As Chapter 9 showed, punk was in many ways a reaction to disco and to disco's optimistic, unabashed commercialism. However, what happened next was in some ways a hybridization of punk and disco. Synth pop and some New Wave relied on the driving beat of disco, and although disco's upbeat optimism usually got lost somewhere along the way, it soon became clear that the genre lines lacked distinct definition. Anything that had been done before could be done again, albeit with tongue firmly in cheek.

New Wave Takes Shape

As far as basic lineup went, punk looked a lot like metal: drums, bass, and one or more electric guitars. When **Elvis Costello** released *My Aim is True* in 1977, record labels marketed the album as punk despite the electric organ sounds that seemed to automatically disqualify him from that classification. Rather, Costello "drew on punk's spirit but escaped its label," (Marcus 1993, 34). In fact, this idea of differentiating punk from the music that followed took some time. Eventually, listeners recognized that the new sound accepted the notion of *construction* rather than embracing the pure nihilistic destruction of the Sex Pistols.

This is not to say, however, that the bands eventually called "New Wave" were optimists—far from it. Certainly, Costello rooted his lyrics in "revenge and guilt" (Marcus 1993, 25), but after punk had torn pop music to pieces, nothing could be done in quite the same way again. If punk had destroyed the old wave—rock & roll carried down from R&B, loaded with Chuck Berry riffs and crowd-pleasing personalities—then it was New Wave's job to start building something anew from the mess. By this time, "punk" had become something image-conscious and even almost marketable.

Punk's commercialization particularly revolted artists such as **David Byrne** of the **Talking Heads**, who argued "Let's see if we can just throw all that out, start from square one" (Reynolds 2005, 161). Although the Talking Heads were not necessarily happy with the New Wave label, as time went on the band absorbed influences from African field recordings and ethnomusicologists as well as from contemporary funk artists, a clear break with its punk predecessors.

Admittedly, the distinction between punk and New Wave is subjective, but a few musical elements help tell the two apart. New Wave songs tend to be more hook-driven and melodic, and its recordings sound less rough and fuzzy than punk's had. Although both New Wave and punk preferred the sound of clipped rhythms to the bluesy note bending and relaxed jamming feel of earlier rock & roll, New Wave musicians' thin sound helped differentiate them from punk artists. In fact,

Chapter 10   172

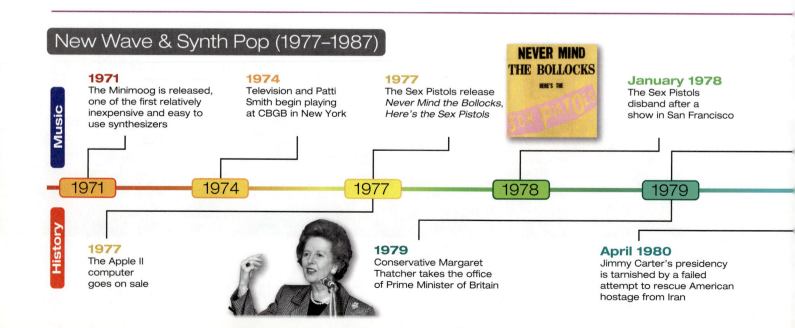

New Wave & Synth Pop (1977–1987)

Music

1971
The Minimoog is released, one of the first relatively inexpensive and easy to use synthesizers

1974
Television and Patti Smith begin playing at CBGB in New York

1977
The Sex Pistols release *Never Mind the Bollocks, Here's the Sex Pistols*

NEVER MIND THE BOLLOCKS HERE'S THE SEX PISTOLS

January 1978
The Sex Pistols disband after a show in San Francisco

| 1971 | 1974 | 1977 | 1978 | 1979 |

History

1977
The Apple II computer goes on sale

1979
Conservative Margaret Thatcher takes the office of Prime Minister of Britain

April 1980
Jimmy Carter's presidency is tarnished by a failed attempt to rescue American hostage from Iran

Byrne wanted New Wave to sound like "a little well-oiled machine where everything was transparent, all the working parts visible" (Reynolds 2005, 159). The self-consciousness of these decisions differentiated New Wave from its forebears.

NEW WAVE IN NEW YORK

Although the Ramones and the Talking Heads lived and worked in New York at the same time, the former was clearly more "punk" than the latter. Never mind the Ramones' big pop harmonies—the willful stupidity of their lyrics distanced them from the carefully wrought lyrics of most New Wave bands. Originally from Queens, New York, the Ramones offered a sound that was a bit less chaotic and furious than that of the Sex Pistols. However, their bare-bones sound still hearkened back to a hard rock revival. A far cry from the clever wordplay of Costello and Byrne, the Ramones epitomized the visceral effect of punk through such driving tracks as "Teenage Lobotomy" and "Beat on the Brat."

On the flip side, the Talking Heads largely typified the quintessential American New Wave band. Its members had become friends at the Rhode Island School of Design, an influence apparent in album art as well as in musical style. Witness their cerebral, sometimes surreal pop songs, with world influences and tightly constrained playing that in no way reflected the no-holds-barred energy of the Ramones. Anxious rather than ecstatic, the Talking Heads embodied the New Wave self-consciousness that thrived as a reaction to punk's visceral energy.

Indeed, the Talking Heads' music seemed to bear no resemblance to that of the Ramones. However, the two groups had some things in common. Both took part in the burgeoning New York Bowery underground scene, and both found a home on **Sire Records**. Founded in 1966 as an

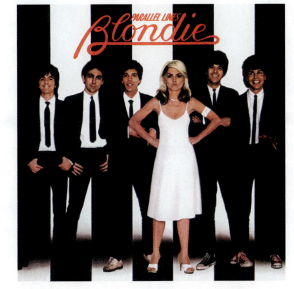

independent label, Sire Records became an early supporter of Bowery bands thanks to label owner Seymour Stein, one of the first to acknowledge the importance of the new musical movement.

Back in the Bowery and just a few blocks from where the Talking Heads shared a loft, music club **CBGB** was making a stir promoting shows by the Ramones and other bands of the nascent New York punk scene. In fact, the real impetus behind the American postpunk music scene was not any one musical style or record label; instead, clubs like CBGB allowed the scene to happen. Opened by Hilly Kristal in the Lower East Side of Manhattan in 1973, CBGB & OMFUG provided the venue for many of these postpunk bands to experiment, a somewhat unusual venture in an age when many clubs—and many audiences—tended toward conservatism.

BLONDIE AND TELEVISION

Among the punk-influenced acts to perform at CBGB was New York group Blondie. Taking their names from the bleached locks of singer Debbie Harry, Blondie became one of the most commercially successful American bands to bear the New Wave label. Like some of their contemporaries, Blondie drew on

<<< Led by the versatile voice of frontwoman Deborah Harry, **Blondie became one of New Wave's best-known acts.**

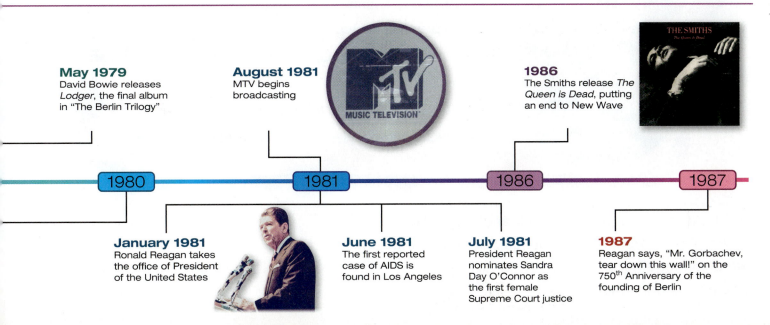

May 1979
David Bowie releases *Lodger*, the final album in "The Berlin Trilogy"

August 1981
MTV begins broadcasting

1986
The Smiths release *The Queen is Dead*, putting an end to New Wave

1980   1981   1986   1987

January 1981
Ronald Reagan takes the office of President of the United States

June 1981
The first reported case of AIDS is found in Los Angeles

July 1981
President Reagan nominates Sandra Day O'Connor as the first female Supreme Court justice

1987
Reagan says, "Mr. Gorbachev, tear down this wall!" on the 750th Anniversary of the founding of Berlin

TOM VERLAINE Television guitarist who is largely credited with bringing punk and postpunk to CBGB.

Jamaican musical forms including reggae and **dub**; unlike those same contemporaries, Blondie also reached out to many other styles. The album *Parallel Lines* (1978) demonstrates their diverse influences, with the hard-edged rock of "One Way or Another" juxtaposed against the disco-styled "Heart of Glass." One of Blondie's most distinctive aspects, however, was their intense seriousness. Just as punk rockers did, Blondie embraced irony—particularly in the image of Debbie Harry, who was both a bleached-blond sex symbol but also cooly detached from the audience, alluring and also off-putting. While punk bands may have abused their listeners and audience members in a rejection of the traditional rock model, Blondie created space with

a winking combination of ironic sex appeal and true pop sensibility in a tongue-in-cheek nod to that same rock star symbolism.

Talking Heads frontman David Byrne credited the guitarist of rock band Television, **Tom Verlaine**, with bringing punk to CBGB, saying that they "persuaded Hilly Kristal to allow them to play for the door at what was then a biker bar on the Bowery" (Kristal 2005). Although other punk guitarists made a point of simplifying their guitar riffs, Verlaine never tried to hide his chops, roaring through such tracks as "Marquee Moon." Television ultimately had a much bigger impact in the United Kingdom than in the United States, in part thanks to Verlaine's electric guitar work. Seeming to take more from New York downtown music than from the blues tradition, Verlaine's style in some ways echoed the efforts of Talking Heads and Sex Pistols to break away from the blues without echoing these other bands' sounds.

Punk or Postpunk?

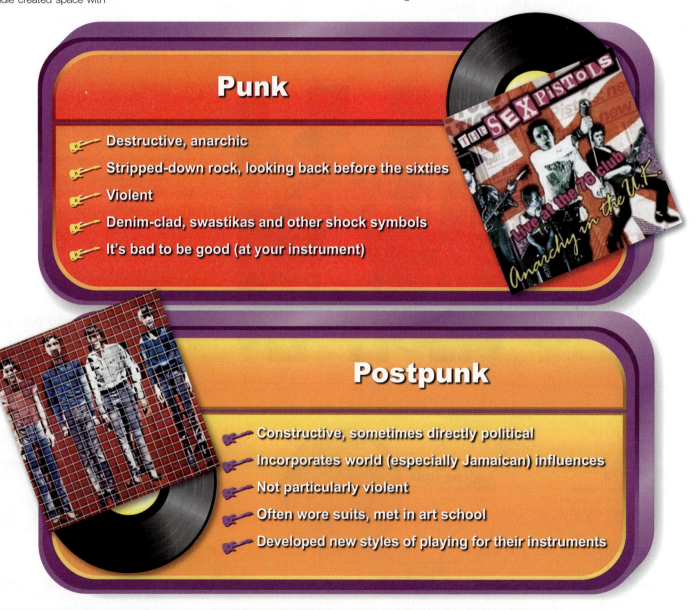

Punk

- Destructive, anarchic
- Stripped-down rock, looking back before the sixties
- Violent
- Denim-clad, swastikas and other shock symbols
- It's bad to be good (at your instrument)

Postpunk

- Constructive, sometimes directly political
- Incorporates world (especially Jamaican) influences
- Not particularly violent
- Often wore suits, met in art school
- Developed new styles of playing for their instruments

∧ **The distinction between punk and postpunk** can be confusing, in part because albums like
∧ the Talking Heads' *More Songs About Buildings and Food* came out while the Sex Pistols
were still together and punk was going strong. These two bands can tell us something
about their differences.

Hilly Kristal

Founder of the club CBGB, Hilly Kristal was a staple of New York City's New Wave music scene. However, Kristal did not originally intend for CBGB & OMFUG to be a punk and postpunk venue; in fact, the club's name stood for Country Blue Grass Blues and Other Music for Urban Gourmandizers. Bearded and sporting a mass of curly hair, Kristal himself did not fit either the punk or the New Wave look. Although he confessed that he was "a little shy" (Kristal 2005), his club became a home for underground rock, or "street rock," as punk was then known.

Kristal's philosophy offered some points in regard to music and musicians. CBGB's sound system was one of the best around for a rock venue, which made both the experiences of playing and listening more satisfying (Weiss 2005). Additionally, Kristal saw musicians as artists rather than as commercial vehicles, and thus "encouraged bands to do their own thing" (Kristal 2005). Unlike many club owners, Kristal booked only bands that played original material. Byrne later noted that the club was never empty, because once a band had played there, Kristal usually let the band's members in for free. At minimum, this practice guaranteed an audience—if not necessarily a paying one—and, at its best, fostered a community of like-minded and supportive musicians.

West Coast and Cleveland Punk

Well after the CBGB scene had been established in New York, the punk and New Wave movements found their way to the West Coast where they took on a new form. John Doe of Los Angeles band X later recalled that he had seen Talking Heads and Blondie on a visit to New York but decided that he "didn't wanna try to weasel my way into something that was already set up" (Spitz & Mullen 2001, 95), and instead moved to Los Angeles. Although X had more in common with punk than with New York New Wave, they called the whole Los Angeles scene "punk," "New Wave," or whatever else they could come up with.

The Germs' vocalist Darby Crash became a poster child for the L.A. punk movement. Despite releasing very few recordings, the Germs became known for its raging, adrenal music and chaotic live performances, in which Crash—born Jan Paul Breahm—sometimes threw food at the audience or even cut himself. He also put out cigarettes on people's wrists, which was known as a "Germ burn" (Adato 2000). In 1980, Crash took a heroin overdose as part of a suicide pact with his girlfriend Casey Cola. Cola managed to survive after being dead for about three minutes, but Crash died at the age of 22. (Spitz & Mullen 2001, 271). His death foreshadowed the end of the first wave of L.A. punk.

Compared to this wild side of punk, the L.A. New Wave scene was much tamer. Oingo Boingo originally started as cabaret act The Mystic Knights of the Oingo Boingo, transformed into one of the scene's premier New Wave bands. The songwriting of group member Danny Elfman largely shaped the group's New Wave style. After the demise of Oingo Boingo in 1995, Elfman found great success as a composer for both film and television, contributing to such films as *Batman* and *The Nightmare Before Christmas* as well as the long-running television show *The Simpsons*.

The musical sounds emanating from the coasts also affected other areas of the country. In Cleveland, Ohio, the spirit of punk caught on with the band Pere Ubu. With the post-industrial urban landscape as a backdrop, Pere Ubu released a few albums featuring Cleveland on the cover. *Dub Housing*, generally considered one of their finest works, combines remarkably modern-sounding dissonant soundscapes that abound with guitars, synthesizers, and manic vocals. Such unique sounds helped Pere Ubu carve out a spot between L.A. and New York that stands as an expression of late 1970s mid-American urban life.

WHAT ROLE DID BRITAIN PLAY IN CRAFTING THE NEW WAVE SOUND?

The British Post-Pistols

Because the Sex Pistols were one of the punk's biggest names, the accompanying London punk scene became one of the most vibrant. However, the postpunk bands that hailed from Britain did not bear the same uninhibited fury that the Sex Pistols had shown. Despite early efforts to market him as punk, Elvis Costello would never have gone so far as to yell "I am an Antichrist"—at least, not directly. Some acts, such as The Police, achieved commercial success with mixes of ska and dub influences infused with pop sensibilities. Even as the punk scene declined, a few stragglers including The Stranglers remained, while bands such as the Buzzcocks and XTC embraced pure New Wave. A final "pure pop" contingent fleshed out the British scene, exemplified by Nick Lowe's *Jesus of Cool* (1978) (U.S. title *Pure Pop for Now People*). Like American music, British music varied greatly while still maintaining strong links from one artist to the next.

TOP OF THE CHARTS
WHAT'S HOT!
1977

1. "Tonight's The Night (Gonna Be Alright)" – Rod Stewart
2. "I Just Want To Be Your Everything" – Andy Gibb
3. "Best Of My Love" – Emotions
4. Love Theme From "A Star Is Born" – Barbra Streisand
5. "Angel In Your Arms" – Hot
6. "I Like Dreamin'" – Kenny Nolan
7. "Don't Leave Me This Way" – Thelma Houston
8. "(Your Love Has Lifted Me) Higher and Higher" – Rita Coolidge
9. "Undercover Angel" – Alan O'Day
10. "Torn Between Two Lovers" – Mary MacGregor

ELVIS COSTELLO

In the late 1970s, Elvis Costello epitomized British New Wave and post-punk. Born in London, Costello moved to Liverpool as a teenager and attended his last two years of secondary school there. Although he wasn't able to see the Clash and the Sex Pistols play in his hometown, he listened to their records when they came out and was influenced by the punk sound. These influences contributed to his early classification as punk, despite his having a much less vicious sound than the Sex Pistols.

Nevertheless, his lyrics reflected the blunt scream of punk and have been acknowledged as some of the best in either punk or New Wave in their use of wordplay and creative vocabulary. As you read earlier in the chapter, Costello thought that the lyrics of his first single "Less Than Zero," an attack on British fascist politician Oswald Mosley, were "utterly obscure to American" ears—and this belief had serious consequences during his legendary *Saturday Night Live* performance as a last-minute replacement for the Sex Pistols.

Although Costello was not allowed back on *SNL* for over a decade, his next two albums, *This Year's Model* and *Armed Forces*, performed well both critically and commercially. **Robert Christgau** ranked *This Year's Model* at the top of his *Village Voice Pazz & Jop Critics Poll*, while *Rolling Stone* trumpeted about *Armed Forces* that "The songs are so brief they barrel right by, leaving an impression of jubilant and spiteful energies at war with each other . . . There's an overload of cleverness on the LP" (Rolling Stone 1979). Costello's personal style also attracted attention, in part because of its sharp contrast to the denim and studs of punk. Costello's sharp-suited, bespectacled appearance earned him multiple comparisons to Buddy Holly—albeit his was a Buddy Holly with an ax to grind. Indeed, Costello built on aspects of punk's sound to create a lyrical, stylish package all his own.

BRITISH SUCCESSES, PUNK HOLDOUTS, AND NEW WAVE

Founded by drummer Stewart Copeland, guitarist Andy Summers, and bassist and singer Sting, The Police became the most commercially successful band of the British New Wave movement. Like many other New Wave bands, the Police blended reggae and ska influences into a reverb-drenched sound that reflected the production techniques of dub. This departure from the blues roots preferred by the groups of the 1960s in favor of reggae, jazz, and dub was a hallmark of New Wave music. Although reggae had some exposure in the United Kingdom, the genre remained relatively unknown in the United States

ROCK TECHNOLOGY ►►► The Synthesizer

Classical and avant-garde musicians alike had used the synthesizer since the mid-20th century, but some even earlier models existed. Patented in 1928, the Ondes-Martenot—an early electronic musical instrument—has appeared occasionally in classical works, and in more recent times in the works of Radiohead's Jonny Greenwood. However, the synthesizer achieved widespread use in the early 1970s when prog rock bands such as Yes began to appear. Yes keyboardist Rick Wakeman played several synthesizers simultaneously as quickly as possible.

The development of second-generation synthesizers such as the **Minimoog** brought the instrument to its full pop musician potential. A descendent of the huge, complicated Moog Modular synthesizer, the Minimoog compressed a portion of the larger synthesizer into a single faceplate, with controls allowing for easy access to sound-morphing parameters. Synth pop pioneer **Gary Numan** described his initial efforts at turning "punk songs into electronic songs" with the

Minimoog as "fat and doomy" (Reynolds 2005, 298). Another late-1970s synthesizer, the inexpensive Wasp, had a totally flat keyboard with about two dozen knobs to control the sound. Like the Minimoog, the Wasp was monophonic: tracks had to be layered to achieve the complexity that New Wave artists wanted. After the Linn Drum Computer appeared as the first programmable drum machine that could realistically replicate acoustic drum sounds, musicians experimented with the drum signal to create futuristic effects. Since these first synthesizer users developed a style tailored for the synthesizer, the instrument has become a near-ubiquitous element of pop music.

<<< The Minimoog synthesizer **was one of the first made for** the average musician.

before The Police's huge success. Some have credited the band with bringing reggae's particular sound and production style to a new, much larger audience.

Even though The Police had several big hits, two stand out. In 1978, the group released "Roxanne." This track, a catchy, reggae-infused love song directed at a prostitute, won some recognition in Britain. Soon, the group became rock superstars on both sides of the Atlantic, winning fans and critics over with such albums as *Zenyatta Mondatta* (1980) and *Synchronicity* (1983). *Synchronicity* single "Every Breath You Take," a subtle exploration of the line between love and obsession, beat out Michael Jackson's "Billie Jean" for the 1983 Grammy for Song of the Year.

By 1985, the group had split, and lead singer Sting embarked on a critically and commercially celebrated solo career during which he has explored pop, world, and classical forms. Sporadic Police reunion sets dotted the years, including a brief 2003 set marking the group's induction into the Rock & Roll Hall of Fame. A sold-out reunion tour followed in 2007.

Punk Holdouts

By the late 1970s, the Sex Pistols may have been gone, but punk was not entirely dead. Some British and American punk bands, including the Dictators, continued in the wake of the Sex Pistols. Started in upstate New York, the Dictators hung on to the shock-heavy politics of the Sex Pistols and the Ramones.

One way in which punk groups tried to distance themselves from rock was by eliminating African American influences from their music. In fact, the entire punk scene, especially the later punk scene, was predominantly white. Although many of these groups brandished swastikas as a method of shock, the acts reflected a desire for confusion and anarchy rather than a considered political position.

Another punk hanger-on was British group the Stranglers. Never fully a part of the punk scene, the Stranglers instead focused on the London pub rock scene. Despite playing loud, fast rock, the group never achieved the widespread success of the Sex Pistols, the Clash, or many of the other London punk bands.

The Buzzcocks and XTC

Formed in Manchester, England, in 1976, the Buzzcocks cut their first EP spending less than $100 on its recording (Marcus 1993, 377). Released in 1977, this debut EP *Spiral Scratch* featured the song "Boredom," with its ranting, sarcastic lyrics and two-note guitar solo. The record was so successful that it sold 16,000 copies without major label support (Reynolds 2005, 27), and the group was so successful in its hometown that it presented the Sex Pistols as its opening act when the London punks first played in Manchester.

Fellow British band XTC helped define the nation's New Wave sound. A year after signing with Virgin in 1977, XTC released *White Music*, which included the singles "Radios in Motion" and "This is Pop?" With a more joyful sound than many of the earlier punk groups, XTC

melded the nervous energy of the Talking Heads with the high-energy punk of the Buzzcocks.

PURE POP IN BRITAIN AND THE UNITED STATES

"Pure pop" contributed something entirely new to the New Wave movement. Named for the American title of Nick Lowe's album *Jesus of Cool* (aka *Pure Pop for Now People*), this style of pop was explicitly fun. However, it was knowingly fun, self-consciously drawing attention to its own status as a commodity. Like his childhood friend Elvis Costello, Lowe infused many of his songs with biting, cynical criticism, readily heard in such songs as "Music for Money," an attack on the music industry. After the release of *Jesus of Cool*, Lowe married Carlene Carter, country singer and stepdaughter to Johnny Cash. During the 1980s, Lowe worked as a producer for the record label Stiff, a major producer of both punk and new wave music.

Lowe had written and recorded the song "(What's So Funny 'Bout) Peace, Love and Understanding" with his band Brinsley Schwarz in 1974. Four years later, Costello rerecorded the track as the close to *Armed Forces*. In describing the tune, critic Greil Marcus wrote "The song is ... so full of irony you can feel the stuff oozing out of the speakers" (Marcus 2004, 357). Both Lowe's pop sounds and his independent, do-it-yourself style of producing had unmistakable influences on the later postpunk and New Wave scene.

Likewise, singer-songwriter John Hiatt provided many more hits for others than he ever had himself. Starting out at the age of 18 as a songwriter for Tree Publishing, Hiatt found early success when rock band Three Dog Night covered his song "Sure as I'm Sittin' Here" and sent it to number 16 on the charts. After being signed and subsequently dropped by Epic Records after two unsuccessful releases, Hiatt moved to Los Angeles. There, he continued to work as a songwriter and tried to make it as a performer. He eventually received a contract with MCA and released the 1979 album *Slug Line*. An album in the same vein as Costello's work, *Slug Line* garnered better critical reception than had his Epic recording, with critic Christgau even writing, "This hard-working young pro may yet turn out to be an all-American Elvis C." (Christgau 1979). Hiatt had more than a stylistic connection to Costello; on his first A&M release, 1987's *Bring the Family*, Nick Lowe played bass. One of the album's songs, "Thing Called Love," was successfully covered in 1989 by Bonnie Raitt and became a pop hit.

New Wave Pure Pop

Despite their New Wave connections, Lowe and Hiatt had come at the "pure pop" ideal from a more pub rock-influenced perspective. Others

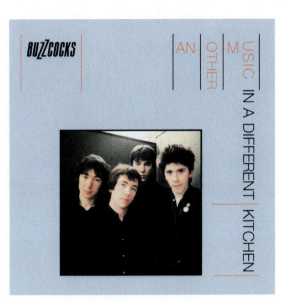

∧
∧ **The Buzzcocks** were one of
∧ the top **British New Wave bands,** especially in their hometown of Manchester.

hailed from a New Wave angle. Sex Pistols impresario Malcolm McLaren put together Bow Wow Wow, a New Wave proto-supergroup comprising members of Adam and the Ants and 15-year-old vocalist Annabella Lwin. Soon, however, Lwin went solo and the group re-formed as Chiefs of Relief. The group blended elements of rock, hip-hop, and electronic music. California girl group the Go-Go's began with punk influences but had moved toward a poppier sound by the time they recorded their first album, *Beauty and the Beat*, in 1981. Finally, the B-52s were an unabashedly fun band from Athens, Georgia. After gaining fame during the New Wave era by playing at New York City clubs Max's Kansas City and CBGB, the B-52s achieved mass success with their 1989 tune "Love Shack." Although disco had largely faded as a commercial force by the 1980s, dance music was also still finding an audience. Michael Jackson's 1982 record *Thriller*, for example, is the second best-selling album of all time (RIAA, 2009).

Chapter 10

Synth Pop

As New Wave developed, artists began working with ever more complex arrangements and instrumentation. The development of affordable, easy-to-use synthesizers created a qualitative shift in the way that producers and musicians approached their music. Other 1970s musicians such as glam rockers had not tried to master the large, impossibly complicated synthesizers of the day. By the time New Wave broke, synthesizers had become simple enough to allow all kinds of musicians to use them. What's more, the instruments held the possibility of entirely new sounds and rhythms. Soon, a style emerged to take advantage of these possibilities: synth pop.

Certainly, a handful of progressive rock bands had already used the synthesizer, but the simplification of synthesizer technology democratized the instrument, allowing less technically inclined players equal opportunities to employ synthesized sounds. These musicians had a greater concern for making great dance beats than for playing as many notes as possible, allowing a truly "pop" sound to emerge. As synthesizers became more sophisticated, players held complete real-time control over all sorts of aspects, including the timbre and qualities of the sound produced. Earlier prog rock users had often tried to replicate acoustic instruments—using programmed sounds to mimic the tones of brass instruments, for example—but synth pop pioneers purposely emphasized the artificiality of the sounds. By exploring the outer limits of the synthesizer's potential rather than fitting the synthesizer to a pre-existing mold, synth pop artists employed this unconventional instrument to its fullest extent.

∧
∧ **Brian Eno and David Bowie**
∧ collaborated on *Low*, the first album of Bowie's "Berlin Trilogy," which **helped define the sound that would become popular in synth pop.**

SYNTHETIC DREAMS

Behind all the technological and stylistic innovations of synth pop musicians was a deep desire to make music sound synthetic, even inhuman. When quality synthetic drum sounds appeared, these artists immediately distorted them. As drum machines replaced real drummers and sequencers stood in for real keyboard players, bands began having fewer members. Synth pop band Human League produced fully automated shows during which programmed music played while band members mingled with the audience, signing autographs (Reynolds 2005, 297). This mechanized aesthetic of automation and non-human production became the driving force behind synth pop.

Synth Pop Muses: Eno and Bowie

Former Roxy Music keyboardist **Brian Eno** may be considered the father of the musical form that would become synth pop. Electronic experimental group Cabaret Voltaire was among many groups that were inspired by Eno's work. In fact, Eno believed that the synthesizer was not necessarily an instrument in the same way that "regular" instruments were, because it didn't have to play notes. On his first solo album *Here Come the Warm Jets* (1974), Eno featured an early, playful use of the synthesizer with a bouncy synth solo over an almost entirely conventional rock guitar line on the song "Paw-Paw Negro Blowtorch."

Eno equally influenced later synth pop artists through his work with David Bowie on the albums *Low*, *"Heroes,"* and *Lodger*. Commonly called Bowie's "Berlin Trilogy," these albums inspired later artists. Synth pop pioneer Gary Numan was even accused of being a Bowie clone because of how closely he imitated the Berlin Trilogy. Although Eno did not necessarily record each album of the Berlin Trilogy, he collaborated closely with Bowie on all of them. In certain segments, Eno's work shows through even more than Bowie's does. Synth pop artists—traced back to Bowie and Eno—viewed the future of music as based upon sounds rather than on instruments. Indeed, later musicians used the synthesizer to embark on solo projects lacking even a basic backing band.

Eno's later involvement with the Talking Heads, especially its leader David Byrne, expanded the idea that there was more to music than instruments. Using samples of conservative and evangelical Christian talk radio, the pair made strange "polyrhythmic collages" (Reynolds 2005, 165) on *My Life in the Bush of Ghosts*. The focus on rhythm and on removing sounds from their natural contexts—not to mention processed acoustic percussion sounds—played huge roles in synth pop. Eno worked to create soundscapes from repeated (looped) segments that would each be singable in its own right but also formed hybrid complex polyrhythmic textures. This textural style influenced music for years to come.

Berlin

During the 1920s, Berlin had risen to become Europe's foremost center for arts and culture: Expressionist painters, Bauhaus architects, and other modern creative forces contributed to a thriving cultural center. Although the Nazi government and World War II that followed this era tamped down artistic expression, by the late 1970s the democratic city of West Berlin had become an island in the middle of the Eastern Bloc, and its cultural history intrigued artists, including David Bowie and Iggy Pop. Indeed, as punk simultaneously exploded and imploded, the cool—even cold—Berlin sound presaged the future of music. Both Bowie and Brian Eno produced recordings in and drew inspiration from Berlin. Seeing how Berlin survived in the amid the repressive Eastern Bloc pushed Bowie and Eno toward expression through textures rather than words, as exemplified by the Berlin Trilogy (Reynolds 2005, 5). The German bands that provided much of Berlin's musical backdrop employed this textural approach, with a particularly futuristic emphasis on industrialization and mechanization.

Bowie and Eno's relocation to Berlin "chimed with the postpunk feeling that America—or at least *white* America—was politically and musically reactionary . . . postpunk looked to places other than the rock 'n' roll heartland" (Reynolds 2005, 5). If punk reached back to the very roots of rock & roll, then postpunk reached back *past* rock, detaching itself from the birthplace of rock itself.

WELCOME TO THE MACHINE

The inhuman and post-human feel of synth pop follow logically from the ways that artists explored the synthesizer's potential. By moving beyond music that replicates human-produced sound, synthesizers allowed artists to stake out new territory. Crucial to this post-human philosophy is the notion that the human performer can become a part of the machine, responding to and moving in tandem with the synthesized beats. Synth pop band the Human League released albums with titles like *Reproduction*, a reference at once sexual and mechanical. These albums dealt with material culled from the world of science fiction as in the *Reproduction* single "Empire State Human," which told about a man who kept growing. The synth pop pioneers ventured as far away from reality as possible.

We are all Berliners

Kraftwerk — German electropop group, who pioneered uses of synthesizers to create droning artificial beats.

Brian Eno — Based many of his operations out of Berlin, and was influential on the sound of British musicians who would record in Berlin, producing many of their albums.

David Bowie — Famous for his "Berlin Trilogy," helped in many ways by Brian Eno, which he included the albums *Low*, "*Heroes*", and *Lodger*, all made between 1977–1979.

Ultravox — Recorded their album *Systems of Romance* (1978) in Germany, and said that they "just seemed to be Germanic." Later (after a lineup shuffle) made the album *Vienna*, celebrating the fallen Hapsburgs.

Spandau Ballet — Named after a prison in western Berlin that held Rudolf Hess and Albert Speer. Songs included "Muscle-bound," with a confusing fascist/communist message.

The New Wave obsession with Germany grew even more intense in the larger genre of synth pop. **Many bands traced some kind of influence back to Germany,** and especially to Berlin.

DIE MENSCH MASCHINE: KRAFTWERK

The Düsseldorf-based electronic band **Kraftwerk** (a German word meaning *factory*) became Germany's best-known band of the era. Basing their music on minimally repeating and usually non-syncopated figures, Kraftwerk employed achingly slow chord changes—usually only one every 30 seconds or so, creating machine-like rhythms. With the addition of its almost entirely monotonic vocals, the band created a feeling of totally static motion, like seeing gears go around and around but going nowhere in particular. Some have acknowledged Kraftwerk's rhythms as the musical equivalent of Andy Warhol's screen-printed Campbell's Soup cans, and the name Kraftwerk itself nods to the idea of art as industrial production.

Despite this obsession with the rote, Kraftwerk made remarkable contributions to electronic technology and culture. Two of the group's members played "electronic percussion," a system of playing electronic samples with homemade percussion triggers. Likewise, the group performed single "Taschenrechner" ("Pocket Calculator") entirely on modified calculators. These performance techniques contributed greatly to their popularity both at home and abroad. *Die Mensch Maschine* (1978, *The Man Machine*) focused on the relationships between humans and technology. One of the few lyrics in the six-minute opening track, "Die Roboter," repeats "Wir sind die Roboter," or "We are robots." *The Man Machine's* music slowly morph from fairly realistic high-register string-like synthesized sounds into entirely unbelievable robot voices and sweeping artificial textures. Throughout the development of synth pop, Kraftwerk—and Germany in general—continued to exert a noticeable influence.

Post-Human: Gary Numan

One of the preeminent artists in the synth pop genre, Gary Numan helped fuse rock and electronic music. Numan's first encounter with a synthesizer came during the summer of 1978 recording sessions with his band Tubeway Army. The band in the studio before them had left behind a Minimoog, and when Numan started to experiment with it he began to get ideas for its possible uses in rock music. The Moog's fat sound recalled the low, distorted guitar riffs of metal group Black Sabbath (Reynolds 2005, 298), and Numan became a guitarist who included synthesizers as another element in the rock group.

Soon, Tubeway Army's album titles, particularly its final album *Replicas,* began to evoke the mechanical nature of the synthesizer. Most of Numan's songs stemmed from a dystopian universe that he had originally created in a failed attempt at a novel. In this science fiction universe, humans build an all-powerful Machine to keep the peace; eventually, the Machine decides that—for the sake of peace—the humans must be destroyed. Numan's first album without Tubeway Army, *The Pleasure Principle* (1979), had no guitars at all, but instead relied heavily on synthesizers. Its continued employment of a bass guitarist and a drummer, however, rooted Numan in rock rather than electronic dance music.

Just a small step from Numan's fantasy world lay the ideas of fascism, and Numan was not alone in his interest in fascist politics. The fascination with both the machine and Berlin created an ideology removed from the swastikas of the Ramones and other punk rockers. Although the punk movement had tended to use swastikas and other controversial symbols for shock value, accompanying fascist symbols with portraits of Marx or the Union Jack, this movement was more anarchy than fascism. Electropop rejected anarchy, although like punk, the genre was loud and distorted. For synth pop musicians, fascism took on a Neo-Nazi air in part because of their obsession with the glamour of Germany—exemplified by David Bowie's Berlin Trilogy—combined with the mechanical rhythms of forward-looking German band Kraftwerk.

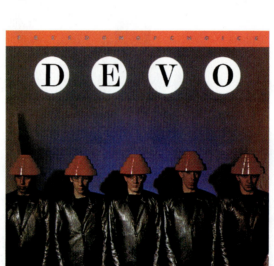

∧
∧ **Devo had a theory of human**
∧ **de-evolution,** and made jerky, jarring music that matched this belief.

DEVO-LUTION

Ohio band Devo, formed by Kent State grads Jerry Casale and Mark Mothersbaugh, took their name from the theory of de-evolution, which argues that humanity has actually regressed rather than progressed. Both Casale and Mothersbaugh had marched in the infamous 1970 Kent State protest against the Vietnam War during which Ohio National Guardsmen opened fire on students. Instead of joining the Weather Underground, they decided to "make some kind of wacked-out creative Dada art response" (Reynolds 2005, 77). They employed the synthesizer as a tool to make disgusting noises rather than beautiful textures. Using their music to help them escape their native Akron, Ohio, they eventually made it to Germany. There, they recorded their Brian Eno-produced debut *Q: Are We Not Men? A: We Are Devo!* (1978). On later Top 20 hit "Whip It," Devo continued its political and social commentary through—what else?—a music video.

ULTRAVOX

Although British synth band Ultravox fit more with punk than with New Wave, they recorded their album *Systems of Romance* (1978) in

Germany. Claiming that they wanted to get away from "Americanisms" in rock, Ultravox rejected blues riffs or scales. Instead, they declared that they "just seemed to be Germanic" (Reynolds 2005, 300) even before they went to that country. *Systems* included such songs as "I Want to Be a Machine" and "My Sex," which lifts the plot of 1973 J.G. Ballard novel *Crash* to describe a car crash victim who can only become sexually aroused through car crashes. However, this album—and all of their albums—failed to sell well, causing Ultravox to be dropped by their label in 1978. Lead singer John Foxx then went solo with the entirely synthesized album *Metamatic* (1980).

But it was another Ultravox member, Billy Currie, who continued to follow the group's path of European obsession all the way to the distant past. Back in London, Currie started hanging out at a nightclub called Billy's and followed this scene when it moved to the larger Blitz. There, the so-called "Blitz kids" exemplified the glamorous, slightly confused style that came to define the period, with pillbox hats, toy-soldier coats, and futuristic makeup and hair styles (Reynolds 2005, 301).Currie went on to re-form Ultravox with a new lead singer and released the album *Vienna*, once called "the sonic equivalent of dry ice" (Reynolds 2005, 302). "First they wanted to be machines, now they want to have roots," (Christgau 1980) cried one critic, while others condemned the album's "familiar and banal electronic effects" (*Rolling Stone* 1981).

The Later New Romantics

Eventually, the Blitz scene evolved into the **New Romantic** movement. Although this movement remained a fairly minor one, its reactionary culture and politics combined with a futuristic ethos made it unique. Further, the whole movement put on aristocratic airs; such pretenses as word-of-mouth gigs and selective doormen became staples of the scene. In addition to Ultravox, other New Romantic bands helped define the era for at least a certain cummerbund-wearing subset. Founded by New Romantic poster boy Boy George, Culture Club followed on George's work with Bow Wow Wow

at one of Malcolm McLaren's Rainbow venue. Although Boy George perhaps became best known for his cross-dressing, Culture Club scored six Top 10 hits in the United States and seven in the United Kingdom, making them one of the most commercially successful New Romantic groups.

Known for their costuming and romantic flair, the punkier Adam and the Ants also had ties to McLaren. In fact, McLaren convinced the Ants to fire Adam and form the group Bow Wow Wow with a different singer. Adam, however, hired a new set of Ants and soldiered on, releasing such singles as "Stand and Deliver."

Probably the best example of a band that looked almost exclusively to the Eastern Bloc, Spandau Ballet even took its name from the West Berlin prison where Nazi leaders Rudolf Hess and Albert Speer had been condemned, eliciting praise from neo-fascist magazine *Bulldog* (Reynolds 2005, 302). In videos for singles from their debut *Journeys to Glory* (1981), singer Tony Hadley croons in fallen dungeons ("To Cut a Long Story Short") and on snow-capped mountains ("Musclebound"). However, Spandau Ballet did not have an international hit until the heavily soul-influenced single "True" in 1983. By that time, the New Romantic movement had all but faded out, and synth pop had evolved into a more sophisticated version of dance pop.

>>> **The New Romantics,** a movement started in London, **cared at least as much about clothing** as about the music itself.

WHAT WAS THE PLACE OF DANCE MUSIC IN POSTPUNK AND NEW WAVE?

Dance Pop: What Have I Done to Deserve This?

In 1981, a mutual love of synthesizers encouraged Neil Tennant and Chris Lowe to start a band. Blatantly up-front about the group's commercial motivation, the **Pet Shop Boys'** first successful single on EMI was titled "Opportunities (Let's Make Lots of Money)." This new breed of satirical electronic dance-floor pop was coupled with a sexual drive that, while in some ways mimicking the glam of Bowie and the New Romantics, was also aware of its own potential as a marketing strategy. Although both the Pet Shop Boys were homosexuals, they downplayed this aspect so they could draw their largely heterosexual audiences to sympathize with a wide range of sexual identities.

The strategy worked, and their album *Actually* (1987) achieved mass international success bolstered by the darkly cynical tracks "Rent" ("I love you/You pay my rent") and "What Have I Done to Deserve This?" Unlike the New Romantics, the Pet Shop Boys continued making albums well into the next century, albeit with mixed success. Most prominent of their post-*Actually* albums were *Very* (1993) and *Yes* (2009).

The Human League and Depeche Mode

The Pet Shop Boys was not the only group to make waves with dance-influenced synth pop. After David Bowie declared in 1979 that watching The Human League was "like watching 1980" (Reynolds 2005, 296), the band couldn't quite live up to the hype. But Buzzcocks and Stranglers

PET SHOP BOYS, *ACTUALLY*

In 1987, the Pet Shop Boys' *Actually* rose to huge critical and commercial success. The group's ironic stance towards their music is perhaps exemplified by the album's cover art: while Tennant stares straight ahead, Lowe yawns, eyes closed. However, for all their satirical edge, the Pet Shop Boys made impeccable dance pop and helped push the boundaries of the genre without removing their feet from the dance floor. In *Actually*, rather than attempting the escapism favored by the New Romantics, the Pet Shop Boys drew attention to the "urban, lonely, and bored yuppies of the late '80s" (Erlewine 2009). The romantic message of the album's fourth single, "Heart," is tempered by Terrant's vocals.

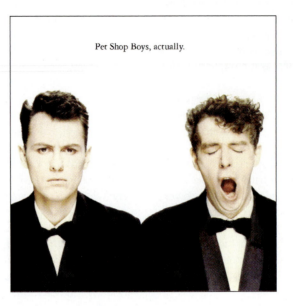

From another group, its message might have been taken at least somewhat seriously, but Tennant's delivery is so flawlessly banal that the words become almost a joke.

Actually also offered technological innovation through the use of the Fairlight sampling system. By using Fairlight synthesizers, which allowed musicians to record and play sound samples through their keyboards, on their albums, the Pet Shop Boys allowed totally new textures and sounds, like the strange scream sound and realistic-sounding bongo drums on the first track, "One More Chance," to invade their music in the era before user-friendly sampling systems were common.

---

producer Martin Rushent whisked the group away to his rural electronic studio, and the Human League shed two of its members and emerged with the single "The Sound of the Crowd." Even with a combination of synthesized toms and sampled screaming sounds, the song managed to hit the Top 20 in the UK.

Another British group, Depeche Mode, was instrumental in bringing sampling into synth pop. Although the group began as peppy New Romantics, they quickly grew darker after turning to synthesizers. Their 1984 album *Some Great Reward* went completely electronic, and exemplified the industrial sound that found success well into the 1990s.

HOW DID MTV CHANGE THE WAY THAT MUSIC WAS RECEIVED?

I Want My MTV

For better or for worse, the birth of MTV on August 1, 1981, marked a momentous cultural shift that stretched well beyond the medium of video itself. Music video had been around for a long time: the Beatles' *A Hard Day's Night* and *Help!* were both produced to fulfill the demand for televised Beatles appearances (Reynolds 2005, 337), not to mention the made-for-TV band the Monkees. In fact, former Monkee Michael Nesmith thought up the idea of MTV, creating the program *Popclips* that appeared on cable channel Nickelodeon. Eventually, Nesmith sold the idea of an entire channel devoted to music videos, although he didn't see the process the entire way through himself.

In the early 1980s, radio programming was fairly conservative, with "classic rock" stations playing well-worn hits. Radio adopted new trends slowly, particularly because no national media outlet existed solely for music to be broadcast and disseminated to the

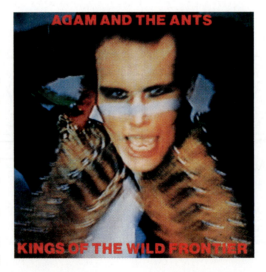

∧ ∧ ∧ **New Romantic bands like Adam and the Ants fared especially well on MTV,** partly due to their visual appeal.

entire country. Through **MTV**, a single network suddenly broadcasted new, cutting-edge music nationwide. Despite this accomplishment, MTV's reach remained somewhat limited; only 25 percent of American homes had cable when cable channel MTV debuted. Furthermore, cable companies in entertainment hubs New York and Los Angeles did not carry the channel. MTV's "I Want My MTV" promotional campaign changed all of that; the channel ran network advertisements in which stars such as Pete Townshend and Mick Jagger urged viewers to call their cable companies and demand that they begin broadcasting MTV. It worked. In 1982, both New York and Los Angeles began carrying the channel.

VIDEO MADE THE TV STAR

The bands of the early 1980s—often made up of art school grads with their ironic humor and mastery of the short form pop song—seemed practically predestined to succeed in video form. Add in such preferred gender-bending activities as dressing up in dandy pirate costumes, and audiences were almost guaranteed. The sartorial splendor of acts like the Pet Shop Boys, whose video for "What Did I Do To Deserve This?" features the pair dressed in tuxedos and surrounded by showgirls, invariably worked on the small screen.

New Wave bands also particularly succeeded because British or European music videos were particularly inventive and well made. Some American bands such as Devo had already been making arty music videos for years, so all MTV had to do was ask for them to hand them over for free. No longer confined to either playing national tours or hoping that a radio station picked them up, Blondie and the Talking Heads had similar success in reaching a national audience. Certainly, Devo and Debbie Harry were more effective on video than strictly on the radio. Despite these successes, the videos of the early years of MTV were rarely the high-budget affairs that characterize music videos today. However, that didn't mean that they were cheap, and indie labels found that even the cheapest video production was out of reach. Of course, as all things in the music business go, this sparked a backlash.

MTV short for music television, the cable channel was one of the only nationwide distribution systems for music at the beginning of its inception.

<<< **MTV,** with its emphasis on visual media, **diminished the importance of radio to rock music.**

R.I.P.
Radio Star
1926-1981

- **Focus on visual performance**
- **Indie labels didn't have the budget for music videos**
- **"Authenticity" is challenged**
- **Videos are primarily (at least at first) British and European**

VIDEO KILLS THE RADIO STAR

MTV proclaimed its mission from the first: Its premiere broadcast video was the Buggles' "Video Killed the Radio Star." To be fair, by the early 1980s the "radio star" in question had already declined; radio stations generally played classic rock and other tried-and-true hits. Certainly, however, video may have killed the *American* star—at least, a certain type of American star. By 1981, the music scene had already declared punk dead— although the genre would have a second wave as 1990s grunge—and new American music had few artistic outlets. New Wave and synth pop bands of the era, however, thrived in the video format with their telegenic looks and natural artistry. So, did video "kill" the radio star, or did MTV simply change what we knew as "music?"

Flashpoints ISSUES in ROCK

Did Video Kill Rock?

Did video really kill the radio star? Thinking of rock alone, video undoubtedly had an impact, especially regarding the virtue of authenticity. Some rock critics condemned the use of electronic instruments such as synthesizers and drum machines as "white-collar work" (Reynolds 2005, 347) as being inauthentic rock. However, successful video artists were often New Wave and synth pop bands that employed new methods of production. These types of bands already looked both to the future and to Britain and Europe, where music video had already gained a foothold. This "inauthentic" music sat at odds with critical opinions of what rock should be; the problem was that American musicians and record companies simply hadn't quite caught up. Come 1983, Michael Jackson released the video for the title single from his multi-platinum 1982 album *Thriller.* Arguably, this video—with its miniature plot, synchronized dancing, and zombies in full costume—changed the way that music videos worked. When pop singer Madonna released the video for "Like a Virgin" in 1984, American musicians seemed to be taking the medium back.

Bruce Springsteen's "Dancing in the Dark," from his 1984 album *Born in the U.S.A.,* spawned a music video the year it came out. A far cry from the synthesized dance music hated by music critics, Springsteen's "Dancing in the Dark" was nonetheless layered with synthesizers. But by this time, "rock" was becoming a loose term, and critics didn't level the charges of inauthenticity at Springsteen that they did at other bands of the era. In fact, record labels may have actually ramped up their efforts at American working-class authenticity through the use of visual, rather than aural, media. Toward the end of the video for "Dancing in the Dark," Springsteen picks a girl wearing a patriotic American T-shirt—none other than a young Courteney Cox—out of the crowd and dances with her on stage. Any skepticism about video was now being met with even greater efforts by the record labels to assure listeners—and now viewers—of the authenticity of their acts. Once records labels figured out that "authenticity" could sell, they did what they had previously done with "classic" rock: They figured out how to concoct it.

Scenes and Styles of Synthesized Pop, 1974–1978

Style name	Characteristics	Representative Albums
Synth pop	Uses keyboards to sound synthetic, rather than to imitate acoustic instruments.	Brian Eno, *Here Come the Warm Jets* (1974) Kraftwerk, *Trans-Europe Express* (1977) Gary Numan, *The Pleasure Principle* (1979)
New Romanticism	Second wave of synth pop, which focused on the futuristic and European elements, as well as retro costuming.	Ultravox, *Vienna* (1980) Adam and the Ants, *Prince Charming* (1981) Spandau Ballet, *Journeys to Glory* (1983) Culture Club, *Colour By Numbers* (1983)
Dance Pop	Well-made synthesized pop, which doubles as dance music. Generally has more artistry and less "cheese" than the New Romantics.	The Human League, *Dare!* (1981) Depeche Mode, *Some Great Reward* (1984) The Pet Shop Boys, *Actually* (1987)

∧∧∧ Bands like Kraftwerk, Spandau Ballet and Depeche Mode represent the diverse styles of synthesized pop.

The Band with a Thorn in its Side: The Smiths

In 1980s Britain, as synth pop and New Wave stormed the charts, a contingent of underground musicians nevertheless looked to break away from what had by then become the status quo. Formed in opposition to both synth pop and New Wave, the **Smiths** were arguably the best British band of the 1980s, with nearly unparalleled influence on later generations both lyrically and musically. In fact, they were an 80s band only "in the sense of being *against* the eighties" (Reynolds 2005, 392).

FORMATION AND INITIAL SUCCESS

Although the Smiths' founders **Johnny Marr** and **Steven Patrick Morrissey** were in many ways quite opposite—Marr a technically brilliant guitarist, laying down his tracks in the studio, and Morrissey a lost Romantic reading Oscar Wilde—the story of their meeting demonstrates the necessity of their collaboration. Neither *just* Morrissey nor *just* Marr could have brought the Smiths similar success.

∧∧ The 1986 album *The Queen Is Dead* was a breakthrough for the Smiths, offering the best of Morrisey's lyrics and Johnny Marr's guitar playing.

Morrissey once said that Johnny Marr simply showed up with his guitar one day. At the time of this fabled meeting, Morrissey had been drawing unemployment and living like a hermit for some time, despite having a fascination with the music world that had inspired him to write a book on the New York Dolls. Marr, on the other hand, had played in various rock groups and had almost scored a record deal with pure pop pioneer Nick Lowe. Morrissey and Marr hit it off and began writing songs, enlisting the drummer from local band the Fall to record a demo with them. After a year of performing around Manchester with replacement drummer Mike Joyce and bassist Andy Rourke, the Smiths had gained some local popularity. This lineup stuck throughout the Smiths' career, with Joyce and Rourke holding down the rhythm for Morrissey and Marr's songs.

Self-titled debut album *The Smiths* appeared in 1984 soon after their first single "Hand In Glove." The song, containing veiled references to homosexuality and a not-so-veiled naked man on the cover, instantly set the tone for the band. From the bluesy harmonica to the driving rhythm section to the melancholy, literary vocals, the song was a clear reaction against the synth pop sounds of the 1980s.

The Smiths' real breakthrough came with their 1986 album *The Queen Is Dead*. Their first effort to chart in the United States, the album featured the Smiths at their best. Morrissey's lyrics are equal parts morose, bitter, and witty; on "Frankly, Mr. Shankley," he tells his imaginary boss—reportedly inspired by a head honcho at the group's record label—that "I didn't realize that you wrote poetry, I didn't realize you wrote such bloody awful poetry," and "I want to go down in musical history." Equally, Marr's guitar hits a lighthearted, moderate tempo offbeat, a sound that probably had not been heard for years in the wake of the dominant late-1970s fast punk guitar sound.

MORRISSEY'S CONTROVERSIAL SEXUALITY

Morrissey drew nearly as much attention for his sexuality as for his musicality. He declared himself chaste, stating that he was a member of "the fourth sex," and thus negating both the Bowie model of glam cross-dressing as well as the macho oversexed model ubiquitous in the rock of earlier decades. Because of his proclaimed chastity, he became an easy object of both same- and opposite-sex desire. Morrissey himself promoted his controversial asexuality, often discussing it in interviews; his proclamation of chastity was absolutely a public one. Whatever the purpose of these maneuvers, the singer used them from the beginning. In a 1984 interview with British music newspaper *New Musical Express* (*NME*), Morrissey said that he had a "non-sexual stance," and that "Everybody has the same sexual needs" (NME 1984).

Morrissey's lyrical work also made a huge impression on later generations of songwriters. Having immersed himself in the wry, forlorn works of Oscar Wilde, Morrissey channeled the writer into a new century. His lyrics combined at times over-the-top self-pity, rarely meant what they said, and dwelled on the completely morose. The song "Heaven Knows I'm Miserable Now," with lines like "I was looking for a job, and then I found a job, and heaven knows I'm miserable now," even bordered on self-parody. The Smiths and Morrissey found an

audience with the similarly disillusioned youth of Thatcher's economically depressed England.

The Smiths' Continued Influence

Luckily for the band, many people shared their disaffection with contemporary England. According to Morrissey, their success was no surprise because "The Smiths speak absolutely for now, singing about the way people live as opposed to the way people don't live" (*Rolling Stone* Oct. 1986). The sound of the Smiths continued into the next generation as well. As early as 1986, Rolling Stone recognized Johnny Marr's sonically thick, layered "wall o' guitars" (*Rolling Stone* Sept. 1986), which gained marked popularity among bands of the late 1980s and early 1990s such as My Bloody Valentine and Jesus & Mary Chain. Marr also brought strong guitar playing back to rock after the five-year absence of the sound since the Talking Heads' choppy guitar-driven album, *Talking Head: 77*. In much the same way, Morrissey made Roxy Music-style crooning fashionable again. After melody had been all but lost in the previous decade of music, from the Sex Pistols to Kraftwerk, Morrissey brought well-crafted melodies back into rock music.

All of these features of the Smiths cropped up again in American alternative rock of the 1990s and beyond: the melancholy lyrics laced with wit, the overdubbed wall of guitars, and the outsider status. In fact, after the 1987 demise of the band, Morrissey went on to a successful solo career in the 1990s. Johnny Marr has cropped up in the lineups of bands including the The and Modest Mouse, another iconic indie rock band that attained critical and commercial success. The Smiths' influence would be felt far beyond Britain, partly because of their own fame but also because of the fame of their younger musical followers. However, one of their greatest achievements remains breaking the New Wave cycle: they seemed to come out of nowhere, giving over-synthed listeners a breath of fresh air and the chance to try something new.

<<< **The Smiths' influenced later generations of performers** and helped bring melody back to rock music.

Review

Summary

HOW DID PUNK'S DESTRUCTIVE FOCUS CREATE NEW OPTIONS FOR LATER MUSICIANS? 172

- Punk's disavowal of all of the 1960s' influences allowed New Wave artists to adopt new styles, both musically and lyrically.

- Indie and D.I.Y. bands were able to break into the scene because of the clear break from the standard ways of making and releasing music.

WHAT ROLE DID BRITAIN PLAY IN CRAFTING THE NEW WAVE SOUND? 175

- Many of the initial New Wave artists were British, including Elvis Costello. Britain generally had a quicker response time in adopting new musical styles.

- Britain's proximity to mainland Europe gave it close contact to Germany, which was a center of synth pop and electronic music. Brian Eno played a large part in this, relocating most of his operation to Berlin.

- London's club called the Blitz housed the New Romantic/Blitz Kid/Futurist movement, which eventually gave way to more intelligent electronic dance music.

WHAT WAS THE PLACE OF DANCE MUSIC IN POSTPUNK AND NEW WAVE? 181

- After punk largely destroyed dance music, New Wave and synth pop brought it back in huge ways, mostly through electronic beats. Rather than tracing dance back to blues-influenced swing music, however, synth pop and New Wave combined a dance rhythm with European, especially Germanic, influences.

- Yet, dance music was often laced with irony. The Pet Shop Boys, for instance, made heavily commercial music that was chock full of self-aware clichés. Also, the focus was not so much on optimism and excitement as it was on boredom and disillusionment.

HOW DID MTV CHANGE THE WAY THAT MUSIC WAS RECEIVED? 182

- Most importantly, MTV was one of the only national distribution channels for music. In the beginning, since U.S. musicians rarely made videos, MTV would get their videos from British and European acts, which gave the channel a bit of an experimental style. Likewise, Devo and other artistic bands made videos as well, so these were incorporated into the playlist. Later, once record companies figured out that there was money to be made, it became much harder for independent and experimental groups to get on MTV.

- The visual element was important as well, partly for the way that it made the images of even fairly minor musicians ubiquitous. Also, there began to be an art of the music video, which required a three-minute storyline or gag to keep popularity and interest up.

- Charges of inauthenticity began to be leveled at MTV, with critics complaining that it makes the record industry focus on looks rather than "authentic" rock & roll. Of course, authenticity quickly became its own industry, as evidenced by Bruce Springsteen's music videos.

- Bands such as the Smiths rebelled against synth pop and New Wave sounds through the use of witty, morose lyrics and the "wall o' guitars."

Key Terms

postpunk music in the immediate aftermath of punk rock that recognizes either punk's influence or the way in which punk denied other influences 172

New Wave the British movement that came out of punk, also associated with U.S. bands like the Talking Heads 172

synth pop an originally British movement that used synthesizers instead of guitars, drawing heavily on European styles 172

Elvis Costello seminal British New Wave/postpunk musician who combined the sarcasm and energy of punk with a biting lyrical style 172

David Byrne lead singer and producer of the Talking Heads who later went on to a long-lasting solo career 172

Talking Heads American postpunk band who met at the Rhode Island School of Design and were part of the developing New York postpunk scene, often playing at CBGB 172

Sire Records record label that signed the Ramones and the Talking Heads, as well as handled the U.S. distribution for The Smiths 173

CBGB club in New York's seedy Bowery district that housed the New Wave and punk scenes. 173

dub musical genre that developed from the practice of re-recording reggae songs as primarily instrumental tracks 174

Tom Verlaine Television guitarist who is largely credited with bringing punk and postpunk to CBGB 174

Robert Christgau "Dean of American rock critics," Christgau wrote for the *Village Voice* for much of his career 176

Brian Eno legendary producer, performer, and creator of the ambient music genre 178

Minimoog a descendent of the legendary Moog Modular and one of the first affordable, easy-to-use synthesizers 176

Gary Numan mastermind behind synth band Tubeway Army who created a whole dystopian universe in which to set his songs *176*

Kraftwerk German group influential in the creation of synth pop *180*

New Romantics also called Futurists, or Blitz kids, these European-obsessed synth pop audiences combined retro and futuristic costuming and favored electronic dance music *181*

Pet Shop Boys one of the founders of more cerebral dance pop comprising singer Neil Tennant and keyboard/synth programmer Chris Lowe *181*

MTV short for music television, the cable channel was one of the only nationwide distribution systems for music at the beginning of its inception *182*

The Smiths seminal 1980s band who broke through the New Wave and late punk noise to produce some of the best albums of the era *184*

Johnny Marr the Smiths guitarist credited with bringing guitar-driven rock back to the mainstream *184*

Morrissey controversial singer for the Smiths famous for his dry, witty lyrics and his declaration of celibacy *184*

Sample Test Questions

1. Which artist was not involved with Malcolm McLaren?
   a. Adam and the Ants
   b. The Sex Pistols
   c. Elvis Costello
   d. Bow Wow Wow

2. Which band/artist is an example of synth pop?
   a. Talking Heads
   b. The Police
   c. The Smiths
   d. Gary Numan

3. Which album was not one of Bowie's "Berlin Trilogy"?
   a. *The Rise and Fall of Ziggy Stardust*
   b. *Low*
   c. *Lodger*
   d. *"Heroes"*

4. Which New York club housed many young New Wave and punk bands?
   a. Village Vanguard
   b. Blitz
   c. Roxy
   d. CBGB

5. Which European city proved an inspiration for much of the New Wave music and culture?
   a. Amsterdam
   b. Berlin
   c. Paris
   d. St. Petersburg

ESSAY QUESTIONS

6. How did Brian Eno's approach to the synthesizer influence later musicians?

7. How did the New Romantics/Blitz kids/Futurists use fashion?

8. What were some world music influences that found their way into postpunk music, and how were they used?

9. What was MTV's initial effect on musical styles in the United States?

10. What were the ways that The Smiths broke from the prevailing tradition, and how did the band influence later bands?

WHERE TO START YOUR RESEARCH PAPER

For an interview with Elvis Costello, go to
http://www.elviscostello.info/articles/r/rolling_stone.820902a.html

For more information on the Talking Heads, go to
http://www.rockhall.com/inductee/talking-heads

For more information on Brian Eno, go to
http://music.hyperreal.org/artists/brian_eno/

For frequently asked questions about Kraftwerk, go to
http://kraftwerkfaq.com/index.html

To read about the history of the synthesizer, with information on many models, go to http://120years.net/

For a history of L.A. punk, as well as details on many L.A. punk bands, go to http://www.punk-information.com/History.htm

For information on the New Romantics, as well as a video showcase, go to http://www.squidoo.com/new-romantics

To read about the history of MTV, go to
http://www.spiritus-temporis.com/mtv/

For an archive of all of the Smiths' interviews, go to
http://foreverill.com/interviews/

ANSWERS: 1. c; 2. d; 3. a; 4. d; 5. b

Remember to check www.thethinkspot.com for additional information, downloadable flashcards, and other helpful resources.

HOW DID ALTERNATIVE ROCK GET THE WORD OUT?

HOW DID THE ROCK UNDERGROUND INFLUENCE ROCK DURING THE 1980s?

HOW DID ALTERNATIVE ROCK TRY TO CHANGE THE WORLD?

"More than

any other U2 album, *The Joshua Tree* has the power and allure to seduce and capture a mass audience on its own terms. Without making a show of its eclecticism, it features assertive rock ('Where the Streets Have No Name'), raw frenzy ('Bullet the Blue Sky'), delicacy ('One Tree Hill'), chugging rhythms ('I Still Haven't Found What I'm Looking For') and even acoustic bluesiness ('Running to Stand Still') – all of it unmistakably U2.

"But if this is a breakthrough, it's a grim, dark-hued one. At first, refreshingly honest, romantic declarations alternate with unsettling religious imagery. Then things get blacker. The raging, melodramatic 'Bullet the Blue Sky' ties Biblical fire and brimstone with American violence overseas and at home. In the stomping, harmonica-spiked rocker 'Trip Through Your Wires,' what looks like salvation could easily be evil seduction; 'One Tree Hill' is a soft, haunting benediction on a U2 crew member who died in a motorcycle accident; and 'Red Hill Mining Town' echoes Peter Gabriel's 'Don't Give Up' in its unsparing look at personal relationships savaged by economic hardship—here, the aftermath of the largely unsuccessful British miners' strike of 1984.

"But for all its gloom, the album is never a heavy-handed diatribe. After the first few times through 'Running to Stand Still,' for instance, you notice the remarkable music: the wholly unexpected blues slide guitar, the soft, Nebraska-style yelps, the ghostly harmonica. It sounds like a lovely, peaceful reverie—except that this is a junkie's reverie, and when that realization hits home, the gentle acoustic lullaby acquires a corrosive power that recalls 'Bad,' from the last LP.

"*The Joshua Tree* is an appropriate response to these times, and a picture bleaker than any U2 has ever painted: a vision of blasted hopes, pointless violence and anguish. But this is not a band to surrender to defeatism. Its last album ended with a gorgeous elegy to Martin Luther King Jr.; *The Joshua Tree* closes with a haunting ode to other victims. 'Mothers of the Disappeared' is built around desolate images of loss, but the setting is soothing and restorative – music of great sadness but also of unutterable compassion, acceptance and calm. *The Unforgettable Chill*, you might call this album, and unforgettable is certainly the right word."

—Steve Pond, *Rolling Stone*, April 1987

ALTERNATIVE ROCK (1982–1987)

CHAPTER 11

HOW DID ALTERNATIVE ROCK GET THE WORD OUT?

When Steve Pond reviewed U2's **The Joshua Tree** in 1987, alternative rock was on the verge of crossing over to the mainstream to become big business. Live Aid had placed **U2** and other alternative bands before audiences of tens of millions worldwide, and the Irish group was selling huge numbers of recordings on both sides of the Atlantic. At this juncture, U2 had the rare opportunity to look back at its early career and define its mission and musical orientation. Powered by such now-legendary rock anthems as "Where the Streets Have No Name" and "I Still Haven't Found What I'm Looking For," *The Joshua Tree* was destined to be a classic album—one that concisely and powerfully defined the group and its sound. Almost any alternative rock band might have hoped for such a masterstroke, regardless of whether that band was making it big on a major label or still chugging from one venue to the next in a beat-up old van. Alternative rock was about searching, but never quite finding, what you were looking for.

Alternative Rock's Three Trajectories

By 1982, it was clear that rock & roll had survived young adulthood with surprisingly good health. Neither the turbulence of the early 1960s nor the psychedelic adventures of the end of that decade nor even the onslaughts of disco and punk had managed to inflict lasting damage on rock. In fact, from the perspective of the marketplace, things had never looked better.

The dawn of the alternative music era was—by the nature of the name itself—an admission that the era of rock & roll revolutions was over. Mainstream rock was here to stay, operating on a perpetual motion machine of greatest hits, reunion tours, and increasingly conservative record labels. Visionaries waiting for the next Beatles or Rolling Stones to turn the world upside-down no longer propelled the industry. Instead, music executives were becoming more sophisticated about defining their audiences and targeting them with their particular product. During the 1980s, alternative rock bands were less interested in dismantling the status quo than they were in living and even prospering by their own, edgier rules. And, as some were discovering, those edgy rules could be good business.

The term alternative rock is an umbrella term first popularized by the early 1990s' touring Lollapalooza Festival, which promoted some of the biggest alternative acts of the era such as the Butthole Surfers, the Henry Rollins Band, Living Colour, and Nine Inch Nails. (For more on the Butthole Surfers, see Chapter 12.) Jane's Addiction

>>> **Perry Farrell of Jane's Addiction** organized the first Lollapalooza Festival in 1991 for **the "alternative nation" of underground rock fans.**

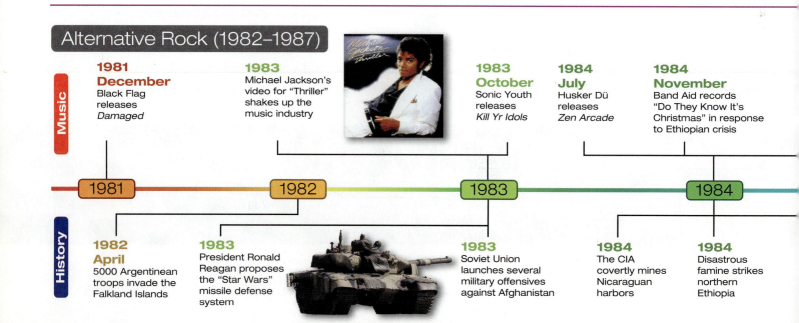

Alternative Rock (1982–1987)

Music

1981 December
Black Flag releases *Damaged*

1983
Michael Jackson's video for "Thriller" shakes up the music industry

1983 October
Sonic Youth releases *Kill Yr Idols*

1984 July
Husker Dü releases *Zen Arcade*

1984 November
Band Aid records "Do They Know It's Christmas" in response to Ethiopian crisis

1981 — 1982 — 1983 — 1984

History

1982 April
5000 Argentinean troops invade the Falkland Islands

1983
President Ronald Reagan proposes the "Star Wars" missile defense system

1983
Soviet Union launches several military offensives against Afghanistan

1984
The CIA covertly mines Nicaraguan harbors

1984
Disastrous famine strikes northern Ethiopia

(and, later, Porno for Pyros) front man Perry Farrell, who organized the initial 1991 Lollapalooza Festival, is credited with coining the term "alternative nation" to describe alternative music's audience: young Americans seeking to capture some of the integrity and political awareness of the late 1960s. As a musical movement, however, alternative rock arose from three different musical trajectories with roots in the early 1980s: punk, college radio, and the desire for creative and commercial independence.

PUNK ATTITUDE

Punk's attitude infused alternative music from the start. Even in the postpunk era, punk rock's rejection of commercialism and mainstream popular culture remained an active force in music. That rejection took many forms, including satire and political activism, in addition to the music itself. The sneering iconoclasm of the Sex Pistols and the earnest leftist political agenda of the Clash had sparked momentum among musicians who, at the very least, wanted to go against the mainstream.

COLLEGE RADIO

The U.S. alternative music movement owed much of its popularity to college radio stations. Like many of the independent radio stations of the early 1950s, American college radio stations were willing to experiment with new sounds, cross traditional boundaries, and offer airtime to bands that had been largely ignored by commercial stations. Radio stations such as Princeton's WPRB and the University of Massachusetts' WAMH were among those that began to include cutting-edge local talent and other new music, a harking back to the small independent stations that broke new acts in the 1950s. Bands such as R.E.M. and the Smiths received their initial boosts from small but enthusiastic radio audiences both on and off campus.

INDIE ROCK

As college rock stations spread the word during the 1980s and early 1990s, alternative music grew into its own as a specific genre with a mainstream audience. Although mainstream rock bands such as Van

THE JOSHUA TREE Irish group U2's epochal fifth album that came to define the mission and restlessness at the core of alternative music.
U2 an Irish alternative rock band.

Halen and Poison may have been happy to forget their first couple of gigs in small, nearly deserted local venues, alternative rock bands—even successful ones such as Nirvana and the Pixies—were fiercely proud of their low-key origins. (You will learn more about both of these alternative acts in Chapter 12.) They had a reason to be proud: Their fan bases had been built through touring, not through the distribution strategies of major labels. Alternative rock bands were also proud of the audiences that they found in those small venues. Rather than appealing to testosterone-fueled armies of young listeners in the way that Van Halen might, indie rock found its audience in disaffected outsiders who might be more likely to sing about their inability to get girls than to boast about their latest on-the-road conquest.

Indie rockers who did sign with major labels frequently strove to retain artistic control. Although punk groups including the Clash, the MC5, and the Sex Pistols all fought battles with their labels over the content of their songs, major labels did little to censor or tone down later indie bands such as Nirvana or the Butthole Surfers. To hang onto their outsider status in the face of corporate backing, however, indie bands maintained a strong anti-corporate stance. For example, Kurt Cobain of Nirvana—a seminal group who brought alternative rock solidly into the mainstream in 1991—maintained indie appeal by wearing a "Corporate Rock Sucks" T-shirt. (For more about Nirvana and its influence on music, see Chapter 12.)

U2: Band of the 1980s and Today

Admittedly, the term "alternative rock" is difficult to pin down. But by the end of the 1980s, that nebulous genre had its own superstars: Irish group U2. The quartet rode to worldwide success on the tripod of postpunk, college radio stations, and indie zeitgeist. A band that seems

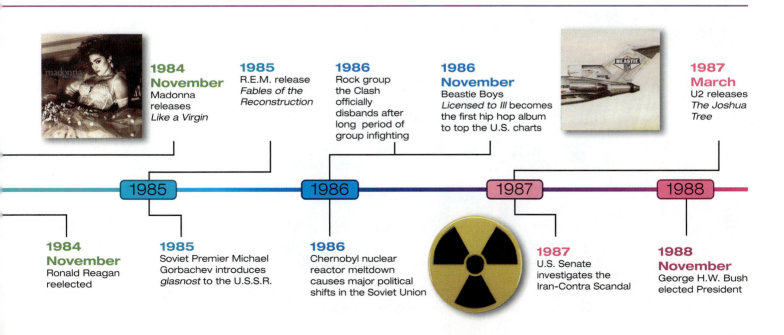

1984 November Madonna releases *Like a Virgin*

1985 R.E.M. release *Fables of the Reconstruction*

1986 Rock group the Clash officially disbands after long period of group infighting

1986 November Beastie Boys *Licensed to Ill* becomes the first hip hop album to top the U.S. charts

1987 March U2 releases *The Joshua Tree*

1985 — 1986 — 1987 — 1988

1984 November Ronald Reagan reelected

1985 Soviet Premier Michael Gorbachev introduces *glasnost* to the U.S.S.R.

1986 Chernobyl nuclear reactor meltdown causes major political shifts in the Soviet Union

1987 U.S. Senate investigates the Iran-Contra Scandal

1988 November George H.W. Bush elected President

>>> **Irish rock group U2** brought platinum sales and stadium rock **to the alternative music scene.**

to toss the traditional template for rock superstars on its head, U2 enjoyed commercial success throughout the 1980s and beyond while maintaining their artistic edge and without burning out or relying on reunion tours.

RISE TO STARDOM

U2's rise to the top of the alt charts was quick and, to many, shocking. In the late 1970s, the four members—singer Paul "Bono" Hewson, guitarist Dave "the Edge" Evans, bassist Adam Clayton, and drummer Larry Mullen, Jr.—were students at Dublin, Ireland's Mount Temple High School. Caught up in the wave of postpunk, the four used what skills they had to craft a distinctive sound. Incapable of playing elaborate lead guitar solos, the Edge

developed his signature reverb-laden chord style ringing with echoing, shimmering notes, while Mullen and Clayton formed a straight-ahead, ramped-up rhythm section. That quickly beating, multi-layered sound created the textured background for Bono's urgent, high-pitched voice.

During the members' final year of high school, U2 got its first big break in a talent contest sponsored by Irish beer-makers Guinness. Paul McGuinness, then manager of British punk act the Stranglers, soon offered to manage the fledgling group. Although the group initially failed its audition for CBS records in 1978, the following year the label released the group's first limited-run EP, *U2 Three*. That initial failure turned to success as the EP soon reached the top of the Irish charts in 1979.

The group's full-length debut, *Boy* (1980), attracted some attention in the United States with the hit "I Will Follow." Energetic live performances added to U2's growing reputation. On their third album, *War* (1982), U2 addressed political themes concerning the Troubles in Northern Ireland. That album took the group to the top of the British charts and reached number 12 in the United States. Their follow-up effort, *The Unforgettable Fire* (1984), saw U2 paying tribute to Martin Luther King, Jr., with their first American Top 40 hit, "Pride (In the Name of Love)." By 1985, U2's star had risen so dramatically that Rolling Stone named the group "Band of the Eighties."

POLITICS AND POPULARITY

Legendary appearances at concert event Live Aid (1985) and six-city Amnesty International benefit tour Conspiracy of Hope (1986) helped cement U2's stature as a politically aware band. Although *Rolling Stone* noted the album's dark outlook in the review that you read at the beginning of the chapter, the album *The Joshua Tree* (1987) spawned such major hits

The Edge, U2	A shimmering sound focusing on texture and melody, achieved through use of reverb and single notes	
Greg Ginn, Black Flag	Loud and fast, without effects or pedals but with high, bending notes	
Lee Ranaldo, Sonic Youth	Uses dissonance, alternative tunings, and experiments with improvised and random insertions (for instance, a screw inserted on a fretboard) to create textures and sounds	
J Mascis, Dinosaur Jr.	High volume, extensive use of pedals—distortion, wah-wah, flanger, volume, and sound effects—to create a "sonic veil"	

<<< **The alternative music era** ushered in **a generation of guitar innovators** rather **than guitar heroes.**

as "I Still Haven't Found What I'm Looking For" and "With or Without You" and propelled U2 into the stratosphere of musical stardom. Ultimately, the album won two Grammy awards and inspired a triumphant world tour.

Unlike many bands, U2 seemed destined to perform in arenas from their beginnings. The anthemic qualities of their songs, with their sing-along choruses and sweeping reach, appealed to the masses in a way that punk or no-wave did not. In an age of dissolution and cynicism permeating the music industry and the political divides of the Reagan era, U2 offered a brand of political idealism that had been absent from the music industry since the late 1960s. Professed Christian Bono cared less about revolution and more about obtainable achievements, an outlook well suited to the more confined, less epic battles of the 1980s. Although punk bands such as the Clash and former Beatle George Harrison had explored similarly political themes through recordings and concerts, Bono's approach to political issues was more measured, non-ideological, and, on the practical level, more committed than these sometimes chaotic or sporadic efforts. In a decade during which Reagan-style capitalism prevailed on a broad scale, U2's left-leaning politics gave post-baby boomers a chance to feel good, as though they were part of a larger movement reminiscent of those of the 1960s. Woodstock had disappeared in a haze of pot smoke and fond memories with little to offer in the way of actual accomplishments, but U2's sharpened, guided approach gave leftism a newly honed edge.

It was no coincidence then that U2's own musical vision of rock & roll stemmed in part from a guitarist who took "**the Edge**" as his stage name. Spare, distinctive, eloquent, and accessible, the Edge's textured guitar licks defined the sound of an era. Subtly subversive, the band—like its music—retained its bite without resorting to self-indulgence or self-destruction. This successful combination in many ways defined the voice and the music of what Perry Farrell eventually dubbed the "alternative nation."

R.E.M.: Kings of College Rock

While U2 offered an explicitly political agenda to anyone who cared to read their songs' lyrics, **R.E.M.** charted a somewhat different route to

the world of mainstream alternative rock. More cryptically subversive, R.E.M. substituted personal politics for U2's broader ambitions. In contrast to U2's global perspective, R.E.M.'s haunted, self-directed diffidence relied on a particularly American tone to shake the underground.

Hailing from the college town of Athens, Georgia, **Michael Stipe**, an itinerant army brat who discovered punk by listening to artists such as Television, Wire, and Patti Smith, fronted R.E.M. Bassist Bill Berry and drummer Mike Mills were two high school buddies from Macon, Georgia, and budding guitarist and fanatical album collector Peter Buck worked at a local record store. In April 1980, the group—then called the Twisted Kites—played its first show in a converted Episcopalian church. (Later, the group selected the name R.E.M. at random after flipping through a dictionary.) During the year and a half that the group toured the South as a psychedelic garage band, Buck developed his distinctive guitar style marked by spread-out chords, while Stipe began to hone his cryptic, sometimes obscure lyricism. The group's first single, "Radio Free Europe," had an initial indie label run of only 1,000 copies, but thanks to college radio airplay received enough publicity to attract the attention of larger indie I.R.S. A well-received EP, *Chronic Town*, preceded R.E.M.'s 1983 debut, *Murmur*.

In some respects, R.E.M. stood as U2's foil. Instead of being broadly anthemic, Stipe brought an understated but ever-present passion to his reserved, almost incoherently run-together vocal style; in fact, some jokingly referred to *Murmur* as *Mumble*. Yet reviewers praised the album highly. In a year that saw such classics as Michael Jackson's *Thriller* and Police's *Synchronicity*, *Rolling Stone* honored *Murmur* as the best album of 1983.

FABLES OF THE RECONSTRUCTION by R.E.M.

On 1985's *Fables of the Reconstruction*, R.E.M. took alternative rock on a sonic tour of the American landscape. Perhaps it seems odd that the group did so in England, where legendary folk producer Joe Boyd recorded the album. Laced with creepy sonic textures, ringing guitars, and enigmatic lyrics, the album offered a breakthrough for a group that was using its alt-rock eclecticism to recreate a vision of America. Michael Stipe's often hazy, difficult-to-understand lyrics made the work a rumination not only on the people but also on the haunting history of the South itself. Even the album's title harked back to the post-Civil War Reconstruction era, a time of immense cultural and political change for the erstwhile Confederacy, that set the stage for the 20th-century South. However, this reference remained typically ambiguous, with the placement of the title on the album's cover allowing dual interpretations; the album's title could equally be read

as *Fables of the Reconstruction* or *Reconstruction of the Fables.*

The song "Can't Get There From Here," a strange dialogue between dislocated voices, summed up the spirit of dislocation that infused alternative rock's music and audience. At its heart, *Fables of the Reconstruction* did for alternative rock what albums such as the Eagles' *Hotel California* did for the mainstream.

ROCK PLACES

Athens, Georgia

College town Athens, Georgia—located some 80 miles northeast of sprawling southern metropolis Atlanta—became a breeding ground for alternative rock during the 1980s. As the home of the University of Georgia, the town bustled with the young people who formed much of alternative's early audience. Student-run college station WUOG engaged those listeners' ears with tracks by contemporary cutting-edge bands, including the Athens' own B-52s and R.E.M. (For more on the B-52s, see Chapter 10.) Both local and national bands performed at local venues such as the 40 Watt Club (pictured here with R.E.M. on stage), which moved into progressively larger spaces as alternative music attracted more and more fans. Numerous independent record stores catered to hordes of dedicated fans. By the late 1980s, Athens' bustling creative scene had grown to include a magazine, *Flagpole*, dedicated entirely to local music happenings.

Even as the geographical focus of alternative musical innovation shifted from college towns such as Athens to the grunge mecca of Seattle in the early 1990s, the Georgia community tenaciously held onto its independent scene. Some of the groups recording for influential independent record label Elephant Six clustered around the city during the 90s, including Neutral Milk Hotel and Olivia Tremor Control. Today, Athens' music scene continues to thrive.

MICHAEL STIPE: BREAKING THE ROCK STAR MOLD

Detached and mumbling, Michael Stipe began to define a new brand of rock star. Instead of wanting to steal your girlfriend or destroy the world, he was a mumbling shoegazer who seemed to take you into his confidence without quite playing all his cards. Guitarist Buck backed up Stipe's distinctive singing with a ringing, rhythmically varied sonic attack. The combined effect created moody, introverted, and bizarrely captivating recordings and live shows that have continued to this day. Unusual clothing choices and dramatic—even mask-like—make-up contribute to Stipe's onstage persona.

R.E.M.'s album sales increased steadily, and their 1985 album *Fables of the Reconstruction* sold 300,000 copies. But the band's influence spread wider and deeper than even these strong sales figure imply, in part because of exhausting tour commitments that included unknown underground bands as opening acts. By the mid-1980s, many American alternative bands had taken up R.E.M.'s musical style. In true Stipe-ian fashion, the band achieved mainstream success without trying too hard. Backed by the strength of Top 10 single "The One I Love," 1987 album *Document* went platinum. The following year, R.E.M. left the indie labels behind, upgrading from I.R.S. to Warner Brothers for a signing fee of 6 million dollars. Major label debut *Green*, a diverse release that ranged from bright pop ("Stand") to driving rock ("Orange Crush") to jangling folk ("The Wrong Child") followed in 1988. By the next year, R.E.M.—like U2—packed stadiums rather than just small Southern clubs.

This crossover success continued with singles such as "Losing My Religion" from 1991 album *Out of Time* and "Everybody Hurts" from 1992 release *Automatic for the People* making their way into heavy rotation on both radio and MTV. The former track, with introspective lyrics hauntingly delivered over a melodic, acoustic background, solidified R.E.M. as a mainstream force, while the latter found Stipe abandoning his trademark obtuse lyrical and vocal style for a cleanly, powerfully expressed emotional cry for strength in times of difficulty. This ability to create both tightly controlled rock tunes and intellectually and emotionally complex lyrical voyages has contributed greatly to the group's continuing artistic and commercial success to the present day.

By the 21st century, Stipe's political streak became more clearly defined as he took on causes such as AIDS awareness and sexual politics. Nevertheless, R.E.M.'s political slant was subtler than U2's or The Clash's, a more personal iconoclasm that didn't require combat boots or global change. The group did what some of the major forces in rock & roll had done before by opening doors and spreading influences that many would not have otherwise accepted. In brief, R.E.M. worked to recover the roots of American music by connecting with the voice of an intelligent—if disenchanted—generation.

CASHING IN OR SELLING OUT?

As one of the first alternative bands to make the transition to a major label, R.E.M. had to answer to accusations that they had sold out. At a 1987 Butthole Surfers show, singer and ex-R.E.M. fan Gibby Haynes protested R.E.M.'s move to the majors by burning dollar bills onstage while the band tore through a hard-driving version of "The One I Love." Haynes' message was clear. Poppy tune "The One I Love" had been R.E.M.'s ticket to the big time, and for the group's members it undeniably paid off financially. But at the same time, R.E.M. had brought alternative American music to new, mainstream audiences.

SELLING ALBUMS WITHOUT SELLING OUT: BRUCE SPRINGSTEEN

If some considered R.E.M. sellouts, how could you make it big without compromising your artistic vision? Alternative rockers had few role models, but New Jersey rocker Bruce Springsteen never lost his integrity or creative control. By 1984, Springsteen's popularity was peaking with the release of his seventh album, *Born in the U.S.A.*, and he was filling arenas with his traditionally American brand of accessible, sing-along rock.

But as Springsteen himself admitted, moving to the mainstream carried its own dangers. As Springsteen moved to megastardom, he underwent a personal makeover and began cultivating a masculine sex appeal. The musician himself maintained his credentials as a left-of-center liberal, but *Born in the U.S.A.'s* album cover with a buff,

patriotic Springsteen standing in front of an American flag seemed to fit too easily into the iconography of the Reagan era. In fact, until Springsteen put on the brakes, title track "Born in the U.S.A." was slated to be the theme song of the 1984 Republican Convention. It was a cautionary tale for the world of alternative rock; Springsteen and other megastars could maintain their integrity, but in the rock & roll marketplace, integrity may not count for much. "Born in the U.S.A." was an antiwar song, but some took it as an anthem for Reagan-era neo-conservative patriotism.

HOW DID THE ROCK UNDERGROUND INFLUENCE ROCK DURING THE 1980s?

American Hardcore Shakes Up the Musical Underground

Throughout the late 1980s and the early 1990s, the mainstream gradually absorbed alternative music and the alternative nation. But there was a lot more leading up to this more mainstream alternative rock than just U2 and R.E.M. Beginning in the late 1970s, a burgeoning underground music scene began to move from one city to the next to form a movement that became known as hardcore. Although hardcore had no real geographical center, the genre's name describes the character of its musicians and fans across the nation: committed, passionate, and determined to go against the grain of the Reagan-era United States.

Hardcore bands never filled arenas with tens of thousands of fans, nor did their record sales hit platinum—or even gold—levels. While other politically minded acts such as R.E.M., The Clash, U2, and Bruce Springsteen considered filling arenas and selling millions of albums to be consistent with their personal values, American hardcore groups prided themselves on maintaining a certain edge and intensity. This relatively small network of musicians and enthusiasts was ready to choose the road less taken without much hesitation.

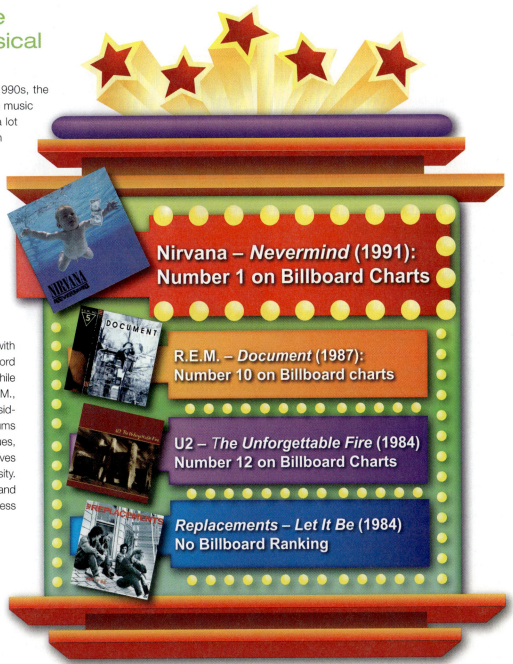

Nirvana – *Nevermind* (1991): Number 1 on Billboard Charts

R.E.M. – *Document* (1987): Number 10 on Billboard charts

U2 – *The Unforgettable Fire* (1984) Number 12 on Billboard Charts

Replacements – *Let It Be* (1984) No Billboard Ranking

>>> After a decade of struggling, **alternative rock hit the big time with Nirvana.**

SONIC YOUTH: BREAKING THE NOISE BARRIER

The confluence of New York City's artistic and musical underground during the early 1980s gave rise to pioneering group Sonic Youth. After the demise of New York's punk scene, a small but influential coterie of bands with names like Teenage Jesus & the Jerks and DNA gave up on the straight-ahead beat of rock & roll to experiment instead with noise, dissonance, and textured layers of sound. At this time, college dropouts Lee Ranaldo and Thurston Moore moved to New York City, where the active New York arts scene quickly absorbed them. There, Moore met artist Kim Gordon, a denizen of the no-wave scene who had taken up the bass. Along with Ranaldo and local drummer Richard Edson, Sonic Youth began to make a name for themselves on the city's alternative music scene.

The band's influences crossed the musical spectrum. One significant and perhaps unexpected influence was modernist composer **John Cage**, who had jolted the classical music world during the 1960s and 70s by refusing to distinguish "music" from "noise." Like Cage, who created "prepared pianos" by placing paper, erasers, drills, or anything else on hand between the instrument's hammers and strings to attain new sounds, Moore and Ranaldo inserted drumsticks and screwdrivers under guitar strings and drilled holes through wah-wah pedals to create new sounds. Through its use of alternate tunings and improvisations, Sonic Youth developed an idiosyncratic and inimitable style; the group's live performances channeled the energy of 1970s punk groups while Kim Gordon's vocals recalled the aggressive yet emotional style of Patti Smith. (For more on Patti Smith and other 1970s New York artists, see Chapter 9.)

Through the early 1980s, Sonic Youth had a small but dedicated local following at clubs such as CBGB. (For more on CBGB, see Chapters 9 and 10.) However, an initial tour of the South and Midwest was less than successful (Azerrad 2001, 240) given the somewhat uncompromising nature of Sonic Youth's work. But European tours in 1983 found receptive audiences and won the band attention for its often riotous shows. In 1986, Sonic Youth finally arose from the New York arts ghetto with *EVOL*, recorded for the punk SST label. Two years later, Enigma released the group's seminal *Daydream Nation*. By 1990, Sonic Youth had joined the major label Capitol Records for the release of their album *Goo*. And then what had seemed previously

unthinkable occurred: a noise-rock band with roots in hardcore, John Cage, and the Stooges made it to the Billboard Top 100.

Although Sonic Youth's influence may be difficult to define, it is unquestionably widespread. The band itself—like its tunings—is impossible to imitate. Extensive touring and a solid work ethic not only gave the group wide exposure, but also contributed to their influence on contemporary alternative acts such as Dinosaur Jr., Mudhoney, and Nirvana. (For more on these bands, see Chapter 12.) But, as bassist Kim Gordon made clear, Sonic Youth's legacy can be easily boiled down: "We were influential in showing people that you can make any kind of music you want" (Barry 2008).

BAD BRAINS: FUSION PUNK

Epochal band **Bad Brains** created much of the musical foundation for hardcore—but, ironically, the group didn't fit easily into the brash, chaotic hardcore movement. Composed of singer H.R., guitarist Dr. Know, bassist Darryl Aaron Jenifer, and drummer Earl Hudson, the African American group from the largely black neighborhood of Capitol Heights

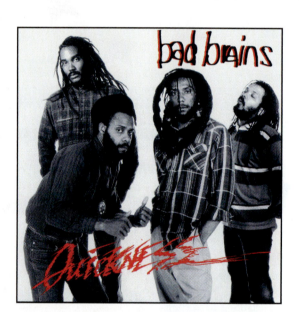

^^^ D.C.'s Bad Brains **broke speed limits and mixed genres.**

near Washington, D.C., Bad Brains stood apart from the largely white hardcore musical community and started out with a definite agenda: the creation of a new, visceral sound out that pulled from jazz, punk, metal, reggae, and other influences. Musically, the band was tightly disciplined in a way that few other hardcore bands were; spiritually, they also adhered strictly to the tenets of Rastafarianism.

A Mix of Influences

Initially a jazz fusion band shopping around for a new musical style, Bad Brains found its niche after its manager introduced the group to the music of the Ramones, Wire, the Sex Pistols, the Clash, and Eater. "We were listening to the Ramones," says H.R., "And we wanted to do it faster" (Barry 2008). This desire led to a hybrid of speed-metal and groove that took the punk sensibilities of the late 1970s to a new, immensely faster dimension. Although early hardcore had relied on the straightforward rock sound of basic I-IV-V power chords, Bad Brains began experimenting with minor and diminished chords, stretching the limits of the genre at a time when many Americans were discovering the simplicity of hardcore punk.

The group's first single, "Pay to Cum" (1980), careened at a high tempo while inserting jazzy guitar riffs in a chorus that floated off into a brief atmospheric whimper. Shortly after the release of "Pay to Cum," Bad Brains became entranced by reggae after watching Bob Marley perform. Never ones to do anything by half measures, the band's members adopted the Rastafarian religion, and reggae became an important musical element of Bad Brains' albums and live shows. These shows exhibited many of the group's unique abilities. H.R.'s driven performances were intensely energetic, while Dr. Know's jazzy variation on speed metal guitar playing raised the technical bar for hardcore performers. The rhythm section of Earl Hudson and

WHAT'S HOT!

AUGUST 8, 1987

1. "I Still Haven't Found What I'm Looking For" – U2
2. "I Want Your Sex" – George Michael
3. "Shakedown" – Bob Seger
4. "Heart and Soul" – T'Pau
5. "Luka" – Suzanne Vega
6. "Rhythm is Gonna Get You" – Gloria Estefan
7. "Who's That Girl" – Madonna
8. "Cross My Broken Heart" – The Jets
9. "Alone" – Heart
10. "Wot's It to Ya" – Robbie Nevil

Darryl Jenifer verged on the chaotic without actually veering into the abyss.

Even though they never reached the pinnacle of mainstream crossover success, Bad Brains became legends of the musical underground. By the early 1980s, Bad Brains had relocated to New York City, where they attracted the attention of some major musical figures. In 1983, the Cars' Rick Ocasek produced the group's *Rock for Light*. However, the 1986 SST release *I Against I* shows the group at its most musically flexible, injecting a melodic, metallic, and somewhat slower tone into the music.

But each of these triumphs was followed by a breakup or, sometimes, a breakdown, which could usually be attributed to their volatile singer, H.R., whose charismatic persona and inimitably energetic, high-speed performance style helped define the group's public image. Even though the group broke up for good in 1995, Bad Brains left a legacy of musical proficiency for their hardcore music followers, pushing the limits of hardcore punk in a way that no others have done.

TEEN IDLES KICK OFF A MOVEMENT

During the early 1980s, Washington, D.C., became a focal point for the development of the hardcore underground. Who was the movement's catalyst?

A handful of teenagers—Ian MacKaye, Jeff Nelson, Nathan Strejcek, and Geordie Grindle—who discovered punk rock partly through Georgetown University's radio station WGTB. Inspired, they formed the band the Teen Idles in 1980.

The quartet started to play whatever small local venues allowed them in. The group's raw, high-energy thrash was gently mocked by the city's older new wavers, who dismissed them as "teeny punks"— kids who were too young to drink and didn't indulge in drugs. The Teen Idles, however, wore that label with pride. Although barely known, the group headed out on a mini-tour during the summer of 1980. Upon their return, the Teen Idles recorded an EP, *Minor Disturbance*, on their own **Dischord Records** label. The tracks' speed and ferocity drew on Los Angeles hardcore, but their lyrics seemed to come from another world. Mocking the pretensions of the D.C. scene, the EP invited younger rockers to create their own musical moment. The word spread, and new bands soon turned D.C. into a hardcore haven.

MINOR THREAT: BREAKING THE AGE LIMIT

When Minor Threat formed in 1981, the band's name was disingenuous. The Teen Idles' Ian MacKaye and Jeff Nelson recruited guitarist Lyle Preslar and bassist Brian Baker. This quintet produced straightforward music with simple chords and shouted vocals. Neither as technically proficient as Bad Brains nor as creatively experimental as Sonic Youth, Minor Threat gained its reputation for speed, intensity, and accuracy. Passionate advocacy compensated for MacKaye's limited vocal range. Minor Threat always prided themselves on being out of step and unpretentious.

∧ ∧ **Although** underground groups like the Teen Idles **never sold as many albums as R.E.M. or U2,** they had a major influence on musical culture of the decade.

In its own subversive way, the group was a political one. As MacKaye himself puts it, rage fueled the groups' members: "The evolution of punk rock had grown from these silly kids to being embattled silly kids to being embittered silly kids, then embittered kids and then violent embittered kids. It kept getting ratcheted up" (Azerrad 2001, 129). MacKaye's blunt lyrics gave voice to white teenage angst and pent-up energy, confronting the kinds of local and even personal issues prevalent within the hardcore scene itself. Propelled by MacKaye's shouted yet oddly melodic vocals, the track "Minor Threat" called to peers who wanted to grow up too quickly, while "Screaming at a Wall" was directed at stubborn friends. In "Filler," MacKaye directed his lyrics at a friend whose religious girlfriend had hijacked his mind. Most importantly, the songs provided a bonding experience for the band and listeners, easy to sing along with and easy for most audience members to sympathize with. As MacKaye sang, he frequently handed the microphone over to audience members.

Straightedge Rock & Roll

In some ways, Minor Threat was as notable for what its members did not do as for what they did. The group's philosophy, which appeared in the song "Straightedge," included a message of avoidance: no drugs, cigarettes, or alcohol. While some mocked this choice as a new form of rock & roll Puritanism, MacKaye insisted that the object of his anger was consumer culture, which he claimed caused people to mindlessly indulge when they could just as easily find entertainment from their own resources. Minor Threat extended that philosophy to its live shows. By setting a maximum ticket price of $5 and avoiding the lavish trappings of rock & roll theater, the group tried to return the music to an all-ages listening experience rather than just as a vehicle for selling drinks and an image.

Minor Threat's insistence on independent thinking extended to their business decisions. The group released all of its EPs—*Minor Threat* (1981), *In My Eyes* (1981), *Out of Step* (1983), and *Salad Days* (1983)—on their own Dischord Records, which in time became one of the hardcore movement's creative centers. Dischord Records used mail order and networking to gradually build up a dependable fan base. Twenty-eight years later, Dischord continues to go strong.

FUGAZI TAKES THE BATON

By 1983, Minor Threat and what had turned into hardcore tribalism had gradually lost its shine for MacKaye, and the group disbanded. MacKaye soon became the front man for Embrace, employing a more introspective lyrical approach that set the stage for what would become emo several years later. (You will learn more about emo in Chapter 15.) In 1986, MacKaye teamed up with Guy Picciotto, singer and guitarist for Rites of Spring, another proto-emo band. With drummer Brendan Canty and bassist Joe Lally, the four formed Fugazi, playing their first show at D.C.'s Wilson Center in 1987. The volatile Picciotto and the principled and stubborn MacKaye were at the center of the band's chemistry. As a Dischord band, Fugazi continued to follow the tradition set by Minor Threat: $5 ticket price, low-cost touring, and no drugs or alcohol. However, MacKaye strove to dismantle what he called the "ritualistic" elements of hardcore: the **slam dancing**, **stage diving**, and unthinking adherence to a musical structure that had turned the hardcore scene into its own small army.

∧∧∧ One of the most **influential voices on the hardcore scene,** singer and guitarist **Ian McKaye (front)** founded the **Teen Idles, Minor Threat** (pictured here on the cover of their *Salad Days* EP), **and Fugazi.**

The band favored dub and reggae influenced rhythms over the thrash-beat of most hardcore bands, placing guitar riffs over this textured rhythmic background. After releasing two EPs, Fugazi made its full-length debut with 1990's *Repeater.* By then, the band had created a carefully integrated, democratic sound marked by a tight rhythm section. Over the next decade, Fugazi sold over 2 million records, including the notable releases *Steady Diet of Nothing* (1991) and *In on the Kill Taker* (1993).

Fugazi also added a new element to the hardcore scene: a political conscience. While in Minor Threat, MacKaye had been content to direct his wrath at those around him, but in Fugazi he openly endorsed a leftist political agenda. The band embraced such causes as vegetarianism, animal rights, and AIDS research, among others.

BLACK FLAG DECLARES WAR

While Washington's bands remained focal points for East Coast hardcore, California's **Black Flag** became equally important to the genre.

In 1979, Los Angeles' suburban Orange County gave rise to what became known as hardcore: a music that, in the words of writer Barney Hoskins was "younger, faster, angrier, full of the pent-up rage of dysfunctional Orange County adolescents who'd had enough of living in a bland Republican paradise" (Azerrad 2001, 13). As the flagship band of this underground scene, Black Flag came to define and dominate the hardcore scene in the early 1980s.

Black Flag founder Greg Ginn drew on his wide-ranging taste in music to develop the template for what would become hardcore—a heavy, rhythm-based guitar played over a blistering drum attack, with the vocalist shouting lyrics depicting a nightmarish version of Reagan-era United States. The group's first EP, *Nervous Breakdown*, appeared in January 1979 and featured vocalist Keith Morris screaming out the sardonic lyrics. Ginn's brother, artist Ray Pettibon, provided unsettling drawings to accompany the band's mix of paranoia, anger, and dark humor. At first, bassist Chuck Dukowski and drummer Robo filled out the band, although multiple personnel changes—most notably, the addition of vocalist Henry Rollins—marked the group's seven-year history.

Black Flag's sound was a distinctly American variation on British punk, with a brutal, dark sense of humor and a violent undercurrent. The band became the center of the emerging Los Angeles area hardcore scene, in which concerts would frequently turn into brawls—often between police and concertgoers. By 1981, Black Flag and other hardcore bands had been banned by many Los Angeles clubs. With their hometown options limited, Black Flag began touring up and down the West Coast, sometimes ranging as far as Texas and Chicago. These

American alternative rock in the 1980s was not restricted to a single scene or geographic area.

The map contains the following labels:

- Seattle, Washington — **Mudhoney**
- San Francisco, California — **The Dead Kennedys**
- San Pedro, California — **The Minutemen**
- Hermosa Beach, California — **Black Flag**
- Phoenix, Arizona — **The Meat Puppets**
- Minneapolis, Minnesota — **The Replacements, Husker Dü**
- San Antonio, Texas — **Butthole Surfers**
- Chicago, Illinois — **Big Black, Naked Raygun**
- Boston, Massachussets — **Mission of Burma**
- Amherst, Massachussets — **Dinosaur Jr.**
- Washington, D.C. — **Bad Brains**
- Athens, Georgia — **R.E.M.**

ROCK TECHNOLOGY ▶▶▶ The Van

During the early years of the alternative music movement, distribution was no easy task. Without the support of major labels, bands relied on the postal services, phone calls, constant touring, and friendships to get the word out. Bands like Black Flag exhibited the stamina and determination of Lewis and Clark to embark on extended, low-budget tours through the American heartland, often playing to tiny—and sometimes hostile—audiences.

Although in the world of conventional rock & roll, tours were money losers whose purpose was to support album sales, those same tours were the only way to make money in the musical underground. Without the label dollars to foot the bills for massive, costly buses, under-

ground bands navigated their trusty (and cheap!) vans across the country on sometimes exhausting tours. However, the van had its disadvantages. Long miles in tight quarters frequently caused friction between band members. Unforeseen breakdowns caused abbreviated or even canceled tour dates. And on more than one occasion, exhausted drivers careened off the road. D. Boon, an iconic underground figure and member of the Minutemen (see below), died in a van accident. Black Flag's Henry Rollins penned an entire memoir about touring in vans, aptly entitled *Get in the Van*. In the end, however, whether the van was the best way or the worst way was irrelevant. For American underground bands, it was the only way.

extended tours, which often visited tiny, dingy clubs holding audiences numbering only in the dozens, in some ways aggressively blazed the path for the hardcore movement by spreading the message of this alternative underground movement.

Henry Rollins

After going through several singers, Black Flag recruited **Henry Garfield,** a Washington, D.C., vocalist with hardcore band S.O.A. When Black Flag made its first East Coast tour in 1981, Garfield—a close friend of Ian MacKaye—auditioned for the band in New York City. He quit his job at a Georgetown ice cream store, changed his name to Henry Rollins, and headed for the West Coast to become Black Flag's most memorable front man. First appearing on Black Flag's 1982 *Damaged* LP, a classic rant against police, consumer culture, materialism, and whatever else the band members had in their heads, Rollins demonstrated a charismatic, aggressive persona that blended well with Black Flag's anarchic nihilism. He quickly became the face of hardcore's angry side, often weaving together screeds with intense confessionals.

Ginn's musical vision constantly shifted, and, over the next several years, Black Flag gradually moved to the slower, more metallic droning roar of 1984's *My War*. Eventually, however, the group disbanded. Although Rollins made a career as a cult personality, hardcore was never able to reconcile itself with mass popularity in the way that U2 and R.E.M. could. For artists such as Greg Ginn and Ian MacKaye, that lack of popularity was a point of pride.

∧
∧ **Henry Rollins,** Black Flag's
∧ charismatic lead singer, **champions the alternative movement** with both his music and poetry.

THE MINUTEMEN

If Black Flag was the nihilistic voice of the suburbs, then the Minutemen gave a voice to the working class. D. Boon and Mike Watt were two friends who grew up in the Navy-occupied public housing projects of San Pedro, 30 miles outside Los Angeles. Both avid fans of popular and populist rock groups such as Creedence Clearwater Revival and Van Halen, Boon and Watt developed a complex network of musical influences that turned the Minutemen into one of hardcore's most flexible and original voices. The pair also shared contempt for the

bands that monopolized 1970s arena rock. "If it weren't for those type of bands, we would never have had the nerve to be a band," said Watt (Azerrad 2001, 65).

After being exposed to punk during the late 1970s, Boon and Watt began to formulate their own approach to hardcore. A brief stint as the Reactions preceded the duo's teaming up with drummer George Hurley to form the Minutemen. Their first EP, the seven-song *Paranoid Time* (1980), was just six minutes and forty two seconds long. However, that was all it took to introduce the Minutemen's almost folksy musical style, punctuated with political rants and played at breakneck speed. Follow-up release *The Punch Line* (1980) featured a similar brevity but experimented with a funky complexity informed by jagged melodies and pulsing rhythms. With their next record, *What Makes a Man Start Fires* (1982), the Minutemen added melody and a high-pitched, somewhat twangy guitar style to their sound. However, the group's musical reputation peaked with 1983's 45-song double LP, *Double Nickels on the Dime*. With tracks such as "History Lesson Pt. 2" proclaiming the life-changing nature of punk rock and "Do You Want New Wave or Do You Want the Truth?" delving into the relationship between abstract truth and concrete words, the album combined seemingly disparate jazz, punk, and even polka to create a surprisingly coherent, unique sound. Their 1987 album, *Three Way Tie for Last*, was even more eclectic, with a cover of Creedence Clearwater Revival's "Have You Ever Seen the Rain?" and a Neil-Young-esque style that was beginning to spread across the punk horizon.

Jamming Econo

In addition to their music, the Minutemen brought a new phrase to the punk lexicon: *jamming econo*. This concept meant making albums with tiny budgets, touring without a crew, and finding ways to make recording a low-cost enterprise. This less-angry, practical approach proved influential, both financially and artistically. Like Fugazi, the Minutemen relied on constant touring along with an open approach to new musical influence to build up a fan base. Indeed, the band seemed ready to crack the mainstream in the wake of a tour opening for R.E.M. But the Minutemen's rise was brought to a sudden and tragic halt in December 1985 when D. Boon died in an automobile accident. That event abrupt stopped one of indie music's most idealistic and inventive bands.

HUSKER DÜ

Minneapolis, Minnesota's **Husker Dü** become one of the few hardcore bands that made it on a major label, a transition that paved the way for later leaps from indie to major by such groups as Nirvana and the Pixies. Husker Dü's uncompromising music nevertheless had the punk-pop structure that bands such as the Buzzcocks (see Chapter 10) used to great effect on the other side of the Atlantic. With tightly constructed songs infused with layers of distorted, loud guitar riffs and surprisingly catchy vocal lines, the group melded the attitude of punk with the songsmithing of pop-rock.

The band originated in 1979 as part of Minneapolis' burgeoning rock scene. Guitarist and singer Bob Mould was working at a record store where he met drummer Grant Hart. The two joined forces with bassist Greg Norton and immediately began to develop a strong local following. Husker Dü did not blend seamlessly in the hardcore scene, however. Their music was quirkier and poppier than most, not to mention that they were technically more adept players with major label aspirations. But the group was able to work the existing, active hardcore network to its advantage. Thanks to constant touring and the assistance of college radio stations, Husker Dü became well known in the indie community.

Husker Dü brought a new level of artistic achievement to hardcore on its 1984 double album, *Zen Arcade*. Recorded in 40 studio hours, the 25-song album is a concept album describing the story of a young boy who joins a cult. The group toyed with traditional punk—loud, fast, energetic conceits such as pounding drums and shouting vocals—to devise a new sound. Long instrumentals, piano solos, acoustic guitar, and covers of songs such as Bo Diddley's 1965 hit "I Want Candy" all indicated that hardcore was coming into its own as an eclectic, integrative form of music with mainstream potential.

$13 Million · $30,000 · $3,300 · $1,200 · $15,000

Guns N' Roses · Sonic Youth · Husker Dü · The Minutemen · R.E.M.

Chinese Democracy · Daydream Nation · Zen Arcade · Double Nickels on the Dime · Murmur

∧
∧ After a decade of high production values, **the American hardcore movement**
∧ showed   that you didn't need to be a millionaire **to make a great record.**

HOW DID ALTERNATIVE ROCK TRY TO CHANGE THE WORLD?

> **LIVE AID** international music festival organized in 1985 to raise funds for Ethiopian refugees.

The Rock Benefit Concert

Unlike some earlier bands, alternative musicians never really tried to define a generation or overthrow the established order. However, alternative music was at its best inherently dynamic. Just as band members didn't accept established musical rules as they were written, they didn't accept the world as it was put before them. Some considered alternative music a path to change and even hoped to use the genre as an instrument of change through live performances, a concept little explored in earlier decades. The successes and failures of these ambitions were central to the alternative era.

LIVE AID, FARM AID, AND BAND AID

Although rock benefit concerts didn't begin with the alternative music era, June 1985's **Live Aid** marked the birth of a new era of "benefit rock" that borrowed some elements from George Harrison's 1971 Concert for Bangladesh. Organized by promoter Bob Geldof, Live Aid had two purposes: to raise funds for famine relief in Ethiopia and to put on a two-stadium, 400-million-viewer bonanza.

Participating rock musicians—including Queen, U2, Elvis Costello, David Bowie, the Who, Paul McCartney, Madonna, Bob Dylan, the Rolling Stones, Crosby Stills, Nash & Young, Black Sabbath, Led Zeppelin, Duran Duran, and others—clearly took those dual goals into consideration. Most of the acts were rock superstars eager to rehabilitate their images as selfish, greedy entertainers. Live Aid's promoters become more sophisticated than had previous benefit organizers; with a world-wide audience, the concerts raised £150 million for famine relief, considerably more than the several hundred thousand drummed up by the Concert for Bangladesh.

British acts composed much of the Live Aid lineup. However, American musicians had their chance with Farm Aid. Organized by Willie Nelson, Neil Young, and John Mellencamp, the concert benefited struggling American farmers. Held in 1985 in Champaign, Illinois, Farm Aid was reportedly spurred by a remark that Bob Dylan had made at Live Aid about the need to rescue family farms in the United States. Over the past 25 years, many additional Farm Aid concerts have taken place, with Nelson, Young, and Mellencamp still among the major performers; this annual event now ranks as the longest-running concert series in the United States. As of 2009, these concerts have raised over $35 million to support family farms and encourage small-scale agricultural practices throughout the United States.

During this era, the rock benefit concert became its own self-promulgating industry that has continued to this day. A crop of charity singles dedicated to raising funds for "deserving" causes sprang up, although these tunes were of varying quality and often leant toward the sentimental. For example, 1984's "Do They Know It's Christmas?" by Band Aid benefited the Ethiopian Relief Fund. Performed by a

ROCK PEOPLE

Sir Bob Geldof

Born in 1954, Bob Geldof became one of rock music's primary philanthropists during the 1980s. After the 1975 formation of the Boomtown Rats—which performed such punk numbers as "Looking After Number One" and the poppier "I Don't Like Mondays"—the band enjoyed moderate success in the United Kingdom but never broke through in the United States. In 1984, Geldof's career in philanthropy

began when he watched a BBC documentary on Ethiopian refugees, inspiring him to compose "Do They Know It's Christmas?" about the crisis. Performed by Band Aid, an ad hoc group that included major British pop stars, the song became an instant hit and went on to become the best-selling single in UK history.

In 1985, Geldof organized Live Aid, which raised tens of millions for impoverished Africans. In recognition of his efforts, Geldof was nominated for a Nobel Prize and later knighted. After the Boomtown Rats disbanded in 1986, the singer went on to a relatively successful solo career. However, philanthropy remained his primary focus. In 1999, Geldof teamed up with Bono, Jimmy Page, Wyclef Jean, and other contemporary stars for Net Aid, a multimedia simulcast that also raised millions in famine relief.

>>> **In addition to his work as** a musician and philanthropist, **Bob Geldoff starred** in the 1982 film version of **Pink Floyd's** *The Wall*.

The outpouring of creativity during the alternative era meant that it was only a matter of time before musicians and audience members began to ask whether that energy could be put to good use. In the late 1980s, efforts to employ rock & roll as a force to create a better, healthier, cleaner world spawned countless organizations, festivals, and foundations. The Clash worked to spread leftist political agenda through their music, and U2's Bono spoke out about the African AIDS epidemic. Bob Geldof's Live Aid was a massive outpouring of support for Ethiopia. On a local level, the Washington D.C. hardcore movement's positivist approach became the nexus for political change through rock. Even on the right, bands have used their music to promote their political agendas.

But for every rock-oriented political rally or benefit, a chorus of skeptical voices emerged. Some commented that George Harrison's Concert for Bangladesh at Madison Square Garden offered little in the way of long-term humanitarian relief. Others noted that Live Aid participants' motivations may not have been as idealistic as they claimed—after all, getting to play on a telecast to an audience of 60 million has its own advantages. Still others noted that, regardless of their humanitarian impulses, audiences at rock concerts wish to be entertained, not mobilized to change history. Memories are frequently as short as the songs; rock & roll feeds on energy, but it may not be the energy needed to change the world.

So, does rock really make a difference? Or are musicians just trying to soothe their consciences?

>>> The two Live Aid concerts **took place simultaneously in** London and Philadelphia.

plethora of rock superstars, the Bob Geldof–penned song immediately shot up to number one on the pop charts. Another famous charity single, "We Are the World," also raised money for poverty relief. Recorded in 1985 by USA for Africa, its performers included such major American stars as Michael Jackson, Lionel Richie, Bruce Springsteen, Diana Ross, Ray Charles, Paul Simon, Stevie Wonder, and Willie Nelson, among others. The trend continues today with such 21st century events as Live 8. With each benefit concert—whether it's for AIDS relief or environmental awareness—debates inevitably ensue about where the money goes or whether the whole thing is publicity stunt.

Although many benefit concert participants are traditional rock stars without any connection to alternative music, the prevalence of these shows seems to indicate that, after the self-indulgence of the 1970s, being a rock star wasn't an end in itself. As Bob Dylan—who participated in several of these events himself—has noted, you've "Gotta Serve Somebody." That philosophy may be the core of the alternative music movement, one that connects such disparate elements as Black Flag and U2. In 1974, at the height of the arena rock era, the Rolling Stones' Mick Jagger declared from the pinnacle of superstardom that it was "only rock & roll." Alternative music, however, came around to remind fans that there was a lot more to it than that.

Summary

HOW DID ALTERNATIVE ROCK GET THE WORD OUT? 190

● Alternative rock stemmed from three basic trajectories: punk, college rock, and the indie networking system.

● Ireland's U2 and the United States' R.E.M. brought alternative rock to the mainstream. Unlike earlier generations of rock stars, however, alternative music bands were ambivalent about what fame and major labels could offer. Some of them looked to Bruce Springsteen, who shared their concerns about preserving his integrity and maintaining artistic control.

HOW DID THE ROCK UNDERGROUND INFLUENCE ROCK DURING THE 1980s? 195

● While R.E.M. and U2 were marching to the tops of their respective charts, the American rock underground was shaking things up. Bands such as New York City's Sonic Youth cultivated a sophisticated relationship between art and music, taking from influences as diverse as John Cage and Minor Threat. Bad Brains incorporated reggae and jazz in their version of hardcore, setting the template for rock & roll that was both fast and technically sophisticated.

● The Washington, D.C., hardcore scene was a thriving one. Bands such as Minor Threat challenged the accepted wisdom about the so-called rock & roll lifestyle and used independent Dischord Records to distribute music from the American underground. Minor Threat singer Ian MacKaye later formed Fugazi.

● California also had an energetic scene. The uncompromising, angry, and nihilistic Black Flag was among California's hardcore groups. Henry Rollins took over as the group's singer in 1981 and became a long-standing influential alternative figure. The Minutemen used a low-cost, working class mentality to spread their eclectic, interesting version of alternative rock.

● Minneapolis's Husker Dü and the Replacements were among the first indie bands to leap to the major labels, although both groups had limited success.

● During the same era, Britain produced alternative bands releasing music laden with Goth and literary references. The Cure, Bauhaus, and Kate Bush each formulated tightly controlled musical visions.

HOW DID ALTERNATIVE ROCK TRY TO CHANGE THE WORLD? 204

● After George Harrison set a precedent in 1971 with his Concert for Bangladesh, the 1980s saw a proliferation of massive benefit concerts such as Live Aid and Farm Aid.

The former, organized by Bob Geldof of the Boomtown Rats in 1985, raised tens of millions for Ethiopian refugees. The latter, organized by Willie Nelson, John Mellencamp, and Neil Young, became a long-standing festival to help struggling American farmers.

● Like alternative rock, these benefit concerts seem to indicate that rock & roll has a larger purpose than mere entertainment.

Key Terms

The Joshua Tree Irish group U2's epochal fifth album that came to define the mission and restlessness at the core of alternative music 190

U2 an Irish alternative rock band 190

The Edge U2 guitarist who developed a textured, reverb-laden guitar sound 193

R.E.M. an American alternative rock band that started out as a garage band 193

Michael Stipe R.E.M.'s enigmatic and influential lead singer 193

John Cage minimalist American composer whose experimentalism influenced Sonic Youth 196

Bad Brains D.C.-based band that helped define the hardcore sound 196

Dischord Records Washington, D.C., hardcore record label started by Ian MacKaye and Jeff Nelson of Minor Threat 197

slam dancing a violent dance style that became popular at early 1980s hardcore shows 198

stage diving a jump from stage to crowd made by performers that became common at early 1980s hardcore shows 198

Black Flag Hermosa, California-based hardcore band that became a powerful force in American alternative rock 198

Henry Garfield D.C.-based singer for S.O.A. who, as Henry Rollins, became the singer for Black Flag and, later, the Henry Rollins Band 200

Husker Dü Minneapolis-based hardcore band that incorporated a poppier, more accessible sound than most of their contemporaries 201

Paul Westerberg front man for popular American hardcore band The Replacements 202

Kate Bush English singer-songwriter whose influential incorporation of performance art, music, and literary influences created a musical form all its own 202

Goth rock bleak atmospheric rock pioneered by Bauhaus 203

Live Aid international music festival organized in 1985 to raise funds for Ethiopian refugees 204

Sample Test Questions

1. Who of the following was NOT an influential guitarist of the alternative era?
   a. The Edge
   b. Greg Ginn
   c. Keith Richards
   d. Lee Ranaldo

2. Which of these bands did NOT record on a major label?
   a. R.E.M.
   b. Fugazi
   c. Husker Dü
   d. The Replacements

3. Which of these statements is correct?
   a. The Replacements were from New York City.
   b. The Cure was a reggae band.
   c. The Minutemen's *Double Nickels on the Dime* was recorded in England.
   d. Fugazi refused to play venues that charged more than $5 per ticket.

4. Which of the following about Bob Geldof is NOT true?
   a. He was a singer.
   b. He was knighted.
   c. He won the Nobel Peace prize.
   d. He is a published writer.

5. Which of the following bands was based in the United States?
   a. The Cure
   b. The Boomtown Rats
   c. Kate Bush
   d. R.E.M.

ESSAY

6. Discuss the impact that alternative music had on rock & roll.

7. Did alternative music of 1980s have a mission?

8. What factors contributed to the alternative phenomenon in the United States?

9. Why did many alternative bands originate in Athens, Georgia?

10. Discuss how several major American alternative bands reflected the social and political climate of 1980s United States.

WHERE TO START YOUR RESEARCH PAPER

For an overview of the alternative era in rock, go to
http://www.britannica.com/EBchecked/topic/80244/Alternative-rock

For an in-depth biography of U2, go to
http://www.rollingstone.com/artists/U2/biography

For an in-depth biography of R.E.M., go to
http://www.rollingstone.com/artists/R.E.M./biography

For more information about the music history of Athens, Georgia, go to
http://athensmusic.net/

To research past and present Billboard 100 charts, go to
http://www.billboard.com/bbcom/index.jsp

To learn more about individual record albums, go to
http://www.allmusic.com

For an overview of the history of rock music, go to
http://encarta.msn.com/encyclopedia_761558548/rock_music.html

ANSWERS: 1. c; 2. b; 3. a; 4. c; 5. d

Remember to check www.thethinkspot.com for additional information, downloadable flashcards, and other helpful resources.

WHAT ELEMENTS DID GRUNGE BORROW FROM PUNK ROCK TO MAKE A NEW MUSICAL GENRE?

WHAT WERE THE MOST IMPORTANT BANDS THAT GREW OUT OF THE SEATTLE SCENE?

HOW WERE OTHER SIMULTANEOUS MOVEMENTS AFFECTED BY GRUNGE?

"Then

the room roars. Nirvana is onstage. I can just see the tippy tops of their pointed little heads. They begin with the song "Aneurysm," there's a quick lurch left, and I'm lifted off my feet, carried forward on an exoskeletal tide, as the entire room starts shrieking and stomping martially in unison along with the band. The beat slows down, and Kurt approaches the mike, by which time, along with everyone else, I think I'm actually holding my breath. *Come on over and do the twist*. He cracks the hard *t* like a bullet—ping!—and the audience moans. "Aaaahhh-ow!" *Overdo it and have a fit!* . . .

"My feet don't find the ground for a full minute and a half, and by the time they do I've been carried away on a tide of flesh. Everyone's bumping heedlessly into one another, skin slapping sinew . . . And yet our bodies have suddenly lost all sexual properties and have become mere tissue. It has happened at last: we are finally free of suggestion. . . .

"An hour later we burst out on the pavement, sopping wet. Nirvana fans were pouring out all around us. The alley was full of hefty boys in backward ball caps, all shirtless, their faces glowing red with the mysterious exertions inside. Many of them had no shoes on; my own legs were mud-spattered, and my green frock had somehow acquired a big hole nowhere near a seam. We milled about dazedly in the warm Hawaiian night—almost satiated, almost postcoital. . . .

"And then, I remember—I will always remember—looking up at the lights of the high-rise Hilton Hawaiian Village and thinking: Somewhere behind one of those cubelike balconies, Kurt and Courtney were anticipating their imminent wedding, while all around them, surrounded and confusing, Middle America in its rawest, ugliest, newlywed state slept peacefully, entirely unaware of the monster in its midst."

—Gina Arnold, *Route 666: On the Road to Nirvana*,
New York: St. Martin's Press, 1993, xi–xii

209

AMERICAN PUNK: THE SECOND WAVE (1987–1994)

CHAPTER 12

WHAT ELEMENTS DID GRUNGE BORROW FROM PUNK ROCK TO MAKE A NEW MUSICAL GENRE?

In the 1980s, there was still a thriving (albeit underground) punk scene in a few pockets of the country, including Bad Brains and Minor Threat in Washington, D.C., Black Flag in Hermosa Beach, California, and Hüsker Dü and the Replacements in Minneapolis. Many of these bands played faster and louder than the original punk outfits—the Sex Pistols, the Clash, and the Ramones—but rather than achieving international spectacle, they went even further underground, setting up their own independent labels and putting on all-ages shows.

But there was something different going on in the Pacific Northwest, where punk had taken hold and independent labels were releasing music from local bands. One of these indie labels, Sub Pop Records, started in 1987, "inventing" **grunge** with the band Green River. The relative isolation of the Pacific Northwest helped the area foster a community free to interpret punk rock in its own way.

Beginnings of a Seattle Scene

The Seattle scene in the mid-1980s was the most productive and unusual offspring of the punk movement, and certainly the most commercially profitable. The "Seattle sound," later dubbed "grunge," was not fast and intense like the hardcore punk of D.C. or Southern California; instead, it was slow and intense. Borrowing musical influences from heavy metal, an attitude from punk, and a few pop influences especially for melody and song structure, the Seattle bands created an entirely new sound.

The Seattle sound eventually crept over the Atlantic, as evidenced by an article in *Melody Maker* featuring Nirvana: "Britain is being swamped in a deluge of long hair, hoary old Black Sabbath licks and American upstarts from Seattle" (Rocco 1998, 11). Although punk rock rejected the 1960s, the article compares the band repeatedly to Jimi Hendrix, especially regarding the use of noise and feedback. Again, punk was fast and intense, and hardcore punk was faster and more intense, so it seemed like the only way to go was exactly the opposite direction: less precision, slower tempos, and more noise. The Seattle sound became as much a collection of influences—mid-1960s influences that were possible to claim because hardcore punk had declared them off-limits—as it was a community of musicians in itself.

HARDCORE PUNK AND GRUNGE

Yet, before the name "grunge" was attached to their sound, the Seattle bands still took the trouble to label themselves as punk. "We never considered anybody to be grunge. . . I always thought we were a punk band" (Heylin 2007, 596), said Steve Turner, lead guitarist and founder of Seattle band Mudhoney. However, bands in Seattle, lacking the more dogmatic punk scene that had developed in D.C. and California, were

>>> In the late 1980s and early 1990s, **Seattle's nascent grunge scene,** of which the Crocodile Café (pictured here) was a part, **became an international phenomenon.**

American Punk: The Second Wave (1987–1994)

Music

1985
Green River releases *Come on Down* EP, often called the first grunge record

GREEN RIVER

1986
Sub Pop releases the *Sub Pop 100* compilation, highlighting local bands

1988 March
The Pixies release *Surfer Rosa*

1990
Early riot grrrl band Bikini Kill is formed by Kathleen Hanna

1991 August
Pearl Jam releases *Ten*, their debut and top seller to date

PEARL JAM

| 1985 | 1986 | 1987 | 1988 | 1989 |

History

1989 June
The demonstration in Tiananmen Square is violently put down by Chinese troops

1989 November
The Berlin Wall falls

1991
The Persian Gulf War begins and ends

able to experiment with other influences. Krist Novoselic, bassist for Nirvana, said, "I liked prog-rock, and then I discovered punk-rock" (Heylin 2007, 598), pointing to a pre-punk influence that would have been unheard of in the earlier punk scene. Prog rock, with its emphasis on technical skill (see Chapter 8), was generally shunned during the visceral days of punk.

In time, the Seattle punk scene grew increasingly away from the established punk scenes in larger cities, partly because, as Steve Turner put it, "[Hardcore punk] became this rigid style of music and dress code and dance-fight. . . We weren't arty, but we weren't wearing leather jackets" (Heylin 2007, 600). The Seattle punk rockers weren't necessarily concerned with making hardcore punk more artful, but they could still see the ways in which the hardcore scene was becoming a fixed idea in the minds of its participants. Most of all, the foundation of grunge seemed to be an unconscious act: unconscious of the "right" influences—and unconscious of the influences deemed off-limits by hardcore punk rockers.

Source of Inspiration: The Pixies

The grunge bands took their inspiration from many types of music and places. But it was the Boston-based mid-1980s band the **Pixies** who probably most closely resembled the Seattle bands, in part because of their disparate, wide-ranging influences. The Pixies started in Boston around 1986, although guitarist Joey Santiago and singer/guitarist Charles Thompson knew each other in college. Thompson, who went by the stage name Black Francis, said that he read an interview with J. Mascis, the guitarist and singer for Dinosaur Jr., and "he said since I didn't know a lot of punk rock, I was innocent, that I could just do whatever" (Frank and Ganz 2006, 10). This was partly true, as Thompson had grown up in a conservative, Christian Pentecostal church and counts Christian rock founder Larry Norman among his influences, going as far as to take the title of the band's 1987 EP *Come on, Pilgrim* from a line that Norman would say at his concerts: "Come on, pilgrim, you know He loves you!" (Frank and Ganz 2006, 83). Thompson also admittedly drew from 1970s groups like the Cars, a fellow Boston band that would have been anathema to the hardcore punk groups of the era.

At the same time, Kim Deal and her twin sister, Kelley, were playing wedding gigs around Boston when Kim answered an ad placed by the Pixies in the local paper looking for a bassist. Although she had been playing guitar for 10 years, Deal ended up playing bass with the Pixies. (She would later play lead guitar in the Breeders, where her sister sang and played guitar as well.) Santiago, Thompson, and Deal rehearsed as a trio for a while, then auditioned drummers, eventually hiring David Lovering, a local electronic engineering student.

ABRASIVE AND MELODIC

One of the things that set the Pixies' sound apart was their ability to be paradoxically abrasive and melodic at the same time. In their song "Bone Machine," on the **Steve Albini**-produced *Surfer Rosa* (1988), Thompson and Deal sing a harmonized, almost a capella "Your bone's got a little machine" before the guitars come back in and Thompson lets out an unearthly scream. Much of this song follows the same pattern, alternating between Thompson's and Deal's harmonized two-line chorus and their nearly-shouted, deafening verses. Still, there are a few tracks on this album that line up more closely with the contemporary hardcore punk movement, particularly "Something Against You," which is mostly just heavily distorted guitars and Thompson screaming through what sounds like an electric megaphone.

The Pixies' influence was felt throughout the entire grunge era, especially in the sound of Nirvana. Kurt Cobain, in a 1994 interview for *Rolling Stone*, said that when he wrote "Smells Like Teen Spirit" for 1991's *Nevermind*, he was "trying to write the ultimate pop song. I was basically

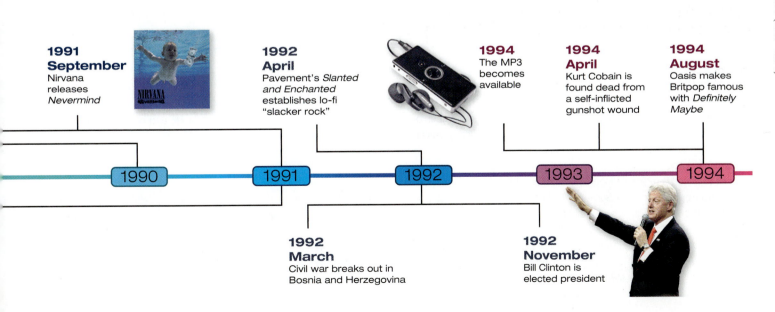

1991 September Nirvana releases *Nevermind*

1992 April Pavement's *Slanted and Enchanted* establishes lo-fi "slacker rock"

1994 The MP3 becomes available

1994 April Kurt Cobain is found dead from a self-inflicted gunshot wound

1994 August Oasis makes Britpop famous with *Definitely Maybe*

1990 1991 1992 1993 1994

1992 March Civil war breaks out in Bosnia and Herzegovina

1992 November Bill Clinton is elected president

trying to rip off the Pixies. . . We used their sense of dynamics, being soft and quiet and then loud and hard."

This use of contrast between soft and quiet and loud and hard is apparent in a number of songs. "Tame," the second track on the Pixies' 1989 LP *Doolittle*, begins as quiet as 1991's "Smells Like Teen Spirit," then explodes and gets quiet and intense again. Nirvana's "Lithium," also from *Nevermind*, follows almost the exact same structure as "Tame," with a quiet verse and a one-word, screamed chorus. In addition to the dynamic similarities between Nirvana and the Pixies, Cobain also developed a throat-ravaging scream much like Thompson's. In the song "Territorial Pissings," from 1991's *Nevermind*, Cobain's one-line chorus culminates in a scream, much like Thompson's extreme contrasts between his screams and his melodic singing in "Tame."

The Pixies' *Doolittle* furthered the band's juxtaposition of pop and punk. Where their previous album, *Surfer Rosa*, was much more harsh and abrasive, *Doolittle* included pop songs, such as "Here Comes Your Man," about to go off the rails. Incidentally, this album came out

the year that Nirvana's first, *Bleach* (1989), was released. Nirvana would go on to select Steve Albini to produce their final album *In Utero* (1993), in large part because of Albini's work in producing the Pixies' *Surfer Rosa*.

After releasing four full-length albums in four years, the Pixies broke up after 1991's *Trompe Le Monde*, just as Nirvana was releasing *Nevermind* and making grunge an international sensation.

Alternative Precursors: The Butthole Surfers

The **Butthole Surfers**, with album names like *Rembrandt Pussyhorse* (1986), *Locust Abortion Technician* (1987), and *Hairway to Steven* (1988), were another important precursor and source of inspiration for the grunge bands, but they were never really destined for mainstream success. Formed in 1981 in San Antonio, Texas, the band was virtually uncategorizable from the beginning. They combined shock tactics with a punk/metal fusion, although they also employed psychedelic sounds in some of their albums. Eventually, they scored a hit with the song "Pepper," from *Electriclarryland* (1996), which reached number 38 on the pop charts and number one on the alternative charts. Their fusion of punk and metal was influential on a number of Seattle bands, particularly Soundgarden, who were described as a fusion of "Led Zeppelin and the Butthole Surfers" (Azerrad 2001, 439).

<<< The Pixies were **one of the most influential forerunners** of the grunge movement.

WHAT WERE THE MOST IMPORTANT BANDS THAT GREW OUT OF THE SEATTLE SCENE?

Seattle Goes Subterranean

The Seattle scene was initially catalyzed by the label **Sub Pop Records** (a shortening of "Subterranean Pop"). One of the first of a number of now-legendary Seattle independent labels, Sub Pop signed early Seattle acts Green River (later, Mudhoney), Soundgarden, and Nirvana. Sub Pop's most important impact, especially in the early years, was an attempt to assert a regional identity for the music they were releasing. In 1986, Sub Pop released the *Sub Pop 100* compilation, which included songs by various rock groups (not all of them local), such as Portland's Wipers and Seattle's U-Men. 1988 saw the release of the sequel to this, the *Sub Pop 200*, which featured many more local bands, among them Tad, Nirvana (pre-*Bleach*), Mudhoney, Soundgarden, Green River, and others. This compilation is still in circulation, partly because many of the tracks are early singles of songs unavailable elsewhere.

Early Seattle Bands

A number of early Seattle bands set the stage for the grunge movement, some of which were on the Sub Pop label, and some of which would experience some mainstream success.

THE MELVINS

The most important early band on the Sub Pop label was the **Melvins**. Kurt Cobain idolized these fellow Aberdeen, Washington, residents, and worked as a local roadie for some of their shows, eventually enlisting the Melvins' drummer, Dale Crover, to play on his and Krist Novoselic's early demos as Nirvana (Rocco 1998, 11). The Melvins were local legends, in part because of their sludgy sound, influenced equally by the early metal of Black Sabbath as well as by the hardcore punk bands of the era.

Although the Melvins pioneered the sound, other groups (Soundgarden and Nirvana, especially), who combined the sound of the Melvins with a more traditional pop song structure would soon overshadow them. Members of the Melvins helped form other bands, particularly Matt Lukin, who became the bassist for Mudhoney.

In 1993, the Melvins moved to Atlantic Records, in part because of the success of Nirvana and Soundgarden, but they were dropped in 1996. The band currently releases records on indie label Ipecac Recordings.

SOUNDGARDEN

One of the most successful early Seattle bands was **Soundgarden**, which formed in 1984. More than other bands, Soundgarden relied on the early metal riffs of Black Sabbath and Led Zeppelin, while retaining the punk do-it-yourself (DIY) ethos. Bruce Pavitt, one of the founders of the Sub Pop label, was friends with the Soundgarden members through high school and college, so Soundgarden was one of Sub Pop's early bands. Although Soundgarden was discovered by Sub Pop, California indie label SST released the band's first record,

Ultramega OK (1988). Soundgarden then became the first distinctly Seattle band to "cross over" to a major label, releasing their 1989 album *Louder Than Love* on A&M.

Soundgarden was mostly marketed as a metal band, however, until Nirvana broke through with *Nevermind* (the same month as Soundgarden's *Badmotorfinger*, in October 1991) and grunge became a viable category. Soundgarden fit well with grunge, partly because of their altered guitar tunings, like the famous drop-D grunge tuning that allows the guitarist to play the metal "power chord" with a single finger. Soundgarden lead singer Chris Cornell also became the closest thing that Seattle had to a hunk—at least until Cobain became a teen idol. The band's breakout record, *Superunknown* (1994), had hits like "Black Hole Sun" and "Spoonman." Even Cobain said that Soundgarden was "obviously metal" and praised their rejection of sexist tendencies "common among metal bands of the period" (Rocco 1998, 56).

This was the strange fusion of the early grunge bands: They accepted and rejected aspects of both metal and punk rock, two genres that seemed similar but were socially segregated. It took an off-the-map city like Seattle to forget that one had to make the choice between being a punk and a metalhead.

GREEN RIVER AND MUDHONEY

Green River, a Seattle band named after a famous Washington State serial killer, were active from 1984 to 1987 and released what is often called the first grunge record, the EP

Band: The Melvins
Record: *Gluey Porch Treatments* (1987)
Sound: Slow, sludgy punk and metal

Band: Green River
Record: *Come on Down* EP (1985)
Sound: Steve Turner's noise-heavy lead guitar

Band: Soundgarden
Record: *Screaming Life* (1987)
Sound: Chris Cornell's sarcastic vocals and Kim Thayil's heavy metal guitars

<<< **The early days of grunge** in Seattle were difficult to describe, in part because the claim of **"first grunge record" or "first grunge band" is complicated.** These early bands all helped to **shape the scene,** through their live shows as well as their records.

Come on Down (1985), with Sub Pop. After this, the band went on to release another EP of studio recordings on Sub Pop called *Dry as a Bone* (1987), although they still failed to gain success outside Seattle. Some call this album the true originator of "grunge," as the Sub Pop catalogue referred to it as "ultra-loose GRUNGE that destroyed the morals of a generation" (Heylin 2007, 606). Eventually, bassist Jeff Ament and rhythm guitarist Stone Gossard went on to form the bands Mother Love Bone, and later, Pearl Jam, while front man Mark Arm and guitarist Steve Turner went further into grunge, forming the band **Mudhoney** in 1988.

Mudhoney's 1988 single "Touch Me I'm Sick" made the band Sub Pop's best-known act. However, like many other Seattle bands, Mudhoney left Sub Pop, moving to Reprise Records in 1992. Their first major-label album, *Piece of Cake* (1992), made it clear that their major-label status would not give them a major-label sound. Turner retained the noise-rock solos reminiscent of Sonic Youth, and the blaring feedback on punk tracks like "Ritzville" is as low-budget

>>> Arguably the first grunge band, **Green River's members went on to form Mudhoney and Pearl Jam.**

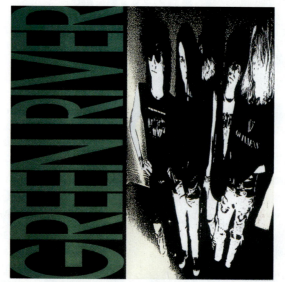

sounding as ever. By this time, the Sub Pop grunge sound had clearly made its way out of the indie labels and into the majors.

Nirvana

In the Seattle suburb of Aberdeen, Washington, Kurt Cobain dropped out of school in 1985 with his friend Krist Novoselic and set about watching "hundreds of Melvins practices" (Rocco 1997, 10), referring to the local Aberdeen band. Inspired, the two formed what would become Seattle's quintessential grunge band, **Nirvana**, in 1987.

Nirvana, embracing the DIY punk ethos and the indie rock world belief that the less money spent, the better an album will be, recorded their first full-length album, *Bleach* (1989), for just $606.17 on the Sub Pop label. While other Seattle bands—Soundgarden and Mudhoney in particular—fused metal riffs with punk rock, Nirvana incorporated a certain amount of pop sensibility into their music, leading to well-crafted songs rather than just sounds. Many early articles about the band, well before its release of *Bleach*, mention Cobain's songwriting as one of the band's defining aspects, which was the feature that most likely helped launch Nirvana onto the worldwide scene.

However, the band's members were not totally satisfied with Sub Pop, mostly because of its limited distribution system (Rocco 1997, 28). Although *Bleach* was poised to become a huge hit (and was, especially after *Nevermind*'s success) it could barely be found in stores. Switching to a major label would allow Nirvana to get their records into K-Marts, which seemed to be the only way to reach "small towns like Aberdeen" (Rocco 1997, 28), as Cobain put it. Although Sub Pop was looking to sign distribution deals with various major companies at the time—and it would later sell 49 percent of the company to Warner—Nirvana decided that if they were going to be on a major label, they may as well choose the label themselves. They signed with DGC Records in 1990.

ROCK PEOPLE

Bruce Pavitt and Jonathan Poneman (Sub Pop Records)

Bruce Pavitt moved to Olympia, Washington, with two friends (future members of the band Soundgarden) to attend the young Evergreen State College, a college that refused to give grades and encouraged students to design their own majors. Although he (like his friends) didn't graduate, Pavitt started a **fanzine** to highlight Northwest rock and punk acts, calling it *Subterranean Pop*. In addition, he

had a show on local public radio station KCMU and a column in a local music paper, and his compilation LP *Sub Pop 100* was an early effort at putting Northwest punk bands alongside established indie acts like Sonic Youth. Jonathan Poneman, meanwhile, was also working as a disc jockey on KCMU.

In April 1988, both Pavitt and Poneman quit their day jobs and went into business, forming Sub Pop, with Poneman financing the album *Screaming Life* by Soundgarden and giving the record label its start. Serving as an unofficial label for the Seattle music scene in general, in the early years, the white-on-black

SUB over the black-on-white POP logo helped the label sell more T-shirts than it did records. Pavitt and Poneman began a mail-order subscription program, where fans would buy a monthly subscription to limited-edition seven-inch singles. Sub Pop went on to sign Mudhoney and Nirvana, while also working the British press on behalf of their bands, flying *Melody Maker*'s Everett True out to Seattle. True's article called Seattle "the most vibrant, kicking music scene encompassed in one city for at least 10 years" (Rocco 1997, 4). Sub Pop had become the world's window into Seattle.

NIRVANA'S *NEVERMIND*

Nirvana's *Nevermind* (1991) was a game-changer in the grunge movement. At the same time, it seemed to be somewhat of a battle between Nirvana (Cobain, especially) and their new record label, DGC Records, a subsidiary of Geffen. "Take all the high end off the snare," the producer Butch Vig recalls Cobain saying, indicating that he wanted the mix to sound muddy rather than crisp and "well-produced" (Heylin 2007, 612). As Cobain sometimes said, "Punk rock is freedom," but this freedom seemed not to include the freedom to succeed. *Nevermind* has sold well over 10 million copies, making it a commercial success by any measure.

The famous cover of *Nevermind* features a naked baby swimming toward a

dollar on a fishhook, as if to suggest the idea that everyone is on the verge of selling out. The songs continue that message, characterizing the typical fan (on "In Bloom") as someone who sings along to the band's songs without really understanding the lyrics. It helps that the song is a sing-along masterpiece, directly attacking the listener singing along. In some ways, the closest parallel to *Nevermind* is the album that offered inspiration in its title, the Sex Pistols' *Never Mind the Bollocks* (see Chapter 9). Both broke a new sound and mentality to the world, and at the same time they both were looked to as indications that the genre had sold itself out.

NEVERMIND THE LABELS

Nirvana's breakthrough success came with the release of their 1991 album *Nevermind*. With this, and with their hit "Smells Like Teen Spirit," they tried to show the hypocrisy of the "indie" ideology: Unknown doesn't mean good, nor does commercial success mean that a band has failed. But even though Cobain explained his pragmatic reasons for moving to a major label—to get the music out there—the success of the image as well as the music came as a shock to the rather secluded Northwesterners. Dave Grohl, Nirvana's drummer who joined the band shortly before the recording of *Nevermind*, said, "When we went to make [*Nevermind*], I had such a feeling of us versus them . . . And all of a sudden, they're all buying our record" (Heylin 2007, 612). *Nevermind* was not necessarily a bad record—the problem for the grunge and indie artists was that it was *too* perfect—so when it was picked up by the national media, it became an easily accessible entry into a previously forbidding genre.

IN UTERO AND COBAIN'S SUICIDE

For their next album, 1993's *In Utero*, the band elected to use Steve Albini as their engineer, partly because Cobain liked the minimal, hard sound on the Pixies' *Surfer Rosa*. However, a quick listen to the album makes a certain aspect of the mix clear: due to protests from their label DGC, the band hired Scott Litt, producer of R.E.M., to remix the songs "Heart Shaped Box" and "All Apologies." The difference is

∧ Nirvana's **early success with** ∧ *Bleach* put them in a position ∧ to **choose a new label.**

immediately apparent, as these two songs have an undeniably cleaner sound than the others.

In the years following *Nevermind*, Cobain became increasingly miserable with his own success. Cobain's angst may stem in large part from the way that success was perceived in the Northwest indie rock world. One of the founding fathers of Northwest music, **Calvin Johnson**, started the label K Records in 1982 to release local Olympia, Washington, bands, often on limited-edition 100-cassette runs. Cobain had lived in Olympia for some time and very likely drew upon this DIY ethos of music. However, this idea that success was something to be avoided conflicted directly with Cobain's pop impulse and his desire to have his songs heard by people in small towns across the country.

In 1994, Kurt Cobain was found dead of a self-inflicted gunshot wound. His tragic death shocked both his fans and the rock music industry, as you will read in Chapter 14. Many fans did not want to accept that Cobain had killed himself and searched for others to blame (see p. 219). A month later, Nirvana's live performance *MTV Unplugged in New York* sold over 300,000 copies in its first week. It seemed most of all that Cobain was unprepared to deal with the band's massive success. Although he worked hard for success since the early days of the band, it turned out that he wasn't completely happy with success when it came. Even if Cobain hated the way that grunge had become a mass commodity, the record labels and broadcast outlets still fed the fire. In the years to come, Soundgarden, Pearl Jam, and others would be commercially successful with one form of grunge or another, but none would achieve the level of fame—and critical respect—of Nirvana and Cobain.

PEARL JAM seminal grunge band with front man Eddie Vedder that has released nine LPs and is still playing today.

RIOT GRRRL a movement of women, based around homemade zines and bands, with the goal of providing support to women and subverting the male-dominated punk scene.

BIKINI KILL early riot grrrl band that originated as a fanzine; led by Kathleen Hanna, who later joined Le Tigre.

Pearl Jam

When the band Green River split up and guitarist Steve Turner and front man Mark Arm formed Mudhoney, Green River's two remaining members decided to continue making music together as well. Guitarist Stone Gossard and bassist Jeff Ament formed the band Mother Love Bone with vocalist Andrew Wood, who promptly overdosed on heroin before their first album was released. Gossard and Ament then recruited lead guitarist Mike McCready and enlisted Soundgarden's Matt Cameron to play drums on a demo, which found its way to singer Eddie Vedder. Vedder joined the band, now known as **Pearl Jam**, and with drummer Dave Krussen they released *Ten* in 1991, hitting number two on the Billboard 200 chart. Still performing today, Pearl Jam has released nine LPs, the most recent of which was 2009's *Backspacer*.

PEARL JAM VS. NIRVANA

Vedder was a California surfer and Kurt Cobain was a flannel-clad young man from the Washington forest, so the media stoked a sometimes false rivalry between the two bands. The rivalry was partly fueled by the members themselves; Cobain's backhanded compliment to the band's rejection of misogyny was that "[e]ven Pearl Jam, who were obvious cock rock poseurs down on the Strip last year" (Rocco 1997, 56) were better than the heavy metal bands. However, Vedder and Cobain reconciled their differences shortly before Cobain's suicide. Pearl Jam's album *Vs.* (1993) had come out the year before, selling over a million copies in the first week—over five times that of *In Utero*—and Vedder was beginning to feel the pressure that Cobain felt. Eight days after Cobain's death, Vedder gave an interview with the *Los Angeles Times*, saying "I understand what Kurt was talking about . . . You just can't do it if you can't be real," (Hilburn 1994). These comments (and others) largely defused the media rivalry, putting it to rest.

VEDDER AND THE MEDIA

One of the key differences between Vedder and Cobain was that Vedder was easier for the media to deal with. Although, like Cobain, he was often negative, Vedder was not nihilistic the way Cobain could be.

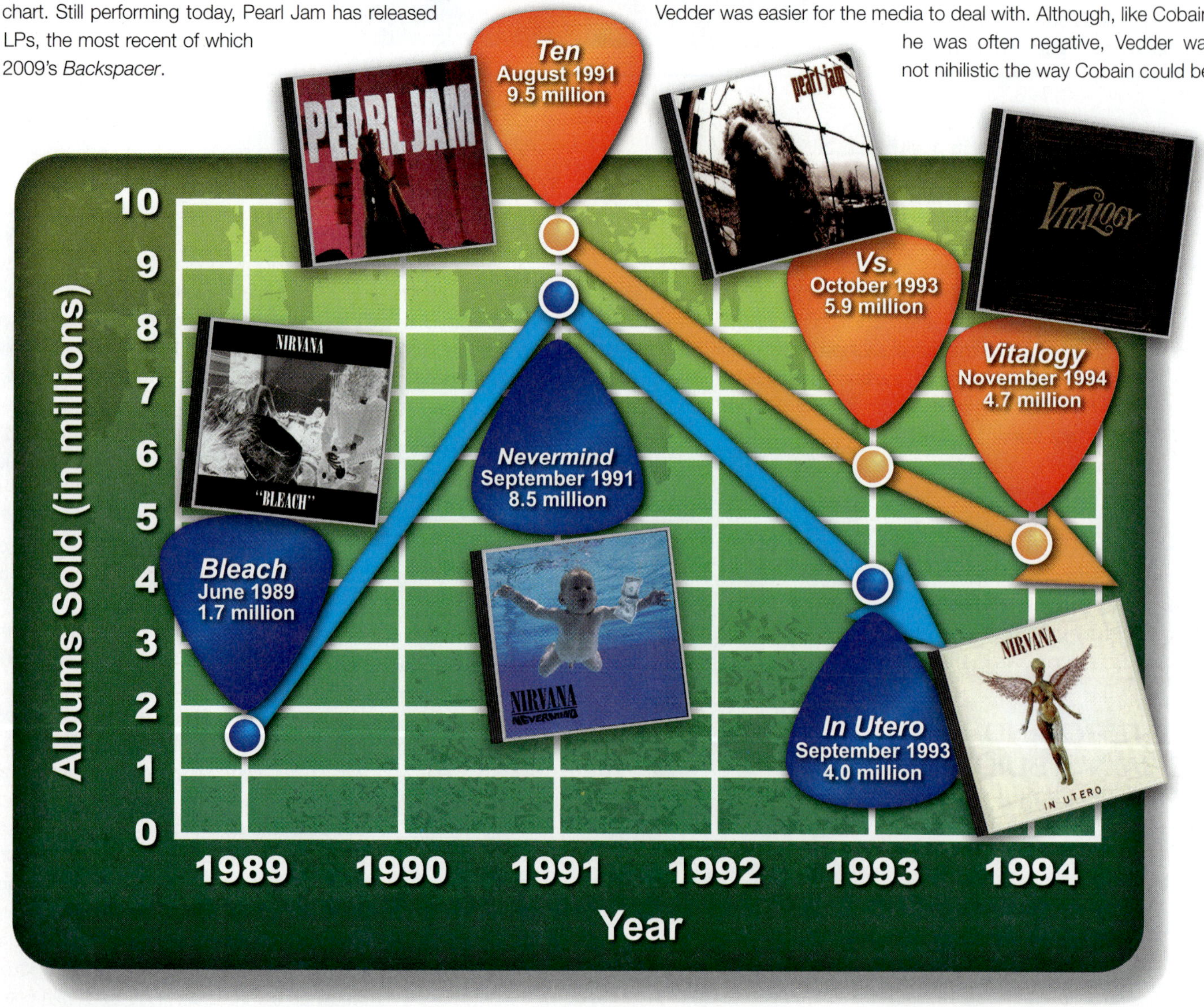

Ten
August 1991
9.5 million
Vs.
October 1993
5.9 million
Vitalogy
November 1994
4.7 million
Bleach
June 1989
1.7 million
Nevermind
September 1991
8.5 million
In Utero
September 1993
4.0 million
Albums Sold (in millions)
0 1 2 3 4 5 6 7 8 9 10
1989 1990 1991 1992 1993 1994
Year

> Although Nirvana is almost universally regarded as the seminal grunge band, **Pearl Jam sold many more of its first three albums than Nirvana did.**

Where Cobain sometimes distrusted his fans, speculating that many of them were into Nirvana because it was the "cool" thing to do, Vedder was "a missionary" (Hilburn 1994), closer to Springsteen or Bono in his unabashedly commercial goals.

Another reason that Vedder tended to work better with the media was that he took on outside causes more readily. As the spokesman for Pearl Jam, he railed against the wasteful cardboard packaging of CDs and supported political causes like opposing Washington State's bill to ban the sale of music with "erotic lyrics" to minors (Rocco 1997, 163). The cause that Vedder was most invested in, however, was an effort to break up the Ticketmaster monopoly. Ticketmaster charges a service fee on every ticket it sells, and it is often the sole vendor of tickets for any given concert, a practice that Vedder and his band mates felt was unfair to fans. This stands as "the band's most public defeat" (Colapinto 1996), and it began when Vedder demanded that Ticketmaster donate one dollar of every service fee for Pearl Jam's concerts to charity; Ticketmaster promptly added an extra one dollar fee to the ticket price itself. Pearl Jam tried to continue booking the rest of its concert tour (supporting *Vitalogy*, in 1994) without Ticketmaster, but it was nearly impossible to find venues that were not exclusively associated with the ticketing giant. Pearl Jam went on to bring a Federal anti-trust suit against the company, which was dropped in 1994. Eventually, the band stopped the fight after their fellow crusaders, most notably R.E.M., decided to go on tour using Ticketmaster, because, according to R.E.M.'s guitarist Peter Buck, doing otherwise would "cripple" the band (Colapinto 1996).

TOP OF THE CHARTS
WHAT'S HOT!
NOVEMBER 6, 1993

1. *Vs.* – Pearl Jam
2. *Counterparts* – Rush
3. *Bat Out of Hell II: Back Into Hell* – Meatloaf
4. *In Utero* – Nirvana
5. *It's On (Dr. Dre) 187um Killa* (EP) – Eazy-E
6. *Common Thread: The Songs of the Eagles* – Various Artists
7. *Music Box* – Mariah Carey
8. *River of Dreams* – Billy Joel
9. *In Pieces* – Garth Brooks
10. *janet.* – Janet Jackson

HOW WERE OTHER SIMULTANEOUS MOVEMENTS AFFECTED BY GRUNGE?

Riot Grrrls

Although grunge bands outwardly and explicitly rejected the misogyny of heavy metal bands, they were still predominantly all-male bands. However, there was another movement happening in and around Seattle at the time, and it was at least as subversive as grunge: the **riot grrrl** movement. Like hip-hop, which was developing in other parts of the country, the riot grrrl scene was not just a musical movement, but a cultural and artistic movement as well as a specifically feminist one. The movement constituted bands (usually punk and grunge), self-published fanzines, and other DIY efforts, all focused on a variety of feminist and other political topics.

One of the features of the riot grrrl bands was their use of an angry, aggressive sound and harsh vocals. Because one of the aspects of the scene—as put forward by bands Bikini Kill and Bratmobile—was of women taking control over their music and its presentation (Leonard 2007, 115), it was no surprise that these artists would depart from the mainstream Mariah Carey-style diva that was the persona of so many female artists of the time. Just as Kurt Cobain made an effort to show a somewhat feminine

>>> Bikini Kill's **Kathleen Hanna** helped shape the riot grrrl movement through both her writing and her music.

side, the riot grrrls knowingly used distorted guitars in an effort to break away from the preconceptions of "girl" music.

Of course, there were already women in alternative music in some places, particularly Kim Deal of the Pixies and the Breeders and Kim Gordon of Sonic Youth. However, as many of the riot grrrl founders were involved with the indie music scene—Bikini Kill's drummer Tobi Vail dated Kurt Cobain before founding the band—it made sense that the independent scene would be their focus.

BIKINI KILL

One of the pioneer riot grrrls bands out of Olympia was **Bikini Kill**. Deriving the band's name from a fanzine she had started, lead singer Kathleen Hanna teamed up with fellow Evergreen State College alum Tobi Vail in 1990 to form the band. The first release from the band was a self-released cassette called *Revolution Girl Style Now!* (1991). Their 1992 debut EP on the Kill Rock Stars indie label, *Bikini Kill*, was produced by Fugazi/Minor Threat front man Ian MacKaye. The EP included a few songs from their cassette as well as recordings made in D.C. and Olympia along with a live track.

Because Evergreen was a liberal arts school, many of the riot grrrl movement's founding members, including Hanna and Vail, were familiar with feminist literature, gay and queer critical theory, and any number of political and social movements. Bikini Kill therefore "managed to mix academic theory with basic rhythms" (Raha 2005, 208); when they released their 1993 song "Rebel Girl," it was only natural for it to turn into a sort of manifesto. This subverted the genre in more ways than one, replacing the "stereotypical female-female jealousy with physical and emotional attraction" (Raha 2005, 207).

The band's feminist leanings could be heard in other songs, including "Suck My Left One" (found on both *Revolution Girl Style Now!* and the *Bikini Kill* EP), which explicitly recounts surviving sexual abuse as a child. In fact, the band would even invite audience members to talk on stage about surviving sexual abuse. Hanna would also flash the audience, then point out her own cellulite or write "bitch" and "slut" on her body, seemingly defusing any attempt at "labeling" her by literally labeling herself (Raha 2005, 207).

Although the confrontational politics of Bikini Kill were on display, this was partly because of the band's desire to provide a safe and supportive environment for young women. Vail wrote in her zine *Jigsaw* that "punk rock is for and by boys mostly," so they wanted to create something separate from that. One of the ways they did this was to create "grrrl-only" areas at the front of the stage, an area that was usually off limits to women because of the violence of the mosh pits at punk concerts. The "grrrl-only" zone was in part a product of the fans themselves: at a Bikini Kill/Fugazi show in 1992, the girls in the mosh pit were being pushed around by the male Fugazi fans. Frustrated, they created a girls-only space—a big circle where they could dance without being threatened by violent male punk rockers.

The media—even the punk rock-friendly media—did not take kindly to the confrontation and gender subversion proffered by Bikini Kill. Feminism was considered confrontational even in the underground movements, and zine editors would still refer to "bitches," "cunts," "man-haters," and "dykes," which was "proof-positive that sexism was still strong in the punk scene" (Sinker 2001, 60). The mainstream media misunderstood the movement in a different way, comparing it to Patti Smith

∧
∧
∧ **Bikini Kill** played a crucial role in the riot grrrl movement, which was as much **a feminist philosophy as a musical style.**

(who disavowed any connection to feminism), saying that riot grrrl music "seeks to alienate" (Raha 2005, 162). When the riot grrrl rockers would clear the mosh pits so that girls could be at the front of the stage, they would be accused of alienating the audience, an accusation that was not levied at male punk groups whose mosh pits were entirely male. Either way, Bikini Kill made a definite mark on music with a brand of punk rock that was one of the greatest coherent statements in all of punk.

OTHER SEATTLE RIOTS

Along with Bikini Kill, one of the first riot grrrl bands to come out of Seattle was **7 Year Bitch**, who recorded on C/Z Records, the same label that released the first record by the Melvins. The band released their debut *Sick 'Em* in 1992, but their next album was more widely received. *¡Viva Zapata!* (1994) was a response to the rape and murder of Mia Zapata, the leader of Seattle band the Gits. 7 Year Bitch was vocal in their support for women's protection; following Zapata's murder, drummer Valerie Agnew co-founded Home Alive, a collective to teach self-defense classes to women (Juno 1996, 107).

Heavens to Betsy, an Olympia band that was around from 1991 to 1994, was another first-wave riot grrrl band, made up of singer/guitarist Corin Tucker with drummer Tracy Sawyer. The band had two releases on Kill Rock Stars, a 7-inch single called "These Monsters Are Real" (1993) and a full-length LP, *Calculated* (1994). After releasing another single on Chainsaw Records in 1994, the duo disbanded.

Singer-guitarist Tucker went on to found the band **Sleater-Kinney** with fellow singer-guitarist Carrie Brownstein. Tucker and Brownstein recorded their first two albums, *Sleater-Kinney* (1995) and *Call the Doctor* (1996), with drummer Lora MacFarlane, but after moving to the Kill Rock Stars label, they switched to drummer Janet Weiss and released *Dig Me Out* in 1997. Their recordings were more professionally produced than many of the earlier riot grrrl bands, although Tucker's vocals were still raw

ROCK PLACES

Olympia, Washington

Olympia, the capital of Washington state, is home to Evergreen State College and one of the most vibrant independent musical scenes in any relatively small town. In part, this was due to the types of young adults the college attracted: rebels who wanted to work outside the system. Evergreen did not (and still does not) hand out grades; rather, every professor fills out a narrative evaluation of each student, and vice versa, with no letter or

number attached. The school attracted Bruce Pavitt, co-founder of Sub Pop Records, as well as his two friends, Kim Thayil and Hiro Yamamoto, who went on to form Soundgarden. Calvin Johnson, the founder of the independent label K Records, also went to Evergreen, as did members of the bands Sleater-Kinney and Bikini Kill. Olympia also housed the label Kill Rock Stars. In short, the town and college produced a number of labels and bands that tended to create their own movements.

The town also held a gallery, Reko Muse, that featured art by women, which was connected to the early riot grrrl movement through Kathleen Hanna of Bikini Kill, who helped run it (Raha 2005, 157). In many ways, the ease and interconnectedness of the Olympia scene allowed for movements like the riot grrrls to take hold; the small scene encouraged the movement to be not only about music, art, literature, *or* politics, but to be about all of these things at once.

and powerful. Sleater-Kinney recorded a few more records on Kill Rock Stars and one on Sub Pop before disbanding in 2006.

OREGON GRRRLS

Although they were part of the "Seattle scene" in terms of playing many of their concerts there, riot grrrl band **Bratmobile** was formed at the University of Oregon in Eugene by Molly Neuman and Allison Wolfe. The two met at the college and began to trade music with each other, Wolfe providing the Seattle-based punk and grunge, Neuman providing Public Enemy and other political works. Upon deciding that nothing was really happening in Eugene, they started a zine and connected with the scene in Olympia. They began to talk up their "band," Bratmobile (a band that didn't yet exist), which evidently fooled Calvin Johnson enough for him to invite them to play on the same ticket as Bikini Kill in 1991. Kill Rock Stars owner Slim Moon saw the band (with drummer Molly Neuman) and released their single "Girl Germs" on a compilation. Kill Rock Stars would eventually release Bratmobile's first full-length album, *Pottymouth* (1993), as well.

Bratmobile toured with Sleater-Kinney and Heavens to Betsy in 1992, their poppier punk and personal lyrics standing out among the garage-rock rails against systemic oppression that characterized many riot grrrl bands. Carving out their own sound was important to them: "[I]f some punk guy tells me to listen to the Ramones to be in a band, I'm gonna do the opposite" said singer Wolfe. Although Bratmobile was somewhat criticized for the musical differences it had with other riot grrrl bands, Wolfe defends them by saying, "As long as there's a myriad of ways to be sexist there's going to be myriad ways to respond" (Raha 2005, 214).

It is important to note that riot grrrl was not just contained in the Northwest. One of the most remarkable things about the movement was that women who wanted to start their own zine or band would start it in a separate city. The semi-official Riot Grrrl Press, from Olympia, would then aid in the interconnection of these zines and bands by copying and distributing any riot grrrl-based zine that was sent to it (Leonard 2007, 118).

COURTNEY LOVE AND HOLE

While riot grrrl is generally considered a fully cultural movement—encompassing zines, art, lifestyle, and music—some people or bands were attached tangentially to the movement, usually by the media. One such person was **Courtney Love**, the lead singer of the L.A. band **Hole** and the wife of Kurt Cobain (whom she married in 1992). Although Love was originally part of the Seattle scene, she found lead guitarist and songwriter Eric Erlandson through an L.A. newspaper ad in 1989. The band's debut full-length album, *Pretty on the Inside* (1991), was produced by Don Fleming, producer for Sonic Youth, and Kim Gordon, Sonic Youth's bassist (Raha 2005, 178). Throughout the years, the bass and drum seats would change regularly, with Love and Erlandson making up the core of the band.

The band's second album, *Live Through This* (1994), was released on Geffen's DGC label and had a bit smoother sound that was better suited to rock radio. Although Love was not a member of the riot grrrl

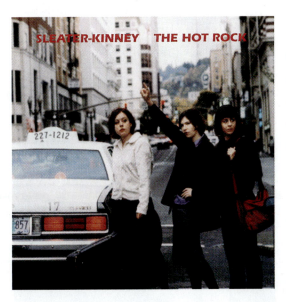

<<< Sleater-Kinney was one of the most critically acclaimed and commercially successful bands to come out of the riot grrrl movement.

movement, in that she did not participate in zines and released her music on a major label, she became somewhat of a symbol for the movement—albeit one the movement was ambivalent about—because she was the most public female voice to sing about feminism.

Live Through This was released four days after Cobain's suicide, and even though (or perhaps because) it was a huge critical and commercial success, there were people who claimed that Cobain had written many of the songs or that Love had ripped off Cobain. Although Cobain had rejected this idea in earlier years, the accusations were further fueled when, during Cobain's memorial, a recording of Love reading Cobain's suicide note was played to the crowd. Addressing the fans gathered at Cobain's memorial in Seattle, Love said that the note was "addressed to most of you," and sneered at both the crowd and Cobain's words, often interjecting her own comments into her reading. A personal low point for a woman with more than her share of public low points, she responded to Cobain's quotation of Neil Young's line, "better to burn out than fade away," with "God! You asshole" (Love 1994).

Critics and journalists lambasted Love after Cobain's death, claiming that she drove him to suicide or even that she killed him herself. The 1998 film *Kurt and Courtney*, which would have been shown at the Sundance Festival were it not for a problem with music licensing, spliced together interviews with people hostile to Love—ex-lovers, an anonymous musician named "El Duce" who claims he was offered $50,000 to kill Cobain, and a private eye "obsessed with proving" Love had something to do with Cobain's death (Ansen 1998). Of course, this was all in the name of "documentary," and even though filmmaker Nick Broomfield claimed that he expected to be sympathetic toward Love, the film was bent against her, and her publicists tried to stop it. There were other conspiracy theorists as well; notably, Love's own father

L7 another L.A. riot grrrl band closely associated with third-wave feminism, they were directly confrontational with their images and lyrics.

HUGGY BEAR one of the few U.K. exponents of the riot grrrl movement; they were tightly associated with the Olympia scene, especially Bikini Kill.

BABES IN TOYLAND Minneapolis band not directly attached to the riot grrrl movement, but are often connected with it by the media.

PAVEMENT founders of "slacker rock," Pavement's sound was purposefully lo-fi; lead singer Stephen Malkmus would go on to a long indie rock career.

SLACKER ROCK rock subgenre characterized by its DIY, lo-fi sound, and blasé attitude.

BECK a slacker rock beacon, Beck mashed together many styles, including blues, hip-hop, and rapping.

started Rock for Choice in 1991, which was a series of concerts benefiting women's health clinics and abortion-rights politics featuring artists Pearl Jam, Red Hot Chili Peppers, Joan Jett, Iggy Pop, and many others.

HUGGY BEAR

As the riot grrrl movement quickly spread across the country, it spread to other countries as well. **Huggy Bear** was a U.K.-based band that latched onto the riot grrrl scene very early on. Contrary to many riot grrrl bands, Huggy Bear included two male members, one of whom shared vocal duties with the female singer. One of the early markers of the riot grrrl movement, a shared LP between Huggy Bear and Bikini Kill titled *Our Troubled Youth/Yeah Yeah Yeah Yeah*, was released on Kill Rock Stars in 1993.

Although the band shared many traits with its American counterparts, it contrasted its situation with the one in the United States, saying that the underground music scene in London had gone seriously downhill (Raphael 1995, 151). It was this background that made Huggy Bear fiercely independent, shunning the spotlight to the extent that they were almost anonymous. Band members often refused to be photographed and would not give interviews or even their names; instead, they wanted to focus on putting their music (and their message) front and center.

BABES IN TOYLAND

Coming out of Minneapolis, the band **Babes in Toyland** was not directly attached to the riot grrrl movement as many other female bands were. Rather, they were more intertwined with the grunge movement, working with producer Jack Endino (L7, Nirvana, Soundgarden) and Lee Ranaldo, a member of Sonic Youth. After they signed to Reprise, Ranaldo produced their first album, *Fontanelle* (1992). This was a product of the relationship that the band had developed with Sonic Youth while touring Europe as their supporting act. They preferred to identify themselves as "grunge," but are often connected with the riot grrrl movement by the media. However, the

wrote the book *Who Killed Kurt Cobain?*, inexplicably attacking his daughter. All of these make a case for the sexism that still runs rampant in rock culture, both despite and fueled by third-wave feminism and riot grrrl. Critics noted that she became a lightning rod for criticism, the most controversial female artist since Yoko Ono. (Raha 2005, 178). Either way, Love's public image allowed her a platform for expressing feminist ideas while subjecting her to the abuse that comes with this position.

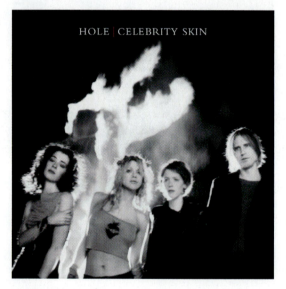

^
^ Courtney Love was one of
^ **the most prominent female figures in alternative rock** in the early 1990s.

L7

Another L.A. band closely associated with riot grrrl feminism was **L7**. They formed in Los Angeles in 1985, recording their self-titled first album with the label Epitaph, and played a show in Seattle hoping to get a contract with Sub Pop. The label responded by signing the group, releasing their *Smell the Magic* LP in 1990. L7 were directly confrontational when it came to their images and their lyrics: the merchandise related to *Smell the Magic* pictured a woman with her legs spread and a man's head between them, inverting the images of male rock bands that had been popular in rock and metal. The band also

Flashpoints ISSUES in ROCK

Huggy Bear and the Barbi Twins on the BBC

On Valentine's Day, 1993, Huggy Bear played "Her Jazz," one of their signature songs, on the then popular BBC television show *The Word*. The band hung around in the studio after performing, and the program began to air a filmed segment on the "Barbi Twins," two American pinup models. Huggy Bear, whose members had built much of their careers on fighting sexism and empowering women, began to heckle the presenter, who then said,

"If these garbagey bands don't want to come on the show, that's fine by me" (Raphael 1995, 147). The band was subsequently thrown out of the studio and later said that their protests were a response to the "trite, casual sexism" of the show (Raphael 1995, 147). This incident would gain them both fame and notoriety, putting them on the cover of *Melody Maker* and bringing the riot grrrl movement to the United Kingdom.

	Year Founded	First Release	Relevant Artists	Current Status
Sub Pop Records	1986, Seattle	*Sub Pop 100* (LP Compilation)	Soundgarden, Nirvana, Mudhoney	Active, but without co-founder Bruce Pavitt
Kill Rock Stars	1991, Portland	*KRS-101*, with Kathleen Hanna and founder Slim Moon	Bikini Kill, the Melvins, Bratmobile, Huggy Bear, Sleater-Kinney	Active, but founder Moon left for Nonesuch Records
SST	1978, Los Angeles	*Nervous Breakdown* 7-inch by Black Flag	Black Flag, Sonic Youth, the Meat Puppets, Bad Brains	Active, with founder Greg Ginn

∧∧∧ Independent record labels were instrumental in the development of grunge.

band did not necessarily participate actively in the zine scene, nor did they have particularly "feminist" lyrics or identify themselves as such. They were simply women making rock music.

Slacker Rock

Although grunge largely overshadowed almost all other music movements during these eight years, there were alternatives that especially affected successive musical styles.

PAVEMENT

One of the most important bands that never quite made it to a mainstream movement was **Pavement**, whose debut LP *Slanted and Enchanted* (1992) single-handedly founded the "**slacker rock**" genre. The band started as a studio collaboration between the two guitarists and songwriters Stephen Malkmus and Scott Kannberg, but became a band during the early 1990s. The initial band also included bassist Mark Ibold, 40-something ex-hippie drummer Gary Young (who owned the studio where the band recorded), and a second drummer, Bob Nastanovich. They released a few singles as well as a

∧∧∧ **Pavement,** led by Stephen Malkmus, **pioneered the distinctive lo-fi sound** that would be popular in the 1990s.

7-inch EP titled *Slay Tracks: (1933–1969)* (1989), recorded for about $800. There were only a few hundred copies of this EP, but it managed to make its way to influential British DJ John Peel. The band released more singles, finally playing live concerts in 1991.

There were two clear aspects of Pavement that found their way into mainstream music, especially in the mid-1990s. The first was its DIY "lo-fi" sound, which gave the impression of home recording or recording without much production at all. (This sound may not have been entirely on purpose, as *Slanted and Enchanted* was recorded in drummer Young's studio.) The second was a widespread ironic sensibility. The band's style is less despairing than the self-deprecation of Cobain and veers toward the lighter, ironic side of things rather than the dark seriousness and black humor of grunge.

BECK

The multi-talented **Beck** also became a slacker rock beacon, in part because of a single song. Beck's debut LP, *Mellow Gold* (1994), mashed together too many styles to count; the single "Loser," off this album, has an old bottleneck slide blues

BRITPOP the movement of bands such as Oasis and Blur who were generally sunnier and poppier than grunge, looking back toward the British pop music tradition.

SUEDE band at the vanguard of the Britpop movement; they inspired many later groups—Oasis and Blur, specifically—who went on to widespread fame.

SHOEGAZE rock subgenre characterized by its "wall of guitars" sound; the name refers to shoegaze bands' habit of staring at the floor as they play.

OASIS Britpop band whose two main voices were the Gallagher brothers, Liam and Noel.

MP3 method of encoding audio files, patented in 1994, that first made widespread distribution of music over the Internet possible.

BLUR 1990s Britpop band that combined Damon Albarn's wry social commentary with incurably catchy melodic hooks.

PULP Britpop band formed by Jarvis Cocker in 1978 that fused a range of musical styles from glam to indie rock.

lick, hip-hop style drum loops, and lackadaisical, self-conscious rapping. Beck was born Beck David Campbell, but then took the last name of his mother, Bibbe Hansen. A high school dropout, he moved to New York, then to Los Angeles, playing acoustic songs between the sets of rock bands. After signing a record contract with Geffen and releasing *Mellow Gold* in 1994, Beck saw the anthem "Loser" make it to the Top 20 and even hit number one on the modern rock charts. After his debut album, Beck continued to release successful records, always changing styles: *Odelay* (1996), the more folksy *Mutations* (1998), the soul- and funk-inspired *Midnite Vultures* (1999), the almost totally acoustic *Sea Change*

(2002), and a return to the sound of *Odelay* with *Guero* (2005). Many of these albums were both critically and commercially successful, with his influence continuing through the 1990s and into the next decade.

In June 2009, Beck brought the DIY ethos of slacker rock to a new project called Record Club, in which he and other musicians gathered to record a cover of an album in one day. According to Beck, nothing is practiced ahead of time, and "there is no intention to 'add to' the original work" (Hansen 2009). For their first two lo-fi reinterpretations, the Record Club has tackled the Velvet Underground's first album, *The Velvet Underground and Nico* (see Chapter 8), and Leonard Cohen's debut, *Songs of Leonard Cohen* (see Chapter 5).

Britpop

While the United States was mired in the darker outlook of alternative rock, there was a sunnier scene going on across the Atlantic. **Britpop**, as it came to be called, brought the short form pop song back onto the airwaves—with some notable changes. Partly because of the influence of U.S. alternative rock, Britpop often had darkly ironic lyrics that were critical of the status quo.

The band **Suede** was at the vanguard of the Britpop movement. In the late 1980s, as Britain was consumed by the noise and textures of **shoegaze**, Suede began releasing three-minute pop singles. At the time, surrounded by U.S. alternative rockers, Suede stood alone in their desire to be somewhat old-fashioned. Probably in part because of the singular identity of the group, their first album, *Suede* (1993), was the fastest-selling debut album in U.K. history. Although the group never caught on in the grunge-swept United States, later groups indebted to them—Oasis and Blur, specifically—would go on to widespread fame.

The Effects of Grunge

Slacker Rock
Rough productions is desirable now; cynicism is good; irony can be commercial

Riot Grrrl
Zine culture; broke down some of the misogyny of punk/metal; created local scenes

Britpop
Nirvana still mastered pop structures; audiences may have wanted something happier; Blur's ironic lyrics were more humorous than grunge's

GRUNGE

OASIS

Formed by singer Liam Gallagher and his Manchester schoolmates in the early 1990s, **Oasis** really became a band when songwriter and guitarist Noel Gallagher, Liam's brother, joined in 1993. The newly minted band rehearsed for about a year before releasing the debut album, *Definitely Maybe* (1994). One of the other most enduring aspects of Oasis was the frequent arguments between the Gallagher brothers, which were often written about in the British tabloids. Although they were not necessarily a revolutionary band, hits like "Champagne Supernova" and "Wonderwall" show undeniable melodic gifts.

Oasis distilled British pop so well that they were frequently accused of ripping off the Beatles to the point of plagiarism. Even with the occasional lambasting in the press, Oasis' popularity with the wider public was not diminished; they beat out the more progressive British rockers Radiohead and Muse to win *NME*'s "Best British Band" award in 2009, one of the top awards for the British music weekly (Jonze 2009). After seemingly unending threats, Noel Gallagher quit the band for good in August 2009, right before a show in the middle of their European tour, saying he could not work "a day longer" with Liam (Itzkoff 2009).

BLUR

According to British tabloids, Britpop was a battle between Oasis and their London rivals, **Blur**. The first single from Blur, "She's So High," off their 1991 debut *Leisure*, did relatively well, and "There's No Other Way," also on the debut LP, made it to number five on the Billboard modern rock chart. Their real breakthrough, however, was their followup album, *Modern Life Is Rubbish*, released in 1993. Much more traditionally poppy than their debut, *Modern Life* retained the guitar influence of the band's much earlier shoegazing days (when the band was called Seymour), while lead man Damon Albarn's wry lyrics and clever songwriting helped keep things fresh.

Blur undoubtedly offered a more jaundiced, witty look at life than was provided in many other Britpop bands, particularly Oasis. Their album *Parklife* (1994), which entered the charts at number one, began with the song "Girls & Boys," a riff

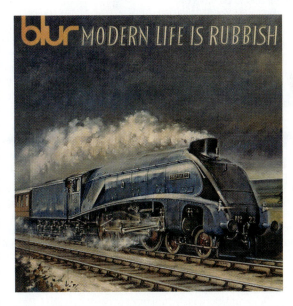

∧
∧ **Blur** was one of the most
∧ successful Britpop bands, partly
due to Damon Albarn's witty lyrics.

on Europop. The song was a perfect imitation of confused new wave dance-pop, synths and all. Like the Kinks' Ray Davies, Albarn and Blur combined wry social commentary with incurably catchy melodic hooks.

Also like Ray Davies, Damon Albarn did not stop making music when the band called it quits after their 2003 album *Think Tank*. Even before Blur disbanded, Albarn had formed a combination cartoon/band called Gorillaz, and in 2000 released their *Tomorrow Comes Today* EP, containing the hit single "Clint Eastwood." A sort of studio hip-hop supergroup, Gorillaz featured multiple producers, each with a cartoon alter ego. Del tha Funkee Homosapien and Dan "The Automator" Nakamura were on the self-titled first album, while the second album, *Demon Days* (2005), featured collaborations with Danger Mouse and De La Soul.

PULP

Pulp was formed by Jarvis Cocker in 1978, when he was 15. From 1981 to 1991, the band (consisting of Cocker and a constantly rotating lineup) released a folk-influenced debut album, *It* (1984); a series of singles followed by two months where Cocker was injured and confined to a wheelchair; and two more albums, until their breakthrough came when *NME* named a single from their 1992 album *Separations* (recorded in 1989) the "Single of the Week." This single, "My Legendary Girlfriend," recorded with the first incarnation of Pulp that would see its way through more than one album, solidified the style (which fused a range of influences from glam to indie rock) that would give them later success.

Two albums later, *Different Class* (1995), held the most incisive political commentary of all the Britpop bands; the songs that aren't about class are about sex. And yet the band's fusion of styles never seems to let up: In one half paragraph in his article on the band, Fricke references inspirations as diverse as Phil Spector, Duran Duran, the Pet Shop Boys, the Clash, and David Bowie. The album was a huge success commercially, going platinum in its second week, and critically topping many of the year's best lists.

Britpop would go on to be seen more generally as a secondary movement, especially against the cultural behemoth of grunge, but it was able to hold its own as it turned from a retro movement to a self-contained style all its own.

ROCK TECHNOLOGY ▶▶▶ The MP3

First available in 1994, the **MP3** format for encoding music continues to influence music today. In an era before high-speed Internet and cheap digital storage, the small size of MP3-encoded files was a boon to some in the music industry. Suddenly, distribution problems of independent labels seemed to be solved. In fact, in 1999, well after Nirvana switched from Sub Pop to DGC in order to get their music heard, Sub Pop became one of the first labels to release songs in MP3 format. Sub Pop has since bolstered its vinyl sales (still popular, especially on independent labels) by offering free MP3 downloads for any album purchased on vinyl.

Of course, the MP3 (sometimes a catchall term used for other digital music formats) has also been a thorn in the side of the record industry, from file-sharing programs like Napster (see Chapter 16) to the present day. The Recording Industry Association of America claims that digital music piracy results in $12.5 billion in economic losses annually, in addition to job losses and other hardships (RIAA 2009). Whether these statistics are accurate is impossible to tell, but one thing is certain: The qualitative shift that came with the MP3 format is here to stay.

Summary

WHAT ELEMENTS DID GRUNGE BORROW FROM PUNK ROCK TO MAKE A NEW MUSICAL GENRE? 210

- Grunge took much of the anti-establishment attitude from punk, but did not adhere to punk's strong belief in rejecting all music from the 1960s and earlier.

- Grunge tried to change the misogyny of both heavy metal and punk rock, but this was mostly just in speech (and lyrics). Grunge bands were still largely all-male.

- Punk rock's energy translated well to the local grunge scenes, but grunge tended to slow everything down and adopt more metal-oriented riffs. Also, instead of a crisp, fast sound, grunge tended to be more disorganized.

- The grunge bands took their inspiration from many types of music and places, but it was the Boston-based band the Pixies who probably most closely resembled and inspired the Seattle bands, in part because of their disparate, wide-ranging influences and juxtaposition of loud and soft, pop and punk.

- The Butthole Surfers' shock tactics and fusion of punk and metal were influential on a number of Seattle bands, particularly Soundgarden.

WHAT WERE THE MOST IMPORTANT BANDS THAT GREW OUT OF THE SEATTLE SCENE? 212

- Many of the early Seattle-area indie labels, like Sub Pop, initially focused on punk or punk-like music. The punk rock ethos of independence led many grunge bands to stay with indie labels even if the major labels might pay better.

- A number of early Seattle bands set the stage for the grunge movement, some of which were on the Sub Pop label, and some of which would experience some mainstream success. These bands included the Melvins, Soundgarden, Green River, and Mudhoney.

- The quintessential grunge band to come out of Seattle was Nirvana, fronted by Kurt Cobain.

- Pearl Jam, led by singer Eddie Vedder, was another hugely popular grunge band to come out of Seattle.

HOW WERE OTHER SIMULTANEOUS MOVEMENTS AFFECTED BY GRUNGE? 217

- Riot grrrl, one of the most prominent movements simultaneous to grunge, was in part a reaction to grunge. However, the indie labels that riot grrrls distributed their music on were often affiliated with grunge or punk in some way. The riot grrrl movement was also a direct descendent from punk rock in the way that they used the entire independent world—zines, record labels, and art alike—to achieve an entire culture based on a movement.

- Although grunge largely overshadowed almost all other music movements during the time, there were alternatives that affected successive musical styles, most importantly the slacker rock established by Pavement.

- Britpop was affected in an oblique way by grunge, partly because it was a reaction to the grunge movement. Although Britain was being overrun by flannel-wearing grunge musicians, Britpop artists like Suede, Oasis, Blur, and Pulp tried to resurrect the three-minute single in a more traditional sense than grunge.

Key Terms

grunge a style of music that fused punk, heavy metal, and more traditional pop styles 210

The Pixies Boston-based precursors to grunge, which drew on many different influences to create a sound that was both abrasive and melodic, and highly influential 211

Steve Albini seminal engineer of both the Pixies' *Surfer Rosa* and Nirvana's *In Utero*, who recreated a feeling of live performance in the studio 211

Butthole Surfers important precursors and source of inspiration for grunge bands, which combined shock tactics with a punk/metal/psychedelic fusion 212

Sub Pop Records an independent Seattle record label that signed influential grunge bands Green River, Nirvana, and Soundgarden, among others 212

The Melvins early Seattle band, influential on Nirvana, that were a staple of the local rock scene; they were in part responsible for the slow, sludgy sound of grunge 212

Soundgarden one of the most successful early Seattle bands, which relied on the early metal riffs of Black Sabbath and Led Zeppelin, while retaining the punk DIY ethos 213

Green River Seattle band that released what is often called the first grunge record, the EP *Come on Down*, in 1985 213

Mudhoney one of the earliest grunge bands, which formed after the previous band Green River (which also spawned Pearl Jam) broke up 214

fanzine an amateur magazine published by fans, often for little or no financial gain 214

Nirvana seminal and immensely popular grunge band whose front man Kurt Cobain became a beacon of the movement 214

Calvin Johnson founder of indie label K Records and tangential to the riot grrrl movement, he was a proponent of zealous independence in music 215

Pearl Jam seminal grunge band with front man Eddie Vedder that has released nine LPs and is still playing today 216

riot grrrl a movement of women, based around homemade zines and bands, with the goal of providing support to women and subverting the male-dominated punk scene 217

Bikini Kill early riot grrrl band that originated as a fanzine; led by Kathleen Hanna, who later joined Le Tigre 217

7 Year Bitch one of the first riot grrrl bands to come out of Seattle; the band was vocal in their support for women's protection 218

Heavens to Betsy first-wave riot grrrl band from Olympia made up of singer and guitarist Corin Tucker with drummer Tracy Sawyer 218

Sleater-Kinney riot grrrl band formed by fellow singer and guitarists Corin Tucker and Carrie Brownstein 218

Bratmobile poppy riot grrrl band, started in Eugene, Oregon, that released records on Kill Rock Stars *219*

Courtney Love lead singer of L.A. band Hole and wife of Kurt Cobain, Love was probably the most prominent female lead singer of the era's punk and rock bands *219*

Hole L.A. band formed by Courtney Love and Eric Erlandson *219*

L7 another L.A. riot grrrl band closely associated with third-wave feminism, they were directly confrontational with their images and lyrics *220*

Huggy Bear one of the few U.K. exponents of the riot grrrl movement; they were tightly associated with the Olympia scene, especially Bikini Kill *220*

Babes in Toyland Minneapolis band not directly attached to the riot grrrl movement, but are often connected with it by the media *220*

Pavement founders of "slacker rock," Pavement's sound was purposefully lo-fi; lead singer Stephen Malkmus would go on to a long indie rock career *221*

slacker rock rock subgenre characterized by its DIY, lo-fi sound, and blasé attitude *221*

Beck a slacker rock beacon, Beck mashed together many styles, including blues, hip-hop, and rapping *221*

Britpop the movement of bands such as Oasis and Blur who were generally sunnier and poppier than grunge, looking back toward the British pop music tradition *222*

Suede band at the vanguard of the Britpop movement; they inspired many later groups—

Oasis and Blur, specifically—who went on to widespread fame *222*

shoegaze rock subgenre characterized by its "wall of guitars" sound; the name refers to shoegaze bands' habit of staring at the floor as they play *222*

Oasis Britpop band whose two main voices were the Gallagher brothers, Liam and Noel *223*

Blur 1990s Britpop band that combined Damon Albarn's wry social commentary with incurably catchy melodic hooks *223*

Pulp Britpop band formed by Jarvis Cocker in 1978 that fused a range of musical styles from glam to indie rock *223*

MP3 method of encoding audio files, patented in 1994, that first made widespread distribution of music over the Internet possible *223*

Sample Test Questions

1. What Aberdeen grunge band was most influential on the young Kurt Cobain?
   a. The Pixies
   b. The Melvins
   c. Green River
   d. Soundgarden

2. An aspect of the Pixies that Cobain tried to emulate was
   a. their surf/punk fusion.
   b. Frank Black's whisper singing.
   c. their extreme dynamic contrasts.
   d. their provocative advertising.

3. Which band did NOT begin on an independent label?
   a. Nirvana
   b. Soundgarden
   c. Mudhoney
   d. Pearl Jam

4. Why were riot grrrl zines an important part of the movement?
   a. Female-published zines were already accepted more widely than female-fronted bands.
   b. The political motivations of the movement mandated an independent publishing outlet.
   c. Male punk and grunge bands would often allow riot grrrl bands to open the show in exchange for favorable press.
   d. There were not enough existing fan zines in Olympia, where the movement partly began.

5. How did the DIY ethos of punk rock translate to other genres?
   a. Singer/songwriters published homemade recordings during the "lo-fi" craze.
   b. Britpop bands tended to do their own artwork.
   c. Grunge bands felt that, to gain radio play, they needed to hire professionals, unlike punk.
   d. Riot grrrl stayed on indie labels even though, much like punk, there was a huge major-label craze to sign riot grrrl bands.

ESSAY

6. There were some influences that grunge accepted that hardcore punk had declared "off-limits." How did these help shape the sound and the song structures of grunge?

7. What role did independent labels play in fostering the grunge scene?

8. What was the role of the media in spreading grunge?

9. How did riot grrrl bands reach a wider audience? What was their larger purpose?

10. How were other musical movements (that may bear little similarity to grunge in terms of style) influenced or impacted by grunge?

WHERE TO START YOUR RESEARCH PAPER

For old Sub Pop merchandising and advertising, go to http://ogami.subpop.com/history/intro.html

For a Kill Rock Stars timeline, go to http://www.killrockstars.com/about/timeline.php

For the full Nirvana discography with Cobain's liner notes, go to http://www.livenirvana.com/digitalnirvana/discography/main/index.html

For an archive of articles published on Soundgarden, go to http://web.stargate.net/soundgarden/articles/

For more information on riot grrrl zines, go to http://grrrlzines.net/

For information on Kathleen Hanna and the Riot Grrrl Manifesto, go to http://kathleenhanna.cjb.net/

ANSWERS: 1. b; 2. c; 3. d; 4. b; 5. a.

Remember to check **www.thethinkspot.com** for additional information, downloadable flashcards, and other helpful resources.

HOW DID HIP HOP GET ITS START?
HOW DID HIP HOP GAIN MAINSTREAM RECOGNITION?
WHAT ARE THE DIFFERENT BRANCHES OF HIP HOP AND RAP?

"On January 9, 1988, 44 members of the rap community huddled into a rental photo studio on Broadway in New York City. The invitation had gone out just two or three days prior—calling all hip hoppers—and now here they were, uncommonly punctual ("We only had the studio for one afternoon," remembers photographer Dorothy Low) and united. The affair had a low-rent vibe—the studio was free as long as it received a credit. But it also had the makings of an event. The shoot was for a *Village Voice* cover, to herald, with due pomp and ceremony, the Hip Hop Nation. . . .

"It was a year of landmark albums—Public Enemy's *It Takes a Nation of Millions to Hold Us Back*, Boogie Down Productions' *By All Means Necessary*, EPMD's *Strictly Business.* It was a year of spectacular, mercurial singles—Rob Base & D.J. E-Z Rock's "It Takes Two," De La Soul's otherworldly "Plug Tunin'," Stetsasonic's robust "Sally." But mostly it was a year of momentous, sudden change . . . MTV launched *YO! MTV Raps*, leapfrogging over both urban radio and BET to give the music a beachhead. As TV exposure remade the music's audience, new jack swingers like Bobby Brown and Teddy Riley's group, Guy, remade black pop music in hip hop's image. . . .

"The year was a creative bubble; you could only blow it once. That photo from January 1988 declared art and genius to be in the music; in the emerging industry, they lay in the individual musicians. Soon the culture split along a dozen axes, never so strong again."

—John Leland, "The Pinnacle,"
In *The Vibe History of Hip Hop*, ed. A. Light, 192–193.
New York: Three Rivers Press, 1999

HIP-HOP AND RAP (1973–)

CHAPTER 13

HOW DID HIP HOP GET ITS START?

HIP HOP a cultural and musical movement beginning in the 1970s that included graffiti, rap music, and break dancing.

RAP vocals overlaid against turntable techniques executed by a DJ.

GRIOTS West African poets and singers who traveled about and passed on oral traditions.

DJ KOOL HERC called the "Godfather" of hip hop, a DJ that is credited for introducing the turntable style to the United States.

BEAT-MATCHING changing the speed of one track to match the tempo of another.

MIXING weaving two tracks together to form one song.

SCRATCHING moving a record back and forth while using the fade control to create unique sounds.

DRUMMING creating a drumming sound with scratching techniques.

THE BREAK a technique in which records are scratched to isolate the drumbeats from music.

BREAK-DANCING a popular form of dance including spinning on one's head.

What is Hip Hop?

The year 1988, which is the year John Leland refers to at the beginning of this chapter, was a pivotal time in rock and hip hop history. A form of music, once heard only in urban areas, was bursting out of every television and radio across the United States and the rest of the world, and performers like Queen Latifah, Niggaz With Attitude (N.W.A), Tone-Loc, and Chuck D (Public Enemy) were bringing their experiences and rhymes to the masses.

The history of rock is often told in a linear fashion when, in reality, it is more three-dimensional, with a multiplicity of independent events taking place, at overlapping times, in different communities and regions. The past four chapters traced the history of punk and other forms of rock that evolved outside the limelight but seized center stage. This chapter will look at another vital and vibrant style of music that evolved independently and rapidly rose to prominence.

Hip hop is often used synonymously with **rap**, but the two have different connotations. Hip hop generally refers to the subculture that includes rap music, graffiti art, and break dancing, whereas rap generally refers to the music created in this culture. Rap's main characteristic is spoken rhyming words—often boastful and witty—over a steady beat. Rap and hip hop have roots in African traditions. In West Africa, **griots**—traveling poets and singers—passed on the oral traditions of the culture for hundreds of years. Talking blues and jazz poetry are two other genres of music that spring from the griot tradition and also contribute to the origins of rap. The people of Surinam in Africa enjoyed interplay between folktales and songs, in a musical form that they call *cutsingi* (Szwed 1999, 6). Hip hop and rap grew out of the culture of speaking poetry over music.

"THE GODFATHER" OF HIP HOP AND HIP HOP'S BEGINNINGS

In the 1970s, DJs at block parties began manipulating turntables to extend the percussion "hook" of funk and soul records. **DJ Kool Herc**, often referred to as "The Godfather" of hip hop, is usually credited with originating the style. Born in Jamaica, Herc brought the techniques of manipulating the turntable with him to New York. These techniques included **beat-matching**, **mixing**, **scratching**, and **drumming**. In beat-matching, a disc jockey changes the speed or duration of one track to match the tempo of another track being played, resulting in mixing, or playing two records simultaneously. Scratching involves moving a record back and forth as it's playing, often cutting in from an existing beat and allowing the DJ something like an instrumental solo; a combination of scratches that creates a percussive rhythm is called drumming. Kool Herc never actually recorded any of his works. However, as Havelock Nelson writes, "Every rapper who ever successfully dropped a verse on tape owes part of his or her career to Kool Herc" (Nelson 1999, 17).

DJ Kool Herc initially scratched records to isolate the drum solos from the rest of the track—known as **the break**—so that people could dance to the track for a longer period. In the 1970s **break-dancing** was

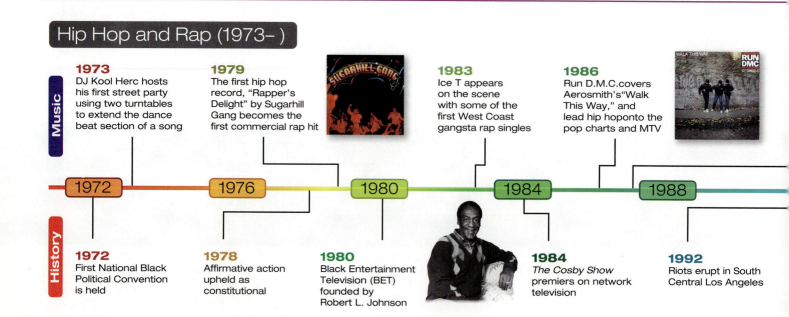

Hip Hop and Rap (1973–)

Music

1973 DJ Kool Herc hosts his first street party using two turntables to extend the dance beat section of a song

1979 The first hip hop record, "Rapper's Delight" by Sugarhill Gang becomes the first commercial rap hit

1983 Ice T appears on the scene with some of the first West Coast gangsta rap singles

1986 Run D.M.C. covers Aerosmith's "Walk This Way," and lead hip hop onto the pop charts and MTV

1972 — 1976 — 1980 — 1984 — 1988

History

1972 First National Black Political Convention is held

1978 Affirmative action upheld as constitutional

1980 Black Entertainment Television (BET) founded by Robert L. Johnson

1984 *The Cosby Show* premiers on network television

1992 Riots erupt in South Central Los Angeles

a popular pastime, as rival gangs battled in clubs using break-dancing moves to outmaneuver one another so they could avoid being thrown out. Break-dancing moves include spinning on one's head, flips, and other gymnastic feats. It was only later that this music added a verbal layer when an MC, or master of ceremonies, began rapping to the altered songs.

Hip hop is part of the larger sociocultural formation of hip hop aesthetics. DJ Afrikaa Bambaataa has identified five pillars that support the hip hop culture: **tagging**, break-dancing, MCing, DJing, and **beatboxing**.

OLD-SCHOOL HIP HOP (C. 1979–1984)

"Old-school hip hop" refers to the rap music created from the late 1970s until the early 1980s. For more than a decade it was largely based on the East Coast, in New York City. It wasn't until N.W.A's *Straight Outta Compton* (1988) that hip hop became a West Coast phenomenon as well. In hip hop's developing years, important figures included "The Godfather" DJ Kool Herc, Kurtis Blow, Afrikaa Bambaataa, and Grandmaster Flash & the Furious Five.

Kurtis Blow

Kurtis Blow was born Kurtis Walker in Harlem, New York. In 1979, the major label Mercury signed Blow (Chang 2005, 132), producing one of the first commercial hip hop LPs. His two early singles, "Christmas Rappin" and "The Breaks," were both platinum-selling hits. "The Breaks" is a rap about accepting what happens in life; Blow recounts many things, from being cheated on by a girlfriend to an unfortunate IRS audit, and dismisses them all as "the breaks." The sparse rhythm section includes Caribbean percussion as well as a funk trio, and instead of rapping over sampled beats, Blow used live musicians.

Over the next seven years, Blow released eight other albums, but none matched the influence of his first. Although he now focuses

on inner-city social issues, later groups have covered his songs, notably Run-D.M.C., who covered Blow's "Hard Times."

Afrika Bambaataa

Like many early hip hop artists, Afrika Bambaataa grew up in the Bronx River Projects, a low-income housing development, and came from an activist family. Bambaataa won an essay contest, and his prize—a tour of Africa—completely changed his perspective on life. Upon his return, he formed a peace-making organization called the Bronx River Organization. Inspired by DJ Kool Herc, he began hosting parties as a way to calm gang tensions; many credit Bambaataa with "naming" hip hop music.

His electronic-tinged single "Planet Rock" was a club hit in 1982, hitting number 48 on the Billboard charts that year. Bambaataa was seemingly influenced by everything, as his single "Looking for the Perfect Beat" employs scratching, New Wave–influenced synths, funk, and Jamaican dub-style production techniques. Although none of these songs made it onto the charts, they influenced later artists. His songs were also sampled frequently (Rolling Stone 2009), and received frequent tributes from later bands like Rage Against the Machine.

Grandmaster Flash and the Furious Five

Grandmaster Flash and the Furious Five consisted of DJ Grandmaster Flash and

∧
∧ Some claim Afrika Bambaataa
∧ "named" hip hop.

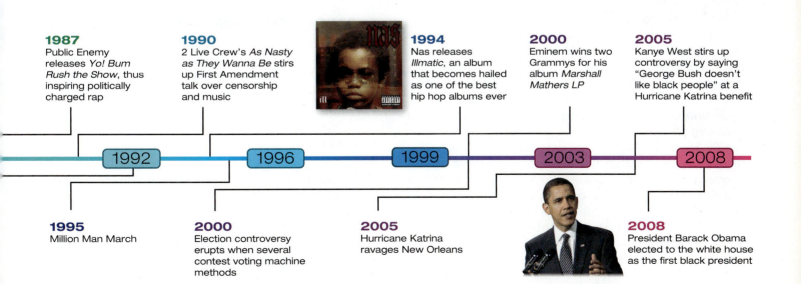

1987
Public Enemy releases *Yo! Bum Rush the Show*, thus inspiring politically charged rap

1990
2 Live Crew's *As Nasty as They Wanna Be* stirs up First Amendment talk over censorship and music

1994
Nas releases *Illmatic*, an album that becomes hailed as one of the best hip hop albums ever

2000
Eminem wins two Grammys for his album *Marshall Mathers LP*

2005
Kanye West stirs up controversy by saying "George Bush doesn't like black people" at a Hurricane Katrina benefit

1992   1996   1999   2003   2008

1995
Million Man March

2000
Election controversy erupts when several contest voting machine methods

2005
Hurricane Katrina ravages New Orleans

2008
President Barack Obama elected to the white house as the first black president

South Bronx

In the early days of hip hop, most of the artists either lived in or were born in New York City's South Bronx. The South Bronx was devastated in 1929 by the building of the Cross-Bronx Expressway, which displaced 60,000 Bronx residents. Although the white residents who had lived in the area moved to the suburbs, many of the poor African American and Latino families could not afford to move. As 600,000 manufacturing jobs disappeared, more people fled the area, and as whole buildings emptied of residents, slumlords hired arsonists to burn them down for the insurance money. This led to the policy of "benign neglect," or the assumption that people in the Bronx didn't want social services anyway, which resulted in seven fire companies being removed from the Bronx in 1968. Over the course of the next decade 43,000 housing units were lost.

All this set the stage for the arrival of a population intent on inexpensive, local entertainment. Bronx residents relied on DJs, who were cheaper than live bands, to provide dance music, and the early hip hop DJs honed their skills at these parties. DJ Kool Herc and Grandmaster Flash both played in these early Bronx parties, and Afrika Bambaataa threw his own parties as a way to soothe inter-gang relations. Kurtis Blow, the first commercially successful rapper, performed at these parties as well.

However, hip hop culture in the South Bronx was more than music. The Bronx also became a hub for graffiti art, as Tats Cru, Fab 5 Freddy, and Friendly Freddy all became well-known graffiti artists. Fab 5 Freddy went on to host "Yo! MTV Raps," which, in 1988, was the first hip hop video show on television (Chang 2005, 10–15).

five rappers: Melle Mel, Kidd Creole, Cowboy, Scorpio, and Raheim. Melle Mel was the main songwriter for the group. Their 1982 album *The Message* was the first popular politically conscious hip hop record. The lyrics to the title track describe inner-city life, poverty, and violence. The song hit number four in the R&B chart and number 62 in the pop chart, and sold half a million copies in one month.

One of the group's other hits, "White Lines (Don't Do It)" (1983), was an anti-drug song about the disparity between poor black inner city kids caught doing drugs and wealthy white business people who do drugs. Like "The Message," the song's lyrics reflect the group's interest in political and social commentary. The group's message was backed up by technique, as Flash often used three turntables at once, flawlessly matching beats on two turntables while scratching on the third.

HOW DID HIP HOP GAIN MAINSTREAM RECOGNITION?

Mainstream Recognition for Hip Hop

As hip hop began to go mainstream, tensions grew between rap and disco. Disco was popular as a form of black music during the 1970s, but it began to fade in popularity around the same time that hip hop music began to climb the charts. In July 1979, the disco backlash came to a head at Disco Demolition Night, an anti-disco event headed by DJ Steve Dahl. That year "Disco Sucks" T-shirts were everywhere; simultaneously, the **Sugarhill Gang** became the first rap group to achieve a crossover hit (Greenberg 1999).

The song by the Sugarhill Gang that created all the sensation was "Rapper's Delight." The Sugarhill Gang was formed for the purpose of recording this song, which was itself calculated to cash in on the (then unrecorded) hip hop craze. The song is based on a riff from the disco group Chic's hit "Good Times," although it was rerecorded rather than sampled. The song seems to have been the brainchild of Sylvia Robinson of Sugar Hill Records. "Rapper's Delight" quickly permeated popular culture. Today, its opening words are among the most recognizable of classic hip hop lyrics. When the writers of "Good Times" threatened to sue,

the band credited them (Niles Rodgers and Bernard Edwards from Chic) as co-writers of the song.

NEW-SCHOOL HIP HOP (C. 1983)

As time passed, a new, more radio-conscious school of hip hop evolved. Although old-school hip hop was performed live for parties and was engineered for dancing, the new-school hip hop replaced break beats (DJing) to a large extent with drum machines. Just like with old-school hip hop, new-school hip hop was largely based in New York City.

Run-D.M.C.

Run-D.M.C. was a rap group composed of Joseph Simmons ("DJ Run"), Jason Mizell ("Jam Master Jay"), and Darryl McDaniels ("D.M.C."). Many claim that Run-D.M.C. is one of the most influential groups in the history of hip hop. Run-D.M.C. tended to use more rock-oriented samples, rather than soul, funk, and disco ones. "Walk this Way" (1986), perhaps their most famous song, features Aerosmith's Steven Tyler and Joe Perry in rerecorded takes of Aerosmith's song of the same name. Although many hip hop groups were crippled by sampling lawsuits, this active collaboration helped rap break into the pop charts, as well as rejuvenate Aerosmith's career; the music video for the song shows the two groups literally breaking down a wall between them. Rap artists had already rummaged through the African American funk, soul, and disco hits, but after Run-D.M.C., groups began to sample music from white-dominated rock as well.

LL Cool J

As rap artists began sampling more rock in their work, the subject matter of hip hop lyrics also shifted. **LL Cool J**, born in Queens, New York, in 1968, introduced love ballads into the hip hop repertoire, which also helped broaden hip hop's audience. LL Cool J stands for "Ladies Love Cool James." LL Cool J is best known for his album, *Mama Said Knock You Out* (1990), which includes the songs "I Need Love" and "Around the Way Girl." While his earlier albums were more pop oriented, including sappy love ballads, this album was much harder sounding, possibly to counteract the accusations that he had sold out. LL Cool J's pose as a boxer in the music video for his "comeback" song and the revamped, hardened lyrics proved a chart success. LL Cool J was less politically radical than many other hip hop artists, performing at President Bill

SUGARHILL GANG often credited with creating the first hip hop record and bringing hip hop into the mainstream with "Rapper's Delight."

RUN-D.M.C. musical group using more rock-oriented samples, famous for "Walk This Way" cover of Aerosmith's hit song.

LL COOL J rap artist whose earlier works are more romantic, but his "Mama Said Knock You Out" was a breakthrough hit.

BEASTIE BOYS hip hop trio from Queens, who had the first number one rap record with *Licensed to Ill*.

Clinton's first inauguration in 1993 (Michel 1999, 88). His rap career has spanned more than 20 years.

Beastie Boys

One of the first white rap groups to come onto the hip hop scene was the **Beastie Boys**. The group offered somewhat clownish, humorous lyrics. Their music suggested that hip hop and rap aren't just about race, but about class and the contemporary urban experience. They began as a punk rock group in 1979, but after they began rapping, they became much more well-known through recorded singles and live performances.

Top Five Greatest Selling Hip Hop Albums

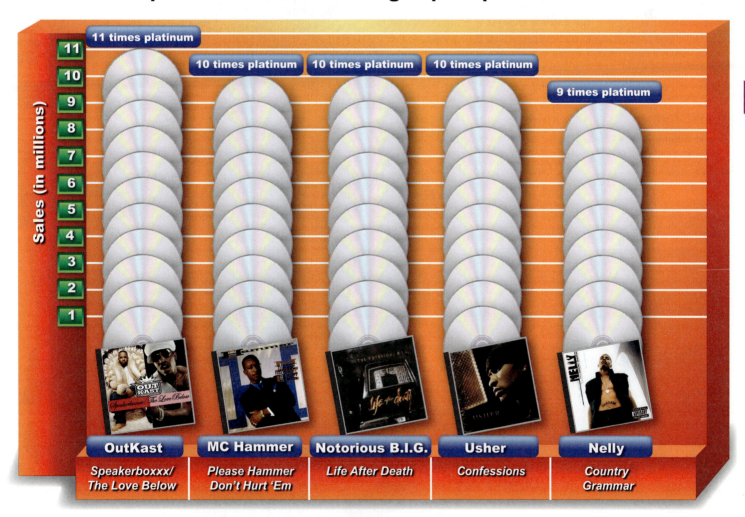

Sales (in millions)

| 11 times platinum | 10 times platinum | 10 times platinum | 10 times platinum | 9 times platinum |

| **OutKast** | **MC Hammer** | **Notorious B.I.G.** | **Usher** | **Nelly** |
| *Speakerboxxx/ The Love Below* | *Please Hammer Don't Hurt 'Em* | *Life After Death* | *Confessions* | *Country Grammar* |

∧∧∧ **Hip Hop's sales demonstrate its popularity.** The platinum award is given for every 1,000,000 copies sold.

ROCK TECHNOLOGY ▶▶▶ "Two Turntables and a Microphone" and "The Wheels of Steel"

"Two turntables and a microphone" refers to a setup including two phonograph record players that are connected to a mixer. While the setup became ubiquitous with hip hop, it was actually created around 1946 by British DJ Jimmy Savile (Broughton 2004). Initially, DJs used this set up to switch between two dance tracks, but in the 1970s, hip hop artists began using the setup to match beats between tracks while a live MC rapped into the microphone. "The Wheels of Steel" refers to the turntables themselves. This term comes from the single "The Adventures of Grandmaster Flash on the Wheels of Steel," which featured Grandmaster Flash creating a collage of songs using three turntables and scratching techniques.

Although the original turntable artists used phonograph records, modern turntables are often just controllers for a wide array of electronic devices, like "scratchable" CD and MP3 players.

When they released their debut album in 1986, *Licensed to Ill*, it quickly became the first hip hop album to top the charts. This album contained the hits "Fight for Your Right" and "No Sleep 'Till Brooklyn." which, like Run-D.M.C.'s work, featured rock samples and generally apolitical party music.

RAP'S GOLDEN AGE (LATE 1980s–EARLY 1990s)

For fans of this **golden age of rap**, the records of these few short years bring it all together: socially and politically engaged lyrics, masterful use of samples and beats, and imaginative songwriting. During this time, the diverse styles of rap, from De La Soul to Public Enemy, were just becoming apparent through many groundbreaking albums. The genre was becoming a clear cultural and economic force.

Public Enemy

Public Enemy, led by Chuck D and Flavor Flav, is considered one of the most important and controversial hip hop groups in the genre's history. The middle-class Chuck D modeled his persona on intellectual (and theatrical) black public figures, personified by Malcolm X, while Flavor Flav provided comic relief, albeit with a fiercely serious undercurrent. Controversy aside, their debut *It Takes a Nation of Millions to Hold Us Back* (1988) is considered one of the defining albums in hip hop history. The album's tracks, including "Don't Believe the Hype," merged funk beats and party lyrics with social statements. They even sampled other recent rap groups, turning the Beastie Boys' "Fight For Your Right to Party" into a political rallying cry, "Party For Your Right to Fight."

Public Enemy's sound was forged in the days before hip hop artists had to license every sample used on an album; *Nation of Millions* was like a rhythmic musical sound collage, stripped of many of the discernible aspects of popular music such as chord changes or melodies. Chuck D has never stopped being revolutionary; in 1998, he released the group's album *Bring the Noise 2000* for free on the group's Web site, but was forced to remove it because Def Jam Records legally owned the recording.

KRS-One

KRS-One, born Lawrence Krishna Parker, was homeless at age 13. Eventually, he met Scott La Rock, a social worker and DJ, and together they formed the group Boogie Down Productions. After Boogie Down's first album, *Criminal Minded* (1987), Scott La Rock was murdered. Taking a closer look at the problems facing urban youth, KRS-One then joined the ranks of the political-philosophical rappers with *By All Means Necessary* (1988) and *Ghetto Music: The Blueprint of Hip Hop* (1989). *Criminal Minded*, however, was still a landmark album in terms of its use of black ghetto slang and attempts to speak the way that people spoke on the streets (Watkins 2005, 240).

Many referred to KRS-One as "The Philosopher" because he served as one of hip–hop's most thoughtful and articulate voices. In 1988, KRS-One founded the Stop the Violence Movement as a response to mounting

Public Enemy's in-your-face politics redefined the role that rap artists could play in contemporary society.

violence in black and hip hop communities. In addition, he founded The Temple of Hip Hop, billed as a ministry, archive, school, and society for those involved in the hip hop movement. He sees hip hop as a total way of life, almost antithetical to the genre's commercial power, and continues to be involved in the movement.

De La Soul

De La Soul's *3 Feet High and Rising* (1989) is one of hip hop's most respected albums. Unlike KRS-One and Public Enemy, who created serious, politically aware music, De La Soul's trio of Kelvin Mercer, David Jude Jolicoeur, and Vincent Mason focused on clever and amusing wordplay. De La Soul's one-minute track "Transmitting Live From Mars" sampled the 60s band the Turtles, leading to a lawsuit—which the Turtles won—determining that any samples used have to be legally cleared and credited.

In contrast to many of the groups popular during the late 1980s, De La Soul concentrated on a message of peace. In "Me, Myself, and I," the trio advocates being comfortable and proud of one's individuality. De La Soul's second album, *De La Soul is Dead* (1991), exhibited a less playful sound and a more serious tone. The band has released music sporadically since, with *The Grind Date* (2004) as their last disc of new releases.

Eric B. & Rakim

Eric B. and Rakim has been hailed as perhaps the most gifted of the MC/DJ combos. Their debut, *Paid in Full* (1987), marked a shift in hip hop through its emphasis on funk samples (especially from the works of James Brown). The two became instant stars, and the album—recorded in only one week—raised the level of artistry and technique in rap. Rather than feature an intense and quick rapping style, like Public Enemy and other groups, Rakim used a calm and steady rapping style that made it easier for the audience to understand the words. This calm delivery became popular as an alternative to Chuck D's manic style, and the East Coast's reputation for innovative hip hop was secured.

Eric B. and Rakim delivered three more albums: *Follow the Leader* (1988), *Let the Rhythm Hit 'Em* (1990), and *Don't Sweat the Technique*

(1992). The duo's contract with MCA was almost complete, but tension arising from the record's production both broke up the group and ended the contract.

A Tribe Called Quest

A Tribe Called Quest, made up of Q-Tip, Phife Dawg, Ali Shaheed Muhammad, and Jarobi was part of a collective of rap groups that became known as "The Native Tongues Posse." Like fellow artists De La Soul, A Tribe Called Quest was not interested in political statements, violence, or profit making. Their debut album, *People's Instinctive Travels and the Paths of Rhythm* (1990), featured mostly lighthearted rhymes and a jazz influence. For example, their track "Bonita Applebaum" featured an electric piano loop not far from jazz fusion. Although their album offered an alternative to activist rappers, it didn't receive much recognition until later in their career.

Their second album, *The Low End Theory* (1991), performed better on the charts and focused more on social issues with songs such as "The Infamous Date Rape" and "Skypager," and their next album, *Midnight Marauders* (1993), was their best-selling album. This album hit the Top 10 and sparked singles such as "Award Tour" and "Electric Relaxation." The group broke up in 1998, but reunited in 2004 and again in 2008.

CLASSIC RECORDINGS ▶▶▶

FEAR OF A BLACK PLANET by Public Enemy

Although their first album, *Nation of Millions*, was a masterpiece of sonic collage and "organized noise" (Watkins 2005, 117), their second, *Fear of a Black Planet* (1990), is largely considered their most influential (and controversial) work. The album "honed the targets of the [group's] first two albums into a more focused attack on white racism and the need for the black community to organize its response" (Light 1999, 172). Despite—or because of—its attack on white culture, the album took Public Enemy into the Top 10 on the charts.

Although most of the record was outwardly confrontational, the media latched onto two of their songs: the under-a-minute "Meet the G That Killed Me," interpreted as homophobic, and "Welcome to the Terrordome," which Chuck D claimed was also grossly misinterpreted. The problem was compounded by their security force leader Professor Griff's remark that "Jews are wicked," after which Chuck D tried to defuse the situation by apologizing for Griff and saying that he was offended by Griff's remark as well.

WHAT ARE THE DIFFERENT BRANCHES OF HIP HOP AND RAP?

GANGSTA RAP a subgenre that sensationalized the gang lifestyle and featured lyrics depicting the experiences of inner-city youth.

ICE-T West Coast gangsta rapper often credited with inventing gangsta rap due to his song "6 in the Mornin'."

N.W.A one of the most controversial rap groups of all time, whose lyrics depict police brutality and retaliation.

After its golden age, hip hop began to split into different directions and genres. Although the early days of the genre are still legendary, many of the branches of hip hop have also had a tremendous influence on pop culture and rock history.

Gangsta Rap

Gangsta rap originated on the West Coast. With its advent in the late 1980s, hip hop broke into two categories: East Coast, with its increasingly complex rhythms and lyrics, and West Coast gangsta rap. Gangsta rap was both "the most influential style in all of pop music in this decade" (Alvarez 1999, 285) and one of the most controversial art forms. It has received criticism from politicians on both sides of the divide, religious leaders, and prominent figures of all races. Violence, drugs, misogyny, more violence, and chronicling of inner-city gang life are all characteristics of gangsta rap.

ICE-T

In 1991, **Ice-T** released an album titled *OG: Original Gangster*. Although Ice-T had been around for a while, this album in particular gained notoriety. Besides being hailed as one of the most important, defining albums in the subgenre of gangsta rap, the album was released just before Ice-T and his heavy metal band, Body Count, sparked nationwide controversy with the song "Cop Killer."

Ice-T was born in Newark, New Jersey, but raised by an aunt in South Central Los Angeles. In high school, the young Tracy Marrow (Ice-T's birth name) became obsessed with rap. After serving in the U.S. Army, Ice-T returned to L.A., but it took a while for him to build his reputation as a rapper. Finally, in 1986 he recorded the album *Rhyme Pays*. Some say that a song from that album, "6 in the Mornin'," shows that Ice-T invented gangsta rap. The song's lyrics capture the life and experiences of living in a violent environment.

When *OG: Original Gangster* was released in 1991, the subgenre was already going strong. Ice-T's next move was to form a heavy metal band, Body Count, that would play music while he rapped lyrics. In 1992, "Cop Killer" was released as a single, which created a huge controversy, in part because some public figures believed Ice-T's lyrics advocated killing policemen. In June, the Combined Law Enforcement Associations of Texas called for a boycott of Time Warner products—the label that released Ice-T's recordings—if the corporation did not remove the song from the group's debut album. Over the next several months, more law enforcement agencies called for action against Time Warner, and both Vice President Dan Quayle and President George H. W. Bush denounced "Cop Killer" as offensive. Of course, people were still buying

the record, and the publicity made Ice-T a household name. The controversy ended when Ice-T decided to take "Cop Killer" off the *Body Count* CD (Johnson 1999, 289).

N.W.A, *STRAIGHT OUTTA COMPTON* (1988)

N.W.A (Niggaz With Attitude) was a group active between 1986 and 1991. Like Ice-T, they are credited with defining the gangsta rap subgenre. After N.W.A split up, the group's most famous members—Dr. Dre, Ice Cube, and Eazy-E—went on to become some of the most well-known figures in hip hop history. In part, this was because the group took the hard-line musical chaos of Public Enemy to a new level, incorporating police sirens and gunshot sound effects in their music from the beginning. Yet, they did it all while seemingly deaf to Chuck D's message: "Straight Outta Compton," their first single, was openly antagonistic.

From the beginning, N.W.A courted controversy. Their debut album, *Straight Outta Compton* (1988), displayed the anger, confusion, and violence prevalent among young urban African Americans. In the title single, each rapper's self-aggrandizing introduction seems ready to give an answer to New York's South Bronx in the form of the West Coast post-industrial wasteland. Each rapper "portrayed himself as an untouchable rebel without a cause. Police, girls, rivals—none of them could get in Cube's game" (Chang 2005, 319).

However, it was the second track on the album that stirred up so much controversy that the federal government got involved. In the second track, "Fuck Tha Police," each MC took the stand in a mock-trial to protest the disparity in police treatment of black and white youths. The lyrics of the first verse of the song were coupled with gunshot sound effects and outright threats against the police department, leading some right-wing politicians to claim that N.W.A was telling fans to kill the police. In one incident, police departments across the South and Midwest faxed each other the song's lyrics. Tour dates were abruptly cancelled. Cops refused to provide security for N.W.A shows in Toledo and Milwaukee. In Cincinnati, federal agents subjected the crew to drug searches, asking if they were L.A. gang members, using their tour as a front to expand their crack-selling operations. The national 200,000-member Fraternal Order of Police voted to boycott groups that advocated assaults on officers of the law. But in Detroit, where local police showed up in intimidatingly large numbers, the crowd chanted "Fuck the police" all night, and the crew decided to try performing the song anyway. As Cube began the song, the cops rushed the stage and the group fled (Chang 2005, 325–326).

Representing Breaks Down

As the group ascended in sales and notoriety, they seemed to demand that the hip hop progressives—embodied in the East Coasters Public Enemy and KRS-One—pick sides in the battle against the white majority. However, it became clear that it was largely suburban white teenagers who were buying N.W.A's gangsta rap. The *New York Times* criticized N.W.A's "self-parody," and their "stereotypes of rappers as sex-starved buffoons" (Watkins

2005, 95). On the one hand, the group was "representing" the streets of Compton, but on the other, this representation was becoming caricature.

In early 1990, Ice Cube left the group to pursue what would become a very successful solo career. The group's final album, *Efil4zaggin* (1991), or Niggaz4life spelled backward, was characterized by Dr. Dre's funky beats and high production quality. Dr. Dre went on to an even more successful solo career, and his production work ranged from discovering Eminem to producing Snoop Doggy Dogg.

Hip Hop Controversies

Ice T and Body Count in "Cop Killer" Controversy

1992

"Cop Killer" ruffles feathers with law enforcement agencies, causing them to call for action. Ice T eventually removed the track from his album.

N.W.A. Frustrates Feds
1989

The rap song "Fuck tha Police" stepped on the toes of the FBI. The controversy helped stir buzz for their album, which went on to sell more than 2 million copies.

Tupac Shakur, Snoop Doggy Dogg, Death Row Records and Interscope Vex Veep
1993

Tupac managed to upset the Vice President Dan Quayle and President George H. W. Bush. Time Warner dropped Death Row and Interscope from their lineup, but Universal picked them up.

2 Live Crew Scandalizes Floridians
1990

"Me So Horny" upset the sensitivities of Florida families and the Supreme Court. The case charging the Crew with "obscenity" and attempting to make it a crime to sell the record was eventually dismissed.

Eminem Makes GLAAD Sad
2000

Eminem upset many—including The Gay and Lesbian Alliance Against Defamation and the National Organization for Women—with his music that sensationalized beating women and homosexuals. Elton John performed the offending song, "Stan" at the Grammy awards with him that year, causing more outrage.

SNOOP DOGGY DOGG West Coast artist famous for his slow delivery and chronic marijuana use.

DEATH ROW RECORDS West Coast hip hop label created by Dr. Dre and Suge Knight in 1991.

CYPRESS HILL most successful Latino hip hop group; glorified marijuana use.

TUPAC SHAKUR (2PAC) West Coast gangsta rapper prone to trouble; murdered in Las Vegas in a drive-by shooting.

BAD BOY RECORDS East Coast record company created by Sean "Diddy" Combs in 1993.

THE NOTORIOUS B.I.G./BIGGIE SMALLS East Coast rapper murdered in a drive-by shooting in L.A.

JAY-Z rap's ultimate businessman; sees himself as a business and is proud of his entrepreneurial status.

SNOOP DOGGY DOGG

Dr. Dre's solo debut *The Chronic* (1992) was done in collaboration with Cordazar Calvin Broadus—otherwise known as **Snoop Doggy Dogg**. In return, Dre produced Snoop's debut album, *Doggystyle* (1993) for **Death Row Records**, the label founded by Dr. Dre and entrepreneur Suge Knight in 1991. *The Chronic*, the first album produced for Death Row, was certified platinum three times in a year, while *Doggystyle* made it to platinum four times in seven months.

In *Doggystyle*, Snoop Doggy Dog rhymed more slowly than previous rappers, contrasting with the clipped rhythms of the East Coast. His voice was also much softer, far from the near-yell of Ice Cube. Snoop Dogg was a member of the notorious gang the Crips, which, along with the Bloods, helped define the territory of the West Coast hip hop scene (Forman 2002, 178). Gang violence became a real part of hip hop when, in 1993, Snoop Dog's bodyguard, Phillip Wolderman, was murdered. Snoop went on tour with Lollapalooza in 1997, further exemplifying the crossover appeal of gangsta rap.

CYPRESS HILL

Cypress Hill was among the first Latino hip hop groups to have success. From Southern California, the group glorified the use of marijuana, as did Dr. Dre and Snoop Dogg. The group consisted of B-Real, DJ Muggs, Eric Bobo, and Sen Dog.

The first singles from their debut *Cypress Hill* (1991) were "The Phuncky Feel One" and "How I Could Just Kill a Man." Their music received play in a new place for gangsta rap acts: college radio. The successes of their first album lead to appearances on the Lollapalooza rock tour in 1992, while their second album, *Black Sunday*, debuted at the top of the Billboard 200 charts in 1993. The first single from this album, "Insane in the Brain," brought the group crossover success, but it was their last hit single. The band dissolved in 1996 and 1997, but came back in 2001 with a more rock-oriented feel.

TUPAC SHAKUR (A.K.A. 2PAC)

Tupac Shakur was a charismatic figure in West Coast hip hop and one of the best selling hip hop artists in the world. He was born in East Harlem but moved to Marin City, California, in 1988. There he began his career as a backup dancer for the musical group Digital Underground, with whom he made his first appearance on their 1991 record *This Is an EP Release*. But it was his album *2Pacalypse Now* (1991) that shot him to stardom. The album addressed many of the social issues of the day: police brutality, teenage pregnancy, drug use, and poverty. Controversy over the album grew when a boy in Texas shot a state trooper and claimed that listening to it spawned his actions. The album went gold, likely helped by both the single "Brenda's Got A Baby" and attacks from Republican Vice President Dan Quayle (AMG 2009).

The day before Tupac was found guilty of sexual assault, November 30, 1994, he was shot in the lobby of a New York City recording studio but survived. He accused Sean Combs, Andre Harrell, Biggie Smalls, and Randy Walker of being involved in the shooting. As a result of his conviction, Tupac served eight months of a four-and-a-half-year prison sentence, and upon his release recorded the 27-song album *All Eyez on Me* (1996) (Smith 1999, 303). The album went quintuple-platinum, fueled in part by the song "California Love." Although Shakur was now one of the largest stars in hip hop, he decided to go into acting and produced two films, *Bullet* and *Gridlock'd*, before he was murdered in 1996.

East Coast Figures

Part of what fueled artists like Snoop Dogg and Tupac was the rivalry between East and West Coast artists. While West Coast rap was going through its gangsta rap phase, East Coast rap was known for its lyrical style. The rivalry was focused mostly between the West Coast's Tupac and Death Row Records and the East Coast's The Notorious B.I.G. and **Bad Boy Records**. Sean "Diddy" Combs founded Bad Boy Records in 1993. When B.I.G.'s record was a success, Death Row looked for new talent as a way to compete against its rival.

∧∧∧ **Before his death,** Biggie Smalls was king **of the East Coast rappers.**

THE NOTORIOUS B.I.G.

The Notorious B.I.G., also known as **Biggie Smalls**, was the larger-than-life figure central to the East Coast rap scene in the same way that Tupac was central to the West Coast. His music featured a slow, easy flow; he was a natural storyteller. His debut album, *Ready to Die* (1994) had instant success and stole some thunder from the West Coast crew. Three singles from this album—"Juicy," "Big Poppa," and "One More Chance"—all did well on the charts. Much like the West Coast rappers, Smalls embraced misogyny with "One More Chance," in which women ask for one more chance while he boasts about his abilities in bed. This album also bears the clear mark of a post–Snoop Dog world, where the chaotic beats of N.W.A and Public Enemy have given way to laidback grooves, albeit with a less laconic delivery.

On March 8, 1997, just weeks before the scheduled release of Biggie's second album, *Life After Death*, Biggie appeared at the Soul Train Awards in Los Angeles to present an award. Later that night, he was returning to his hotel when a car pulled up next to the Suburban carrying him and its driver shot four bullets into his chest. Smalls died on the way to the hospital. His second album, released 15 days after his death, hit number one on the charts upon its release. Sean Combs, as Puff Daddy, released a song, "I'll Be Missing You," featuring those who had been involved in Biggie's life in 1997.

JAY-Z

Jay-Z, born Shawn Corey Carter, was a popular rapper, especially during the early 2000s. He is also well-known for being an entrepreneur, as shown by the Kanye West track "Diamonds," where he sings "I'm not

East Coast vs. West Coast

West Coast		East Coast
Voicing concern over inner city issues—violence, gang life, poverty, etc.	**Focus**	Lyrical dexterity
Death Row Records	**Primary Record Company**	Bad Boy Records
Tupac Shakur	**Well-Known Artist**	Notorious B.I.G.
Tupac Shakur murdered in 1996	**Controversy**	Notorious B.I.G. murdered in 1997
Birthplace of gangsta rap	**Claim to Fame**	Birthplace of hip hop music
Mostly sampled from funk hits, the tempo was slowed down and female backgrounds vocals	**Beats**	Beats for a while were being sampled from James Brown, more detached and highly compressed drums
Dr. Dre – The Chronic	**Landmark Album**	Nas – *Illmatic*

∧∧∧ The rivalry between East Coast and West Coast artists lead to different styles of music, as well as controversies involving artists like Notorious B.I.G. and Tupac.

THE WU-TANG CLAN innovative group of nine eclectic rappers inspired by Chinese culture.

DJ JAZZY JEFF & THE FRESH PRINCE duo famous for kitschy raps such as "Parents Just Don't Understand" and "I Think I Can Beat Mike Tyson."

MC HAMMER a true rags-to-riches-to-rags again story, Hammer was enormously successful commercially yet wound up broke.

a businessman; I'm a *business*, man!" Jay-Z popularized the rags-to-riches narrative in hip hop; it makes sense, as Jay-Z is the CEO of Roc-A-Fella Records, former president of Def Jam Records, and owner of the New York Nets. He embodies the role of hip hop CEO, and his songs reflect this, extolling the virtues of intelligence and business savvy.

Jay-Z is one of the most financially successful hip hop artists. His debut album, *Reasonable Doubt* (1996), established him as a driven businessman as well as a hit machine, and his next album, *In My Lifetime, Volume 1* (1997), confirmed this with platinum status and lyrics that chronicled a dark period of his life. However, it was Jay-Z's third album, *Vol. 2 . . . Hard Knock Life* (1998) that launched him into superstar status. The many singles, including "Can I Get A. . ." and "Hard Knock Life (Ghetto Anthem)" drove the album to win the Best Rap Album Grammy, as well as selling over 5 million copies.

After the release of *The Black Album* (2003), Jay-Z retired from making new studio albums for several years, but he worked on side projects, including the founding of record labels and an urban clothing brand, Rocawear. Jay-Z has also been very active as a philanthropist, most notably contributing money, along with Sean Combs, to Hurricane Katrina relief efforts.

HOUSE OF PAIN

House of Pain, consisting of Everlast, DJ Lethal, and Danny Boy, offered working-class narratives with an Irish immigrant twist. Their biggest hit,

"Jump Around" (1992), featured lyrics that have been heard at many clubs across the world. Although their first album and single brought them success, later albums didn't do as well, and the group eventually split up. Two members, Everlast and DJ Lethal, would enjoy further success in the music business—the former with a solo career and the latter through his part in the rap-rock group Limp Bizkit.

THE WU-TANG CLAN

The Wu-Tang Clan is a group of rappers based in New York City consisting of nine artists: RZA, GZA, Raekwon, U-God, Ghostface Killah, Inspectah Deck, Method Man, Masta Killa, and Ol' Dirty Bastard. Each had a solo career and solo projects outside the Wu-Tang, which drove the group and the individual members to success. Strong influences from martial arts cinema and Chinese culture helped form a mythological framework for the group. After their debut album, *Enter the Wu-Tang (36 Chambers)*, released in 1993, established their identities, each solo artist continually referenced the group on solo projects, extending their mythology in many different directions. The gritty sound of the album established the RZA as one of the preeminent producers and artists in hardcore hip hop.

Pop Rap

Although East and West Coast rappers were battling for the top of the charts, another movement was on the rise: the pop rap movement. As hip hop proved to be commercially viable, new genre aimed directly at the pop charts, leading to everything from TV sitcoms to the reality show *Hammertime*.

DJ JAZZY JEFF & THE FRESH PRINCE

DJ Jazzy Jeff & The Fresh Prince brought hip hop into everyone's living rooms with the sitcom, *The Fresh Prince of Bel Air*. The duo first

Flashpoints **ISSUES in ROCK**   ## The Murder of Tupac Shakur

Tupac Shakur (pictured on left) didn't get much of a chance to enjoy his time as a rapper at the top of the charts. On September 6, 1996, Tupac left the MGM Grand in Las Vegas and got into a scuffle with a Crips gang member, Orlando Anderson, in the lobby. A short time later, at around 11:15 pm, he was gunned down in a drive-by shooting. Death Row Records president Suge Knight (pictured on right) was hit by the shrapnel, but was otherwise unharmed. Tupac, on the other hand, died of internal bleeding.

Because of a feud arising from Biggie Smalls' claim that he slept with Tupac's wife, it was thought that Smalls might have been involved in the shooting, but Smalls had

alibis for his whereabouts at the time. As gangsta rap was becoming more popular, the extreme persona of N.W.A was giving way to much more seriously violent music, no longer purely for shock value. The commercial potential of violence led rappers to project streetwise, tough-guy images that have been considered as possible causes of rap violence. As rappers initially sought to "represent" the violence of Compton, they were now acting it out in full force. Are violent lyrics always reprehensible, or do they draw attention to issues that would otherwise be hidden? Do they exacerbate the violence, or only uncover it?

Sean "Puffy" Combs

Sean "Puffy" Combs, also known as "Puff Daddy," "P. Diddy," and now just "Diddy," is a major player in East Coast rap. Founder of Bad Boy Records (1993) and a rap artist in his own right, Diddy produced B.I.G.'s works as well as many other acts. After the shooting of his friend and main act Biggie Smalls, Combs achieved what was perhaps his greatest commercial success as a solo artist with the track "I'll Be Missing You," featuring Biggie's wife Faith Evans, a tribute to B.I.G.

Although Combs is one of the most commercially successful people in the hip hop industry, he has been accused of linking popular samples to mediocre hits, most

notably in his track "Come With Me," featuring Rage Against the Machine guitarist Tom Morello playing Led Zeppelin's "Kashmir" riff. In 2001, Combs was indicted in a shooting in a New York club, both because he had an unauthorized firearm and because his driver said Combs bribed him to claim it as his own (*New York Times* 2001). Combs was acquitted and continues producing. In addition to his production and rap career, Sean Combs has a clothing line, Sean John, and he owns a restaurant chain called Justin's.

performed together at a Philadelphia house party in 1986, when Will Smith was 18 and Jeff Townes was 19. Their first album, *Rock the House* (1986) performed moderately well, but their second album, *He's the DJ, I'm the Rapper* (1988), and their single "Parents Just Don't Understand" put them on the map as multi-platinum stars. Their third album, *And in This Corner* (1989), showed signs of dwindling popularity, and two albums later they split up. Since the 1990s, Will Smith has had a successful solo and acting career, while DJ Jazzy Jeff became a producer of R&B and soul.

MC HAMMER

MC Hammer, born Stanley Kirk Burrell, had a whirlwind success story. He was born in Oakland, California, and self-produced his first album, *Feel My Power* (1987), which Capitol retitled *Let's Get it Started* (1988). This album went multi-platinum with singles like "Turn This Mutha Out." However, MC Hammer's third album, *Please Hammer, Don't Hurt 'Em* (1990), spent 21 weeks at the number one slot on Billboard's charts and is the highest-selling rap album of all time, with 10 million copies sold. His single "U Can't Touch This" featured a beat from Rick James' "Super Freak" and spawned a video that introduced baggy "Hammer pants" to the world. MC Hammer dolls went on the market, and a Saturday morning cartoon, *Hammerman*, featured MC Hammer's voice. This self-promotion created a critical backlash among those who felt that Hammer was not a "legitimate" rap star but merely cashing in on the movement. He had one more successful album, *Too Legit To Quit* (1991), before his amassed fortune had been spent and his new rags-to-riches-to-

> ∧
> ∧ After the duo split up, Will Smith
> ∧ went on to become a successful
> actor and commercial solo artist.

rags story was born when he declared bankruptcy. Hammer has made several attempts at a comeback, and in summer 2009 starred in his own reality show, *Hammertime*, on the A&E channel.

VANILLA ICE

Vanilla Ice, born Robert Van Winkle, is perhaps the most maligned man in all of hip hop. Even so, "Ice Ice Baby" (1991) was a huge hit with an infectious hook. The song sampled "Under Pressure" by Queen and David Bowie, and it is one of the most recognizable in hip hop, although it sparked controversy because it did not initially credit Bowie and Queen. Vanilla Ice had one of the hardest crashes in hip hop history, ending with a 1991 arrest for threatening a homeless man and the starring role in the unsuccessful film *Cool as Ice*. Nevertheless, Vanilla Ice inspired others, including one white boy from Boston, Massachusetts—Marky Mark Wahlberg—whose brother was in the hottest group around.

MARKY MARK AND THE FUNKY BUNCH

Marky Mark and the Funky Bunch had a huge commercial impact; when their album came out, it quickly topped the charts. Part of the reason for this was that the lead rapper, Marky Mark's older brother, Donnie Wahlberg, was a member of New Kids on the Block, an extremely popular boy band. When Marky Mark's debut album, *Music for the People* (1991), was released with his single "Good Vibrations," he had a number one hit. Besides being known for the one-hit wonder status of "Good

Genres and Subgenres of Rap

Category	Characteristics	Sub-Genres	Exemplary Performers
East Coast hip hop	Noted for its emphasis on lyrics and lyrical ability, complex wordplay, and metaphors	Mafioso rap, alternative hip hop, hardcore hip hop, jazz rap	Nas
West Coast hip hop	Less cohesive as a whole than East Coast hip hop, focused a bit more on dance beats and the inner city lifestyle	Gangsta rap, underground rap, Latin rap, nerdcore hip hop, G-funk	N.W.A
Southern rap	More club-oriented, strong dance beats	Dirty South, Miami bass, crunk, New Orleans hip hop	Arrested Development
Detroit hip hop	Music originating in Detroit, often quite controversial	Acid rap	Eminem
Pop rap	Commercially successful hip hop with a strong pop music influence	N/A	DJ Jazzy Jeff and the Fresh Prince
Political hip hop	Politically aware rap that takes on a social or political theme and discusses it	N/A	Public Enemy
Rapcore	A fusion of rap and rock with punk rock	Nu metal, rock rap, metal rap	Rage Against the Machine
Trip hop	Electronic music featuring a down-tempo beat	Shackgroove, trip rock	Portishead

Rap split off into many genres and sub-genres during its golden age.

Vibrations," Marky Mark was known for showing off his physique in his underwear for Calvin Klein. Mark Wahlberg eventually left hip hop stardom and, like Ice-T and Ice Cube, went on to pursue a very successful acting career, being nominated for an Academy Award in 2008 for a role in Martin Scorsese's *The Departed*.

SALT-N-PEPA

Salt-n-Pepa was a best-selling female rap trio originally hailing from Queens. Cheryl James ("Salt"), Sandra Denton ("Pepa"), and Deidra Roper ("Spinderella") received some attention for their first album, *Hot, Cool, and Vicious* (1986), but it wasn't until a remix of "Push It" was created by a San Francisco DJ that the trio made waves and received a Grammy nomination. Their sound mixed girl-group harmonies with rapping, and they became one of the earliest groups to cross over onto the pop charts. They continued their success with *Blacks' Magic* (1990), which was funkier, and *Very Necessary* (1993), whose hits "Whatta Man" and "Shoop" propelled it into the Billboard Top 10, a remarkable feat for a group once thought of as a one-hit wonder.

From Between the Coasts

Although a big part of the media focus was on the rivalry between East and West Coast rap, a wide diversity of artists sprang up between the coasts as well.

ATLANTA HIP HOP

One of the largest concentrations of hip hop was—and still is—in Atlanta. Arrested Development, OutKast, and Goodie Mob are all from Atlanta and help define that city's sound. Atlanta had a large black middle class, and its hip hop tended to opt for a "gentler, more cultural nationalist" (Sarig 2007, 110) vibe influenced by De La Soul and A Tribe Called Quest.

Arrested Development

Arrested Development, a Grammy-award winning rap group from Atlanta, sought to provide a "positive" Afrocentric response to gangsta rap. The group's first album, *3 Years, 5 Months, and Two Days in the Life Of. . .* (1990), included the hit "Tennessee," with its spiritual lyrics about speaking to God. This contrasts with the harsh lyrics and language of gangsta rap, and it topped the *Village Voice*'s *Pazz & Jop* critics' poll. Their follow-up album, *Zingalamaduni* (1994), received critical praise but didn't do well in sales, and the band broke up shortly after their 1995 tour.

Goodie Mob

"Goodie Mob" was said to stand for "The GOOD DIE Mostly Over Bullshit." This group's debut, *Soul Food* (1995), won much acclaim from critics at the time. This album, originally conceived as a compilation rather than the work of an actual group, touched on issues of social justice, public housing, and prison overpopulation—it was no "wholesome Atlanta-style protest" (Sarig 2007, 137), but rather had hints of Public Enemy. Member Cee-Lo left the group in 2000 and formed the group Gnarls Barkley with DJ Danger Mouse, whose hit "Crazy" (2006) was important in its own right because of its success as a digital single.

OutKast

OutKast, or André Benjamin (André 3000) and Antwan Patton (Big Boi), are considered the kings of the Atlanta scene, with their combination of soul, funk, and constant reference to the black Southern experience. OutKast became celebrities with *Southernplayalisticadillacmuzik* (1994) when they were just out of their teens. They continued to be successful, with their song "Hey Ya!" spending 32 weeks on the charts, from the album *Speakerboxxx/The Love Below* (2003), which spent 56 weeks on the Billboard 200. The group won the 2004 Grammy Award for Album of the Year, becoming only the second hip hop act to receive such an honor (the first was Lauryn Hill's album *The Miseducation of Lauryn Hill* in 1999).

THE MIDWEST AND NEW ORLEANS

Atlanta was not the only off-coast hip hop machine. Hip hop came from all over the post-industrial Midwest, as well as the logical home of party music, New Orleans.

Kanye West

Kanye West is a Chicago-based producer-turned-MC. His first album, *The College Dropout,* featured gospel–hip hop fusion in "Jesus Walks," "All Falls Down," and "Through the Wire." His second album, *Late Registration* (2005), continued in Sean Combs' tradition of hiring a popular performer (in this case, Jamie Foxx) to cover a legendary artist (Ray Charles), leading to the massive hit "Gold Digger," a critical and commercial winner. Kanye West was noted for talking about

TOP OF THE CHARTS

WHAT'S HOT!

NOVEMBER 28, 1998

1. "Nobody Supposed To Be Here" – Deborah Cox
2. "Doo Wop (That Thing)" – Lauryn Hill
3. "Lately" – Divine
4. "Love Like This" – Faith Evans
5. "How Deep Is Your Love" – Dru Hill Featuring Redman
6. "Can I Get A. . ." – Jay-Z Featuring Amil (of Major Coinz)
7. "Trippin" – Total Featuring Missy Elliott
8. "All The Places (I Will Kiss. . .)" – Aaron Hall
9. "Love Me" – 112 Featuring Mase
10. "Hard Knock Life (Ghetto Anthem)" – Jay-Z

Summary

HOW DID HIP HOP GET ITS START? 228

- Rap and hip hop are sometimes used as synonyms, but hip hop often refers to the cultural phenomenon, including break-dancing and graffiti, whereas rap refers to music featuring vocal overlays and sampled DJed tracks.
- The vocal style of hip hop can be traced back to African call-and-response traditions.
- DJs invented the style through manipulating turntables to make a song more danceable, extending the "break."
- Old-school hip hop was almost solely an East Coast phenomenon for nearly a decade.

HOW DID HIP HOP GAIN MAINSTREAM RECOGNITION? 230

- The Sugarhill Gang is largely credited with breaking the mainstream barrier with their song "Rapper's Delight" in 1979.
- New-school hip hop originated around 1983. It was more radio-conscious than old-school hip hop, focusing less on dancing and more on songs.
- Rap's golden age lasted from the late 80s until the early 90s.

WHAT ARE THE DIFFERENT BRANCHES OF HIP HOP AND RAP? 234

- Gangsta rap was the most controversial branch, calling first-amendment rights into question.
- An important feature of gangsta rap, in addition to its West Coast focus, is its emphasis on narrating the life of a young person living in the inner city.
- East Coast rap posed a formidable rivalry to West Coast rap—most notably the rivalry between Tupac and Biggie Smalls and their respective production companies, Death Row Records and Bad Boy Records.
- Pop rap has received an enormous amount of backlash. DJ Jazzy Jeff and the Fresh Prince, MC Hammer, and Salt-n-Pepa are all examples of this rap genre.
- The activity going on in the South and Midwest in rap was extremely diverse. The rap artists Arrested Development, Goodie Mob, OutKast, Kanye West, Lil Wayne, and Eminem traverse the musical spectrum.
- The British scene is radically different from the U.S. scene, with a pronounced electronica influence.
- Trip hop fuses hip hop with ambient music, R&B samples, and down-beat electronica.
- Rap rock, rap metal, and rapcore are three more recent subgenres that have fused hip hop with alternative rock and metal.

Key Terms

hip hop a cultural and musical movement beginning in the 1970s that included graffiti, rap music, and break dancing *228*

rap vocals overlaid against turntable techniques executed by a DJ *228*

griots West African poets and singers who traveled about and passed on oral traditions *228*

DJ Kool Herc called the "Godfather" of hip hop, a DJ that is credited for introducing the turntable style to the United States *228*

beat-matching changing the speed of one track to match the tempo of another *228*

mixing weaving two tracks together to form one song *228*

scratching moving a record back and forth while using the fade control to create unique sounds *228*

drumming creating a drumming sound with scratching techniques *228*

the break a technique in which records are scratched to isolate the drumbeats from music *228*

break-dancing a popular form of dance including spinning on one's head *228*

tagging painting one's name or affiliation as graffiti *229*

beatboxing making drumbeats with one's mouth *229*

old-school hip hop refers to the rap music created in the late 1970s until the early 1980s *229*

Sugarhill Gang often credited with creating the first hip hop record and bringing hip hop into the mainstream with "Rapper's Delight" *230*

Run-D.M.C. musical group using more rock oriented samples, famous for "Walk This Way" cover of Aerosmith's hit song *230*

LL Cool J rap artist whose earlier works are more romantic, but his "Mama Said Knock You Out" was a breakthrough hit *231*

Beastie Boys hip hop trio from Queens, who had the first number one rap record with *Licensed to Ill* *231*

golden age of rap a period from the late 80s through early 90s when rap was flourishing *232*

Public Enemy controversial group espousing black militant politics, but also very influential *232*

KRS-One member of Boogie Down Productions, known for statements about education *232*

De La Soul witty, playful group offering respite from some of the more serious acts popular during the golden age *233*

Eric B. & Rakim duo famous for their album *Paid in Full* and for popularizing the use of James Brown and funk in sampling *233*

A Tribe Called Quest group fusing hip hop and jazz during rap's Golden Age *233*

gangsta rap a subgenre that sensationalized the gang lifestyle and featured lyrics depicting the experiences of inner-city youth *234*

Ice-T West Coast gangsta rapper often credited with inventing gangsta rap due to his song "6 in the Mornin' " *234*

N.W.A one of the most controversial rap groups of all time, whose lyrics depict police brutality and retaliation *234*

Snoop Doggy Dogg West Coast artist famous for his slow delivery and chronic marijuana use *236*

Death Row Records West Coast hip hop label created by Dr. Dre and Suge Knight in 1991 *236*

Cypress Hill most successful Latino hip hop group; glorified marijuana use *236*

Tupac Shakur (2Pac) West Coast gangsta rapper prone to trouble; murdered in Las Vegas in a drive-by shooting *236*

Bad Boy Records East Coast record company created by Sean "Diddy" Combs in 1993 *236*

The Notorious B.I.G./Biggie Smalls East Coast rapper murdered in a drive-by shooting in L.A. *236*

Jay-Z rap's ultimate businessman; sees himself as a business and is proud of his entrepreneurial status *237*

The Wu-Tang Clan innovative group of nine eclectic rappers inspired by Chinese culture *238*

DJ Jazzy Jeff & The Fresh Prince duo famous for kitschy raps such as "Parents Just Don't Understand" and "I Think I Can Beat Mike Tyson" *238*

MC Hammer a true rags-to-riches-to-rags again story, Hammer was enormously successful commercially yet wound up broke *239*

Arrested Development Atlanta-based rap group wishing to bring positive Afrocentric response to gangsta rap *241*

Lil Wayne young prodigy when it comes to rap music, hailed as one of the best artists in his generation of performers *242*

Eminem white rap artist reaching heights of stardom and controversy beginning in the early 2000s *242*

Brithop British hip hop *242*

trip hop a combination of strings, electronic, and rap-like lyrics inspired by hip hop music and coming from of Bristol, England; includes Portishead *243*

Massive Attack Bristol trip hop group that has been credited with starting the subgenre *243*

rap rock a combination of various rock influences with hip hop lyrics; an example is Rage Against the Machine *243*

rap metal a combination of heavy metal music and rap lyrics; sometimes also known as nü metal; an example is Limp Bizkit *243*

rapcore a combination of hardcore punk and rap music; an example is Linkin Park *243*

Sample Test Questions

1. Which of the following DJs was credited with the term "The Godfather" of hip hop?
   a. DJ Kool Herc
   b. DJ Jazzy Jeff
   c. DJ Lethal
   d. DJ Run

2. Which of these statements is NOT correct?
   a. The Sugarhill Gang is credited with creating the first mainstream rap song.
   b. Tupac Shakur was killed from injuries related to a drive by shooting in Las Vegas
   c. N.W.A has avoided controversy as a popular multi-genre rap group.
   d. Vanilla Ice is often despised because of his "poser" gangsta style and lyrics.

3. Which song is most likely to spark a great controversy among police officers?
   a. Vanilla Ice "Ice Ice Baby"
   b. Snoop Doggy Dog "Gin and Juice"
   c. N.W.A "Straight Outta Compton"
   d. Public Enemy "Fight the Power"

4. Which of the following was NOT become involved in the East Coast/West Coast rivalry?
   a. Tupac Shakur
   b. Suge Knight
   c. Biggie Smalls
   d. The Streets

5. In 1990, how did Public Enemy stir up controversy?
   a. A song called "Cop Killer"
   b. An anti-Semitic remark
   c. A sexual abuse case
   d. An unpopular gang affiliation

ESSAY

6. Discuss the influence of hip hop on rock & roll.
7. Why did East Coast and West Coast rap have a rivalry?
8. What are some of the characteristics of gangsta rap? Why were these controversial?
9. Why did so many rap artists come from the South Bronx and inner-city L.A.?
10. Choose any artist from the old-school hip hop era and discuss the contributions made and the influences that artist had upon other artists.

WHERE TO START YOUR RESEARCH PAPER

To research the most current hip hop news, go to
http://www.daveyd.com

To research rap and hip hop slang, go to
http://www.rapdict.org/Main_Page

To research hip hop lyrics, go to http://ohhla.com/all.html

To research rap music history, go to
http://www.yale.edu/ynhti/curriculum/units/1993/4/93.04.04.x.html

To research old-school hip hop, go to
http://www.oldschoolhiphop.com

ANSWERS: 1. a; 2. c; 3. c; 4. d; 5. b

Remember to check www.thethinkspot.com for additional information, downloadable flashcards, and other helpful resources.

WHY WAS 1994 AN IMPORTANT YEAR IN THE HISTORY OF ROCK MUSIC?

HOW HAVE GIRL GROUPS AND BOY BANDS INFLUENCED THE HISTORY OF ROCK?

HOW HAS ROCK & ROLL BEEN CHANGED BY AGGRESSIVE MARKETING TO YOUNGER AUDIENCES?

"I received

a vinyl copy of that wonderfully classic scripture [the "very-out-of-print first Raincoats LP"] with a personalized dust sleeve covered with xeroxed lyrics, pictures, and all the members' signatures. There was also a touching letter from Anna [sic: Ana Da Silva, founding member of the band]. It made me happier than playing in front of thousands of people each night, rock-god idolization from fans, music industry plankton kissing my ass, and the million dollars I made last year. It was one of the few really important things that I've been blessed with since becoming an untouchable boy genius. . . .

"A big "f**k you" to those of you who have the audacity to claim that I'm so naive and stupid that I would allow myself to be taken advantage of and manipulated.

"I don't feel the least bit guilty for commercially exploiting a completely exhausted Rock Youth Culture because, at this point in rock history, Punk Rock (while still sacred to some) is, to me, dead and gone. We just wanted to pay tribute to something that helped us to feel as though we had crawled out of the dung heap of conformity. To pay tribute like an Elvis or Jimi Hendrix impersonator in the tradition of a bar band. I'll be the first to admit that we're the 90's version of Cheap Trick or the Knack but the last to admit that it hasn't been rewarding.

"At this point I have a request for our fans. If any of you in any way hate homosexuals, people of different color, or women, please do this one favor for us—leave us the fuck alone! Don't come to our shows and don't buy our records.

"Last year, a girl was raped by two wastes of sperm and eggs while they sang the lyrics to our song "Polly." I have a hard time carrying on knowing there are plankton like that in our audience. Sorry to be so anally P.C. but that's the way I feel.

Love,

Kurdt (the blond one)"

—Kurt Cobain, liner notes from *Incesticide*, 1992

SMOOTH SOUNDS, SLICK PACKAGING: THE PERSISTENCE OF POP (1994–)

CHAPTER 14

WHY WAS 1994 AN IMPORTANT YEAR IN THE HISTORY OF ROCK MUSIC?

The Death of Rock & Roll?

The alleged death of rock & roll has been a long-standing debate in the world of rock music. Is rock & roll truly "dead?" Did the death knell ring in 1994, or was it yet another example of fans mistakenly associating the death of a single performer with the end of an entire genre of music? And who is to say that the world's soon-to-be greatest rock & roll band isn't currently jamming in their parents' garage, just a few short years away from being discovered and adored by the masses?

Rock musicians and their fans alike were talking about the death of the genre long before 1994 came around. Don McLean speaks of the "the day the music died" in his classic 1971 folk rock song "American Pie." There are many interpretations of these lyrics, the most common of which refer to the 1959 plane crash that killed rock & roll icons Ritchie Valens, the Big Bopper, and Buddy Holly (McLean's major musical influence). Other critics argue that the song cryptically refers to the death of rock & roll as a genre. Since McLean has steadfastly refused to discuss the actual meaning of the song's lyrics, the debate is unlikely to be settled any time soon, although the general theme of the song is repeatedly expressed among households across the country. Every generation, some parents denounce their children's music and declare that rock & roll is officially dead—a comforting thought to eradicate the threatening new sounds emerging from their children's iPods. Yet every generation, a new brand of rock & roll emerges—from the British Invasion bands of the 1960s, to the heavy metal bands of the 1970s, to the industrial metal bands of the 1980s, to the alternative bands of the 1990s. The deaths of rock & roll giants such as Elvis, John Lennon, and Kurt Cobain prompted many critics to declare the end of an era (the week that Lennon was murdered, *Time* magazine carried the headline "When the Music Died"), but the genre is too big to be attached to any one individual. Nonetheless, 1994 marked the 25th anniversary of the Woodstock music festival and the death of rock star Kurt Cobain—two events that caused many fans and critics to question the direction in which rock & roll was headed.

1994: WOODSTOCK'S 25TH ANNIVERSARY

The 25th anniversary of the Woodstock music festival caused a lot of reflection on the past history of rock & roll and a lot of speculation about the future trajectory of the genre. Woodstock was a monumental event in rock & roll history, and it left a footprint that is still clearly visible today. To celebrate the anniversary of the fabled Woodstock, a slew of bands, promoters, and record company types decided to organize "Woodstock '94." This was to be a major festival featuring current bands to celebrate the spirit of rock & roll felt at the original Woodstock. Although the festival had some great performances, it was certainly not on a par with the original Woodstock.

Woodstock '94

The original 1969 Woodstock festival is remembered for its spirit of peace, happiness, camaraderie, and a prolific musical lineup that included 1960s icons Jimi Hendrix, The Who, and Janis Joplin (see Chapter 7 for more details of the original Woodstock). Woodstock '94 was originally billed as a two-day festival, but was ultimately extended to three. The posters advertising the festival paid homage to the original Woodstock advertisement, with the slogan "two more days of peace and music." The festival was held in Saugerties, New York, the location that the original Woodstock organizers had tried, unsuccessfully, to book for the festival.

Music festivals were much more common in 1994 than they had been in 1969, which probably contributed to the significantly smaller crowd. The

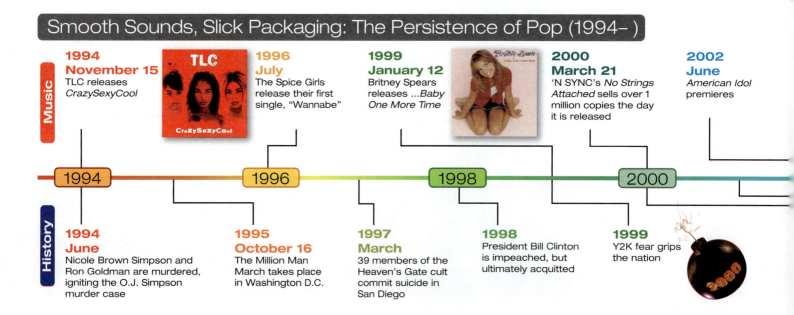

Smooth Sounds, Slick Packaging: The Persistence of Pop (1994–)

Music

1994
November 15
TLC releases *CrazySexyCool*

1996
July
The Spice Girls release their first single, "Wannabe"

1999
January 12
Britney Spears releases ...*Baby One More Time*

2000
March 21
'N SYNC's *No Strings Attached* sells over 1 million copies the day it is released

2002
June
American Idol premieres

1994 — 1996 — 1998 — 2000

History

1994
June
Nicole Brown Simpson and Ron Goldman are murdered, igniting the O.J. Simpson murder case

1995
October 16
The Million Man March takes place in Washington D.C.

1997
March
39 members of the Heaven's Gate cult commit suicide in San Diego

1998
President Bill Clinton is impeached, but ultimately acquitted

1999
Y2K fear grips the nation

> >>> While **Woodstock '94** was a success overall, many felt that the **commercialism involved** took away from the original spirit of the 1969 Woodstock festival.

original Woodstock drew approximately 500,000 people, while Woodstock 1994 drew a modest 255,000. Although a huge crowd by most standards, it paled in comparison to the incredible sprawling mass of people drawn to the original festival. There was a lengthy list of popular performers, and the event went off without any major tragedies. However, the true spirit of the Summer of '69 was not recreated, in part because commercialism has so greatly changed the face of the music industry.

The original Woodstock cost $3 million to put on, and tickets sold for $18. Woodstock '94 cost $30 million, and tickets were $135 and had to be purchased in pairs. Vending at the original Woodstock mostly consisted of peace activist Wavy Gravy and fellow members of the Hog Farm Collective—affiliates of a long-running hippie commune that also provided security for the festival—giving out free meals to as many people as humanly possible. Woodstock '94 had a slew of corporate sponsors, including Pepsi, Apple Computer, and Häagen-Dazs. The promoters also allowed pay-per-view broadcasts of the concert live in 27 countries, raking in over $5 million from viewer fees. In a move that further challenged the spirit of "peace and music," the promoters of Woodstock '94 filed an 80-million-dollar lawsuit against a group attempting to put on a festival called Bethel '94, to be held on the original Woodstock grounds. The suit was settled out of court, and the Bethel festival was eventually cancelled. In response to this, 12,000 people showed up at the sight spontaneously, and original Woodstock veteran Arlo Guthrie, as well as several others, gave free, impromptu performances.

The commercialism of the event turned many people off, and some performers, including Pearl Jam and Neil Young, refused invitations to play at it. Although the festival certainly deviated from the original formula

and was obviously not the groundbreaking event that was the original Woodstock, fans remained relatively peaceful, the bands put on some memorable performances, and DVDs of the festival are still available today. A contemporary *Time* magazine review concluded that Woodstock '94 had been "less than a cultural milestone, but more than a concert" (Farley and Thigpen 1994).

DID THE DEATH OF KURT COBAIN EQUAL THE DEATH OF ROCK?

The 1994 suicide of Nirvana front man Kurt Cobain caused shock waves throughout the rock & roll scene. Cobain's articulation of the fears and frustrations of Generation X identified him as the spokesperson for millions of teenagers worldwide. Despite his general distaste for fame and the music industry in general, Cobain was an icon whose turbulent home life reflected that of many of his fans (see Chapter 12). Music critic Anthony DeCurtis described the band's hit 1991 album *Nevermind* as "a defining moment in rock history," arguing that "Nirvana announced the end of one rock & roll era and the start of another" (DeCurtis 1994).

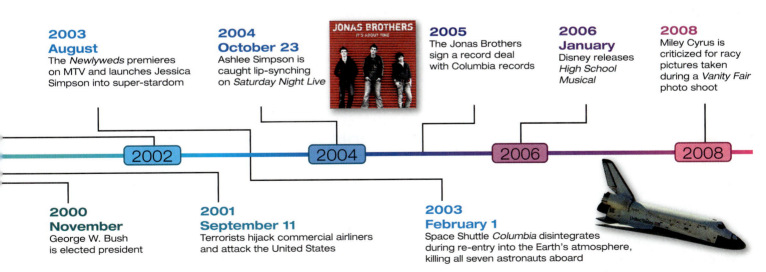

2003 August
The *Newlyweds* premieres on MTV and launches Jessica Simpson into super-stardom

2004 October 23
Ashlee Simpson is caught lip-synching on *Saturday Night Live*

2005
The Jonas Brothers sign a record deal with Columbia records

2006 January
Disney releases *High School Musical*

2008
Miley Cyrus is criticized for racy pictures taken during a *Vanity Fair* photo shoot

2002 2004 2006 2008

2000 November
George W. Bush is elected president

2001 September 11
Terrorists hijack commercial airliners and attack the United States

2003 February 1
Space Shuttle *Columbia* disintegrates during re-entry into the Earth's atmosphere, killing all seven astronauts aboard

MADONNA best selling female rock performer of the 20th century; her career has so far spanned almost three decades and covered a wide variety of musical styles and performances.

PRO TOOLS software program for recording and editing music; particularly useful in enhancing vocals through the use of pitch correction and vocal effects.

As we noted earlier, Cobain's death from a self-inflicted gunshot wound prompted fans and critics to herald the death of music itself. A glimpse at various Internet postings unveils comments such as, "It is too damn bad that Rock is dead. For me, Rock died the day that Kurt Cobain was murdered. I mean name me one really good rock album that actually mattered since 1994" (Dettmar 2006, 138). Despite fans' gloomy proclamations, equating the death of Cobain with the death of rock is both superficial and inaccurate. Throughout the next three chapters, we will examine the three main directions that rock & roll has taken over the past 15 years.

Since 1994: Three Main Streams in Rock & Roll

It is difficult to classify music that is being made currently; it always takes the distance of a few years to look at current music and put a label on it. Since 1994, it seems that there have been three major trends in rock & roll music:

1. The persistence of pop
2. A new accommodation of strong emotional content into evolving musical styles
3. The rise of musical appropriation, brought into rock by hip-hop

DOMESTICATION OF ROCK & ROLL

The history of rock & roll is, in some sense, the history of its various domestications; various segments of the larger culture have been at work for more than half a century trying to contain the sometimes anarchic energy of rock & roll. Rock music is by its very nature something of a wild beast. Although there are obvious musical differences

between 1950s rock musicians such as Chuck Berry and 1970s punk rockers such as Sid Vicious, the music stems from a similar rambunctious spirit of fun and rebellion. The boy bands and girl bands that rose to pop chart prominence in the 1990s seemed to indicate that the watered-down, clean-cut version of rock & roll music had finally risen to prominence over the often over-the-top, rebellious antics of some of the genre's more colorful and outrageous personalities over the years. However, it is important to remember that prepackaged, media-friendly acts have been popular almost as long as the genre itself.

Record company executives quickly learned that creating media-friendly ensemble acts—groups that were inoffensive, safe, and typically easy on the eyes—was an effective moneymaking tactic. For example, the Monkees were a manufactured group created in the mid-1960s at the height of Beatlemania (see Chapter 6). Formed of four Beatles look-alikes in Los Angeles for a television series, the show's producers hoped that they could ride the coattails of their British counterparts' success. Initially, the band was given so little control over their music that they were not even allowed to play their own instruments, although they later earned the right to produce their own material.

∧
∧ **Kurt Cobain's untimely**
∧ **death** in 1994 caused fans and critics alike to proclaim **the death of rock & roll.**

MADONNA

One contemporary pop star who most definitely isn't a prefabricated ensemble act is Madonna. The best selling female rock performer of the 20th century, **Madonna** has enjoyed a musical career that has spanned several decades. Arguably one of the first female pop stars to have complete control over her music and image, the Michigan-born performer has experimented with various multimedia, including movies, television, videos, fashion, and books, making her one of the most recognizable names in the world.

A major part of Madonna's appeal has been her chameleon-like ability to change appearances and genres. She has been compared to David Bowie in this regard (see Chapter 8 for a detailed analysis of Bowie's music), and she is as much a provocateur as a traditional performing artist. Able to change personae as easily as other performers might change outfits, Madonna has portrayed herself as a virginal innocent, a Marilyn Monroe-like sex symbol, a cold, androgynous robot, and, in her

ROCK TECHNOLOGY ▶▶▶ Pro-Tools and Music Editing in the Recording Studio

With rapidly improving technology in the music industry, the days of vocal talent being an absolute necessity for creating a hit record are long gone. Music editing software has become so advanced that almost anyone can be made to sound good in the studio.

Pro Tools is a software program for recording and editing music. Initially developed by Berkeley graduates Peter Gotcher and Evan Brooks to edit sounds for a sampling keyboard in the early 1980s, the system now enables the enhancement of vocal tracks to a point where the original singer's voice is all but unrecognizable. Pro Tools can perform vocal tuning, pitch correction, and add a whole host of effects to vocal tracks

to make them sound better. The obvious advantage is a streamlined, professional sound. But are programs such as Pro Tools destroying the integrity of the vocalist?

Critics argue that modern pop stars are attractive youngsters with mediocre singing abilities whose lack of natural talent can be covered up in the studio. As we will discuss later in the chapter, doctoring people's voices in the studio may cause major problems during live performances. As artists such as Milli Vanilli and Ashlee Simpson have discovered to their cost, technology cannot always be relied upon. When sound systems fail onstage, no amount of music software is able to compensate for raw natural talent.

First Top 40 hit with "Holiday"	Release of *True Blue*, which tops the US charts	Release of number one hit *Like a Prayer*	Release of *Ray of Light*	Release of *Confessions on a Dance Floor*
1983	**1986**	**1989**	**1998**	**2005**

1984	**1986**	**1992**	**2003**
Release of first number one album, *Like a Virgin*	Film career tanks with the release of critically-panned movie *Shanghai Surprise*	Release of top sellers *Sex* and *Erotica*	Release of *American Life*

∧ ∧ ∧ Part of **Madonna's appeal** comes from her ability to constantly **recreate her own image.**

more recent material (*Ray of Light*, 1998; *American Life*, 2003), a spiritual being and doting mother. Jeffrey Katzenberg, former chairman of Walt Disney Studios, explains: "Every two years she comes up with a new look, a new way of presenting herself, a new attitude, a new act, and a new design. And every time it is successful" (McGregor 1997).

Rising to superstardom with the release of *Like a Virgin,* which hit number one on both the singles and album charts in 1984, Madonna's success reached its peak in the mid-late 1980s with *True Blue* (1986) and *Like a Prayer* (1989). Having already courted controversy with her use of Catholic images in the video for *Like a Prayer*, she adopted an overtly sexual image in

1992 with the soft-core pornographic book "Sex" featuring hundreds of erotic photos of herself and other celebrities and the accompanying album *Erotica*. Madonna's complex explorations of sex and sexuality in *Erotica* (1992), metaphysical musings in *Ray of Light* (1998), and social commentary in *American Life* (2003) illustrate her ability to immerse herself in a chosen project before moving into a completely different style for the next album. Although this technique has caused some reviewers to dismiss the pop star's ever-changing interests as superficial, it highlights her talent for remaining one step ahead of musical trends—a capacity that highlights the "one-trick pony" nature of some of the later boy band and girl band groups in the 1990s.

HOW HAVE GIRL GROUPS AND BOY BANDS INFLUENCED THE HISTORY OF ROCK?

Girl Groups

The all-girl musical group has been a popular fixture on the music scene since the early 1960s. Groups such as the Chantels ("Maybe," 1958), the Shirelles ("Will You Still Love Me Tomorrow?," 1961), the Ronettes ("Be My Baby," 1963), and the Crystals ("Uptown," 1962) enjoyed huge success among crossover audiences before the British Invasion bands stormed the charts in the mid-1960s. Teaming up

with some of the greatest pop songwriters of the era, including Gerry Goffin and Carole King, Ellie Greenwich and Jeff Barry, and Cynthia Weil and Barry Mann, the groups formulated the classic girl-group sound with their loose harmonies mixing elements of R&B and pop. The original girl groups featured an identifiable lead vocal with a harmony arrangement and sang songs about the ups and downs of young love—a formula that would continue throughout the girl-group revival of the 1990s.

OCCASIONAL REVIVALS OF THE GIRL GROUP

Once the British Invasion landed in the mid-1960s, the popularity of girl groups began to wane, with only the Supremes and Martha and the Vandellas making any noticeable impact on the charts. In the 1980s, sporadic revivals of the genre occurred, with a few breakout girl groups enjoying some popularity and recognition.

The **Go-Go's** emerged from the punk/new wave explosion as a commercially successful all-girl group in the early '80s. Their roots were mostly in punk rock, but they refined their sound to one that was more commercially viable and scored a couple of major hits from their 1982 album *Beauty and the Beat* with "Our Lips Are Sealed" and "We Got the Beat." Lead singer Belinda Carlisle's girlish lead vocals recalled the earlier girl group sound, complemented by the group harmonies and rather basic rock accompaniments. Carlisle later launched a successful solo career, charting a string of mainstream pop hits in the late 1980s, including the 1987 number one single "Heaven is a Place on Earth."

The **Bangles**—made up of sisters Debbi and Vicki Peterson on drums and guitar respectively, singer/guitarist Susanna Hoffs, and bassist Annette Zilinskas (later replaced by Michael Steele)—started as more of a 60s rock/neo-folk sounding outfit, but only achieved chart success when they traded their original sound for a more heavily produced '80s pop style sound. Slightly harder edged and more serious than the tongue-in-cheek Go-Go's, the Bangles' rich vocal harmonies over '60s-tinged guitar riffs earned them a record deal with Columbia in 1983. The band released studio debut *All Over the Place* the following year, which earned critical acclaim (if not commercial success) for its fusion of British Invasion-style rock and West Coast pop.

Pop superstar Prince, then going by the name Christopher Tracy, was a fan of the band and gave them his song "Manic Monday."

∧ In the 1990s, **all-female groups**
∧ **like TLC and En Vogue** revived
the successful **girl-group formula**
from the 1960s.

The single charted at number two in 1986 and paved the way for the follow-up smash "Walk Like an Egyptian," which went straight to the top of the charts the same year. Both hits appeared on breakthrough sophomore album *A Different Light* (1986), a slickly produced record that marked the band's transition from '60s-influenced pop rock to a more synthesized, radio-friendly sound (demonstrated by the heavy drum machines on "Walk Like an Egyptian" and "Walking Down Your Street.") Third album *Everything* (1988) spawned the number one hit ballad "Eternal Flame," but tensions within the band were already running high. Susanna Hoffs' appearance in B-movie *The Allnighter* added to the drama when the media began to focus on her as an individual rather than on the band as a whole, and the group eventually split in 1989.

In the early '90s, two girl groups found success by developing a smooth, R&B-inflected pop sound reminiscent of the Supremes: **En Vogue** and **TLC**. Stylish vocal quartet En Vogue consisted of former Miss Black California Cindy Herron, Maxine Jones, Dawn Robinson, and Terry Ellis. The group enjoyed huge commercial success with their 1992 album, *Funky Divas*, which covered a wide variety of styles, including soul, hip-hop, pop, and dance. Three of the album's singles hit the Top 10, including "My Lovin' (You're Never Going to Get It)," a sassy, full-throated assertion of feminine power that incorporated a sample of the guitar riff from James Brown's "The Payback." Sophisticated Aretha Franklin remake "Giving Him Something He Can Feel" and rock-infused "Free Your Mind" also neared the top of the charts, causing the album to go multiplatinum. Unlike many girl groups, En Vogue shared the lead vocals and intentionally made sure that no one band member was labeled the "star."

TLC's sassy vibe and wild fashion sense, coupled with good song-writing and performance skills, earned them a great deal of success. Their second album, *CrazySexyCool* (1994), a smooth, polished effort that combined rap and R&B, signified the band's coming of age. Generating four Top 10 singles, including the slinky "Creep" and Prince-inspired morality tale ballad "Waterfalls," the album sold over 11 million copies in the United States alone and won a Grammy for best R&B Album. In 1999, the Atlanta, Georgia-based trio topped the chart with the million-selling *Fanmail*, a smooth collection of urban soul that replicated the sounds of the group's sophomore effort. The album's most popular track, the sarcastic feminist kiss-off "No Scrubs," earned the band their third number one hit and became one of the group's signature songs. As well known for their chaotic personal lives as they were for their music, the group came to a tragic end in 2002 when rapper Lisa "Left Eye" Lopes was killed in a car accident.

THE SPICE GIRLS

Although the girl group phenomenon certainly hadn't died out by the mid-'90s, the **Spice Girls** changed the face of the girl group formula, exploding off the British stage to become an international sensation. The Spice Girls were not just another run-of-the-mill girl singing group; they had a recipe for success that made them the biggest band to come out of England since the Beatles. Dance pop music was the vehicle for their popularity, but the Spice Girls' key to success was the infusion of their music with an independent, feminist stance and a celebration of female friendship and good times. Their light "girl power" message, encouraging female empowerment, today reads like a cartoonish domestication of the angrier riot grrrl message put forward by all-female punk bands in the early 90s such as Bikini Kill and Bratmobile (see Chapter 12).

Appealing primarily to adolescent and younger girls, the Spice Girls were a manufactured group, created when producers Bob and Chris Herbert ran an ad in *Stage* magazine that read, "Wanted: Streetwise, outgoing, ambitious, and dedicated girls to play in a band." The ad successfully drew in four of the five members, although the band soon broke free of their original management and signed with Virgin Records in 1995. A mass marketing campaign introducing the individual band members created for each of the girls a specific identity that would remain with them for the duration of the group's life span: Geri Halliwell became "Ginger Spice," Victoria Adams (later Victoria Beckham upon her marriage to soccer star David Beckham) became "Posh Spice," Melanie Brown became "Scary Spice," Melanie Chisholm became "Sporty Spice," and Emma Bunton became "Baby Spice." Together, the girls put forward a message emphasizing the importance of female friendships. Debut single "Wannabe," which reached the top of the UK charts in 1996 and hit the number one spot on the U.S. charts a year later. The single was released on the group's debut album *Spice* (1996), a collection of bright, bouncy dance-pop anthems infused with hip-hop beats. The girls' charisma and enthusiasm compensated for their limited vocal abilities and, aided by an impressive marketing machine, *Spice* became Europe's best-selling album of 1997.

In addition to spreading feminist empowerment, the Spice Girls embodied the image of "Cool Britannia" that was emerging in the late 1990s. After 18 years of Conservative government, the success of Tony Blair and his New Labour party in the 1997

∧
∧ **The Spice Girls' positive message**
∧ **of female empowerment** helped
make them the **biggest English**
band since the Beatles.

general election marked a trend toward a younger, cooler Britain. Having suffered a diminution of its powers on the world stage, Britain became fashionable again, and the superhero-like costumes worn by the Spice Girls supported the pro-British message. The Union Jack dress worn by Geri Halliwell at the 1997 Brit Awards received worldwide media attention and eventually raised more than $60,000 when it was sold at a charity auction.

Proving their media awareness, as well as an ability to poke fun at their own public image, the Spice Girls created a takeoff of the 1960s pop films (including the Beatles' *Hard Day's Night*) with their 1997 film *Spiceworld: The Movie*. Coinciding with the release of an album of the same name, the movie featured cameos from numerous celebrities and helped three singles from the album reach the US Top 20. The group's success began to falter with the release of R&B-inflected *Forever* (2000), and the band announced their separation several months later. Its members have all since pursued solo careers with varying degrees of success and reunited in 2007 for a sold-out comeback tour.

As of 2009, the Spice Girls' four albums have sold more than 60 million copies worldwide. Their success paved the way for the all-girl group pop and teen pop that have followed in their wake.

DESTINY'S CHILD

Destiny's Child rose to prominence in the late '90s as the dominant female singing group in the United States. Often involved in well-publicized feuds in the media and abrupt personnel changes, the Texas-based group became a veritable hit-generating machine when they finally stabilized at the turn of the century.

Known for their elaborate vocal harmonies and athletic choreography, Destiny's Child achieved their first hit single in 1997 with the seductive R&B track "No, No, No," which reached number three on the charts. Two years later, their album *The Writing's on the Wall* created four Top 40 hits, including number one singles "Bills, Bills, Bills" and "Say My Name." The band's updated Motown characteristics drew inevitable comparisons with the Supremes, with lead vocalist Beyoncé Knowles frequently compared to Diana Ross (even before her performance as a Ross-like character in the 2006 film *Dreamgirls*).

<<< **Beyoncé Knowles,** formerly of Destiny's Child, refers to her **provocative on-stage persona as Sasha Fierce.**

that demonstrates the contrast between the singer's vulnerable, romantic self ("If I Were a Boy") and her sassy, sexually aggressive onstage persona ("Single Ladies").

BRITNEY SPEARS

A controversial pop culture icon, **Britney Spears** has become one of the most successful female vocalists of the 21st century. Blessed with girl-next door looks and a decent singing voice, Spears burst onto the music charts in 1998 with her debut single ". . . Baby One More Time," a sexually suggestive song that raised concerns about the possible masochistic invitation in the lyrics "Hit me." Coupled with the video's Catholic schoolgirl outfits, Spears's image as a sex symbol was firmly established from the outset—a far cry from her early days as a contestant on *Star Search* and as a Mouseketeer on the *New Mickey Mouse Club*. Balancing a fine line between wholesome innocence ("Lucky," 2000 and "I'm Not a Girl, Not Yet a Woman," 2002) and titillating sexuality ("Oops! . . . I Did It Again," 2000 and "I'm a Slave 4 U," 2001), Spears became a controversial pop phenomenon, prompting endless debates about her suitability as a role model for teenage girls and displaying the darker side of "girl power."

Following a series of controversial personnel changes in 1999 that resulted in two former band members launching a lawsuit against Beyoncé's father, manager Matthew Knowles, the group ultimately became a trio. Releasing subtle feminist anthems "Independent Women" (2000) and "Survivor" (2001), the band retained the sentiments of female empowerment without the sloganeering and gimmickry of the Spice Girls.

Some of the Spice Girls have enjoyed minor success as solo acts, while Beyoncé Knowles has virtually dropped her last name and become a household name as a solo artist/actress, paving the way for some of the largest solo pop acts of recent years. Debut album *Dangerously in Love* (2003), which Knowles co-wrote and co-produced, incorporated elements of reggae, hip-hop, and funk into its dance numbers. Of these, catchy lead single "Crazy in Love" became one of the most successful singles of the decade, reaching the number one spot on both sides of the Atlantic and selling more than 5 million copies worldwide. The album went on to win five Grammy awards and reached multi-platinum status. When Destiny's Child disbanded after the release of their 2005 greatest hits album, Knowles focused her attention on her budding solo career. She has subsequently released two further albums: the forceful, upbeat *B'Day* (2006) and *I Am . . . Sasha Fierce* (2008), a two-disc set

Like many other teen pop stars, Spears's career was micromanaged from the beginning to ensure maximum publicity, incorporating advertising campaigns, promotional tie-ins, and even a mall tour before the release of her first album. However, unlike other stars, Spears has been a willing collaborator in her career path, making independent decisions and actively seeking a more mature sound for her third album, *Britney* (2001) on which she co-wrote five of the

CLASSIC RECORDINGS ⟩⟩⟩

SURVIVOR by Destiny's Child

Destiny's Child had a strong position in the world of pop music at the beginning of the new millennium. With singles "Bills, Bills, Bills" and "Say My Name" both hitting the top of the charts, it seemed that no one was going to challenge their position as the top group in the contemporary R&B scene. When third studio album *Survivor* was released in May 2001, it debuted at number one on the Billboard 200 chart, selling 663,000 units in its first week. The album stayed at the top of the Billboard chart for two weeks upon its release.

Following its release, *Survivor* created four major hit singles for Destiny's Child. Attitude-filled "Bootylicious," a catchy pop tune with Michael Jackson-inspired vocal stylings, and dance floor juggernaut "Independent Women Part 1," a feminist anthem with swirling vocal harmonies, were both number one hits. The album's title track, penned by Beyoncé Knowles, won the Grammy award in 2001 for "Best R&B Vocal for Duo or Group." Their cover of the Bee Gee's ballad, "Emotion," which

included the sophisticated arrangement of the original combined with gospel-tinged vocal harmonies, also did well as a single. Other tracks on the album featured Latin influences ("Sexy Daddy"), R&B balladry ("Brown Eyes"), and light, airy pop ("Happy Face").

Despite the album's success, it received mixed reviews from the critics, with *Entertainment Weekly* magazine classifying it as a "premature, but inevitable growing-pains album" (Browne 2001). Many reviewers felt that the album seemed contrived, and lacked some of the original soul of the group's previous records. The group had been going through lots of internal conflict, and Beyoncé's message behind the title-track "Survivor" (allegedly inspired by a DJ's gag about the band members voting each other off the island per the popular CBS reality series) seemed to be that the group had triumphed over a tumultuous time. Despite some gripes from reviewers about the sincerity of the record, *Survivor* solidified Destiny's Child's position as the top all-female R&B group of the era.

Top-Selling Female Solo Artists

	Gold singles (more than 500,000 units)	Platinum singles (more than 1,000,000 units)	Multi-platinum singles (more than 2,000,000 units)
Mariah Carey	23	10	22
Madonna	26	6	21
Whitney Houston	18	7	10
Janet Jackson	21	5	22
Beyoncé Knowles	15	7	23
Rihanna	10	9	0
Aretha Franklin	18	0	10
Britney Spears	8	4	0
Barbara Streisand	8	5	0

> ∧ ∧ ∧ **Britney Spears** ranks eighth among female solo artists with the most gold, platinum, and multi-platinum singles.

songs. Although its singles weren't as successful as previous efforts, the album itself became her third straight number one hit record. A sharp, self-reflexive concept album, *Britney* featured revealing personal songs about the singer's experiences—she's "Lonely," she feels "Overprotected," and she's "Not a Girl, Not Yet a Woman." By follow-up effort, *In the Zone* (2003), Spears had shed her girlish image completely, rejecting sappy love songs and sugarcoated big hooks in favor of husky, hip-hop—infused dance tracks such as "Showdown." The album reached number one on the Billboard chart, and the energetic dance track "Toxic" earned Spears a Grammy for Best Dance Recording.

Unfortunately for Britney Spears, success came with a side of chaos. In a pattern that is becoming entirely too common for contemporary pop stars, her personal life turned into a sort of media reality show. Spears's personal problems, some of them undoubtedly exacerbated by constant media exposure, were plastered all over the covers of tabloid magazines and on television news stations, culminating in several stints in rehab and various psychiatric facilities. Despite constant blows to her public image, Spears won "Album of the Year" for her fifth album *Blackout* (2007) at the Europe Music Awards in 2008, and achieved her first number one hit in nearly a decade with the thumping, stuttering dance track "Womanizer" (2008).

CHRISTINA AGUILERA

A former *Star Search* contestant and Mouseketeer on the *New Mickey Mouse Club*, **Christina Aguilera** followed the exact same trajectory to stardom as fellow Mouseketeer Britney Spears. Despite obvious similarities, Aguilera's vocal range and power earned her comparisons with divas such as Whitney Houston and Mariah Carey, and she beat out both Britney Spears and Macy Gray to win the 2000 Best New Artist Grammy award. A mixture of engaging ballads and catchy, light R&B dance numbers, Aguilera's self-titled debut album entered the charts at number one upon its release in 1999 and sold over 8 million copies in the United States alone, with hit single "Genie in a Bottle" remaining at the top spot for five weeks. Follow-up single "What a Girl Wants," was the first number one single of 2000, and earned Aguilera a spot performing at a White House Christmas Gala and the Super Bowl half-time show.

Whereas Britney Spears consistently straddled the line between childish innocence and womanly sexuality, never quite escaping her Disney identity, Aguilera took an overtly sexual approach from the outset, bragging to one interviewer that her genital piercings had "gotten a lot of compliments," before quickly adding "from my gynecologist" (Heath 2001). Embracing her status as a sex symbol, she appeared topless on the cover of second album *Stripped* (2002), posed nude for an issue of *Rolling Stone*, and unabashedly pranced around stage while performing the album's raunchy debut single "Dirrty." Developing into a more mature style while retaining her provocative image, Aguilera transitioned into more sophisticated material, exploring jazz and blues influences in the style of Etta James and Billie Holiday for 2006 album *Back to Basics*. In 2008, she commemorated 10 years in the music business with the release of *Keeps Getting Better: A Decade of Hits*.

SIMON COWELL

Much of the success of music reality shows *Pop Idol* and *American Idol* can be attributed to the acerbic wit of talent judge **Simon Cowell**, whose blunt criticisms of contestants and scathing commentary keep viewers tuning in week after week. Already a successful A&R executive, record producer, and entrepreneur when he joined the British program *Pop Idol*'s judging panel in 2001, Cowell has since

become one of the most recognizable faces on both British and American television.

Brought up in a wealthy family in Hertfordshire, England, Cowell's father was a music industry executive and his mother was a ballet dancer and socialite. Despite being ousted from several boarding schools on account of his poor behavior, Cowell was able to use his father's music connections to secure a low-level position at EMI Music Publishing, where he began to work his way up the corporate ladder. "From my first day on the job I began planning and scheming my way to the top of the business," he later wrote in his memoir (Cowell 2003). Quitting to form E&S Music with former EMI boss Ellis Rich, the label had a few major hits, but Cowell's first real success in the music industry came with EMI subsidiary Fanfare Records. Helping to build the company into a successful indie pop label, Cowell enjoyed several years of success, most notably with pop star

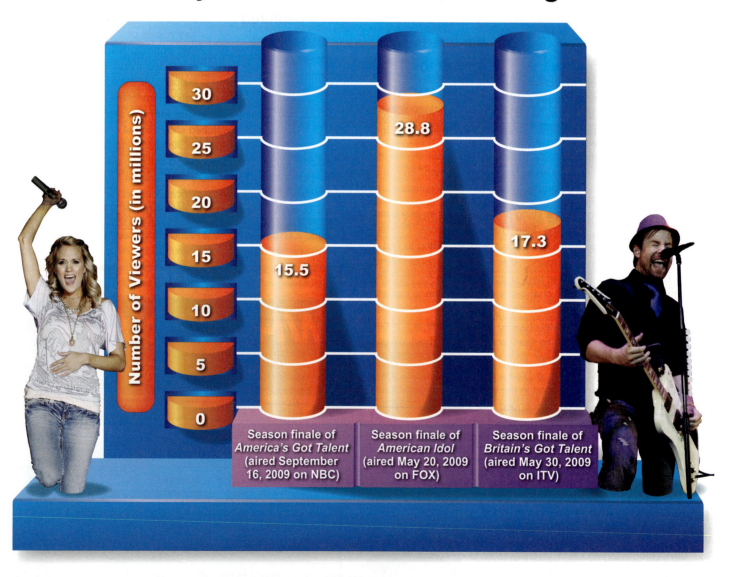

Reality Music Show Viewer Ratings

∧ Interactive music talent shows such as *American Idol* and *America's Got Talent*
∧ frequently top viewer ratings lists.

>>> *American Idol* judge **Simon Cowell** has become one of the **most recognizable faces** on both British and American **television.**

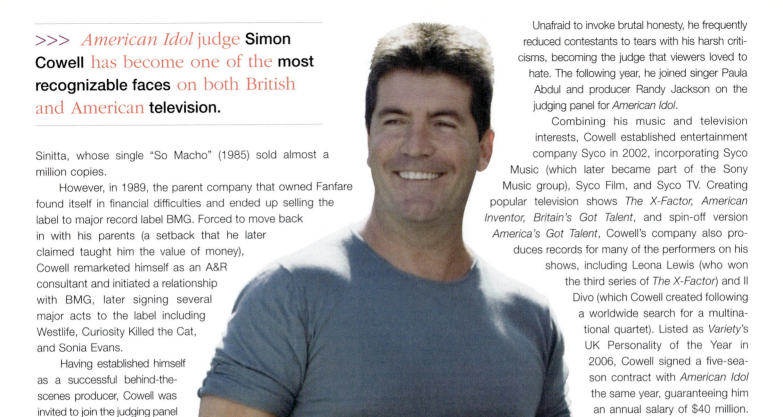

Sinitta, whose single "So Macho" (1985) sold almost a million copies.

However, in 1989, the parent company that owned Fanfare found itself in financial difficulties and ended up selling the label to major record label BMG. Forced to move back in with his parents (a setback that he later claimed taught him the value of money), Cowell remarketed himself as an A&R consultant and initiated a relationship with BMG, later signing several major acts to the label including Westlife, Curiosity Killed the Cat, and Sonia Evans.

Having established himself as a successful behind-the-scenes producer, Cowell was invited to join the judging panel on *Pop Idol* in 2001, where he earned himself a reputation as the show's "Mr. Nasty."

Unafraid to invoke brutal honesty, he frequently reduced contestants to tears with his harsh criticisms, becoming the judge that viewers loved to hate. The following year, he joined singer Paula Abdul and producer Randy Jackson on the judging panel for *American Idol*.

Combining his music and television interests, Cowell established entertainment company Syco in 2002, incorporating Syco Music (which later became part of the Sony Music group), Syco Film, and Syco TV. Creating popular television shows *The X-Factor, American Inventor, Britain's Got Talent*, and spin-off version *America's Got Talent*, Cowell's company also produces records for many of the performers on his shows, including Leona Lewis (who won the third series of *The X-Factor*) and Il Divo (which Cowell created following a worldwide search for a multinational quartet). Listed as *Variety*'s UK Personality of the Year in 2006, Cowell signed a five-season contract with *American Idol* the same year, guaranteeing him an annual salary of $40 million. In 2007, he earned the number 21 spot on *Forbes*' Celebrity 100 Power List.

HOW HAS ROCK & ROLL BEEN CHANGED BY AGGRESSIVE MARKETING TO YOUNGER AUDIENCES?

The Disneyfication of Pop Rock

If the rock & roll aimed at teenagers in the 1960s and 1970s was considered dangerous and threatening, today's parents are positively rejoicing over the plethora of G-rated pop tunes emerging from Disney's vault of so-called tween stars. Although dismissed by many as kiddie pop, there is no denying the profitability of acts such as Miley Cyrus, the Cheetah Girls, and the Jonas Brothers, whose albums frequently outsell those of "serious" rock acts like My Chemical Romance. With Miley Cyrus tour tickets among the most expensive on the resale market of any pop act (one front row seat in Uniondale, New York, was sold by a scalper for $3,429), Disney's marketing gurus are already looking for the next tween star to promote to the lucrative 8- to 12-year-old market.

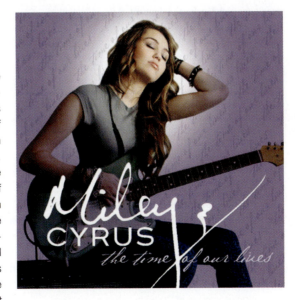

∧
∧ **Miley Cyrus' "racy" photo shoot**
∧ for Vanity Fair caused **outrage among the parents** of young fans.

MILEY CYRUS

When **Miley Cyrus** became an overnight sensation among pre-teens in 2006 with the launch of the Disney Channel's *Hannah Montana* series, the name rang bells among older brothers and sisters who recalled a mullet-sporting country singer named Billy Ray Cyrus and his number one hit single "Achy Breaky Heart" (1992). Whatever success Billy Ray enjoyed in his singing career is small potatoes in comparison to the tidal wave of success enjoyed by his daughter. Miley, better known to the masses as "**Hannah Montana**," brings in an estimated $1 billion a year for the Disney Company.

Born Destiny Hope Cyrus, the teen star earned the moniker "Smiley" due to her cheerful disposition as a child, a nickname that stuck when it was shortened to Miley. Starring in several minor acting roles, including a part in the Tim Burton film *Big Fish* (2003), Cyrus got her big break when

THE JONAS BROTHERS

Another part of the Disney franchise, the **Jonas Brothers** are tween-friendly pop stars whose sellout tours promote a respectable brand of rock & roll not unlike that of '90s teen boy band Hanson (although Hanson had no connection to Disney). Committed evangelical Christians, the brothers all wear purity rings to signify their vow to abstain from premarital sex, promoting a wholesome, family-friendly image that is reflected in their music.

she was cast in the title role of *Hannah Montana*, a television series about a girl leading a double life as an ordinary kid during the day and a multi-platinum pop star at night. A soundtrack from the series was released in 2006, featuring a mixture of teen-pop, rock, and country-inflected songs and including a duet with Cyrus' father. Its success prompted several more Hannah Montana releases, but with the launch of *Breakout* 2009, Cyrus finally had a more sophisticated album under her own name. Veering toward Avril Lavigne-type punk pop, the album vented Cyrus's teenage frustrations through tracks such as "Breakout" and "7 Things."

Like Britney Spears, Cyrus has found it difficult to shake her Disney identity, holding her back from developing into more mature work. A 2008 photo shoot for *Vanity Fair* caused a huge public outcry when 15-year-old Cyrus appeared in the magazine clutching a satin bed sheet across her otherwise naked torso. Although tame by most people's standards, the photos prompted such outrage that Disney Chief Executive Robert Iger met with Cyrus and her family and Cyrus issued an apology to her fans, claiming she was "embarrassed" by the pictures. Although viewing figures for Hannah Montana sharply declined immediately following the incident, the shoot does not appear to have done any long-term damage to Cyrus's popularity and in 2009 she made number 29 on *Forbes'* Celebrity 100 list.

^
^ The *High School Musical*
^ franchise has become a
major moneymaker for Disney.

Given an early start into the world of music by their musical parents, Joseph, Kevin, and Nicholas Jonas began singing and songwriting at a young age. Youngest brother, Nicholas, was a particularly strong singer, and by the age of seven had already had a taste of fame performing on Broadway. Attracting the attention of executives at Columbia Records, the trio was signed in 2005 and released a hook-filled, sing-along debut album *It's About Time* a year later. Despite the album's modest success, the brothers were dropped by Columbia and picked up by Disney-owned Hollywood Records—a move that rocketed them to stardom. Their second, self-titled album, released in 2007, was supported by appearances on various Disney Channel programs, and a nationwide tour that sold out from coast to coast. Appearances on reality television show *Jonas Brothers: Living the Dream* and Disney Channel television movie *Camp Rock* (2008) have helped establish the band as one of the most popular teen acts in recent years. Their latest release, *Lines, Vines, and Trying Times* (2009) takes the band in a more mature direction, replacing tween-dream innocence with angst-filled songs that demonstrate an increased stylistic range. However, like their fellow Disney rockers, the Jonas Brothers maintain their wholesome image, reflected through songs such as "Fly With Me" and "Keep It Real."

ROCK PLACES

Los Angeles

Since the film industry arrived in Los Angeles at the beginning of the 20th century, it has been regarded as the entertainment hub of the United States. Home not only to major film production companies, but also to musical landmarks such as Capitol Records, the city is one of the most important places in the world for the recorded music industry. With an ever-increasing interconnection between the television and music industries, Los Angeles is becoming even more important in the pop rock music scene.

With L.A.-based television shows such as *Hannah Montana* spawning teen pop stars that can sell out venues all over the country, Disney-owned **Hollywood Records** is becoming a serious force to be reckoned with in the music industry. Founded in 1989, the company releases many of the soundtracks from films made by Disney or Disney-owned studios and, as of 2008, became part of the Disney Music Group. Although its roster primarily includes young Disney Channel stars such as Miley Cyrus, the Jonas Brothers, Selena Gomez, and *High School Musical's*

Vanessa Hudgens, the label features a surprising number of experienced artists. Duran Duran, Queen, and George Michael have all been signed to Hollywood Records at some point in their careers.

Despite an increasingly family-friendly image, the L.A. music scene is still associated with some traditional sex, drugs, and rock & roll. Hollywood music tours offer visitors the chance to see the hotel where Janis Joplin died, visit West Hollywood's legendary Troubadour Club, and see where Led Zeppelin partied with their groupies.

THE *HIGH SCHOOL MUSICAL* FRANCHISE

When **High School Musical** was released in 2006, it became the most successful Disney Channel Original Movie ever produced. Initially watched by 7.7 million viewers, the film went on to win Emmys for Outstanding Children's Programming and Outstanding Choreography, it and launched the careers of teen stars Vanessa Hudgens and Zac Efron. The original soundtrack made the number one spot on the Billboard 200 chart twice (in March 2006), became the best-selling album in the United States in 2006, and eventually went quadruple platinum.

Based on a modern adaptation of Romeo and Juliet, *High School Musical* focuses on two high-school juniors from rival cliques, who come together over a love of music. Promoting Disney's family values about following your heart and rejecting peer pressure, the film's use of exciting song and dance numbers appealed to tween audiences all over the world. Featuring squeaky-clean lyrics, the soundtrack combines various genres, from Broadway-type numbers such as the

jaunty, piano-driven "What I've Been Looking For" to Disney-style power ballads ("When There Was Me and You"), to modern hip-hop tunes ("Get'cha Head in the Game").

Not a company to miss a marketing opportunity, Disney quickly capitalized on *High School Musical*'s success, turning it into a veritable business franchise of its own. *High School Musical 2* debuted as a cable telecast on the Disney Channel in August 2007, attracting over 18 million viewers in the United States and becoming the number one cable telecast of all time. It was followed by *High School Musical 3: Senior Year*, which holds the record for the highest-grossing movie musical in its opening weekend, netting over $80,000,000 worldwide. The latest installment in the series, *High School Musical 4: East Meets West*, is reportedly scheduled to air in 2010.

HIGH-SCHOOL MUSICAL Disney production that is extremely popular with pre-teen and young teenage audiences.

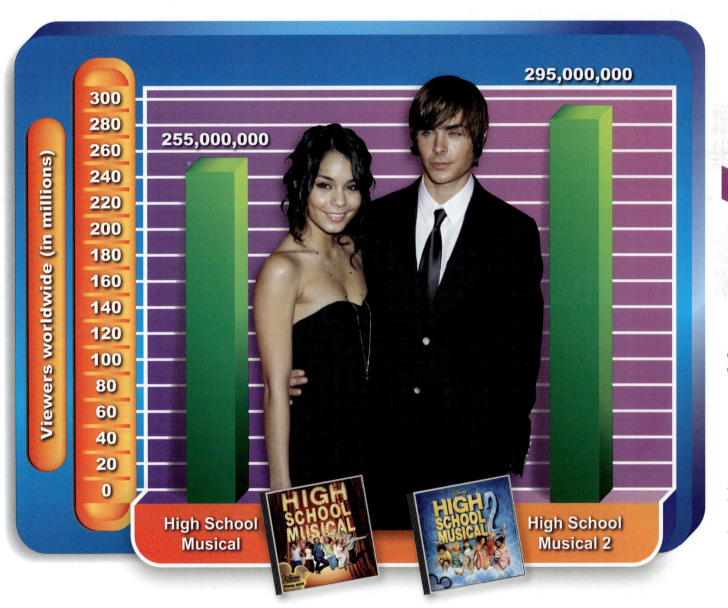

High School Musical is **hugely popular,** generating millions of viewers **all around the world.**

14

Summary

WHY WAS 1994 AN IMPORTANT YEAR IN THE HISTORY OF ROCK MUSIC? 248

- The 25ᵗʰ anniversary of the Woodstock music festival was in 1994, and the celebration of this anniversary resulted in a lot of reflection about rock music's history and the direction it was headed.
- Nirvana front man Kurt Cobain's untimely death shocked the rock music community and created a lot of speculation about the death of rock & roll.
- Cobain's death definitely signified a sea change in the rock music industry.
- In the decade and a half since 1994, there have been three main streams of rock & roll: the persistence of pop, the accommodation of strong emotional content to evolving musical styles, and the rise of musical appropriation brought into rock by hip-hop.

HOW HAVE GIRL GROUPS AND BOY BANDS INFLUENCED THE HISTORY OF ROCK? 251

- The original 1960s girl groups featured an identifiable lead vocal with a harmony arrangement and sang songs about the ups and downs of young love—a formula that continued throughout the girl-group revival of the 1990s.
- In the 1980s, sporadic revivals of the girl group genre occurred, with a few breakout girl groups such as the Go-Go's and the Bangles enjoying some popularity and recognition.

- The popularity of the Spice Girls, with their feminist "girl power" message sparked a wave of girl group acts in the 1990s, including Destiny's Child, and solo pop acts such as Britney Spears, Christina Aguilera, and Jessica Simpson.
- The Jackson Five set the precedent for all future boy bands, but the genre's 1990's revival was largely due to the role Lou Pearlman played in creating the Backstreet Boys and 'N Sync.
- Other notable 1990s boy bands include 98 Degrees, Take That, and Westlife.
- TV shows such as *Pop Idol* and *American Idol* are playing a more active role in creating rather than just popularizing stars.

HOW HAS ROCK & ROLL BEEN AFFECTED BY AGGRESSIVE MARKETING TO YOUNGER AUDIENCES? 261

- The "Disneyfication" of rock & roll has tapped into an extremely valuable market: the pre-teen and young teenage market.
- Miley Cyrus/Hannah Montana is the hottest concert ticket around; arena shows sell out in seconds, and scalpers are making huge profits off parents willing to pay virtually any price to get their kid into the show.
- Disney is working its way into the pop rock world with acts such as Hannah Montana and the Jonas Brothers. These acts are incredibly profitable because they are multimedia crossover acts, covering television shows, movies, and live concerts. Album and DVD sales and spin-off merchandise are also filling Disney's coffers.

Key Terms

Madonna best selling female rock performer of the 20th century; her career has so far spanned almost three decades and covered a wide variety of musical styles and performances 250

Pro Tools software program for recording and editing music; particularly useful in enhancing vocals through the use of pitch correction and vocal effects 250

The Go-Go's emerged from the punk/new wave explosion as a commercially successful all-girl group in the early 80s 252

The Bangles girl group that started as more of a 60s rock/neo-folk sounding outfit, but traded their original sound for a more heavily produced 80s pop sound 252

En Vogue girl group that achieved huge commercial success with 1992 album *Funky Divas* 252

TLC early to mid-90s girl group whose sassy vibe and wild fashion sense, coupled with good song-writing and performance skills, earned them a great deal of success 252

The Spice Girls manufactured girl group that spread a message of feminist empowerment and became the most successful English band since the Beatles 252

Destiny's Child rose to prominence in the late 90s as the dominant female singing group in the United States 253

Britney Spears one of the most successful female vocalists of the 21ˢᵗ century and controversial pop culture icon 254

Christina Aguilera female vocalist; won Best New Artist Grammy award in 2000 for her outstanding vocal range and power 255

Jessica Simpson gospel singer who achieved mainstream pop success with debut album *Sweet Kisses*; starred in MTV reality series *Newlyweds* following her marriage to 98 Degrees singer Nick Lachey 256

Ashlee Simpson little sister of Jessica Simpson; infamously caught in an embarrassing lip-synching incident on *Saturday Night Live* that tarnished her career as a singer 256

lip-synching miming to a pre-recorded backing track 256

The Backstreet Boys first boy band of the 90s to become hit-generating international superstars 257

'N Sync boy band act that dominated the pop scene of the late 90s; put together by producer Lou Pearlman 257

98 Degrees adult contemporary boy band that appealed to a slightly more mature audience; straddled the line between soul and pop *257*

Lou Pearlman boy band Svengali who guided the Backstreet Boys and 'N Sync to chart-topping success *258*

Westlife Irish boy band created by pop impresario Louis Walsh; holds the Guinness World Record for most successful new chart act *259*

Pop Idol British television talent show that premiered in 2001; "pop stars of tomorrow" voted on by the television-watching audience *259*

American Idol U.S. *Pop Idol* spin-off launched in 2002; remains one of the most popular shows on American television *259*

Simon Cowell British television producer and *American Idol* judge; listed at number 21 on *Forbes*' Celebrity 100 Power List in 2007 *260*

Miley Cyrus/Hannah Montana Disney's superstar of television show *Hannah Montana*; became an overnight musical sensation with

tour tickets among the most expensive on the resale market *261*

Jonas Brothers wholesome members of the Disney franchise; the brothers promote abstinence and project a family-friendly image *262*

Hollywood Records Disney-owned music label launched in 1989 that primarily features teen stars associated with the Disney Channel *262*

High-School Musical Disney production that is extremely popular with pre-teen and young teenage audiences *263*

Sample Test Questions

1. 1994 marked the 25th anniversary of which major music festival?
   a. Lollapalooza
   b. Woodstock
   c. Monterey Pop Festival
   d. Newport Folk Festival

2. Which of these statements is correct?
   a. The Milli Vanilli lip-synching scandal was the first time an artist mimed to a pre-recorded backing track.
   b. The 1990s was the first decade to witness the creation of media-friendly ensemble acts.
   c. *Pop Idol* and *American Idol* were among the first music shows to create, rather than popularize new acts.
   d. Lou Pearlman was the first producer to put together a manufactured boy band.

3. The Spice Girls were primarily known for:
   a. bitter feuds within the group.
   b. promoting "girl power."
   c. an overtly sexual image.
   d. appearing on a reality show.

4. What was the name of the producer who put together The Backstreet Boys and 'N Sync?
   a. Phil Spector
   b. Lou Pearlman
   c. Dante Alexander
   d. Simon Cowell

5. Which of the following teen-oriented musical acts is NOT part of the Disney franchise?
   a. The Jonas Brothers
   b. Hannah Montana
   c. Hanson
   d. Vanessa Hudgens

ESSAY

6. Discuss the significance of 1994 and the impact of Kurt Cobain's death on rock & roll.

7. How has editing software such as Pro Tools affected the authenticity of rock music?

8. Discuss the impact of shows such as *Pop Idol* and *American Idol* on the music industry.

9. Consider whether pop stars such as Miley Cyrus have a responsibility to promote a particular image to young fans.

10. Has the watered-down, clean-cut version of rock & roll music finally triumphed over its original rebellious roots?

WHERE TO START YOUR RESEARCH PAPER

To learn more about the life, career, and untimely death of Nirvana front man Kurt Cobain, go to
http://www.biography.com/articles/Kurt-Cobain-9542179

To research past and present Billboard *100* charts, go to
http://www.billboard.com/bbcom/index.jsp

To learn more about Pro Tools, go to
http://www.digidesign.com/

To learn more about Woodstock '94, go to
http://www.well.com/woodstock/wstockconf/

To learn more about the Spice Girls, go to
http://www.thespicegirls.com/

To read more about Hannah Montana, go to
http://tv.disney.go.com/disneychannel/hannahmontana/

ANSWERS: 1. b; **2.** c; **3.** b; **4.** b; **5.** c

Remember to check www.thethinkspot.com for additional information, downloadable flashcards, and other helpful resources.

HOW DID A NEW GENERATION UPDATE SOME OLDER STYLES OF ROCK & ROLL?
HOW DID ROCK & ROLL BECOME EVEN MORE PERSONAL?
HOW DOES ROCK & ROLL CONTINUE TO UPDATE ITSELF?

"The days of whine and poses may be over, but don't tell that to Radiohead singer Thom Yorke. He has survived the demise of grunge with all of his anxiety and disillusionment intact. Which hardly means that his group's music hasn't matured. On the contrary, Radiohead are one of the few guitar-based bands of the mid-'90s that has grown by leaps and bounds. . . .

"On *OK Computer*, Radiohead take the ideas they had begun toying with on *The Bends* into the stratosphere. At a time when they could have played it safe, selling their psychedelic souls for more radio-friendly rock & roll, Radiohead have released a concept album whose theme—based on rock's age-old fear of the imminence of a world run by computers—unfolds gradually during the course of the album's 12 songs.

"*OK Computer* is not an easy listen. From guitarist Jonny Greenwood's menacing riff that introduces the opener, 'Airbag,' to Yorke's fragile pleas to 'slow down' on the final track, 'The Tourist,' each song takes time to reveal itself as a narrative link to the album's ultimately spiritual message. In the suite 'Paranoid Android,' acoustic and electric instruments float understatedly through the mix as Yorke sings, through clenched teeth, lines like 'Ambition makes you look very ugly.' Complex tempo changes, touches of dissonance, ancient choral music and a King Crimson-like melodic structure propel the song to its conclusion, where Yorke sings in a pleading voice, 'God loves his children.'

"There are moments on 'Paranoid Android when Yorke sounds as though he's conjuring the spirit of Queen's Freddie Mercury. On several other tracks, Radiohead also draw from the past for inspiration. Yorke's throwaway words to 'Karma Police' ('This is what you get when you mess with us') are rescued by the layered, 'Strawberry Fields Forever' vibe of the music. 'Let Down' is driven by Byrds-like chiming guitars. And the Eno-esque ambience of 'Fitter Happier'—based around a computerized voice intoning platitudes like 'Comfortable/Not drinking too much/Regular exercise at the gym . . . / Calm, fitter, healthier and more productive'—gives the song a claustrophobic, Doll's House feel. . . .

"[T]he music on *OK Computer* has a surreal, cinematic quality . . . [and] hints at some kind of dark spiritual crossroad. In the delicate 'No Surprises,' Yorke announces, 'This is my final fit, my final bellyache.' Where Radiohead might go from here is anyone's guess, but *OK Computer* is evidence that they are one rock band still willing to look the devil square in the eyes."

—Mark Kemp, "Radiohead: OK Computer." *Rolling Stone*, July 10, 1997

HYPHENATED-ROCK & EXPLORATIONS OF THE POSTMODERN SELF (1994–)

CHAPTER 15

HOW DID A NEW GENERATION UPDATE SOME OLDER STYLES OF ROCK & ROLL?

Progressive Rock, Reborn

During the 1980s and well into the mid-1990s, many thought that progressive rock was part of the distant past, never to be revisited again. After all, some considered the music overly ornate, even flamboyant. With songs that could easily surpass the 15-minute mark, clearly progressive rock would never appeal to everyone.

By the time 1994 rolled around, however, a second wave of progressive rock had begun to take shape. Although the progressive music of the 1990s had changed considerably, certain elements, such as elaborate concept albums, lengthy songs that didn't mesh well with the standard MTV format, and the use of orchestration, connected the present with the past. In many cases, the musicians of the 1990s were not as technically polished as their counterparts of decades gone by. As a result, musical virtuosity became less of a focal point; there were no extended guitar, keyboard, or drum solos on the records or during live performances. The influence of improvised jazz or traditional classical arrangements also played a less prominent role in the songwriting of the 1990s.

In addition, the lyrical content of the music had taken on a darker, more introspective tone. Songs tended to feature fewer fantastic or mystical elements and were, instead, more grounded or personal in nature. The idealistic hippie influence of the past had given way to a more realistic, punk-inspired pessimism. The new wave of progressive rock didn't only pay homage to the past—it also embraced the present, employing the sounds and technologies of modern music as the building blocks of a revised art form.

RADIOHEAD

Of the new wave of **experimental rock** music, **Radiohead** was—and continues to be—the most accomplished. Drawing from such diverse influences as house music, dance music, classic rock, post-punk, ambient, 20th-century classical, and modern jazz, Radiohead has continually pushed the boundaries of what progressive music can be. As you read in the review at the beginning of the chapter, many have acknowledged the band's 1997 *OK Computer* as the definitive statement of postmodern alienation. The album featured themes of paranoia, melancholy, and release, with Thom Yorke's frail falsetto issuing a faint suggestion of human resilience in the face of inhuman forces.

Although the band's debut *Pablo Honey* (1993) gave little indication of what was to come from Radiohead, second effort *The Bends* (1995) saw the group finally hit its stride. *The Bends* became both a commercial success and a turning point in the development of the band's aesthetics. Balancing a heavy rock sound with interesting musical experimentation and melodic ballads ("High and Dry"), Radiohead evolved toward more multilayered rock, exploring cryptic lyrics and

<<< **Radiohead's seminal 1997 release *OK Computer*** firmly established the group as one of the most experimental and innovative **in modern rock & roll.**

Hyphenated Rock & Explorations of the Postmodern Self (1994–)

Music

2000
The Dandy Warhols release *Thirteen Tales from Urban Bohemia*

2001
Weezer, Tenacious D, and Jimmy Eat World begin 13 date mini-tour

2002
June
Korn begins summer tour in Wilkes-Barre, Pennsylvania

2002
September
The Yeah Yeah Yeahs perform in Seattle

1998 — 2000 — 2001 — 2002 — 2003

History

1998
President Bill Clinton impeached

2001
January
George W. Bush certified as election winner by Congress

2001
September 11
Terrorists attack New York and Washington, D.C.

2001
October
U.S. attacks begin in Afghanistan

larger themes of fame and insignificance through Thom Yorke's haunting, melancholy vocals. Although the spacey sounds of "Planet Telex" hinted at the direction the band would take on later albums, *The Bends* was ultimately a guitar rock album (albeit a melancholic, anguished rock album), full of forceful guitar riffs and chiming arpeggios. Demonstrating further maturation of style, the band stripped away many of the obvious elements of guitar rock and expanded on its experimental electronic soundscapes for breakthrough album *OK Computer* (1997), which won a Grammy for Best Alternative Music recording. With each subsequent release, Radiohead has experienced enormous artistic evolution, continuing to expand its sound even on its seventh studio album, 2007's *In Rainbows*. The band's music, particularly early works such as *The Bends*, had an undeniable influence on Britpop bands such as Coldplay, Muse, and Travis.

In addition to their creative influences, Radiohead has also been extremely influential in changing the way that the music industry operates by offering alternatives to the standard sales model. With the release of *In Rainbows*, the band decided to allow its fans to download the album at a price of their choosing. The resultant commercial success proved to many doubters that music fans were willing to pay for music in a way that benefited musicians rather than their corporate labels. You will learn more about how this decision affected the music industry in Chapter 16.

COLDPLAY

Many bands owe some of their success to the influence of Radiohead. Among these groups, **Coldplay** is probably the most notable example both in terms of Radiohead's impact on the group's sound and in terms of the commercial success that Coldplay has enjoyed as a result. Although Coldplay's music offers a more pop-oriented, MTV-friendly sound than much of Radiohead's more experimental material, the band utilizes some of the same ambitious song structures and has also mastered the art of the power ballad.

Formed at the University College of London in 1996, Coldplay engendered a simple acoustic style that included catchy, melodic hooks and elements of anthemic rock. Radiohead's release of the overly experimental *Kid A* (2000) left a gap in the market for a bona fide rock band, and UK audiences turned to Coldplay's debut album

Parachutes (2000) to fill the void. Although lead single "Shiver" did not have much of an impact, follow-up release "Yellow" climbed the charts on both sides of the Atlantic, becoming one of the first power-ballad hits of the new millennium. The band solidified their position as the go-to band for melodic guitar-centric rock with second album *A Rush of Blood to the Head* (2002), which spawned several award-winning hits, including psychedelic rock song "Clocks." To date, Coldplay has won seven Grammy Awards and has hit the top of the Billboard albums chart three times.

GODSPEED YOU! BLACK EMPEROR

Another experimental band that has updated the classic progressive sound is Canada's **Godspeed You! Black Emperor**. A fully instrumental outfit with a seemingly ever-changing roster of musicians, Godspeed You! Black Emperor abandons standard rock song structure for long, orchestral-inspired songs. Although the band does use the standard four-instrument rock & roll arrangement in its music, it also incorporates strings and brass instruments. The resulting slightly sentimental, slightly somber compositions have earned the band an audience of loyal listeners since its inception in 1994. The band has also become known for integrating visual elements into its live shows, projecting films behind the musicians as part of the performance. For audiences in attendance, this lends the music additional layers of depth.

Though neither as popular nor as commercially successful as either Radiohead or Coldplay, Godspeed You! Black Emperor won critical esteem for its 2000 release, *Lift Your Skinny Fists Like Antennas to*

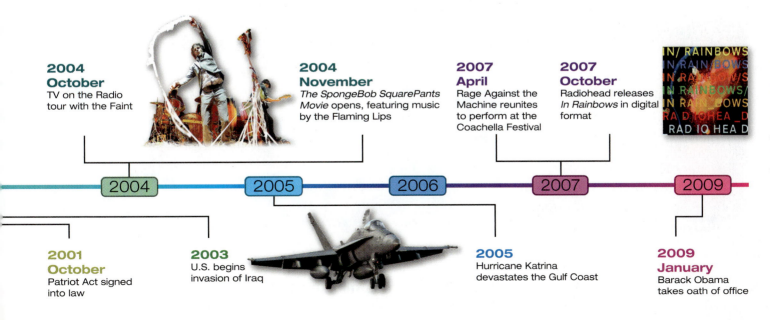

2004 October TV on the Radio tour with the Faint

2004 November *The SpongeBob SquarePants Movie* opens, featuring music by the Flaming Lips

2007 April Rage Against the Machine reunites to perform at the Coachella Festival

2007 October Radiohead releases *In Rainbows* in digital format

2004 — 2005 — 2006 — 2007 — 2009

2001 October Patriot Act signed into law

2003 U.S. begins invasion of Iraq

2005 Hurricane Katrina devastates the Gulf Coast

2009 January Barack Obama takes oath of office

SIGUR RÓS an experimental rock band from Iceland known for its atmospherics and unique vocal stylings.

TV ON THE RADIO an experimental rock band that incorporates soul, rock, and jazz in its sound.

NEO-PSYCHEDELIA a lo-fi update of psychedelic rock that embraced organic experimentation and modern forms of music.

Heaven, considered the band's strongest release. Structurally and conceptually closer to a symphony than a conventional rock album, the album unfolds over the span of two CDs but features only four total tracks. Its length and structure hearken back to the 1974 Yes album *Tales from Topographic Oceans*. Instrumental except for sampled voice inserts, the tracks on each disc are ordered in suites, with typical sections building on short, repeated themes from bass, violin, or guitar. Between these themes, the group incorporates sound-art sequences using cymbals, guitars, and field recordings of public

announcements and radio preachers. Each track rises and falls from delicate introductory passages to grand climaxes, creating a dense, emotional musical soundscape that earned the band a reputation as prog-rock innovators.

SIGUR RÓS

Similar in approach to Godspeed You! Black Emperor, Icelandic group **Sigur Rós** has developed a style of songwriting that incorporates dramatic composition with moody atmospherics. The group has toured with both Radiohead and Godspeed You! Black Emperor, first gaining widespread attention as an opening act for Radiohead during the latter group's European tour in the year 2000.

Although debut effort *Von* (1997) made few musical waves—perhaps due to its limited Iceland-only release—the group gave a clearer picture of its developing sound and pushed further away from mainstream rock & roll on its 1999 follow-up *Ágætis Byrjun*. With lush string arrangements and the addition of horns on some tracks, critics viewed the album

Radio Unfriendly Experimental Rock Songs

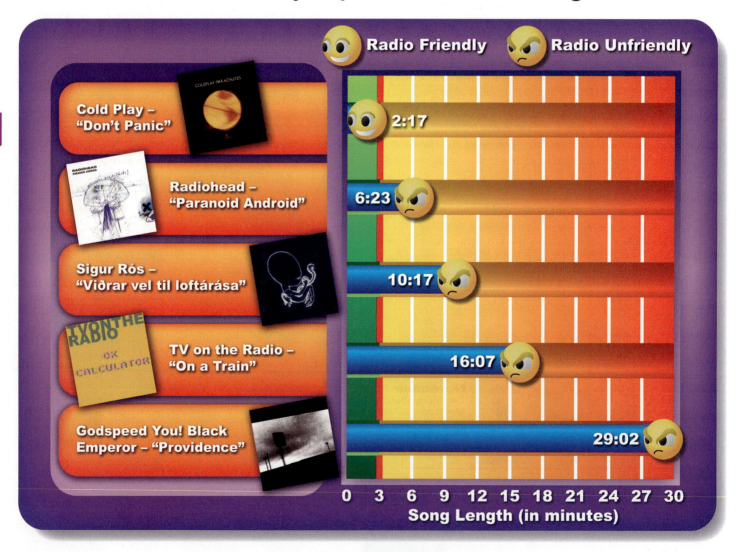

Radio Friendly   Radio Unfriendly

Cold Play – "Don't Panic" — 2:17

Radiohead – "Paranoid Android" — 6:23

Sigur Rós – "Viðrar vel til loftárása" — 10:17

TV on the Radio – "On a Train" — 16:07

Godspeed You! Black Emperor – "Providence" — 29:02

Song Length (in minutes)
0 3 6 9 12 15 18 21 24 27 30

∧
∧ **Experimental rock challenges the conventions of popular music, one of which is the radio-friendly three-minute song.**

RETURN TO COOKIE MOUNTAIN by TV on the Radio

TV on the Radio's strong EPs and full-length debut had made for high expectations for 2006's *Return to Cookie Mountain*. Expanding on the sound established with its 2004 release *Desperate Youth, Blood Thirsty Babes*, *Return to Cookie Mountain* offers a more polished realization of the band's musical ideas.

The song "I Was A Lover," with its densely layered tracks and syncopated beat, gets the album off to a promising start. Guest vocals by David Bowie on the song "Province" serve as an indication that the band has gained not only notice, but also the approval of past musical explorers. Indeed, the album often evokes Bowie's ambitious development of funk and soul on *Station to Station* (1976). Later on, "Wolf Like Me" provides the album's closest offering to conventional rock with its poppy melodies, while "A Method" explores a layered vocal delivery that hints at folk and gospel influences. In all, *Return to Cookie Mountain* cemented the band's reputation for delivering music that challenges listeners and inspires critics.

as being overly precious and ornate. The band received similar complaints of pretense when they released third album ( ) (2002) with no title and eight untitled songs. Equally lengthy as the band's previous offerings, ( ) was a more somber version of *Ágætis Byrjun*, but otherwise used many of the same funereal tempos and elegant, if over-the-top arrangements.

Although many of Sigur Rós's songs are sung in the band's native Icelandic, singer and guitarist Jon Thor Birgisson also sings some tunes in a made-up language dubbed Hopelandic. Much like scatting in jazz, this contributes to the band's overall depth of sound. Also unique to Sigur Rós is Birgisson's occasional use of a bow when playing his electric guitar, a technique that gives the music an ethereal tone.

TV ON THE RADIO

Brooklyn-based band **TV on the Radio** blends elements of soul, guitar rock, funk, and jazz to create a gritty, dense, industrial sound. The group's innovative use of instrumental dissonance with vocal harmonies brings urban sensibilities to the progressive sound. Giving an indication of the band's progressive rock bearings, the title of the band's first, self-released album *OK Calculator* (2002) is a nod to the Radiohead album *OK Computer*.

One of the things that makes TV on the Radio unique among its peers is its blending of progressive music with hip-hop—tinged and electronic-inspired effects— elements that are not commonly associated with the genre. The band's ability to use these elements so effectively to create a new sound tapestry has contributed greatly to its growing popularity.

Because of its singular approach to music, TV on the Radio has been a critical favorite since the release of 2003 debut, the *Young Liars* EP. The band's following releases have been no less favored. Although the band has not yet achieved mainstream popularity, TV on the Radio performs at such large music festivals as Lollapalooza, Coachella, and Bonnaroo.

The band has also made television appearances on popular shows including *Saturday Night Live* and *The Colbert Report*. *The Colbert Report* host Stephen Colbert recognized that the band has not yet been unable to take full advantage of its status as a critical darling; when the group came on his show to perform the song "Dancing Choose" in February 2009. Colbert—in his usual joking fashion—quipped to the band that "you can't eat critical acclaim" (Colbert Nation 2009). Even so, TV on the Radio's latest release, *Dear Science* (2008) was named album of the year by both *Spin* and *Rolling Stone*.

Neo-Psychedelia

Contrary to popular belief, psychedelia didn't die in the 1970s when the last of the hippies traded in their tie-dyed shirts for disco outfits or signed up for corporate jobs. The sound may have taken a backseat to other types of music for a brief period during the 1970s and 80s, but the psychedelic style and sound had regained momentum by the time the 1990s came around. The roots of **neo-psychedelia** spring from the psychedelic bands of the 1960s, whose sound was as much fueled by drugs and the quest for mind expansion as it was a product of its political and social times.

Although the neo-psychedelic bands were no less experimental than their progressive counterparts, the lo-fi musical experimentation of neo-psychedelic bands had a more organic nature than that of hi-fi, high-density, experimental rock acts. Although progressive rock is often seen as being overly ambitious, neo-psychedelic music approaches songwriting with a studied lack of pretense.

Some neo-psychedelic bands favored lengthy, improvised jam sessions, while others favored a more condensed, even pop-oriented approach. Although psychedelic bands of earlier decades influenced their modern counterparts to a large degree, the bands of the 1990s also took cues from contemporary forms of music in building their sound. Here, too, the music was a product of its social and political times, and

Oxford, UK

Long-time conventional wisdom had held that a band needed to relocate to one of the well-known music hubs such as London, New York, or Los Angeles if it ever expected to have any hope of getting noticed. Music scenes, however, are just too prolific and full of talent for the music industry to ignore. Beginning in the 1990s, one such scene has been Oxford in the United Kingdom. Home to many bands—most notably Supergrass and Radiohead—Oxford remains a vibrant music scene to this day.

A haven for independent musicians, Oxford had an impressive number of live music venues that attracted up-and-coming young bands in the early 1990s. Alternative Oxford band Ride was beginning to gain national attention, drawing music fans to venues on the local pub circuit. These venues included the famous Jericho's Tavern, where Radiohead played their first gig in 1986, and the Zodiac, where the band filmed the video for their first single "Creep." By the late 1980s, Oxfordshire and the Thames Valley had an active indie scene, centering on shoegazing bands such as

Ride, Chapterhouse, and Slowdive. So-named because of the musicians' tendency to maintain a motionless onstage posture and stare at their shoes, shoegazing bands produced a popular brand of alternative rock typified by the use of guitar effects and indistinguishable vocal melodies. The success of these bands paved the way for later indie bands on the Oxford music scene, including Supergrass and Radiohead. Today, the indie music scene continues to thrive in Oxford with bands such as Goldrush, who organize Oxfordshire's annual independent music festival, the Truck Festival.

the musical themes changed as a result. Spacey, flowery, or even non-sensical themes sometimes gave way to the more jaded outlook and approach of the 1990s.

THE DANDY WARHOLS

Originally from Portland, Oregon, the **Dandy Warhols** helped bring the neo-psychedelic sound back into the mainstream during the 1990s. With songs highlighted by singer Courtney Taylor-Taylor's blasé vocal delivery and often smirking, ironic lyrics, the Dandy Warhols merge unabashed pop sensibilities and the psychedelic sound. Incorporating electronics, aggressive guitar tones, and an uncharacteristically polished production into its music, the band drew comparisons with psychedelic pop band the Velvet Underground when they appeared on the music scene in the mid-1990s. Openly citing the Velvets as a major influence, the group's debut album *Dandy's Rule, OK?* (1995) featured the songs "Lou Weed" and "Ride" (tongue-in-cheek pastiches of the band's namesakes). Although the band acquired an underground cult following, they did not achieve mainstream success until the release of third album *Thirteen Tales from Urban Bohemia* (2000). The album's hit single "Bohemian Like You," a wry social commentary with an impressive guitar riff, initially gained a fan base through college radio,

before launching the band into the mainstream. The group opened for David Bowie on his 2003 tour, and recently collaborated with Dire Straits vocalist Mark Knopfler for sixth studio album *Earth to the Dandy Warhols* (2008).

DIG!

The long-standing but generally amicable rivalry between the Dandy Warhols singer Courtney Taylor-Taylor and singer Anton Newcombe of the Brian Jonestown Massacre, another neo-psychedelic band, gave rise to the 2004 documentary *DIG!* Shot over seven years, the feature-length documentary was culled from 1,500 hours of footage and tracked the developing careers of the two bands and their respective front men.

>>> **The Dandy Warhols** brought the neo-psychedelic sound to the mainstream with their **pop approach to the music.**

Newcombe, a brilliant and prolific songwriter in his own right, was often considered the more authentic of the two, creating songs that seemed truer to the spirit of the 1960s psychedelic movement. Taylor-Taylor, on the other hand, was known for crafting songs that appealed to fans of the 1960s-style psychedelic music but that also had commercial appeal. Eventually, Newcombe's dedication to his creative idealism and artistic independence caused him to destroy multiple opportunities for financial success, while Taylor-Taylor's willingness to toe the corporate line launched the Dandy Warhols onto the Billboard charts. The bands' philosophical differences ultimately put them at irreconcilable odds.

THE FLAMING LIPS

Originally forming in Oklahoma in 1983, the **Flaming Lips** began to gain mainstream popularity in the mid-1990s before achieving cult status in the early 2000s. Often drawing from sci-fi and Japanimation (cartoon-style animation from Japan) as influences, the band's songs can seem goofy or childlike while carrying an underlying poignancy. Melodic, spacious, and full of the fuzzy tones and swirling sounds for which psychedelic bands have become known, the band's songs have become infamous for their spacey lyrics and bizarre titles—"Psychiatric Exploration of the Fetus with Needles" from 1995 album *Clouds Taste Metallic* being a prime example. Over the years, the band has also gained a reputation for its theatrical live performances, which often employ large props, dancers, confetti, balloons, light shows, and audience interaction (Serpick 2006).

Having suffered a series of personal setbacks in the mid-1990s, including the departure of guitarist Ronald Jones and a hit-and-run accident involving bassist Michael Ivins, the Flaming Lips regained their stride with the ultra-melodic 1998 album *The Soft Bulletin*. In 2002, the group won a Grammy award for Best Rock Instrumental Performance for its song "Approaching Pavonis Mons by Balloon (Utopia Planitia)," and repeated the feat four years later for "The Wizards Turns On . . ." In early 2009, the song "Do You Realize??" was declared the official rock song of the state of Oklahoma (Aswad 2009). That September, the band made an appearance on *The Colbert Report* to promote the release of its latest album, *Embryonic*. After the show aired, the band took a page out of Radiohead's playbook and made the album available for fans to stream for a limited time on *The Colbert Report* Web site.

PHISH

Following in the footsteps of the Grateful Dead, **Phish** has embraced psychedelic **jam-band** aesthetics, taking its fans on a new and different ride with each show. Formed at the University of Vermont in 1983, guitarist/vocalist Trey Anastasio, drummer Jon Fishman, keyboardist Page McConnell, and bassist Mike Gordon comprise the quartet and developed an eclectic form of rock & roll that incorporated elements of jazz, country, bluegrass, and pop. Anastasio's casual, conversational lead style drew inevitable comparisons with Grateful Dead front man Jerry Garcia. The Phish guitarist cites Garcia a major influence, stating, "He taught me subtlety, the emotional power of a quiet phrase. I saw a Dead show . . . in 1982 that was a life-changing event for me" (Anastasio, 1999).

Fully embracing the spontaneous nature of live shows, the band used them as opportunities to explore uncharted regions of sound, as well as a chance to incorporate goofy elements such as vacuum cleaners, trampolines, and a giant hotdog into their concerts. Because of this approach, no two Phish shows are the same. Fans have thus been known to follow the band on tour and see them several times in succession at different places around the country. The band's efforts to push musical boundaries has led them to embrace many different styles of music, including hip-hop. During a 2004 Brooklyn show, Jay-Z appeared as a guest performer while the band provided the accompanying music to his songs.

Phish officially broke up in August 2004, following the release of critically panned studio album *Undermined*. The band reunited in 2009, performing three sold-out shows in Virginia, followed by a reunion tour and the release of the group's 11th album *Joy* (2009).

>>> **The Flaming Lips** has developed a reputation for its elaborate live shows.

THE STROKES a pop-oriented New York garage rock band.

BABYSHAMBLES a garage rock band from the UK known as much for its music as its singer's lifestyle.

THE ARCTIC MONKEYS a top-selling garage rock band from the UK.

YEAH YEAH YEAHS a female-fronted New York garage rock band that draws from punk influences.

PJ HARVEY a highly influential musician whose music transcends all genres and definitions.

TOP OF THE CHARTS
WHAT'S HOT!
OCTOBER 8, 2005

1. "Gold Digger" – Kanye West featuring Jamie Foxx
2. "Shake It Off" – Mariah Carey
3. "Like You" – Bow Wow featuring Ciara
4. "Photograph" – Nickelback
5. "My Humps" – The Black Eyed Peas
6. "We Belong Together" – Mariah Carey
7. "Wake Me Up When September Ends" – Green Day
8. "Play" – David Banner
9. "Don't Cha" – The Pussycat Dolls featuring Busta Rhymes
10. "Beverly Hills" – Weezer

THE STROKES

The release of the **Strokes** debut album *Is This It?* (2001) consolidated the public's renewed interest in punk rock. Heavily influenced by proto-punk bands such as the Velvet Underground as well as classic rockers such as Buddy Holly and John Lennon, the New York band offered a scruffy brand of late 70s rock that owed much of its retro feel to in-studio treatments and engineering effects. *Is This It?* featured raw, world-weary vocals, infectious, pop-inflected melodies, and spiky guitar riffs that found favor with music critics on both sides of the Atlantic (although the band were particularly hyped by the UK press).

The Strokes' profile continued to rise throughout 2002, during which the band toured with The White Stripes, Weezer, and the Rolling Stones. The band's second album *Room on Fire* (2003) stuck to the template of the band's first album, albeit in a slightly more polished format. With its members all working on solo projects, the band has been on hiatus since shortly after the release of its 2006 album, *First Impressions of Earth*.

BABYSHAMBLES

Formed in London in 2004 and fronted by singer and guitarist Pete Doherty, **Babyshambles** plays a brand of neo-pub rock that has a very rough, almost primitive sound not unlike that of Doherty's previous project, the Libertines. Combining a DIY attitude toward music-making with a flair for adding a poetic touch to their lyrics, Babyshambles are the sensitive underbelly of garage rock. Both the band's first album, *Down in Albion* (2005), and follow-up release, *Shotter's Nation* (2007), earned marked critical acclaim in the United Kingdom and the United States.

These days, however, Doherty may be better known for his tabloid antics than for his music. With several run-ins with the law due to drug addiction and a reputation for volatile romantic

ROCK TECHNOLOGY ⟫⟫ The iPod

The shift toward a new era in personal music players began with digital music files, a technological leap forward in the way that music could be stored, played, and distributed. With the help of the Internet and the widespread use of high-speed connections, music could be easily transmitted via computer, meaning that it no longer had to be purchased at a physical record store. Recognizing that the market was ripe for a new device that could make the most of this innovation in music technology, Apple created the iPod.

Like its predecessors—the cassette-based Walkman and portable CD Discman—the iPod, which was launched in 2001, dominates the realm of portable music devices. What makes the iPod different from its precursors, however, is its ability to break down genre barriers. No longer forced to purchase an entire album, users can cherry-pick individual songs and download them onto their computer, creating playlists that combine any number of musical genres. It has also proven to be an effective space-saver. Unlike previous, more cumbersome technologies that required owners to tote their music collection around with them, the all-inclusive iPod has a relatively large storage capacity and utilizes digital files to store and play music without the need for several LPs, cassettes, or CDs.

With the iPod, music fans can listen to music *and* watch it. Many iPod models incorporate video technology into their design, allowing owners to download and watch music videos, movies, television shows, or play games such as *iQuiz Music Trivia*. With all of these features in one handheld device, the iPod has moved beyond all other portable music technologies. By 2007, Apple had sold more than 100 million iPods, making it the fastest selling music player in history.

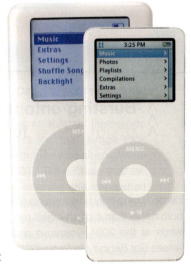

relationships, Doherty has in some ways become famous for everything except for his music; indeed, this negative coverage has often overshadowed the band and its music. Doherty's problems have largely served to stifle the band's progress, preventing Babyshambles from living up to its full potential, both in terms of musical advancement and output.

THE ARCTIC MONKEYS

Also from the UK, the **Arctic Monkeys** has a fuller, more refined pop sound than Doherty's outfit, with the usual fuzzed-out tones of garage rock more subdued. Although the Arctic Monkeys' lyrical content is relatively lowbrow in comparison to the poetic leanings of Babyshambles, front man Alex Turner's canny observations of working-class England earned the band almost instantaneous success. Debut album, *Whatever People Say I Am, That's What I'm Not* (2006), holds the record as being the fastest-selling British debut album of all time. With a dose of the Strokes' world-weary attitude, and punk elements from the Libertines and Franz Ferdinand, the album offered an unpretentious mixture of succinct guitar riffs, racing drums, and snarly, wordy lyrics.

The band's second release, *Favourite Worst Nightmare* (2007), featured louder instruments and faster tempos than its predecessor and earned the band critical acclaim for its developing depth. Similar accolades were heaped on third release *Humbug* (2009), a heavier, more abstract album that retained Turner's snide social observations.

THE YEAH YEAH YEAHS

The **Yeah Yeah Yeahs** specialize in New York City punk-infused, lo-fi garage rock in the tradition of the Ramones and Patti Smith. Fronted by singer, Karen O, the art punk trio formed in 2000, supporting the White Stripes and the Strokes before releasing their first full-length album, *Fever to Tell* in 2003.

Like the Strokes, the Yeah Yeah Yeahs have elements of the Velvet Underground in their sound, but also cite rockabilly singer Jon Spencer and alternative rock band Sonic Youth as major influences. With each release, the band moves farther away from its garage roots and into new and unexplored territory. Third and most recent album, *It's Blitz!* (2009), is almost new wave in its orientation at times, with synth-infused songs that are more danceable and less anthemoriented than the band's first two releases, 2003's *Fever to Tell* and 2006's *Show Your Bones*.

Defying All Categories: PJ Harvey

PJ Harvey—short for Polly Jean Harvey—is one of the most influential singer-songwriters in modern music. With a career that spans almost two decades, Harvey is known for writing songs that can be dark, mysterious, alluring, and, at times, even charming. As early as 1992 debut *Dry*, Harvey laid the groundwork for becoming an eventual underground phenomenon. Subsequent albums, including the raw-edged break-up epic *Rid of Me* (1993) and more mature *Stories from the City, Stories from the Sea* (2000) ensured her place in alternative rock. Sometimes aggressive, sometimes upbeat and jangly, and sparse at other times, Harvey's sound reflects influences as diverse as punk, new wave, classical, jazz, alternative, and folk. Not one to focus on pop hooks or to be overly concerned with widespread appeal, Harvey's music has remained under the radar for many casual music listeners.

Over her extensive career, Harvey has recorded nearly a dozen albums. Most recently, Harvey released *A Woman a Man Walked By* in 2009, a collaborative effort with John Parish. A mixed bag of upbeat songs and slower, more introspective music, the album features tunes such as the dissonant and aggressive "Pig Will Not" with more temperate and melodic tracks such as "Passionless, Pointless." Featuring an expansive production quality with layered arrangements throughout, the album closes with "Cracks in the Canvas," a short, melodic tune with wandering vocals.

Noteworthy Garage Rock Revival Albums

Artist	Title	Year
The White Stripes	*Elephant*	2003
The Strokes	*Is This It*	2001
The Hives	*Veni Vidi Vicious*	2000
The Vines	*Highly Evolved*	2002
Babyshambles	*Shotter's Nation*	2007
The Arctic Monkeys	*Favourite Worst Nightmare*	2007
Yeah Yeah Yeahs	*Fever To Tell*	2003

Review

Summary

HOW DID A NEW GENERATION UPDATE SOME OLDER STYLES OF ROCK & ROLL? 268

● Experimental rock music took the established sounds of the progressive music of the 1960s and 1970s and gave them a more contemporary feel by drawing from different genres of modern music combined with a more streamlined, rock-oriented approach.

● Neo-psychedelic music updated its sound by incorporating modern recording techniques and by drawing from other types of modern rock such as punk and electronic music as influences.

● Both forms of music also embraced contemporary attitudes, highlighted by a sense of irony or pessimism in their lyrical content.

HOW DID ROCK & ROLL BECOME EVEN MORE PERSONAL? 274

● Influenced by the emo style, many artists embraced a musical approach that was emotionally evocative in both its sound and its lyrical content.

● Lyrics became more personal and introspective, even confessional in nature.

HOW DOES ROCK & ROLL CONTINUE TO UPDATE ITSELF? 277

● By combining established styles of modern music that were once considered incompatible such as rap and rock, new sounds such as nü metal began to emerge during the 1990s.

● Such techniques of incorporating other styles of music into established genres give the music a different feel and sense of originality.

Key Terms

experimental rock an update of progressive rock that embraces modern forms of music and contemporary attitudes and challenges traditional pop rock sensibilities *268*

Radiohead the most commercially successful of the experimental rock bands *268*

Coldplay Britpop band that achieved widespread success because of its similarities to mid-1990s Radiohead *269*

Godspeed You! Black Emperor a Canadian experimental rock band known for implementing a visual aspect to its live performances *269*

Sigur Rós an experimental rock band from Iceland known for its atmospherics and unique vocal stylings *270*

TV on the Radio an experimental rock band that incorporates soul, rock, and jazz in its sound *271*

neo-psychedelia a lo-fi update of psychedelic rock that embraced organic experimentation and modern forms of music *271*

The Dandy Warhols a neo-psychedelic band known for its pop orientation and blending of psychedelic and alternative music *272*

The Flaming Lips a neo-psychedelic band known for its live performances *273*

Phish a jam band that incorporated neo-psychedelic music into its sound *273*

jam band band that features extensive musical improvisation in its performances and crosses genre boundaries *273*

emo short for "emotional" or "emocore," it is a style of music characterized by its personal, introspective themes *274*

Ian MacKaye an influential member of the D.C. punk scene whose bands would influence the emo sound *274*

Jawbreaker a forerunner of the emo sound that laid much of the foundation for future bands *274*

Sunny Day Real Estate a Seattle band that influenced the emo sound *274*

Weezer a highly successful and influential emo band *274*

Jimmy Eat World a popular emo band that found mainstream success *275*

Death Cab for Cutie a popular and successful emo band *276*

Dashboard Confessional a popular emo band known for its revealing lyrical content *276*

Fall Out Boy a band with catchy hooks that plays in the emo tradition *276*

My Chemical Romance a band that performs a highly polished form of emo *277*

nü metal a style of music that incorporates elements of metal, alternative rock, rap, and punk *277*

Tool a precursor to the nü metal sound that blended progressive music, alternative rock, and metal *278*

Rage Against the Machine a precursor to the nü metal sound that blended rap, punk, and heavy riffs *278*

Godsmack a nü metal band with a more traditional metal sound *278*

Korn a popular nü metal band known for its bottom-heavy sound *278*

Slipknot band that blended shock rock and nü metal *279*

shock rock a style of music that often incorporates dark lyrics, harrowing imagery, and a spirit of rebelliousness in its music *279*

Marilyn Manson a shock rock performer *279*

Linkin Park one of the more commercially successful nü metal bands *280*

garage rock simple raw form of rock & roll created by amateurish American bands in the 1960s; a recent garage rock revival incorporates punk into its rough, bluesy sound *280*

The White Stripes a highly influential and successful garage rock band from Detroit *280*

The Strokes a pop-oriented New York garage rock band *282*

Babyshambles a garage rock band from the UK known as much for its music as its singer's lifestyle *282*

The Arctic Monkeys a top-selling garage rock band from the UK *283*

Yeah Yeah Yeahs a female-fronted New York garage rock band that draws from punk influences *283*

PJ Harvey a highly influential musician whose music transcends all genres and definitions *283*

Sample Test Questions

1. Which band gained mainstream recognition as an opening act for Radiohead?
   a. Rage Against the Machine
   b. TV on the Radio
   c. Godspeed You! Black Emperor
   d. Sigur Rós

2. Which of the following bands does NOT fall into the garage rock category?
   a. The White Stripes
   b. Sunny Day Real Estate
   c. The Strokes
   d. Babyshambles

3. Which band had a great influence on nü metal bands?
   a. The Dandy Warhols
   b. The Brian Jonestown Massacre
   c. Tool
   d. Fall Out Boy

4. Neo-psychedelia is characterized by a sound that is
   a. lo-fi.
   b. hi-fi.
   c. complex.
   d. aggressive.

5. Jimmy Eat World falls into the category of
   a. neo-psychedelia.
   b. emo.
   c. garage rock.
   d. nü metal.

ESSAY

6. Compare recent progressive bands to their earlier counterparts. What are some similarities and differences?

7. Do you find emo to be more emotional than other forms of music, or is this a misleading description? Explain your answer.

8. Do you think the political messages of Rage Against the Machine had an influence on its audience?

9. How has the iPod changed the way you listen to music?

10. Which style of music mentioned in this chapter has had the greatest impact on you? How?

WHERE TO START YOUR RESEARCH PAPER

For a list of some of Radiohead's lesser-known influences, go to
http://www.rollingstone.com/news/story/18060334/radioheads_secret_influences_from_fleetwood_mac_to_thomas_pynchon

To see a timeline of the iPod from 2001 to 2008, go to
http://www.gizmodo.com/5047665/7-years-of-ipod-what-you-paid-and-what-you-got

To learn about the movie *DIG!*, go to http://www.digthemovie.com

To read a female musician's perspective on misogyny in modern music, go to http://www.independent.co.uk/arts-entertainment/music/news/patronising-sexist-sickening-lily-allen-lashes-out-425885.html

To explore emo culture, go to http://www.luv-emo.com

ANSWERS: 1. d; 2. b; 3. c; 4. a; 5. b

WHAT IS THE ROLE OF APPROPRIATION IN POPULAR MUSIC?
WHAT WAS THE IMPACT OF THE DIGITAL SAMPLER?
WHAT WAS NAPSTER AND HOW DID IT AFFECT DIGITAL DISTRIBUTION?

"Those

headphones on our students bother teachers because they seem to symbolize a voluntary deafness and a concomitant isolation. Allan Bloom put it most memorably, if artlessly, when he complained in *The Closing of the American Mind* that "as long as they [our students] have the Walkman on, they cannot hear what the great tradition has to say. And, after its prolonged use, when they take it off, they find they are deaf." If anything, the musical isolation of students (and, truth be told, some of their teachers) has become even more pronounced since Bloom pronounced his dire warning. If music before the age of mechanical reproduction was of necessity a communal activity, today music consumption tends to be the most private of acts. . . .

"Much of the communal activity of rock-music consumption has been driven underground. Given the copyright maximalism of legislation like the Sonny Bono Copyright Term Extension Act and the hyperactive enforcement regime of the Recording Industry Association of America . . . our students are understandably nervous about advertising their interest in sharing music. The slipperiness of music ownership was dramatized by a delicious, small irony of the Lollapalooza I attended [in 2006]: The most popular song of the festival was last summer's ubiquitous hit "Crazy," by Gnarls Barkley. It was performed by Jack White's band the Raconteurs and by Kanye West, in addition to Gnarls Barkley themselves, the duet of veteran hip-hop artist Cee-Lo and DJ Danger Mouse.

Danger Mouse became famous precisely for "stealing" music—for a brilliant, unauthorized mash-up of *The Beatles* (aka *The White Album*) and Jay-Z's *The Black Album*, which Danger Mouse called, logically enough, *The Grey Album*, and which was available, following an injunction brought by the Beatles' Apple Corps, only on the black (or perhaps "grey") market. Now that he's moving CD's for Downtown Records, a new "indie" label distributed in a collaborative venture of Warner Brothers and Atlantic, however, Danger Mouse's sins seem to have been forgiven.

"[Today,] the "'mix tape' culture celebrated in Nick Hornby's *High Fidelity* is alive and well, even if the format is now CD or MP3. "I'll burn it for you," which would have suggested something very different when I was in college, is the pass phrase of this new communitarian, or at least communal, impulse. And if this all sounds like a subculture—well, a subculture is just a community with a bad reputation. . . .

"To think of our students as simply (i)Pod people, like the mindless, alien drones in *Invasion of the Body Snatchers,* as Allan Bloom and Andrew Sullivan do, is to look complacently at just half the story. A strong desire for community, albeit an ephemeral, shifting community, is the other half. . . . To see the iPod as an agent of isolation rather than a symptom of, or a clever adaptation to, that isolation is to confuse cause and effect."

—Kevin Dettmar, "Earbuds and Mosh Pits," *The Chronicle of Higher Education*, June 1, 2007

REMIX CULTURE

CHAPTER 16

WHAT IS THE ROLE OF APPROPRIATION IN POPULAR MUSIC?

MASHUPS a genre of music that uses existing songs to make new ones, whether that is as simple as combining two different songs or as elaborate as a three-minute track containing samples from more than 20 different songs.

IPOD portable music player created by Apple in 2001 that plays MP3s stored on its hard drive.

REMIX CULTURE a society that allows and encourages works of art derived from other works of art; term coined by Lawrence Lessig.

READYMADE a found object considered art because presented and perceived in an artistic context.

ANDY WARHOL pop artist who rose to prominence in the 1960s and has had a lasting cultural influence on contemporary artists and musicians.

APPROPRIATION the artistic use of another's work in the creation of a new piece.

Remixes and Mashups

The 21st century has seen a steady progression in music toward greater possibilities for individual expression—especially for those music listeners with access to a computer. From slapped-together parodies like **mashups** between Nirvana and Beyoncé ("Smells like Booty") or Limp Bizkit and Cookie Monster ("I Did It All for the Cookie") to the unlimited potential for individual mixes provided by the **iPod** and iMix software to concerts where all audience members wear headphones, private musical worlds and the greater sonic community have collided in ways never seen before.

Despite some fears that the iPod isolates people by putting each listener in a tiny, impenetrable bubble, music fans are using new technology to communicate with one another and enter into a dialogue with the music they love. Bands like Radiohead have released new albums first online as digital downloads. Other musical artists, such as Tom Petty and the Heartbreakers, offer online-only musical experiences; for example, during the weeks leading up to the release of a sprawling four-disc live anthology, that group offered special downloads with early access to half the album's tracks enhanced by selected retrospective materials. Practically every artist working today has a Web site on which news posts, message boards, and blogs provide vehicles for musicians and fans to interact. In this manner, bands have used the Internet to open up more lines of communication directly with their fans. Some of these fans have in turn become digital artists themselves—some by making mashups, some by creating their own music videos, and still others by making visual art inspired by their favorite music.

Remix culture—a society that allows and encourages works derived from other works of art—is the gift of technology. Hip-hop, electronica, *techno brega* (a form of electronic music melding '80s songs with contemporary, "cheesy" dance beats), and many other types of artistic creations remix and sample the work of other artists to form something new and distinct.

VISUAL PREDECESSORS

Visual art in the 20th century incorporated found objects as early as 1917, the year that Marcel Duchamp introduced the idea of the **readymade**, or found art. According to Duchamp, the readymade is a found object considered art because it is presented and received in an artistic context. Duchamp's most famous readymade is *Fountain*, which consists of a urinal hung upside down on a gallery wall with the signature R. Mutt on it.

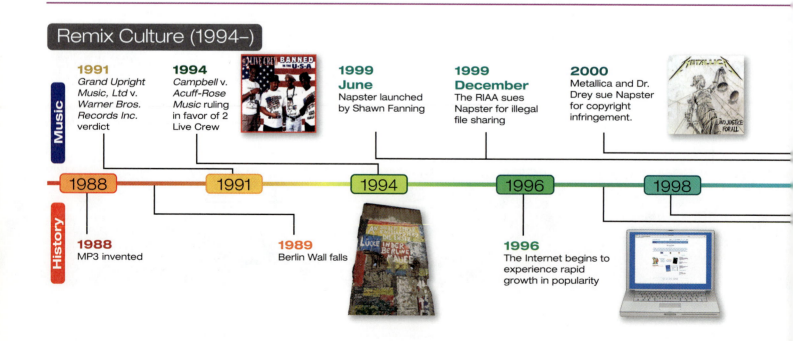

Remix Culture (1994–)

Music

1991 *Grand Upright Music, Ltd v. Warner Bros. Records Inc.* verdict

1994 *Campbell* v. *Acuff-Rose Music* ruling in favor of 2 Live Crew

1999 June Napster launched by Shawn Fanning

1999 December The RIAA sues Napster for illegal file sharing

2000 Metallica and Dr. Drey sue Napster for copyright infringement.

1988   1991   1994   1996   1998

History

1988 MP3 invented

1989 Berlin Wall falls

1996 The Internet begins to experience rapid growth in popularity

Andy Warhol

Whereas Duchamp appropriated non-art objects in an attempt to widen or destroy the existing definitions of art, later artists such as **Andy Warhol** took the concept further by taking images or ideas of existing things and recreating as well as recontextualizing them. For example, in his iconic silk-screened *Campbell's Soup Cans* (1962), Warhol appropriated someone else's creation—the familiar red-and-white design of the Campbell's soup logo—and presented it as art, creating a separate canvas for each of the then-available Campbell's flavors. This sort of **appropriation**, or the artistic use of another's work in the creation of a new piece, is a central strategy in postmodern art.

When Warhol initially exhibited his *Campbell's Soup Cans*, he presented each canvas in two ways: hung on the gallery wall and set on grocery store-style shelves, offering two distinct contexts for the same work. By putting the pieces in different contexts light, Warhol challenged contemporary notions of art and commercialism while celebrating popular culture. In removing the act of creation from the production of art, Warhol shook up long-held beliefs about the painter as original thinker/creator and set the stage for later generations of artists to reinterpret existing materials for their own creative ends.

Taking appropriation a step further, Warhol for his last significant artistic output made a series of paintings entitled *The Last*

Andy Warhol (1928–1987), American, "Campbell's Soup Can", 1962, Saatchi Collection, London/A.K.G., Berlin/Superstock (c) 2009 The Andy Warhol Foundation for the Visual Arts, Inc./Artists Rights Society (ARS), New York.

∧
∧ Andy Warhol's appropria-
∧ tion of other artists' works prefigured a similar trend in popular music.

Supper (1986), based on a cheap black-and-white reproduction of Leonardo da Vinci's famous *Last Supper*. In this original painting, Jesus is performing the miracle of transubstantiation, turning the wine into blood and bread into his flesh—in other words turning one thing into another. Warhol in turn reinterpreted this event through the lens of da Vinci, creating enormous silk-screened canvases—one covered an area nearly 10 feet by 33 feet—splashed with blocks of color, camouflage prints, and even repeating rows of the same image. In his painting, da Vinci is turning the Bible story into a painting. By turning da Vinci's painting into a set of his own paintings, featuring his own distinctive style, Warhol further transubstantiates, or remixes, the event.

Sherrie Levine

In 1979, appropriation artist Sherrie Levine photographed classic Walker Evans photographs—pictures documenting the Great Depression—and presented them as her own work. Her photographs, which she showed at the Metro Pictures Gallery under the title "After Walker Evans" in 1980, were identical to the originals; unlike Warhol's appropriations, which at least transferred an image from one medium (for example, a three-dimensional soup can) to another medium (a two-dimensional silk-screened canvas), Levine's photographs had not been altered in any way. In 2001, artist Michael Mandiberg scanned and uploaded reproductions of Levine's photographs, encouraging the public to download and print the photographs along

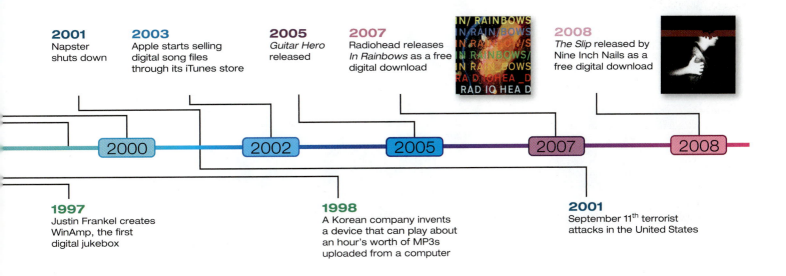

2001
Napster shuts down

2003
Apple starts selling digital song files through its iTunes store

2005
Guitar Hero released

2007
Radiohead releases *In Rainbows* as a free digital download

2008
The Slip released by Nine Inch Nails as a free digital download

1997
Justin Frankel creates WinAmp, the first digital jukebox

1998
A Korean company invents a device that can play about an hour's worth of MP3s uploaded from a computer

2001
September 11th terrorist attacks in the United States

2000 2002 2005 2007 2008

with certificates of authenticity proclaiming the printouts to be genuine Mandibergs. On his Web site, Mandiberg explains, "This is an explicit strategy to create a physical object with cultural value, but little or no economic value."

FAIR USE

Appropriation does not come without its risks. Andy Warhol was sued by various artists whose work he appropriated. Sherrie Levine was sued by the estate of Walker Evans. Michael Mandiberg was not sued because, according to a spokesperson for the Metropolitan Museum of Art (which owns both the Walker Evans photographs and the Sherrie Levine photographs), "He's not a major publisher, so we really don't care." Appropriations artists tend to claim fair use in these cases. But what is fair use, and what does it actually allow?

The Copyright Act of 1976A

The short answer is that no one can be entirely certain what constitutes **fair use** without a court decision qualifying a reproduction as such. The long answer is much more complex. Courts base fair-use decisions on the Copyright Act of 1976A, which granted all reproduction and distribution rights for a particular creative work to the copyright holder of that work while allowing others to use small portions of that work in the pursuit of other purposes, such as education, satire, or news reporting. According to this ruling, there are four factors to consider when determining whether a given use is fair use:

1. the purpose and character of the use, including whether such use is of a commercial nature or is for nonprofit educational purposes;

2. the nature of the copyrighted work;

3. the amount and substantiality of the portion used in relation to the copyrighted work as a whole; and

4. the effect of the use upon the potential market for or value of the copyrighted work.

Fair Use in Action: Culture versus Commerce

Intent is a factor that determines the legality of using copyrighted material. In the case of the Michael Mandiberg digital reproductions, Mandiberg has stated that his purpose was to create culturally significant artists' objects and not make money. This economic aspect informs fair use rulings as well; burning an album that you downloaded on iTunes to a CD to listen to in your car is fair use, but selling copies of that same CD to your classmates to make a few bucks is blatant copyright infringement. In the former case you are not impeding the copyright holder's opportunity to make money from his or her work, but in the latter case you are preventing that person from making a fair profit. Andy Warhol's paintings of soup cans have no impact on the sales of actual Campbell's soup—but a review of a memoir that contains all the memoir's juiciest bits might very well hurt sales of the book.

Mashups Versus Remixes

A mashup uses existing songs to make new ones

A remix takes one song and incorporates new elements, often to make it more dance oriented.

Fair Use in Action: Purpose and Content

Purpose also plays a major role. When television program *The Soup* shows a five-second clip from *The Tyra Banks Show* and makes a joke about it, the usage of that clip is considered fair use because it uses a small portion of a longer copyrighted work for its own purpose— parody—without negatively impacting the original creator's exclusive right to broadcast the work in its entirety. Equally, the status of the copyrighted work affects fair use. In the case of much nonfictional written material, the information cannot be copyrighted; only the way in which it is expressed is protected. For example, in an academic paper, it is considered fair use to quote briefly from another work to make a critical point. However, it would be considered copyright infringement to use a substantial portion of another work without crediting the original author.

Fair Use in Action: How Much is Too Much?

The amount and cultural importance of what is reused also determine whether something falls under fair use. This factor gets a lot of samplers into trouble. Imagine that a DJ wants to sample Mick Jagger singing "I can't" from the Rolling Stones' 1965 single "(I Can't Get No) Satisfaction." The original song is three minutes and 44 seconds long, but the sampling is less than three seconds. The "amount" in question is minuscule and therefore falls under fair use, right? Wrong.

Lawyers for the Rolling Stones would likely argue that the sample, however short, contains a substantial part of the song because the phrase is iconic and distills the essence of the song in that fragment. This provision, more than any other, has become the greatest legal barrier to the practice of fair use. It means that there is no safe length—that even two seconds might contain too much of the song's "substantiality" while longer clips of different substance might be perfectly acceptable.

The biggest problem with fair use may be that it is a defense; you invoke it as a response to being sued by a copyright holder. Only courts can ultimately decide what constitutes fair use, and the consequences for copyright infringements can be costly. Even if your use is ultimately found to be fair, a protracted lawsuit is prohibitively expensive. Because of this, many music companies and artists view sampling music as not worth the risk. The cost of mounting a successful defense on fair use grounds has led music scholar Joanna Demers to declare, "For the majority of musicians who appropriate, fair use is dead" (Demers 2006, 121).

Beg, Borrow, and Steal: The Legacy of Appropriation in Popular Music

Rock was born of appropriation: Its earliest stars stole from the blues, from musicians whose ethnicity denied them a large audience of screaming teenagers. Elvis admitted straightforwardly that he had appropriated his music: "The colored folks been singing it and playing it just like I'm doin' now, man, for more years than I know" (Dettmar 1999, 25). And it didn't stop there; rock has fed on itself and other genres throughout its history, with references to predecessors. For example, in a rather involved referential sequence, the long fade-out in the Beatles' "All You Need Is Love" alludes to both Bach's "Two-Part Invention #8 in F" and "Greensleeves." The song also contains a short musical conversation between the Beatles about the band's history. John Lennon sings a fragment from "Yesterday," a song written by Paul McCartney, and McCartney responds by starting to sing the chorus of the Beatles' 1963 hit, "She Loves You," written by John Lennon.

COVER SONGS

Rock & roll has a rich history of covers. At the most basic level, a cover song is a song written by and originally recorded by someone else. But, of course, covers can be creative endeavors in their own right—they can transform a song, giving it new meaning and purpose. For example, when Aretha Franklin covered the Beatles' "Eleanor Rigby," she put the song into the first person rather than third person, and thereby gave Eleanor a voice. When Placebo covered Kate Bush's "Running Up That Hill," they appropriated her song for the queer community. The song's narrative has a woman expressing her desire to swap places; when bisexual Brian Molko sings it with Placebo, the same desire has a different meaning and a different cultural context.

When Pat Boone put out *In a Metal Mood: No More Mr. Nice Guy*, an album of hard rock and heavy metal covers, he put a new spin on every song he covered. For example, he changes Metallica's "Enter Sandman" from a menacing (if somewhat ridiculous) lullaby into a thoroughly goofy swing number. William Shatner's spoken word versions of popular songs ranging from Bob Dylan's "Mr. Tambourine Man" (for more on Bob Dylan, see Chapter 5) to Pulp's "Common People" (for more on Pulp, see Chapter 12) lent the originals a different, somewhat campier voice. These are only a few examples of songs transformed when performed by other artists.

A Nod to the Past

Some rock bands, of course, merely take elements from others' songs and styles. On Nirvana's 1991 best-selling album *Nevermind*, the track "Something in the Way" is a song apparently about a man who lives under a bridge and is incredibly unhappy. But "Something in the Way" is built around the Beatles' "Something." "[T]he chorus is effectively the same as the opening bars of 'Something,' only shifted into a minor key" (Dettmar 1999, 5–6). While the Beatles' song sweetly describes being attracted by the alluring way a woman moves, Kurt Cobain's song contains no lover. There's no "she"—there's just something in the way—and "that certain something no longer hovers tantalizingly just out of reach but is completely, cruelly unattainable" (Dettmar 1999, 6). A complete understanding of the song relies on the listener's background knowledge of rock; what Cobain swiped from the Beatles both enriches his own music and ties it into the tradition of rock & roll.

WHAT WAS THE IMPACT OF THE DIGITAL SAMPLER?

A Little Bit of This, a Little Bit of That: Sampling

With the advent of the digital sampler, it became a simple matter not just to allude to another song, but actually to "sample" it. In other words, it became possible to appropriate the musical DNA of other compositions as the building blocks of one's own music. Sampling has become a mainstay of hip-hop and electronica. Artists such as the Sugar Hill Gang, Grandmaster Flash, David Byrne, and Brian Eno were among the early samplers. Grandmaster Flash's "The Adventures of Grandmaster Flash on the Wheels of Steel" was an influence for many later sampling artists.

SAMPLING IN HIP-HOP

The availability and use of sampling helped shape hip-hop and rap for more than a decade—sampling was backbeat, appropriation, and/or homage. Most samples were not licensed from the original artists or record labels; licensing would be prohibitively expensive even if permission was granted, and it is entirely likely that some permissions would be refused.

Shawn Fanning

In June of 1999, 18-year-old college dropout **Shawn Fanning** launched Napster, a digital file-sharing service that within months had attracted better than 50 million users. Napster allowed people to exchange MP3s with relative ease—you only had to search, select a result, and hope for the best. Suddenly, instead of paying $18.99 for a CD, music fans could download entire albums without ever leaving home—for free. Some artists—among them Limp Bizkit, the Offspring, Prince, and Chuck D of Public Enemy—were excited by the possibilities. Prince declared, "What's currently going on can only be viewed as an exciting new development in the history of music."

The Beastie Boys were firmly in favor of this new digital distribution; in August of 1998, they used their Web site to facilitate downloads of tracks from their summer tour. Mark Kates, who ran their label at the time, says of Fanning, "Shawn did not seek to bring down the modern record business. He was a music lover and he wanted to share music with his friends. I kept telling people, 'We have to follow the audience. They're going to tell us what to do, because they need it more than we do.' . . . When the audience is actually creating

the technology, the business has to adapt" (Kot 2009, 28).

However, not everyone agreed with the idea that music wants to be free. In December 1999, six months after Fanning debuted the program, the RIAA filed suit against Napster, declaring that "nearly every hit song by every significant recording artist can be found on Napster" and seeking $20 million in damages. The suits weren't the only ones lining up against Napster. In April 2000, Metallica sued Napster for copyright infringement. Soon after this, hip-hop producer Dr. Dre also filed suit against Napster. Both Dre and Metallica's Lars Ulrich provided Napster with lists of users who were swapping their songs: 240,000 names from Dr. Dre and 335,000 Metallica fans busted by the band.

On April 29, 2000, an opinion piece from Chuck D appeared in the *New York Times*. Referencing the lawsuits by Metallica and Dr. Dre, he declared that "I believe that artists should welcome Napster. We should think of it as a new kind of radio—a promotional tool that can help artists who don't have the opportunity to get their music played on mainstream radio or on MTV." After denouncing the record industry's practices and their effects on artists, he closes by asking, "Will the corporations that dominate concede to sharing the musical marketplace?" In July 2001, he got his answer, when Napster shut down. It declared bankruptcy the following year. The company's logo and name were sold, later to be used by a pay service.

Although Napster (in its original incarnation) didn't last long—it was operational for just over a year—its legacy lives on in Gnutella, Grokster, Kazaa, Lime Wire, Morpheus, and other peer-to-peer networks. These second-generation services are less vulnerable to lawsuits because they are not centralized the way that Napster was; users are in direct communication rather than connecting through a central server. Napster may have gone the way of the dodo, but Fanning's service has had a permanent effect on the way that music reaches listeners.

it and doing something new with it. I don't think I'm creating competition for the artists; it's just further spreading the message."

Gillis releases his music on the label Illegal Art, which specializes testing the boundaries of U.S. copyright law, distributing music that makes extensive use of samples. Gillis cites 1990s grunge as an influence; if these guys, who hardly looked like rock stars, could make it big, surely anyone can. Because Girl Talk albums are made up primarily of samples, getting permissions for and paying royalties on every sample is simply not feasible. *Feed the Animals* uses 322 samples; the source material ranges from Afrika Bambaataa to the Yeah Yeah Yeahs, from Avril Lavigne to Wilson Pickett. But the album isn't regarded as purely derivative. The magazine *Blender* named *Feed the Animals* their number two best album of 2008.

Feed the Animals is essentially one long song broken up into several tracks, and it is almost entirely made up of samples, with minor supplemental instrumentation provided by Gillis. The flip side of the impossibility of getting comprehensive permissions for a Girl Talk album is the unprofitability of taking Gillis to court—even if the courts ruled that 100 percent of royalties from *Feed the Animals* had to be paid to those who had been sampled, after that money had been split 322 ways, it would hardly be worth litigating over.

<<< **Nine Inch Nails' latest album,** 2008's *The Slip,* **was released for free online** as a gift to fans.

Girl Talk himself is optimistic about the future of sampling in rock & roll. "I think we're approaching an era where there's a consistent dialogue going on between artists and consumers. . . . . I feel that it's not stealing sales from anyone; it's turning people on to the music." His view of sampling might bring comfort to sampled artists, if not the labels and publishers who hold the rights to their work. If listeners love a baseline they hear in Girl Talk, track it down, and then acquire the original, everyone wins—except, perhaps, those reluctant to see the music industry change.

THIS ONE'S ON ME: MORE FREE DIGITAL DISTRIBUTION

Trent Reznor, the front man for the industrial rock band Nine Inch Nails, is another rock star who values digital distribution and the connection it can provide for artists and fans—as well as the escape it can permit from the music industry, about which he has grown very cynical. In concert in 2007, he ranted against the industry and its practices: "Now my record label all around the world hates me, because I yelled at them, I called them out for being greedy . . . I didn't get a chance to check, has the price come down at all? I see a no, a no, a no. . .

Okay, well, you know what that means—steal it. Steal away. Steal and steal and steal some more and give it to all your friends and keep on stealin'. Because one way or another, these [industry executives] . . . will get it through their head that they're ripping people off and that that's not right."

Industrial music began as experimental music that used the most primitive type of sampling: editing tape. It is "most abrasive and aggressive fusion of rock and electronic music," and began as a genre hostile to the idea of listenability (AllMusic.com). That hostility has softened over time—Reznor himself is credited with combining industrial with traditional song structures and helping the style gain popularity. But Nine Inch Nails retain the abrasiveness and totalitarian imagery traditionally associated with industrial rock; their 2007 release *Year Zero* is described by Reznor as a concept album predicting what the American government's policies will lead

CLASSIC RECORDINGS ▶▶▶

THE GREY ALBUM by Danger Mouse

The Grey Album is the creation of DJ **Danger Mouse** (Brian Burton); it is a mashup album that uses a cappella vocal tracks from Jay-Z's *Black Album* (2003) and instrumental tracks and loops from *The Beatles* (otherwise known as *The White Album*). Burton released three thousand promotional copies of *The Grey Album* in December 2003; in February 2004, EMI—holder of the rights to the *White Album*—sent Burton a cease-and-desist notice. EMI also threatened legal action against any person who sold or distributed files from *The Grey Album*. In response, there was a public protest known as "Grey Tuesday" on March 5, 2004; led by Downhill Battle and Kimbrew McLeod, the event involved Web sites offering the entire album free for downloading and radio stations playing *The Grey Album* throughout the day. Although some who participated in "Grey Tuesday" received cease-and-decease letters from EMI, no charges were filed in connection with the event.

Danger Mouse stopped selling or distributing *The Grey Album* in March 2004, but the album remained available for download online.

"I don't want to disrespect the Beatles," Burton explained in an interview with MTV. "I knew my friends wouldn't think it was sacrilege, so I just made sure it was something I would dig myself."

Although *The Grey Album* was never put to the test in court, it remains one of the most sophisticated mashup efforts to date. It is also responsible for the inauguration of downloading and electronic distribution as a form of social protest.

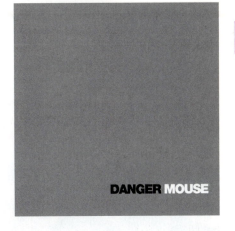

FEED THE ANIMALS by Girl Talk

Released in 2008, *Feed the Animals* is the brainchild of mashup artist Girl Talk (Gregg Gillis). *Feed the Animals* was released on the Web site Illegal Art; as with Radiohead's *In Rainbows*, downloaders were allowed to choose set their own price for the album. If they chose $0.00, they were asked to explain why, selecting from the options: "I may donate later"; "I can't afford to pay"; "I don't really like Girl Talk"; "I don't believe in paying for music"; "I have already purchased this album"; "I don't value music made from sampling"; "I am part of the press, radio, or music industry"; or "other reasons." If users paid $10, they were able to acquire a CD copy of the album. Gillis, in an interview with the *Washington Post*, explained why he preferred this method of

distribution: "I want to get the music out to as many people as quickly as possible." He added, "With the name your price thing, I don't have any specific stats on me, but I'm pretty sure that the majority of people got it for free. Which is cool to me."

Your Parents' Basement

Digital recording and engineering tools make it possible to make professional-sounding music almost anywhere. Mashup artist DJ Danger Mouse made *The Grey Album* while he was living in his mother's basement. No longer are albums created exclusively in recording studios or during live performances. An individual sitting at a computer with a pair of headphones can accomplish the same feat in the privacy of her parents' home. As Moby (Richard Hall), the creator of *Play*—the first album to have every song licensed—put it, "Some people can be larger than life rock stars, and I love them, but I'm just a bald jerk who makes music in his bedroom and hopes that someone might listen to it."

Musicians can also recording a rock podcast in the basement. Some musicians, especially those who specialize in remixes or electronica, choose to release their music this way. Other rock podcasts are commentary by and for fans, updates on band news, and/or discussions of music.

Your parents' basement is also the traditional setting for playing Rock Band or Guitar Hero. These games allow players to live the rock & roll dream. In fact, in the original Guitar Hero, the first venue is called

"The Basement." The Guitar Hero and Rock Band franchises allow players to stand in their parents' basement, close their eyes, and sing "Wayward Son" as though thousands of adoring fans were longing to hear it.

The basement is a rock place for consumers in a new way as well. Sitting at a computer is more and more the way that fans obtain music, whether they purchase songs from iTunes, illegally download them from peer-to-peer networks, or purchase old-fashioned compact disks from retailers. Record stores are no longer necessary. Fans can sit at their computer and read music magazines like *Rolling Stone* or perhaps a blog operated by their favorite musician. Even if the computer isn't used to create music, it is a great asset to a music fan. Online forums and message boards allow for music discussions that go on for months, examine every possible facet of an issue, and have contributions from fans around the world.

Part of the allure of the iPod is that it makes every place a rock place, even the basement. Fans of music can take their tunes anywhere, from the dentist's office to

a public restroom to the Greyhound bus. In that case, the basement may become a musical HQ: a place to recharge the iPod, organize and expand its music library, and get recommendations from the Internet. Having listened to new tunes while out and about, a music fan can return to the basement to write reviews, make recommendations, check for new releases, and download more new music. Your parents' basement is rock central—and it's a beautiful thing.

music." When all music was restricted to live performance, there were relatively few occasions for listening to music. When music became available at home by means of the radio, the record player, and subsequent technology, there were more occasions for listening to music.

But now that portable, personal music players are ubiquitous, people can listen to music while waiting in line at McDonald's. Fans can listen to music while waiting for clothes at the Laundromat. Individuals can listen to music alone in bed at night without disturbing roommates or partners. Downloadable ringtones is a logical extension of the idea that music is meant to be consumed everywhere. The idea of hearing a low-resolution clip from a song every time you get a phone call is apparently a powerful one. Ringtone sales now amount to nearly a half-billion dollars annually in the United States.

Activate Star Power: Rock Band and Guitar Hero

Remix is ultimately about interactivity, with consumers of music becoming producers. The hip-hop DJs of the South Bronx are consider one of the first groups to do this—to take their record collections and create

something new through sampling, remixing, and scratching. In this manner they escaped the passive consumption of music and made music conform to the contours of their own lives and desires. Much like the first DJs, mashup artists, electronica musicians, and pop stars have taken the history of rock into their own hands, reshaping it according to their needs and dreams.

One cultural offshoot of remix culture is the **Rock Band** and **Guitar Hero** video games. These games allow players to hold small plastic instruments, forget their humble surroundings, and totally rock out alongside rockers such as Joan Jett, Black Sabbath, and Aerosmith. Released in September 2009, the Beatles edition of Rock Band allows teens to participate in the re-interpretation of the legacy of the baby boomer's most venerated act. Although music video games are nothing new—the PaRappa the Rapper franchise is both critically acclaimed and popular, and Gitaroo Man had massive underground success—Guitar Hero and Rock Band take the genre to a new level, configuring players into bands and requiring them to play rock & roll standards.

Allowing players to feel the thrill of being an arena rock hero is no accident. Both Rock Band and Guitar Hero rely on technology developed by Harmonix Studios, a technology company founded by MIT graduates who studied under digital composer and innovator Tod

Machover. As early as the 1970s, Machover began developing what he called "hyperinstruments"—electronically enhanced instruments aimed at boosting the types of sounds that instruments could produce. In time, this nugget of an idea grew to include those who had little musical training or skill, but wished to create their own technically proficient music. Music video games encapsulate this democratic idea: The power and thrill of playing rock music is not limited only to musicians, but extended to music lovers of all types.

The Rock Nation

Some baby boomers—the first generation to grow up with rock & roll as the dominant popular music—wring their hands at the increasing dissemination (some would say "dilution") of rock & roll: Bob Dylan has made Cadillac commercials, and "Layla" is now just another ringtone. But there is another way to regard how rock is growing, changing, and coming to permeate more and more aspects of people's lives. Now more than ever, rock fans have figured out how to become more active, engaged, involved, and intelligent consumers of rock & roll. With the help of new technology, they have figured out how to make rock music their own and better fit it into the contours of their lives. As people fill all the crannies of their lives with music, it is able to affect

daily lives in ways that baby boomers could not have dreamed of in their youth.

In his book *High Fidelity,* Nick Hornby talks about the ways in which music speaks to the lives of fans: the protagonist, Rob, constantly talks about his life in musical references, and at one point his love interest Laura reaches out to him in the same way: "Yeah, you're all right. But you're not perfect, and you're certainly not happy. So what happens if you *get* happy, and yes I know that's the title of an Elvis Costello album, I used the reference deliberately to catch your attention, do you take me for a complete idiot?" (Hornby 1995, 271) Laura is adopting Rob's habit of using rock music to speak for him so that he can better hear her; she is speaking his language, the language of rock, the language that now fills the air in every venue of American life. More and more, Americans "have our ears on" all the time, constantly surrounded by and hearing rock, and that's a gift.

∧ Music games like **Guitar Hero and Rock Band** allow players
∧ to **take part in the thrill of performing in a rock band.**

16

Review

Summary

WHAT IS THE ROLE OF APPROPRIATION IN POPULAR MUSIC? 288

- Remix culture—aided by new technology—allows and encourages sampling and new works (such as mashups) created from other works of art.

- Appropriation in popular culture has a long history that includes visual artists such as Marcel Duchamp, Andy Warhol, and Sherrie Levine.

- Covers that take a song and give it a new twist are examples of appropriation in rock & roll.

WHAT WAS THE IMPACT OF THE DIGITAL SAMPLER? 291

- With the advent of the digital sampler, it became a simple matter not just to allude to another song, but actually to "sample" it: to use the musical DNA of another composition as one of the building blocks of one's own.

- Sampling became a mainstay of hip-hop and electronica.

- 2 Live Crew's use of a Roy Orbison sample in their parody "Pretty Woman" was ruled fair use, but rapper Biz Markie's sampling of

Gilbert O'Sullivan song "Alone Again (Naturally)" without permission was ruled illegal. This last decision made artists and record companies more wary of sampling.

WHAT WAS NAPSTER AND HOW DID IT AFFECT DIGITAL DISTRIBUTION? 295

- Napster was a digital file-sharing service that allowed people to exchange MP3s and attracted 50 million users.

- In December 1999, the RIAA filed suit against Napster, declaring that "nearly every hit song by every significant recording artist can be found on Napster" and seeking $20 million in damages.

- In July 2001, Napster shut down. It declared bankruptcy the following year. The company's logo and name were sold, later to be used by a pay service.

- Digital distribution and the continued availability of pirated music on the Internet had changed the musical industry, making the old model less profitable.

- Large music festivals, portable MP3 players, and games like Guitar Hero make it easier for music fans to integrate music into every facet of their lives.

Key Terms

mashups a genre of music that uses existing songs to make new ones, whether that is as simple as combining two different songs or as elaborate as a three-minute track containing samples from more than 20 different songs 288

iPod portable music player created by Apple in 2001 that plays MP3s stored on its hard drive 288

remix culture a society that allows and encourages works of art derived from other works of art; term coined by Lawrence Lessig 288

readymade a found object considered art because presented and perceived in an artistic context 288

Andy Warhol pop artist who rose to prominence in the 1960s and has had a lasting cultural influence on contemporary artists and musicians 289

appropriation the artistic use of another's work in the creation of a new piece 289

fair use use of intellectual property that is exempt from licensing requirements 290

Grand Upright Music, Ltd v. Warner Bros. Records Inc. ruling that set precedent that sampling was illegal without consent of copyright holder or under fair use 292

Negativland an experimental band from the San Francisco area that became famous for its legal wrangling with U2's record label in the early 1990s 293

RIAA Recording Industry Association of America; a group that represents music distributors and rights holders in the United States 295

Napster a digital file-sharing service that allowed people to exchange MP3s through a central server 295

iTunes computer application that allows users to manage their iPods; it also contains

an online store that sells songs as digital downloads 295

Piratbyrån a Swedish political organization whose primary issue is the importance of free-flowing ideas and culture 295

Girl Talk Gregg Gillis, a mashup artist 297

Shawn Fanning the creator of Napster, the first and biggest file sharing software 298

Danger Mouse Brian Burton, a DJ, producer and mashup artist 299

music festivals musical performances by a number of performers stretched over one or several days 300

Rock Band music-based video game that allows players to live out the fantasy of rock stardom 302

Guitar Hero music-based video game that allows players to live out the fantasy of rock stardom 302

Sample Test Questions

1. Which of the following people created Napster?
   a. Shawn Fanning
   b. Kevin Duffy
   c. Gregg Gillis
   d. Chuck D

2. Which of the following is NOT a portable music player?
   a. the iPod
   b. the Zune
   c. the Zeppo
   d. the Walkman

3. The state of music festivals reflect contemporary changes in rock music by
   a. proving that fans no longer enjoy live music.
   b. booking only acts signed to major labels.
   c. requiring artists to sign waivers allowing others to cover their songs.
   d. reflecting the soaring prices of tickets to music performances.

4. *Grand Upright Music, Ltd v. Warner Bros. Records Inc.* is a legal ruling that
   a. defended 2 Live Crew's sampling as fair use.
   b. prematurely ended Girl Talk's career.
   c. found that Biz Markie's sampling had not been fair use.
   d. set a precedent for the legality of file sharing.

5. Which album was the first to be created entirely from samples?
   a. DJ Shadow's *Endtroducing. . . . .*
   b. DJ Danger Mouse' *The Grey Album*
   c. Girl Talk's *Feed the Animals*
   d. Nine Inch Nails' *The Slip*

ESSAY

6. Discuss the importance of the digital playlist. What does it make possible for the average listener?

7. What do music festivals provide?

8. What is artistic appropriation, and what are its predecessors in visual art?

9. How did *Grand Upright Music, Ltd v. Warner Bros. Records Inc.* impact sampling in popular music?

10. What does digital downloading mean for the future of the music industry? What are its advantages and disadvantages for musicians?

WHERE TO START YOUR RESEARCH PAPER

For information about activism against the music industry, go to Downhill Battle's Web site: http://downhillbattle.org/

For a trailer for and information about Kimbrew McLeod's documentary on remixes, go to http://copyrightcriminals.com/

For the journal of a sampling musician who sometimes comments on the music industry, go to http://www.moby.com/journal

To learn more about Negativland and their copyLEFT activism, go to http://www.negativland.com/index.php?opt5bio&subopt5neglandbio

For more interpretations of kopimi, go to http://www.kopimi.com/kopimi/

For information on a vital alternative to traditional copyright, go to http://creativecommons.org/

To watch the truly excellent copyright, fair use, and sampling documentary *Good Copy Bad Copy*, go to http://video.google.com/videoplay?docid5-4323661317653995812#

Answers: 1. a; 2. c; 3. d; 4. c; 5. a

Remember to check www.thethinkspot.com for additional information, downloadable flashcards, and other helpful resources.

GLOSSARY

Parenthetical numbers refer to the pages on which the term is introduced.

7 Year Bitch   one of the first riot grrrl bands to come out of Seattle; the band was vocal in their support for women's protection (218)

13th Floor Elevators   a band that pioneered psychedelic rock; fronted by singer Roky Erickson (119)

45   seven-inch vinyl record with a single and a backing song ("B-side") that made rock & roll songs available to the youth market (25)

98 Degrees   adult contemporary boy band that appealed to a slightly more mature audience; straddled the line between soul and pop (257)

acid trip   the mind-altering experience of LSD (119)

Alan Freed   Cleveland disc jockey and radio personality known as "Moondog" and credited with bringing rock & roll to a mainstream teenage audience (22)

album   a collection of songs on a 45 or 33 1/3 r.p.m. record (13)

Allen Ginsberg   American poet and member of the Beats (121)

The Almanac Singers   politically progressive U.S. folk act featuring Woody Guthrie and Pete Seeger (75)

Altamont Speedway Free Festival   rock festival held on December 6, 1969, in California near San Francisco; due to tragic events, it is viewed by many as the end of the psychedelic-hippie era (124)

AM radio   broadcasting technology that provides high-fidelity sound over radio airwaves (33)

American Bandstand   national televised dance party that ran from 1957 to 1989 and launched the careers of many clean-cut teen idols (59)

American Idol   U.S. *Pop Idol* spin-off launched in 2002; remains one of the most popular shows on American television (259)

American Society of Composers, Authors, and Publishers (ASCAP)   a membership association that held nearly all publishing rights to recorded music until the 1940s (42)

Andy Warhol   pop artist who rose to prominence in the 1960s and has had a lasting cultural influence on contemporary artists and musicians (289)

The Animals   Northern English band heavily influenced by black American R&B and credited with producing the first folk rock song (101)

appropriation   the artistic use of another's work in the creation of a new piece (289)

The Arctic Monkeys   a top-selling garage rock band from the UK (283)

Aretha Franklin   gospel-influenced Queen of Soul; achieved huge crossover success among white audiences in the late 1960s and early 1970s (135)

Arlan Coolidge   a chairman at the Department of Music at Brown University who supported legislation in the music industry in the late 1950s (42)

Arrested Development   Atlanta-based rap group wishing to bring positive Afrocentric response to gangsta rap (241)

art rock   experimental music genre with avant-garde influences that attempted to elevate rock music into an art form (143)

Arthur "Big Boy" Crudup   born in 1905 in Mississippi, he wrote "That's All Right, Mama," the song that would launch Elvis Presley's career, although he received little credit or compensation for it (30)

Arthur Lee   lead singer and guitarist for Love (118)

Artists and Repertoire   the division in a record company that is responsible for the acquisition of new talent (45)

Ashlee Simpson   little sister of Jessica Simpson; infamously caught in an embarrassing lip-synching incident on *Saturday Night Live* that tarnished her career as a singer (256)

Babes in Toyland   Minneapolis band not directly attached to the riot grrrl movement, but are often connected with it by the media (220)

Babyshambles   a garage rock band from the UK known as much for its music as its singer's lifestyle (282)

The Backstreet Boys   first boy band of the 1990s to become hit-generating international superstars (257)

backward echo   effect obtained during mixing by placing the echo ahead of the sound (141)

Bad Boy Records   East Coast record company created by Sean "Diddy" Combs in 1993 (236)

Bad Brains   D.C.-based band that helped define the hardcore sound (196)

The Bangles   girl group that started as more of a 1960s rock/neo-folk sounding outfit, but traded their original sound for a more heavily produced 80s pop sound (252)

Barry Gibb   lead singer for the Bee Gees whose trademark falsetto gave the group their distinctive sound (155)

Barry McGuire   American singer-songwriter most famous for his hit "Eve of Destruction" (113)

Barry White   R&B crooner, sex symbol, and songwriter whose recordings were influential during the disco era (154)

basket houses   venues at which performers were paid by passing a hat or basket around the audience (78)

Beach Boys   surf rock band that went on to help launch psychedelic and prog rock (81)

Beale Street   Memphis, Tennessee, cultural center for African-American music (29)

Beastie Boys   hip hop trio from Queens, who had the first number one rap record with *Licensed to Ill* (231)

beatboxing   making drumbeats with one's mouth (229)

The Beatles   rock & roll quartet from Liverpool whose popularity launched the British Invasion in the United States (93)

beat-matching   changing the speed of one track to match the tempo of another (228)

beatnik   a member of the Beat Generation, an anti-establishment literary and cultural youth movement of the 1950s (113)

Beck   a slacker rock beacon, Beck mashed together many styles, including blues, hip-hop, and rapping (221)

Benny Goodman   one of the most successful swing band leaders, and a pioneer in integrating his band (8)

Berry Gordy   founder of Motown (65)

Big Bopper   a rock & roll musician also known as Jiles Perry Richardson; killed in a plane crash (50)

Big Brother and the Holding Company   influential psychedelic rock band from San Francisco (116)

Bikini Kill   early riot grrrl band that originated as a fanzine; led by Kathleen Hanna, who later joined Le Tigre (217)

Bill Graham   highly successful concert promoter who managed many of the most important rock acts of the 1960s (114)

Bill Haley and His Comets   covered several popular R&B songs in the early 1950s, best known for "Rock Around the Clock," one of the earliest rock & roll songs (57)

Black Flag   Hermosa, California-based hardcore band that became a powerful force in American alternative rock (198)

Black Sabbath   one of the defining 1970s heavy metal bands, fronted by "prince of darkness" Ozzy Osbourne (141)

Blackboard Jungle   controversial film that showed juvenile delinquency in the 1950s and connected it with rock & roll through the use of its opening song "Rock Around the Clock" (40)

blue notes   "bent" notes, or notes slightly flat of a normal note as played on a piano; played in the country blues era by either stopping the string with a bottleneck slide or bending the string on the fret (12)

bluegrass style of music that melded the format of African American blues and jazz with the Southern string band sound, and featured instrumentalists and "high lonesome" singing (16)

Blur 1990s Britpop band that combined Damon Albarn's wry social commentary with incurably catchy melodic hooks (223)

Bob Dylan legendary musician who began as a folksinger, ushered in folk rock, and enjoyed a long and versatile career (77)

Bob Weir rhythm guitarist for the Grateful Dead (113)

Bratmobile poppy riot grrrl band, started in Eugene, Oregon, that released records on Kill Rock Stars (219)

the break a technique in which records are scratched to isolate the drumbeats from music (228)

break-dancing a popular form of dance including spinning on one's head (228)

Brian Eno legendary producer, performer, and creator of the ambient music genre (178)

Brill Building center of music production in the 1950s, housing record companies, songwriters, and publishers (61)

Brithop British hip hop (242)

Britney Spears one of the most successful female vocalists of the 21st century and controversial pop culture icon (254)

Britpop the movement of bands such as Oasis and Blur who were generally sunnier and poppier than grunge, looking back toward the British pop music tradition (222)

Broadcast Music Incorporated (BMI) a membership association formed as a response to ASCAP's music licensing monopoly (42)

Bruce Springsteen U.S. musician who gave music fans a dose of realism and "authenticity" (147)

B-side the opposite side of a record relative to the "A-side" of a single (13)

Buddy Holly a rock & roll musician who influenced later generations; killed in a plane crash (50)

busking performing music on the street for money (79)

Butthole Surfers important precursors and source of inspiration for grunge bands, which combined shock tactics with a punk/metal/psychedelic fusion (212)

The Byrds an early folk-rock band that achieved success by injecting elements of rock into Dylan songs (83)

Calvin Johnson founder of indie label K Records and tangential to the riot grrrl movement, he was a proponent of zealous independence in music (215)

Carl Perkins born in 1932, singer-guitarist who composed the hit "Blue Suede Shoes" (32)

Carly Simon singer-songwriter married to James Taylor; best known for chart-topping single "You're So Vain" (133)

Carole King singer-songwriter from Brill Building group of early 1960s who went on to enjoy solo success with top-selling album *Tapestry* (133)

The Cavern Club jazz cellar in Liverpool that launched the Beatles and other Merseybeat bands (94)

CBGB club in New York's seedy Bowery district that housed the New Wave and punk scenes (173)

Chas Chandler the Animals' bassist and manager of Jimi Hendrix (116)

Chess Record Studio Chicago recording studio partly responsible for the "Chicago Sound," a new, beat-oriented R&B sound that would eventually become rock & roll (25)

Chic one of disco's most influential bands with hits including "Le Freak" and "Good Times" (154)

Chitlin Circuit collective name given to a number of performance venues throughout the eastern and southern United States that catered to African American artists and audiences during the period of racial segregation (67)

Christina Aguilera female vocalist; won Best New Artist Grammy award in 2000 for her outstanding vocal range and power (255)

Chuck Berry born 1926, a pioneer of rock & roll guitar (28)

The Clash musically and politically brash British punk rockers (162)

Coldplay Britpop band that achieved widespread success because of its similarities to mid-1990s Radiohead (269)

"Colonel" Tom Parker Elvis Presley's manager who marketed him as an icon rather than just a musician (35)

Comiskey Park 1970s home of the Chicago White Sox and site of Disco Demolition Night (156)

country blues a rough style of blues performed by Robert Johnson and others; also called "delta blues," after the Mississippi Delta (10)

Courtney Love lead singer of L.A. band Hole and wife of Kurt Cobain, Love was probably the most prominent female lead singer of the era's punk and rock bands (219)

cover versions current performances of songs that were expected to become hits (later acquired negative connotations related to lack of originality and exploitation) (56)

crooning an exaggerated style of singing that developed with the invention of the electric microphone, allowing for more intimacy than was previously possible with acoustic megaphones (7)

crossover a hit popular with multiple audiences; for example, Roy Acuff's "Great Speckled Bird" was a hit with both popular and country audiences (15)

Cypress Hill most successful Latino hip hop group; glorified marijuana use (236)

D.A. Pennebaker American documentary filmmaker who created the seminal documentary *Monterey Pop* (116)

The Dandy Warhols a neo-psychedelic band known for its pop orientation and blending of psychedelic and alternative music (272)

Danger Mouse Brian Burton, a DJ, producer and mashup artist (299)

Dashboard Confessional a popular emo band known for its revealing lyrical content (276)

Dave Van Ronk a club owner and central figure in the Greenwich Village folk scene (78)

David Bowie early 1970s glam rocker who took the image to extremes, creating controversial, glittery onstage personas such as Ziggy Stardust (132)

David Byrne lead singer and producer of the Talking Heads who later went on to a long-lasting solo career (172)

De La Soul witty, playful group offering respite from some of the more serious acts popular during the golden age (233)

Death Cab for Cutie a popular and successful emo band (276)

Death Row Records West Coast hip hop label created by Dr. Dre and Suge Knight in 1991 (236)

Deep Purple second-wave British Invasion band that shifted to heavy metal music midway through its career (142)

Destiny's Child rose to prominence in the late 1990s as the dominant female singing group in the United States (253)

Detroit Midwestern city in which Motown originated (67)

Dewey Phillips Memphis disc jockey who helped popularize Elvis Presley's music (34)

Dick Clark presenter of *American Bandstand* who helped popularize rock & roll among the white middle classes (59)

Dick Dale musician who worked with guitar manufacturer Leo Fender to develop the reverberation unit that gave surf music its distinctive sound (62)

Dischord Records Washington, D.C., hardcore record label started by Ian MacKaye and Jeff Nelson of Minor Threat (197)

Disco Sucks anti-disco campaign that led to the backlash against disco in 1979 (156)

distortion effect created on an electric guitar when an amplifier's voltage exceeds its maximum power capability, clipping the input signal (100)

DJ Jazzy Jeff & The Fresh Prince duo famous for kitschy raps such as "Parents Just Don't Understand" and "I Think I Can Beat Mike Tyson" (238)

DJ Kool Herc called the "Godfather" of hip hop, a DJ that is credited for introducing the turntable style to the United States (228)

Don McLean a musician who wrote the song "American Pie" and coined the phrase "the day the music died" (50)

Donna Summer American singer who came to prominence during the disco era (153)

Donovan folk singer known as the British Bob Dylan (103)

The Doors acid rock band that fused blues, heavy rock, and Eastern mysticism, and was fronted by Jim Morrison (117)

doo-wop musical genre influenced by gospel, jazz, pop, and blues, and performed by urban vocal harmony groups (64)

double stop two notes played together; rock & roll guitar technique pioneered by Chuck Berry (63)

drumming creating a drumming sound with scratching techniques (228)

Duane Eddy instrumentalist whose innovative guitar work laid the foundation for future rock guitarists (62)

dub musical genre that developed from the practice of re-recording reggae songs as primarily instrumental tracks (173)

Dusty Springfield British soul singer who single-handedly invented British female soul (103)

The Eagles country rock band that straddled the line between mainstream rock, folk rock, and country rock; produced the best-selling album in U.S. history (134)

Ealing Club London R&B club in which the Rolling Stones were introduced to each other (97)

Edgard Varèse 20th-century French experimental composer (119)

The Edge U2 guitarist who developed a textured, reverb-laden guitar sound (193)

electrical recording method of recording that utilizes an amplified microphone to capture and transmit sound to an electromechanical record engraver (7)

Elton John singer-songwriter who first achieved popularity in the 1970s with his sensitive ballads and wild onstage antics (140)

Elvis Costello seminal British New Wave/postpunk musician who combined the sarcasm and energy of punk with a biting lyrical style (172)

Elvis Presley born in Mississippi in 1936, one of the first white musicians to popularize black R&B and blues songs with credibility (29)

Emerson, Lake and Palmer British prog-rock band that was one of the earliest rock & roll supergroups (143)

Eminem white rap artist reaching heights of stardom and controversy beginning in the early 2000s (242)

emo short for "emotional" or "emocore," it is a style of music characterized by its personal, introspective themes (274)

En Vogue girl group that achieved huge commercial success with 1992 album *Funky Divas* (252)

Eric B. & Rakim duo famous for their album *Paid in Full* and for popularizing the use of James Brown and funk in sampling (233)

Etta James influential female R&B singer whose career spans from the 1950s to the present day (64)

The Everly Brothers country-influenced duo famed for their vocal harmonies (61)

experimental rock an update of progressive rock that embraces modern forms of music and contemporary attitudes and challenges traditional pop rock sensibilities (268)

Fabian manufactured teen idol from Philadelphia, promoted on *American Bandstand* (60)

fair use use of intellectual property that is exempt from licensing requirements (289)

Fall Out Boy a band with catchy hooks that plays in the emo tradition (276)

fanzine an amateur magazine published by fans, often for little or no financial gain (214)

feedback sound created when an electric guitar picks up a sound from a speaker connected to an amplifier and regenerates it back through the amplifier (102)

Fender Stratocaster popular electric guitar introduced in 1954 (63)

Fillmore historic music venue in San Francisco (117)

First Rock & Roll Ball a highly successful rock concert held in New York City and organized by Alan Freed, noteworthy for its integrated audience (22)

The Flaming Lips a neo-psychedelic band known for its live performances (273)

folk music simple, sincere music with roots in working-class and African American genres (74)

folk revival the repopularization and modernization of traditional folk music that took place in the United States during the 1950s and 1960s (74)

folk rock genre of music combining characteristics of folk music and rock & roll that emerged in 1965 (74)

folkniks musicians and followers of the 1960s folk revival (74)

The Four Tops Motown male vocal quartet known for its longevity; achieved success under the guidance of songwriting team Holland-Dozier-Holland (68)

Frank Sinatra American singer popular in the 1940s and 1950s (40)

Frank Zappa prolific American rock musician and composer (119)

Frankie Avalon teen idol famous for hit songs "Venus" and "Why;" later crossed into the film industry (68)

Freddie Mercury lead vocalist and frontman for Queen (138)

The Funk Brothers Motown's in-house session musicians; ensured a consistency of sound across all the Motown groups (69)

fuzztone blurred effect produced by increased vibrations or added overtones (102)

gangsta rap a subgenre that sensationalized the gang lifestyle and featured lyrics depicting the experiences of inner-city youth (234)

garage rock simple raw form of rock & roll created by amateurish American bands in the 1960s; a recent garage rock revival incorporates punk into its rough, bluesy sound (280)

Gary Lewis and the Playboys American band fronted by the son of comedian Jerry Lewis (106)

Gary Numan mastermind behind synth band Tubeway Army who created a whole dystopian universe in which to set his songs (176)

Gary Snyder Pulitzer Prize-winning American poet, essayist, and social activist (121)

Genesis British progressive rock band that provided a launching pad for singers Peter Gabriel and Phil Collins (144)

Girl Talk Gregg Gillis, a mashup artist (297)

glam rock fusion of hard rock and pop characterized by performers' flamboyant, glittery costumes (136)

Godsmack a nü metal band with a more traditional metal sound (278)

Godspeed You! Black Emperor a Canadian experimental rock band known for implementing a visual aspect to its live performances (269)

The Go-Go's emerged from the punk/new wave explosion as a commercially successful all-girl group in the early 1980s (252)

golden age of rap a period from the late 1980s through early 1990s when rap was flourishing (232)

"Good Rockin' Tonight" one of the first rock & roll songs about sex, which popularized the "shouting" style of rock & roll when recorded by Wynonie Harris (26)

Goth rock bleak atmospheric rock pioneered by Bauhaus (203)

Grace Slick lead singer of Jefferson Airplane (114)

Grand Upright Music, Ltd v. Warner Bros. Records Inc. ruling that set precedent that sampling was illegal without consent of copyright holder or under fair use (292)

Grateful Dead American rock band formed in 1965 (113)

Green River Seattle band that released what is often called the first grunge record, the EP *Come on Down*, in 1985 (213)

griots West African poets and singers who traveled about and passed on oral traditions (228)

grunge a style of music that fused punk, heavy metal, and more traditional pop styles (210)

Guitar Hero music-based video game that allows players to live out the fantasy of rock stardom (302)

Haight-Ashbury a district in San Francisco associated with 1960s counterculture and psychedelic rock bands (115)

Hank Williams considered one of the most important country singers, he had a string of hits until his early death in 1953 at age 30 (16)

Happy Days a television show in the 1970s that portrayed a sanitized version of life in the 1950s (47)

harmonica neck rack   a device that wrapped around a singer's neck to hold a harmonica in front of the mouth to enable performers to sing while playing guitar and harmonica (96)

Harry Wayne "KC" Casey   disco composer and singer of Top 10 hits including "Boogie Shoes" and "Shake Shake Shake (Shake Your Booty)" (155)

Heavens to Betsy   first-wave riot grrrl band from Olympia made up of singer and guitarist Corin Tucker with drummer Tracy Sawyer (218)

heavy metal   genre of music characterized by extreme volume, distorted timbre, screeching vocals, emphatic beats, and extended guitar solos (140)

Hells Angels Motorcycle Club   worldwide motorcycle gang (125)

Henry Garfield   D.C.-based singer for S.O.A. who, as Henry Rollins, became the singer for Black Flag and, later, the Henry Rollins Band (200)

Herman's Hermits   Manchester pop band known in the United States for their novelty British songs (101)

High School Musical   Disney production that is extremely popular with pre-teen and young teenage audiences (263)

hijacking   release of a cover by a white artist on the heels of a hit by a African American performer (56)

hillbilly   records the country music of the rural South; analogous to "race records" in terms of the audience targeted (10)

hip hop   a cultural and musical movement beginning in the 1970s that included graffiti, rap music, and break dancing (228)

hippie   a member of the counterculture of the 1960s (112)

Hole   L.A. band formed by Courtney Love and Eric Erlandson (219)

Hollywood Records   Disney-owned music label launched in 1989 that primarily features teen stars associated with the Disney Channel (262)

hootenanny   an informal folk music event featuring various musicians (78)

hot music   a catch-all term to describe jazz at its beginning; it referred to the driving, syncopated rhythms of the Dixieland dance bands (8)

hot-rod music   similar to surf music, West Coast music that revolved around cars and the greaser lifestyle (82)

Huggy Bear   one of the few U.K. exponents of the riot grrrl movement; they were tightly associated with the Olympia scene, especially Bikini Kill (220)

Human Be-In   rock and cultural festival held January 14, 1967, in San Francisco's Golden Gate Park (120)

Husker Dü   Minneapolis-based hardcore band that incorporated a poppier, more accessible sound than most of their contemporaries (201)

"The Hustle"   partner dance that became popular during the disco era and was featured prominently in *Saturday Night Fever* (153)

Ian MacKaye   an influential member of the D.C. punk scene whose bands would influence the emo sound (274)

Ice-T   West Coast gangsta rapper often credited with inventing gangsta rap due to his song "6 in the Mornin'" (234)

Iggy Pop   American proto-punk rocker infamous for his wild onstage antics; did not achieve mainstream success until the mid-1990s (139)

Igor Stravinsky   20th-century Russian composer (113)

iPod   portable music player created by Apple in 2001 that plays MP3s stored on its hard drive (288)

Irving Berlin   one of the most successful Tin Pan Alley songwriters; wrote "God Bless America" and "White Christmas," as well as the music for "Annie, Get Your Gun" (5)

iTunes   computer application that allows users to manage their iPods; it also contains an online store that sells songs as digital downloads (295)

The Jackson Five   Motown's youngest superstars who took the recording empire into its second decade with their brand of funky pop-soul (69)

jam band   band that features extensive musical improvisation in its performances and crosses genre boundaries (273)

James Dean   American actor who first achieved popularity in the film *Rebel Without* a Cause, created one of the first personas of the rebellious American teenager, and was admired by Elvis Presley (24)

James Taylor   successful 1970s singer-songwriter whose music exemplified the introspective, self-oriented style of soft rock (132)

Jan and Dean   surf rock band that collaborated with the Beach Boys (81)

Janis Joplin   singer and songwriter, lead singer of Big Brother and the Holding Company (116)

Jawbreaker   a forerunner of the emo sound that laid much of the foundation for future bands (274)

Jay-Z   rap's ultimate businessman; sees himself as a business and is proud of his entrepreneurial status (237)

Jefferson Airplane   San Francisco based-band fronted by Grace Slick (114)

Jerry Garcia   guitarist of the Grateful Dead (113)

Jerry Lee Lewis   born in 1935, pioneering pianist, vocalist, and bad boy during the early days of rock & roll (32)

Jessica Simpson   gospel singer who achieved mainstream pop success with debut album *Sweet Kisses*; starred in MTV reality series *Newlyweds* following her marriage to 98 Degrees singer Nick Lachey (256)

Jim Morrison   lead singer and songwriter for the Doors (117)

Jimi Hendrix   influential guitarist and member of the Jimi Hendrix Experience (116)

Jimmy Eat World   a popular emo band that found mainstream success (275)

Joan Baez   a traditional folksinger and social and political activist who went on to have a career as a singer-songwriter (79)

John Cage   minimalist American composer whose experimentalism influenced Sonic Youth (196)

John Coltrane   American jazz saxophonist and composer (113)

John Hammond   Columbia Records producer and talent scout responsible for helping integrate music and launch the career of Bob Dylan (79)

John Lydon   singer for the Sex Pistols and later Public Image Limited who took the stage name Johnny Rotten (161)

Johnny Marr   the Smiths guitarist credited with bringing guitar-driven rock back to the mainstream (184)

The Jonas Brothers   wholesome members of the Disney franchise; the brothers promote abstinence and project a family-friendly image (262)

Joni Mitchell   singer-songwriter who was a part of the Canadian Invasion and whose long and stylistically diverse career is representative of how singer-songwriters often experimented with different musical styles throughout their careers (86)

The Joshua Tree   Irish group U2's epochal fifth album that came to define the mission and restlessness at the core of alternative music (190)

Joy Division   British postpunk band featuring the somber lyrics and baritone vocals of troubled frontman Ian Curtis (165)

Judy Collins   song interpreter who popularized many Joni Mitchell and Leonard Cohen songs (96)

jukebox   a machine used to play records often found in clubs, diners, and restaurants in the 1950s (50)

Kate Bush   English singer-songwriter whose influential incorporation of performance art, music, and literary influences created a musical form all its own (202)

Ken Kesey   American writer and political activist associated with 1960s counterculture (112)

The Kingston Trio   an early popular folk band that gained popularity by eschewing political topics (76)

The Kinks   London band that popularized the power chord (99)

Korn   a popular nü metal band known for its bottom-heavy sound (278)

Kraftwerk   German group influential in the creation of synth pop (180)

KRS-One   member of Boogie Down Productions, known for statements about education (232)

L7 another L.A. riot grrrl band closely associated with third-wave feminism, they were directly confrontational with their images and lyrics (220)

Lead Belly an African American folksinger who was one of the first to bring traditional folk music to a mainstream audience (74)

Led Zeppelin influential 1970s heavy metal band led by former Yardbirds guitarist Jimmy Page (140)

Leo Fender radio repairman who revolutionized the guitar sound by developing a solid-bodied electric guitar (25)

Leonard Cohen Canadian poet, novelist, and musician whose style is marked by dark, personal lyrics (86)

Lil Wayne young prodigy when it comes to rap music, hailed as one of the best artists in his generation of performers (242)

Linkin Park one of the more commercially successful nü metal bands (280)

lip-synching miming to a pre-recorded backing track (256)

Little Richard born Richard Penniman in 1932, a flamboyant rock & roll showman with major 1950s hits, including "Long Tall Sally" and "Tutti Frutti" (27)

Live Aid international music festival organized in 1985 to raise funds for Ethiopian refugees (204)

Liverpool British port city on the Northwest coast, home of Merseybeat (93)

LL Cool J rap artist whose earlier works are more romantic, but his "Mama Said Knock You Out" was a breakthrough hit (231)

Lonnie Donegan British musician known as the "King of Skiffle" (92)

Lou Pearlman boy band Svengali who guided the Backstreet Boys and 'N Sync to chart-topping success (258)

Lou Reed singer in the Velvet Underground, later began a solo career that incorporated the glam rock image (137)

Louis Jordan a pioneer of "jump blues," who also had a huge influence on rock & roll (17)

Madonna best-selling female rock performer of the 20th century; her career has so far spanned almost three decades and covered a wide variety of musical styles and performances (250)

The Mamas and the Papas a harmonic quartet emblematic of commercial folk (81)

Marc Bolan one of the early pioneers of 1970s British glam rock, lead singer of T. Rex (137)

Marilyn Manson a shock rock performer (279)

Martha and the Vandellas earthier girl-group alternative to the Supremes, achieved hit status with "Dancing In the Street" (77)

mashups a genre of music that uses existing songs to make new ones, whether that is as simple as combining two different songs or as elaborate as a three-minute track containing samples from more than 20 different songs (288)

Massive Attack Bristol trip hop group that has been credited with starting the subgenre (243)

MC Hammer a true rags-to-riches-to-rags-again story, Hammer was enormously successful commercially yet wound up broke (239)

Me Decade nickname given to the 1970s by writer Tom Wolfe that came to characterize the self-absorption and hedonism of the era (154)

The Melvins early Seattle band, influential on Nirvana, that were a staple of the local rock scene; they were in part responsible for the slow, sludgy sound of grunge (212)

Merseybeat combination of skiffle, doo-wop, and soul originating from the Mersey area of the UK (93)

Michael Stipe R.E.M.'s enigmatic and influential lead singer (193)

Mike Oldfield Composer who experimented with electronic rock, creating the legendary 49-minute instrumental composition Tubular Bells (145)

Miley Cyrus/Hannah Montana Disney's superstar of television show Hannah Montana; became an overnight musical sensation with tour tickets among the most expensive on the resale market (261)

Minimoog a descendant of the legendary Moog Modular and one of the first affordable, easy-to-use synthesizers (176)

Mississippi Delta location in the American South, where the acoustic delta blues would first emerge with singers like Robert Johnson and Son House (23)

mixing weaving two tracks together to form one song (228)

Moby Grape a popular psychedelic band in the 1960s (115)

Mods fashion-conscious British teens who wore Italian-style clothes and rode customized scooters (100)

The Monkees American band specifically manufactured for television following the success of the Beatles' film *A Hard Day's Night* (107)

Monterey International Pop Music Festival three-day concert held in 1967 that was attended by 200,000 people (121)

Moog Synthesizer digital keyboard used to create background for disco hits (152)

MOR middle-of-the-road, or popular music (45)

Morrissey controversial singer for the Smiths famous for his dry, witty lyrics and his declaration of celibacy (184)

Motown style of music originating in Detroit that combined elements of soul, jazz, and pop (65)

Mott the Hoople American glam rock band that achieved a cult homosexual following in the 1970s (138)

MP3 method of encoding audio files, patented in 1994, that first made widespread distribution of music over the Internet possible (223)

MTV short for music television, the cable channel was one of the only nationwide distribution systems for music at the beginning of its inception (182)

Muddy Waters migrating blues musician who was among the first to integrate amplified electric guitar sounds into music and record songs that would become rock & roll standards (25)

Mudhoney one of the earliest grunge bands, which formed after the previous band Green River (which also spawned Pearl Jam) broke up (214)

multitrack recording recording with more than two tracks simultaneously to enable various musical elements to be recorded on separate tracks (147)

multi-track tape recording the process of recording multiple "tracks" (often each a single instrument) onto different sections (by width) of a reel of magnetic tape; allows for independent control of each instrument after it has already been recorded, and also lets performers "double" themselves on a different track, a process called "overdubbing" (16)

music festivals musical performances by a number of performers stretched over one or several days (300)

My Chemical Romance a band that performs a highly polished form of emo (277)

N.W.A one of the most controversial rap groups of all time, whose lyrics depict police brutality and retaliation (234)

Napster a digital file-sharing service that allowed people to exchange MP3s through a central server (295)

Negativland an experimental band from the San Francisco area that became famous for its legal wrangling with U2's record label in the early 1990s (293)

Neil Sedaka performer and songwriter known for hits about the joys and angst of teenage love (61)

Neil Young a singer-songwriter and rock musician who was a part of the Canadian Invasion and achieved popularity as part of the group Crosby, Still, Nash, and Young (85)

neo-psychedelia a lo-fi update of psychedelic rock that embraced organic experimentation and modern forms of music (271)

New Romantics also called Futurists, or Blitz kids, these European-obsessed synth pop audiences combined retro and futuristic costuming and favored electronic dance music (181)

New Wave the British movement that came out of punk, also associated with U.S. bands like the Talking Heads (172)

Newport Folk Festival a major annual folk music concert that has launched numerous folk careers (74)

Nirvana seminal and immensely popular grunge band whose front man Kurt Cobain became a beacon of the movement (214)

The Notorious B.I.G./Biggie Smalls East Coast rapper murdered in a drive-by shooting in L.A. (236)

novelty record a humorous parody (46)

'N Sync boy band act that dominated the pop scene of the late 90s; put together by producer Lou Pearlman (257)

nü metal a style of music that incorporates elements of metal, alternative rock, rap, and punk (277)

Oasis Britpop band whose two main voices were the Gallagher brothers, Liam and Noel (223)

old-school hip hop refers to the rap music created in the late 1970s until the early 1980s (229)

Oscar Hammerstein II an American songwriter who testified for ASCAP in the ASCAP-BMI hearings of 1958 (42)

overdubbing process of merging additional musical elements with previously recorded tracks (147)

Owsley Stanley sound engineer for the Grateful Dead and underground LSD chemist (114)

Pablo Casals a Spanish cellist and conductor (46)

Pat Boone second-biggest selling artist of the 1950s after Elvis, popularized R&B hits for mass audiences (56)

Paul Anka Canadian songwriter and performer associated with the Brill Building sound (61)

Paul Revere and the Raiders American band that played up the humorous aspect of the anti-British Invasion by wearing Revolutionary War costumes (106)

Paul Westerberg front man for popular American hardcore band The Replacements (202)

Pavement founders of "slacker rock," Pavement's sound was purposefully lo-fi; lead singer Stephen Malkmus would go on to a long indie rock career (221)

payola the practice of play for pay on radio stations (43)

Pearl Jam seminal grunge band with front man Eddie Vedder that has released nine LPs and is still playing today (216)

pedal steel guitar type of electric guitar played horizontally; pedal steel is mostly commonly heard in U.S. country music (113)

Pet Shop Boys one of the founders of more cerebral dance pop comprising singer Neil Tennant and keyboard/synth programmer Chris Lowe (181)

Pete Seeger played with Woody Guthrie in the Almanac Singers; later went on to form the first commercially successful urban folk group, the Weavers (12)

Peter, Paul, and Mary a folksinging ensemble that achieved success by performing traditional folk songs and Dylan songs in a more accessible style (80)

Petula Clark British solo pop singer whose hit song "Downtown" made her famous in the United States (103)

Phil Ochs a traditional folksinger best known for his protest songs (80)

Philadelphia International Records record label created by Philadelphia-based songwriting duo Kenny Gamble and Leon Huff that introduced the Sound of Philadelphia (136)

Phish a jam band that incorporated neo-psychedelic music into its sound (273)

pickup small microphone attached to vibrating surface that captures mechanical vibrations and converts them into an electric signal (63)

Pink Floyd English band that began as a psychedelic band (120)

Piratbyrån a Swedish political organization whose primary issue is the importance of free-flowing ideas and culture (295)

The Pixies Boston-based precursors to grunge, which drew on many influences to create a sound that was both abrasive and melodic, and highly influential (211)

PJ Harvey a highly influential musician whose music transcends all genres and definitions (283)

Pop Idol British television talent show that premiered in 2001; "pop stars of tomorrow" voted on by the television-watching audience (259)

pop music shortened name of "popular music" (40)

postpunk music in the immediate aftermath of punk rock that recognizes either punk's influence or the way in which punk denied other influences (172)

power chord a chord containing only the root and fifth of the scale (100)

Pro Tools software program for recording and editing music; particularly useful in enhancing vocals through the use of pitch correction and vocal effects (250)

progressive rock musical genre associated with prominent keyboards, complex metric shifts, fantastical or abstract lyrics, and elements of classical, jazz, or world music (143)

protest song a type of folk song that uses music to deliver a topical message (75)

psychedelic pop pop music inspired by hallucinogens or "mind-expanding" drugs such as LSD (103)

pub rock back-to-basics rock movement that drew on country and blues influences and paved the way for punk, postpunk, and New Wave in the United Kingdom (161)

Public Enemy controversial group espousing black militant politics, but also very influential (232)

Pulp Britpop band formed by Jarvis Cocker in 1978 that fused a range of musical styles from glam to indie rock (223)

Queen London glam rock band that created a mock-operatic sound and was known for its extravagant theatrical performances (138)

R.E.M. an American alternative rock band that started out as a garage band (193)

r.p.m. revolutions per minute, or the speed at which a record rotates on a turntable; the quicker the speed, the less information can be encoded per square inch of vinyl (6)

race records any record marketed toward a predominantly African American audience (9)

radio network a series of linked commercial radio stations, allowing for live broadcasts to be transmitted across the country (6)

Radiohead the most commercially successful of the experimental rock bands (268)

Rage Against the Machine a precursor to the nü metal sound that blended rap, punk, and heavy riffs (278)

ragtime a "rag" is a derivation of an African American term describing the process of syncopating a piece of music (6)

Ram Dass American Hindu spiritual teacher (121)

The Ramones quartet from Queens that created the template for short, fast punk rock songs (160)

rap metal a combination of heavy metal music and rap lyrics; sometimes also known as nü metal; an example is Limp Bizkit (243)

rap vocals overlaid against turntable techniques executed by a DJ (228)

rapcore a combination of hardcore punk and rap music; an example is Linkin Park (243)

rave-up lengthy, ad hoc jamming session within a song (102)

Ray Charles soul singer whose full-throated vocal style in the early 1950s would influence rock & roll singing style (25)

readymade a found object considered art because presented and perceived in an artistic context (288)

remix culture a society that allows and encourages works of art derived from other works of art; term coined by Lawrence Lessig (288)

reverb unit device that simulates the way sounds naturally reflect and fade away in enclosed spaces (63)

rhythm & blues term describing many different styles of blues-influenced music and used as a euphemism for "race records" after Billboard stopped using the term in 1949; often abbreviated R&B (16)

RIAA Recording Industry Association of America; a group that represents music distributors and rights holders in the United States (295)

Richard Thompson guitarist, singer, and songwriter for British band Fairport Convention (127)

Ricky Nelson teen idol who used his role on the TV sitcom *The Adventures of Ozzie and Harriet* to promote his music (61)

riff a repeated musical phrase, used often in jazz and swing music, and later in rock & roll (10)

riot grrrl a movement of women, based around homemade zines and bands, with the goal of providing support to women and subverting the male-dominated punk scene (217)

Ritchie Valens a rock & roll musician famous for "La Bamba"; killed in a plane crash (50)

Robert Christgau "Dean of American rock critics," Christgau wrote for the Village Voice for much of his career (176)

rock & roll a term first used to describe sexual intercourse that, in the 1950s, became the term for the popular, youth-oriented music trend that was sweeping the nation (22)

Rock Band music-based video game that allows players to live out the fantasy of rock stardom (302)

rock opera a musical work presenting a storyline told over multiple parts (101)

rock rap a combination of various rock influences with hip hop lyrics; an example is Rage Against the Machine (243)

Rockers British teen subculture with an affinity for leather, motorcycles, and American rock & roll (100)

"Rocket '88" song recorded by Ike Turner and his band in 1951, pioneered the use of distortion (26)

The Rolling Stones London R&B "bad boy" band created in the opposite image of the Beatles (97)

Ross Bagdasarian a songwriter and creator of Alvin and the Chipmunks (46)

Run-D.M.C. musical group using more rock oriented samples, famous for "Walk This Way" cover of Aerosmith's hit song (230)

Sam Phillips head of Sun Studio, responsible for helping launch the career of Elvis Presley (29)

Sandy Denny vocalist for British band Fairport Convention (127)

scratching moving a record back and forth while using the fade control to create unique sounds (228)

Senator Joseph McCarthy a Wisconsin senator who held hearings on alleged communists in the 1940s and 1950s (46)

Sex Pistols British band that was one of the most influential groups in the punk movement (152)

Shawn Fanning the creator of Napster, the first and biggest file sharing software (298)

shock rock a style of music that often incorporates dark lyrics, harrowing imagery, and a spirit of rebelliousness in its music (279)

shoegaze rock subgenre characterized by its "wall of guitars" sound; the name refers to shoegaze bands' habit of staring at the floor as they play (222)

Showman amp Fender amp with more than 100 watts of power, enabling the electric guitar to be played at high volume (62)

Sigur Rós an experimental rock band from Iceland known for its atmospherics and unique vocal stylings (270)

Simon and Garfunkel highly successful folk-rock act that paved the way for later singer-songwriters (94)

Simon Cowell British television producer and American Idol judge; listed at number 21 on Forbes' Celebrity 100 Power List in 2007 (260)

singer-songwriters musicians who write and perform their own songs, which often feature personal and sincere lyrics (85)

single a 78 or 45 r.p.m. record, containing an A-side and a B-side; usually the A-side was the one referred to as the "single" (13)

Sire Records record label that signed the Ramones and the Talking Heads, as well as handled the U.S. distribution for the Smiths (173)

sitar Indian stringed instrument (126)

sit-ins nonviolent occupations of an area for the purpose of protest (121)

skiffle simple three-chord style featuring an instrumental lineup of guitar and/or banjo, and homemade instruments (92)

slacker rock rock subgenre characterized by its DIY, lo-fi sound and blasé attitude (221)

slam dancing a violent dance style that became popular at early 1980s hardcore shows (198)

Sleater-Kinney riot grrrl band formed by fellow singer and guitarists Corin Tucker and Carrie Brownstein (218)

Slipknot band that blended shock rock and nü metal (279)

The Slits all-female punk group led by 14-year-old singer Arianna Foster (164)

The Smiths seminal 1980s band who broke through the New Wave and late punk noise to produce some of the best albums of the era (184)

Snoop Doggy Dogg West Coast artist famous for his slow delivery and chronic marijuana use (236)

soft rock melodic rock music that stresses themes of vulnerability in a confessional, introspective style (132)

song pluggers employees of Tin Pan Alley publishing companies paid to promote their employers' songs around the city, in places ranging anywhere from department stores to saloons (5)

Soul Train first black-oriented music variety show on American television; ran for 35 years (135)

Soundgarden one of the most successful early Seattle bands, which relied on the early metal riffs of Black Sabbath and Led Zeppelin, while retaining the punk DIY ethos (213)

The Spice Girls manufactured girl group that spread a message of feminist empowerment and became the most successful English band since the Beatles (252)

stadium rock commercialized genre of music that fused elements of progressive rock, hard rock, and heavy metal; designed to be performed in a large stadium (145)

stage diving a jump from stage to crowd made by performers that became common at early 1980s hardcore shows (198)

standards songs with predictable forms written during the Golden Age that were commonly interpreted by many performers (6)

Stax Records Memphis record label founded in 1960 by brother-and-sister team Jim Stewart and Estelle Axton; Motown's main rival (135)

Steve Albini seminal engineer of both the Pixies' *Surfer Rosa* and Nirvana's *In Utero*, who recreated a feeling of live performance in the studio (211)

Steve Dahl Chicago DJ who organized the Disco Demolition night at Chicago's Comiskey Park (156)

The Stooges proto-punk 1970s band fronted by Iggy Pop (139)

string band a country band, usually with banjo, mandolin, guitars, fiddle, string bass, or any combination thereof (16)

The Strokes a pop-oriented New York garage rock band (282)

Studio 54 famous Manhattan dance club that became the center of disco culture in the late 1970s (153)

Sub Pop Records an independent Seattle record label that signed influential grunge bands Green River, Nirvana, and Soundgarden, among others (212)

Suede band at the vanguard of the Britpop movement; they inspired many later groups—Oasis and Blur, specifically—who went on to widespread fame (222)

The Sugarhill Gang often credited with creating the first hip hop record and bringing hip hop into the mainstream with "Rapper's Delight" (230)

Summer of Love summer 1967, a time at which the hippie era was at its peak (112)

Sun Studio Memphis recording studio run by Sam Phillips that became the focus point for the crossover of music from R&B to rock & roll (23)

Sunny Day Real Estate a Seattle band that influenced the emo sound (274)

supergroups bands comprised of musicians already famous for their performances as individuals or in other groups (102)

The Supremes Motown's most successful female vocal group, later known as Diana Ross and the Supremes (66)

surf music music popularized by the surfing culture in California and characterized by twanging guitar riffs and high harmony vocals (62)

sustain length of a held note (102)

Sweet Philly Soul soul music originating from Philadelphia characterized by smooth vocals and lush orchestral sounds (136)

Syd Barrett founding member of Pink Floyd (120)

syncopated describing the state in which the accent of a measure of music falls either between the beat or on a beat not normally accented (6)

synth pop an originally British movement that used synthesizers instead of guitars, drawing heavily on European styles (172)

synthesizer   electronic instrument that combines simple wave-forms to produce a wide variety of sounds (101)

tagging   painting one's name or affiliation as graffiti (229)

The Talking Heads   American postpunk band who met at the Rhode Island School of Design and were part of the developing New York postpunk scene, often playing at CBGB (172)

tambura   Indian stringed instrument (126)

Tamla Records   music label owned by Berry Gordy, subsidiary of Motown Records (65)

teen idol   white teen heartthrob of the 1950s (68)

The Temptations   Motown male vocal quintet that achieved chart success in the 1960s with several hits written by Smokey Robinson (68)

Timothy Leary   American writer, psychologist, and vocal advocate of psychedelic drug use (112)

Tin Pan Alley   area of Manhattan around 28th Street where much of the sheet music for the popular vaudeville tunes of the early 20th century were written (4)

TLC   early to mid-1990s girl group whose sassy vibe and wild fashion sense, coupled with good song-writing and performance skills, earned them a great deal of success (252)

Tom Verlaine   Television guitarist who is largely credited with bringing punk and postpunk to CBGB (174)

Tool   a precursor to the nü metal sound that blended progressive music, alternative rock, and metal (278)

tremolo   lever on an electric guitar that produces a wavering effect in a musical tone (62)

A Tribe Called Quest   group fusing hip hop and jazz during rap's Golden Age (233)

trip hop   a combination of strings, electronic, and rap-like lyrics inspired by hip hop music and coming from of Bristol, England; includes Portishead (243)

Tupac Shakur (2Pac)   West Coast gangsta rapper prone to trouble; murdered in Las Vegas in a drive-byshooting (236)

The Turtles   folk-rock band that began as a surf rock band and later had a hit with Dylan's "It Ain't Me Babe" (84)

"Tutti Frutti"   an early rock & roll song popularized by Little Richard after its original sexually explicit lyrics were tamed into nonsense sounds (27)

TV on the Radio   an experimental rock band that incorporates soul, rock, and jazz in its sound (271)

twang   reverberating, treble-heavy guitar sound (62)

U2   an Irish alternative rock band (190)

Vance Packard   a journalist and social critic in the 1950s who took part in the ASCAP-BMI hearings of 1958 (43)

The Velvet Underground   American garage band formed in the 1960s; considered one of the most influential groups in rock history for its substantial impact on punk, glam, and garage rock (137)

The Village People   concept disco band 1970s that released hits including "Macho Man," "In the Navy," and "Y.M.C.A." (156)

W.C. Handy   one of the most successful African American Tin Pan Alley composers, and the artist responsible for bringing some version of the blues to a wide audience (11)

wah-wah pedal   guitar effects pedal that mimics the human voice (117)

Watts riots   large-scale race riot that took place in Watts, California, in August 1965 (119)

Wattstax Music Festival   L.A. music concert held in 1972 to commemorate the Watts riots; popularity reflected growing market appeal of African American artists (135)

The Weavers   a prominent folk group formed by Pete Seeger (76)

Weezer   a highly successful and influential emo band (274)

Westlife   Irish boy band created by pop impresario Louis Walsh; holds the Guinness World Record for most successful new chart act (259)

The White Stripes   a highly influential and successful garage rock band from Detroit (280)

The Who   London Mod band credited with producing the first official rock opera, *Tommy*, and famous for their exciting and unpredictable performances (100)

William "Count" Basie   the pianist and bandleader most closely allied with the blues tradition, exemplified the Kansas City style in that he was inspired by the blues (8)

Winterland Palace   San Francisco concert hall where the Sex Pistols played their last show in January 1978 (162)

Woodstock Music & Art Fair   iconic rock festival held in 1969 near Woodstock, New York; viewed by many as the high point of the psychedelic-hippie era (121)

Woody Guthrie   a pioneer of "urban folk," he combined traditional folk music with an urban, cosmopolitan sensibility (12)

The Wu-Tang Clan   innovative group of nine eclectic rappers inspired by Chinese culture (238)

The Yardbirds   London band best known for their pioneering guitar innovations (102)

The Yeah Yeah Yeahs   a female-fronted New York garage rock band that draws from punk influences (283)

Yes   influential British progressive rock band featuring neoclassical structures and three-part harmonies (143)

The Zombies   Southern English band that fused jazz and rock, laying the groundwork for progressive rock (102)

REFERENCES

AARON, CHARLES. 1999. "KRS-One." In Light, 1999, 145–151.

ADATO, ALLISON. 2000. "Crash and Burn: The Most Untimely Death of a White-Hot Germ." *Los Angeles Times Magazine*. December 3. http://home.earthlink.net/~aladato/darby.html.

ALLMUSIC. "Industrial." http://www.allmusic.com/cg/amg.dll?p=amg&sql=77:141.

ALTERMAN, LORRAINE. 1968. "Who Let the Kinks In?" *Rolling Stone*, December 18.

ALTSCHULER, GLENN. 2003. *All Shook Up: How Rock 'n' Roll Changed America*. New York: Oxford University Press.

ALVAREZ, GABRIEL, 1999. "Gangsta Rap in the '90s." In Light, 1999, 285–295.

AMG DATA SOLUTIONS. *All Music*. http://allmusic.com.

ANASTASIO, TREY. 1999. "Jerry Garcia." *Rolling Stone*. February 18.

ANSEN, DAVID. 1998. "'Bad' Courtney Is Back." *Newsweek*, Feb. 2, 1998. http://www.newsweek.com/id/114048.

ARNOLD, GINA. 1997. *Kiss This: Punk in the Present Tense*. New York: St. Martin's Griffin.

THE ART DIRECTORS CLUB. 1994. "Andy Warhol." http://www.adcglobal.org/archive/hof/1994/?id=212

ASBURY, EDITH EVANS. 1957. "Rock 'n' Roll Teen-Agers Tie Up the Times Square Area" The New York Times, February 23.

ASWAD, JEM. 2009. "Flaming Lips' 'Do You Realize??' Named Official Rock Song of Oklahoma." MTV Networks. March 3.

ATHENSMUSIC.NET. 2004. *Athens Music History Tour*. http://athensmusic.net/newsdesk_info.php?newsPath=3&newsdesk_id=84.

AUSTEN, JAKE. 2005. *TV-go-go: Rock on TV from American Bandstand to American Idol*. Chicago: Chicago Preview Press.

AZERRAD, MICHAEL. 2001. *Our Band Could Be Your Life: Scenes from the American Indie Underground 1981–1991*. New York: Little, Brown and Company.

BACON, TONY, and KEITH BADMAN. 2004. *The Beach Boys: The Definitive Diary of America's Greatest Band, on Stage and in the Studio*. San Francisco: Backbeat Books.

BAIO, ANDY. 2008. "Girl Talk's Feed the Animals: The Official Sample List." http://waxy.org/2008/10/feed_the_animals_official_sample_list/

BANGS, LESTER. 1970. Led Zeppelin III. *Rolling Stone*. November 26. http://www.rollingstone.com/artists/ledzeppelin/albums/album/104760/review/6067705/led_zeppelin_iii.

BARRY, JOHN. 2008. I Against I. *Baltimore City Paper*, October 15, http://www.citypaper.com/music/story.asp?id=16871.

BARTHES, ROLAND. 1977. "From Work to Text." *Image—Music—Text*. New York: Hill and Wang.

BBC. 2001. "Bands In Oxford." BBC. http://www.bbc.co.uk/dna/h2g2/A522370&clip=1.

BECKER, SCOTT MARC. 1999. "Sharps & flats." Salon.com. http://www.salon.com/ent/music/review/1999/06/08/moby/.

BELZ, CARL. 1972. *The Story of Rock*. 2nd ed. New York: Harper Colophon Books.

BILLBOARD. 2007 "Independent Albums." Billboard.com. http://www.billboard.com/#/charts/independent-albums?chartDate=2007-05-05.

BISHOP, BUZZ. 2002. "Moby Didn't Feel Pressure To Follow Up 'Play,' '18' Bows At Number Four." Yahoo Music. http://new.music.yahoo.com/moby/news/moby-didnt-feel-pressure-to-follow-up-play-18-bows-at-number-four—12054910.

BONNAROO. 2009. "TV on the Radio." Bonnaroo. http://www.bonnaroo.com/artists/tv-on-the-radio.aspx.

BORLAND, JOHN. 2000. "Rapper Chuck D throws weight behind Napster." CNet News. http://news.cnet.com/2100-1023-239917.html.

BOZZA, ANTHONY. 2000. "NSynchronicity," *Rolling Stone*, March 30, 55.

BRACKER, MILTON. 1957. "Experts Propose Study of 'Craze'," The New York Times, February 23.

BRIAN, GREG. 2008. "First Grammy Awards in 1959: The Internal Battle Between Easy Listening and Rock N' Roll Begins." http://www.associatedcontent.com/article/589869/first_grammy_awards_in_1959_the_internal_pg2.html?cat=33.

BROADLEY, ERIN. 2009. "Buddyhead Redux." *LA Weekly*. July 15.

BROCKEN, MICHAEL. 2003. *The British Folk Revival, 1944–2002*. Aldershot: Ashgate.

BRONSON, FRED. 2003. *The Billboard Book of Number One Hits*, Rev. ed. New York: Billboard Books.

BROUGHTON, F. 2004. "Jimmy Savile." Interview on DJhistory.com., May 20. http://www.djhistory.com/interviews/jimmy-savile.

BROWNE, DAVID. 2001. "Review: Survivor (Destiny's Child)." *Entertainment Weekly*. May 7. http://www.ew.com/ew/article/0,,108583,00.html.

BUCKLEY, PETER. 2003. *The Rough Guide to Rock: The Definitive Guide to More Than 1200 Artists and Bands*. London: Rough Guides.

BUTCHER, MIKE. 2009. "SXSW – where everybody knows your Twitter name." http://uk.techcrunch.com/2009/03/18/sxsw-where-everybody-knows-your-twitter-name/.

CANTWELL, ROBERT. 1996. *When We Were Good: The Folk Revival*. Cambridge: Harvard University Press.

CHANG, JEFF. 2005. *Can't Stop Won't Stop*. New York: St. Martin's Press.

CHAPPLE, STEVE, AND REEBEE GAROFALO. 1977. *Rock 'n' Roll Is Here to Pay: The History and Politics of the Music Industry*. Chicago: Nelson-Hall.

CHRISTGAU, ROBERT. *Consumer Guide*. 1969–2009. http://www.robertchristgau.com/get_artist.php.

CHUCK D. 2000. " 'Free' Music Can Free the Artist." http://www.daveyd.com/FullArticles%5Carticle N339.asp.

CLARK, DICK, AND RICHARD ROBINSON. 1976. *Rock, Roll, and Remember*. New York: Thomas Y. Crowell Company.

CLARKE, DONALD. 2008. *The Rise and Fall of Popular Music*. http://www.donaldclarkemusicbox.com/rise-and-fall/index.php.

COACHELLA. 2009. "TV on the Radio." http://www.coachella.com/event/lineup/tv-on-the-radio.

COHN, LAWRENCE, ed. 1993. *Nothing But the Blues: The Music and the Musicians*. New York: Abbeville Publishing Group.

COLAPINTO, JOHN. 1996. "Cover Story: Pearl Jam's Mystery Man." *Rolling Stone*, Nov. 28, 1996. http://www.rollingstone.com/news/story/5937954/cover_story_pearl_jams_mystery_man/print.

COLBERT NATION. 2009. "February 9, 2009: TV on the Radio." http://www.colbertnation.com/the-colbert-report-videos/218124/february-09-2009/tv-on-the-radio.

COLEMAN, RAY. 1984. *Lennon*. New York: McGraw-Hill.

CONSIDINE, J. D. 1990. "Led Zeppelin." *Rolling Stone*. September 20.

CONTRERAS, FELIX. 2006. "Family of 'Lion Sleeps Tonight' Writer to Get Millions." From National Public Radio, *All Things Considered*. March 24. http://www.npr.org/templates/story/story.php?storyId=5300359.

COOPER, SEAN. 2009. MTV. http://www.mtv.com/music/artist/fatboy_slim/artist.jhtml.

COWELL, SIMON. 2003. "*I Don't Mean to be Rude, But...*" New York: Broadway Books.

COYLE, M. 2002. "Hijacked Hits and Antic Authenticity: Cover Songs, Race, and Postwar Marketing." In *Rock Over the Edge: Transformations in Popular Music Culture*. eds. Roger Beebe, Denise Fulbrooke, and Ben Saunders. Durham, N. C.: Duke University Press.

CROSS, CHARLES R. 2006. *Room Full of Mirrors: A Biography of Jimi Hendrix*. New York: Hyperion.

DAWSON, JIM. 2005. *Rock Around the Clock: The Record that Started the Rock Revolution*. San Francisco. Backbeat Books.

DECURTIS, ANTHONY. 1994. "Kurt Cobain, 1967–1994." *Rolling Stone*. June 2.

DECURTIS, ANTHONY, ed. 1992. *Present Tense: Rock & Roll and Culture*. Durham, NC. Duke University Press.

DEMERS, JOANNA. 2006. *Steal This Music*. University of Georgia Press.

DETTMAR, KEVIN. 2006. *Is Rock Dead?* New York: Routledge.

DETTMAR, KEVIN, ed. 2009. *The Cambridge Companion to Bob Dylan*. Cambridge: Cambridge University Press.

DETTMAR, KEVIN AND WILLIAM RICHEY. 1999. *Reading Rock and Roll*. New York: Columbia University Press.

DOCTOROW, CORY. 2006. "Mashup best-of 2006 album." http://www.boingboing.net/2007/01/11/mashup-bestof-2006-a.html.

DOHERTY, THOMAS. 2002. *Teenagers and Teenpics: The Juvenilization of American Movies in the 1950s*. Philadelphia. Temple University Press.

DOWNHILL BATTLE HOMEPAGE. http://downhillbattle.org/.

DUNCAN, ANDRÉA M. 1999. "Future Shock: Trip Hop and Beyond." In Light 1999, 366–367.

DYLAN, BOB. 2004. *Chronicles: Volume One*. New York: Simon & Schuster.

EDER, BRUCE. 2009. "Peter, Paul and Mary." All Music. http://www.allmusic.com/cg/amg.dll?p=amg&sql=11:fifpxqq5ldhe~T1.

ELDER, ROB. 2001. "Down on the Peacock Farm." Salon.com. November 16. http://dir.salon.com/story/people/feature/2001/11/16/kesey99/index.html.

EHRENREICH, BARBARA, ELIZABETH HESS, AND GLORIA JACOBS. 1992. "Beatlemania: Girls Just Want to Have Fun." In *The Adoring Audience: Fan Culture and Popular Media*, ed. Lisa A. Lewis, 84–106. London and New York: Routledge.

ELLERTSON, PETER. 2005. "Sacred Harp Singing in a Living History Environment." Midwest Open Air Museums Coordinating Council. November 10. http://www.sci.edu/faculty/ellertsen/livinghistory.html.

ELROD, BRUCE C. *Your Hit Parade & American Top Ten Hits: A Week-by-Week Guide To the Nation's Favorite Music, 1935–1994*. Ann Arbor: Popular Culture Ink.

ELVIS PRESLEY ENTERPRISES. 2009. In Discover Elvis. Retrieved August 18, 2009, from www.elvis.com/elvisology/quotes/byelvis.asp.

EMERSON, KEN. 2005. *Always Magic in the Air: The Bomp and Brilliance of the Brill Building Era*. New York: Penguin Books.

ENNIS, PHILIP. 1992. *The Seventh Stream: The Emergence of Rocknroll in American Popular Music*. Hanover, NH: Wesleyan University Press.

ERLEWINE, STEPHEN THOMAS. 2009. "Hole: *Live Through This*." Allmusic Guide. http://www.allmusic.com/cg/amg.dll?p=amg&sql=10:fjftxqrgldae.

ERLEWINE, STEPHEN THOMAS. 2009. "Oasis: *Definitely Maybe*." Allmusic Guide. http://www.allmusic.com/cg/amg.dll?p=amg&sql=10:3ifox-qwhldde.

ERLEWINE, STEPHEN THOMAS. 2009. "Pet Shop Boys: *Actually*." Allmusic Guide. http://www.allmusic.com/cg/amg.dll?p=amg&sql=10:g9fqxqr5ldhe.

EVERETT, WALTER. 2001. *The Beatles as Musicians*. 2 vols. New York: Oxford. Fitzgerald, Scott. 1996. *The Jazz Age*. New York: New Directions.

FARLEY, CHRISTOPHER JOHN, AND THIGPEN, DAVID E. 1994. "MUSIC: Woodstock Suburb." *Time*. August 22. http://www.time.com/time/magazine/article/0,9171,981316-3,00.html.

FEED THE ANIMALS DOWNLOAD LOCATION. http://74.124.198.47/illegal-art.net/__girl__talk__feed__the__anima.ls__/.

FLAMING LIPS BLOG. 2009. "Embryonic set to stream on ColbertNation.com." http://www.flaminglips.com/blog?page=1.

FLICK, LARRY. 2002. "Declining Sales in 2002 Trigger Desire for Less Hype, Better Records, Fresh Blood." *Billboard*. December 28, 17.

FORMAN, M. 2002. *The 'Hood Comes First: Race, Space, and Place in Rap and Hip Hop*. Middletown: Wesleyan University Press.

FOSTER, TOM. 2006. "Carling Take Over Zodiac." *The Oxford Student*. November 9.

FRANK, JOSH & CARYN GANZ. 2006. *Fool the World: The Oral History of a Band Called Pixies*. New York: St. Martin's Griffin.

FRICKE, DAVID. 1998. "Different Class: Pulp: Review." *Rolling Stone*, February 2. http://www.rollingstone.com/reviews/album/125517/review/5941861/differentclass.

FRIEDLANDER, PAUL. 2008. *Rock and Roll: A Social History*. 2nd ed. Boulder, Colorado: Westview Press.

GARELICK, JON. 2003. "Rock's Visionary: Sam Phillips, 1923–2003." The Boston Phoenix. August 8–14.

GAROFALO, REEBEE. 2008. *Rockin' Out: Popular Music in the USA*. 4th ed. Upper Saddle River, NJ: Pearson Prentice Hall.

GAYLOR, BRETT. 2009. *Rip! A Remix Manifesto*.

GILLET, CHARLIE. 1996. *The Sound of the City: The Rise of Rock and Roll*. 2nd ed. New York: Da Capo Press.

GILLIS, GREGG. 2008. "Girl Talk/Gregg Gillis On New Album, Music Industry." *The Washington Post*. http://www.washingtonpost.com/wp-dyn/content/discussion/2008/07/16/DI2008071601445.html.

GLOCK, ALLISON. 2006. "Nick Lachey: King of Pain," *Rolling Stone*, April 21.

GOOD COPY BAD COPY. 2007. http://video.google.com/videoplay?docid=4323661317653995812#.

GORDON, DEVIN. 2003. "Confessions Of An Emo Punk." *Newsweek*. August 25.

GOULD, JONATHAN. 2007. *Can't Buy Me Love: The Beatles, Britain, and America*. New York: Harmony Books.

GRAHAM, BILL, AND ROBERT GREENFIELD. 2004. *Bill Graham Presents: My Life Inside Rock and Out*. Cambridge: Da Capo.

GRAMMY. 2009. "Grammy Award Winners." http://www.grammy.com/GRAMMY_Awards/Winners/Results.aspx.

GRAND UPRIGHT V. WARNER. 780 F. Supp. 182 (S.D.N.Y. 1991) http://cip.law.ucla.edu/cases/case_grandwarner.html.

GRAVY, WAVY. 2002. "Wavy's Biography." http://www.wavygravy.net/bio/biography.html.

GREENBERG, STEVE. 1999. "Sugar Hill Records." In Light 1999, 23–33.

GURALNICK, PETER. 1994. *Last Train to Memphis*. New York: Back Bay Books.

HAJDU, DAVID. 2002. *Positively 4th Street: The Lives and Times of Joan Baez, Bob Dylan, Mimi Baez Farina and Richard Farina*. New York: North Point.

HAMPTON, DREAM. 1999. "Bad Boy." In Light 1999, 339–349.

HANSEN, BECK. 2009. "Songs of Leonard Cohen 'Suzanne.'" Record Club Web site. http://www.beck.com/record_club.

HARVEY, MIKE. 2009. "Single-mother digital pirate Jammie Thomas-Rasset must pay $80,000 per song." *Times Online*. http://technology.timson-line.co.uk/tol/news/tech_and_web/article6534542.ece.

HEATH, CHRIS. 2001. "Has Anyone Seen Christina," *Rolling Stone*, November 14, 55.

HERMES, WILL, AND MICHEL, SIA, eds. 2005. *Spin: 20 Years of Alternative Music*. New York: Three Rivers Press.

HEYLIN, CLINTON. 2007. *Babylon's Burning: From Punk to Grunge*. New York: Conongate.

HILBURN, ROBERT. 1994. "He Didn't Ask for All of This." *Los Angeles Times*. May 1. http://articles.latimes.com/1994-05-01/entertainment/ca-52475_1_pearl-jam-concert.

HOLM-HUDSON, KEVIN. 2002. *Progressive Rock Reconsidered*. New York: Routledge.

HORNBY, NICK. 1995. *High Fidelity*. New York: Riverhead Books.

HOWARD, ALAN AND MCLEAN, DON. 2009. "American Pie." http://www.don-mclean.com.

HUFFMAN, LARRY. 2009. "Bell Laboratories and the Development of Electrical Recording." *From Leopold Stokowski and the Philadelphia Orchestra: Their Story and Their Recordings 1917 to 1940*. http://www.stokowski.org/Development_of_Electrical_Recording.htm.

ITZKOFF, DAVE. 2009. "Arts, Briefly: Noel Gallagher Says He's Leaving Oasis." *New York Times*. August 28. http://www.nytimes.com/2009/08/29/arts/music/29arts-NOELGALLAGHE_BRF.html?_r=1&scp=1&sq=noel%20gallagher&st=cse.

JACKSON, JOHN A. 2004. *A House on Fire: The Rise and Fall of Philadelphia Soul*. New York: Oxford University Press.

JANA, REENA. 2001. "Is It Art, or Memorex?" http://www.wired.com/culture/lifestyle/news/2001/05/43902.

JOHNSON, MARTIN. "'Cop Killer' and Sister Souljah: Hip Hop Under Fire." In Light 1999, 288–289.

JONZE, TIM. 2009. "Oasis win best band at NME awards." *The Guardian*. February 26. http://www.guardian.co.uk/music/2009/feb/26/oasis-win-nme-awards.

JUNO, ANDREA. 1996. *Angry Women in Rock*. New York: Juno Books.

KAYE, LENNY. 1971. "Led Zeppelin IV." *Rolling Stone*. December 23. http://www.rollingstone.com/artists/ledzeppelin/albums/album/236870/review/5946018/led_zeppelin_iv.

KOPIMI HOMEPAGE. http://www.kopimi.com/kopimi/.

KOT, GREG. 2009. *Ripped: How the Wired Generation Revolutionized Music*. New York: Scribner.

KOZINN, ALLAN. 1995. *The Beatles*. London: Phaidon.

KRAVETS, DAVID. 2007. "RIAA Juror: 'We Wanted to Send a Message.'" *Wired*. October 9. http://www.wired.com/threatlevel/2007/10/riaa-juror-we-w/.

KRISTAL, HILLY. 2005. *CBGB and OMFUG: Thirty Years from the Home of Underground Rock*. New York: Harry N. Abrams, Inc.

LAING, DAVE. 1985. *One Chord Wonders: Power and Meaning in Punk Rock*. Milton Keynes, UK: Open University Press.

LANKFORD, JR., RONALD D. 2005. *Folk Music U.S.A.: The Changing Voice of Protest*. New York: Schirmer.

LELAND, JOHN. 1999. "The Pinnacle: 1988." In Light 1999, 192–193.

LEONARD, MARION. 2007. *Gender in the Music Industry: Rock, Discourse, and Girl Power*. Burlington, VT: Ashgate Publishing Company.

LEVIATHANT. 2007. Nine Inch Nails Hotline. http://www.theninhotline.net/news/archives/backissue.php?y=07&m=9#1189989696

LEVY, STEVEN. 2006. *The Perfect Thing: How the iPod Shuffles Commerce, Culture, and Coolness*. New York: Simon and Schuster Paperbacks.

LIGHT, ALAN, 1999. "Public Enemy." In Light 1999, 165–175.

LIGHT, ALAN, ed. 1999. *The Vibe History of Hip Hop*. New York: Three Rivers Press.

LOLLAPALOOZA. 2009. "TV on the Radio." http://2009.lollapalooza.com/band/tv-on-the-radio.

LOLLAPALOOZA HOMEPAGE. 2009. http://2009.lollapalooza.com/.

LORNELL, KIP. 2004. *The NPR Curious Listener's Guide to American Folk*. New York: Penguin.

LOVE, COURTNEY. 1994. Speech at Cobain's memorial. April 10. http://gos.sbc.edu/l/love.html.

MACAN, EDWARD. 1997. *Rocking the Classics: English Progressive Rock and the Counterculture*. New York: Oxford University Press.

MACKAYE, IAN. 1986. "Ian MacKaye - 1986 - Emocore is stupid." YouTube. http://www.youtube.com/watch?v=mbdh0Qm_5A0.

MANDIBERG, MICHAEL. 2001. http://www.aftersherrielevine.com/.

MARCUS, GREIL. 1993. *Ranters and Crowd Pleasers: Punk in Pop Music, 1977–92*. New York: Doubleday.

MARTIN, LINDA & KERRY SEGRAVE. 1993. *Anti-Rock: The Opposition to Rock 'n' Roll*. Connecticut. Da Capo Press.

MAY, E.N. 2009. "Rock History 101: Phil Ochs's 'I Ain't Marching Anymore.' " http://consequenceofsound.net/2009/01/08/rock-history-101-phil-ochss-i-aint-marching-anymore.

MCALEER, DAVE. 1999. *All Music Book of Hit Singles Top 20 Charts from 1954 to the Present-day*. San Francisco: Miller Freeman Books.

MCCARTNEY, PAUL. 2009. "Musicians on Brian." BrianWilson.com. http://www.brianwilson.com/brian/musicians.html.

MCGREGOR, JOCK. 1997. "Madonna: Icon of Postmodernity." Facing the Challenge.org. http://www.facingthechallenge.org/madonna.php.

MCLEOD, KEMBREW. 2009. *Copyright Criminals*. http://www.kembrew.com.

MCNEIL, LEGS. 1996. *Please Kill Me: The Uncensored Oral History of Punk Rock*. New York: Grove Press.

MEDIA OF ALAN FREED. 1998. Freed's Last Goodbye. http://www.alanfreed.com/media.html.

MICHEL, SIA. 1999. "L.L. Cool J," In Light 1999, 81–89.

MITCHELL, JONI. 1983. Interview by Dave Fanning. RTE Radio, May.

MORRIS, CHRIS. 2009. "Making It Look Easy: The Art of Frank Sinatra." *Sinatra.com*. http://www.sinatra.com/legacy/making-it-look-easy.

MOBY. 2009. "if you're in the music business (and for your sake i hope you're not…) you probably know about bob lefsetz." http://www.moby.com/node/8507.

MOBY. 2009. "the riaa have sued Jammie Thomas-Rasset of minnesota for $2,000,000 for illegally downloading music." http://www.moby.com/journal/2009-06-20/riaa-have-sued-jammie-thomas-rasset-minn.html.

MTV. "*Rage Builds 'Evil Empire'*." 1996. MTV Networks. May 3. http://www.mtv.com/news/articles/1433600/19960503/rage_against_the_machine.jhtml.

MTV NEWS. 2004. "*Grey Album* Producer Danger Mouse Explains How He Did It." http://www.mtv.com/news/articles/1485693/20040311/jay_z.jhtml?headlines=true/.

NATIONAL PARK SERVICE. "Jazz Origins in New Orleans, 1895–1927." http://www.nps.gov/archive/jazz/Jazz%20History_origins_1895_1927.htm.

NEAL, R. 2004 "Turntablism 101: The Turntable as an Instrument?" *CBS Sunday Morning Home*. March 28. http://www.cbsnews.com/stories/2004/03/25/sunday/main608774.shtml.

NEGATIVLAND homepage. http://www.negativland.com/index.php?opt=bio&subopt=neglandbio.

NELSON, HAVELOCK. 1999. "DJ Kool Herc." In Light 1999, 16–17.

NEW MUSICAL EXPRESS. 1984. "A Suitable Case for Treatment." December 22/29. http://foreverill.com/interviews/1984/suitable.htm.

NEWSWEEK. 1963. "The Milk Drinkers." August 12.

NEW YORK TIMES. 2001. "Combs Trial Jurors Consider Gun Case Against Rap Star." Katherine E. Finkelstein and Dexter Filkins. March 15. http://www.nytimes.com/2001/03/15/nyregion/combs-trial-jurors-consider-gun-case-against-rap-star.html.

NEW YORK TIMES. 2008. Pareles, Jon. "Frustration and Fury: Take It. It's Free." http://www.nytimes.com/2008/06/08/arts/music/08pare.html?_r=2&pagewanted=1.

NILSON, PER. 1988. *The Wild One: The True Story of Iggy Pop*. London: Omnibus Press.

NORMAN, PHILIP. 1982. *Shout! The Beatles in Their Generation*. New York: Warner Books.

OCHS, PHIL. 1967. "It Ain't Me, Babe." The Village Voice. August 12.

PALMER, ROBERT. 1996. *Dancing in the Streets*. London: BBC Books.

PALMER, ROBERT. 1995. *Rock & Roll: An Unruly History*. New York: Harmony Books.

PARVEZ, D. 2003. "Lollapalooza: Then and now." *Seattle Post-Intelligencer*. http://www.seattlepi.com/pop/136299_lollapalooza23.html.

POSNER, GERALD. 2002. *Motown: Music, Money, Sex, and Power*. New York: Random House.

POWERS, NICOLE. 2009. "Moby: Wait For Me." http://suicidegirls.com/interviews/Moby%3A+Wait+For+Me/.

PRICE, STEVEN. 2007. *1001 Greatest Things Ever Said About California*. Guilford, Connecticut: Lyons Press.

PUNKNEWS.ORG. 2001. "Jimmy Eat World - Bleed American" Punknews.org. http://www.punknews.org/review/328.

RAFERTY, BRIAN. 2008. "Album of the Year: TV on the Radio." *Spin*. December 15.

RAHA, MARIA. 2005. *Cinderella's Big Score: Women of the Punk and Indie Underground*. Emeryville, CA: Seal Press.

RAPHAEL, AMY. 1995. *Grrrls: Viva Rock Divas*. New York: St. Martin's Griffin.

REDDINGTON, HELEN. 1988. *The Lost Women of Rock* Cornwall: MPG Books, Ltd.

REYNOLDS, SIMON. 2005. *Rip it Up and Start Again: Postpunk 1978–1984*. New York: Penguin Books.

RIAA (RECORDING INDUSTRY ASSOCIATION OF AMERICA). 2009. "Gold & Platinum – August 23, 2009." August 23. http://www.riaa.com/goldandplatinumdata.php?table=tblTop100.

RIAA (RECORDING INDUSTRY ASSOCIATION OF AMERICA). 2009. "Piracy: Online and On the Street." http://www.riaa.com/physicalpiracy.php.

RICHARDSON, MARK. 2006. "Girl Talk." *Pitchfork Media*. http://pitchfork.com/features/interviews/7522-girl-talk/.

ROCCO, JOHN, ed. 1998. *The Nirvana Companion: Two Decades of Commentary*. New York: Schirmer Books.

ROCK AND ROLL HALL OF FAME AND MUSEUM. 2007. "The Mamas and the Papas." http://www.rockhall.com/inductee/the-mamas-and-the-papas.

ROLLING STONE. 2001. "Afrika Bambaataa" http://www.rollingstone.com/artists/afrikabambataa/biography.

ROLLING STONE. 1979. "Elvis Costello: *Armed Forces* Review." Janet Maslin, March 22. http://www.rollingstone.com/reviews/album/14936209/review/5942893.

ROLLING STONE. 1986. "Keeping Up With The Smiths." David Fricke. October 9. http://www.rollingstone.com/artists/thesmiths/articles/story/9532295/keeping_up_with_the_smiths.

ROLLING STONE. 2008. "The 50 Best Albums of 2008." Rolling Stone. http://www.rollingstone.com/news/story/24958695/albums_of_the_year.

ROLLING STONE. 1986. "The Smiths: *The Queen Is Dead*: Music Reviews: Rolling Stone." Mark Coleman. September 11. http://www.rollingstone.com/artists/thesmiths/albums/album/234723/review/5940416/the_queen_is_dead.

ROLLING STONE. 1981. "Ultravox: *Vienna*: Music Reviews: Rolling Stone." Debra Rae Cohen. March 5. http://www.rollingstone.com/artists/ultravox/albums/album/212496/review/5945641/vienna.

ROLLING STONE. 2006. "Whatever People Say I Am, That's What I'm Not: Arctic Monkeys: Review:" http://www.rollingstone.com/reviews/album/9199780/review/9359479/whateverpeoplesayiamthatswhatimnot.

ROMAINE, JAMES. 2003. "Transubstantiating the Culture: Andy Warhol's Secret."

ROMANOWSKI, PATRICIA, AND HOLLY GEORGE-WARREN, eds. 1995. *The New Rolling Stone Encyclopedia of Rock and Roll*. Rev. ed. New York: Fireside.

SARIG, RONI. 2007. *Third Coast: OutKast, Timbaland, and How Hip Hop Became a Southern Thing*. Cambridge: Da Capo Press.

SCADUTO, ANTHONY. 1973. *Bob Dylan*. New York: Signet.

SCAGGS, AUSTIN. 2007. "Bonnaroo." *Rolling Stone*. http://www.rollingstone.com/news/coverstory/20200609/page/23.

SCHEERER, MARK. 2001. "DJ Moby finds inspiration in old Southern music." CNN. http://archives.cnn.com/2000/SHOWBIZ/Music/02/08/moby/.

SCHIPPER, HENRY. 1990. "Dick Clark." *Rolling Stone*. April 19.

SCHMUCKLI, CLAUDIA. 1999. "Andy Warhol: *The Last Supper*." http://pastexhibitions.guggenheim.org/warhol/.

SCOTT, ANDREW. 2001. "The Swift Rise and Rapid Demise of Harry Herbert Pace's 'Black Swan Records.' " *All About Jazz*. http://www.allaboutjazz.com/articles/arti0101_03.htm.

SEAGRAVE, KERRY. 1994. *Payola in the Music Industry: A History, 1880–1991*. Jefferson, NC: McFarland.

SERPICK, EVAN. 2006. "The Flaming Lips Get Spectacular." *Rolling Stone*. April 28.

SHAPIRO, PETER, ed. 2000. *Modulations: A History of Electronic Music*. New York: Caipirinha Publications.

SHAW, ARNOLD. 1970. *The World of Soul*. New York: Cowles.

SHELTON, ROBERT. 1986. *No Direction Home: The Life and Music of Bob Dylan*. New York: William Morrow.

SHORE, MICHAEL, AND DICK CLARK. 1985. *The History of American Bandstand*. New York: Ballantine Books.

SINKER, DANIEL. 2001. *We Owe You Nothing: Punk Planet: The Collected Interviews*. New York: Akashic Books.

SMITH, DANYEL. 1999. "Tupac Shakur." In Light 1999, 297–305.

SMITH, ETHAN. 2002. "Organization Moby." *Wired*. May. http://www.wired.com/wired/archive/10.05/moby.html.

SOUTH BY SOUTHWEST HOMEPAGE. http://sxsw.com/.

SPITZ, MARC AND BRENDEN MULLEN. 2001. *We Got The Neutron Bomb: The Untold Story of L.A. Punk*. New York: Three Rivers Press.

SPITZ, ROBERT STEPHEN. 1989. *Barefoot in Babylon*. New York: The Viking Press.

STARR, LARRY AND CHRISTOPHER WATERMAN. 2003. *American Popular Music: From Minstrelsy to MTV*. New York: Oxford University Press.

STEERE, MIKE. 2008. "'Guitar Hero' Guru Makes Music with Robots." *CNN.com*. http://www.cnn.com/2008/TECH/science/08/25/RoboticOrchestra/index.html.

STILLMAN, KEVIN. 2006. "'Word to your mother.'" *Iowa State Daily*. http://www.iowastatedaily.com/articles/2006/02/27/news/20060227-archive5.txt.

STUESSY, JOE, AND SCOTT LIPSCOMB. 2009. *Rock and Roll: Its History and Stylistic Development*. 6th ed. Upper Saddle River, NJ: Pearson Prentice Hall.

SUDDATH, CLAIRE. 2009. "Greg Kot: How the Internet Changed Music." *Time*. May 21.

SULLIVAN, JAMES. 1997. "*Endtroducing. . . . .*" http://www.synthesis.net/music/interview/item-185/1997-05-01-endtroducing.

SZATMARY, DAVID P. 2010. *Rockin' in Time: A Social History of Rock-and-Roll*. 7th ed. Upper Saddle River, NJ: Prentice Hall.

SZWED, JOHN F. 1999. "The Real Old School." In Light 1999, 3–11.

TAYLOR, CHARLES. 2006. "All joys equal in this critic's book," *Los Angeles Times*. December 24. http://articles.latimes.com/2006/dec/24/entertainment/ca-hampton24pg=3.

TIME. 1950. "Music: Good Night, Irene." August 14. http://www.time.com/time/magazine/article/0,9171,858914,00.html.

TIME. 1975. The Backstreet Phantom of Rock. *Time.com*. October 27. http://www.time.com/time/magazine/article/0,9171,913583-1,00.html.

THOMSON, ELIZABETH AND DAVID GUTMAN, eds. 1996. *The Bowie Companion*. Cambridge, MA: Da Capo Press.

THOMPSON, GORDON. 2008. *Please Please Me: Sixties British Pop, Inside Out*. New York: Oxford University Press.

TRAGER, OLIVER. 2004. *Keys to the Rain: The Definitive Bob Dylan Encyclopedia*. New York: Billboard Books.

TRUST, GARY. 2009. "Chart Beat Wednesday: Linkin Park, Eagles, Shakira." *Billboard*. August 19.

TURNER CLASSIC MOVIES. 2009. Notes for Blackboard Jungle. http://www.tcm.com/tcmdb/title.jsp?stid=1206&category=Notes.

TYRANGIEL, JOSH. 2006. "*Endtroducing. . . . .*" *Time*. http://www.time.com/time/2006/100albums/0,27693,Endtroducing,00.html.

WALT, VIVIENNE. 2007. "Postcard: Paris." *Time*. July 19.

WATKINS, S. CRAIG. 2005. *Hip Hop Matters: Politics, Pop Culture, and the Struggle for the Soul of a Movement*. Boston: Beacon Press.

WEINGARTEN, MARK. 2000. *Station to Station: The History of Rock 'n' Roll on Television*. New York: Pocket Books.

WEISS, DAVID. 2005. "NY Metro Report: The Sound of CBGB." *Mix*. December 1. http://mixonline.com/mag/audio_new_york_metro_46/.

WEUSI, JITU K. 1996. "The Rise and Fall of Black Swan Records." http://www.redhotjazz.com/blackswan.html.

WHITE, CHARLES. 1984. *The Life and Times of Little Richard*. New York: Pocket Books.

WICKE, PETER. 1987. *Rock Music: Culture, Aesthetics and Sociology*. Cambridge: Cambridge University Press.

WILSON, BRIAN. 2007. "An Evening with Brian Wilson: The Palace Theatre in Manchester, England—September 23, 2007." Interview by Robert Stevens. Manchester, England.

WILSON, GREG. 2004. "Norman Cook: A Conversation." http://www.electrofunkroots.co.uk/interviews/norman_cook.html.

WOLFE, TOM. 1976. "The 'Me' Decade and the Third Great Awakening," *New York*. August 23.

WOLK, DOUGLAS. 2002. "Barely Legal." *The Village Voice*. http://www.villagevoice.com/2002-02-05/music/barely-legal/

ZETUMER, JOSH. 2001. "Jimmy Eat World album leaves familiar taste." *Daily Trojan*. September 19.

PHOTO CREDITS

INDEX

320